The Keto Bible More Than A Keto Diet Cookbook

the Ultimate Guide for the Keto Diet with 1000 Flavorful Recipes for Beginners and Advanced Ketoers

Ketone Academy

Disclaimer Notice:

Please note the information contained within this document is for educational and entertainment purposes only. All effort has been executed to present accurate, up to date, reliable, complete information. No warranties of any kind are declared or implied. Readers acknowledge that the author is not engaged in the rendering of legal, financial, medical or professional advice. The content within this book has been derived from various sources. Please consult a licensed professional before attempting any techniques outlined in this book.

By reading this document, the reader agrees that under no circumstances is the author responsible for any losses, direct or indirect, that are incurred as a result of the use of the information contained within this document, including, but not limited to, errors, omissions, or inaccuracies.

Table of Content

Chapter 6 Poultry 49

Chapter 8 Beef and Lamb 84

Chapter 9 Fish and Seafood 101

Chapter 15 Egg and Dairy 173

Chapter 16 Side Dishes 178

Chapter 17 Smoothies....................185

The 28-Day Keto Challenge

Week 1

Meal Plan	Breakfast	Lunch	Dinner	Snack/ Dessert	Motivational Quotes
Day-1	**Chorizo, Kale, and Avocado Eggs** calories: 275 fat: 23.1g protein: 12.9g carbs: 7.7g net carbs: 4.1g fiber: 3.6g	**Pumpkin and Cauliflower Curry** calories: 501 fat: 44.0g protein: 7.0g carbs: 19.0g net carbs: 9.0g fiber: 10.0g	**White Wine Pork with Cabbage** calories: 512 fat: 32.6g protein: 42.9g carbs: 9.3g net carbs: 5.9g fiber: 3.4g	**Turkey Stuffed Mini Peppers** calories: 200 fat: 17.1g protein: 7.8g carbs: 2.9g net carbs: 2.0g fiber: 0.9g	Don't let a stumble in the road be the end of your journey.
Start simple. Keep it simple, especially when you are starting out. The best way to start keto for beginners is to use a simple framework for your meals: Pick a protein+Pick a (low carb) veggie +Add fat.					

Start simple.

Keep it simple, especially when you are starting out. The best way to start keto for beginners is to use a simple framework for your meals:

Pick a protein+Pick a (low carb) veggie +Add fat.

Meal Plan	Breakfast	Lunch	Dinner	Snack/ Dessert	Motivational Quotes
Day-2	**Cheddar Bacon and Egg Frittata** calories: 326 fat: 28.1g protein: 14.9g carbs: 2.5g net carbs: 2.1g fiber: 0.4g	**Seared Scallops with Sausage** calories: 835 fat: 61.9g protein: 55.9g carbs: 10.5g net carbs: 9.4g fiber: 1.1g	**Leek and Pumpkin Turkey Stew** calories: 357 fat: 27.0g protein: 21.0g carbs: 11.0g net carbs: 7.0g fiber: 4.0g	**Cheese Bites with Pickle** calories: 200 fat: 15.6g protein: 11.4g carbs: 4.8g net carbs: 3.8g fiber: 1.0g	When you eat crap, you feel crap.

Remove temptations.

One of the easiest keto diet tips to implement is to get rid of foods you need to avoid. It's much easier to stick to your goals if you're not constantly fighting temptation.

Meal Plan	Breakfast	Lunch	Dinner	Snack/ Dessert	Motivational Quotes
Day-3	**Bacon and Jalapeño Egg Muffins** calories: 301 fat: 23.8g protein: 19.8g carbs: 3.8g net carbs: 3.3g fiber: 0.5g	**Chicken Thigh Green Salad** *pg119* calories: 455 fat: 29.1g protein: 40.2g carbs: 6.6g net carbs: 2.8g fiber: 3.8g	**Texas Chili** calories: 488 fat: 38.1g protein: 25.9g carbs: 17.1g net carbs: 10.2g fiber: 6.9g	**Cheese and Shrimp Stuffed Celery** calories: 127 fat: 6.1g protein: 13.4g carbs: 4.2g net carbs: 3.7g fiber: 0.5g	Every step is progress, no matter how small.

Stock your fridge.

Along with getting rid of all the bad stuff, fill your fridge with plenty of good stuff:

Healthy fats, Leafy greens, Low-carb vegetables, Meat, Poultry, Seafood, Full-fat dairy, Eggs, Low-carb fruit.

Day-4	Avocado and Berry Smoothie	Salmon and Cucumber Panzanella	Chipotle Tomato and Pumpkin Chicken Chili	Chocolate Almond Bark	With the new day comes new strength and new thoughts.
	calories: 446 fat: 43g protein: 7g carbs: 16g net carbs: 9g fiber: 7g	calories: 339 fat: 21.6g protein: 28.6g carbs: 5.3g net carbs: 3.2g fiber: 2.1g	calories: 390 fat: 30.0g protein: 22.0g carbs: 14.0g net carbs: 9.0g fiber: 5.0g	calories: 118 fat: 13.0g protein: 1.0g carbs: 1.0g net carbs: 0g fiber: 1.0g	

Stock your pantry.

Don't forget to stock your pantry with keto staples, too! Pantry ingredients are most prone to be high in carbs, but here are the types of items you'll want to keep:

Herbs & spices, Low-carb condiments, Nuts & seeds, Sugar-free sweeteners, Low carb flours, Sugar-free beverages.

Day-5	Cinnamon-Cream-Cheese Almond Waffles	Cauliflower Egg Bake	Chipotle Beef Spare Ribs	Pecan Pralines	The past cannot be changed, the future is yet in your power.
	calories: 308 fat: 24.1g protein: 11.9g carbs: 9.6g net carbs: 7.8g fiber: 1.8g	calories: 237 fat: 13.6g protein: 20.2g carbs: 7.1g net carbs: 4.8g fiber: 2.3g	calories: 396 fat: 32.8g protein: 20.9g carbs: 3.7g net carbs: 3.0g fiber: 0.7g	calories: 86 fat: 9.0g protein: 1.0g carbs: 1.0g net carbs: 0g fiber: 1.0g	

Ease into it.

If you're starting a keto diet coming from eating a lot of carbs and sugar, cutting it all out cold turkey may be a shock. It can cause (temporary) keto flu symptoms and cravings, and while these can be manageable, it doesn't mean that's the only way.

Day-6	Broccoli and Ham Egg Bake	Colden Gazpacho Soup	Duo-Cheese Pork and Turkey Patties	Cinnamon Crusted Almonds	You will never win if you never begin.
	calories: 345 fat: 27.9g protein: 11.0g carbs: 8.9g net carbs: 4.2g fiber: 4.7g	calories: 528 fat: 46g protein: 8g carbs: 7g net carbs: 4g fiber: 3g	calories: 514 fat: 35.2g protein: 44.2g carbs: 2.5g net carbs: 2.2g fiber: 0.3g	calories: 385 fat: 33.9g protein: 13.0g carbs: 13.0g net carbs: 4.9g fiber: 8.1g	

Carbs are a limit.

This means you set the maximum that you can consume per day, If you go under this number, that's okay! It's not a hard goal, just a limit.

Day-7	Avocado Sausage Stacks	Sriracha Shrimp Sushi Rolls	Beef and Pimiento in Zucchini Boats	Strawberries Coated with Chocolate Chips	It does not matter how slowly you go, as long as you don't stop.
	calories: 388 fat: 22.9g protein: 16.1g carbs: 9.6g net carbs: 5.1g fiber: 4.5g	calories: 220 fat: 10.2g protein: 18.6g carbs: 2.0g net carbs: 0.9g fiber: 1.1g	calories: 334 fat: 24.0g protein: 17.9g carbs: 7.6g net carbs: 6.9g fiber: 0.7g	calories: 216 fat: 18.0g protein: 4.0g carbs: 11.0g net carbs: 6.0g fiber: 5.0g	

Protein is a goal.

This means you want to reach this number each day, so try not to go below the goal. Going over a little bit is also okay, but a large excess in protein might convert to glucose and kick you out of ketosis.

Week 2

Meal Plan	Breakfast	Lunch	Dinner	Snack/Dessert	Motivational Quotes
Day-1	**Dill-Cream-Cheese Salmon Rolls** calories: 251 fat: 16.1g protein: 17.8g carbs: 8.7g net carbs: 7.0g fiber: 1.7g	**Sausage and Leek Soup** calories: 385 fat: 31.2g protein: 20.9g carbs: 5.1g net carbs: 3.9g fiber: 1.2g	**Chicken Thigh and Kale Stew** calories: 277 fat: 22.0g protein: 17.0g carbs: 6.0g net carbs: 4.0g fiber: 2.0g	**Romano and Asiago Cheese Crisps** calories: 110 fat: 7.5g protein: 8.4g carbs: 2.0g net carbs: 1.6g fiber: 0.4g	Take it one meal at a time.

Fat is a lever.

After your carb limit and protein goal, the remaining calories you need for the day come from fat. This is what keeps you satisfied and provides the majority of your energy source.

You can use fat as a lever, increasing it up or down, based on your goals. Increase it if you're hungry, decrease it to lose weight, but remember you can't go too low (don't get caught in the outdated "fat is bad" trap), since it's your main energy source.

Meal Plan	Breakfast	Lunch	Dinner	Snack/Dessert	Motivational Quotes
Day-2	**Mushroom and Kale Tofu Scramble** calories: 470 fat: 38.7g protein: 24.9g carbs: 7.6g net carbs: 4.9g fiber: 2.7g	**Dijon Crab Cakes** calories: 316 fat: 24.3g protein: 15.2g carbs: 1.8g net carbs: 1.5g fiber: 0.3g	**Pinwheel Beef and Spinach Steaks** calories: 491 fat: 41.0g protein: 28.0g carbs: 2.1g net carbs: 2.0g fiber: 0.1g	**Cream Cheese Fat Bombs** calories: 66 fat: 6.9g protein: 0g carbs: 0g net carbs: 0g fiber: 0g	You are your only limit.

Portions do matter.

Even though calories and portions are not the primary focus of a ketogenic lifestyle, they still matter. It's still possible not to lose weight, or even gain weight, on keto if you consume too much – this would be the case with any diet. The key to remember is that fat is a lever.

Meal Plan	Breakfast	Lunch	Dinner	Snack/Dessert	Motivational Quotes
Day-3	**Cheese and Egg Spinach Nests** calories: 231 fat: 17.6g protein: 12.2g carbs: 5.4g net carbs: 4.1g fiber: 1.3g	**Cheese Stuffed Spaghetti Squash** calories: 220 fat: 17.6g protein: 9.0g carbs: 6.8g net carbs: 5.9g fiber: 0.9g	**Creamy Dijon Pork Filet Mignon** calories: 302 fat: 16.5g protein: 34.1g carbs: 2.2g net carbs: 2.1g fiber: 0.1g	**Meaty Jalapeños** calories: 190 fat: 13.3g protein: 12.6g carbs: 4.8g net carbs: 3.6g fiber: 1.2g	What you plant now, you will harvest later.

Eat only when hungry.

There is no need to eat when you are not hungry! Simply focus on hitting your protein goal when you do get hungry and eat, but otherwise let your body signal when to eat.

	Cream Cheese Almond Muffins	Spinach and Bacon Salad	Beef Tripe with Onions and Tomatoes	Peanut Butter and Chocolate Fat Bombs	
Day-4	calories: 321 fat: 30.5g protein: 4.1g carbs: 8.1g net carbs: 5.9g fiber: 2.2g	calories: 402 fat: 34.6g protein: 12.9g carbs: 11.1g net carbs: 7.4g fiber: 3.7g	calories: 341 fat: 26.9g protein: 21.9g carbs: 2.7g net carbs: 1.0g fiber: 1.7g	calories: 70 fat: 7.1g protein: 1.0g carbs: 1.9g net carbs: 1.9g fiber: 0g	Leap, and the net will appear.

Salting your food generously to avoid the keto flu.

The keto flu is temporary and avoidable. The short version is, make sure you get enough electrolytes (especially sodium, potassium and magnesium) to avoid the keto flu. Salting your food generously is one of the best things you can do here; some people even add sea salt to their water. Easing into it slowly can also help.

	Easy Peanut Butter Smoothie	Sardines with Zoodles	Bell Pepper Turkey Casserole	Caprese Sticks	
Day-5	calories: 486 fat: 40g protein: 30g carbs: 11g net carbs: 6g fiber: 5g	calories: 432 fat: 28.2g protein: 32.3g carbs: 7.1g net carbs: 5.4g fiber: 1.7g	calories: 465 fat: 28.5g protein: 45.4g carbs: 4.5g net carbs: 4.2g fiber: 0.3g	calories: 142 fat: 8.3g protein: 12.8g carbs: 3.2g net carbs: 2.2g fiber: 1.0g	Don't stop until you're proud.

Stay hydrated.

Drinking water is great for anyone, but especially if you are in ketosis. Eating carbs causes us to store more water in our bodies, while a keto diet flushes out more water, so it's even more crucial to drink enough. Aim for 16 cups per day.

	Zucchini and Carrot Coconut Bread	Almond and Rind Crusted Zucchini Fritters	Hazelnut Haddock Bake	Posset	
Day-6	calories: 176 fat: 10.6g protein: 11.5g carbs: 4.5g net carbs: 1.7g fiber: 2.8g	calories: 462 fat: 36.0g protein: 27.5g carbs: 7.6g net carbs: 4.8g fiber: 2.8g	calories: 786 fat: 56.9g protein: 64.9g carbs: 9.5g net carbs: 8.4g fiber: 1.1g	calories: 520 fat: 54.8g protein: 3.0g carbs: 6.0g net carbs: 6.0g fiber: 0g	You get what you focus on, so focus on what you want.

Make easy keto recipes for beginners.

Keto recipes are not 100% required to stick to a keto lifestyle, but they sure make it easier and more enjoyable! Once you have the basics down, introducing your old comfort food favorites in keto form, like keto bread or keto casseroles, can help you stick to it long term.

	Mushroom and Broccoli Quiche	Tuna Omelet Wraps	Pork Medallions	Strawberry Mousse	
Day-7	calories: 486 fat: 39.6g protein: 24.6g carbs: 7.1g net carbs: 6.2g fiber: 0.9g	calories: 480 fat: 37.8g protein: 26.8g carbs: 9.9g net carbs: 6.3g fiber: 3.6g	calories: 529 fat: 31.7g protein: 51.1g carbs: 6.2g net carbs: 3.7g fiber: 2.5g	calories: 160 fat: 15.9g protein: 0.9g carbs: 4.0g net carbs: 3.0g fiber: 1.0g	Never let your fear decide your future.

Use sweeteners responsibly.

Cutting out sugar isn't easy, but it's worth it! Weight loss is the motivator for many people looking for keto diet tips, but the improved energy, focus, mood, and other "NSV's" (non-scale victories) turn out to be a pleasant surprise for many people. And getting rid of those sugar cravings feels so good.

Week 3

Meal Plan	Breakfast	Lunch	Dinner	Snack/Dessert	Motivational Quotes
Day-1	**Egg and Ham Muffins** calories: 366 fat: 28.1g protein: 13.6g carbs: 1.3g net carbs: 1.0g fiber: 0.3g	**Zucchini and Beef Lasagna** calories: 346 fat: 17.9g protein: 40.2g carbs: 5.5g net carbs: 2.8g fiber: 2.7g	**Salmon Fillets with Broccoli** calories: 564 fat: 36.8g protein: 53.9g carbs: 8.3g net carbs: 5.9g fiber: 2.4g	**Super Coconut Cupcakes** calories: 164 fat: 16.8g protein: 2.2g carbs: 1.6g net carbs: 0.7g fiber: 0.9g	A little progress each day adds up to big results.

Get support.

Starting out on a new way of eating isn't easy, and you don't have to do it alone! Find support in keto forums and possibly within your family.

Meal Plan	Breakfast	Lunch	Dinner	Snack/Dessert	Motivational Quotes
Day-2	**Raspberry and Kale Smoothie** calories: 436 fat: 36g protein: 28g carbs: 11g net carbs: 6g fiber: 5g	**Mediterranean Tomato and Zucchini Salad** calories: 242 fat: 22.1g protein: 6.4g carbs: 6.9g net carbs: 5.1g fiber: 1.8g	**Creamy Pepper Loin Steaks** calories: 450 fat: 19.1g protein: 62.2g carbs: 6.0g net carbs: 4.9g fiber: 1.1g	**Bacon-Wrapped Poblano Poppers** calories: 184 fat: 14.1g protein: 8.9g carbs: 5.8g net carbs: 5.0g fiber: 0.8g	There's no such thing as failure: either you win, or you learn.

Plan your meals.

You can make your own plan, whether that's planning for the week ahead like I do or simply looking at the day ahead in the morning. If you use a tracking app, some people find it helpful to enter what you'll eat ahead of time so to help you plan better.

Meal Plan	Breakfast	Lunch	Dinner	Snack/Dessert	Motivational Quotes
Day-3	**Swiss Chard, Sausage, and Squash Omelet** calories: 557 fat: 51.6g protein: 32.2g carbs: 12.9g net carbs: 7.4g fiber: 5.5g	**Coconut Shrimp Stew** calories: 325 fat: 20.9g protein: 22.8g carbs: 6.2g net carbs: 5.1g fiber: 1.1g	**Chicken Drumsticks in Capocollo** calories: 486 fat: 33.7g protein: 39.1g carbs: 3.6g net carbs: 2.6g fiber: 1.0g	**Mocha Mousse** calories: 126 fat: 11.9g protein: 0g carbs: 3.1g net carbs: 2.0g fiber: 1.1g	Quit slacking and make shit happen.

Choose the keto lifestyle for you.

At the end of the day, these keto diet tips will help anyone wanting to jump start their keto journey, but it doesn't mean there's a one-size-fits-all solution. Different people do low carb in different ways, that's okay! There are many ways to do it. All of them have benefits and can be effective, so do what works best for you!

	Coconut and Seed Bagels	Beef and Veggie Stuffed Butternut Squash	Chive-Sauced Chili Cod	BLT Cups	
Day-4	calories: 425 fat: 19.0g protein: 33.2g carbs: 3.3g net carbs: 0.5g fiber: 2.8g	calories: 405 fat: 14.5g protein: 33.8g carbs: 20.7g net carbs: 12.3g fiber: 8.4g	calories: 450 fat: 35.2g protein: 20.1g carbs: 7.0g net carbs: 6.4g fiber: 0.6g	calories: 93 fat: 8.2g protein: 2.6g carbs: 1.5g net carbs: 1.1g fiber: 0.4g	When you feel like quitting, think about why you started.

Skip the exogenous ketones and one big thing you don't need in your pantry? Exogenous ketones, diet supplements, and processed products labeled "keto". Always read labels and check if the actual ingredients are keto friendly. While ketones are a controversial topic and some people have found that they help a little, they are absolutely not necessary to have success. Your body will produce ketones on its own if you restrict carbs enough.

	Tomato and Bacon Cups	Broccoli Cheddar Soup	Roasted Pork Shoulder	Anise Cookies	
Day-5	calories: 426 fat: 45.1g protein: 16.1g carbs: 5.5g net carbs: 4.2g fiber: 1.3g	calories: 395 fat: 33.1g protein: 16.9g carbs: 7.2g net carbs: 5.9g fiber: 1.3g	calories: 500 fat: 35.4g protein: 40.1g carbs: 2.6g net carbs: 2.1g fiber: 0.5g	calories: 143 fat: 12.9g protein: 3.6g carbs: 5.1g net carbs: 2.7g fiber: 2.4g	Keep going.

Apply a couple of these keto tips and tricks at a time.

Keto diet is a big shift of lifestyle and dieting habits, so give yourself ample time to adjust, test the water gradually, tip by tip and keto trick by trick, you will notice yourself making a big change in your life.

	Sausage Quiche	Beef and Broccoli Casserole	Cheddar Bacon Stuffed Chicken Fillets	Chicken and Spinach Meatballs	
Day-6	calories: 341 fat: 28.1g protein: 16.9g carbs: 6.2g net carbs: 2.9g fiber: 3.3g	calories: 435 fat: 21.1g protein: 50.9g carbs: 13.5g net carbs: 5.5g fiber: 8.0g	calories: 400 fat: 23.8g protein: 41.3g carbs: 3.6g net carbs: 2.4g fiber: 1.2g	calories: 210 fat: 12.4g protein: 19.4g carbs: 4.5g net carbs: 4.0g fiber: 0.5g	One pound at a time.

Cut out foods gradually.

Eliminate all sugars first, such as soda and candy, then complex carbs like bread and pasta, and starchy veggies and fruit last. Don't force yourself too much by plunge into the keto diet, be patient.

	Spinach-Cucumber Smoothie	Goat Cheese Eggplant Casserole	Russian Beef and Dill Pickle Gratin	Chocolate Lava Cake	
Day-7	calories: 353 fat: 32g protein: 15g carbs: 9g net carbs: 6g fiber: 3g	calories: 476 fat: 41.4g protein: 18.4g carbs: 7.2g net carbs: 3.6g fiber: 3.6g	calories: 585 fat: 48.1g protein: 40.9g carbs: 8.5g net carbs: 5.2g fiber: 3.3g	calories: 169 fat: 15.7g protein: 4.4g carbs: 6.0g net carbs: 3.4g fiber: 2.6g	If you know you can do better, then do better.

Listen to your body's signals and be patient.

If you finished your meal and are still hungry, try drinking some water, brushing your teeth, distracting yourself with something fun to do, or just waiting 20 minutes for your brain to catch up. If you're still hungry after that, try a salty, water-packed snack, like olives or pickles.

Week 4

Meal Plan	Breakfast	Lunch	Dinner	Snack/ Dessert	Motivational Quotes
Day-1	**Creamy Ricotta Almond Cloud Pancakes** calories: 406 fat: 30.5g protein: 11.4g carbs: 8.8g net carbs: 6.4g fiber: 2.4g	**Tilapia Tacos with Cabbage Slaw** calories: 261 fat: 20.1g protein: 13.9g carbs: 5.5g net carbs: 3.6g fiber: 1.9g	**Bacon and Beef Stew** calories: 591 fat: 36.1g protein: 63.1g carbs: 8.1g net carbs: 5.6g fiber: 2.5g	**Penuche Bars** calories: 180 fat: 18.4g protein: 1.7g carbs: 3.1g net carbs: 2.0g fiber: 1.1g	Eliminate the mindset of can't — because you can do anything.

Include coconut oil in your diet.

Eating coconut oil can help you get into ketosis. It contains fats called medium-chain triglycerides (MCTs). Unlike most fats, MCTs are rapidly absorbed and taken directly to the liver, where they can be used immediately for energy or converted into ketones.

Meal Plan	Breakfast	Lunch	Dinner	Snack/ Dessert	Motivational Quotes
Day-2	**Gruyere and Mushroom Lettuce Wraps** calories: 471 fat: 43.9g protein: 19.4g carbs: 6.5g net carbs: 5.3g fiber: 1.2g	**Lemony Prawn and Arugula Salad** calories: 215 fat: 20g protein: 8g carbs: 3g net carbs: 2g fiber: 1g	**Chicken, Pepper, and Tomato Bake** calories: 411 fat: 20.6g protein: 50.0g carbs: 6.2g net carbs: 4.7g fiber: 1.5g	**Hazelnut Pudding** calories: 342 fat: 33.1g protein: 6.5g carbs: 7.4g net carbs: 4.4g fiber: 3.0g	Keep an open mind and a closed refrigerator.

Ramp up your physical activity.

A growing number of studies have found that being in ketosis may be beneficial for some types of athletic performance, including endurance exercise, In addition, being more active can help you get into ketosis. When you exercise, you deplete your body of its glycogen stores.

Meal Plan	Breakfast	Lunch	Dinner	Snack/ Dessert	Motivational Quotes
Day-3	**Pesto Bacon and Avocado Mug Cakes** calories: 512 fat: 38.3g protein: 16.3g carbs: 10.3g net carbs: 4.4g fiber: 5.9g	**Greek Tilapia with Tomatoes and Olives** calories: 183 fat: 15.0g protein: 22.9g carbs: 7.9g net carbs: 6.2g fiber: 1.7g	**Lamb Shanks with Wild Mushrooms** calories: 474 fat: 35.9g protein: 30.9g carbs: 11.1g net carbs: 5.0g fiber: 6.1g	**Cream Cheese Stuffed Mushrooms** calories: 104 fat: 9.8g protein: 2.6g carbs: 2.0g net carbs: 1.5g fiber: 0.5g	The secret of change is to focus all of your energy not on fighting the old, but on building the new.

Increase your healthy fat intake.

Consuming plenty of healthy fat can boost your ketone levels and help you reach ketosis.

Indeed, a very low-carb ketogenic diet not only minimizes carbs, but is also high in fat.

Ketogenic diets for weight loss, metabolic health and exercise performance usually provide between 60–80% of calories from fat.

Meal Plan	Breakfast	Lunch	Dinner	Snack/ Dessert	Motivational Quotes
Day-4	**Vanilla Mascarpone Cups** calories: 182 fat: 13.6g protein: 10.4g carbs: 3.8g net carbs: 3.6g fiber: 0.2g	**Italian Sausage and Okra Stew** calories: 315 fat: 25.1g protein: 16.1g carbs: 16.8g net carbs: 6.9g fiber: 8.9g	**Pork Ragout** calories: 390 fat: 24.2g protein: 33.0g carbs: 5.3g net carbs: 4.1g fiber: 1.2g	**Peanut and Chocolate Balls** calories: 330 fat: 32.5g protein: 6.8g carbs: 7.5g net carbs: 4.9g fiber: 2.6g	Success is no accident: it is hard work and perseverance.

Try a short fast or a fat fast.

"Fat fasting" is another ketone-boosting approach that mimics the effects of fasting.

It involves consuming about 1,000 calories per day, 85–90% of which come from fat. This combination of low calorie and very high fat intake may help you achieve ketosis quickly.

Maintain Adequate Protein Intake Achieving ketosis requires a protein intake that is adequate but not excessive.

Day-5	Triple Cheese and Bacon Zucchini Balls	Beef and Mushroom Soup	Pistachio Nut Salmon with Shallot Sauce	Wrapped Asparagus with Prosciutto	It has to be hard so you'll never ever forget.
	calories: 406 fat: 26.7g protein: 33.3g carbs: 8.6g net carbs: 5.7g fiber: 2.9g	calories: 316 fat: 18.9g protein: 30.1g carbs: 5.0g net carbs: 4.0g fiber: 1.0g	calories: 564 fat: 47.0g protein: 34.0g carbs: 8.1g net carbs: 6.0g fiber: 2.1g	calories: 120 fat: 6.5g protein: 10.1g carbs: 6.2g net carbs: 3.2g fiber: 3.0g	

Test ketone levels and adjust your diet as needed.

Like many things in nutrition, achieving and maintaining a state of ketosis is highly individualized. Therefore, it can be helpful to test your ketone levels to ensure you're achieving your goals.

Day-6	Avocado Smoothie with Mixed Berries	Chinese Flavor Chicken Legs	Balsamic Glazed Meatloaf	Almond Fudge Bars	Food can be both enjoyable and nourishing.
	calories: 336 fat: 25g protein: 8g carbs: 18g net carbs: 12g fiber: 6g	calories: 366 fat: 14.6g protein: 51.1g carbs: 3.4g net carbs: 2.4g fiber: 1.0g	calories: 375 fat: 25g protein: 23g carbs: 13g net carbs: 12g fiber: 1g	calories: 80 fat: 6.9g protein: 0.6g carbs: 4.6g net carbs: 3.5g fiber: 1.1g	

Whatever you do, don't beat yourself up!

I am human. I had a moment of failure. And I will probably fail again. That's okay. What's important is that I keep on trying. In the immortal words of Taylor Swift, shake it off!

Day-7	Mozzarella and Chorizo Omelet	Duo-Cheese Broccoli Croquettes	Pork Cutlets with Juniper Berries	Caribbean Baked Wings	Start where you are. Use what you have. Do what you can.
	calories: 452 fat: 36.4g protein: 30.1g carbs: 5.4g net carbs: 2.9g fiber: 2.5g	calories: 324 fat: 24.1g protein: 19.9g carbs: 5.8g net carbs: 3.5g fiber: 2.3g	calories: 370 fat: 20.5g protein: 40.2g carbs: 1.2g net carbs: 1.0g fiber: 0.2g	calories: 287 fat: 18.6g protein: 15.5g carbs: 5.1g net carbs: 3.3g fiber: 1.8g	

Don't excuse your behaviour. Own it.

we all fail sometimes, and we do. But that doesn't mean you shouldn't hold yourself accountable. It isn't someone else's fault that you scarfed down that pizza or dove head first into a plate of Oreos. Be an adult and recognize that you did this to yourself and the consequences suck. And then ask yourself why.

Chapter 1 Keto Crash Course

While most fad diets focus vaguely on "eating clean," or hitting a calorie deficit, the ketogenic diet focuses on enacting a particular biological shift in the body. By removing the body's default energy source, the carbohydrate, and replacing it with fats, the ketogenic diet eventually shifts the body into a metabolic state called ketosis. That's the wonderful thing about this approach. A person in ketosis begins to burn fat for energy rather than carbohydrates. The keto diet trains the human body to eliminate stores of fat, whereas a normal human diet, high in carbohydrates, requires us to burn through our carbs before we can even begin to burn fat and lose weight.

It takes approximately four days of eating less than 50 grams of carbohydrates per day, plus eating lots of saturated and unsaturated fats, to enter a state of ketosis. At that point, the body experiences a drastic decrease in blood sugar and insulin levels. It also begins to transform fat into ketones in the liver, and these ketones are terrific for supporting neurological health. The ketogenic diet is medically recommended to diabetic and prediabetic patients and has been linked to a reduction in heart disease and epileptic seizures. Ketosis is also a fairly speedy way to begin dropping excess fat from the body, making it all the more attractive to weight-loss dieters.

Anyone interested in beginning their journey toward achieving and maintaining ketosis likely has lots of questions after discovering this strategic nutritional approach, most of which revolve around the dos and don'ts of eating. The table below gives you an at-a-glance idea of the basic structure of the keto diet:

A New Energy Source

When you deprive your body of energy from carbohydrates, it's forced to turn back to what was stored. It only does this when that deprivation is there, however. Even if you're eating a limited amount of carbohydrates daily, your body is still going to use that up first and then it will turn to what was stored.

A keto diet aims to eliminate what was stored by depriving the body of carbohydrates.

When there aren't any carbohydrates to use, there isn't glucose in your body to break down. It's here that you enter ketosis. This is done by converting fat into ketones, which become the body's new source of energy.

Keto is the term used to describe ketogenic diets. At first it might appear you have to completely give up eating since there are carbs in many foods. However, the aim of a keto diet is to provide nutritious, low-carb food that still provides protein and fat for energy. Adding healthy fats and proteins aids in your body's process of energy building, which is why it's important to choose food that has multiple benefits. If your body has no stored fat to go to, it can turn towards muscles and even organs, so healthy fats and proteins assist in protecting these important parts of your body.

While eating nothing but cream cheese and bacon sounds appealing at first, it's not the only source of fat and protein to follow. Don't fret! That's the point of this cookbook—so you don't have to fear trying a new diet.

Keto Diet Rules

To be clear, a person on the keto diet need not completely eradicate carbohydrates from their diet—only decrease them to such a small degree that they do not disrupt the process of ketosis. A good rule of thumb for dividing your macronutrients as a ketogenic eater is to consume 75% fats, 20% protein, and 5% carbohydrates. Remember, carbs are in lots of different food items that we don't generally think of as carby, so reaching that 5% figure will likely be satisfied without excessive effort. Below, I've

KETO FOODS TO ENJOY

HIGH FAT / LOW CARB (BASED ON NET CARBS)

MEATS & SEAFOOD
- Beef (ground beef, steak, etc.)
- Chicken
- Crab
- Crawfish
- Duck
- Fish
- Goose
- Lamb
- Lobster
- Mussels
- Octopus
- Pork (pork chops, bacon, etc.)
- Quail
- Sausage (without fillers)
- Scallops
- Shrimp
- Veal
- Venison

DAIRY
- Blue cheese dressing
- Burrata cheese
- Cottage cheese
- Cream cheese
- Eggs
- Greek yogurt (full-fat)
- Grilling cheese
- Halloumi cheese
- Heavy (whipping) cream
- Homemade whipped cream
- Kefalotyri cheese
- Mozzarella cheese
- Provolone cheese
- Queso blanco
- Ranch dressing
- Ricotta cheese
- Unsweetened almond milk
- Unsweetened coconut milk

VEGETABLES
- Alfalfa sprouts
- Asparagus
- Avocados
- Bell peppers
- Broccoli
- Cabbage
- Carrots (in moderation)
- Cauliflower
- Celery
- Chicory
- Coconut
- Cucumbers
- Garlic (in moderation)
- Green beans
- Herbs
- Jicama
- Lemons
- Limes
- Mushrooms
- Okra
- Olives
- Onions (in moderation)
- Pickles
- Pumpkin
- Radishes
- Salad greens
- Scallions
- Spaghetti squash (in moderation)
- Tomatoes (in moderation)
- Zucchini

NUTS & SEEDS
- Almonds
- Brazil nuts
- Chia seeds
- Flaxseeds
- Hazelnuts
- Macadamia nuts
- Peanuts (in moderation)
- Pecans
- Pine nuts
- Pumpkin seeds
- Sacha inchi seeds
- Sesame seeds
- Walnuts

FRUITS
- Blackberries
- Blueberries
- Cranberries
- Raspberries
- Strawberries

KETO FOODS TO AVOID

LOW FAT / HIGH CARB (BASED ON NET CARBS)

MEATS & MEAT ALTERNATIVES
- Deli meat (some, not all)
- Hot dogs (with fillers)
- Sausage (with fillers)
- Seitan
- Tofu

DAIRY
- Almond milk (sweetened)
- Coconut milk (sweetened)
- Milk
- Soy milk (regular)
- Yogurt (regular)

NUTS & SEEDS
- Cashews
- Chestnuts
- Pistachios

VEGETABLES
- Artichokes
- Beans (all varieties)
- Burdock root
- Butternut squash
- Chickpeas
- Corn
- Edamame
- Eggplant
- Leeks
- Parsnips
- Plantains
- Potatoes
- Sweet potatoes
- Taro root
- Turnips
- Winter squash
- Yams

FRUITS &
- Apples
- Apricots
- Bananas
- Boysenberries
- Cantaloupe
- Cherries
- Currants
- Dates
- Elderberries
- Gooseberries
- Grapes
- Honeydew melon
- Huckleberries
- Kiwifruits
- Mangos
- Oranges
- Peaches
- Peas
- Pineapples
- Plums
- Prunes
- Raisins
- Water chestnuts

KETO COOKING STAPLES
1. Pink Himalayan salt
2. Freshly ground black pepper
3. Ghee (clarified butter, without dairy; buy grass-fed if you can)
4. Olive oil
5. Grass-fed butter

KETO PERISHABLES
1. Eggs (pasture-raised, if you can)
2. Avocados
3. Bacon (uncured)
4. Cream cheese (full-fat; or use a dairy-free alternative)
5. Sour cream (full-fat; or use a dairy-free alternative)
6. Heavy whipping cream or coconut milk (full-fat; I buy the coconut milk in a can)
7. Garlic (fresh or pre-minced in a jar)
8. Cauliflower
9. Meat (grass-fed, if you can)
10. Greens (spinach, kale, or arugula)

*Vegetables grown above ground (i.e., cucumber, peppers, celery, avocado, tomato, etc.) are generally low in starch and keto-safe, but root vegetables (i.e., carrots, beets, radishes, potatoes) tend to be high in carbohydrates.

Now you know what ketosis is, how to achieve it, and how to stock your kitchen to make it a true lifestyle. Lastly, I want to equip you with the supplementary tool of intermittent fasting. Intermittent fasting is simply the practice of going without food for anywhere between sixteen and twenty-four hours for three-five days out of the week. Intermittent fasting, or IF, works really well with ketosis because the body is already trained to use its stores of fat as fuel for moving us throughout our days.

Think about it: the human body stores fat. You may well be all too uncomfortably familiar with the locations of those fat storages on your own body! This allows the body in ketosis to fast for longer periods without suffering from unpleasant consequences such as grogginess, fatigue, irritability, and headaches, all of which are signs of low blood sugar, by the way. That's because the body, when burning calories, the traditional way, relies on external energy sources to maintain daily operations. The body in ketosis needs fuel as well, but it has a much larger reservoir to draw from when no fuel is being provided.

If you've ever sat down to a meal high in fats, such as a breakfast laden with fried eggs and sausages, you've likely experienced that full feeling that lasts for hours. On the ketogenic diet, that feeling comes after every single meal. With consistently even blood sugar levels, low insulin, and lots of ketones in the body, you simply won't feel the need to eat as often, and intermittent fasting will feel natural.

There's one catch, however: if you're planning on keeping yourself in a large calorie deficit while in ketosis, fasting may not be for you. The entire premise of IF is to eat freely without restricting calories during eating periods so that fasting periods are sustainable and beneficial. Being in a state of calorie deficit is not necessarily a bad thing, but can become dangerous when paired with a regular IF schedule. Think of calorie deficits and intermittent fasting as an either/or situation rather than a both/and.

Before beginning a practice of intermittent fasting, you'll also need to recognize yourself as the ultimate authority on your own body. Every person is different, and no one knows your system like you do. That means that you should never be fasting on principle while simultaneously enduring warning signals from your body. Even if you're doing everything right, your body may begin to demand fuel. In that case, go ahead and eat! No pressure. As with any diet, be sensible. The whole point is to make you healthier, not to harm you. Please also be mindful of any warning signs in your thought patterns and emotions while fasting. If you begin to exhibit signs of disordered eating such as binging, purging, extreme restricting, or even revolving your life and thoughts around food and meals in general, consider letting go of your fasting regimen and eating without restriction for a while. This should help to cleanse the mind of any harmful or obsessive thoughts, and, when you feel that you have a strong footing again, you can consider returning to the practice mindfully and perhaps with the help of a nutrition professional.

The FDA recommends a daily caloric intake between 2,000 and 2,500 for adults.

Keto Diet Pyramid

So, when you apply Keto diet principles into your food selection, you will find there is a hierarchy among different foods.

There are foods that are the epitome of Keto diet, which contain high and healthy fat, and/or low carbs. And there are foods that should be consumed with careful calculation, and you may also need to put some foods into the no-fly zone.

Keto Food Pyramid

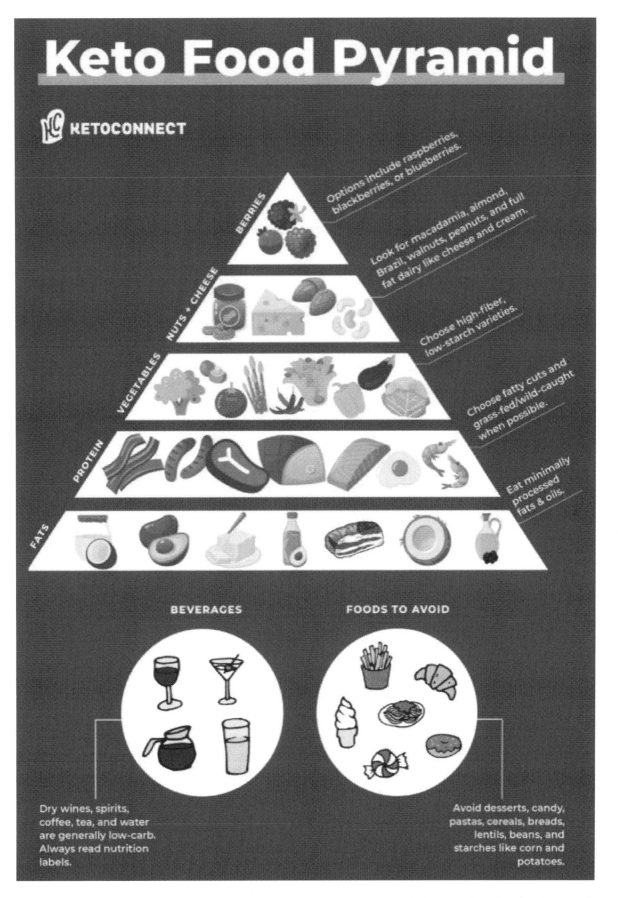

KETOCONNECT

BERRIES — Options include raspberries, blackberries, or blueberries.

NUTS + CHEESE — Look for macadamia, almond, Brazil, walnuts, peanuts, and full fat dairy like cheese and cream.

VEGETABLES — Choose high-fiber, low-starch varieties.

PROTEIN — Choose fatty cuts and grass-fed/wild-caught when possible.

FATS — Eat minimally processed fats & oils.

BEVERAGES

Dry wines, spirits, coffee, tea, and water are generally low-carb. Always read nutrition labels.

FOODS TO AVOID

Avoid desserts, candy, pastas, cereals, breads, lentils, beans, and starches like corn and potatoes.

Understanding What Ketones and Ketosis is

The Ketogenic diet supports the body in losing weight by creating a metabolic state known as ketosis. During ketosis, the body begins to convert its fat stores into much-needed energy: when this happens ketones are released.

Under normal circumstances, the body will use sugar as its primary source of energy. Our bodies break down the glucose into simple sugars and use it for energy, storing the excess in the liver for later use. When there is not enough sugar in the body (obtained from eating carbs) the body will look to alternatives and begin to burn fat. To help the body along the liver turns the fat into ketones (acid) and pumps them into your bloodstream to allow your tissues and muscles to utilize them.

As the keto diet restricts the number of carbohydrates you consume to 1.7 to 1.8 ounces per day your body gradually begins to run out of energy. This process takes three to four days. After which you begin to breakdown the fat and proteins in the body which enables those to lose weight.

How the Keto Diet Affects Hormones

The ketones in your body affect the cholecystokinin, the hormone which is responsible for allowing you to feel full. They also impact the hunger hormone, ghrelin.

Cholecystokinin is responsible for regulating the amount of food we eat. The ketones in the body increase the levels of this hormone allowing us to feel satisfied after meals. The hormone may even help those to cut meals while eating.

Ghrelin encourages us to eat and this hormone is released within the stomach. When the stomach is satisfied with food, the level of ghrelin in the body drops again. When you are in ketosis this hormone is suppressed, therefore leaving you less inclined to go searching for your next meal.

Apart from the impact that the keto diet has on hormones that affect appetite, it can support those who struggle with hormonal imbalances. A keto diet is rich in good fats that support hormonal balance and help with the production of hormones. The reason for this is that they are the basis of testosterone, progesterone, and estrogen, all of which begin to dramatically change with age.

Keto also manages the production of cortisol, the stress hormone. If the stressors in our life are not managed correctly, the body is inclined to keep churning out cortisol. The influx of cortisol in the body robs it of progesterone, testosterone, and estrogen. If this is the case you are at risk of experience imbalances related to low sex drive, high blood sugar levels, burnout, and loss of muscle. Foods such as dark, leafy greens, and a selection of berries that the keto diet includes, can help normalize the levels of cortisol in the body.

The diet may not be ideal for all but it has shown significant results for those who struggle with hormone imbalances and symptoms that come with aging.

Keto and the Role It Has on Insulin and Blood Sugar Levels

Because of the limited intake of carbohydrates while on the keto diet, blood sugar levels are less inclined to spike: this allows the levels of blood sugar to stabilize, which may support those who suffer from Type 2 diabetes.

Keto may even help reduce the blood sugar levels to such a point where medication may be reviewed (Felman as cited by Medical News Today, 2019).

How to Prepare for Your Keto Lifestyle

Starting a new diet or lifestyle can be challenging. However, the keto diet is one of the easiest to implement. With that being said, there are a few steps to take beforehand to maximize success.

The first step is to mentally prepare for the changes coming. It's important to psychologically prepare and visualize the journey ahead. For many, writing down goals and aspirations proves helpful. Avoiding foods or unhealthy habits you once enjoyed will be even more difficult if the end goals are not clear. During this step, write down all of the reasons a change is necessary. After reading about the benefits, be sure to include which apply most and are the most intriguing. If the main goal is to lose weight, right down all the reasons that's desired and how you will feel once that goal is achieved.

Once a list has been prepared, put it in a safe place to reference when times get hard. It's also recommended to keep a weekly log. Not only will it be easier to make adjustments for quicker results, but your progress can be tracked. Seeing the positive changes from week to week is encouraging! Not all changes will be physical, so a short entry detailing other positive changes is necessary. Staying in tune with goals weekly and monitoring the positive changes will help you to keep going!

Related to the above, before you start keto, it is also recommended to go for a check-up with your health care provider and run some common blood work for cholesterol, creatinine, a complete blood count, your fasting blood glucose, and hemoglobin A1c (Bourdua-Roy, et al., n.d.). These results are important as low-carb diets can have adverse indications and these can only be seen when you visit the lab and get the results. Ideally, get your bloods tested every 3 months.

The second step is to consider telling a close friend or partner all the goals you wish to achieve. An accountability partner may be helpful but isn't necessary if you feel uncomfortable. Talking with an accountability partner or someone in a similar situation can increase motivation. Sharing frustrations or goals is healthy for mental health and creates a release that subdues stress.

Lifestyle changes aren't always easy and sharing wins and defeats can make the journey easier. If you're comfortable sharing your lifestyle change, it may be easier in social settings to stick to the keto guidelines and avoid temptations. However, not all situations will prompt questions from others, and most of the time, many won't notice the skipped treat or breadstick. If you prefer to keep your changes private, step one will be of extra benefit.

The third step to take before starting the keto diet is to clean out the pantry or do some rearranging. If you're living with others, it might not be possible to get rid of treats or temptations. In that situation, consider keeping your food in a special location where other people's food isn't visible. For example, your own personal pantry can be created and does not have to be in a traditional "pantry" location. In the refrigerator, keep your food organized and in one location. This will help prevent the urge to cheat or binge. The keto diet is safe and healthy for most and it's possible for the entire household/family to participate. For example, chips, bread, treats, and more can still be enjoyed with some modifications. Replace unhealthy foods with keto approved foods. If you're living alone or making the lifestyle change with your partner, donate the unhealthy foods and get them out of sight! If you're able, control what foods are in the house so less temptations are possible.

By taking these three steps, your chances of a successful keto diet will increase. Staying focused and persistent will yield results! Don't forget to track your progress and make adjustments as necessary. Stick to the keto guidelines put forth in this eBook and be sure to reward success in a healthy way!

Chapter 2 Ketosis, Keto Flu, and Exercise

When starting the keto diet, there's a few things to be aware of. This chapter will outline what to expect in the early stages and explain how to avoid unwanted symptoms in the starting weeks. The importance of ketosis will be explained, and tips for troubleshooting are outlined. Exercising on keto is important, but not all forms are suitable. This chapter will go through the best exercises for success and introduce fasting, a technique that archives results faster!

What is Ketosis and Why Does It Matter?

Ketosis is the metabolic process that occurs when fat is used as the main fuel source. Normally, the human body relies on carbs, sugar, or starchy foods to produce glucose for energy. By eliminating carbs, the body is forced to find a new source. The focus then turns to fats that are obtained through eating and even the fat stores within the body. When fat is relied upon, a process occurs within the liver that converts fat into ketones, usable energy. Fat itself cannot be used and must be converted into ketones. Ketones are a form of acid that supply energy and then leave the body through urinating. The presence of ketones signal that the body is breaking down fat and no longer primarily relying on glucose. When enough ketones are present, the body is said to be in a state of ketosis, which is a completely natural metabolic state and is safe in most cases. If you have a pre-existing medical condition, it's important to consult with a physician before starting the keto diet.

Achieving ketosis is different for everyone and relies on many factors, some unexplainable. Ketosis is easier for some to achieve than others. For those who ate a high carb diet before starting keto, the process may take longer than someone eating a generally low-to-moderate carb diet. In general, it takes about 2 to 4 days if the individual is eating 20 to 50 grams of carbs per day (Raman, 2019). For some following the same carb guidelines, it can take up to a week or longer.

Determining ketosis can be done using a number of methods. The keto flu is one way to know a change is occurring. This flu is discussed later in this chapter but triggers a variety of symptoms that can mean the body is transitioning into ketosis. However, the most effective way to measure ketones and determine ketosis is through a test.

There are three types of ketones, which are known as acetoacetate, acetone, and beta-hydroxybutyrate. These ketones can be present and measured through urine, breath, or blood. Ketone strips are available for purchase and measure acetoacetate levels through a urine sample. This test can be done in the comfort of your home. The strip will turn various shades of purple or pink and gage the amount of ketones leaving the body. Depending on the color, ketosis can be determined. Darker colors usually indicate higher levels of ketones, but the directions on the testing strips will explain. Testing trips are an affordable and easy way to know if the body is in ketosis.

Other testing devices include ketone breath meters or a blood ketone meter, which are said to be more accurate. Acetone and beta-hydroxybutyrate are the ketones specifically measured in those tests. The directions on either test will explain the indicators to look for to determine if the body is in ketosis or not. Test kits are usually available in most health shops or pharmacies. Asking a pharmacist in your local drug store may also prove helpful.

If ketosis is not being achieved, there are adjustments that can be made. In some cases, keto supplements may be necessary to help you enter ketosis. This option should be discussed with a physician or medical first. Stress may also hinder ketosis so it's important to stick to a routine and get adequate rest. Meditation, yoga, and breathing exercises can also help to manage stress. For others not battling stress, the first place to start is a food journal. Tracking proteins, fats, and carb intake at first is imperative to achieving ketosis. Because everybody is different, small adjustments may need to be made at the macro level. If macros are not being tracked, it's hard to see what's not working. Start lowering carb intake and increasing fat or protein consumption to see if ketones increase. A common mistake participants make is not consuming enough fat or calories in the beginning stages. Too much protein can also hinder ketosis in some. It's best to start or work towards the standard macros of 75% fats, 20% protein, and only 5% carbs and adjust as necessary.

Keto Flu and What to Do

When starting the keto diet, participants are undergoing internal changes in the first few weeks. The body is learning and is forced to use fat as fuel, instead of carbs. The transition sometimes leads to undesirable side effects. The keto flu is the result of switching fuel sources and adjusting to a new lifestyle. The symptoms of keto flu are fatigue, headaches, irritability, brain fog, dizziness, cravings, nausea, and muscle cramps. Some experience all symptoms, some experience a few, and some report not feeling any. However, most people report feeling one or many of these symptoms during the first three to five days. Some symptoms may last up to two weeks.

While you should be aware of the keto flu and what it entails, it's not something to fear. While the body adapts, there are things that can be done to ease the symptoms. Keto flu cannot be completely avoided by all, but it can certainly be managed. The number one tip is to increase salt and water intake. Salt and water are responsible for most keto issues, as the body becomes dehydrated. Frequent urination takes place during the first stages of keto because the body has a hard time storing water. During the first few weeks of keto, if a headache, lethargy, nausea, dizziness, or other symptoms start to come on, immediately drink a glass of water with half a teaspoon of salt stirred in. This trick should help alleviate symptoms within 15 to 30 minutes for most. Sipping on bone broth, consommé, bouillon, chicken stock, or beef stock can also do the trick. Be sure to consume as much liquid as possible during the first stages of keto to avoid symptoms.

When first starting keto, be sure to take it easy on exercise. Avoid putting additional stress on the body and hold off on new workout routines. While light exercise can ease keto flu symptoms and allow it to pass faster, higher intensity workouts should be avoided. Light walks, swimming, biking, and yoga are activities suitable for the beginning stages. It's important to get a good night's sleep and feel as rested as possible while the body adjusts to burning fat.

By being mindful and taking a few additional steps, keto flu can be avoided or managed. If symptoms persist, allow a few more days to see if the body regulates. The keto flu will pass and it's important to stay focused (and not give up) during this time!

Exercise and Fasting on Keto

In the beginning stages of the keto diet, it's understandable that exercising may be different or more challenging. When the body is going through changes and switching energy sources, some workouts may be challenging. It's not advised to skip physical activity altogether, but do know that exercise will come easier after the body has regulated.

According to an article by Rachael Link (2020), a registered dietician and journalist for Healthline, the keto diet has the ability to enhance athletic performance. Link explains that in terms of endurance, the keto diet has proven beneficial. The metabolic state of ketosis improves the body's ability to use fat for energy and sustain the body longer during physical activity. Examples of endurance activities include body weight squats, lunges, push-ups, sit-ups, and planks. Aerobic exercises such as walking, jogging, swimming, biking, and yoga are also suitable activities.

Physical activity or exercise on the keto diet will boost fat burning, according to Link. This means results are visible faster, but it will also lead to better body composition. Muscle tone and definition are easier achieved by implementing exercise and healthy eating. Luckily, the keto diet has shown to speed up muscle recovery leading to less soreness and inflammation.

All exercise falls into two categories: aerobic and anaerobic. The exercises mentioned before are aerobic exercises, which means "with air." During those types of exercises, the body produces energy by using oxygen. With anaerobic, the body produces energy without oxygen and the word translates to "without air." Carbs are the main source of energy for high intensity activities. Therefore, large amounts of anaerobic activity aren't suggested while on the keto diet without supervision. Examples of anaerobic activities include high intensity training such as sprinting, boxing, jumping rope, or HIIT classes.

In terms of fasting, the most popular way to fast in the keto diet is through intermittent fasting. While there are many different types of fasting methods, intermittent fasting is by far the most popular. Intermittent fasting (IF) is not associated with the keto diet and is effective in its own way; however, combined with keto can increase the number of benefits you reap as you reap IF benefits as well as those from following keto. This type of fasting is the technique of eating within a restricted time frame and refraining from food or drink during the other time frame. Water is always allowed throughout the entire fast, and other herbal drinks are allowed in most cases. Coffee is also allowed. However, all of these beverages must be consumed plain, without sweetener, milk, honey, etc.

Intermittent fasting can be done in different ways. While some will fast only five days out of the week, some will implement intermittent fasting only occasionally. The 16/8 method is used by most and creates an eight-hour eating window within 24 hours. The eight-hour eating window can be at any time. Some wish to abstain from food in the morning and eat for a longer period into the night. Others prefer to start eating early in the day and cut off eating at a certain point in the late afternoon. The eight-hour eating window should be decided on preference and doesn't make a huge difference. In the beginning stages, abstaining from food for 16 hours may be too challenging and adjustments can be made at first. It's important to note that sleeping counts during the 16-hour refraining period and should be used as an advantage. Although eating is done during a certain time frame, a caloric deficit does not occur. This means that the same number of calories must be consumed and eating less calories is not a part of intermittent fasting or keto.

According to Jillian Kubala (2018), a registered dietitian and nutritionist, there are many benefits to implementing intermittent fasting and the Keto diet at the same time, and you can implement it into your weekly or monthly routine. Kubala explains that intermittent fasting may help to reach ketosis quicker because fasting encourages the body to use fat as fuel, just like the keto diet. The two working together help regulate insulin and glycogen stores. Combining intermittent fasting and the keto diet may also lead to more fat burn than the keto diet alone. Intermittent fasting boosts metabolism and encourages the body to go deeper into the fat store for energy. In fact, an eight-week study found that men who practiced the 16/8 method lost nearly 14% more body fat than those following a normal eating pattern (Moro et al., 2016). Other benefits of intermittent fasting include the regulation of hormones, better cellular repair, and gene expression.

Chapter 3 Eating and Maintaining a Keto Diet

Research has indicated that lowering your carbohydrate intake and upping the intake of healthy fats can be effective in supporting patients with epilepsy, those looking to lose weight and diabetics (Spritzler as cited by Healthline, 2017).

On the keto diet, carbohydrates are limited to between 0.7 and 1.7 ounces per day. This may seem difficult to accomplish, but it is doable and you will easily be able to include a variety of nutrient-rich foods into your diet daily that meet the diet requirements.

Foods to Enjoy

There is a varied range of foods that you can enjoy while on a keto diet. Meat is an easy keto-friendly option, as it is naturally low in carbohydrates. Stay away from processed meats and opt for grass-fed whenever you gain. Seafood is also healthy for you; you may want to consider eating smaller fish varieties such as mackerel, herring, and sardines.

Eggs, butter, and heavy cream are also allowed. Be sure to pay attention to the amount of milk you drink as one glass contains 0.5 ounces of carbohydrates. You can flavor your food with fresh herbs and an assortment of high-fat oils, such as olive and coconut.

Whether fresh or frozen, berry fruits and leafy green vegetables can be included in your diet. Always opt for vegetables grown above ground.

Meats and Seafood

- Seafood (3.5 ounces = 20.28 g protein, 2 g fat, and 0 g carbohydrates)
- Beef (3.5 ounces = 20.52 g protein, 5.71 fat, and 0 g carbohydrates)
- Chicken (3.5 ounces = 20.33 g protein, 2.7 g fat, and 0 g carbohydrates)
- Pork (3.5 ounces = 25.61 g protein, 11.06 g fat, and 0 g carbohydrates)
- Game (3.5 ounces = 22.95 g protein, 1.45 g fat, and 0 g carbohydrates)

Dairy

- Butter
- Eggs
- Heavy cream
- Soft cheeses (camembert, brie, gouda, and colby)
- Hard cheeses (parmesan, mozzarella, cheddar, and Swiss cheese)

Nuts and Seeds

Nuts can be consumed as long as it is in moderation. It is easy to overeat nuts, so be mindful when snacking on them. Consider sprinkling them over salads and roast vegetables to add texture, rather than feasting on a bowl of them. Choose pecan or macadamia nuts if you are looking for a light snack.

1.7 ounces of nuts contain 21.15 g protein, 49.93 g fat, and 21.55 g carbohydrates.

- Almonds
- Brazil nuts
- Macadamia nuts
- Walnuts
- Pecans
- Pumpkin seeds
- Chia seeds
- Flaxseeds
- Hemp seeds

Fruits and Vegetables

The average nutritional count per 3.5 ounces of these foods is 2 g protein, 14.66 g fat, and 8.53 g carbohydrates. As mentioned, always opt for dark, leafy green vegetables and those that grow above the ground.

- Lettuce
- Greens
- Avocado
- Eggplant
- Mushroom
- Tomato
- Broccoli
- Cauliflower
- Zucchini
- Cucumber
- Berry fruits

Foods to Avoid

Foods that are processed and laden with starch and sugar are generally bad for you and should be avoided when on the ketogenic diet. All these foods carry high amounts of carbohydrates and may affect the outcome of the diet.

Meats and Seafood

- Bacon
- Processed meats
- Glazed meats
- Breaded meats

Dairy

- Condensed milk
- Margarine
- Fat-free or low-fat yogurt
- Creamed cottage cheese

Nuts and Seeds

- Almonds
- Hazelnuts
- Pistachios
- Cashews
- Pine nuts
- Peanuts

Fruits and Vegetables

- Sweet potato
- Potato
- Carrots
- Beetroot
- Pumpkin
- Parsnips
- Celeriac
- Citrus fruits (oranges, nectarines, tangerines)
- Banana
- Pineapple
- Apple
- Mango
- Peaches
- Grapes
- Pear
- Beans and lentils

Other

- Sugar
- Cakes, bakes, pastries
- Sodas
- Sports drinks
- Fruit juices
- Breakfast cereals
- Ice cream
- Beer
- Wine
- Bread
- Rice
- Pasta

There are quite a few common non-keto foods that you might like to think are safe, but they are not. These include: popcorn, beets, dried fruits, sweet potatoes, cantaloupe melon, squash, oranges, quinoa, grapes, peaches, rice, watermelon, plums, pineapple, peanuts, cranberries, mangoes, green peas, chickpeas/humous, dried or cooked beans (pinto/ borlotti/kidney etc.)

Pantry Essentials

It is time to restock your kitchen cupboards and pantry with the following items. All of these ingredients form the basis of many delicious and tasty keto meals.

Vegetables	Fruits	Oils	Protein	Non-Perishables
Leafy greens	Blackberries	Olive oil	Chicken	Canned coconut milk
Cauliflower	Raspberries	Coconut oil	Lamb	Full-cream ranch dressing
Broccoli	Strawberries	MCT oil	Beef	Jerky
Asparagus	Blueberries	Dairy	Pork	Bone broth
Bell peppers	Olives	Eggs	Seafood	Peanut butter
Mushrooms	Avocado	Butter	Chia seeds	Pork rinds
Zucchini	Tomatoes	Heavy whipping cream	Flaxseeds	Monk fruit sweetener
Brussel sprouts	Lemon	Hard and soft cheese	Walnuts	Almond flour
Eggplants	Limes	Yogurt	Pecans	Cocoa powder

Zero Carb Drinks

Probably the greatest sacrifice you will have to make while on a ketogenic diet, is to give on sugar in your favourite drinks. The good news is that the following alcohols have zero carbs!

- Gin
- Rum
- Vodka
- Whiskey
- Martini
- Tequila

You should stick to these healthier drinks though.

- Water
- Unsweetened Tea
- Unsweetened Coffee
- Club Soda
- Diet Soda (be cautious, as artificial sweeteners can affect low carb weight loss)
- Sugar Free Sparkling Water
- Herbal Tea

Keto Food Swaps

- Cauliflower rice instead of regular rice
- Zucchini chips instead of potato chips
- Almond flour instead of breadcrumbs
- Avocado halves or large field mushrooms instead of 'burger buns
- Zucchini "noodles" instead of regular noodles
- Mashed broccoli instead of mashed potato
- Turnip fries instead of potato fries

Best Keto Sweeteners (and three to avoid)

1. Stevia

Stevia is a natural sweetener derived from the Stevia rebaudiana plant. It contains little to no calories or carbs. Stevia is available in both liquid and powdered form and can be used to sweeten everything from drinks to desserts. Because it's much sweeter than regular sugar, recipes require less stevia to achieve the same flavour. For each cup (200 grams) of sugar, substitute only 1 teaspoon (4 grams) of powdered stevia.

2. Sucralose

Sucralose is an artificial sweetener that is not metabolized, meaning it passes through your body undigested and thus doesn't provide calories or carbs. Splenda is the most common sucralose-based sweetener on the market and popular because it lacks the bitter taste found in many other artificial sweeteners.

While sucralose itself is calorie-free, Splenda contains maltodextrin and dextrose, two carbs that supply about 3 calories and 1 gram of carbs in each packet. Sucralose is not a suitable substitute for sugar in recipes that require baking. For best results, swap about 1 1/3 cups (267 grams) of erythritol for each cup (200 grams) of sugar.

3. Xylitol

Xylitol is another type of sugar alcohol commonly found in products like sugar-free gum, candies and mints. It's as sweet as sugar but contains just 3 calories per gram and 4 grams of carbs per teaspoon. Xylitol can be easily added to tea, coffee, shakes or smoothies. It also works well in baked goods. Because xylitol is as sweet as regular sugar, you can exchange it for sugar in a 1:1 ratio.

Three Sweeteners to Avoid on a Keto Diet

These alternative sweeteners are high in carbs, they can increase blood sugar levels, and interrupt ketosis:

1. Maltodextrin

This highly processed sweetener is produced from starchy plants like rice, corn or wheat and it contains the same amounts of calories and carbs as regular sugar.

2. Honey

This is high in calories and carbs and may not be suitable for a keto diet.

3. Maple syrup

This is high in sugar and carbs.

Great News for Beer-Lovers!

Drinking large amounts of beer is not good for you, whether you are on a keto diet or not. You don't need to quit altogether. Sometimes it's nice to have a beer when you are socializing. These are the best brews for keto-dieters:

	Calories	Carbs	ABV
Budweiser Select	55	1.9	2.4%
Corona Premier	90	2.6	4%
Bud Select	99	3.1	4.3%
Natural Light	95	3.2	4.2%
Busch Light	95	3.2	4.1%
Miller Lite	96	3.2	4.2%
Beck's Premier Light	64	4	2.3%
Amstel Light	95	5	3.5%
Corona Light	99	5	4.5%
Coors Light	102	5	4.2%
Bud Light	110	6.6	4.2%
Heineken Light	99	7	3.3%

Maintaining the Keto Diet

1. **Keep away from non-keto foods.**

   Don't fool yourself by bingeing on non-keto foods to give yourself a "reward." The occasional treat is fine. Be wary of creating bad habits.

2. **Make and stick to a meal plan.**

   Being unprepared will result in bad choices. Shop with a meal plan, and buy only what you need. Do not buy treats and non-keto food items in your regular shop. Find some good keto cookbooks and use the recipes. Be bold! Try new foods, as long as they are part of the keto plan.

3. **Monitor your protein.**

   You must stick to the given ratios. Don't overdo or underdo the proteins. They are essential. But you have to eat the right proteins. A good keto cookbook will help you to do this at each meal.

4. **Set and Track your goals.**

   You must have a plan. Consult with a trainer and nutritionist if you are not sure what you are doing. Get them to help you to set some realistic achievable goals, then map and track those goals each week. This will give you encouragement when you feel like lapsing back to bad habits.

5. **Take more exercise.**

   Obviously, when your body hits ketosis, you will lose weight. But to sustain weight loss, if that is one of your goals, you need to ramp up the exercise regime. For the sake of your overall well-being, you also need to exercise regularly. Don't overdo it, and don't engage in activities that you dislike or find boring. Pick some activities that you enjoy and make them part of your routine.

Chapter 4 Breakfasts

Chorizo, Kale, and Avocado Eggs

Prep time: 7 minutes | Cook time: 13 minutes | Serves 4

1 teaspoon butter
1 red onion, sliced
4 ounces (113 g) chorizo, sliced into thin rounds
1 cup chopped kale

1 ripe avocado, pitted, peeled, chopped
4 eggs
Salt and black pepper to season

Preheat oven to 370ºF (188ºC). Melt butter in a cast iron pan over medium heat and sauté the onion for 2 minutes. Add the chorizo and cook for 2 minutes more, flipping once. Introduce the kale in batches with a splash of water to wilt, season lightly with salt, stir and cook for 3 minutes. Mix in the avocado and turn the heat off. Create four holes in the mixture, crack the eggs into each hole, sprinkle with salt and black pepper, and slide the pan into the preheated oven to bake for 6 minutes until the egg whites are set or firm and yolks still runny. Season to taste with salt and pepper, and serve right away with low carb toasts.

calories: 275 | fat: 23.1g | protein: 12.9g | carbs: 7.7g | net carbs: 4.1g | fiber: 3.6g

Coconut and Seed Bagels

Prep time: 5 minutes | Cook time: 20 minutes | Serves 4

½ cup coconut flour
6 eggs, beaten in a bowl
½ cup vegetable broth
¼ cup flax seed meal
¼ cup chia seed meal
1 teaspoon onion powder

1 teaspoon garlic powder
1 teaspoon dried parsley
1 teaspoon chia seeds
1 teaspoon sesame seeds
1 chopped onion

Preheat the oven to 350ºF (180ºC). Mix the coconut flour, eggs, broth, flax seed meal, chia seed meal, onion powder, garlic powder, and parsley. Spoon the mixture into a donut tray. In a small bowl, mix the chia seeds, sesame seeds, and onion, and sprinkle on the batter. Bake the bagels for 20 minutes. Serve the bagels with creamy pumpkin soup.

calories: 425 | fat: 19.0g | protein: 33.2g | carbs: 3.3g | net carbs: 0.5g | fiber: 2.8g

Bacon and Jalapeño Egg Muffins

Prep time: 10 minutes | Cook time: 20 minutes | Serves 6

12 eggs
¼ cup coconut milk
Salt and black pepper to taste
1 cup grated Cheddar cheese

12 slices bacon
4 jalapeño peppers, seeded and minced

Preheat oven to 370ºF (188ºC). Crack the eggs into a bowl and whisk with coconut milk until combined. Season with salt and pepper, and evenly stir in the Cheddar cheese. Line each hole of a muffin tin with a slice of bacon and fill each with the egg mixture twothirds way up. Top with the jalapeño peppers and bake in the oven for 18 to 20 minutes or until puffed and golden. Remove, allow cooling for a few minutes, and serve with arugula salad.

calories: 301 | fat: 23.8g | protein: 19.8g | carbs: 3.8g | net carbs: 3.3g | fiber: 0.5g

Tomato and Bacon Cups

Prep time: 10 minutes | Cook time: 23 minutes | Serves 6

12 bacon slices
2 tomatoes, diced
1 onion, diced
1 cup shredded Cheddar cheese

1 cup mayonnaise
12 low carb crepes/pancakes
1 teaspoon dried basil
Chopped chives to garnish

Fry the bacon in a skillet over medium heat for 5 minutes. Remove and chop with a knife. Transfer to a bowl. Add in Cheddar cheese, tomatoes, onion, mayonnaise, and basil. Mix well set aside. Place the crepes on a flat surface and use egg rings to cut a circle out of each crepe. Grease the muffin cups with cooking spray and fit the circled crepes into them to make a cup. Now, fill the cups with 3 tablespoons of bacon-tomato mixture. Place the muffin cups on a baking sheet, and bake for 18 minutes. Garnish with the chives, and serve with a tomato or cheese sauce.

calories: 426 | fat: 45.1g | protein: 16.1g | carbs: 5.5g | net carbs: 4.2g | fiber: 1.3g

Cheddar Bacon and Egg Frittata

Prep time: 9 minutes | Cook time: 16 minutes | Serves 4

10 slices bacon
10 fresh eggs
3 tablespoons butter, melted
½ cup almond milk

Salt and black pepper to taste
1½ cups Cheddar cheese, shredded
¼ cup chopped green onions

Preheat the oven to 400ºF (205ºC) and grease a baking dish with cooking spray. Cook the bacon in a skillet over medium heat for 6 minutes. Once crispy, remove from the skillet to paper towels and discard grease. Chop into small pieces. Whisk the eggs, butter, milk, salt, and black pepper. Mix in the bacon and pour the mixture into the baking dish. Sprinkle with Cheddar cheese and green onions, and bake in the oven for 10 minutes or until the eggs are thoroughly cooked. Remove and cool the frittata for 3 minutes, slice into wedges, and serve warm with a dollop of Greek yogurt.

calories: 326 | fat: 28.1g | protein: 14.9g | carbs: 2.5g | net carbs: 2.1g | fiber: 0.4g

Dill-Cream-Cheese Salmon Rolls

Prep time: 10 minutes | Cook time: 0 minutes | Serves 3

3 tablespoons cream cheese, softened
1 small lemon, zested and juiced

3 teaspoons chopped fresh dill
Salt and black pepper to taste
3 (7-inch) low carb tortillas
6 slices smoked salmon

In a bowl, mix the cream cheese, lemon juice, zest, dill, salt, and black pepper. Lay each tortilla on a plastic wrap (just wide enough to cover the tortilla), spread with cream cheese mixture, and top each (one) with two salmon slices. Roll up the tortillas and secure both ends by twisting. Refrigerate for 2 hours, remove plastic, cut off both ends of each wrap, and cut wraps into wheels.

calories: 251 | fat: 16.1g | protein: 17.8g | carbs: 8.7g | net carbs: 7.0g | fiber: 1.7g

Mushroom and Kale Tofu Scramble

Prep time: 5 minutes | Cook time: 26 minutes | Serves 4

2 tablespoons butter
1 cup sliced white mushrooms
2 cloves garlic, minced
16 ounces (454 g) firm tofu,

pressed and crumbled
Salt and black pepper to taste
½ cup thinly sliced kale
6 fresh eggs

Melt the butter in a non-stick skillet over medium heat, and sauté the mushrooms for 5 minutes until they lose their liquid. Add the garlic and cook for 1 minute. Crumble the tofu into the skillet, season with salt and black pepper. Cook with continuous stirring for 6 minutes. Introduce the kale in batches and cook to soften for about 7 minutes. Crack the eggs into a bowl, whisk until well combined and creamy in color, and pour all over the kale. Use a spatula to immediately stir the eggs while cooking until scrambled and no more runny, about 5 minutes. Plate, and serve with low carb crusted bread.

calories: 470 | fat: 38.7g | protein: 24.9g | carbs: 7.6g | net carbs: 4.9g | fiber: 2.7g

Cheese and Egg Spinach Nests

Prep time: 13 minutes | Cook time: 22 minutes | Serves 4

2 tablespoons olive oil
1 clove garlic, grated
½ pound (227 g) spinach, chopped
Salt and black pepper to taste

2 tablespoons shredded Parmesan cheese
2 tablespoons shredded gouda cheese
4 eggs

Preheat oven to 350°F (180°C). Warm the oil in a non-stick skillet over medium heat; add the garlic and sauté until softened for 2 minutes. Add the spinach to wilt for about 5 minutes, and season with salt and black pepper. Allow cooling. Grease a baking sheet with cooking spray, mold 4 (firm and separate) spinach nests on the sheet, and crack an egg into each nest. Sprinkle with Parmesan and gouda cheese. Bake for 15 minutes just until the egg whites have set and the yolks are still runny. Plate the nests and serve right away with low carb toasts and coffee.

calories: 231 | fat: 17.6g | protein: 12.2g | carbs: 5.4g | net carbs: 4.1g | fiber: 1.3g

Cream Cheese Almond Muffins

Prep time: 10 minutes | Cook time: 20 minutes | Serves 4

2 drops liquid stevia
2 cups almond flour
2 teaspoons baking powder
½ teaspoon salt
8 ounces (227 g) cream

cheese, softened
¼ cup melted butter
1 egg
1 cup unsweetened almond milk

Preheat oven to 400°F (205°C) and grease a 12-cup muffin tray with cooking spray. Mix the flour, baking powder, and salt in a large bowl. In a separate bowl, beat the cream cheese, stevia, and butter using a hand mixer and whisk in the egg and milk. Fold in the flour, and spoon the batter into the muffin cups two-thirds way up. Bake for 20 minutes until puffy at the top and golden brown, remove to a wire rack to cool slightly for 5 minutes before serving. Serve with tea.

calories: 321 | fat: 30.5g | protein: 4.1g | carbs: 8.1g | net carbs: 5.9g | fiber: 2.2g

Mushroom and Broccoli Quiche

Prep time: 15 minutes | Cook time: 55 to 60 minutes | Serves 6

12 eggs
1½ cups shredded Cheddar cheese
1½ cups almond milk
½ teaspoon dried thyme
Quiche Pastry:
¾ cup almond flour
A pinch of salt
2 ounces (57 g) cold butter
½ teaspoon baking powder

Salt to taste
¼ cup sliced mushrooms
½ cup chopped broccoli
1 clove garlic, minced

1 tablespoon cold water
2 eggs
Cooking spray

Preheat the oven to 370°F (188°C). In a large bowl, mix all the crust ingredients until dough is formed. Press it into a greased baking dish and bake for 20-25 minutes until lightly golden. Spread the Cheddar cheese in the pie crust. Beat the eggs with the almond milk, thyme, and salt, then, stir in the mushrooms, broccoli, and garlic. Pour the ingredients into the pie crust and bake in the oven for 35 minutes until the quiche is set. Remove and serve sliced with a tomato and avocado salad.

calories: 486 | fat: 39.6g | protein: 24.6g | carbs: 7.1g | net carbs: 6.2g | fiber: 0.9g

Vanilla Mascarpone Cups

Prep time: 5 minutes | Cook time: 15 minutes | Serves 6

¾ cup mascarpone cheese
¼ cup natural yogurt
3 eggs, beaten
1 tablespoon walnuts, ground

4 tablespoons erythritol
½ teaspoon vanilla essence
⅓ teaspoon ground cinnamon

Set oven to 360°F (182°C) and grease a muffin pan. Mix all ingredients in a bowl. Split the batter into the muffin cups. Bake for 12 to 15 minutes. Remove and set on a wire rack to cool slightly before serving.

calories: 182 | fat: 13.6g | protein: 10.4g | carbs: 3.8g | net carbs: 3.6g | fiber: 0.2g

Egg and Ham Muffins

Prep time: 15 minutes | Cook time: 25 minutes | Serves 9

2 cups chopped smoked ham
⅓ cup grated Parmesan cheese
¼ cup almond flour
9 eggs

⅓ cup mayonnaise, sugar-free
¼ teaspoon garlic powder
¼ cup chopped onion
Sea salt to taste

Preheat your oven to 370°F (188°C). Lightly grease nine muffin pans with cooking spray and set aside. Place the onion, ham, garlic powder, and salt, in a food processor, and pulse until ground. Stir in the mayonnaise, almond flour, and Parmesan cheese. Press this mixture into the muffin cups. Make sure it goes all the way up the muffin sides so that there will be room for the egg. Bake for 5 minutes. Crack an egg into each muffin cup. Return to the oven and bake for 20 more minutes or until the tops are firm to the touch and eggs are cooked. Leave to cool slightly before serving.

calories: 366 | fat: 28.1g | protein: 13.6g | carbs: 1.3g | net carbs: 1.0g | fiber: 0.3g

Bacon and Zucchini Hash

Prep time: 10 minutes | Cook time: 15 minutes | Serves 1

1 medium zucchini, diced
2 bacon slices
1 egg
1 tablespoon coconut oil

½ small onion, chopped
1 tablespoon chopped parsley
¼ teaspoon salt

Place the bacon in a skillet and cook for a few minutes, until crispy. Remove and set aside. Warm the coconut oil and cook the onion until soft, for about 3-4 minutes, occasionally stirring. Add the zucchini, and cook for 10 more minutes until zucchini is brown and tender, but not mushy. Transfer to a plate and season with salt. Crack the egg into the same skillet and fry over medium heat. Top the zucchini mixture with the bacon slices and a fried egg. Serve hot, sprinkled with parsley.

calories: 341 | fat: 26.7g | protein: 17.3g | carbs: 7.3g | net carbs: 6.5g | fiber: 0.8g

Almond Shake

Prep time: 5 minutes | Cook time: 0 minutes | Serves 1

1½ cups almond milk
2 tablespoons almond butter ½
teaspoon almond extract
½ teaspoon cinnamon
2 tablespoons flax meal

1 tablespoon collagen peptides
A pinch of salt
15 drops of stevia
A handful of ice cubes

Add almond milk, almond butter, flax meal, almond extract, collagen peptides, a pinch of salt, and stevia to the bowl of a blender. Blitz until uniform and smooth, for about 30 seconds. Add a bit more almond milk if it's very thick. Then taste, and adjust flavor as needed, adding more stevia for sweetness or almond butter to the creaminess. Pour in a smoothie glass, add the ice cubes and sprinkle with cinnamon.

calories: 325 | fat: 26.9g | protein: 19.1g | carbs: 8.1g | net carbs: 6.0g | fiber: 2.1g

Zucchini and Carrot Coconut Bread

Prep time: 15 minutes | Cook time: 55 minutes | Serves 4

1 cup shredded carrots
1 cup shredded zucchini, squeezed
⅓ cup coconut flour
1 teaspoon vanilla extract
6 eggs
1 tablespoon coconut oil

¾ teaspoon baking soda
1 tablespoon cinnamon powder
½ teaspoon salt
½ cup Greek yogurt
1 teaspoon apple cider vinegar
½ teaspoon nutmeg powder

Preheat the oven to 350ºF (180ºC) and grease the loaf pan with cooking spray. Set aside. Mix the carrots, zucchini, coconut flour, vanilla extract, eggs, coconut oil, baking soda, cinnamon powder, salt, Greek yogurt, vinegar, and nutmeg. Pour the batter into the loaf pan and bake for 55 minutes. Remove the bread after and let cool for 5 minutes. Preserve the bread and use it for toasts, sandwiches, or served with soups and salads.

calories: 176 | fat: 10.6g | protein: 11.5g | carbs: 4.5g | net carbs: 1.7g | fiber: 2.8g

Broccoli and Ham Egg Bake

Prep time: 5 minutes | Cook time: 20 minutes | Serves 4

2 heads broccoli, cut into small florets
2 red bell peppers, seeded and chopped
¼ cup chopped ham

2 teaspoons butter
1 teaspoon dried oregano plus extra to garnish
Salt and black pepper to taste
8 fresh eggs

Preheat oven to 425ºF (220ºC). Melt the butter in a frying pan over medium heat; brown the ham, stirring frequently, about 3 minutes. Arrange the broccoli, bell peppers, and ham on a foil-lined baking sheet in a single layer, toss to combine; season with salt, oregano, and black pepper. Bake for 10 minutes until the vegetables have softened. Remove, create eight indentations with a spoon, and crack an egg into each. Return to the oven and continue to bake for an additional 5 to 7 minutes until the egg whites are firm. Season with salt, black pepper, and extra oregano, share the bake into four plates and serve with strawberry lemonade (optional).

calories: 345 | fat: 27.9g | protein: 11.0g | carbs: 8.9g | net carbs: 4.2g | fiber: 4.7g

Avocado Sausage Stacks

Prep time: 5 minutes | Cook time: 15 minutes | Serves 6

6 Italian sausage patties
4 tablespoons olive oil
2 ripe avocados, pitted
2 teaspoons fresh lime juice

Salt and black pepper to taste
6 fresh eggs
Red pepper flakes to garnish

In a skillet, warm the oil over medium heat and fry the sausage patties about 8 minutes until lightly browned and firm. Remove the patties to a plate. Spoon the avocado into a bowl, mash with the lime juice, and season with salt and black pepper. Spread the mash on the sausages. Boil 3 cups of water in a wide pan over high heat, and reduce to simmer. Crack each egg into a small bowl and gently put the egg into the simmering water; poach for 2 to 3 minutes. Use a perforated spoon to remove from the water on a paper towel to dry. Repeat with the other 5 eggs. Top each stack with a poached egg, sprinkle with chili flakes, salt, black pepper, and chives. Serve with turnip wedges.

calories: 388 | fat: 22.9g | protein: 16.1g | carbs: 9.6g | net carbs: 5.1g | fiber: 4.5g

Avocado-Coconut Protein Shake

Prep time: 5 minutes | Cook time: 0 minutes | Serves 4

3 cups flax milk, chilled
3 teaspoons unsweetened cocoa powder
1 medium avocado, pitted, peeled, sliced
1 cup coconut milk, chilled

3 mint leaves plus extra to garnish
3 tablespoons erythritol
1 tablespoon low carb Protein powder
Whipping cream for topping

Combine the flax milk, cocoa powder, avocado, coconut milk, 3 mint leaves, erythritol, and protein powder into the smoothie maker, and blend for 1 minute to smooth. Pour the drink into serving glasses, lightly add some whipping cream on top, and garnish with 1 or 2 mint leaves. Serve immediately.

calories: 266 | fat: 15.6g | protein: 11.9g | carbs: 7.8g | net carbs: 4.0g | fiber: 3.8g

Cinnamon-Cream-Cheese Almond Waffles

Prep time: 15 minutes | Cook time: 10 minutes | Serves 6

Spread:

8 ounces (227 g) cream cheese, at room temperature
1 teaspoon cinnamon powder
3 tablespoons Swerve brown

sugar
Cinnamon powder for garnishing

Waffles:

5 tablespoons melted butter
1½ cups unsweetened almond milk
7 large eggs

¼ teaspoon liquid stevia
½ teaspoon baking powder
1½ cups almond flour

Combine the cream cheese, cinnamon, and Swerve with a hand mixer until smooth. To make the waffles, whisk the butter, milk, and eggs in a medium bowl. Add the stevia and baking powder and mix. Stir in the almond flour and combine until no lumps exist. Let the batter sit for 5 minutes to thicken. Spritz a waffle iron with a non-stick cooking spray. Ladle a ¼ cup of the batter into the waffle iron and cook until golden, about 10 minutes in total. Repeat with the remaining batter. Slice the waffles into quarters; apply the cinnamon spread in between each of two waffles and snap. Sprinkle with cinnamon powder and serve.

calories: 308 | fat: 24.1g | protein: 11.9g | carbs: 9.6g | net carbs: 7.8g | fiber: 1.8g

Eggs Stuffed Avocados

Prep time: 5 minutes | Cook time: 10 minutes | Serves 4

2 large avocados, halved and pitted
4 small eggs

Salt and black pepper to season
Chopped parsley to garnish

Preheat the oven to 400ºF (205ºC). Crack each egg into each avocado half and place them on a greased baking sheet. Bake the filled avocados in the oven for 8 or 10 minutes or until eggs are cooked. Season with salt and pepper, and garnish with parsley.

calories: 235 | fat: 19.2g | protein: 8.1g | carbs: 8.7g | net carbs: 2.0g | fiber: 6.7g

Crabmeat Egg Bake

Prep time: 5 minutes | Cook time: 10 minutes | Serves 3

1 tablespoon olive oil
6 eggs, whisked
Salt and black pepper to taste
¾ cup crème fraiche
½ cup scallions, chopped
½ teaspoon garlic powder

1 (6-ounce / 170-g) can crabmeat, flaked
For the Salsa:
Salt and black pepper to taste
½ teaspoon fresh dill, chopped

Set a sauté pan over medium heat and warm olive oil. Crack in eggs and scramble them. Stir in crabmeat and season with salt and black pepper; cook until cooked thoroughly. In a mixing dish, combine all salsa ingredients. Equally, split the egg/crabmeat mixture among serving plates; serve alongside the scallions and salsa to the side.

calories: 335 | fat: 26.1g | protein: 21.0g | carbs: 4.8g | net carbs: 4.2g | fiber: 0.6g

Carrot and Ham Egg Frittata

Prep time: 15 minutes | Cook time: 26 minutes | Serves 4

2 tablespoons butter, at room temperature
½ cup green onions, chopped
2 garlic cloves, minced
1 jalapeño pepper, chopped

1 carrot, chopped
8 ham slices
8 eggs, whisked
Salt and black pepper, to taste
½ teaspoon dried thyme

Set a pan over medium heat and warm the butter. Stir in green onions and sauté for 4 minutes. Place in garlic and cook for 1 minute. Stir in carrot and jalapeño pepper, and cook for 4 more minutes. Remove the mixture to a lightly greased baking pan, with cooking spray, and top with ham slices. Place in the eggs over vegetables and ham; add thyme, black pepper, and salt for seasoning. Bake in the oven for about 18 minutes at 360ºF (182ºC). Serve warm alongside a dollop of full-fat natural yogurt.

calories: 311 | fat: 26.3g | protein: 15.3g | carbs: 4.5g | net carbs: 3.8g | fiber: 0.7g

Cream Cheese Salmon Omelet Roll

Prep time: 10 minutes | Cook time: 5 minutes | Serves 1

½ avocado, sliced
2 tablespoons chopped chives
½ package smoked salmon, cut into strips
1 spring onions, sliced

3 eggs
2 tablespoons cream cheese
1 tablespoon butter
Salt and black pepper, to taste

In a small bowl, combine the chives and cream cheese; set aside. Beat the eggs in a large bowl and season with salt and black pepper. Melt the butter in a pan over medium heat. Add the eggs to the pan and cook for about 3 minutes. Flip the omelet over and continue cooking for another 2 minutes until golden. Remove the omelet to a plate and spread the chive mixture over. Arrange the salmon, avocado, and onion slices. Wrap the omelet and serve immediately.

calories: 512 | fat: 47.8g | protein: 36.8g | carbs: 13.0g | net carbs: 5.7g | fiber: 7.3g

Colby Broccoli Frittata

Prep time: 8 minutes | Cook time: 12 minutes | Serves 4

2 tablespoons olive oil
½ cup onions, chopped
1 cup broccoli, chopped
8 eggs, beaten
½ teaspoon jalapeño pepper,

minced
Salt and red pepper, to taste
¾ cup colby cheese, grated
¼ cup fresh cilantro, to serve

Set an ovenproof frying pan over medium heat and warm the oil. Add onions and sauté until caramelized. Place in the broccoli and cook until tender. Add in jalapeño pepper and eggs; season with red pepper and salt. Cook until the eggs are set. Scatter colby cheese over the frittata. Set oven to 370ºF (188ºC) and cook for approximately 12 minutes, until frittata is set in the middle. Slice into wedges and decorate with fresh cilantro before serving.

calories: 249 | fat: 17.2g | protein: 17.5g | carbs: 6.7g | net carbs: 6.1g | fiber: 0.6g

Swiss Chard, Sausage, and Squash Omelet
Prep time: 6 minutes | Cook time: 4 minutes | Serves 1

2 eggs
1 cup Swiss chard, chopped
4 ounces (113 g) sausage, chopped
2 tablespoons ricotta cheese

4 ounces (113 g) roasted squash
1 tablespoon olive oil
Salt and black pepper, to taste
Fresh parsley to garnish

Beat the eggs in a bowl, season with salt and pepper; stir in the swiss chard and the ricotta cheese. In another bowl, mash the squash and add to the egg mixture. Heat ¼ tablespoon of olive oil in a pan over medium heat. Add sausage and cook until browned on all sides, turning occasionally. Drizzle the remaining olive oil. Pour the egg mixture over. Cook for about 2 minutes per side until the eggs are thoroughly cooked and lightly browned. Remove the pan and run a spatula around the edges of the omelet; slide it onto a warm platter. Fold in half, and serve sprinkled with fresh parsley.

calories: 557 | fat: 51.6g | protein: 32.2g | carbs: 12.9g | net carbs: 7.4g | fiber: 5.5g

Mozzarella and Chorizo Omelet
Prep time: 8 minutes | Cook time: 7 minutes | Serves 1

2 eggs
6 basil leaves
2 ounces (57 g) Mozzarella cheese
1 tablespoon butter

1 tablespoon water
4 thin slices chorizo
1 tomato, sliced
Salt and black pepper, to taste

Whisk the eggs along with the water and some salt and pepper. Melt the butter in a skillet and cook the eggs for 30 seconds. Spread the chorizo slices over. Arrange the tomato and Mozzarella over the chorizo. Cook for about 3 minutes. Cover the skillet and cook for 3 minutes until omelet is set. When ready, remove the pan from heat; run a spatula around the edges of the omelet and flip it onto a warm plate, folded side down. Serve garnished with basil leaves and green salad.

calories: 452 | fat: 36.4g | protein: 30.1g | carbs: 5.4g | net carbs: 2.9g | fiber: 2.5g

Rosemary Turkey Sausage Egg Muffins
Prep time: 5 minutes | Cook time: 15 minutes | Serves 3

1 teaspoon butter
6 eggs
Salt and black pepper, to taste
½ teaspoon dried rosemary

1 cup pecorino romano cheese, grated
3 turkey sausages, chopped

Preheat oven to 400ºF (205ºC) and grease muffin cups with cooking spray. In a skillet over medium heat add the butter and cook the turkey sausages for 4-5 minutes. Beat 3 eggs with a fork. Add in sausages, cheese, and seasonings. Divide between the muffin cups and bake for 4 minutes. Crack in an egg to each of the cups. Bake for an additional 4 minutes. Allow cooling before serving.

calories: 422 | fat: 34.2g | protein: 26.4g | carbs: 2.1g | net carbs: 2.1g | fiber: 0g

Feta Spinach Frittata
Prep time: 15 minutes | Cook time: 25 minutes | Serves 4

5 ounces (142 g) spinach
8 ounces (227 g) crumbled Feta cheese
1 pint halved cherry tomatoes

10 eggs
3 tablespoons olive oil
4 scallions, diced
Salt and black pepper, to taste

Preheat your oven to 350ºF (180ºC). Drizzle the oil in a casserole and place in the oven until heated. In a bowl, whisk the eggs along with the black pepper and salt, until thoroughly combined. Stir in the spinach, Feta cheese, and scallions. Pour the mixture into the casserole, top with the cherry tomatoes and place back in the oven. Bake for 25 minutes until your frittata is set in the middle. When done, remove the casserole from the oven and run a spatula around the edges of the frittata; slide it onto a warm platter. Cut the frittata into wedges and serve with salad.

calories: 462 | fat: 35.1g | protein: 25.9g | carbs: 8.2g | net carbs: 6.1g | fiber: 2.1g

Aioli Eggs with Tuna and Veggies
Prep time: 15 minutes | Cook time: 0 minutes | Serves 8

8 eggs, hard-boiled, chopped
28 ounces (794 g) tuna in brine, drained
½ cup lettuces, torn into pieces
½ cup green onions, finely
Aioli:
1 cup mayonnaise
2 cloves garlic, minced

chopped
½ cup Feta cheese, crumbled
⅓ cup sour cream
½ tablespoon mustard

1 tablespoon lemon juice
Salt and black pepper, to taste

Set the eggs in a serving bowl. Place in tuna, onion, mustard, cheese, lettuce, and sour cream. To prepare aioli, mix in a bowl mayonnaise, lemon juice, and garlic. Add in black pepper and salt. Stir in the prepared aioli to the bowl to incorporate everything. Serve with pickles.

calories: 356 | fat: 22.6g | protein: 29.6g | carbs: 2.2g | net carbs: 1.7g | fiber: 0.5g

Sausage Quiche
Prep time: 15 minutes | Cook time: 40 minutes | Serves 6

6 eggs
12 ounces (340 g) raw sausage roll
10 cherry tomatoes, halved
2 tablespoons heavy cream
2 tablespoons Parmesan

cheese
¼ teaspoon salt
A pinch of black pepper
2 tablespoons chopped parsley
5 eggplant slices

Preheat your oven to 370ºF (188ºC). Grease a pie dish with cooking spray. Press the sausage roll at the bottom of a pie dish. Arrange the eggplant slices on top of the sausage. Top with cherry tomatoes. Whisk the eggs along with the heavy cream, salt, Parmesan cheese, and black pepper. Spoon the mixture over the sausage. Bake for about 40 minutes until browned around the edges. Serve warm, sprinkled with parsley.

calories: 341 | fat: 28.1g | protein: 16.9g | carbs: 6.2g | net carbs: 2.9g | fiber: 3.3g

Creamy Ricotta Almond Cloud Pancakes

Prep time: 5 minutes | Cook time: 5 minutes | Serves 4

1 cup almond flour
1 teaspoon baking powder
2½ tablespoons Swerve
⅓ teaspoon salt
1¼ cups ricotta cheese
⅓ cup coconut milk
2 large eggs
1 cup heavy whipping cream

In a medium bowl, whisk the almond flour, baking powder, Swerve, and salt. Set aside. Crack the eggs into the blender and process on medium speed for 30 seconds. Add the ricotta cheese, continue processing it, and gradually pour the coconut milk in while you keep on blending. In about 90 seconds, the mixture will be creamy and smooth. Pour it into the dry ingredients and whisk to combine. Set a skillet over medium heat and let it heat for a minute. Then, fetch a soup spoonful of mixture into the skillet and cook it for 1 minute. Flip the pancake and cook further for 1 minute. Remove onto a plate and repeat the cooking process until the batter is exhausted. Serve the pancakes with whipping cream.

calories: 406 | fat: 30.5g | protein: 11.4g | carbs: 8.8g | net carbs: 6.4g | fiber: 2.4g

Double Cheese Omelet

Prep time: 10 minutes | Cook time: 0 minutes | Serves 2

3 tablespoons olive oil
4 eggs, beaten
Salt and black pepper, to taste
¼ teaspoon paprika
¼ teaspoon cayenne pepper
½ cup Asiago cheese,
shredded
½ cup Cheddar cheese, shredded
2 tablespoons fresh basil, roughly chopped

Set a pan over medium heat and warm the oil. Season eggs with cayenne pepper, salt, paprika, and black pepper. Transfer to the pan and ensure they are evenly spread. Top with the Asiago and Cheddar cheeses. Slice the omelet into two halves. Decorate with fresh basil, to serve.

calories: 491 | fat: 44.5g | protein: 22.8g | carbs: 4.8g | net carbs: 4.6g | fiber: 0.2g

Gruyere and Mushroom Lettuce Wraps

Prep time: 10 minutes | Cook time: 10 minutes | Serves 4

Wraps:
6 eggs
2 tablespoons almond milk
1 tablespoon olive oil
Sea salt, to taste
Filling:
1 teaspoon olive oil
1 cup mushrooms, chopped
Salt and black pepper, to taste
½ teaspoon cayenne pepper
8 fresh lettuce leaves
4 slices Gruyere cheese
2 tomatoes, sliced

Mix all the ingredients for the wraps thoroughly. Set a frying pan over medium heat. Add in ¼ of the mixture and cook for 4 minutes on both sides. Do the same thrice and set the wraps aside, they should be kept warm. In a separate pan over medium heat, warm 1 teaspoon of olive oil. Cook the mushrooms for 5 minutes until soft; add cayenne pepper, black pepper, and salt. Set 1-2 lettuce leaves onto every wrap, split the mushrooms among the wraps and top with tomatoes and cheese.

calories: 471 | fat: 43.9g | protein: 19.4g | carbs: 6.5g | net carbs: 5.3g | fiber: 1.2g

Double Cheese and Egg Stuffed Avocados

Prep time: 5 minutes | Cook time: 15 minutes | Serves 4

3 avocados, halved and pitted, skin on
½ cup Feta cheese, crumbled
½ cup Cheddar cheese, grated
2 eggs, beaten
Salt and black pepper, to taste
1 tablespoon fresh basil, chopped

Set oven to 360ºF (182ºC) and lay the avocado halves in an ovenproof dish. In a mixing dish, mix both types of cheeses, black pepper, eggs, and salt. Split the mixture equally into the avocado halves. Bake thoroughly for 15 to 17 minutes. Decorate with fresh basil before serving.

calories: 343 | fat: 30.5g | protein: 11.2g | carbs: 17.5g | net carbs: 7.4g | fiber: 10.1g

Cacao Nib Nut Granola

Prep time: 5 minutes | Cook time: 30 minutes | Serves 6

½ cup chopped raw pecans
½ cup flax seeds
½ cup superfine blanched almond flour
½ cup unsweetened dried coconut
¼ cup chopped cacao nibs
¼ cup chopped raw walnuts
¼ cup sesame seeds
¼ cup sugar-free vanilla-flavored protein powder
3 tablespoons granulated erythritol
1 teaspoon ground cinnamon
⅛ teaspoon kosher salt
⅓ cup coconut oil
1 large egg white, beaten

Preheat the oven to 300ºF (150ºC). Line a 15 by 10-inch sheet pan with parchment paper. Place all of the ingredients in a large bowl. Stir well until the mixture is crumbly and holds together in small clumps. Spread out on the parchment-lined pan. Bake for 30 minutes, or until golden brown and fragrant. Let the granola cool completely in the pan before removing. Store in an airtight container in the refrigerator for up to 2 weeks.

calories: 442 | fat: 40.0g | protein: 15.0g | carbs: 14.0g | net carbs: 4.0g | fiber: 10.0g

Cinnamon Cream Cheese Pancakes

Prep time: 5 minutes | Cook time: 12 minutes | Makes 4 pancakes

2 ounces (57 g) cream cheese (¼ cup), softened
2 large eggs
1 teaspoon granulated
erythritol
½ teaspoon ground cinnamon
1 tablespoon butter, for the pan

Place the cream cheese, eggs, sweetener, and cinnamon in a small blender and blend for 30 seconds, or until smooth. Let the batter rest for 2 minutes. Heat the butter in a 10-inch nonstick skillet over medium heat until bubbling. Pour ¼ cup of the batter into the pan and tilt the pan in a circular motion to create a thin pancake about 6 inches in diameter. Cook for 2 minutes, or until the center is no longer glossy. Flip and cook for 1 minute on the other side. Remove and repeat with the rest of the batter, making a total of 4 pancakes.

calories: 396 | fat: 35.0g | protein: 17.0g | carbs: 3.0g | net carbs: 3.0g | fiber: 0g

Spinach Fontina Chorizo Waffles
Prep time: 10 minutes | Cook time: 5 minutes | Serves 6

6 eggs
6 tablespoons almond milk
1 teaspoon Spanish spice mix or allspice
Sea salt and black pepper, to taste
3 chorizo sausages, cooked, chopped
1 cup Fontina cheese, shredded

Using a mixing bowl, beat the eggs, Spanish spice mix, black pepper, salt, and almond milk. Add in shredded cheese and chopped sausage. Use a nonstick cooking spray to spray a waffle iron. Cook the egg mixture for 5 minutes. Serve alongside homemade sugar-free tomato ketchup.

calories: 315 | fat: 24.9g | protein: 20.1g | carbs: 1.4g | net carbs: 1.4g | fiber: 0g

Pesto Bacon and Avocado Mug Cakes
Prep time: 6 minutes | Cook time: 2 minutes | Serves 2

¼ cup flax meal
1 egg
2 tablespoons heavy cream
2 tablespoons pesto
Filling:
2 tablespoons cream cheese
4 slices bacon
¼ cup almond flour
¼ teaspoon baking soda
Salt and black pepper, to taste

½ medium avocado, sliced

Mix together the dry muffin ingredients in a bowl. Add egg, heavy cream, and pesto, and whisk well with a fork. Season with salt and pepper. Divide the mixture between two ramekins. Place in the microwave and cook for 60-90 seconds. Leave to cool slightly before filling. Meanwhile, in a skillet, over medium heat, cook the bacon slices until crispy. Transfer to paper towels to soak up excess fat; set aside. Invert the muffins onto a plate and cut in half, crosswise. To assemble the sandwiches: spread cream cheese and top with bacon and avocado slices.

calories: 512 | fat: 38.3g | protein: 16.3g | carbs: 10.3g | net carbs: 4.4g | fiber: 5.9g

Roquefort Kielbasa Waffles
Prep time: 15 minutes | Cook time: 5 minutes | Serves 2

2 tablespoons butter, melted
Salt and black pepper, to taste
½ teaspoon parsley flakes
½ teaspoon chili pepper flakes
4 eggs
½ cup Roquefort cheese, crumbled
4 slices kielbasa, chopped
2 tablespoons fresh chives, chopped

In a mixing bowl, combine all ingredients except fresh chives. Preheat waffle iron and spray with a cooking spray. Pour in the batter and close the lid. Cook for 5 minutes or until golden-brown, do the same with the rest of the batter. Decorate with fresh chives and serve while warm.

calories: 471 | fat: 40.2g | protein: 24.5g | carbs: 3.0g | net carbs: 2.8g | fiber: 0.2g

Gruyere and Parmesan Cauliflower Burgers
Prep time: 10 minutes | Cook time: 33 minutes | Serves 6

1½ tablespoons olive oil
1 onion, chopped
1 garlic clove, minced
1 pound (454 g) cauliflower, grated
6 tablespoons coconut flour
½ cup Gruyere cheese, shredded
1 cup Parmesan cheese
2 eggs, beaten
½ teaspoon dried rosemary
Sea salt and ground black pepper, to taste

Set a cast iron skillet over medium heat and warm oil. Add in garlic and onion and cook until soft, about 3 minutes. Stir in grated cauliflower and cook for a minute; allow cooling and set aside. To the cooled cauliflower, add the rest of the ingredients; form balls from the mixture, then, press each ball to form burger patty. Set oven to 400ºF (205ºC) and bake the burgers for 20 minutes. Flip and bake for another 10 minutes or until the top becomes golden brown.

calories: 415 | fat: 33.7g | protein: 12.9g | carbs: 9.7g | net carbs: 7.6g | fiber: 2.1g

Pumpkin Coffee Latte
Prep time: 5 minutes | Cook time: 0 minutes | Serves 1

6 ounces (170 g) brewed hot coffee
1 tablespoon coconut oil
1 tablespoon granulated erythritol
1 tablespoon solid-pack pumpkin purée
1 tablespoon unsalted butter
¼ teaspoon pumpkin pie spice

Place all of the ingredients in a small blender and blend until smooth. Pour into a 10-ounce (283-g) mug and serve immediately.

calories: 225 | fat: 35.1g | protein: 0g | carbs: 3.0g | net carbs: 2.0g | fiber: 1.0g

Strawberry Kefir Smoothie
Prep time: 5 minutes | Cook time: 0 minutes | Serves 1

¾ cup unsweetened vanilla-flavored almond milk
¼ cup full-fat unsweetened kefir, store-bought or homemade
1 tablespoon granulated erythritol, or more to taste
¼ teaspoon pure vanilla extract
4 medium-sized fresh strawberries, hulled, plus 1 fresh strawberry for garnish (optional)
3 ice cubes

Place all of the ingredients in a blender and blend until smooth and creamy. Taste and add more sweetener if desired. Pour into a 12-ounce (340-g) glass and serve immediately. If desired, rest a strawberry on the rim for garnish.

calories: 74 | fat: 3.9g | protein: 2.9g | carbs: 4.8g | net carbs: 4.0g | fiber: 0.8g

Triple Cheese and Bacon Zucchini Balls

Prep time: 20 minutes | Cook time: 10 minutes | Serves 6

4 cups zucchini, spiralized
½ pound (227 g) bacon, chopped
6 ounces (170 g) cottage cheese, curds
6 ounces (170 g) cream cheese
1 cup Fontina cheese
½ cup dill pickles, chopped, squeezed
2 cloves garlic, crushed

1 cup grated Parmesan cheese
½ teaspoon caraway seeds
¼ teaspoon dried dill weed
½ teaspoon onion powder
Salt and black pepper, to taste
1 cup crushed pork rinds
Cooking oil

Thoroughly mix zoodles, cottage cheese, dill pickles, ½ cup of Parmesan cheese, garlic, cream cheese, bacon, and Fontina cheese until well combined. Shape the mixture into balls. Refrigerate for 3 hours. In a mixing bowl, mix the remaining ½ cup of Parmesan cheese, crushed pork rinds, dill, black pepper, onion powder, caraway seeds, and salt. Roll cheese ball in Parmesan mixture to coat. Set a skillet over medium heat and warm 1-inch of oil. Fry cheeseballs until browned on all sides. Set on a paper towel to soak up any excess oil.

calories: 406 | fat: 26.7g | protein: 33.3g | carbs: 8.6g | net carbs: 5.7g | fiber: 2.9g

Chia Walnut Coconut Pudding

Prep time: 5 minutes | Cook time: 5 minutes | Serves 1

½ teaspoon vanilla extract
½ cup water
1 tablespoon chia seeds
2 tablespoons hemp seeds
1 tablespoon flax seed meal

2 tablespoons almond meal
2 tablespoons shredded coconut
¼ teaspoon granulated stevia
1 tablespoon walnuts, chopped

Put chia seeds, hemp seeds, flaxseed meal, almond meal, granulated stevia, and shredded coconut in a nonstick saucepan and pour over the water. Simmer over medium heat, occasionally stirring, until creamed and thickened, for about 3-4 minutes. Stir in vanilla. When the pudding is ready, spoon into a serving bowl, sprinkle with walnuts and serve warm.

calories: 335 | fat: 29.1g | protein: 15.1g | carbs: 14.5g | net carbs: 1.4g | fiber: 13.1g

Pepperoni Ciabatta

Prep time: 10 minutes | Cook time: 5 minutes | Serves 6

10 ounces (283 g) cream cheese, melted
2½ cups Mozzarella cheese, shredded
4 large eggs, beaten
3 tablespoons Romano cheese, grated

½ cup pork rinds, crushed
2½ teaspoon baking powder
½ cup tomato purée
12 large slices pepperoni

Combine eggs, Mozzarella cheese and cream cheese. Place in baking powder, pork rinds, and Romano cheese. Form into 6 chiabatta shapes. Set a nonstick pan over medium heat. Cook each ciabatta for 2 minutes per side. Sprinkle tomato purée over each one and top with pepperoni slices to serve.

calories: 465 | fat: 33.5g | protein: 31.2g | carbs: 10.5g | net carbs: 9.2g | fiber: 1.3g

Chapter 5 Vegetables

Pumpkin and Cauliflower Curry
Prep time: 15 minutes | Cook time: 7 to 8 hours | Serves 6

1 tablespoon extra-virgin olive oil
4 cups coconut milk
1 cup diced pumpkin
1 cup cauliflower florets
1 red bell pepper, diced
1 zucchini, diced
1 sweet onion, chopped
2 teaspoons grated fresh ginger
2 teaspoons minced garlic
1 tablespoon curry powder
2 cups shredded spinach
1 avocado, diced, for garnish

Lightly grease the insert of the slow cooker with the olive oil. Add the coconut milk, pumpkin, cauliflower, bell pepper, zucchini, onion, ginger, garlic, and curry powder. Cover and cook on low for 7 to 8 hours. Stir in the spinach. Garnish each bowl with a spoonful of avocado and serve.

calories: 501 | fat: 44.0g | protein: 7.0g | carbs: 19.0g | net carbs: 9.0g | fiber: 10.0g

Indian White Cabbage Stew
Prep time: 8 minutes | Cook time: 22 minutes | Serves 3

6 ounces (170 g) Goan chorizo sausage, sliced
2 cloves garlic, finely chopped
1 teaspoon Indian spice blend
1 pound (454 g) white cabbage, outer leaves removed and finely shredded
¾ cup cream of celery soup

Heat a large-sized wok over a moderate flame. Now, sear the Goan chorizo sausage until no longer pink; reserve. Cook the garlic and Indian spice blend in the pan drippings until they are aromatic. Now, stir in the cabbage and cream of celery soup. Turn the temperature to medium-low, cover, and continue simmering an additional 22 minutes or until tender and heated through. Add the reserved Goan chorizo sausage; ladle into individual bowls and serve. Enjoy!

calories: 236 | fat: 17.7g | protein: 9.8g | carbs: 6.1g | net carbs: 3.7g | fiber: 2.4g

Cauliflower Egg Bake
Prep time: 10 minutes | Cook time: 25 minutes | Serves 6

1½ pounds (680 g) cauliflower, broken into small florets
½ cup Greek yogurt
4 eggs, beaten
6 ounces (170 g) ham, diced
1 cup Swiss cheese, preferably freshly grated

Place the cauliflower into a deep saucepan; cover with water and bring to a boil over high heat; immediately reduce the heat to medium-low. Let it simmer, covered, approximately 6 minutes. Drain and mash with a potato masher. Add in the yogurt, eggs and ham; stir until everything is well combined and incorporated. Scrape the mixture into a lightly greased casserole dish. Top with the grated Swiss cheese and transfer to a preheated at 390ºF (199ºC) oven. Bake for 15 to 20 minutes or until cheese bubbles and browns. Bon appétit!

calories: 237 | fat: 13.6g | protein: 20.2g | carbs: 7.1g | net carbs: 4.8g | fiber: 2.3g

Cottage Kale Stir-Fry
Prep time: 10 minutes | Cook time: 10 minutes | Serves 3

½ tablespoon olive oil
1 teaspoon fresh garlic, chopped
9 ounces (255 g) kale, torn into
pieces
½ cup Cottage cheese, creamed
½ teaspoon sea salt

Heat the olive oil in a saucepan over a moderate flame. Now, cook the garlic until just tender and aromatic. Then, stir in the kale and continue to cook for about 10 minutes until all liquid evaporates. Fold in the Cottage cheese and salt; stir until everything is heated through. Enjoy!

calories: 94 | fat: 4.5g | protein: 7.0g | carbs: 6.2g | net carbs: 3.5g | fiber: 2.7g

Spiced Cauliflower Cheese Bake
Prep time: 20 minutes | Cook time: 20 minutes | Serves 4

½ teaspoon butter, melted
1 (½-pound / 227-g) head cauliflower, broken into florets
½ cup Swiss cheese, shredded
½ cup Mexican blend cheese, room temperature
½ cup Greek yogurt
1 cup cooked ham, chopped
1 roasted chili pepper, chopped
½ teaspoon porcini powder
1 teaspoon garlic powder
1 teaspoon shallot powder
½ teaspoon cayenne pepper
¼ teaspoon dried sage
½ teaspoon dried oregano
Sea salt and ground black pepper, to taste

Preheat the oven to 340ºF (171ºC). Coat the bottom and sides of a casserole dish with ½ teaspoon of melted butter. Empty the cauliflower into a pot and cover it with water. Let it cook for 6 minutes until it is tender. Mash the cauliflower with a potato masher. Stir in the cheese until the cheese has melted. Add Greek yogurt, chopped ham, roasted pepper, and spices. Place the mixture in the prepared casserole dish; bake for 20 minutes. Let it sit for about 10 minutes before cutting. Serve.

calories: 189 | fat: 11.3g | protein: 14.9g | carbs: 5.7g | net carbs: 4.6g | fiber: 1.1g

Creamy Spinach
Prep time: 5 minutes | Cook time: 5 minutes | Serves 4

1 tablespoon butter, room temperature
1 clove garlic, minced
10 ounces (283 g) spinach
½ teaspoon garlic salt
¼ teaspoon ground black pepper, or more to taste
½ teaspoon cayenne pepper
3 ounces (85 g) cream cheese
½ cup double cream

Melt the butter in a saucepan that is preheated over medium heat. Once hot. Cook garlic for 30 seconds. Now, add the spinach; cover the pan for 2 minutes to let the spinach wilt. Season with salt, black pepper, and cayenne pepper. Stir in cheese and cream; stir until the cheese melts. Serve immediately.

calories: 167 | fat: 15.1g | protein: 4.4g | carbs: 5.0g | net carbs: 3.3g | fiber: 1.7g

Zucchini Casserole

Prep time: 15 minutes | Cook time: 45 minutes | Serves 4

Nonstick cooking spray
2 cups zucchini, thinly sliced
2 tablespoons leeks, sliced
½ teaspoon salt
Freshly ground black pepper, to taste
½ teaspoon dried basil
½ teaspoon dried oregano
½ cup Cheddar cheese, grated
¼ cup heavy cream
4 tablespoons Parmesan cheese, freshly grated
1 tablespoon butter, room temperature
1 teaspoon fresh garlic, minced

Start by preheating your oven to 370ºF (188ºC). Lightly grease a casserole dish with a nonstick cooking spray. Place 1 cup of the zucchini slices in the dish; add 1 tablespoon of leeks; sprinkle with salt, pepper, basil, and oregano. Top with ¼ cup of Cheddar cheese. Repeat the layers one more time. In a mixing dish, thoroughly whisk the heavy cream with Parmesan, butter, and garlic. Spread this mixture over the zucchini layer and cheese layers. Place in the preheated oven and bake for about 40 to 45 minutes until the edges are nicely browned. Sprinkle with chopped chives, if desired. Bon appétit!

calories: 156 | fat: 12.8g | protein: 7.5g | carbs: 3.6g | net carbs: 2.8g | fiber: 0.8g

Mushroom Stroganoff

Prep time: 5 minutes | Cook time: 10 minutes | Serves 3

2 tablespoons olive oil
½ shallot, diced
3 cloves garlic, chopped
12 ounces (340 g) brown mushrooms, thinly sliced
2 cups tomato sauce

Heat the olive oil in a stockpot over medium-high heat. Then, sauté the shallot for about 3 minutes until tender and fragrant. Now, stir in the garlic and mushrooms and cook them for 1 minute more until aromatic. Fold in the tomato sauce and bring to a boil; turn the heat to medium-low, cover, and continue to simmer for 5 to 6 minutes. Salt to taste and serve over cauliflower rice if desired. Enjoy!

calories: 137 | fat: 9.3g | protein: 3.4g | carbs: 7.1g | net carbs: 5.3g | fiber: 1.8g

Bell Pepper and Tomato Sataraš

Prep time: 5 minutes | Cook time: 15 minutes | Serves 3

3 teaspoons olive oil
1 onion, chopped
2 garlic cloves, minced
3 bell peppers, seeded and sliced
1 tomato, puréed

Heat the olive oil in a saucepan over moderate flame. Then, sweat the onion until translucent. Stir in the garlic and bell peppers and sauté for 2 minutes more or until aromatic. Stir in the puréed tomato. Cover, reduce the temperature to medium-low and continue to cook for 12 minutes or until the peppers have softened and the cooking liquid has evaporated. Salt to taste and serve in individual bowls. Bon appétit!

calories: 84 | fat: 4.6g | protein: 1.6g | carbs: 6.5g | net carbs: 4.7g | fiber: 1.8g

Cheese Stuffed Spaghetti Squash

Prep time: 15 minutes | Cook time: 50 to 60 minutes | Serves 4

½ pound (227 g) spaghetti squash, halved, scoop out seeds
1 teaspoon olive oil
½ cup Mozzarella cheese, shredded
½ cup cream cheese
½ cup full-fat Greek yogurt
2 eggs
1 garlic clove, minced
½ teaspoon cumin
½ teaspoon basil ½ teaspoon mint
Sea salt and ground black pepper, to taste

Place the squash halves in a baking pan; drizzle the insides of each squash half with olive oil. Bake in the preheated oven at 370ºF (188ºC) for 45 to 50 minutes or until the interiors are easily pierced through with a fork. Now, scrape out the spaghetti squash "noodles" from the skin in a mixing bowl. Add the remaining ingredients and mix to combine well. Carefully fill each of the squash half with the cheese mixture. Bake at 350ºF (180ºC) for 5 to 10 minutes, until the cheese is bubbling and golden brown. Bon appétit!

calories: 220 | fat: 17.6g | protein: 9.0g | carbs: 6.8g | net carbs: 5.9g | fiber: 0.9g

Romano Zucchini Cups

Prep time: 10 minutes | Cook time: 15 minutes | Serves 4

1 teaspoon sea salt
1 (½-pound / 227-g) zucchini, grated
½ cup almond flour
2 eggs, beaten
1 cup Romano cheese, grated

Place the salt and grated zucchini in a bowl; let it sit for 15 minutes, squeeze using a cheesecloth and discard the liquid. Now, stir in the almond flour, eggs, and Romano cheese. Spritz a 12-cup mini-muffin pan with cooking spray. Bake in the preheated oven for 15 minutes until the surface is no longer wet to the touch. Let them cool about 5 minutes to set up. Bon appétit!

calories: 225 | fat: 18.0g | protein: 13.4g | carbs: 3.0g | net carbs: 1.5g | fiber: 1.5g

Paprika Riced Cauliflower

Prep time: 4 minutes | Cook time: 6 minutes | Serves 4

1 tablespoon butter
1 pound (454 g)cauliflower florets
2 cloves garlic, minced
1 tablespoon smoked paprika
Flaky salt, to taste

Melt the butter in a frying pan over a moderate flame. Pulse the cauliflower in your food processor until your cauliflower has broken down into rice-sized chunks approximately 6 seconds. Add the cauliflower rice to the frying pan and cook, covered, for 5 minutes. Stir in the garlic and smoked paprika. Continue to sauté an additional minute or so. Season with salt to taste and serve immediately. Bon appétit!

calories: 57 | fat: 3.2g | protein: 2.3g | carbs: 6.1g | net carbs: 3.8g | fiber: 2.3g

Riced Cauliflower Stuffed Bell Peppers

Prep time: 15 minutes | Cook time: 45 minutes | Serves 6

2 tablespoons vegetable oil
2 tablespoons yellow onion, chopped
1 teaspoon fresh garlic, crushed
½ pound (227 g) ground pork
½ pound (227 g) ground turkey
1 cup cauliflower rice
½ teaspoon sea salt
¼ teaspoon red pepper flakes, crushed
½ teaspoon ground black pepper
1 teaspoon dried parsley flakes
6 medium-sized bell peppers, seeded and cleaned
½ cup tomato sauce
½ cup Cheddar cheese, shredded

Heat the oil in a pan over medium flame. Once hot, sauté the onion and garlic for 2 to 3 minutes. Add the ground meat and cook for 6 minutes longer or until it is nicely browned. Add cauliflower rice and seasoning. Continue to cook for a further 3 minutes. Divide the filling between the prepared bell peppers. Cover with a piece of foil. Place the peppers in a baking pan; add tomato sauce. Bake in the preheated oven at 380ºF (193ºC) for 20 minutes. Uncover, top with cheese, and bake for 10 minutes more. Bon appétit!

calories: 245 | fat: 12.8g | protein: 16.6g | carbs: 3.3g | net carbs: 2.3g | fiber: 1.0g

Mozzarella Italian Peppers

Prep time: 7 minutes | Cook time: 13 minutes | Serves 5

4 tablespoons canola oil
1 yellow onion, sliced
1⅓ pounds (605 g) Italian peppers, seeded and sliced
1 teaspoon Italian seasoning mix
Sea salt and cayenne pepper, to season
2 balls buffalo Mozzarella, drained and halved

Heat the canola oil in a saucepan over a medium-low flame. Now, sauté the onion until just tender and translucent. Add in the peppers and spices. Cook for about 13 minutes, adding a splash of water to deglaze the pan. Divide between serving plates; top with cheese and serve immediately. Enjoy!

calories: 175 | fat: 11.0g | protein: 10.4g | carbs: 7.0g | net carbs: 5.1g | fiber: 1.9g

White Wine-Dijon Brussels Sprouts

Prep time: 10 minutes | Cook time: 10 minutes | Serves 3

6 ounces (170 g) smoked bacon, diced
12 Brussels sprouts, trimmed and halved
¼ teaspoon ground bay leaf
¼ teaspoon dried oregano
¼ teaspoon dried sage
¼ teaspoon freshly cracked black pepper, or more to taste
Sea salt, to taste
½ cup dry white wine
1 teaspoon Dijon mustard

Heat up a nonstick skillet over medium-high heat. Once hot, cook the bacon for 1 minute. Add the Brussels sprouts and seasoning and continue sautéing, adding white wine and stirring until the bacon is crisp and the Brussels sprouts are tender. It will take about 9 minutes. Then, stir in the mustard, remove from the heat, and serve immediately. Enjoy!

calories: 298 | fat: 22.4g | protein: 9.6g | carbs: 6.4g | net carbs: 3.4g | fiber: 3.0g

Cumin Green Cabbage Stir-Fry

Prep time: 10 minutes | Cook time: 20 minutes | Serves 2

2 tablespoons olive oil
1 (1-inch) piece fresh ginger, grated
½ teaspoon cumin seeds
1 shallot, chopped
½ cup chicken stock
¾ pound (340 g) green cabbage, sliced
¼ teaspoon turmeric powder
½ teaspoon coriander powder
Kosher salt and cayenne pepper, to taste

Heat the olive oil in a saucepan over medium heat; then, sauté the ginger and cumin seeds until fragrant. Add in the shallot and continue sautéing an additional 2 to 3 minutes or until just tender and aromatic. Pour in the chicken stock to deglaze the pan. Add the cabbage wedges, turmeric, coriander, salt, and cayenne pepper. Cover and cook for 15 to 18 minutes or until your cabbage has softened. Make sure to stir occasionally. Serve in individual bowls and enjoy!

calories: 169 | fat: 13.0g | protein: 2.6g | carbs: 7.0g | net carbs: 2.9g | fiber: 4.1g

Almond and Rind Crusted Zucchini Fritters

Prep time: 13 minutes | Cook time: 2 minutes | Serves 2

2 tablespoons olive oil
3 eggs, whisked
1 teaspoon garlic, pressed
½ pound (227 g) zucchini, grated
⅓ cup almond meal
2 tablespoons pork rinds
¼ teaspoon paprika
Sea salt and ground black pepper, to taste
½ cup Swiss cheese, shredded

Add the grated zucchini to a colander. Add ½ teaspoon of salt, toss and let it sit for 10 minutes. After that, drain the zucchini completely using a cheese cloth. Heat the olive oil in a skillet over medium-high flame. In a mixing bowl, combine the zucchini with the remaining ingredients until everything is well incorporated. Make the fritters, flattening them with a spatula; cook for 2 minutes on both sides. Bon appétit!

calories: 462 | fat: 36.0g | protein: 27.5g | carbs: 7.6g | net carbs: 4.8g | fiber: 2.8g

Chinese Cauliflower Rice with Eggs

Prep time: 7 minutes | Cook time: 8 minutes | Serves 3

½ pound (227 g) fresh cauliflower
1 tablespoon sesame oil
½ cup leeks, chopped
1 garlic, pressed
Sea salt and freshly ground black pepper, to taste
½ teaspoon Chinese five-spice powder
1 teaspoon oyster sauce
½ teaspoon light soy sauce
1 tablespoon Shaoxing wine
3 eggs

Pulse the cauliflower in a food processor until it resembles rice. Heat the sesame oil in a pan over medium-high heat; sauté the leeks and garlic for 2 to 3 minutes. Add the prepared cauliflower rice to the pan, along with salt, black pepper, and Chinese five-spice powder. Next, add oyster sauce, soy sauce, and wine. Let it cook, stirring occasionally, until the cauliflower is crisp-tender, about 5 minutes. Then, add the eggs to the pan; stir until everything is well combined. Serve warm and enjoy!

calories: 132 | fat: 8.8g | protein: 7.2g | carbs: 6.2g | net carbs: 4.4g | fiber: 1.8g

Broccoli and Cauliflower Mash

Prep time: 2 minutes | Cook time: 13 minutes | Serves 3

½ pound (227 g) broccoli florets
½ pound (227 g) cauliflower florets
Kosher salt and ground black pepper, to season
½ teaspoon garlic powder
1 teaspoon shallot powder
4 tablespoons whipped cream cheese
1½ tablespoons butter

Microwave the broccoli and cauliflower for about 13 minutes until they have softened completely. Transfer to a food processor and add in the remaining ingredients. Process the ingredients until everything is well combined. Taste and adjust the seasoning. Bon appétit!

calories: 163 | fat: 12.8g | protein: 4.7g | carbs: 7.2g | net carbs: 3.7g | fiber: 3.5g

Braised Cream Kale

Prep time: 4 minutes | Cook time: 11 minutes | Serves 5

2 tablespoons olive oil
1 shallot, chopped
6 cups kale, torn into pieces
½ teaspoon fresh garlic, minced
2 tablespoons dry white wine
¼ teaspoon red pepper flakes, crushed
Sea salt and ground black pepper, to taste
½ cup double cream

Heat the olive oil in a large, heavy-bottomed sauté pan over moderate heat. Now, sauté the shallot until it is tender or about 4 minutes. Stir in the kale and continue to cook for 2 minutes more. Remove any excess liquid and stir in the garlic; continue to cook for a minute or so. Add a splash of wine to deglaze the pan. Then, add the red pepper, salt, black pepper, and double cream to the pan. Turn the heat to simmer. Continue to simmer, covered, for a further 4 minutes. Serve warm and enjoy!

calories: 130 | fat: 10.5g | protein: 3.7g | carbs: 6.1g | net carbs: 3.1g | fiber: 3.0g

Italian Tomato and Cheese Stuffed Peppers

Prep time: 15 minutes | Cook time: 10 minutes | Serves 2

1 tablespoon canola oil
1 garlic clove, pressed
½ cup celery, finely chopped
½ Spanish onion, finely chopped
4 ounces (113 g) pork, ground
Sea salt, to taste
1 teaspoon Italian seasoning mix
2 sweet Italian peppers, seeded and halved
1 large-sized Roma tomato, puréed
½ cup Cheddar cheese, grated

Heat the canola oil in a sauté pan over medium-high heat. Now, sauté the garlic, celery, and onion until they have softened. Stir in the ground pork and cook for a further 3 minutes or until no longer pink. Sprinkle with salt and Italian seasoning mix. Divide the filling mixture between the pepper halves. Add the puréed tomato to a lightly greased baking dish; place the stuffed peppers in the baking dish. Bake in the preheated oven at 390°F (199°C) for 20 minutes. Top with the Cheddar cheese and bake an additional 4 to 6 minutes or until the cheese is bubbling. Serve warm and enjoy!

calories: 312 | fat: 21.4g | protein: 20.2g | carbs: 5.7g | net carbs: 3.8g | fiber: 1.9g

Zucchini Fritters

Prep time: 10 minutes | Cook time: 5 minutes | Serves 6

1 pound (454 g) zucchini, grated and drained
1 egg
1 teaspoon fresh Italian parsley
½ cup almond meal
½ cup goat cheese, crumbled
Sea salt and ground black pepper, to taste
½ teaspoon red pepper flakes, crushed
2 tablespoons olive oil

Mix all ingredients, except for the olive oil, in a large bowl. Let it sit in your refrigerator for 30 minutes. Heat the oil in a non-stick frying pan over medium heat; scoop the heaped tablespoons of the zucchini mixture into the hot oil. Cook for 3 to 4 minutes; then, gently flip the fritters over and cook on the other side. Cook in a couple of batches. Transfer to a paper towel to soak up any excess grease. Serve and enjoy!

calories: 110 | fat: 8.8g | protein: 5.8g | carbs: 3.2g | net carbs: 2.2g | fiber: 1.0g

Roasted Asparagus

Prep time: 10 minutes | Cook time: 15 minutes | Serves 5

4 tablespoons butter, melted
4 tablespoons Pecorino Romano cheese, grated
1½ pounds (680 g) asparagus, trimmed
½ teaspoon cayenne pepper
Sea salt and cracked black pepper, to taste
1 tablespoon Sriracha sauce
1 tablespoon fresh cilantro, roughly chopped

Toss your asparagus with the melted butter, cheese, cayenne pepper, salt, black pepper, and Sriracha sauce; toss until well coated. Place the asparagus on a roasting pan. Roast in the preheated oven at 420°F (216°C) for 10 minutes. Rotate the pan and continue to cook an additional 4 to 5 minutes. Serve immediately garnished with fresh cilantro. Bon appétit!

calories: 141 | fat: 11.5g | protein: 5.6g | carbs: 5.5g | net carbs: 2.6g | fiber: 2.9g

Mushroom Red Wine Chili

Prep time: 10 minutes | Cook time: 15 minutes | Serves 3

3 ounces (85 g) bacon, diced
1 brown onion, chopped
2 cloves garlic, minced
¾ pound (340 g) brown mushrooms, sliced
3 tablespoons dry red wine
½ teaspoon freshly ground black pepper
1 teaspoon chili powder
2 bay laurels
Sea salt, to taste

Heat a soup pot over a medium-high flame and fry the bacon; once the bacon is crisp, remove from the pot and reserve. Now, cook the brown onion and garlic until they have softened or about 6 minutes. Stir in the mushrooms and sauté them for 3 to 4 minutes longer. Turn the heat to simmer; add the other ingredients and continue to cook for 10 minutes more, until most of the cooking liquid has evaporated. Ladle into bowls and top with the reserved bacon. Bon appétit!

calories: 160 | fat: 11.3g | protein: 6.9g | carbs: 6.0g | net carbs: 4.7g | fiber: 1.3g

Herbed Eggplant

Prep time: 15 minutes | Cook time: 20 minutes | Serves 2

1 teaspoon basil	2 tablespoons coconut aminos
½ teaspoon oregano	1 teaspoon balsamic vinegar
½ teaspoon rosemary	1 tablespoon olive oil
½ teaspoon coarse sea salt	½ teaspoon Sriracha sauce
1 large-sized eggplant, curt into slices lengthwise	¼ cup fresh chives, chopped

Toss your eggplant with the basil, oregano, rosemary, and salt. Place the eggplant on a parchment-lined roasting pan. Roast in the preheated oven at 420ºF (216ºC) approximately 15 minutes. Meanwhile, mix the coconut aminos, vinegar, oil, and Sriracha sauce. Drizzle the Sriracha mixture over the eggplant slices. Place under the preheated broil for 3 to 5 minutes. Garnish with fresh chives and serve warm.

calories: 102 | fat: 7.0g | protein: 1.6g | carbs: 8.0g | net carbs: 3.3g | fiber: 4.7g

Mushroom Mélange

Prep time: 10 minutes | Cook time: 15 minutes | Serves 6

4 tablespoons olive oil	1 cup tomato sauce
1 bell pepper, sliced	½ teaspoon dried oregano
½ cup leeks, finely diced	½ teaspoon chili powder
2 cloves garlic, smashed	½ teaspoon paprika
2 pounds (907 g) brown mushrooms, sliced	½ teaspoon ground black pepper
2 cups chicken broth	Sea salt, to taste

Heat the oil in a heavy-bottomed pot over medium-high flame. Now, sauté bell pepper along with the leeks for about 5 minutes. Stir in the garlic and mushrooms, and continue sautéing an additional minute or so. Add in a splash of chicken broth to deglaze the bottom of the pan. After that, add in the tomato sauce and seasonings. Bring to a boil and immediately reduce the heat to simmer. Partially cover and cook for 8 to 10 minutes more or until the mushrooms are cooked through. Ladle into individual bowls and serve with cauli rice if desired. Bon appétit!

calories: 124 | fat: 9.2g | protein: 4.6g | carbs: 5.8g | net carbs: 4.3g | fiber: 1.5g

Mozzarella Roasted Peppers

Prep time: 5 minutes | Cook time: 15 minutes | Serves 4

2 teaspoons olive oil	¼ teaspoon red pepper flakes
4 Italian sweet peppers, seeded and halved	8 ounces (227 g) Mozzarella cheese
Sat and black pepper, to taste	

Put your oven on broil. Drizzle the pepper halves with olive oil. Season the peppers with salt, black pepper, and red pepper flakes. Top the pepper halves with Mozzarella cheese. Arrange the stuffed peppers on a parchment-lined baking tray. Roast for 12 to 15 until the cheese is browned on top and the peppers are tender and blistered. Bon appétit!

calories: 215 | fat: 15.1g | protein: 13.5g | carbs: 6.7g | net carbs: 4.7g | fiber: 2.0g

Broccoli Cheese

Prep time: 10 minutes | Cook time: 15 minutes | Serves 5

3 tablespoons olive oil	pepper
1 teaspoon garlic, minced	½ teaspoon paprika
1½ pounds (680 g) broccoli florets	½ cup cream of mushrooms soup
½ teaspoon flaky salt	6 ounces (170 g) Swiss cheese, shredded
½ teaspoon ground black	

Heat 1 tablespoon of the olive oil in a nonstick frying pan over a moderate flame. Then, sauté the garlic until just tender and fragrant. Preheat your oven to 390ºF (199ºC). Now, brush the sides and bottom of a casserole dish with 1 tablespoon of olive oil. Parboil the broccoli in salted water until it is crisp-tender; discard any excess water and transfer the boiled broccoli florets to the prepared casserole dish. Scatter the sautéed garlic around the broccoli florets. Drizzle the remaining tablespoon of olive oil; sprinkle the salt, black pepper, and paprika over your broccoli. Pour in the cream of mushroom soup. Top with the Swiss cheese and bake approximately 18 minutes until the cheese bubbled all over. Bon appétit!

calories: 180 | fat: 10.3g | protein: 13.5g | carbs: 7.6g | net carbs: 4.0g | fiber: 3.6g

Parmigiano-Reggiano Cheese Broiled Avocados

Prep time: 10 minutes | Cook time: 5 minutes | Serves 6

3 avocados, pitted and halved	3 tablespoons extra-virgin olive oil
½ teaspoon red pepper flakes, crushed	6 tablespoons Parmigiano-Reggiano cheese, grated
½ teaspoon Himalayan salt	

Begin by preheating your oven for broil. Then, cut a crisscross pattern about ¾ of the way through on each avocado half with a sharp knife. Sprinkle red pepper and salt over the avocado halves. Drizzle olive oil over them and top with the grated Parmigiano-Reggiano cheese. Transfer the avocado halves to a roasting pan and cook under the broiler approximately 5 minutes. Enjoy!

calories: 196 | fat: 18.8g | protein: 2.6g | carbs: 6.4g | net carbs: 1.9g | fiber: 4.5g

Baked Eggplant Rounds

Prep time: 10 minutes | Cook time: 35 minutes | Serves 6

1 pound (454 g)eggplant, peeled and sliced	½ teaspoon salt
2 teaspoons Italian seasoning blend	1½ cups marinara sauce
½ teaspoon cayenne pepper	1 cup Mozzarella cheese
	2 tablespoons fresh basil leaves, snipped

Begin by preheating your oven to 380ºF (193ºC). Line a baking pan with parchment paper. Now, arrange the eggplant rounds on the baking pan. Season with the Italian blend, cayenne pepper, and salt. Bake for 25 to 28 minutes, flipping the rounds half-way through baking time. Next, remove from the oven and top with the marinara sauce and Mozzarella cheese. Bake for 6 to 8 minutes more until Mozzarella is bubbling. Garnish with fresh basil leaves just before serving.

calories: 92 | fat: 4.8g | protein: 5.2g | carbs: 5.2g | net carbs: 2.3g | fiber: 2.9g

Duo-Cheese Broccoli Croquettes

Prep time: 10 minutes | Cook time: 10 minutes | Serves 5

1 pound (454 g) broccoli florets	3 eggs
1 tablespoon fresh parsley, minced	1 cup Romano cheese, preferably freshly grated
½ teaspoon paprika	5 ounces (142 g) Swiss cheese, sliced
Sea salt and ground black pepper, to taste	2 tablespoons olive oil

Pulse the broccoli florets in your food processor until small rice-sized pieces are formed. Mix the chopped broccoli florets with the parsley, paprika, salt, pepper, eggs, and Romano cheese. Shape the mixture into bite-sized balls; flatten the balls with your hands or fork. Heat the olive oil in a frying pan over a moderate flame. Cook for 4 to 5 minutes; turn over, top with the Swiss cheese and continue to cook on the other side for a further 4 minutes or until thoroughly cooked. Bon appétit!

calories: 324 | fat: 24.1g | protein: 19.9g | carbs: 5.8g | net carbs: 3.5g | fiber: 2.3g

Avocado Sauced Cucumber Noodles

Prep time: 15 minutes | Cook time: 0 minutes | Serves 2

½ teaspoon sea salt	1 tablespoon olive oil
1 cucumber, spiralized	½ teaspoon garlic powder
1 California avocado, pitted, peeled and mashed	½ teaspoon paprika
	1 tablespoon fresh lime juice

Toss your cucumber with salt and let it sit for 30 minutes; discard the excess water and pat dry. In a mixing bowl, thoroughly combine the avocado with the olive oil, garlic powder, paprika, and lime juice. Add the sauce to the cucumber noodles and serve immediately. Bon appétit!

calories: 195 | fat: 17.2g | protein: 2.6g | carbs: 7.6g | net carbs: 3.0g | fiber: 4.6g

Fennel Avgolemono

Prep time: 10 minutes | Cook time: 20 minutes | Serves 6

2 tablespoons olive oil	5 cups chicken stock
1 celery stalk, chopped	Sea salt and ground black pepper, to season
1 pound (454 g) fennel bulbs, sliced	2 eggs
1 garlic clove, minced	1 tablespoon freshly squeezed lemon juice
1 bay laurel	
1 thyme sprig	

Heat the olive oil in a heavy-bottomed pot over a medium-high flame. Sauté the celery and fennel until they have softened but not browned, about 8 minutes. Add in the garlic, bay laurel, and thyme sprig; continue sautéing until aromatic an additional minute or so. Add the chicken stock, salt, and black pepper to the pot. Bring to a boil. Reduce the heat to medium-low and let it simmer, partially covered, approximately 13 minutes. Discard the bay laurel and then, blend your soup with an immersion blender. Whisk the eggs and lemon juice; gradually pour 2 cups of the hot soup into the egg mixture, whisking constantly. Return the soup to the pot and continue stirring for a few minutes or just until thickened. Serve warm.

calories: 85 | fat: 6.2g | protein: 2.8g | carbs: 6.0g | net carbs: 3.5g | fiber: 2.5g

Gruyère Celery Boats

Prep time: 10 minutes | Cook time: 35 minutes | Serves 2

1 jalapeño pepper, seeded and minced	3 tablespoons scallions, minced
¼ teaspoon sea salt	½ teaspoon caraway seeds
¼ teaspoon ground black pepper	2 ounces (57 g) Gruyère cheese
1 teaspoon granulated garlic	3 celery stalks, halved

In a mixing bowl, thoroughly combine the minced jalapeño with sea salt, black pepper, garlic, scallions, caraway seeds, and Gruyère cheese. Spread this mixture over the celery stalks. Then, arrange them on a parchment-lined baking tray. Roast in the preheated oven at 360ºF (182ºC) for 35 minutes or until cooked through.

calories: 195 | fat: 17.1g | protein: 2.5g | carbs: 7.0g | net carbs: 2.0g | fiber: 5.0g

Fried Cabbage

Prep time: 10 minutes | Cook time: 15 minutes | Serves 3

4 ounces (113 g) bacon, diced	½ teaspoon cayenne pepper
1 medium-sized onion, chopped	1 pound (454 g) red cabbage, shredded
2 cloves garlic, minced	¼ teaspoon ground black pepper, to season
½ teaspoon caraway seeds	1 cup beef bone broth
1 bay laurel	

Heat up a nonstick skillet over a moderate flame. Cook the bacon for 3 to 4 minutes, stirring continuously; set aside. In the same skillet, sauté the onion for 2 to 3 minutes or until it has softened. Now, sauté the garlic and caraway seeds for 30 seconds more or until aromatic. Then, add in the remaining ingredients and stir to combine. Reduce the temperature to medium-low, cover, and cook for 10 minutes longer; stirring periodically to ensure even cooking. Serve in individual bowls, garnished with the reserved bacon. Enjoy!

calories: 242 | fat: 22.2g | protein: 6.5g | carbs: 6.8g | net carbs: 4.9g | fiber: 1.9g

Spinach and Butternut Squash Stew

Prep time: 10 minutes | Cook time: 30 minutes | Serves 4

2 tablespoons olive oil	1 celery stalk, chopped
1 Spanish onion, peeled and diced	3 cups vegetable broth
1 garlic clove, minced	Kosher salt and freshly cracked black pepper, to taste
½ pound (227 g) butternut squash, diced	4cups baby spinach
	4 tablespoons sour cream

Heat the olive oil in a soup pot over a moderate flame. Now, sauté the Spanish onion until tender and translucent. Then, cook the garlic until just tender and aromatic. Stir in the butternut squash, celery, broth, salt, and black pepper. Turn the heat to simmer and let it cook, covered, for 30 minutes. Fold in the baby spinach leaves and cover with the lid; let it sit in the residual heat until the baby spinach wilts completely. Serve dolloped with cold sour cream. Enjoy!

calories: 150 | fat: 11.6g | protein: 2.5g | carbs: 6.8g | net carbs: 4.5g | fiber: 2.3g

Wax Beans with Tomato-Mustard Sauce

Prep time: 9 minutes | Cook time: 6 minutes | Serves 4

1 tablespoon butter
2 garlic cloves, thinly sliced
½ pound (227 g) wax beans, trimmed
½ cup tomato sauce

2 tablespoons dry white wine
½ teaspoon mustard seeds
Sea salt and ground black pepper, to taste

Melt the butter in a saucepan over a medium-high flame. Now, sauté the garlic until aromatic but not browned. Stir in the wax beans, tomato sauce, wine, and mustard seeds. Season with salt and black pepper to taste. Turn the heat to medium-low, partially cover and continue to cook for 6 minutes longer or until everything is heated through. Bon appétit!

calories: 56 | fat: 3.5g | protein: 1.5g | carbs: 6.0g | net carbs: 3.8g | fiber: 2.2g

Romaine Lettuce Boats

Prep time: 10 minutes | Cook time: 3 minutes | Serves 4

½ pound (227 g) pork sausage, sliced
1 green bell pepper, seeded and chopped
1 garlic clove, minced
½ cup tomato purée
¼ teaspoon ground black

pepper
½ teaspoon fennel seeds
Himalayan salt, to taste
1 head romaine lettuce, separated into leaves
2 scallions, chopped

Preheat a nonstick frying pan over a moderate flame. Then, sear the pork sausage until no longer pink, crumbling with a fork. Stir in the bell pepper and garlic, and continue sautéing an additional minute or so or until fragrant. Fold in the tomato purée. Season with black pepper, fennel seeds, and salt. Stir well and continue to cook for 2 minutes more; remove from the heat. Arrange the lettuce boats on a serving platter. Then, top each boat with the sausage mixture. Garnish with scallions and serve immediately. Bon appétit!

calories: 231 | fat: 18.1g | protein: 10.2g | carbs: 5.6g | net carbs: 3.5g | fiber: 2.1g

Peasant Stir-Fry

Prep time: 10 minutes | Cook time: 20 minutes | Serves 5

2 tablespoons olive oil
1 yellow onion, sliced
3 garlic cloves, halved
8 bell peppers, seeded and cut into strips
1 tomato, chopped

½ teaspoon ground black pepper
½ teaspoon paprika
½ teaspoon kosher salt
2 eggs

Heat the olive oil in a frying pan over medium-low heat. Now, sweat the onion for 3 to 4 minutes or until tender. Now, stir in the garlic and peppers; continue sautéing for 5 minutes. Then, add in the tomato, black pepper, paprika, and kosher salt. Partially cover and continue to cook for a further 6 to 8 minutes. Fold in the eggs and stir fry for another 5 minutes. Serve warm and enjoy!

calories: 115 | fat: 7.5g | protein: 3.4g | carbs: 6.0g | net carbs: 4.5g | fiber: 1.5g

Zucchini Noodles with Mushroom Sauce

Prep time: 10 minutes | Cook time: 10 minutes | Serves 3

1½ tablespoons olive oil
3 cups button mushrooms, chopped
2 cloves garlic, smashed
1 cup tomato purée
1 pound (454 g) zucchini,

spiralized
Salt and ground black pepper, to taste
⅓ cup Pecorino Romano cheese, preferably freshly grated

Heat the olive oil in a saucepan over a moderate flame. Then, cook the mushrooms until tender and fragrant or about 4 minutes. Stir in the garlic and continue to sauté an additional 30 seconds or until just tender and aromatic. Fold in the tomato purée and zucchini. Reduce the heat to medium-low, partially cover and let it cook for about 6 minutes or until heated through. Season with salt and black pepper to taste. Divide your zoodles and sauce between serving plates. Top with Pecorino Romano cheese and serve warm. Bon appétit!

calories: 161 | fat: 10.5g | protein: 10.0g | carbs: 7.4g | net carbs: 4.0g | fiber: 3.4g

Queso Fresco Avocado Salsa

Prep time: 5 minutes | Cook time: 0 minutes | Serves 4

2 tomatoes, diced
3scallions, chopped
1 poblano pepper, chopped
1 garlic clove, minced
2 ripe avocados, peeled, pitted and diced

1 tablespoon extra-virgin olive oil
2 tablespoons fresh lime juice
Sea salt and ground black pepper, to season
¼ cup queso fresco, crumbled

Place the tomatoes, scallions, poblano pepper, garlic and avocado in a serving bowl. Drizzle olive oil and lime juice over everything. Season with salt and black pepper. To serve, top with crumbled queso fresco and enjoy!

calories: 189 | fat: 16.0g | protein: 3.6g | carbs: 6.9g | net carbs: 2.7g | fiber: 4.2g

Za'atar Chanterelle Stew

Prep time: 15 minutes | Cook time: 50 minutes | Serves 4

½ teaspoon Za'atar spice
4 tablespoons olive oil
½ cup shallots, chopped
2 bell peppers, chopped
1 poblano pepper, finely chopped
8 ounces (227 g) Chanterelle

mushroom, sliced
½ teaspoon garlic, minced
Sea salt and freshly cracked black pepper, to taste
1 cup tomato purée
3 cups vegetable broth
1 bay laurel

Combine the Za'atar with 3 tablespoons of olive oil in a small saucepan. Cook over a moderate flame until hot. Set aside for 1 hour to cool and infuse. In a pot, heat the remaining olive oil. Sauté the shallots and bell peppers until just tender and fragrant. Stir in the poblano pepper, mushrooms, and garlic; continue to sauté until the mushrooms have softened. Add in the salt, black pepper, tomato purée, broth, and bay laurel. Once your stew begins to boil, turn the heat down to a simmer. Let it simmer for about 40 minutes until everything is thoroughly cooked. Ladle into individual bowls and drizzle each serving with Za'atar oil. Serve.

calories: 156 | fat: 13.8g | protein: 1.4g | carbs: 6.0g | net carbs: 3.1g | fiber: 2.9g

Goat Cheese Eggplant Casserole

Prep time: 10 minutes | Cook time: 25 minutes | Serves 3

1 (1-pound / 454-g) eggplant, cut into rounds
2 bell peppers, seeded and quartered
2 vine-ripe tomatoes, sliced
3 tablespoons olive oil
Sea salt and freshly ground black pepper, to taste
½ teaspoon red pepper flakes, crushed
½ teaspoon sumac
½ cup sour cream
1½ cups goat cheese
2 tablespoons green onions, chopped

Place your eggplant and peppers in a baking pan. Top with the sliced tomatoes. Drizzle olive oil over the vegetables. Season with salt, black pepper, crushed red pepper, and sumac. Bake in the preheated oven at 420ºF (216ºC) for 15 minutes. Rotate the pan and bake an additional 10 minutes. Top with sour cream and goat cheese. Garnish with green onions and serve. Enjoy!

calories: 476 | fat: 41.4g | protein: 18.4g | carbs: 7.2g | net carbs: 3.6g | fiber: 3.6g

Provençal Ratatouille

Prep time: 15 minutes | Cook time: 35 minutes | Serves 6

2 tablespoons olive oil
2 garlic cloves, finely minced
1 red pepper, sliced
1 yellow pepper, sliced
1 green pepper, sliced
1 shallot, sliced
1 large-sized zucchini, sliced
3 tomatoes, sliced
1 cup vegetable broth
Sea salt, to taste
½ teaspoon dried oregano
½ teaspoon dried parsley flakes
½ teaspoon paprika
½ teaspoon ground black pepper
6 eggs

Start by preheating your oven to 400ºF (205ºC). Brush the sides and bottom of a baking pan with olive oil. Layer all vegetables into the prepared pan and cover tightly with foil. Pour in the vegetable broth. Season with salt, oregano, parsley, paprika, and ground black pepper. Bake for about 25 minutes. Create six indentations in the hot ratatouille. Break an egg into each indentation. Bake until the eggs are set or about 9 minutes. Enjoy!

calories: 440 | fat: 45.0g | protein: 6.4g | carbs: 5.6g | net carbs: 4.6g | fiber: 1.0g

Green Cabbage with Tofu

Prep time: 5 minutes | Cook time: 15 minutes | Serves 3

6 ounces (170 g) tofu, diced
½ shallot, chopped
2 garlic cloves, finely chopped
1 (1½-pound / 680-g) head green cabbage, cut into strips
½ cup vegetable broth

Heat up a lightly oiled sauté pan over moderate heat. Now, cook the tofu until brown and crisp; set aside. Then, sauté the shallot and garlic until just tender and fragrant. Add in the green cabbage and beef bone broth; stir to combine. Reduce the heat to medium-low and continue cooking an additional 13 minutes. Season with salt to taste, top with reserved tofu and serve warm. Bon appétit!

calories: 168 | fat: 11.7g | protein: 10.5g | carbs: 5.2g | net carbs: 2.9g | fiber: 2.3g

Cauliflower Soup

Prep time: 4 minutes | Cook time: 15 minutes | Serves 4

2 green onions, chopped
½ teaspoon ginger-garlic paste
1 celery stalk, chopped
1 pound (454 g) cauliflower florets
3 cups vegetable broth

Heat up a lightly oiled soup pot over a medium-high flame. Now, sauté the green onions until they have softened. Stir in the ginger-garlic paste, celery, cauliflower, and vegetable broth; bring to a rapid boil. Turn the heat to medium-low. Continue to simmer for 13 minutes more or until heated through; heat off. Puree the soup in your blender until creamy and uniform. Enjoy!

calories: 70 | fat: 1.6g | protein: 6.2g | carbs: 7.0g | net carbs: 4.0g | fiber: 3.0g

Mushroom and Bell Pepper Omelet

Prep time: 5 minutes | Cook time: 5 minutes | Serves 4

2 tablespoons olive oil
1 cup Chanterelle mushrooms, chopped
2 bell peppers, chopped
1 white onion, chopped
6 eggs

Heat the olive oil in a nonstick skillet over moderate heat. Now, cook the mushrooms, peppers, and onion until they have softened. In a mixing bowl, whisk the eggs until frothy. Add the eggs to the skillet, reduce the heat to medium-low, and cook approximately 5 minutes until the center starts to look dry. Do not overcook. Taste and season with salt to taste. Bon appétit!

calories: 240 | fat: 17.5g | protein: 12.3g | carbs: 6.1g | net carbs: 4.3g | fiber: 1.8g

Cauliflower Chowder with Fresh Dill

Prep time: 10 minutes | Cook time: 31 minutes | Serves 4

1 tablespoon butter, softened at room temperature
½ stalk celery, chopped
1 white onion, chopped
1 teaspoon ginger-garlic paste
1 pound (454 g) cauliflower florets
Sea salt and white pepper, to taste
1 teaspoon ground sumac
4 cups roasted vegetable broth
1 cup heavy whipping cream
2 tablespoons fresh dill, chopped

Melt the butter in a heavy pot over medium-high heat. Then, sauté the celery and onions for 5 minutes, until just tender and fragrant. Stir in the ginger-garlic paste, cauliflower, salt, white pepper, and sumac; continue to sauté for 1 minute more. Pour in the vegetable broth, bringing to a rapid boil. Immediately turn the heat to medium-low. Cover part-way and continue to simmer for about 25 minutes. Purée the chowder using an immersion blender or food processor until you achieve your desired smoothness. Return the chowder to the pot and fold in the heavy whipping cream. Cook briefly until your chowder is all warmed through. Test and adjust seasonings as needed. Garnish with fresh dill and serve warm.

calories: 172 | fat: 15g | protein: 3g | carbs: 7g | net carbs: 4g | fiber: 3g

Greek-Style Aubergine-Egg Casserole

Prep time: 5 minutes | Cook time: 57 minutes | Serves 5

1 pound (454 g) aubergine, cut into rounds
2 vine-ripe tomatoes, sliced
5 eggs, beaten
1 cup Greek-style yogurt
1½ cups feta cheese, grated

Place the aubergine on a large pan lined with paper towel; toss with 1 teaspoon of sea salt and let it stand for 25 minutes in a colander. Pat your aubergine dry and transfer to a lightly oiled baking sheet. Brush them with olive oil. Bake in the preheated oven at 390°F (199°C) for about 40 minutes, or until they are golden brown. Layer the rounds of roasted aubergine on the bottom of a lightly oiled casserole dish. Top with sliced tomatoes. In a mixing dish, whisk the eggs with the yogurt. Pour the mixture over the prepared vegetables. Top with feta cheese and bake in the preheated oven at 360°F (182°C) for 17 minutes. Enjoy!

calories: 226 | fat: 14g | protein: 16g | carbs: 7g | net carbs:4 g | fiber: 3g

Mexican-Flavored Stuffed Peppers

Prep time: 5 minutes | Cook time: 40 minutes | Serves 3

3 bell peppers, halved, seeded
3 eggs, whisked
1 cup Mexican cheese blend
1 teaspoon chili powder
1 garlic clove, minced
1 teaspoon onion powder
1 ripe tomato, puréed
1 teaspoon mustard powder

Start by preheating your oven to 370°F (188°C). Spritz the bottom and sides of a baking pan with a cooking oil. In a mixing bowl, thoroughly combine the eggs, cheese, chili powder, garlic, and onion powder. Divide the filling between the bell peppers. Mix the tomatoes with mustard powder and transfer the mixture to the baking pan. Cover with foil and bake for 40 minutes, until the peppers are tender and the filling is thoroughly heated. Bon appétit!

calories: 194 | fat: 14g | protein: 13g | carbs: 4g | net carbs: 3g | fiber: 1g

Halloumi Asparagus Frittata

Prep time: 10 minutes | Cook time: 20 minutes | Serves 4

1 tablespoon olive oil
½ red onion, sliced
4 ounces (113 g) asparagus, cut into small chunks
1 tomato, chopped
5 whole eggs, beaten
10 ounces (284 g) Halloumi cheese, crumbled
2 tablespoons green olives, pitted and sliced
1 tablespoon fresh parsley, chopped

Heat the oil in a skillet over medium-high heat; then, cook the onion and asparagus about 3 minutes, stirring continuously. Next, add the tomato and cook for 2 minutes longer. Transfer the sautéed vegetables to a baking pan that is lightly greased with cooking oil. Mix the eggs with cheese until well combined. Pour the mixture over the vegetables. Scatter sliced olives over the top. Bake in the preheated oven at 350°F (180°C) for 15 minutes. Garnish with fresh parsley and serve immediately. Enjoy!

calories: 376 | fat: 29g | protein: 25g | carbs: 4g | net carbs: 3g | fiber: 1g

Cheesy Egg-Stuffed Avocados

Prep time: 5 minutes | Cook time: 15 minutes | Serves 4

2 avocados, pitted and halved
4 eggs
Sea salt and freshly ground black pepper, to taste
1 cup Asiago cheese, grated
½ teaspoon red pepper flakes
½ teaspoon dried rosemary
1 tablespoon fresh chives, chopped

Crack the eggs into the avocado halves, keeping the yolks intact. Sprinkle with salt and black pepper. Top with cheese, red pepper flakes, and rosemary. Arrange the stuffed avocado halves in a baking pan. Bake in the preheated oven at 420°F (216°C) for about 15 minutes. Serve garnished with fresh chives. Enjoy!

calories: 300 | fat: 25g | protein: 15g | carbs: 6g | net carbs: 1g | fiber: 5g

Swiss Zucchini Gratin

Prep time: 10 minutes | Cook time: 10 minutes | Serves 5

10 large eggs
3 tablespoons yogurt
2 zucchinis, sliced
½ medium-sized leek, sliced
Sea salt and ground black
pepper, to taste
1 teaspoon cayenne pepper
1 cup cream cheese
2 garlic cloves, minced
1 cup Swiss cheese, shredded

Start by preheating your oven to 360°F (182°C). Then, spritz the bottom and sides of an oven proof pan with a nonstick cooking spray. Then, mix the eggs with yogurt until well combined. Overlap ½ of the zucchini and leek slices in the pan. Season with salt, black pepper, and cayenne pepper. Add cream cheese and minced garlic. Add the remaining zucchini slices and leek. Add the egg mixture. Top with Swiss cheese. Bake for 40 minutes, until the top is golden brown. Bon appétit!

calories: 371 | fat: 32g | protein: 16g | carbs: 5g | net carbs: 4g | fiber: 1g

Italian Broccoli and Spinach Soup

Prep time: 15 minutes | Cook time: 30 minutes | Serves 3

4 ounces (113 g) broccoli
2 tablespoons sesame oil
1 small-sized onion, chopped
2 garlic cloves, minced
1 teaspoon cayenne pepper
Sea salt and ground black pepper, to taste
1 cup spinach leaves, torn into pieces
1 celery stalk, peeled and chopped
2 cups vegetable broth
1 cup water
1 tomato, puréed
1 jalapeño pepper, minced
1 tablespoon Italian seasonings

Pulse the broccoli in your food processor until rice-sized pieces are formed; work in batches; reserve. Then, heat the oil in a saucepan over medium heat. Then, sauté the onion and garlic for 3 minutes, until tender and aromatic. Add the broccoli and cook for 2 minutes more. Add the remaining ingredients, except the spinach. Bring to a rapid boil and then, immediately reduce the heat to medium-low. Now, simmer the soup approximately 25 minutes. Add spinach, turn off the heat, and cover with the lid; let it wilt. Bon appétit!

calories: 137 | fat: 11g | protein: 6g | carbs: 6g | net carbs: 5g | fiber: 1g

Leek, Mushroom, and Zucchini Stew

Prep time: 5 minutes | Cook time: 15 minutes | Serves 4

½ cup leeks, chopped
1 pound (454 g) brown mushrooms, chopped
1 teaspoon garlic, minced
1 medium-sized zucchini, diced
2 ripe tomatoes, puréed

Heat up a lightly greased soup pot over medium-high heat. Now, sauté the leeks until just tender about 3 minutes. Stir in the mushrooms, garlic, and zucchini. Continue to sauté an additional 2 minutes or until tender and aromatic. Add in the tomatoes and 2 cups of water. Season with Sazón spice, if desired. Reduce the temperature to simmer and continue to cook, covered, for 10 to 12 minutes more. Bon appétit!

calories: 108 | fat: 7.5g | protein: 3.1g | carbs: 7.0g | net carbs: 4.5g | fiber: 2.5g

Cauliflower and Celery Soup

Prep time: 5 minutes | Cook time: 15 minutes | Serves 4

2 green onions, chopped
½ teaspoon ginger-garlic paste
1 celery stalk, chopped
1 pound (454 g) cauliflower florets
3 cups vegetable broth

Heat up a lightly oiled soup pot over a medium-high flame. Now, sauté the green onions for 2 minutes, until they have softened. Stir in the ginger-garlic paste, celery, cauliflower, and vegetable broth; bring to a rapid boil. Turn the heat to medium-low. Continue to simmer for 13 minutes more or until heated through; heat off. Purée the soup in your blender until creamy and uniform. Enjoy!

calories: 69 | fat: 2g | protein: 6g | carbs: 7g | net carbs: 4g | fiber: 3g

Provençal Ratatouille Casserole

Prep time: 15 minutes | Cook time: 1 hour | Serves 6

3 tablespoons extra-virgin olive oil, divided
1 tomato, sliced
2 yellow onions, sliced
3 garlic, sliced
3 bell peppers, sliced
2 medium-sized zucchinis, cut into rounds
1 medium-sized Japanese
eggplant, cut into rounds
1 cup tomato purée
Sea salt and black pepper, to taste
1 tablespoon Herbes de Provence
2 tablespoons fresh cilantro, chopped

Start by preheating your oven to 375ºF (190ºC). Toss the sliced vegetables with the olive oil and brush the sides and bottom of a casserole dish with cooking spray. Arrange the sliced vegetables in alternating patterns in the baking pan. Add the tomato purée, salt, black pepper, and Herbes de Provence. Cover with aluminum foil. Bake in the preheated oven for 30 minutes. Remove the foil and bake for a further 30 minutes or until the tomato purée is bubbling. Garnish with fresh cilantro just before serving. Enjoy!

calories: 104 | fat: 7g | protein: 2g | carbs: 7g | net carbs: 4g | fiber: 3g

Mushroom and Bell Pepper Omelet

Prep time: 5 minutes | Cook time: 10 minutes | Serves 4

2 tablespoons olive oil
1 cup Chanterelle mushrooms, chopped
2 bell peppers, chopped
1 white onion, chopped
6 eggs

Heat the olive oil in a nonstick skillet over moderate heat. Now, cook the mushrooms, peppers, and onion for 5 minutes, until they have softened. In a mixing bowl, whisk the eggs until frothy. Add the eggs to the skillet, reduce the heat to medium-low, and cook for approximately 5 minutes until the center starts to look dry. Do not overcook. Taste and season with salt to taste. Bon appétit!

calories: 239 | fat: 18g | protein: 12g | carbs: 6g | net carbs: 4g | fiber: 2g

Peppery Omelet with Cheddar Cheese

Prep time: 10 minutes | Cook time: 8 minutes | Serves 2

2 tablespoons olive oil
1 onion, sliced
2 bell peppers, chopped
1 jalapeño pepper, chopped
4 eggs, whisked
4 tablespoons full-fat yogurt
½ teaspoon red pepper flakes
Sea salt and ground black pepper, to season
3 ounces (85 g) Cheddar cheese, shredded

Heat the olive oil in a frying pan over a moderate flame. Sauté the onion and peppers for 3 minutes, until tender and fragrant. Then, mix the eggs with the full-fat yogurt. Now, pour the egg mixture into the frying pan. Season with red pepper, salt, and black pepper. Move the pan around to spread it out evenly. Continue to cook for about 5 minutes until the eggs are fully set and the surface is smooth. Top with cheese and serve immediately. Bon appétit!

calories: 439 | fat: 37g | protein: 23g | carbs: 4g | net carbs: 4g | fiber: 0g

Citrus Asparagus and Cherry Tomato Salad

Prep time: 10 minutes | Cook time: 16 minutes | Serves 3

1 pound (454 g) asparagus, trimmed
¼ teaspoon ground black pepper
Flaky salt, to season
3 tablespoons sesame seeds
1 tablespoon Dijon mustard
½ lime, freshly squeezed
3 tablespoons extra-virgin olive oil
2 garlic cloves, minced
1 tablespoon fresh tarragon, snipped
1 cup cherry tomatoes, sliced

Start by preheating your oven to 395ºF (202ºC). Spritz a roasting pan with nonstick cooking spray. Roast the asparagus for about 13 minutes, turning the spears over once or twice. Sprinkle with salt, pepper, and sesame seeds; roast an additional 3 to 4 minutes. To make the dressing, whisk the Dijon mustard, lime juice, olive oil, and minced garlic. Chop the asparagus spears into bite-sized pieces and place them in a nice salad bowl. Add the tarragon and tomatoes to the bowl; gently toss to combine. Dress your salad and serve at room temperature. Enjoy!

calories: 159 | fat: 12g | protein: 6g | carbs: 6g | net carbs: 2g | fiber: 4g

Shirataki Mushroom Ramen

Prep time: 10 minutes | Cook time: 13 to 18 minutes | Serves 4

1½ tablespoons butter, melted
1 pound (454 g) brown mushrooms, chopped
1 teaspoon ginger-garlic paste
½ teaspoon ground cumin
½ teaspoon ground coriander
¼ teaspoon ground black

pepper, or more to taste
Sea salt, to taste
2 tablespoons green onions, chopped
4 cups roasted vegetable broth
8 ounces (227 g) shirataki noodles

Melt the butter in a soup pot over moderate heat. Then, sauté the mushrooms for about 3 minutes or until they are just tender. Stir in the ginger-garlic paste, cumin, coriander, black pepper, salt, and green onions. Pour in the roasted vegetable broth and bring to a boil. Immediately reduce the heat to medium-low. Let it simmer for 8 to 11 minutes. Fold in the shirataki noodles and cook for 2 to 4 minutes more. Serve hot and enjoy!

calories: 76 | fat: 5g | protein: 4g | carbs: 5g | net carbs: 4g | fiber: 1g

Cheesy Veggie Fritters

Prep time: 10 minutes | Cook time: 5 to 6 minutes | Serves 5

1 pound (454 g) cauliflower florets
1 celery stalk, chopped
1 small-sized zucchini, cut into rounds
1 shallot, chopped
Sea salt and freshly ground black pepper, to taste

½ teaspoon cayenne pepper
2 garlic cloves, minced
1 cup Parmesan cheese, shredded
1 egg, beaten
½ cup almond meal
2 tablespoons sesame oil

Pulse the cauliflower florets and celery in a food processor until they've broken down into "rice". Then, pulse the zucchini and shallot in your food processor for 30 to 40 seconds. Mix the grated vegetables with the salt, black pepper, cayenne pepper, garlic, Parmesan cheese, egg, and almond meal. Shape the mixture into small patties. Heat the sesame oil in a frying pan and fry the patties for 5 to 6 minutes until golden brown and thoroughly cooked. Bon appétit!

calories: 173 | fat: 11g | protein: 11g | carbs: 7g | net carbs: 4g | fiber: 3g

Mushroom and Zucchini Stew

Prep time: 5 minutes | Cook time: 15 minutes | Serves 4

½ cup leeks, chopped
1 pound (454 g) brown mushrooms, chopped

1 teaspoon garlic, minced
1 medium-sized zucchini, diced
2 ripe tomatoes, puréed

Heat up a lightly greased soup pot over medium-high heat. Now, sauté the leeks until just tender about 3 minutes. Stir in the mushrooms, garlic, and zucchini. Continue to sauté an additional 2 minutes or until tender and aromatic. Add in the tomatoes and 2 cups of water. Season with Sazón spice, if desired. Reduce the temperature to simmer and continue to cook, covered, for 10 to 12 minutes more. Bon appétit!

calories: 108 | fat: 8g | protein: 3g | carbs: 7g | net carbs: 4g | fiber: 3g

Creamy Summer Stew with Chives

Prep time: 10 minutes | Cook time: 28 minutes | Serves 4

2 teaspoons sesame oil
2 bell peppers, seeded and chopped
1 small-sized shallot, chopped
1 summer zucchini, chopped
4 cups vegetable broth

2 vine-ripe tomatoes
4 tablespoons sour cream, well-chilled
2 tablespoons fresh chives, minced

Heat the sesame oil in a heavy pot over moderate flame. Sauté the bell peppers and shallot for 3 minutes, until just tender and aromatic. Stir in the zucchini, broth, tomatoes, and stir to combine. Bring to a rolling boil. Immediately reduce the heat to medium-low and let it simmer for 25 minutes until everything is thoroughly cooked. Ladle into individual bowls and garnish with sour cream and fresh chives. Enjoy!

calories: 67 | fat: 4g | protein: 2g | carbs: 6g | net carbs: 4g | fiber: 2g

Colby Broccoli Bake

Prep time: 10 minutes | Cook time: 26 minutes | Serves 5

1 pound (454 g) broccoli florets
1 cup yellow onion, sliced
2 cloves garlic, smashed
½ cup heavy cream
1 cup vegetable broth
1 cup Colby cheese, shredded

1 teaspoon cayenne pepper
½ teaspoon dried oregano
½ teaspoon basil
½ teaspoon ground bay laurel
Sea salt and ground black pepper, to taste

Bring a saucepan with salted water to a boil. Parboil your broccoli for 2 to 3 minutes until crisp-tender. Throw the broccoli into a lightly oiled baking dish. Add in the onion and garlic. In a mixing dish, whisk the heavy cream with the vegetable broth. Season with cayenne pepper, oregano, basil, ground bay laurel, salt, and black pepper. Pour the cream mixture over the vegetables in the baking dish. Bake in the preheated oven at 390ºF (199ºC) for 18 minutes. Top with the cheese and continue to bake an additional 6 minutes or until bubbling. Bon appétit!

calories: 194 | fat: 14g | protein: 9g | carbs: 7g | net carbs: 4g | fiber: 3g

Creamy Cabbage and Cauliflower

Prep time: 5 minutes | Cook time: 13 minutes | Serves 4

2 tablespoons olive oil
1 white onion, chopped
½ pound (227 g) savoy cabbage, shredded
½ pound (227 g) cauliflower florets

1 bell pepper
1 cup cream of mushroom soup
1 cup heavy whipping cream
Sea salt and red pepper flakes, to taste

Heat the olive oil in a saucepan over a moderate flame. Now, sauté the onion for 3 minutes, until just tender and fragrant. Stir in the cabbage, cauliflower, bell pepper, and cream of mushroom soup. Reduce the heat to medium-low; let it cook for 8 minutes more until the vegetables have softened. Fold in the heavy whipping cream and continue to simmer for 2 to 3 minutes more. Sprinkle with salt and red pepper to taste. Serve warm.

calories: 256 | fat: 24g | protein: 3g | carbs: 7g | net carbs: 4g | fiber: 3g

Lemony Cucumber-Avocado Salad

Prep time: 5 minutes | Cook time: 0 minutes | Serves 6

1 avocado, peeled, pitted and sliced
½ white onion, chopped
1 Lebanese cucumber, sliced
3 teaspoons fresh lemon juice
2 tablespoons extra-virgin olive oil

Toss all ingredients in a nice salad bowl. Transfer to your refrigerator until ready to serve. Serve well chilled and enjoy!

calories: 149 | fat: 14g | protein: 2g | carbs: 6g | net carbs: 2g | fiber: 4g

Lebanese Tabbouleh Salad

Prep time: 15 minutes | Cook time: 8 minutes | Serves 2

1 cup cauliflower florets
1 tablespoon fresh mint leaves, roughly chopped
1 tablespoon fresh parsley leaves, roughly chopped
½ white onion, thinly sliced
½ cup cherry tomatoes, halved
1 Lebanese cucumber, diced
Pink salt and freshly cracked black pepper, to taste
1 tablespoon hulled hemp seeds
1 tablespoon fresh lemon juice
2 tablespoons extra-virgin olive oil

Pulse the cauliflower florets in your food processor until they're broken into tiny chunks (just bigger than rice). Pat dry with paper towels. Cook in a lightly greased nonstick skillet over medium heat until the cauliflower rice is turning golden or about 8 minutes; transfer to a serving bowl. Add the remaining ingredients and toss to combine well. Adjust the seasonings and serve. Enjoy!

calories: 180 | fat: 16g | protein: 3g | carbs: 7g | net carbs: 4g | fiber: 3g

Mediterranean Cauliflower Quiche

Prep time: 15 minutes | Cook time: 45 minutes | Serves 2

½ pound (227 g) small cauliflower florets
½ cup vegetable broth
2 scallions, chopped
1 teaspoon garlic, crushed
½ cup almond milk
2 eggs, whisked
Sea salt and ground black
pepper, to taste
½ teaspoon paprika
½ teaspoon basil
½ teaspoon oregano
1 ounce (28 g) sour cream
3 ounces (85 g) Provolone cheese, freshly grated

Cook the cauliflower with the vegetable broth over medium-low flame until tender but crispy. Transfer the cauliflower florets to a lightly greased casserole dish. Then, preheat your oven to 360ºF (182ºC). In a mixing dish, thoroughly combine the scallions, garlic, milk, eggs, salt, black pepper, paprika, basil, and oregano. Pour the scallion mixture over the cauliflower florets. Mix the sour cream and Provolone cheese; add the cheese mixture to the top. Cover with foil. Bake in the preheated oven for about 45 minutes, until topping is lightly golden and everything is heated through. Transfer to a cooling rack for 10 minutes before serving. Bon appétit!

calories: 309 | fat: 21g | protein: 21g | carbs: 8g | net carbs: 5g | fiber: 3g

Cheesy Broccoli Bake

Prep time: 5 minutes | Cook time: 27 minutes | Serves 6

6 eggs
6 ounces (170 g) sour cream
1 cup vegetable broth
¾ pound (340 g) broccoli
florets
6 ounces (170 g) Swiss cheese, shredded

Start by preheating your oven to 360ºF (182ºC). Then, spritz a baking pan with nonstick cooking spray. Thoroughly combine the eggs, sour cream, and vegetable broth. Bring a pot with lightly salted water to a boil. Add the broccoli florets to the boiling water and cook for 2 minutes. Arrange the broccoli florets on the bottom of the prepared pan. Pour the egg/cream mixture over the broccoli. Top with the shredded cheese. Bake for 25 to 28 minutes, turning your pan once or twice. Bon appétit!

calories: 241 | fat: 16g | protein: 16g | carbs: 6g | net carbs: 4g | fiber: 2g

Parmesan Zoodles with Avocado Sauce

Prep time: 10 minutes | Cook time: 0 minutes | Serves 2

½ avocado, pitted and peeled
2 tablespoons sunflower seeds, hulled
1 ripe tomato, quartered
2 tablespoons water
Sea salt and ground black pepper, to taste
¼ teaspoon dried dill weed
1 medium-sized zucchini, sliced
2 tablespoons Parmesan cheese, preferably freshly grated

In your blender or food processor, purée the avocado, sunflower seeds, tomato, water, salt, black pepper, and dill until creamy and uniform. Prepare your zoodles using a spiralizer. Top the zoodles with the sauce; serve garnished with Parmesan cheese. Bon appétit!

calories: 164 | fat: 14g | protein: 6g | carbs: 9g | net carbs: 4g | fiber: 5g

Traditional Thai Tom Kha Soup

Prep time: 20 minutes | Cook time: 22 minutes | Serves 2

1 teaspoon coconut oil
1 shallot, chopped
1 clove garlic, minced
½ celery stalk, chopped
½ bell pepper, chopped
1 Bird's eye chili, divined and minced
1 cup vegetable broth
¼ teaspoon stone ground
mustard
Sea salt and freshly cracked black pepper, to season
½ teaspoon ground cumin
½ teaspoon coriander seeds
2 cardamom pods
1 cup full-fat coconut milk
2 tablespoons Thai basil leaves, snipped

In a deep saucepan, heat the coconut oil until sizzling; now, sauté the shallot, garlic, celery, and peppers for 5 minutes, until just tender and fragrant; make sure to stir frequently. Add a splash of broth to deglaze the pan. Add in the remaining broth, mustard, and spices and bring to a rolling boil. Turn the heat to medium-low and let it simmer for 15 minutes or until heated through. After that, pour in the coconut milk and continue to simmer for 2 minutes more. Ladle into soup bowls and serve garnished with fresh Thai basil. Enjoy!

calories: 273 | fat: 27g | protein: 5g | carbs: 6g | net carbs: 5g | fiber: 1g

Double Cheese Kale Bake

Prep time: 10 minutes | Cook time: 30 to 35 minutes | Serves 4

Nonstick cooking spray
6 ounces (170 g) kale, torn into pieces
4 eggs, whisked
1 cup Cheddar cheese, grated
1 cup Romano cheese
2 tablespoons sour cream
1 garlic clove, minced
Sea salt, to taste
½ teaspoon ground black pepper, or more to taste
½ teaspoon cayenne pepper

Start by preheating your oven to 365°F (185°C). Spritz the sides and bottom of a baking pan with a nonstick cooking spray. Mix all ingredients and pour the mixture into the baking pan. Bake for 30 to 35 minutes or until it is thoroughly heated. Bon appétit!

calories: 384 | fat: 29g | protein: 25g | carbs: 6g | net carbs: 4g | fiber: 2g

Braised Mushrooms and Cabbage

Prep time: 15 minutes | Cook time: 13 minutes | Serves 3

2 tablespoons extra-virgin olive oil
½ cup onion, chopped
2 cups brown mushrooms, sliced
1 garlic clove, pressed
¾ pound (340 g) green cabbage, shredded
½ cup cream of mushroom soup
1 bay laurel
Kosher salt, to season
½ teaspoon caraway seeds
½ teaspoon ground black pepper, to taste
1 teaspoon smoked paprika
1 tablespoon apple cider vinegar

Heat the oil in a heavy-bottomed pot over medium-high heat. Now, sweat the onion for 3 minutes, until tender and translucent. Next, stir in the mushrooms; continue to sauté until the mushrooms are caramelized or about 3 minutes. Don't crowd the mushrooms. Stir in the garlic and sauté for 30 seconds longer or until aromatic. Add in the green cabbage, soup, bay laurel, salt, caraway seeds, black pepper, and paprika. Continue cooking for 7 to 8 minutes more or until the cabbage leaves wilt. Ladle into three serving bowls. Drizzle vinegar over each serving and serve warm. Bon appétit!

calories: 133 | fat: 9g | protein: 4g | carbs: 7g | net carbs: 3g | fiber: 4g

Easy Roasted Asparagus with Mayo Sauce

Prep time: 10 minutes | Cook time: 9 to 11 minutes | Serves 5

1½ pounds (680 g) asparagus, trimmed
4 tablespoons olive oil
Sea salt and ground black pepper, to taste
4 tablespoons shallots, minced
½ cup mayonnaise
4 tablespoons sour cream
2 tablespoons coriander, chopped
1 teaspoon fresh garlic, minced

Begin by preheating your oven to 390°F (199°C). Brush the asparagus spears with olive oil. Add the salt, black pepper, and shallots and roast for 9 to 11 minutes in the preheated oven. Meanwhile, mix the remaining ingredients to make the dipping sauce. Serve the asparagus with the mayo sauce on the side and enjoy!

calories: 296 | fat: 28g | protein: 4g | carbs: 7g | net carbs: 4g | fiber: 3g

Creamy Broccoli and Zucchini Soup

Prep time: 10 minutes | Cook time: 25 minutes | Serves 4

3 tablespoons olive oil
2 cups broccoli florets
1 green bell pepper, chopped
1 jalapeño pepper, chopped
1 medium zucchini, cut into chunks
4 cups vegetable broth
Kosher salt and ground black pepper, to taste
½ teaspoon dried dill weed
1 bay laurel

Heat the olive oil in a heavy-bottomed pot over medium-high heat. Now, sauté the broccoli, peppers, and zucchini for 5 minutes, until they have softened. Add in the remaining ingredients and stir to combine. Cook until the soup comes to a boil. Turn the heat to simmer. Partially cover and let it simmer for a further 20 minutes or until heated through. Purée with an immersion blender and serve warm. Bon appétit!

calories: 111 | fat: 10g | protein: 2g | carbs: 4g | net carbs: 2g | fiber: 2g

Spinach and Zucchini Chowder

Prep time: 15 minutes | Cook time: 22 minutes | Serves 4

1 tablespoon olive oil
1 clove garlic, chopped
½ cup scallions, chopped
4 cups water
2 zucchini, sliced
1 celery stalk, chopped
2 tablespoons vegetable bouillon powder
4 ounces (113 g) baby spinach
Salt and ground black pepper, to taste
1 heaping tablespoon fresh parsley, chopped
1 tablespoon butter
1 egg, beaten

In a stockpot, heat the oil over medium-high heat. Now, cook the garlic and scallions until tender or about 4 minutes. Add water, zucchini, celery, vegetable bouillon powder; cook for 13 minutes. Add spinach, salt, black pepper, parsley, and butter; cook for a further 5 minutes. Then, stir in the egg and mix until well incorporated. Ladle into individual bowls and serve warm. Enjoy!

calories: 85 | fat: 6g | protein: 4g | carbs: 4g | net carbs: 3g | fiber: 1g

Italian-Style Zoodles

Prep time: 10 minutes | Cook time: 16 minutes | Serves 3

1 tablespoon butter, melted
2 green onions, chopped
2 green garlic stalks, chopped
2 vine-ripe tomatoes, puréed
Sea salt and ground black pepper, to taste
½ teaspoon cayenne pepper
1 tablespoon Italian seasoning blend
¾ pound (340 g) zucchini, spiralized
1 cup Asiago cheese, shredded

Melt the butter in a frying pan over a moderate flame. Now, sweat the green onions and garlic until just tender and fragrant. Add in the tomatoes and bring to a boil. Add in the salt, black pepper, cayenne pepper, and Italian seasoning blend. Reduce the heat to medium-low and let it cook for 13 minutes or until heated through. Fold in the zoodles and cook for 3 minutes more or until they are crisp-tender. Top with cheese and serve immediately. Bon appétit!

calories: 241 | fat: 17g | protein: 13g | carbs: 6g | net carbs: 3g | fiber: 3g

Peanut Butter Crêpes with Coconut

Prep time: 5 minutes | Cook time: 4 to 5 minutes | Serves 5

4 eggs, well whisked
4 ounces (113 g) cream cheese
A pinch of salt

2 tablespoons coconut oil
3 tablespoons peanut butter
2 tablespoons toasted coconut

Whisk the eggs, cream cheese, and salt in a mixing bowl. Heat the oil in a pancake frying pan over medium-high heat. Fry each pancake for 4 to 5 minutes. Serve topped with peanut butter and coconut. Enjoy!

calories: 248 | fat: 22g | protein: 9g | carbs: 6g | net carbs: 5g | fiber: 1g

Garlicky Creamed Swiss Chard

Prep time: 10 minutes | Cook time: 10 minutes | Serves 6

2 tablespoons butter
1 yellow onion, chopped
2 garlic cloves, minced
½ teaspoon kosher salt
¼ teaspoon ground black pepper
¼ teaspoon dried oregano

¼ teaspoon dried dill
1½ pounds (680 g) Swiss chard
½ cup vegetable broth
2 tablespoons dry white wine
1 cup sour cream

Melt the butter in a saucepan over a moderate flame. Then, sauté the onion until tender and fragrant or about 4 minutes. Stir in the garlic and continue to sauté for 1 minute or until aromatic. Add in the salt, black pepper, oregano, and basil. Fold in the Swiss chard in batches. Pour in vegetable broth and cook for 5 minutes or until Swiss chard wilts. Stir in the wine and sour cream. Stir to combine well and serve.

calories: 149 | fat: 11g | protein: 5g | carbs: 7g | net carbs: 5g | fiber: 2g

Indian Tomato Soup with Raita

Prep time: 20 minutes | Cook time: 20 minutes | Serves 4

1½ tablespoons butter
1 medium-sized leek, sliced
1 red chili pepper, chopped
1 bell pepper, roughly chopped
½ teaspoon cumin seeds
Raita:
1 cup full-fat yogurt
1 cucumber, chopped
¼ cup fresh cilantro, chopped

2 garlic cloves, minced
4 tomatoes, puréed
¼ piece of a stick of cinnamon
½ teaspoon mustard seeds
2 pods cardamom

½ teaspoon powdered coriander

Melt the butter in a heavy-bottomed pot over medium-high heat. Now, sweat the leek and peppers until just tender and fragrant. Stir in the cumin seeds and garlic; continue to sauté an additional 30 seconds; just make sure they do not burn. Stir in the tomatoes, cinnamon, mustard seeds, and cardamom. Bring to a rapid boil and immediately turn the heat to a simmer. Let it simmer for 20 minutes or until heated through. Purée everything together with an immersion blender. Meanwhile, mix all the ingredients for the Raita. Serve the warm tomato soup with the Raita on the side. Enjoy!

calories: 106 | fat: 6g | protein: 4g | carbs:7 g | net carbs: 5g | fiber: 2g

Spinach and Egg Salad

Prep time: 10 minutes | Cook time: 8 minutes | Serves 3

4 eggs
Sea salt and red pepper flakes, to taste
½ pound (227 g) spinach
1 roasted pepper in oil, drained and chopped
1 tomato, diced

2 scallions, sliced
¼ teaspoon dried oregano
½ teaspoon dried basil
2 tablespoons white vinegar
2 tablespoons extra-virgin olive oil

Cook the eggs in a saucepan for about 8 minutes; peel the eggs under running water and carefully slice them. Season the eggs with salt and red pepper. Add the spinach, red pepper, tomato, scallions, oregano, and basil to a nice serving bowl. Drizzle vinegar and olive oil over your vegetables. Top with the boiled eggs. Serve at room temperature or well chilled. Bon appétit!

calories: 156 | fat: 10g | protein: 10g | carbs: 7g | net carbs: 4g | fiber: 3g

Greek Roasted Cauliflower with Feta Cheese

Prep time: 5 minutes | Cook time: 40 minutes | Serves 4

1 pound (454 g) cauliflower, halved
1 medium-sized leek, cut into 2-inch pieces
2 tablespoons olive oil

1 tablespoon Greek seasoning blend
Sea salt and ground black pepper, to taste
1 cup feta cheese, crumbled

Begin by preheating your oven to 390ºF (199ºC). Toss cauliflower and leek with olive oil, Greek seasoning blend, salt, and black pepper. Arrange vegetables on a parchment-lined roasting pan. Transfer to the preheated oven. Roast approximately 20 minutes; turn them over and roast an additional 20 minutes. Top with feta cheese and serve immediately. Enjoy!

calories: 194 | fat: 15g | protein: 7g | carbs: 6g | net carbs: 3g | fiber: 3g

Mozzarella Creamed Salad with Basil

Prep time: 20 minutes | Cook time: 0 minutes | Serves 4

4 ounces (113 g) arugula
4 ounces (113 g) lettuce
4 scallions, sliced
2 green garlic stalks, sliced
½ cup celery rib, chopped
1 cucumber, sliced
1 tomato, sliced
½ cup olives, pitted and halved
½ cup mayonnaise

1 teaspoon stone-ground mustard
2 tablespoons white vinegar
Sea salt and ground black pepper, to taste
½ cup Mozzarella cheese
2 tablespoons fresh basil leaves, snipped

Toss the arugula, lettuce, scallions, green garlic, celery, cucumber, tomato, and olives in a large-sized bowl. In a small mixing dish, whisk the mayonnaise, mustard, vinegar, salt, and black pepper. Add the mayo mixture to the vegetables and toss to combine well. Top with Mozzarella and serve garnished with fresh basil. Enjoy!

calories: 255 | fat: 23g | protein: 7g | carbs: 7g | net carbs: 4g | fiber: 3g

Button Mushroom Stroganoff

Prep time: 20 minutes | Cook time: 22 minutes | Serves 5

2 tablespoons olive oil
½ cup onion, minced
1 tablespoon butter
1½ pounds (680 g) button mushrooms, sliced
1 teaspoon garlic paste
½ teaspoon red curry paste
Sea salt and ground black

pepper, to taste
1 teaspoon dried parsley flakes
½ teaspoon celery seeds
½ teaspoon mustard seeds
½ teaspoon red pepper flakes
2 tablespoons tomato purée
4 cups vegetable stock
1 cup sour cream

Heat the olive oil in a heavy-bottomed soup pot until sizzling. Then, sauté the onion until tender and translucent or about 4 minutes. Then, melt the butter in the same pot and cook the mushrooms for 3 to 4 minutes until just tender. Add in the garlic paste, curry paste, spices, tomato purée, and stock. Bring the mixture to just below boiling point. Turn the heat to simmer and let it cook for 15 minutes longer and stir it all together. Taste, adjust the seasonings and serve warm. Enjoy!

calories: 166 | fat: 13g | protein: 6g | carbs: 7g | net carbs: 5g | fiber: 2g

Chinese Cabbage Stir-Fry

Prep time: 10 minutes | Cook time: 7 minutes | Serves 5

3 tablespoons sesame oil
1 shallot, sliced
2 garlic cloves, minced
1 tablespoon Shaoxing wine
Sea salt and ground black pepper, to taste
½ teaspoon chili sauce, sugar-free

¼ teaspoon rougui (Chinese cinnamon)
½ teaspoon fennel seeds
½ teaspoon Sichuan peppercorns, crushed
1½ pounds (680 g) Chinese cabbage, shredded

Heat the sesame oil in a wok over medium-high heat. Once hot, sauté the shallot and garlic until tender and translucent or about 2 minutes. Add the Shaoxing wine to deglaze the pan. Add in the remaining ingredients. Cook, stirring continuously, until the cabbage leaves are wilted about 5 minutes. Serve with some extra toasted sesame seeds if desired. Enjoy!

calories: 108 | fat: 9g | protein: 2g | carbs: 8g | net carbs: 6g | fiber: 2g

Homemade Coleslaw with Cauliflower

Prep time: 5 minutes | Cook time: 0 minutes | Serves 5

1 cup green cabbage, shredded
1 cup fresh cauliflower, chopped
4 tablespoons shallots, chopped

1 teaspoon garlic, minced
1 teaspoon lime juice
1 teaspoon white wine vinegar
⅓ cup mayonnaise
Sea salt and ground black pepper, to taste

Add the cabbage, cauliflower, shallots, and garlic to a salad bowl. In a small mixing dish, whisk the lime juice, vinegar, mayonnaise, salt, and pepper. Dress the salad and serve immediately. Bon appétit!

calories: 121 | fat: 9g | protein: 3g | carbs: 7g | net carbs: 5g | fiber: 2g

Baked Stuffed Peppers with Olives

Prep time: 10 minutes | Cook time: 32 minutes | Serves 2

1 garlic clove, minced
2 scallions, chopped
3 ounces (85 g) cream cheese
3 eggs
3 ounces (85 g) Provolone cheese, grated
Sea salt and ground black

pepper, to taste
½ teaspoon hot paprika
1 teaspoon coriander
3 bell peppers, seeded and sliced in half
4 Kalamata olives, pitted and sliced

In a mixing bowl, thoroughly combine the garlic, scallions, cream cheese, eggs, provolone cheese, salt, black pepper, paprika, and coriander. Stuff the peppers and place them on a parchment lined baking sheet. Bake in the preheated oven at 370ºF (188ºC) approximately 30 minutes until the peppers are tender. If you want your peppers nicely charred, just place them under the broiler for 2 minutes. Garnish with olives and serve immediately. Bon appétit!

calories: 387 | fat: 30g | protein: 23g | carbs: 5g | net carbs: 4g | fiber: 1g

Broccoli-Cabbage Soup

Prep time: 10 minutes | Cook time: 29 minutes | Serves 6

2 tablespoons extra-virgin olive oil
2 bell peppers, chopped
1 cup broccoli florets
1 shallot, chopped
1 teaspoon garlic, minced
1 pound (454 g) cabbage, shredded

1 cup tomato purée
5 cups vegetable broth
Sea salt and ground black pepper, to taste
½ teaspoon cayenne pepper
½ teaspoon dried dill weed
1 bay laurel

Heat the oil in a heavy-bottomed pot over the highest setting. Now, sauté the bell peppers, broccoli and shallot for about 4 minutes or until they have softened. Add in the remaining ingredients and gently stir to combine well. Turn the heat to medium-low; let it simmer, partially covered, for 25 minutes. Ladle into individual bowls and serve warm. Enjoy!

calories: 82 | fat: 4g | protein: 2g | carbs: 6g | net carbs: 3g | fiber: 3g

Spiced Mashed Cauliflower

Prep time: 5 minutes | Cook time: 5 minutes | Serves 8

½ pound (227 g) cauliflower florets
Sea salt and ground black pepper, to taste
½ teaspoon cayenne pepper

½ teaspoon dried oregano
½ teaspoon dried basil
1 cup heavy whipping cream
5 ounces (142 g) Swiss cheese, grated

Steam the cauliflower for 5 minutes, until tender; pulse in your food processor until it resembles mashed potatoes. Season the mashed cauliflower with salt, black pepper, cayenne pepper, oregano, and basil. In a saucepan, warm the cream and stir in the cheese. Whisk until the cheese is melted. Fold in the mashed cauliflower and stir again. Serve with your favorite keto veggies. Bon appétit!

calories: 129 | fat: 10g | protein: 6g | carbs: 3g | net carbs: 2g | fiber: 1g

Fried Veggies with Eggs

Prep time: 10 minutes | Cook time: 23 minutes | Serves 4

2 tablespoons olive oil
1 shallot, sliced
2 bell peppers, seeded and sliced
2 garlic cloves, minced
½ teaspoon ginger, peeled and minced

1 cup green cabbage, shredded
1 cup broccoli florets
1 cup cauliflower florets
½ cup cream of onion soup
4 eggs

Heat the olive oil in a large-sized frying pan over high heat. Now, fry the shallots and pepper for 3 minutes, until just tender. Add in the garlic and ginger; continue sautéing for 30 seconds more until aromatic. Then, stir in the cabbage, broccoli, cauliflower, and onion soup. Turn the heat to medium-low. Continue to cook for 10 minutes or until tender and thoroughly cooked. Next, make four indentations in the vegetable mixture using the back of a wooden spoon. Crack the eggs into the indentations. Cover your frying pan with a lid. Cook for a further 10 minutes or until the egg whites are firm but the yolks are a little runny. Serve immediately.

calories: 121 | fat: 7g | protein: 7g | carbs: 7g | net carbs: 5g | fiber: 2g

Herbed Cheese Balls with Walnuts

Prep time: 5 minutes | Cook time: 0 minutes | Serves 6

4 ounces (113 g) Neufchatel cheese
4 ounces (113 g) blue cheese
Sea salt and freshly cracked black pepper, to taste
2 tablespoons fresh parsley,

chopped
2 tablespoons fresh cilantro, chopped
8 tablespoons walnuts, finely chopped

Thoroughly combine the cheese, salt, black pepper, parsley, and cilantro in a bowl. Shape into 8 balls and roll them in the chopped walnuts. Refrigerate until ready to serve. Bon appétit!

calories: 183 | fat: 16g | protein: 8g | carbs: 3g | net carbs: 2g | fiber: 1g

Gouda Cauli-Broccoli Casserole

Prep time: 15 minutes | Cook time: 6 hours | Serves 6

1 tablespoon extra-virgin olive oil
1 pound (454 g) broccoli, cut into florets
1 pound (454 g) cauliflower, cut into florets
¼ cup almond flour

2 cups coconut milk
½ teaspoon ground nutmeg
Pinch freshly ground black pepper
1½ cups shredded Gouda cheese, divided

Lightly grease the insert of the slow cooker with the olive oil. Place the broccoli and cauliflower in the insert. In a small bowl, stir together the almond flour, coconut milk, nutmeg, pepper, and 1 cup of the cheese. Pour the coconut milk mixture over the vegetables and top the casserole with the remaining ½ cup of the cheese. Cover and cook on low for 6 hours. Serve warm.

calories: 377 | fat: 32g | protein: 16g | carbs: 12g | net carbs: 6g | fiber: 6g

Italian Pepper and Mushrooms Stew

Prep time: 15 minutes | Cook time: 25 minutes | Serves 5

3 tablespoons extra-virgin olive oil
1 red onion, chopped
2 sweet Italian peppers, chopped
1 poblano pepper, chopped
1 pound (454 g) cremini mushrooms, sliced
2 garlic cloves

2 cups water
1 cup cream of mushroom soup
½ teaspoon ground cumin
½ teaspoon mustard seeds
2 vine-ripe tomatoes, puréed
2 bay laurels
Sea salt and ground black pepper, to taste

Heat the oil in a heavy-bottomed soup pot over medium-high heat. Once hot, sauté the onion and peppers for 3 minutes, until crisp-tender and fragrant. Stir in the mushrooms and garlic and continue to sauté an additional 2 minutes. Add in the remaining ingredients and turn the heat to medium-low. Cook, partially covered, for 20 minutes or until thoroughly cooked. Ladle into individual bowls and serve warm. Enjoy!

calories: 156 | fat: 12g | protein: 5g | carbs: 6g | net carbs: 4g | fiber: 2g

Vegetable Stir-Fry with Seeds

Prep time: 10 minutes | Cook time: 11 minutes | Serves 3

2 tablespoons sesame oil
1 yellow onion, sliced
1 red bell pepper, seeded and sliced
2 garlic cloves, minced
1 tomato, chopped
½ cup cream of mushroom

soup
Sea salt and ground black pepper, to taste
½ teaspoon cayenne pepper
½ teaspoon celery seeds
½ teaspoon fennel seeds

Heat the sesame oil in a wok over medium-high heat. Stir fry the onion and peppers for 3 to 4 minutes. Add in the garlic and continue to cook for 30 seconds more. Add in the remaining ingredients and cook for a further 8 minutes. Taste, adjust seasonings and serve warm. Enjoy!

calories: 118 | fat: 10g | protein: 2g | carbs: 6g | net carbs: 5g | fiber: 1g

Spicy Roasted Eggplant with Avocado

Prep time: 5 minutes | Cook time: 20 to 25 minutes | Serves 7

2 pounds (907 g) eggplant, sliced
3 teaspoons avocado oil
2 tablespoons tahini
1 teaspoon garlic paste

1 tablespoon Dijon mustard
1 tablespoon lemon juice
½ teaspoon harissa
1 avocado, pitted, peeled and mashed

Brush the bottom of a roasting pan with nonstick cooking oil. Arrange the eggplant slices on the prepared roasting pan. Drizzle the eggplant with 2 teaspoons of the avocado oil. Transfer the pan to the preheated oven. Roast in the preheated oven at 420ºF (216ºC) for 15 to 20 minutes. Meanwhile, mix the remaining ingredients, except for the avocado, until everything is well incorporated. Divide this mixture between the eggplant slices. Broil approximately 5 minutes. Top with the mashed avocado and serve warm. Bon appétit!

calories: 94 | fat: 6g | protein: 3g | carbs: 7g | net carbs: 3g | fiber: 4g

Balsamic Zucchini Salad

Prep time: 15 minutes | Cook time: 9 minutes | Serves 5

1½ pounds (680 g) zucchini, sliced
4 tablespoons extra-virgin olive oil, divided
Sea salt and ground black pepper, to taste
½ teaspoon cayenne pepper
½ teaspoon dried dill weed
½ teaspoon dried basil
1 red onion, sliced
1 garlic clove, pressed
2 tomatoes, sliced
1 teaspoon Dijon mustard
1 tablespoon balsamic vinegar
1 tablespoon fresh lime juice
4 ounces (113 g) goat cheese, crumbled

Toss the zucchini with 2 tablespoons of olive oil and spices. Arrange them on a rimmed baking sheet. Roast in the preheated oven at 425ºF (220ºC) until tender about 9 minutes. Toss roasted zucchini with red onion, garlic, and tomatoes. Add the remaining tablespoons of olive oil, mustard, vinegar, and lime juice. Toss to combine and top with goat cheese. Enjoy!

calories: 186 | fat: 14g | protein: 11g | carbs: 7g | net carbs: 5g | fiber: 2g

Broccoli Salad with Tahini Dressing

Prep time: 15 minutes | Cook time: 0 minutes | Serves 2

½ cup broccoli florets
1 bell pepper, seeded and sliced
1 shallot, thinly sliced
½ cup arugula
2 ounces (57 g) Mozzarella cheese
2 tablespoons toasted sunflower seeds

Tahini Dressing:
1 tablespoon freshly squeezed lemon juice
¼ cup tahini (sesame butter)
1 garlic clove, minced
½ teaspoon yellow mustard
½ teaspoon ground black pepper
Pink salt, to taste

Place the cabbage, pepper, shallot, and arugula in a nice salad bowl. Mix all ingredients for the dressing. Now, dress your salad and top with the Mozzarella cheese and sunflower seeds. Serve at room temperature or well chilled. Bon appétit!

calories: 323 | fat: 25g | protein: 16g | carbs: 7g | net carbs: 3g | fiber: 4g

Balsamic Broccoli Salad

Prep time: 10 minutes | Cook time: 22 minutes | Serves 6

6 cups broccoli florets
1 red chili pepper, sliced
1 garlic clove, minced
1 shallot, sliced
½ cup mayonnaise
1 teaspoon Dijon mustard
2 tablespoons balsamic vinegar
1 tablespoon prepared horseradish
Kosher salt and ground black pepper, to taste

Brush the broccoli florets with nonstick cooking spray and roast at 425ºF (220ºC) for about 22 minutes until crisp-tender and little charred. In a salad bowl, toss the roasted broccoli florets, chili pepper, garlic, and shallot. In a small mixing dish, thoroughly combine the remaining ingredients. Dress the salad and serve immediately. Bon appétit!

calories: 170 | fat: 14g | protein: 3g | carbs: 7g | net carbs: 4g | fiber: 3g

Garlicky Voodles with Avocado Sauce

Prep time: 5 minutes | Cook time: 6 minutes | Serves 3

1 zucchini
1 cucumber
2 bell peppers
2 tablespoons olive oil
2 garlic cloves, peeled
1 avocado, peeled and pitted
½ lemon, juiced and zested
2 tablespoons coriander
Kosher salt and ground black pepper, to taste
½ teaspoon red pepper flakes

Spiralize the zucchini, cucumber, and bell peppers by using a spiralizer or a julienne peeler. Heat the olive oil in a wok or a large nonstick skillet. Sauté the voodles in the hot olive oil for about 6 minutes. Then, in your food processor or blender, purée the remaining ingredients until uniform and creamy. Pour the avocado sauce over the voodles and serve. Bon appétit!

calories: 181 | fat: 16g | protein: 2g | carbs: 7g | net carbs: 3g | fiber: 4g

Creamy Vegetable Chowder

Prep time: 15 minutes | Cook time: 36 to 38 minutes | Serves 5

1 tablespoon olive oil
½ cup shallots, chopped
1 cup celery, chopped
1 teaspoon oregano
1½ teaspoon basil
½ teaspoon rosemary
5 cups vegetable broth
1 bay laurel
2 tablespoons cilantro, chopped
Sea salt and ground black pepper, to taste
¼ cup dry white wine
1 cup heavy cream

Heat the olive oil in a large heavy-bottomed pot until sizzling. Then, sweat the shallot and celery until tender and aromatic. Stir in the remaining ingredients, except for the heavy cream. When it comes to the boil, turn the heat to medium-low. Let it simmer, partially covered, for 30 minutes. Lastly, fold in the cream. Continue to simmer an additional 6 to 8 minutes. Bon appétit!

calories: 131 | fat: 13g | protein: 2g | carbs: 3g | net carbs: 2g | fiber: 1g

Double Cheese Braised Vegetables

Prep time: 15 minutes | Cook time: 6 hours | Serves 6

1 tablespoon extra-virgin olive oil
½ head cauliflower, cut into small florets
2 cups green beans, cut into 2-inch pieces
1 cup asparagus spears, cut into 2-inch pieces
½ cup sour cream
½ cup shredded Cheddar cheese
½ cup shredded Swiss cheese
3 tablespoons butter
¼ cup water
1 teaspoon ground nutmeg
Pinch freshly ground black pepper, for seasoning

Lightly grease the insert of the slow cooker with the olive oil. Add the cauliflower, green beans, asparagus, sour cream, Cheddar cheese, Swiss cheese, butter, water, nutmeg, and pepper to the insert. Cover and cook on low for 6 hours. Serve warm.

calories: 207 | fat: 18g | protein: 8g | carbs: 5g | net carbs: 3g | fiber: 2g

Garlicky Cauliflower-Pecan Casserole

Prep time: 15 minutes | Cook time: 6 hours | Serves 6

1 tablespoon extra-virgin olive oil
2 pounds (907 g) cauliflower florets
1 cup chopped pecans
4 garlic cloves, sliced
½ teaspoon salt

½ teaspoon freshly ground black pepper
2 tablespoons freshly squeezed lemon juice
4 hard-boiled eggs, shredded, for garnish
1 scallion, white and green parts, chopped, for garnish

Lightly grease the insert of the slow cooker with the olive oil. In a medium bowl, toss together the cauliflower, pecans, garlic, salt, and pepper. Transfer the mixture to the insert and sprinkle the lemon juice over the top. Cover and cook on low for 6 hours. Garnish with hard-boiled eggs and scallion and serve.

calories: 219 | fat: 17g | protein: 8g | carbs: 11g | net carbs: 6g | fiber: 5g

Slow Cooked Spaghetti Squash

Prep time: 15 minutes | Cook time: 6 hours | Serves 8

1 small spaghetti squash, washed
½ cup vegetable stock
¼ cup butter

Salt, for seasoning
Freshly ground black pepper, for seasoning

Place the squash and chicken stock in the insert of the slow cooker. The squash should not touch the sides of the insert. Cook on low for 6 hours. Let the squash cool for 10 minutes and cut in half. Scrape out the squash strands into a bowl with a fork. When finished, add the butter and toss to combine. Season with salt and pepper and serve.

calories: 98 | fat: 5g | protein: 1g | carbs: 6g | net carbs: 3g | fiber: 3g

Braised Mushrooms with Parsley

Prep time: 10 minutes | Cook time: 6 hours | Serves 8

3 tablespoons extra-virgin olive oil
1 pound (454 g) button mushrooms, wiped clean and halved
2 teaspoons minced garlic

¼ teaspoon salt
⅛ teaspoon freshly ground black pepper
2 tablespoons chopped fresh parsley

Place the olive oil, mushrooms, garlic, salt, and pepper in the insert of the slow cooker and toss to coat. Cover and cook on low for 6 hours. Serve tossed with the parsley.

calories: 58 | fat: 5g | protein: 2g | carbs: 2g | net carbs: 1g | fiber: 1g

Chapter 6 Poultry

Leek and Pumpkin Turkey Stew

Prep time: 20 minutes | Cook time: 7 to 8 hours | Serves 6

3 tablespoons extra-virgin olive oil, divided
1 pound (454 g) boneless turkey breast, cut into 1-inch pieces
1 leek, thoroughly cleaned and sliced
2 teaspoons minced garlic
2 cups chicken broth
1 cup coconut milk
2 celery stalks, chopped
2 cups diced pumpkin
1 carrot, diced
2 teaspoons chopped thyme
Salt, for seasoning
Freshly ground black pepper, for seasoning
1 scallion, white and green parts, chopped, for garnish

Lightly grease the insert of the slow cooker with 1 tablespoon of the olive oil. In a large skillet over medium-high heat, heat the remaining 2 tablespoons of the olive oil. Add the turkey and sauté until browned, about 5 minutes. Add the leek and garlic and sauté for an additional 3 minutes. Transfer the turkey mixture to the insert and stir in the broth, coconut milk, celery, pumpkin, carrot, and thyme. Cover and cook on low for 7 to 8 hours. Season with salt and pepper. Serve topped with the scallion.

calories: 357 | fat: 27.0g | protein: 21.0g | carbs: 11.0g | net carbs: 7.0g | fiber: 4.0g

Italian Turkey Meatballs with Leeks

Prep time: 10 minutes | Cook time: 20 minutes | Serves 4

1 pound (454 g) ground turkey
1 tablespoon Italian seasoning blend
2 cloves garlic, minced
½ cup leeks, minced
1 egg

Throw all ingredients into a mixing bowl; mix to combine well. Form the mixture into bite-sized balls and arrange them on a parchment-lined baking pan. Spritz the meatballs with cooking spray. Bake in the preheated oven at 400°F (205°C) for 18 to 22 minutes. Serve with cocktail sticks and enjoy!

calories: 217 | fat: 11.1g | protein: 24.1g | carbs: 3.4g | net carbs: 2.8g | fiber: 0.6g

Lemony Rosemary Chicken Thighs

Prep time: 10 minutes | Cook time: 14 minutes | Serves 4

8 chicken thighs
1 teaspoon salt
1 tablespoon lemon juice
1 teaspoon lemon zest
1 tablespoon olive oil
1 tablespoon chopped rosemary
¼ teaspoon black pepper
1 garlic clove, minced

Combine all ingredients in a bowl. Place in the fridge for one hour. Heat a skillet over medium heat. Add the chicken along with the juices and cook until crispy, about 7 minutes per side. Serve immediately.

calories: 477 | fat: 31g | protein: 31g | carbs: 3g | net carbs: 3g | fiber: 0g

Chicken with Cream of Mushroom Soup

Prep time: 10 minutes | Cook time: 15 minutes | Serves 2

1 tablespoon olive oil
1 yellow onion, chopped
2 garlic cloves, pressed
2 chicken breast, skinless and boneless, cut into bite-sized pieces
½ cup cream of mushroom soup

Heat the olive oil in a saucepan over medium-high heat. Once hot, sweat the yellow onion until tender and translucent about 3 minutes. Then, cook the garlic until aromatic or about 30 seconds. Then, sear the chicken breast for 3 minutes, stirring frequently to ensure even cooking. Pour in the cream of mushroom soup and stir to combine. Turn the heat to medium-low and let it simmer until the sauce has reduced by half or 6 to 8 minutes longer. Serve immediately.

calories: 336 | fat: 20.7g | protein: 30.7g | carbs: 4.2g | net carbs: 3.7g | fiber: 0.5g

Tikka Masala

Prep time: 10 minutes | Cook time: 25 minutes | Serves 5

1½ pounds (680 g) chicken breasts, cut into bite-sized pieces
1 onion, chopped
10 ounces (283 g) tomato purée
1 teaspoon garam masala
½ cup heavy cream

Heat a wok that is greased with a nonstick cooking spray over medium-high heat. Now, sear the chicken breasts until golden brown on all sides. Add the onions and sauté them for 2 to 3 minutes more or until tender and fragrant. Stir in the tomato purée and garam masala. Cook for 10 minutes until the sauce turns into a dark red color. Fold in the heavy cream and stir to combine. Cook for 10 to 13 minutes more or until heated through. Serve with cauliflower rice if desired and enjoy!

calories: 293 | fat: 17.1g | protein: 29.1g | carbs: 4.8g | net carbs: 3.6g | fiber: 1.2g

Italian Asiago and Pepper Stuffed Turkey

Prep time: 15 minutes | Cook time: 50 minutes | Serves 6

2 tablespoons extra-virgin olive oil
1 tablespoon Italian seasoning mix
Sea salt and freshly ground black pepper, to season
2 garlic cloves, sliced
6 ounces (170 g) Asiago cheese, sliced
2 bell peppers, thinly sliced
1½ pounds (680 g) turkey breasts
2 tablespoons Italian parsley, roughly chopped

Brush the sides and bottom of a casserole dish with 1 tablespoon of extra-virgin olive oil. Preheat an oven to 360°F (182°C). Sprinkle the turkey breast with the Italian seasoning mix, salt, and black pepper on all sides. Make slits in each turkey breast and stuff with garlic, cheese, and bell peppers. Drizzle the turkey breasts with the remaining tablespoon of olive oil. Bake in the preheated oven for 50 minutes or until an instant-read thermometer registers 165°F (74°C). Garnish with Italian parsley and serve warm. Bon appétit!

calories: 350 | fat: 22.3g | protein: 32.1g | carbs: 3.0g | net carbs: 2.4g | fiber: 0.6g

Simple White Wine Drumettes

Prep time: 10 minutes | Cook time: 35 minutes | Serves 4

1 pound (454 g) chicken drumettes
1 tablespoon olive oil
2 tablespoons butter, melted
1 garlic cloves, sliced
Fresh juice of ½ lemon

2 tablespoons white wine
Salt and ground black pepper, to taste
1 tablespoon fresh scallions, chopped

Start by preheating your oven to 450ºF (235ºC). Place the chicken in a parchment-lined baking pan. Drizzle with olive oil and melted butter. Add the garlic, lemon, wine, salt, and black pepper. Bake in the preheated oven for about 35 minutes. Serve garnished with fresh scallions. Enjoy!

calories: 210 | fat: 12.3g | protein: 23.3g | carbs: 0.5g | net carbs: 0.4g | fiber: 0.1g

Chipotle Tomato and Pumpkin Chicken Chili

Prep time: 20 minutes | Cook time: 7 to 8 hours | Serves 6

3 tablespoons extra-virgin olive oil, divided
1 pound (454 g) ground chicken
½ sweet onion, chopped
2 teaspoons minced garlic
1 (28-ounce / 794-g) can diced tomatoes
1 cup chicken broth

1 cup diced pumpkin
1 green bell pepper, diced
3 tablespoons chili powder
1 teaspoon chipotle chili powder
1 cup sour cream, for garnish
1 cup shredded Cheddar cheese, for garnish

Lightly grease the insert of the slow cooker with 1 tablespoon of the olive oil. In a large skillet over medium-high heat, heat the remaining 2 tablespoons of the olive oil. Add the chicken and sauté until it is cooked through, about 6 minutes. Add the onion and garlic and sauté for an additional 3 minutes. Transfer the chicken mixture to the insert and stir in the tomatoes, broth, pumpkin, bell pepper, chili powder, and chipotle chili powder. Cover and cook on low for 7 to 8 hours. Serve topped with the sour cream and cheese.

calories: 390 | fat: 30.0g | protein: 22.0g | carbs: 14.0g | net carbs: 9.0g | fiber: 5.0g

Chicken and Bell Pepper Kabobs

Prep time: 10 minutes | Cook time: 10 minutes | Serves 6

2 tablespoons olive oil
4 tablespoons dry sherry
1 tablespoon stone-ground mustard
1½ pounds (680 g) chicken, skinless, boneless and cubed
2 red onions, cut into wedges
1 green bell pepper, cut into

1-inch pieces
1 red bell pepper, cut into 1-inch pieces
1 yellow bell pepper, cut into 1-inch pieces
½ teaspoon sea salt
¼ teaspoon ground black pepper, or more to taste

In a mixing bowl, combine the olive oil, dry sherry, mustard and chicken until well coated. Alternate skewering the chicken and vegetables until you run out of ingredients. Season with salt and black pepper. Preheat your grill to medium-high heat. Place the kabobs on the grill, flipping every 2 minutes and cook to desired doneness. Serve warm.

calories: 201 | fat: 8.2g | protein: 24.3g | carbs:7.0 g | net carbs: 5.7g | fiber: 1.3g

Asian Turkey and Bird's Eye Soup

Prep time: 10 minutes | Cook time: 15 minutes | Serves 5

2 tablespoons canola oil
2 Oriental sweets peppers, deseeded and chopped
1 Bird's eye chili, deseeded and chopped
2 green onions, chopped

5 cups vegetable broth
1 pound (454 g) turkey thighs, deboned and cut into halves
½ teaspoon five-spice powder
1 teaspoon oyster sauce
Kosher salt, to taste

Heat the olive oil in a stockpot over a moderate flame. Then, sauté the peppers and onions until they have softened or about 4 minutes. Add in the other ingredients and bring to a boil. Turn the heat to simmer, cover, and continue to cook an additional 12 minutes. Ladle into individual bowls and serve warm. Enjoy!

calories: 180 | fat: 7.5g | protein: 21.4g | carbs: 6.7g | net carbs: 5.5g | fiber: 1.2g

Chicken Thigh and Kale Stew

Prep time: 20 minutes | Cook time: 6 hours | Serves 6

3 tablespoons extra-virgin olive oil, divided
1 pound (454 g) boneless chicken thighs, diced into 1½-inch pieces
½ sweet onion, chopped
2 teaspoons minced garlic
2 cups chicken broth

2 celery stalks, diced
1 carrot, diced
1 teaspoon dried thyme
1 cup shredded kale
1 cup coconut cream
Salt, for seasoning
Freshly ground black pepper, for seasoning

Lightly grease the insert of the slow cooker with 1 tablespoon of the olive oil. In a large skillet over medium-high heat, heat the remaining 2 tablespoons of the olive oil. Add the chicken and sauté until it is just cooked through, about 7 minutes. Add the onion and garlic and sauté for an additional 3 minutes. Transfer the chicken mixture to the insert, and stir in the broth, celery, carrot, and thyme. Cover and cook on low for 6 hours. Stir in the kale and coconut cream. Season with salt and pepper, and serve warm.

calories: 277 | fat: 22.0g | protein: 17.0g | carbs: 6.0g | net carbs: 4.0g | fiber: 2.0g

Bell Pepper Turkey Casserole

Prep time: 10 minutes | Cook time: 25 minutes | Serves 5

3 teaspoons olive oil
1 cup bell peppers, sliced
1 yellow onion, thinly sliced
1½ pounds (680 g) turkey breast

Se salt and ground black pepper, to taste
1 cup chicken bone broth
1 cup double cream
½ cup Swiss cheese, shredded

Heat 2 teaspoons of the olive oil in a sauté pan over a moderate flame. Sauté the peppers and onion until they have softened; reserve. In the same sauté pan, heat the remaining teaspoon of olive oil and sear the turkey breasts until no longer pink. Layer the peppers and onions in a lightly greased baking pan. Add the turkey breast; sprinkle with salt and pepper. Mix the chicken bone broth with the double cream; pour the mixture over the turkey breasts. Bake in the preheated oven at 350ºF (180ºC) for 20 minutes; top with the Swiss cheese. Bake an additional 5 minutes or until golden brown on top. Bon appétit!

calories: 465 | fat: 28.5g | protein: 45.4g | carbs: 4.5g | net carbs: 4.2g | fiber: 0.3g

Chicken Drumsticks in Capocollo

Prep time: 10 minutes | Cook time: 35 minutes | Serves 5

2 pounds (907 g) chicken drumsticks, skinless and boneless
1 garlic clove, peeled and halved

½ teaspoon smoked paprika
Coarse sea salt and ground black pepper, to taste
10 thin slices of capocollo

Using a sharp kitchen knife, butterfly cut the chicken drumsticks in half. Lay each chicken drumstick flat on a cutting board and rub garlic halves over the surface of chicken drumsticks. Season with paprika, salt, and black pepper. Lay a slice of capocollo on each piece, pressing lightly. Roll them up and secure with toothpicks. Bake in the preheated oven at 420°F (216°C) for about 15 minutes until the edges of the chicken begin to brown. Turn over and bake for a further 15 to 20 minutes. Bon appétit!

calories: 486 | fat: 33.7g | protein: 39.1g | carbs: 3.6g | net carbs: 2.6g | fiber: 1.0g

Olla Tapada

Prep time: 15 minutes | Cook time: 25 minutes | Serves 3

2 teaspoons canola oil
1 red bell pepper, seeded and chopped
1 shallot, chopped
½ cup celery rib, chopped
½ cup chayote, peeled and cubed
1 pound (454 g) duck breasts,

boneless, skinless, and chopped into small chunks
1½ cups vegetable broth
½ stick Mexican cinnamon
1 thyme sprig
1 rosemary sprig
Sea salt and freshly ground black pepper, to taste

Heat the canola oil in a soup pot (or clay pot) over a medium-high flame. Now, sauté the bell pepper, shallot and celery until they have softened about 5 minutes. Add the remaining ingredients and stir to combine. Once it starts boiling, turn the heat to simmer and partially cover the pot. Let it simmer for 17 to 20 minutes or until thoroughly cooked. Enjoy!

calories: 230 | fat: 9.6g | protein: 30.5g | carbs: 3.3g | net carbs: 2.3g | fiber: 1.0g

Cheddar Bacon Stuffed Chicken Fillets

Prep time: 10 minutes | Cook time: 25 minutes | Serves 2

2 chicken fillets, skinless and boneless
½ teaspoon oregano
½ teaspoon tarragon
½ teaspoon paprika
¼ teaspoon ground black

pepper
Sea salt, to taste
2 (1-ounce / 28-g) slices bacon
2 (1-ounce / 28-g) slices Cheddar cheese
1 tomato, sliced

Sprinkle the chicken fillets with oregano, tarragon, paprika, black pepper, and salt. Place the bacon slices and cheese on each chicken fillet. Roll up the fillets and secure with toothpicks. Place the stuffed chicken fillets on a lightly greased baking pan. Scatter the sliced tomato around the fillets. Bake in the preheated oven at 390°F (199°C) for 15 minutes; turn on the other side and bake an additional 5 to 10 minutes or until the meat is no longer pink. Discard the toothpicks and serve immediately. Bon appétit!

calories: 400 | fat: 23.8g | protein: 41.3g | carbs: 3.6g | net carbs: 2.4g | fiber: 1.2g

Herbed Balsamic Turkey

Prep time: 15 minutes | Cook time: 15 minutes | Serves 2

1 turkey drumstick, skinless and boneless
1 tablespoon balsamic vinegar
1 tablespoon whiskey
3 tablespoons olive oil
1 tablespoon stone ground mustard
½ teaspoon tarragon

1 teaspoon rosemary
1 teaspoon sage
1 garlic clove, pressed
Kosher salt and ground black pepper, to season
1 brown onion, peeled and chopped

Place the turkey drumsticks in a ceramic dish. Toss them with the balsamic vinegar, whiskey, olive oil, mustard, tarragon, rosemary, sage, and garlic. Cover with plastic wrap and refrigerate for 3 hours. Heat your grill to the hottest setting. Grill the turkey drumsticks for about 13 minutes per side. Season with salt and pepper to taste and serve with brown onion. Bon appétit!

calories: 389 | fat: 19.6g | protein: 42.0g | carbs: 6.0g | net carbs: 4.6g | fiber: 1.4g

Thyme Roasted Drumsticks

Prep time: 10 minutes | Cook time: 40 minutes | Serves 6

1 stick unsalted butter, softened
4 cloves garlic, minced
Sea salt and ground black pepper, to taste

1 tablespoon fresh thyme leaves
2 pounds (907 g) chicken drumsticks

In a mixing bowl, thoroughly combine the butter, garlic, salt, black pepper, and thyme. Rub this mixture all over the chicken drumsticks. Lay the chicken drumsticks on a parchment-lined baking tray. Bake in the preheated oven at 390°F (199°C) until an instant-read thermometer reads 165°F (74°C) about 40 minutes. Place under the preheated broiler for 1 to 2 minutes if you'd like the golden, crisp skin. Bon appétit!

calories: 342 | fat: 24.3g | protein: 28.1g | carbs: 1.7g | net carbs: 1.4g | fiber: 0.3g

Turkey and Canadian Bacon Pizza

Prep time: 10 minutes | Cook time: 32 minutes | Serves 4

½ pound (227 g) ground turkey
½ cup Parmesan cheese, freshly grated
½ cup Mozzarella cheese, grated
Salt and ground black pepper, to taste

1 bell pepper, sliced
2 slices Canadian bacon, chopped
1 tomato, chopped
1 teaspoon oregano
½ teaspoon basil

In mixing bowl, thoroughly combine the ground turkey, cheese, salt, and black pepper. Then, press the cheese-chicken mixture into a parchment-lined baking pan. Bake in the preheated oven, at 390°F (199°C) for 22 minutes. Add bell pepper, bacon, tomato, oregano, and basil. Bake an additional 10 minutes and serve warm. Bon appétit!

calories: 361 | fat: 22.6g | protein: 32.5g | carbs: 5.8g | net carbs: 5.2g | fiber: 0.6g

Grilled Rosemary Wings with Leeks

Prep time: 10 minutes | Cook time: 20 minutes | Serves 4

8 chicken wings
2 tablespoons butter, melted
The Marinade:
2 garlic cloves, minced
¼ cup leeks, chopped

2 tablespoons lemon juice
Salt and ground black pepper, to taste
½ teaspoon paprika
1 teaspoon dried rosemary

Thoroughly combine all ingredients for the marinade in a ceramic bowl. Add the chicken wings to the bowl. Cover and allow it to marinate for 1 hour. Then, preheat your grill to medium-high heat. Drizzle melted butter over the chicken wings. Grill the chicken wings for 20 minutes, turning them periodically. Taste, adjust the seasonings, and serve warm. Enjoy!

calories: 132 | fat: 7.9g | protein: 13.3g | carbs: 1.9g | net carbs: 1.6g | fiber: 0.3g

Turkish Chicken Thigh Kebabs

Prep time: 15 minutes | Cook time: 9 to 12 minutes | Serves 2

1 pound (454 g) chicken thighs, boneless, skinless and halved
½ cup Greek yogurt
Sea salt, to taste
1 tablespoon Aleppo red pepper flakes
½ teaspoon ground black pepper

¼ teaspoon dried oregano
½ teaspoon mustard seeds
⅛ teaspoon ground cinnamon
½ teaspoon sumac
2 Roma tomatoes, chopped
2 tablespoons olive oil
1½ ounces (43 g) Swiss cheese, sliced

Place the chicken thighs, yogurt, salt, red pepper flakes, black pepper, oregano, mustard seeds, cinnamon, sumac, tomatoes, and olive oil in a ceramic dish. Cover and let it marinate in your refrigerator for 4 hours. Preheat your grill for medium-high heat and lightly oil the grate. Thread the chicken thighs onto skewers, making a thick log shape. Cook your kebabs for 3 or 4 minutes; turn over and continue cooking for 3 to 4 minutes more. An instant-read thermometer should read about 165°F (74°C). Add the cheese and let it cook for a further 3 to 4 minutes or until completely melted. Bon appétit!

calories: 500 | fat: 23.3g | protein: 61.0g | carbs: 6.2g | net carbs: 4.5g | fiber: 1.7g

Chinese Flavor Chicken Legs

Prep time: 10 minutes | Cook time: 15 minutes | Serves 4

1 tablespoon sesame oil
4 chicken legs
¼ cup Shaoxing wine

2 tablespoons brown erythritol
¼ cup spicy tomato sauce

Heat the sesame oil in a cast-iron skillet over medium-high flame. Now, sear chicken wings until they turn golden in color on all sides; reserve. Then, in the same skillet, add a splash of wine to deglaze the pan. Add in the remaining wine, brown erythritol, and spicy tomato sauce. Bring to a boil and immediately reduce the heat to medium-low. Let it simmer for 5 to 10 minutes until the sauce coats the back of a spoon. Add the reserved chicken legs back to the skillet. Cook for a further 3 minutes or until the chicken is well coated and heated through. Enjoy!

calories: 366 | fat: 14.6g | protein: 51.1g | carbs: 3.4g | net carbs: 2.4g | fiber: 1.0g

Spiced Duck Goulash

Prep time: 15 minutes | Cook time: 5 minutes | Serves 2

2 (1-ounce / 28-g) slices bacon, chopped
½ pound (227 g) duck legs, skinless and boneless
2 cups chicken broth, preferably homemade
½ cup celery ribs, chopped
2 green garlic stalks, chopped
2 green onion stalks, chopped

1 ripe tomato, puréed
Kosher salt, to season
¼ teaspoon red pepper flakes
½ teaspoon Hungarian paprika
½ teaspoon ground black pepper
½ teaspoon mustard seeds
½ teaspoon sage
1 bay laurel

Heat a stockpot over medium-high heat. Fry the bacon until crisp, about 3 minutes. Add in the duck legs and cook until no longer pink. Chop the meat, discarding any remaining skin and bones. Reserve the bacon and meat. Pour in a splash of chicken broth to deglaze the pan. Sauté the celery, green garlic and onions for 2 to 3 minutes, stirring periodically. Add the remaining ingredients to the pot, including the reserved bacon and meat. Stir to combine and reduce the heat to medium-low. Let it cook, covered, until everything is thoroughly heated or about 1 hour. Serve.

calories: 364 | fat: 22.4g | protein: 33.2g | carbs: 5.1g | net carbs: 3.7g | fiber: 1.4g

Turkey and leek Goulash

Prep time: 10 minutes | Cook time: 40 minutes | Serves 6

2 tablespoons olive oil
1 large-sized leek, chopped
2 cloves garlic, minced
2 pounds (907 g) turkey

thighs, skinless, boneless and chopped
2 celery stalks, chopped

Heat the olive oil in a soup pot over a moderate flame. Then, sweat the leeks until just tender and fragrant. Then, cook the garlic until aromatic. Add in the turkey thighs and celery; add 4 cups of water and bring to a boil. Immediately reduce the heat and allow it to simmer for 35 to 40 minutes. Ladle into individual bowls and serve hot. Bon appétit!

calories: 221 | fat: 7.3g | protein: 35.4g | carbs: 2.6g | net carbs: 2.2g | fiber: 0.4g

Mediterranean Chicken with Peppers and Olives

Prep time: 15 minutes | Cook time: 15 minutes | Serves 2

2 chicken drumsticks, boneless and skinless
1 tablespoon extra-virgin olive oil
Sea salt and ground black pepper, to season

2 bell peppers, seeded and halved
1 small chili pepper, finely chopped
2 tablespoons Greek aioli
6 Kalamata olives, pitted

Brush the chicken drumsticks with the olive oil. Season the chicken drumsticks with salt and black pepper. Preheat your grill to moderate heat. Grill the chicken drumsticks for 8 minutes; turn them over and add the bell peppers. Grill them for a further 5 minutes. Transfer to a serving platter; top with chopped chili pepper and Greek aioli. Garnish with Kalamata olives and serve warm. Enjoy!

calories: 400 | fat: 31.3g | protein: 24.5g | carbs: 5.0g | net carbs: 3.9g | fiber: 1.1g

Chicken Mélange

Prep time: 15 minutes | Cook time: 35 minutes | Serves 3

2 ounces (57 g) bacon, diced
¾ pound (340 g) whole
chicken, boneless and
chopped
½ medium-sized leek, chopped
1 teaspoon ginger garlic paste
1 teaspoon poultry seasoning
mix

Sea salt, to taste
1 bay leaf
1 thyme sprig
1 rosemary sprig
1 cup chicken broth
½ cup cauliflower, chopped
into small florets
2 vine-ripe tomatoes, puréed

Heat a medium-sized pan over medium-high heat; once hot, fry
the bacon until it is crisp or about 3 minutes. Add in the chicken
and cook until it is no longer pink; reserve. Then, sauté the leek
until tender and fragrant. Stir in the ginger garlic paste, poultry
seasoning mix, salt, bay leaf, thyme, and rosemary. Pour in
the chicken broth and reduce the heat to medium; let it cook
for 15 minutes, stirring periodically. Add in the cauliflower and
tomatoes along with the reserved bacon and chicken. Decrease
the temperature to simmer and let it cook for a further 15
minutes or until warmed through. Bon appétit!

calories: 353 | fat: 14.4g | protein: 44.1g | carbs: 5.9g | net
carbs: 3.5g | fiber: 2.4g

Buffalo Chicken Bake

Prep time: 10 minutes | Cook time: 55 minutes | Serves 6

1 tablespoon olive oil
2 pounds (907 g) chicken
drumettes
Sauce:
½ cup melted butter

½ cup hot sauce
2 tablespoons white vinegar
¼ teaspoon granulated garlic
Sea salt and ground black, to
season

Start by preheating your oven to 320°F (160°C). Brush a baking
pan with olive oil. Arrange the chicken drumettes in the greased
pan. Prepare the sauce by whisking the melted butter, hot
sauce, white vinegar, garlic, salt and black pepper until well
combined. Pour the sauce over the chicken drumettes. Bake for
55 minutes, flipping the chicken drumettes once or twice. Taste,
adjust the seasonings and serve warm.

calories: 289 | fat: 20.5g | protein: 23.4g | carbs: 1.3g | net
carbs: 1.0g | fiber: 0.3g

Garlicky Drumsticks

Prep time: 10 minutes | Cook time: 1 hour 10 minutes | Serves 5

2 tablespoons olive oil
2 pounds (907 g) chicken
drumsticks, boneless, skinless
Sea salt and ground black
pepper, to taste

2 garlic cloves, minced
½ cup tomato paste
½ cup chicken broth
4 tablespoons rice vinegar
2 scallions, chopped

Start by preheating the oven to 330°F (166°C). Brush the sides
and bottom of a baking pan with olive oil. Arrange the chicken
drumsticks in the baking pan. Add the salt, black pepper, garlic,
tomato paste, chicken broth, and rice vinegar to the pan. Bake
for 1 hour 10 minutes or until everything is heated through.
Garnish with scallions and serve. Bon appétit!

calories: 353 | fat: 22.2g | protein: 33.2g | carbs: 2.6g | net
carbs: 2.0g | fiber: 0.6g

Chicken, Pepper, and Tomato Bake

Prep time: 10 minutes | Cook time: 25 minutes | Serves 3

1 tablespoon olive oil
¾ pound (340 g) chicken
breast fillets, chopped into bite-
sized chunks
2 garlic cloves, sliced
¼ teaspoon Korean chili
pepper flakes
¼ teaspoon Himalayan salt

½ teaspoon poultry seasoning
mix
1 bell pepper, seeded and
chopped
2 ripe tomatoes, chopped
¼ cup heavy whipping cream
¼ cup sour cream

Brush a casserole dish with olive oil. Add the chicken, garlic,
Korean chili pepper flakes, salt, and poultry seasoning mix to
the casserole dish. Next, layer the pepper and tomatoes. Whisk
the heavy whipping cream and sour cream in a mixing bowl.
Top everything with the cream mixture. Bake in the preheated
oven at 390°F (199°C) for about 25 minutes or until thoroughly
heated. Bon appétit!

calories: 411 | fat: 20.6g | protein: 50.0g | carbs: 6.2g | net carbs:
4.7g | fiber: 1.5g

Mediterranean Roasted Chicken Drumettes

Prep time: 15 minutes | Cook time: 20 minutes | Serves 5

2 tablespoons olive oil
1½ pounds (680 g) chicken
drumettes
2 cloves garlic, minced
1 thyme sprig
1 rosemary sprig
½ teaspoon dried oregano

Sea salt and freshly ground
black pepper, to taste
2 tablespoons Greek cooking
wine
½ cup chicken bone broth
1 red onion, cut into wedges
2 bell peppers, sliced

Start by preheating your oven to 420°F (216°C). Brush the sides
and bottom a baking dish with 1 tablespoon of olive oil. Heat the
remaining tablespoon of olive oil in a saucepan over a moderate
flame. Brown the chicken drumettes for 5 to 6 minutes per side.
Transfer the warm chicken drumettes to a baking dish. Add the
garlic, spices, wine and broth. Scatter red onion and peppers
around chicken drumettes. Roast in the preheated oven for
about 13 minutes. Serve immediately and enjoy!

calories: 219 | fat: 9.2g | protein: 28.5g | carbs: 4.2g | net carbs:
3.5g | fiber: 0.7g

Turkey Wing Curry

Prep time: 15 minutes | Cook time: 55 minutes | Serves 4

3 teaspoons sesame oil
1 pound (454 g)turkey wings,
boneless and chopped
2 cloves garlic, finely chopped
1 small-sized red chili pepper,
minced
½ teaspoon turmeric powder
½ teaspoon ginger powder

1 teaspoon red curry paste
1 cup unsweetened coconut
milk, preferably homemade
½ cup water
½ cup turkey consommé
Kosher salt and ground black
pepper, to taste

Heat sesame oil in a sauté pan. Add the turkey and cook until it
is light brown about 7 minutes. Add garlic, chili pepper, turmeric
powder, ginger powder, and curry paste and cook for 3 minutes
longer. Add the milk, water, and consommé. Season with salt
and black pepper. Cook for 45 minutes over medium heat. Bon
appétit!

calories: 296 | fat: 19.6g | protein: 25.6g | carbs: 3.0g | net
carbs: 3.0g | fiber: 0g

Double-Cheese Ranch Chicken

Prep time: 15 minutes | Cook time: 20 minutes | Serves 4

2 chicken breasts
2 tablespoons butter, melted
1 teaspoon salt
½ teaspoon garlic powder
½ teaspoon cayenne pepper
½ teaspoon black peppercorns, crushed
½ tablespoon ranch seasoning

mix
4 ounces (113 g) Ricotta cheese, room temperature
½ cup Monterey-Jack cheese, grated
4 slices bacon, chopped
¼ cup scallions, chopped

Start by preheating your oven to 370ºF (188ºC). Drizzle the chicken with melted butter. Rub the chicken with salt, garlic powder, cayenne pepper, black pepper, and ranch seasoning mix. Heat a cast iron skillet over medium heat. Cook the chicken for 3 to 5 minutes per side. Transfer the chicken to a lightly greased baking dish. Add cheese and bacon. Bake about 12 minutes. Top with scallions just before serving. Bon appétit!

calories: 290 | fat: 19.3g | protein: 25.1g | carbs: 2.5g | net carbs: 2.5g | fiber: 0g

Asiago Drumsticks with Spinach

Prep time: 10 minutes | Cook time: 12 minutes | Serves 2

1 tablespoon peanut oil
2 chicken drumsticks
½ cup vegetable broth
½ cup cream cheese
2 cups baby spinach
Sea salt and ground black

pepper, to taste
½ teaspoon parsley flakes
½ teaspoon shallot powder
½ teaspoon garlic powder
½ cup Asiago cheese, grated

Heat the oil in a pan over medium-high heat. Then cook the chicken for 7 minutes, turning occasionally; reserve. Pour in broth; add cream cheese and spinach; cook until spinach has wilted. Add the chicken back to the pan. Add seasonings and Asiago cheese; cook until everything is thoroughly heated, an additional 4 minutes. Serve immediately and enjoy!

calories: 588 | fat: 46.0g | protein: 37.6g | carbs: 5.7g | net carbs: 4.7g | fiber: 1.0g

Chicken Puttanesca

Prep time: 15 minutes | Cook time: 20 minutes | Serves 5

2 tablespoons olive oil
1 bell pepper, chopped
1 red onion, chopped
1 teaspoon garlic, minced
1½ pounds (680 g) chicken wings, boneless
2 cups tomato sauce

1 tablespoon capers
¼ teaspoon red pepper, crushed
¼ cup Parmesan cheese, preferably freshly grated
2 basil sprigs, chopped

Heat the olive oil in a non-stick skillet over a moderate flame. Once hot, sauté the bell peppers and onions until tender and fragrant. Stir in the garlic and continue to cook an additional 30 seconds. Stir in the chicken wings, tomato sauce, capers, and red pepper; continue to cook for a further 20 minutes or until everything is heated through. Serve garnished with freshly grated Parmesan and basil. Bon appétit!

calories: 266 | fat: 11.3g | protein: 32.6g | carbs: 6.4g | net carbs: 5.1g | fiber: 1.3g

Rind and Cheese Crusted Chicken

Prep time: 10 minutes | Cook time: 10 minutes | Serves 3

2 tablespoons double cream
1 egg
2 ounces (57 g) pork rinds, crushed
2 ounces (57 g) Romano cheese, grated
Sea salt and ground black pepper, to taste

1 teaspoon cayenne pepper
1 teaspoon dried parsley1 garlic clove, halved
½ pound (227 g) chicken fillets
2 tablespoons olive oil
1 large-sized Roma tomato, puréed

In a mixing bowl, whisk the cream and egg. In another bowl, mix the crushed pork rinds, Romano cheese, salt, black pepper, cayenne pepper, and dried parsley. Rub the garlic halves all over the chicken. Dip the chicken fillets into the egg mixture; then, coat the chicken with breading on all sides. Heat the olive oil in a pan over medium-high heat; add butter. Once hot, cook chicken fillets until no longer pink, 2 to 4 minutes on each side. Transfer the prepared chicken fillets to a baking pan that is lightly greased with a nonstick cooking spray. Cover with the puréed tomato. Bake for 2 to 3 minutes until everything is thoroughly warmed. Bon appétit!

calories: 360 | fat: 23.5g | protein: 30.5g | carbs: 5.7g | net carbs: 3.4g | fiber: 1.3g

Greek Drumettes with Olives

Prep time: 10 minutes | Cook time: 20 minutes | Serves 2

1 pound (454 g) chicken drumettes
1 teaspoon Greek seasoning blend

1 tablespoon olive oil
6 ounces (170 g) tomato sauce
6 Kalamata olives, pitted and sliced

Place the chicken drumettes and Greek seasoning blend in a Ziploc bag. Shake the bag, ensuring even coating. Heat the olive oil in a saucepan over medium-high heat. Sear the chicken drumettes until golden brown, flipping them occasionally to ensure even cooking. After that, stir in the tomato sauce and Kalamata olives. Continue to cook until the chicken is tender and everything is thoroughly heated or about 20 minutes. Bon appétit!

calories: 342 | fat: 14.2g | protein: 47.0g | carbs: 3.5g | net carbs: 2.4g | fiber: 1.1g

Lemony Chicken Wings

Prep time: 10 minutes | Cook time: 15 minutes | Serves 4

A pinch of garlic powder
1 teaspoon lemon zest
1 tablespoon lemon juice
½ teaspoon ground cilantro
1 tablespoon fish sauce
1 tablespoon butter

¼ teaspoon xanthan gum
1 tablespoon Swerve sweetener
20 chicken wings
Salt and black pepper, to taste

Combine lemon juice and zest, fish sauce, cilantro, sweetener, and garlic powder in a saucepan. Bring to a boil, cover, lower the heat, and let simmer for 10 minutes. Stir in the butter and xanthan gum. Set aside. Season the wings with some salt and pepper. Preheat the grill and cook for 5 minutes per side. Serve topped with the sauce.

calories: 365 | fat: 25g | protein: 21g | carbs: 4g | net carbs: 4g | fiber: 0g

Rice Wine Duck with White Onion

Prep time: 5 minutes | Cook time: 25 minutes | Serves 6

1½ pounds (680 g) duck breast
1 tablespoon sesame oil
1 white onion, chopped
¼ cup rice wine
3 teaspoons soy sauce

Gently score the duck breast skin in a tight crosshatch pattern using a sharp knife. Heat the sesame oil in a skillet over moderate heat. Now, sauté the onion until tender and translucent. Add in the duck breasts; sear the duck breasts for 10 to 13 minutes or until the skin looks crispy with golden brown color; drain off the duck fat from the skillet. Flip the breasts over and sear the other side for 3 minutes. Deglaze the skillet with rice wine, scraping up any brown bits stuck to the bottom. Transfer to a baking pan; add the rice wine and soy sauce to the baking pan. Roast in the preheated oven at 400°F (205°C) for 4 minutes for medium-rare (145°F / 63°C), or 6 minutes for medium (165°F / 74°C). Serve garnished with sesame seeds if desired. Enjoy!

calories: 264 | fat: 11.4g | protein: 34.2g | carbs: 3.6g | net carbs: 3.0g | fiber: 0.6g

Italian Parmesan Turkey Fillets

Prep time: 10 minutes | Cook time: 15 minutes | Serves 5

2 eggs
1 cup sour cream
1 teaspoon Italian seasoning blend
Kosher salt and ground black
pepper, to taste
½ cup grated Parmesan cheese
2 pounds (907 g) turkey fillets

In a mixing bowl, whisk the eggs until frothy and light. Stir in the sour cream and continue whisking until well combined. In another bowl, mix the Italian seasoning blend with the salt, black pepper, and Parmesan cheese; mix to combine well. Dip the turkey fillets into the egg mixture; then, press them into the Parmesan mixture. Cook in the greased frying pan until browned on all sides. Bon appétit!

calories: 336 | fat: 12.7g | protein: 47.5g | carbs: 5.2g | net carbs: 5.0g | fiber: 0.2g

Roasted Whole Chicken with Black Olives

Prep time: 10 minutes | Cook time: 1 hour 15 minutes | Serves 5

2 pounds (907 g) whole chicken
1 teaspoon paprika
1 teaspoon lemon zest, slivered
Kosher salt and freshly ground
black pepper, to taste
1 cup oil-cured black olives, pitted
4 cloves garlic
1 bunch fresh thyme, leaves picked

Begin by preheating your oven to 360°F (182°C). Then, spritz the sides and bottom of a baking dish with nonstick cooking oil. Sprinkle the chicken with paprika, lemon zest, salt, and black pepper. Bake for 60 minutes. Scatter black olives, garlic, and thyme around the chicken and bake an additional 10 to 13 minutes; a meat thermometer should read 180°F (82°C). Bon appétit!

calories: 236 | fat: 7.4g | protein: 37.1g | carbs: 2.6g | net carbs: 1.6g | fiber: 1.0g

Whole Chicken with Leek and Mushrooms

Prep time: 15 minutes | Cook time: 45 minutes | Serves 4

1 tablespoon olive oil
1½ pounds (680 g) whole chicken, skinless and boneless
2 cups button mushrooms, sliced
1 serrano pepper, sliced
1 medium-sized leek, chopped
1 teaspoon ginger-garlic paste
¼ cup dry red wine
Sea salt and ground black pepper, to season
2 tablespoons capers
1 cup tomato paste

Heat the olive oil in a frying pan over a moderate flame. Fry the chicken until golden brown on all sides or about 10 minutes; set aside. Then, cook the mushrooms, serrano pepper, and leek in the pan drippings. Cook until they have softened or about 6 minutes. After that, stir in the ginger-garlic paste and fry for a further 30 seconds. Add a splash of red wine to deglaze the pan. Add the chicken back to the frying pan. Add in salt, black pepper, capers, and tomato paste; stir to combine well and bring to a rapid boil. Turn the heat to medium-low and let it cook for 30 minutes more or until everything is heated through. Serve immediately.

calories: 425 | fat: 29.1g | protein: 33.4g | carbs: 5.6g | net carbs: 4.4g | fiber: 1.2g

Chicken Thigh Green Chowder

Prep time: 10 minutes | Cook time: 35 minutes | Serves 5

5 chicken thighs
½ cup Italian peppers, deseeded and chopped
½ cup green cabbage, shredded
½ cup celery, chopped
1 shallot, chopped
5 cups roasted vegetable broth
Freshly ground black pepper, to taste
7 ounces (198 g) full-fat cream cheese

Add the chicken thighs, Italian peppers, cabbage, celery, shallot, broth, and black pepper to a soup pot. Cook, partially covered, over a moderate heat for 25 minutes. Shred the chicken, discarding the bones. Fold in the cream cheese, stir and cover. Let it sit in the residual heat for 10 minutes. Ladle into individual bowls and serve warm.

calories: 512 | fat: 37.9g | protein: 35.2g | carbs: 5.3g | net carbs: 4.9g | fiber: 0.4g

Chicken and Mushroom Ramen

Prep time: 15 minutes | Cook time: 30 minutes | Serves 6

1 tablespoon peanut oil
1 pound (454 g) chicken thigs
6 cups water
1 dashi pack
4 ounces (113 g) enokitake or
enoki mushrooms
4 garlic cloves, chopped
2 tablespoons sake
1 tablespoon fresh chives, minced

Heat the peanut oil in a stockpot over medium-high heat. Then, brown the chicken thighs for 4 to 5 minutes per side. Then, add the water, dashi, enoki mushrooms, and garlic to the pot. When the soup reaches boiling, turn the heat to a simmer. Let it cook, partially covered, for 28 minutes. Shred the chicken, discarding the bones and add it back to the pot. Add in the sake and stir to combine. Ladle into soup bowls and garnish with minced chives. Enjoy!

calories: 200 | fat: 13.6g | protein: 14.6g | carbs: 2.3g | net carbs: 1.8g | fiber: 0.5g

Mexican Cotija Chicken Breasts

Prep time: 15 minutes | Cook time: 20 minutes | Serves 6

2 tablespoons olive oil
1½ pounds (680 g) chicken breasts, cut into bite-sized cubes
1 teaspoon garlic, finely chopped
1 Mexican chili pepper, finely chopped
2 ripe tomatoes, puréed

Sea salt and black pepper, to taste
½ teaspoon paprika
½ teaspoon Mexican oregano
4 ounces (113 g) sour cream
6 ounces (170 g) Cotija cheese, crumbled
2 tablespoons fresh chives, chopped

Heat the olive oil in a frying pan over a medium-high flame. Now, brown the chicken breasts for 4 to 5 minutes per side. Then, sauté the garlic and pepper until they are tender and aromatic. Fold in the puréed tomatoes and cook for a further 4 minutes. Season with salt, black pepper, paprika, and Mexican oregano. Transfer the chicken with the sauce to a lightly greased casserole dish. Top with the sour cream and Cotija cheese. Bake in the preheated oven for 12 to 13 minutes or until thoroughly cooked. Garnish with fresh chives and serve warm.

calories: 355 | fat: 23.1g | protein: 29.2g | carbs: 5.9g | net carbs: 5.4g | fiber: 0.5g

Spiced Chicken Breast

Prep time: 10 minutes | Cook time: 30 minutes | Serves 6

6 chicken breasts
4 cloves garlic, minced
½ cup oregano leaves, chopped
½ cup lemon juice

⅔ cup olive oil
¼ cup erythritol
Salt and black pepper, to taste
3 small chilies, minced

Preheat a grill to 350ºF (180ºC). In a bowl, mix the garlic, oregano, lemon juice, olive oil, chilies and erythritol. Set aside. While the spices incorporate in flavor, cover the chicken with plastic wraps, and use the rolling pin to pound to ½-inch thickness. Remove the wrap, and brush the mixture on the chicken on both sides. Place on the grill, cover the lid and cook for 15 minutes. Baste the chicken with more of the spice mixture, and continue cooking for 15 more minutes.

calories: 265 | fat: 9g | protein: 26g | carbs: 4g | net carbs: 3g | fiber: 1g

Hungarian Chicken Thighs

Prep time: 10 minutes | Cook time: 7 to 8 hours | Serves 4

1 tablespoon extra-virgin olive oil
2 pounds (907 g) boneless chicken thighs
½ cup chicken broth
Juice and zest of 1 lemon

2 teaspoons minced garlic
2 teaspoons paprika
¼ teaspoon salt
1 cup sour cream
1 tablespoon chopped parsley, for garnish

Lightly grease the insert of the slow cooker with the olive oil. Place the chicken thighs in the insert. In a small bowl, stir together the broth, lemon juice and zest, garlic, paprika, and salt. Pour the broth mixture over the chicken. Cover and cook on low for 7 to 8 hours. Turn off the heat and stir in the sour cream. Serve topped with the parsley.

calories: 404 | fat: 32g | protein: 23g | carbs: 4g | net carbs: 0g | fiber: 4g

Salsa Turkey Cutlet and Zucchini Stir-Fry

Prep time: 10 minutes | Cook time: 15 minutes | Serves 4

2 tablespoons olive oil
1 pound (454 g) turkey cutlets
1 red onion, sliced
2 garlic cloves, minced
1 chili pepper, chopped
Sea salt and ground black pepper, to taste

½ teaspoon cayenne pepper
½ teaspoon dried basil
1 teaspoon dried rosemary
½ teaspoon cumin seeds
½ teaspoon mustard seeds
1 zucchini, spiralized
½ cup salsa

Heat 1 tablespoon of the olive oil in a frying pan over a moderate flame. Cook the turkey cutlets until they are golden brown or about 10 minutes; shred the meat with two forks and reserve. Heat the remaining tablespoon of olive oil in the same frying pan. Now, sauté the onion, garlic, and chili pepper until they have softened. Add the spices and stir in the reserved turkey. Fold in the zucchini and cook for 3 minutes or until it is tender and everything is cooked through. Serve with salsa on the side. Enjoy!

calories: 211 | fat: 9.1g | protein: 26.1g | carbs: 5.5g | net carbs: 4.4g | fiber: 1.1g

Cheesy Spinach Stuffed Chicken

Prep time: 10 minutes | Cook time: 30 minutes | Serves 6

4 ounces (113 g) cream cheese
3 ounces (85 g) mozzarella slices
10 ounces (283 g) spinach

⅓ cup shredded mozzarella cheese
1 tablespoon olive oil
1 cup tomato basil sauce
3 whole chicken breasts

Preheat your oven to 400ºF (205ºC). Combine the cream cheese, shredded mozzarella cheese, and spinach in the microwave. Cut the chicken a couple of times horizontally and stuff with the spinach mixture. Brush with olive oil. place on a lined baking dish and bake in the oven for 25 minutes. Pour the tomato basil sauce over and top with mozzarella slices. Return to the oven and cook for an additional 5 minutes.

calories: 338 | fat: 28g | protein: 37g | carbs: 7g | net carbs: 3g | fiber: 4g

Herbed Chicken Legs

Prep time: 10 minutes | Cook time: 15 minutes | Serves 5

2 tablespoons butter, softened at room temperature
5 chicken legs, skinless
2 scallions, chopped
1 teaspoon fresh basil, chopped
1 teaspoon fresh thyme,

chopped
1 garlic clove, minced
½ teaspoon black peppercorns, freshly cracked
1 cup vegetable broth
½ teaspoon paprika
Sea salt, to taste

Melt 1 tablespoon of butter in a frying pan over a medium-high flame. Once hot, brown the chicken legs for 4 to 5 minutes per side. Add in the scallions, basil, thyme, and garlic; continue to sauté about a minute or so. Add the remaining tablespoon of butter, black peppercorns, broth, and paprika. Bring to a boil and immediately reduce the heat to simmer. Let it simmer for 10 minutes or until everything is cooked through. Season with salt to taste and serve. Bon appétit!

calories: 371 | fat: 15.9g | protein: 51.0g | carbs: 0.8g | net carbs: 0.5g | fiber: 0.3g

Cooked Chicken in Creamy Spinach Sauce

Prep time: 10 minutes | Cook time: 21 minutes | Serves 4

1 pound (454 g) chicken thighs
1 tablespoon coconut oil
1 tablespoon coconut flour
2 cups spinach, chopped
1 teaspoon oregano
1 cup heavy cream
1 cup chicken broth
1 tablespoon butter

Warm the coconut oil in a skillet and brown the chicken on all sides, about 6-8 minutes. Set aside. Add and melt the butter and whisk in the flour over medium heat. Whisk in the heavy cream and chicken broth and bring to a boil. Stir in oregano. Add the spinach to the skillet and cook until wilted. Add the thighs in the skillet and cook for an additional 15 minutes.

calories: 446 | fat: 38g | protein: 18g | carbs: 3g | net carbs: 2g | fiber: 1g

Ranch Turkey with Greek Aioli Sauce

Prep time: 10 minutes | Cook time: 15 minutes | Serves 4

2 eggs
Kosher salt and ground black pepper, to taste
1 teaspoon paprika
2 tablespoons pork rinds
2 tablespoons flaxseed meal
Sauce:
2 tablespoons Greek aioli
½ cup Greek yogurt

½ cup almond meal
1 pound (454 g)turkey tenders, ½-inch thick
2 tablespoons sesame seeds
2 tablespoons olive oil

Flaky sea salt and freshly ground black pepper, to season

In a mixing bowl, whisk the eggs with salt and black pepper until well combined. In a separate bowl, make the keto breading. Thoroughly combine the paprika, pork rinds, flaxseed meal, and almond meal. Dip the turkey tenders into the egg mixture. Press the turkey tenders into the keto breading. Dip them into the egg mixture again and roll them over the sesame seeds to coat well. Heat the olive oil in a pan over medium-high heat. Once hot, add the turkey tenders and brown for 4 minutes per side. Whisk the sauce ingredients until well incorporated. Serve the turkey tenders with the sauce on the side.

calories: 397 | fat: 27.4g | protein: 32.9g | carbs: 3.8g | net carbs: 2.0g | fiber: 1.8g

Fried Turkey and Pork Meatballs

Prep time: 20 minutes | Cook time: 15 minutes | Serves 4

4 spring onions, finely chopped
2 spring garlic stalks, chopped
2 tablespoons cilantro, chopped
½ pound (227 g) ground pork
½ pound (227 g) ground turkey
1 egg, whisked

½ cup Parmesan cheese, grated
1 teaspoon dried rosemary
½ teaspoon mustard powder
Sea salt and freshly ground black pepper, to season
2 tablespoons olive oil

In a mixing bowl, thoroughly combine all ingredients, except for the olive oil. Shape the mixture into small balls. Refrigerate your meatballs for 1 hour. Then, heat the olive oil in a frying pan over medium-high heat. Once hot, fry the meatballs for 6 minutes until nicely browned. Turn them and cook 6 minutes on the other side. Bon appétit!

calories: 367 | fat: 27.6g | protein: 25.9g | carbs: 3.0g | net carbs: 2.5g | fiber: 0.5g

Chicken Wing and Italian Pepper Soup

Prep time: 15 minutes | Cook time: 50 minutes | Serves 6

1 tablespoon olive oil
6 chicken wings
1 Italian pepper, seeded and sliced
½ cup celery, chopped
½ cup onions, finely chopped
2 sprigs rosemary, leaves
picked
2 sprigs thyme, leaves picked
Sea salt and ground black pepper, to taste
6 cups vegetable stock
1 whole egg

Heat the olive oil in a soup pot over a moderate flame. Brown the chicken wings for 4 to 5 minutes per side or until no longer pink; reserve. Then, cook the Italian pepper, celery and onions in the same pot until they have softened. Stir in the rosemary, thyme, salt, black pepper, and vegetable stock; return the chicken to the pot. Stir with a spoon and bring to a boil. Reduce the heat to medium-low and let it simmer an additional 45 minutes, stirring once or twice. Transfer the chicken to a cutting board and shred the chicken, discarding the bones. Add the egg to the pot and whisk until well combined. Add the chicken back to the pot, stir, and serve warm. Enjoy!

calories: 284 | fat: 18.8g | protein: 25.3g | carbs: 2.5g | net carbs: 2.1g | fiber: 0.4g

Grilled Lemony Chicken Wings

Prep time: 10 minutes | Cook time: 12 minutes | Serves 4

2 pounds (907 g) chicken wings
Juice from 1 lemon
½ cup fresh parsley, chopped
2 garlic cloves, peeled and minced
1 Serrano pepper, chopped
1 tablespoon olive oil
Salt and black pepper, to taste
Lemon wedges, for serving
Ranch dip, for serving
½ teaspoon cilantro

In a bowl, stir together lemon juice, garlic, salt, serrano pepper, cilantro, olive oil, and black pepper. Place in the chicken wings and toss well to coat. Refrigerate for 2 hours. Set a grill over high heat and add on the chicken wings; cook each side for 6 minutes. Remove to a plate and serve alongside lemon wedges and ranch dip.

calories: 326 | fat: 12g | protein: 50g | carbs: 3g | net carbs: 2g | fiber: 1g

Spicy Chicken Skewers

Prep time: 10 minutes | Cook time: 6 minutes | Serves 6

2 pounds (907 g) chicken breasts, cubed
1 teaspoon sesame oil
1 tablespoon olive oil
1 cup red bell pepper pieces
1 tablespoon five spice powder
1 tablespoon granulated sweetener
1 tablespoon fish sauce

Combine the sesame and olive oils, fish sauce, and seasonings in a bowl. Add the chicken, and let marinate for 1 hour in the fridge. Preheat the grill. Take 12 skewers and thread the chicken and bell peppers. Grill for 3 minutes per side.

calories: 297 | fat: 17g | protein: 32g | carbs: 2g | net carbs: 1g | fiber: 1g

Garlicky Sweet Chicken Skewers

Prep time: 10 minutes | Cook time: 10 minutes | Serves 4

For the Skewers:

1 tablespoon coconut aminos
1 tablespoon ginger-garlic paste
1 tablespoon Swerve

Chili pepper to taste
1 tablespoon olive oil
3 chicken breasts, cut into cubes

For the Dressing:

½ cup tahini
½ teaspoon garlic powder

Pink salt to taste
¼ cup warm water

In a small bowl, whisk the coconut aminos, ginger-garlic paste, Swerve, chili pepper, and olive oil. Put the chicken in a zipper bag, pour the marinade over, seal and shake for an even coat. Marinate in the fridge for 2 hours. Preheat a grill to 400ºF (204ºC) and thread the chicken on skewers. Cook for 10 minutes in total with three to four turnings to be golden brown; remove to a plate. Mix the tahini, garlic powder, salt, and warm water in a bowl. Pour into serving jars. Serve the chicken skewers and tahini dressing with cauli fried rice.

calories: 470 | fat: 25g | protein: 52g | carbs: 5g | net carbs: 2g | fiber: 3g

Sri Lankan Curry

Prep time: 15 minutes | Cook time: 25 minutes | Serves 6

2 tablespoons coconut oil
½ teaspoon cumin seeds
½ cup shallot, chopped
1 chili pepper, chopped
2 tablespoons curry paste
1 teaspoon ginger-garlic paste
Kosher salt and freshly ground

black pepper, to taste
1½ pounds (680 g) chicken tenders, cut into chunks
½ cup coconut milk
½ cup chicken broth
2 tablespoons fresh cilantro, chopped

Warm the coconut oil in a large frying pan over a moderate flame. Then, sauté the cumin seeds for 30 seconds or until aromatic. Add in the shallot and chili pepper and continue to sauté for a further 3 minutes or until tender and fragrant. Add in the curry paste, ginger-garlic paste, salt, black pepper, and chicken tenders. Cook for 3 minutes, stirring periodically. Then, pour in the coconut milk and chicken broth; bring to a boil. Immediately turn the heat to simmer and continue cooking for a further for 22 minutes. Serve warm garnished with fresh cilantro. Enjoy!

calories: 371 | fat: 16.0g | protein: 51.0g | carbs: 0.8g | net carbs: 0.6g | fiber: 0.2g

Basil Turkey Meatballs

Prep time: 10 minutes | Cook time: 5 minutes | Serves 4

1 pound (454 g) ground turkey
1 tablespoon chopped sun-dried tomatoes
1 tablespoon chopped basil
½ teaspoon garlic powder
1 egg

½ teaspoon salt
¼ cup almond flour
1 tablespoon olive oil
½ cup shredded mozzarella cheese
¼ teaspoon pepper

Place everything, except the oil in a bowl. Mix with your hands until combined. Form into 16 balls. Heat the olive oil in a skillet over medium heat. Cook the meatballs for 4-5 minutes per each side. Serve immediately.

calories: 310 | fat: 26g | protein: 22g | carbs: 3g | net carbs: 2g | fiber: 1g

Bacon and Chicken Frittata

Prep time: 15 minutes | Cook time: 25 minutes | Serves 4

4 slices bacon
1 pound (454 g) chicken breasts, cut into small strips
1 red bell pepper, chopped
1 onion, chopped
2 garlic cloves, minced
6 eggs

½ cup yogurt
½ teaspoon hot paprika
Sea salt and freshly ground black pepper
½ teaspoon oregano
½ teaspoon rosemary
1 cup Asiago cheese, shredded

In a pan, cook the bacon until crisp, crumbling with a fork; reserve. In the same pan, cook the chicken breasts for 5 to 6 minutes or until no longer pink; reserve. Sauté the pepper, onion, and garlic in the bacon grease. Cook until softened. In a mixing bowl, whisk the eggs with the yogurt, paprika, salt, black pepper, oregano, and rosemary. Add the bacon and chicken back to the pan. Pour the egg mixture over the chicken mixture. Top with Asiago cheese. Bake in the oven at 390ºF (199ºC) for 20 minutes until the eggs are puffed and opaque. Cut a slit in the center of the frittata to check the doneness. Serve.

calories: 485 | fat: 31.7g | protein: 41.8g | carbs: 5.7g | net carbs: 4.9g | fiber: 0.8g

Chicken and Broccoli Marsala

Prep time: 10 minutes | Cook time: 15 minutes | Serves 2

1 tablespoon olive oil
2 chicken fillets
¼ cup marsala wine
1 cup broccoli florets
1 teaspoon fresh garlic, chopped

¼ tomato paste
½ cup double cream
½ teaspoon paprika
Sea salt and ground black pepper, to taste

Heat the olive oil in a frying pan over a moderate flame. Once hot, brown the chicken fillets for 7 minutes on each side. Add a splash of wine to deglaze the pot. Add in the broccoli, garlic, and tomato paste and gently stir to combine. Turn the heat to simmer. Continue to cook an additional 5 minutes. After that, stir in the double cream, paprika, salt, and black pepper. Continue to simmer for 5 minutes more or until heated through. Bon appétit!

calories: 350 | fat: 20.5g | protein: 35.2g | carbs: 4.6g | net carbs: 3.4g | fiber: 1.2g

Roast Herbs Stuffed Chicken

Prep time: 10 minutes | Cook time: 1½ hours | Serves 8

5 pounds (2.3 kg) whole chicken
1 bunch oregano
1 bunch thyme
1 tablespoon marjoram
1 tablespoon parsley

1 tablespoon olive oil
2 pounds (907 g) Brussels sprouts
1 lemon
1 tablespoon butter

Preheat your oven to 450ºF (235ºC). Stuff the chicken with oregano, thyme, and lemon. Roast for 15 minutes. Reduce the heat to 325ºF (163ºC) and cook for 40 minutes. Spread the butter over the chicken, and sprinkle parsley and marjoram. Add the brussels sprouts. Return to the oven and bake for 40 more minutes. Let sit for 10 minutes before carving.

calories: 432 | fat: 32g | protein: 30g | carbs: 10g | net carbs: 5g | fiber: 5g

Hungarian Chicken Paprikash

Prep time: 15 minutes | Cook time: 30 minutes | Serves 5

2 tablespoons olive oil
2 pounds (907 g) chicken drumsticks
½ cup leeks, sliced
1 bell pepper, deseeded and chopped
1 Hungarian wax pepper, chopped

3 garlic cloves, chopped
1 cup tomato purée
4 cups vegetable broth
Sea salt and freshly ground black pepper, to taste
1 tablespoon Hungarian paprika
1 bay laurel

Heat the olive oil in a soup pot over a moderate flame. Once hot, brown the chicken drumsticks for about 7 minutes or until no longer pink; shred the meat and reserve. Then, cook the leeks and peppers in the pan drippings for about 5 minutes or until they have softened. Now, add in the garlic and cook for a minute or so. Add in the tomato purée, vegetable broth, salt, black pepper, Hungarian paprika, and bay laurel. Stir in the reserved chicken and bring to a boil; turn the heat to medium-low, cover, and let it simmer for 22 minutes. Ladle into individual bowls and serve. Enjoy!

calories: 359 | fat: 22.1g | protein: 33.2g | carbs: 4.5g | net carbs: 3.9g | fiber: 0.6g

Chicken and Shallot Mull

Prep time: 10 minutes | Cook time: 30 minutes | Serves 4

2 tablespoons butter
1 pound (454 g) chicken thighs, boneless and skinless
½ cup shallots, chopped
1 celery stalk, chopped
4 cups chicken broth
Sea salt and ground black

pepper, to your liking
½ teaspoon cayenne pepper
½ teaspoon mustard seeds
½ teaspoon celery seeds
1 cup milk
1 tablespoon fresh cilantro, chopped

Melt the butter in a heavy-bottomed pot over a moderate flame. Now, brown the chicken until no longer pink or about 6 minutes. Add in the shallots, celery, broth, salt, black pepper, cayenne pepper, mustard seeds, and celery seeds; stir to combine. Turn the heat to simmer and let it cook for 25 minutes longer or until heated through. Pour in the milk, stir and ladle into soup bowls. Garnish with fresh cilantro and serve warm. Bon appétit!

calories: 342 | fat: 26.6g | protein: 20.8g | carbs: 3.7g | net carbs: 3.4g | fiber: 0.3g

Paprika Chicken with Steamed Broccoli

Prep time: 10 minutes | Cook time: 15 minutes | Serves 6

1 tablespoon smoked paprika
Salt and black pepper to taste
1 teaspoon garlic powder

1 tablespoon olive oil
6 chicken breasts
1 head broccoli, cut into florets

Place broccoli florets onto the steamer basket over the boiling water; steam approximately 8 minutes or until crisp-tender. Set aside. Grease grill grate with cooking spray and preheat to 400°F (205°C). Combine paprika, salt, black pepper, and garlic powder in a bowl. Brush chicken with olive oil and sprinkle spice mixture over and massage with hands. Grill chicken for 7 minutes per side until well-cooked, and plate. Serve warm with steamed broccoli.

calories: 42 | fat: 18g | protein: 50g | carbs: 2g | net carbs: 2g | fiber: 0g

Chicken Breast with Anchovy Tapenade

Prep time: 10 minutes | Cook time: 10 minutes | Serves 2

1 chicken breast, cut into 4 pieces
For the Tapenade:
1 cup black olives, pitted
1 ounce (28 g) anchovy fillets, rinsed
1 garlic clove, crushed
Salt and ground black pepper,

1 tablespoon coconut oil
3 garlic cloves, crushed

to taste
1 tablespoon olive oil
¼ cup fresh basil, chopped
1 tablespoon lemon juice

Using a food processor, combine the olives, salt, olive oil, basil, lemon juice, anchovy, and black pepper, blend well. Set a pan over medium heat and warm coconut oil, stir in the garlic, and sauté for 2 minutes. Place in the chicken pieces and cook each side for 4 minutes. Split the chicken among plates and apply a topping of the anchovy tapenade. Serve immediately.

calories: 155 | fat: 13g | protein: 25g | carbs: 3g | net carbs: 3g | fiber: 0g

Chimichurri Chicken Tender

Prep time: 10 minutes | Cook time: 35 minutes | Serves 5

½ cup fresh parsley, chopped
¼ cup olive oil
4 tablespoons white wine vinegar
2 garlic cloves, minced

1½ pounds (680 g) chicken tenders
Sea salt and ground black pepper, to taste
1 cup sour cream

In a food processor or blender, process the parsley, olive oil, vinegar, and garlic until chunky sauce forms. Now, pierce the chicken randomly with a small knife. Pour half of the chimichurri sauce on top, cover, and refrigerate for 1 hour; discard the chimichurri sauce. Brush the sides and bottom of a baking pan with nonstick cooking spray. Arrange the chicken tenders in the baking pan. Then, season your chicken with salt and black pepper to taste. Pour in the sour cream and bake in the preheated oven at 370°F (188°C) for 35 minutes or until cooked through. Serve with the remaining chimichurri sauce. Bon appétit!

calories: 316 | fat: 29.8g | protein: 29.4g | carbs: 4.0g | net carbs: 3.8g | fiber: 0.2g

Lemony Chicken Skewers

Prep time: 10 minutes | Cook time: 12 minutes | Serves 4

3 chicken breasts, cut into cubes
1 tablespoon olive oil, divided
⅔ jar preserved lemon, flesh removed, drained
2 cloves garlic, minced

½ cup lemon juice
Salt and black pepper to taste
1 teaspoon rosemary leaves to garnish
2 to 4 lemon wedges to garnish

First, thread the chicken onto skewers and set aside. In a wide bowl, mix half of the oil, garlic, salt, pepper, and lemon juice, and add the chicken skewers, and lemon rind. Cover the bowl and let the chicken marinate for at least 2 hours in the refrigerator. When the marinating time is almost over, preheat a grill to 350°F (180°C), and remove the chicken onto the grill. Cook for 6 minutes on each side. Remove and serve warm garnished with rosemary leaves and lemons wedges.

calories: 350 | fat: 11g | protein: 34g | carbs: 6g | net carbs: 4g | fiber: 2g

Pepper, Cheese, and Sauerkraut Stuffed Chicken

Prep time: 15 minutes | Cook time: 30 minutes | Serves 5

2 tablespoons olive oil
5 chicken cutlets
½ teaspoon cayenne pepper
½ teaspoon oregano
Sea salt and ground black pepper, to taste
1 tablespoon Dijon mustard
2 garlic cloves, minced

5 Italian peppers, seeded and chopped
1 chili pepper, chopped
1 cup Romano cheese, shredded
5 tablespoons sauerkraut, for serving

Brush a baking pan with 1 tablespoon of the olive oil. Bruch the chicken cutlets with the remaining tablespoon of olive oil. Season the chicken cutlets with the cayenne pepper, oregano, salt, and black pepper. Spread mustard on one side of each chicken cutlet. Divide the garlic, peppers, and Romano cheese on the mustard side. Roll up tightly and use toothpicks to secure your rolls. Transfer to the prepared baking pan. Bake in the preheated oven at 370ºF (188ºC) for about 30 minutes until golden brown on all sides (an instant-read thermometer should register 165ºF (74ºC)). Spoon the sauerkraut over the chicken and serve. Bon appétit!

calories: 378 | fat: 16.6g | protein: 47.0g | carbs: 5.7g | net carbs: 4.7g | fiber: 1.0g

Bacon on Cheesy Chicken Breast

Prep time: 10 minutes | Cook time: 20 minutes | Serves 4

4 bacon strips
4 chicken breasts
3 green onions, chopped
4 ounces (113 g) ranch dressing

1 ounce coconut aminos
1 tablespoon coconut oil
4 ounces (113 g) Monterey Jack cheese, grated

Set a pan over high heat and warm the oil. Place in the chicken breasts, cook for 7 minutes, then flip to the other side; cook for an additional 7 minutes. Set another pan over medium heat, place in the bacon, cook until crispy, remove to paper towels, drain the grease, and crumble. Add the chicken breast to a baking dish. Place the green onions, coconut aminos, cheese, and crumbled bacon on top, set in an oven, turn on the broiler, and cook for 5 minutes at high temperature. Split among serving plates and serve.

calories: 423 | fat: 21g | protein: 34g | carbs: 4g | net carbs: 3g | fiber: 1g

Dijon Chicken Thighs

Prep time: 10 minutes | Cook time: 16 minutes | Serves 4

½ cup chicken stock
1 tablespoon olive oil
½ cup chopped onion
4 chicken thighs

¼ cup heavy cream
1 tablespoon Dijon mustard
1 teaspoon thyme
1 teaspoon garlic powder

Heat the olive oil in a pan. Cook the chicken for about 4 minutes per side. Set aside. Sauté the onion in the same pan for 3 minutes, add the stock, and simmer for 5 minutes. Stir in mustard and heavy cream, along with thyme and garlic powder. Pour the sauce over the chicken and serve.

calories: 504 | fat: 39g | protein: 33g | carbs: 4g | net carbs: 3g | fiber: 1g

Browned Chicken and Mushrooms

Prep time: 10 minutes | Cook time: 20 minutes | Serves 6

2 cups sliced mushrooms
½ teaspoon onion powder
½ teaspoon garlic powder
¼ cup butter
1 teaspoon Dijon mustard

1 tablespoon tarragon, chopped
2 pounds (907 g) chicken thighs
Salt and black pepper, to taste

Season the thighs with salt, pepper, garlic, and onion powder. Melt the butter in a skillet, and cook the chicken until browned; set aside. Add mushrooms to the same fat and cook for about 5 minutes. Stir in Dijon mustard and ½ cup of water. Return the chicken to the skillet. Season to taste with salt and pepper, reduce the heat and cover, and let simmer for 15 minutes. Stir in tarragon. Serve warm.

calories: 405 | fat: 33g | protein: 25g | carbs: 1g | net carbs: 1g | fiber: 0g

Braised Chicken and Veggies

Prep time: 10 minutes | Cook time: 21 minutes | Serves 4

1 tablespoon butter
1 pound (454 g) chicken thighs
Salt and black pepper, to taste
2 cloves garlic, minced
1 (14 ounce / 397-g) can whole

tomatoes
1 eggplant, diced
10 fresh basil leaves, chopped, extra to garnish

Melt butter in a saucepan over medium heat, season the chicken with salt and black pepper and fry for 4 minutes on each side until golden brown. Remove to a plate. Sauté the garlic in the butter for 2 minutes, pour in the tomatoes, and cook covered for 8 minutes. Add in the eggplant and basil. Cook for 4 minutes. Season the sauce with salt and black pepper, stir and add the chicken. Coat with sauce and simmer for 3 minutes. Serve chicken with sauce on a bed of squash pasta. Garnish with extra basil.

calories: 330 | fat: 22g | protein: 21g | carbs: 13g | net carbs: 7g | fiber: 6g

Turkey Chili

Prep time: 15 minutes | Cook time: 35 minutes | Serves 5

1 pound (454 g) ground turkey
½ pound (227 g) ground pork
4 tablespoons red wine
1 chili pepper, seeded and minced
2medium Italian peppers, seeded and sliced
1 onion, diced

2 cloves garlic, minced
3 cups vegetable broth
1 vine-ripe tomato, crushed
½ teaspoon cayenne pepper
Sea salt and ground black pepper, to your liking
5 ounces (142 g) Monterey Jack cheese, shredded

Preheat a saucepan over medium-high heat. Then, brown the ground meat for 5 minutes, crumbling with a wide spatula. Add in a splash of red wine to scrape up the browned bits that stick to the bottom of the saucepan. Add in the remaining ingredients, except for the Monterey Jack cheese; stir to combine well. When the mixture starts to boil, turn the heat to a medium-low. Let it cook, partially covered, for 30 minutes. Serve with the shredded Monterey Jack cheese. Bon appétit!

calories: 391 | fat: 25.1g | protein: 33.6g | carbs: 4.6g | net carbs: 3.4g | fiber: 1.2g

Veg Stuffed Chicken with Spiralized Cucumber

Prep time: 20 minutes | Cook time: 55 minutes | Serves 4

Chicken:

2 tablespoons butter	1 tomato, chopped
4 chicken breasts	¼ cup goat cheese
1 cup baby spinach	Salt and black pepper, to taste
1 carrot, shredded	1 teaspoon dried oregano

Salad:

2 cucumbers, spiralized	1 tablespoon rice vinegar
2 tablespoons olive oil	

Preheat oven to 390°F (199°C) and grease a baking dish with cooking spray. Place a pan over medium heat. Melt half of the butter and sauté spinach, carrot, and tomato until tender, for about 5 minutes. Season with salt and pepper. Transfer to a medium bowl and let cool for 10 minutes. Add in the goat cheese and oregano, stir and set to one side. Cut the chicken breasts lengthwise and stuff with the cheese mixture and set into the baking dish. On top, put the remaining butter and bake until cooked through for 20-30 minutes. Arrange the cucumbers on a serving platter, season with salt, black pepper, olive oil, and vinegar. Top with the chicken and pour over the sauce.

calories: 618 | fat: 46.4g | protein: 40.6g | carbs: 9.4g | net carbs: 7.6g | fiber: 1.8g

Chicken Thighs with Caesar Salad

Prep time: 15 minutes | Cook time: 15 minutes | Serves 4

Chicken:

4 chicken thighs	2 garlic cloves, minced
¼ cup lemon juice	2 tablespoons olive oil

Salad:

½ cup caesar salad dressing	3 Parmesan cheese crisps
2 tablespoons olive oil	Parmesan cheese, grated
12 bok choy leaves	

Combine the chicken ingredients in a Ziploc bag. Seal the bag, shake to combine, and refrigerate for 1 hour. Preheat the grill to medium heat, and grill the chicken about 4 minutes per side. Cut bok choy leaves lengthwise, and brush it with oil. Grill for about 3 minutes. Place on a serving platter. Top with the chicken, and drizzle the dressing over. Sprinkle with Parmesan cheese and finish with Parmesan crisps to serve.

calories: 530 | fat: 39.0g | protein: 33.0g | carbs: 6.7g | net carbs: 5.0g | fiber: 1.7g

Pesto Turkey with Zucchini Spaghetti

Prep time: 10 minutes | Cook time: 32 minutes | Serves 6

2 cups sliced mushrooms	1 cup diced onion
1 teaspoon olive oil	2 cups broccoli florets
1 pound (454 g) ground turkey	6 cups zucchini, spiralized
1 tablespoon pesto sauce	

Heat the oil in a skillet. Add zucchini and cook for 2-3 minutes, stirring continuously; set aside. Add turkey to the skillet and cook until browned, about 7-8 minutes. Transfer to a plate. Add onion and cook until translucent, about 3 minutes. Add broccoli and mushrooms, and cook for 7 more minutes. Return the turkey to the skillet. Stir in the pesto sauce. Cover the pan, lower the heat, and simmer for 15 minutes. Stir in zucchini pasta and serve immediately.

calories: 273 | fat: 16g | protein: 19g | carbs: 7g | net carbs: 4g | fiber: 3g

Herbed Turkey Breast

Prep time: 25 minutes | Cook time: 7 to 8 hours | Serves 6

3 tablespoons extra-virgin olive oil, divided	2 teaspoons minced garlic
1½ pounds (680 g) boneless turkey breasts	2 teaspoons dried thyme
	1 teaspoon dried oregano
Salt, for seasoning	1 avocado, peeled, pitted, and chopped
Freshly ground black pepper, for seasoning	1 tomato, diced
1 cup coconut milk	½ jalapeño pepper, diced
	1 tablespoon chopped cilantro

Lightly grease the insert of the slow cooker with 1 tablespoon of the olive oil. In a large skillet over medium-high heat, heat the remaining 2 tablespoons of the olive oil. Lightly season the turkey with salt and pepper. Add the turkey to the skillet and brown for about 7 minutes, turning once. Transfer the turkey to the insert and add the coconut milk, garlic, thyme, and oregano. Cover and cook on low for 7 to 8 hours. In a small bowl, stir together the avocado, tomato, jalapeño pepper, and cilantro. Serve the turkey topped with the avocado salsa.

calories: 347 | fat: 27g | protein: 25g | carbs: 5g | net carbs: 2g | fiber: 3g

Chicken in Creamy Mushroom Sauce

Prep time: 10 minutes | Cook time: 26 minutes | Serves 4

1 tablespoon butter	2 cups chicken broth
4 chicken breasts, cut into chunks	15 baby bella mushrooms, sliced
Salt and black pepper to taste	1 cup heavy cream
1 packet white onion soup mix	1 small bunch parsley, chopped

Melt butter in a saucepan over medium heat, season the chicken with salt and black pepper, and brown on all sides for 6 minutes in total. Put in a plate. In a bowl, stir the onion soup mix with chicken broth and add to the saucepan. Simmer for 3 minutes and add the mushrooms and chicken. Cover and simmer for another 20 minutes. Stir in heavy cream and parsley, cook on low heat for 3 minutes, and season with salt and pepper. Ladle the chicken with creamy sauce and mushrooms over beds of cauli mash. Garnish with parsley to serve.

calories: 448 | fat: 38g | protein: 22g | carbs: 4g | net carbs: 2g | fiber: 2g

Traditional Chicken Stroganoff

Prep time: 10 minutes | Cook time: 4 hours | Serves 4

2 garlic cloves, minced	1 pound (454 g) chicken breasts
8 ounces (227 g) mushrooms, chopped	1½ teaspoon dried thyme
¼ teaspoon celery seeds, ground	1 tablespoon fresh parsley, chopped
1 cup chicken stock	Salt and black pepper, to taste
1 cup sour cream	4 zucchinis, spiralized
1 cup leeks, chopped	

Place the chicken in a slow cooker. Place in the salt, leeks, sour cream, half of the parsley, celery seeds, garlic, black pepper, mushrooms, stock, and thyme. Cook on high for 4 hours while covered. Uncover the pot and add the rest of the parsley. Heat a pan with water over medium heat, place in some salt, bring to a boil, stir in the zucchini pasta, cook for 1 minute, and drain. Place in serving bowls, top with the chicken mixture, and serve.

calories: 365 | fat: 22g | protein: 26g | carbs: 11g | net carbs: 4g | fiber: 7g

Turkey and Pumpkin Ragout

Prep time: 15 minutes | Cook time: 8 hours | Serves 6

1 tablespoon extra-virgin olive oil
1 pound (454 g) boneless turkey thighs, cut into 1½-inch chunks
3 cups cubed pumpkin, cut into 1-inch chunks
1 red bell pepper, diced
½ sweet onion, cut in half and sliced
1 tablespoon minced garlic

1½ cups chicken broth
1½ cups coconut milk
2 teaspoons chopped fresh thyme
½ cup coconut cream
Salt, for seasoning
Freshly ground black pepper, for seasoning
12 slices cooked bacon, chopped, for garnish

Lightly grease the insert of the slow cooker with the olive oil. Add the turkey, pumpkin, red bell pepper, onion, garlic, broth, coconut milk, and thyme. Cover and cook on low for 8 hours. Stir in the coconut cream and season with salt and pepper. Serve topped with the bacon.

calories: 418 | fat: 34g | protein: 25g | carbs: 6g | net carbs: 5g | fiber: 1g

Classic Jerk Chicken

Prep time: 15 minutes | Cook time: 7 to 8 hours | Serves 6

½ cup extra-virgin olive oil, divided
2 pounds (907 g) boneless chicken (breast and thighs)
1 sweet onion, quartered
4 garlic cloves
2 scallions, white and green parts, coarsely chopped
2 habanero chiles, stemmed and seeded

2 tablespoons granulated erythritol
1 tablespoon grated fresh ginger
2 teaspoons allspice
1 teaspoon dried thyme
½ teaspoon cardamom
½ teaspoon salt
2 tablespoons chopped cilantro, for garnish

Lightly grease the insert of the slow cooker with 1 tablespoon of the olive oil. Arrange the chicken pieces in the bottom of the insert. In a blender, pulse the remaining olive oil, onion, garlic, scallions, chiles, erythritol, ginger, allspice, thyme, cardamom, and salt until a thick, uniform sauce forms. Pour the sauce over the chicken, turning the pieces to coat. Cover and cook on low for 7 to 8 hours. Serve topped with the cilantro.

calories: 485 | fat: 40g | protein: 27g | carbs: 5g | net carbs: 4g | fiber: 1g

Herbed Turkey with Cucumber Salsa

Prep time: 15 minutes | Cook time: 6 minutes | Serves 4

2 spring onions, thinly sliced
1 pound (454 g) ground turkey
1 egg
2 garlic cloves, minced
Cucumber Salsa:
1 tablespoon apple cider vinegar
1 tablespoon chopped dill
1 garlic clove, minced

1 tablespoon chopped herbs
1 small chili pepper, deseeded and diced
1 tablespoon butter

2 cucumbers, grated
1 cup sour cream
1 jalapeño pepper, minced
1 tablespoon olive oil

Place all turkey ingredients, except the butter, in a bowl. Mix to combine. Make patties out of the mixture. Melt the butter in a skillet over medium heat. Cook the patties for 3 minutes per side. Place all salsa ingredients in a bowl and mix to combine. Serve the patties topped with salsa.

calories: 350 | fat: 23g | protein: 27g | carbs: 7g | net carbs: 5g | fiber: 2g

Parmesan Chicken Wings with Yogurt Sauce

Prep time: 10 minutes | Cook time: 20 minutes | Serves 6

For the Dipping Sauce:
1 cup plain yogurt
1 teaspoon fresh lemon juice
For the Wings:
2 pounds (907 g) chicken wings
Salt and black pepper to taste
Cooking spray

Salt and black pepper to taste

½ cup melted butter
½ cup Hot sauce
¼ cup grated Parmesan cheese

Mix the yogurt, lemon juice, salt, and black pepper in a bowl. Chill while making the chicken. Preheat oven to 400ºF and season wings with salt and black pepper. Line them on a baking sheet and grease lightly with cooking spray. Bake for 20 minutes until golden brown. Mix butter, hot sauce, and Parmesan cheese in a bowl. Toss chicken in the sauce to evenly coat and plate. Serve with yogurt dipping sauce and celery strips.

calories: 371 | fat: 23g | protein: 36g | carbs: 3g | net carbs: 3g | fiber: 0g

Baked Chicken Skewers and Celery Fries

Prep time: 10 minutes | Cook time: 40 minutes | Serves 4

2 chicken breasts
½ teaspoon salt
¼ teaspoon ground black
For the Fries:
1 pound (454 g) celery root
1 tablespoon olive oil
½ teaspoon salt

pepper
1 tablespoon olive oil
¼ cup chicken broth

¼ teaspoon ground black pepper

Set oven to 400ºF (205ºC). Grease and line a baking sheet. In a bowl, mix oil, spices and the chicken; set in the fridge for 10 minutes while covered. Peel and chop celery root to form fry shapes and place into a separate bowl. Apply oil to coat and add pepper and salt for seasoning. Arrange to the baking tray in an even layer and bake for 10 minutes. Take the chicken from the refrigerator and thread onto the skewers. Place over the celery, pour in the chicken broth, then set in the oven for 30 minutes. Serve with lemon wedges.

calories: 579 | fat: 43g | protein: 39g | carbs: 8g | net carbs: 6g | fiber: 2g

Homemade Poulet en Papillote

Prep time: 10 minutes | Cook time: 25 minutes | Serves 4

4 chicken breasts, skinless, scored
1 tablespoon white wine
1 tablespoon olive oil, plus extra for drizzling
1 tablespoon butter
3 cups mixed mushrooms,

teared up
2 cups water
3 cloves garlic, minced
4 sprigs thyme, chopped
3 lemons, juiced
Salt and black pepper, to taste
1 tablespoon Dijon mustard

Preheat the oven to 450ºF (235ºC). In a bowl, evenly mix the chicken, mushrooms, garlic, thyme, lemon juice, salt, black pepper, and mustard. Make 4 large cuts of foil, fold them in half, and then fold them in half again. Tightly fold the two open edges together to create a bag. Now, share the chicken mixture into each bag, top with the white wine, olive oil, and a tablespoon of butter. Seal the last open end securely making sure not to pierce the bag. Put the bag on a baking tray and bake the chicken in the middle of the oven for 25 minutes.

calories: 394 | fat: 13g | protein: 25g | carbs: 6g | net carbs: 5g | fiber: 1g

Creamy-Lemony Chicken Thighs

Prep time: 10 minutes | Cook time: 7 to 8 hours | Serves 6

3 tablespoons extra-virgin olive oil
2 tablespoons butter
1½ pounds (680 g) boneless chicken thighs
½ sweet onion, diced
2 teaspoons minced garlic
2 teaspoons dried oregano
½ teaspoon salt
⅛ teaspoon pepper, depending on taste
1½ cups chicken broth
Juice and zest of 1 lemon
1 tablespoon dijon mustard
1 cup heavy (whipping) cream

Lightly grease the insert of the slow cooker with 1 tablespoon of the olive oil. In a large skillet over medium-high heat, heat the remaining 2 tablespoons of the olive oil and the butter. Add the chicken and brown for 5 minutes, turning once. Transfer the chicken to the insert and add the onion, garlic, oregano, salt, and pepper. In a small bowl, whisk together the broth, lemon juice and zest, and mustard. Pour the mixture over the chicken. Cover and cook on low for 7 to 8 hours. Remove from the heat, stir in the heavy cream, and serve.

calories: 400 | fat: 34g | protein: 22g | carbs: 2g | net carbs: 2g | fiber: 0g

Chicken with Mayo-Avocado Sauce

Prep time: 10 minutes | Cook time: 12 minutes | Serves 4

For the Sauce:
1 avocado, pitted
½ cup mayonnaise
For the Chicken:
1 tablespoon butter
4 chicken breasts
Pink salt and black pepper to
Salt to taste

taste
1 cup chopped cilantro leaves
½ cup chicken broth

Spoon the avocado, mayonnaise, and salt into a small food processor and puree until a smooth sauce is derived. Pour sauce into a jar and refrigerate while you make the chicken. Melt butter in a large skillet, season chicken with salt and black pepper and fry for 4 minutes on each side to golden brown. Remove chicken to a plate. Pour the broth in the same skillet and add the cilantro. Bring to simmer covered for 3 minutes and add the chicken. Cover and cook on low heat for 5 minutes until the liquid has reduced and chicken is fragrant. Dish chicken only into serving plates and spoon the mayoavocado sauce over.

calories: 398 | fat: 32g | protein:24 g | carbs: 9g | net carbs: 4g | fiber: 5g

Slow Cooked Chicken Cacciatore

Prep time: 15 minutes | Cook time: 3 to 4 hours or 6 to 8 hours | Serves 4

¼ cup good-quality olive oil
4 (4-ounce /113-g) boneless chicken breasts, each cut into three pieces
1 onion, chopped
2 celery stalks, chopped
1 cup sliced mushrooms
2 tablespoons minced garlic
1 (28-ounce / 794-g) can sodium-free diced tomatoes
½ cup red wine
½ cup tomato purée
1 tablespoon dried basil
1 teaspoon dried oregano
⅛ teaspoon red pepper flakes

In a skillet over medium-high heat, warm the olive oil. Add the chicken breasts and brown them, turning them once, about 10 minutes in total. Place the chicken in the slow cooker and stir in the onion, celery, mushrooms, garlic, tomatoes, red wine, tomato purée, basil, oregano, and red pepper flakes. Cook it on high for 3 to 4 hours or on low for 6 to 8 hours, until the chicken is fully cooked and tender. Divide the chicken and sauce between four bowls and serve it immediately.

calories: 383 | fat: 26g | protein: 26g | carbs: 11g | net carbs: 7g | fiber: 4g

Parma Ham-Wrapped Stuffed Chicken

Prep time: 10 minutes | Cook time: 23 minutes | Serves 4

4 chicken breasts
1 tablespoon olive oil
3 cloves garlic, minced
3 shallots, finely chopped
1 tablespoon dried mixed herbs
8 slices Parma ham
8 ounces (227 g) cream cheese
2 lemons, zested
Salt, to taste

Preheat the oven to 350ºF (180ºC). Heat the oil in a small skillet and sauté the garlic and shallots with a pinch of salt and lemon zest for 3 minutes; let it cool. After, stir the cream cheese and mixed herbs into the shallot mixture. Score a pocket in each chicken breast, fill the holes with the cream cheese mixture and cover with the cut-out chicken. Wrap each breast with two Parma ham and secure the ends with a toothpick. Lay the chicken parcels on a greased baking sheet and cook in the oven for 20 minutes. Remove to rest for 4 minutes before serving with green salad and roasted tomatoes.

calories: 485 | fat: 35g | protein: 26g | carbs: 3g | net carbs: 2g | fiber: 1g

Bacon Fat Browned Chicken

Prep time: 15 minutes | Cook time: 7 to 8 hours | Serves 8

3 tablespoons coconut oil, divided
¼ pound (113 g) bacon, diced
2 pounds (907 g) chicken (breasts, thighs, drumsticks)
2 cups quartered button
mushrooms
1 sweet onion, diced
1 tablespoon minced garlic
½ cup chicken broth
2 teaspoons chopped thyme
1 cup coconut cream

Lightly grease the insert of the slow cooker with 1 tablespoon of the coconut oil. In a large skillet over medium-high heat, heat the remaining 2 tablespoons of the coconut oil. Add the bacon and cook until it is crispy, about 5 minutes. Using a slotted spoon, transfer the bacon to a plate and set aside. Add the chicken to the skillet and brown for 5 minutes, turning once. Transfer the chicken and bacon to the insert and add the mushrooms, onion, garlic, broth, and thyme. Cover and cook on low for 7 to 8 hours. Stir in the coconut cream and serve.

calories: 406 | fat: 34g | protein: 22g | carbs: 5g | net carbs: 3g | fiber: 2g

Bacon-Wrapped Chicken with Asparagus
Prep time: 10 minutes | Cook time: 40 minutes | Serves 4

6 chicken breasts
Pink salt and black pepper to taste
8 bacon slices
1 tablespoon olive oil

1 pound (454 g) asparagus spears
1 tablespoon fresh lemon juice
Manchego cheese, for topping

Preheat the oven to 400ºF (205ºC). Season chicken breasts with salt and black pepper, and wrap 2 bacon slices around each chicken breast. Arrange on a baking sheet that is lined with parchment paper, drizzle with oil and bake for 25-30 minutes until bacon is brown and crispy. Preheat your grill to high heat. Brush the asparagus spears with olive oil and season with salt. Grill for 8-10 minutes, frequently turning until slightly charred. Remove to a plate and drizzle with lemon juice. Grate over Manchego cheese so that it melts a little on contact with the hot asparagus and forms a cheesy dressing.

calories: 468 | fat: 38g | protein: 26g | carbs: 5g | net carbs: 2g | fiber: 3g

Baked Cheesy Chicken and Spinach
Prep time: 10 minutes | Cook time: 35 minutes | Serves 6

6 chicken breasts, skinless and boneless
1 teaspoon mixed spice seasoning
Pink salt and black pepper to season

2 loose cups baby spinach
1 teaspoon olive oil
4 oz cream cheese, cubed
1¼ cups shredded mozzarella cheese
1 tablespoon water

Preheat oven to 370ºF (188ºC). Season chicken with spice mix, salt, and black pepper. Pat with your hands to have the seasoning stick on the chicken. Put in the casserole dish and layer spinach over the chicken. Mix the oil with cream cheese, mozzarella, salt, and black pepper and stir in water a tablespoon at a time. Pour the mixture over the chicken and cover the pot with aluminium foil. Bake for 20 minutes, remove foil and continue cooking for 15 minutes until a nice golden brown color is formed on top. Take out and allow sitting for 5 minutes. Serve warm with braised asparagus.

calories: 463 | fat: 18g | protein: 48g | carbs: 2g | net carbs: 2g | fiber: 0g

Marinated Chicken with Peanut Sauce
Prep time: 20 minutes | Cook time: 14 minutes | Serves 6

1 tablespoon wheat-free coconut aminos
1 tablespoon sugar-free fish sauce
1 tablespoon lime juice
1 teaspoon cilantro
1 teaspoon minced garlic
Peanut sauce:
½ cup peanut butter
1 teaspoon minced garlic
1 tablespoon lime juice
1 tablespoon water
1 teaspoon minced ginger

1 teaspoon minced ginger
1 tablespoon olive oil
1 tablespoon rice wine vinegar
1 teaspoon cayenne pepper
1 teaspoon erythritol
6 chicken thighs

1 tablespoon chopped jalapeño
1 tablespoon rice wine vinegar
1 tablespoon erythritol
1 tablespoon fish sauce

Combine all chicken ingredients in a large Ziploc bag. Seal the bag and shake to combine. Refrigerate for 1 hour. Remove from fridge about 15 minutes before cooking. Preheat the grill to medium heat and cook the chicken for 7 minutes per side. Whisk together all sauce ingredients in a mixing bowl. Serve the chicken drizzled with peanut sauce.

calories: 492 | fat: 36g | protein: 35g | carbs: 5g | net carbs: 3g | fiber: 2g

Itanlian Chicken Cacciatore
Prep time: 15 minutes | Cook time: 8 hours | Serves 6

3 tablespoons extra-virgin olive oil, divided
2 pounds boneless chicken thighs
Salt, for seasoning
Freshly ground black pepper, for seasoning
1 (14-ounce / 397-g) can stewed tomatoes

2 cups chicken broth
1 cup quartered button mushrooms
½ sweet onion, chopped
1 tablespoon minced garlic
1 tablespoon dried oregano
1 teaspoon dried basil
Pinch red pepper flakes

Lightly grease the insert of the slow cooker with 1 tablespoon of the olive oil. Lightly season the chicken thighs with salt and pepper. In a large skillet over medium-high heat, heat the remaining 2 tablespoons of the olive oil. Add the chicken thighs and brown for about 8 minutes, turning once. Transfer the chicken to the insert and add the tomatoes, broth, mushrooms, onion, garlic, oregano, basil, and red pepper flakes. Cover and cook on low for 8 hours. Serve warm.

calories: 425 | fat: 32g | protein: 27g | carbs: 8g | net carbs: 7g | fiber: 1g

Baked Chicken in Tomato Purée
Prep time: 15 minutes | Cook time: 1½ hours | Serves 4

8 chicken drumsticks
1½ tablespoon olive oil
1 medium white onion, diced
3 medium turnips, peeled and diced
2 green bell peppers, seeded, cut into chunks
2 cloves garlic, minced

¼ cup coconut flour
1 cup chicken broth
1 (28 ounce / 794-g) can tomato purée
1 tablespoon dried Italian herbs
Salt and black pepper, to taste

Preheat oven to 400ºF (205ºC) . Heat the oil in a skillet over medium heat. Season the drumsticks with salt and pepper, and fry in the oil to brown on both sides for 10 minutes. Remove to a baking dish. Sauté the onion, turnips, bell peppers, and garlic in the same oil for 10 minutes. In a bowl, combine the broth, coconut flour, tomato purée, and Italian herbs together, and pour it over the vegetables in the pan. Stir and cook to thicken for 4 minutes. Pour the mixture on the chicken in the baking dish. Bake for around 1 hour. Remove from the oven and serve with steamed cauli rice.

calories: 515 | fat: 34g | protein: 51g | carbs: 15g | net carbs: 7g | fiber: 8g

Stir-Fried Chicken, Broccoli and Cashew
Prep time: 10 minutes | Cook time: 17 minutes | Serves 4

1 chicken breasts, cut into strips
1 tablespoon olive oil
1 tablespoon coconut aminos
1 teaspoon white wine vinegar
1 teaspoon erythritol
1 teaspoon xanthan gum
1 lemon, juiced
1 cup unsalted cashew nuts
2 cups broccoli florets
1 white onion, thinly sliced
Salt and black pepper to taste

In a bowl, mix the coconut aminos, vinegar, lemon juice, erythritol, and xanthan gum. Set aside. Heat the oil in a wok and fry the cashew for 4 minutes until golden-brown. Remove to a paper towel lined plate. Sauté the onion in the same oil for 4 minutes until soft and browned; add to the cashew nuts. Add the chicken to the wok and cook for 4 minutes; include the broccoli, salt, and black pepper. Stir-fry and pour the coconut aminos mixture in. Stir and cook the sauce for 4 minutes and pour in the cashews and onion. Stir once more, cook for 1 minute, and turn the heat off. Serve the chicken stir-fry with some steamed cauli rice.

calories: 325 | fat: 21g | protein: 22g | carbs: 6g | net carbs: 4g | fiber: 2g

Cheesy Spinach Stuffed Chicken
Prep time: 15 minutes | Cook time: 20 minutes | Serves 4

4 chicken breasts, boneless and skinless
½ cup mozzarella cheese
⅓ cup Parmesan cheese
6 ounces (170 g) cream
Breading:
2 eggs
⅓ cup almond flour
1 tablespoon olive oil
cheese
2 cups spinach, chopped
A pinch of nutmeg
½ teaspoon minced garlic

½ teaspoon parsley
⅓ cup Parmesan cheese
A pinch of onion powder

Pound the chicken until it doubles in size. Mix the cream cheese, spinach, mozzarella, nutmeg, salt, black pepper, and Parmesan cheese in a bowl. Divide the mixture between the chicken breasts and spread it out evenly. Wrap the chicken in a plastic wrap. Refrigerate for 15 minutes. Heat the oil in a pan and preheat the oven to 370°F (188°C). Beat the eggs and combine all other breading ingredients in a bowl. Dip the chicken in egg first, then in the breading mixture. Cook in the pan until browned. Place on a lined baking sheet and bake for 20 minutes.

calories: 491 | fat: 36g | protein: 38g | carbs: 6g | net carbs: 4g | fiber: 2g

Spiced Chicken Wings
Prep time: 10 minutes | Cook time: 25 minutes | Serves 4

12 chicken wings, cut in half
1 tablespoon turmeric
1 tablespoon cumin
1 tablespoon fresh ginger, grated
1 tablespoon cilantro, chopped
1 tablespoon paprika
Salt and ground black pepper,
to taste
1 tablespoon olive oil
Juice of ½ lime
1 cup thyme leaves
¾ cup cilantro, chopped
1 tablespoon water
1 jalapeño pepper

In a bowl, stir together 1 tablespoon ginger, cumin, paprika, salt, 1 tablespoon olive oil, black pepper, and turmeric. Place in the chicken wings pieces, toss to coat, and refrigerate for 20 minutes. Heat the grill, place in the marinated wings, cook for 25 minutes, turning from time to time, remove and set to a serving plate. Using a blender, combine thyme, remaining ginger, salt, jalapeno pepper, black pepper, lime juice, cilantro, remaining olive oil, and water, and blend well. Drizzle the chicken wings with the sauce to serve.

calories: 175 | fat: 7g | protein: 21g | carbs: 7g | net carbs: 4g | fiber: 3g

Chicken Garam Masala
Prep time: 15 minutes | Cook time: 26 minutes | Serves 4

1 pound (454 g) chicken breasts, sliced lengthwise
1 tablespoon butter
1 tablespoon olive oil
1 yellow bell pepper, finely chopped
For the Garam Masala:
1 teaspoon ground cumin
1 teaspoon ground coriander
1 teaspoon ground cardamom
1 teaspoon turmeric
1¼ cups heavy whipping cream
1 tablespoon fresh cilantro, finely chopped
Salt and pepper, to taste

1 teaspoon ginger
1 teaspoon paprika
1 teaspoon cayenne, ground
1 pinch ground nutmeg

Set your oven to 400°F (205°C). In a bowl, mix the garam masala spices. Coat the chicken with half of the masala mixture. Heat the olive oil and butter in a frying pan over medium-high heat, and brown the chicken for 3 to 5 minutes per side. Transfer to a baking dish. To the remaining masala, add heavy cream and bell pepper. Season with salt and pepper and pour over chicken. Bake for 20 minutes until the mixture starts to bubble. Garnish with chopped cilantro to serve.

calories: 564 | fat: 50g | protein: 33g | carbs: 6g | net carbs: 5g | fiber: 1g

Chili Chicken Breast
Prep time: 10 minutes | Cook time: 25 minutes | Serves 4

4 chicken breasts, skinless, boneless, cubed
1 tablespoon butter
½ onion, chopped
2 cups chicken broth
8 ounces (227 g) diced tomatoes
2 ounces (57 g) tomato puree
1 tablespoon chili powder
1 tablespoon cumin
½ tablespoon garlic powder
1 Serrano pepper, minced
½ cup shredded cheddar cheese
Salt and black pepper, to taste

Set a large pan over medium-high heat and add the chicken. Cover with water and bring to a boil. Cook until no longer pink, for 10 minutes. Transfer the chicken to a flat surface to shred with forks. In a large pot, pour in the butter and set over medium heat. Sauté onion until transparent for 5 minutes. Stir in the chicken, tomatoes, cumin, serrano pepper, garlic powder, tomato puree, broth, and chili powder. Adjust the seasoning and let the mixture boil. Reduce heat to simmer for about 10 minutes. Divide chili among bowls and top with shredded cheese to serve.

calories: 421 | fat: 21g | protein: 45g | carbs: 7g | net carbs: 5g | fiber: 2g

Baked Cheesy Chicken and Zucchini

Prep time: 15 minutes | Cook time: 35 minutes | Serves 6

2 pound (907 g) chicken breasts, cubed
1 tablespoon butter
1 cup green bell peppers, sliced
1 cup yellow onions, sliced
1 zucchini, cubed
2 garlic cloves, divided
1 teaspoon Italian seasoning
½ teaspoon salt
½ teaspoon black pepper
8 ounces (227 g) cream cheese, softened
½ cup mayonnaise
1 tablespoon Worcestershire sauce (sugar-free)
2 cups cheddar cheese, shredded

Set oven to 370ºF (188ºC) and grease and line a baking dish. Set a pan over medium heat. Place in the butter and let melt, then add in the chicken. Cook until lightly browned, about 5 minutes. Place in onions, zucchini, black pepper, garlic, bell peppers, salt, and 1 teaspoon of Italian seasoning. Cook until tender and set aside. In a bowl, mix cream cheese, garlic, remaining seasoning, mayonnaise, and Worcestershire sauce. Stir in meat and sauteed vegetables. Place the mixture into the prepared baking dish, sprinkle with the shredded cheddar cheese and insert into the oven. Cook until browned for 30 minutes. Serve immediately.

calories: 489 | fat: 37g | protein: 21g | carbs: 6g | net carbs: 5g | fiber: 1g

Garlicky Chicken Thighs

Prep time: 15 minutes | Cook time: 7 to 8 hours | Serves 4

¼ cup extra-virgin olive oil, divided
1½ pounds (680 g) boneless chicken thighs
1 teaspoon paprika
Salt, for seasoning
Freshly ground black pepper, for seasoning
1 sweet onion, chopped
4 garlic cloves, thinly sliced
½ cup chicken broth
2 tablespoons freshly squeezed lemon juice
½ cup greek yogurt

Lightly grease the insert of the slow cooker with 1 tablespoon of the olive oil. Season the thighs with paprika, salt, and pepper. In a large skillet over medium-high heat, heat the remaining olive oil. Add the chicken and brown for 5 minutes, turning once. Transfer the chicken to the insert and add the onion, garlic, broth, and lemon juice. Cover and cook on low for 7 to 8 hours. Stir in the yogurt and serve.

calories: 434 | fat: 36g | protein: 22g | carbs: 5g | net carbs: 4g | fiber: 1g

Coconut-Chicken Breasts

Prep time: 15 minutes | Cook time: 7 to 8 hours | Serves 6

3 tablespoons extra-virgin olive oil, divided
1½ pounds (680 g)boneless chicken breasts
½ sweet onion, chopped
1 cup quartered baby bok choy
1 red bell pepper, diced
2 cups coconut milk
2 tablespoons almond butter
1 tablespoon red thai curry paste
1 tablespoon coconut aminos
2 teaspoons grated fresh ginger
Pinch red pepper flakes
¼ cup chopped peanuts, for garnish
2 tablespoons chopped cilantro, for garnish

Lightly grease the insert of the slow cooker with 1 tablespoon of the olive oil. In a large skillet over medium-high heat, heat the remaining 2 tablespoons of the olive oil. Add the chicken and brown for about 7 minutes. Transfer the chicken to the slow cooker and add the onion, baby bok choy, and bell pepper. In a medium bowl, whisk together the coconut milk, almond butter, curry paste, coconut aminos, ginger, and red pepper flakes, until well blended. Pour the sauce over the chicken and vegetables, and mix to coat. Cover and cook on low for 7 to 8 hours. Serve topped with the peanuts and cilantro.

calories: 543 | fat: 42g | protein: 35g | carbs: 10g | net carbs: 5g | fiber: 5g

Roasted Chicken

Prep time: 15 minutes | Cook time: 7 to 8 hours | Serves 8

¼ cup extra-virgin olive oil, divided
1 (3-pound / 1.4-kg) whole chicken, washed and patted dry
Salt, for seasoning
Freshly ground black pepper,
for seasoning
1 lemon, quartered
6 thyme sprigs
4 garlic cloves, crushed
3 bay leaves
1 sweet onion, quartered

Lightly grease the insert of the slow cooker with 1 tablespoon of the olive oil. Rub the remaining olive oil all over the chicken and season with the salt and pepper. Stuff the lemon quarters, thyme, garlic, and bay leaves into the cavity of the chicken. Place the onion quarters on the bottom of the slow cooker and place the chicken on top so it does not touch the bottom of the insert. Cover and cook on low for 7 to 8 hours, or until the internal temperature reaches 165ºF (74ºC) on an instant-read thermometer. Serve warm.

calories: 427 | fat: 34g | protein: 29g | carbs: 2g | net carbs: 2g | fiber: 0g

Chapter 7 Pork

Pork Paprikash

Prep time: 10 minutes | Cook time: 50 minutes | Serves 4

1 pound (454 g) pork stew meat, cut into bite-sized chunks
1 teaspoon Hungarian spice blend

2 bell peppers, deseeded and chopped
1 red onion, chopped
4 cups chicken bone broth

Heat up a medium-sized stockpot over a medium-high flame. Then, sear the pork for about 5 minutes, stirring periodically to ensure even cooking; add the Hungarian spice blend and reserve. Cook the bell peppers and onion in the pan drippings until they have softened. Pour in the chicken bone broth, stir and bring to a rapid boil. Add the reserved meat back to the stockpot. Immediately turn temperature to simmer. Let it simmer for 45 to 50 minutes. Serve in individual bowls and enjoy!

calories: 271 | fat: 15.6g | protein: 25.4g | carbs: 5.5g | net carbs: 4.8g | fiber: 0.7g

Cream of Onion Pork Cutlets

Prep time: 10 minutes | Cook time: 10 minutes | Serves 4

2 tablespoons olive oil
4 pork cutlets
¼ cup cream of onion soup

½ teaspoon paprika
Sea salt and ground black pepper, to taste

Heat the olive oil in a sauté pan over moderate heat. Once hot, sear the pork cutlets for 5 to 6 minutes, turning once or twice to ensure even cooking. Add in the cream of onion soup, paprika, salt, and black pepper. Cook for a further 3 minutes until heated through. The meat thermometer should register 145ºF (63ºC). Serve in individual plates garnished with freshly snipped chives if desired. Enjoy!

calories: 396 | fat: 24.5g | protein: 40.2g | carbs: 0.9g | net carbs: 0.7g | fiber: 0.2g

Chili Con Carne

Prep time: 15 minutes | Cook time: 45 minutes | Serves 4

2 ounces (57 g) bacon, diced
1 red onion, chopped
1 pound (454 g) ground pork
1 teaspoon ground cumin
2 cloves garlic, minced

1 teaspoon chipotle powder
Kosher salt and ground black pepper, to taste
½ cup beef broth
2 ripe tomatoes, crushed

Heat up a medium stockpot over a moderate flame. Cook the bacon until crisp; reserve. Cook the onion and ground pork in the bacon grease. Cook until the ground pork is no longer pink and the onion just begins to brown. Stir in the ground cumin and garlic and continue to sauté for 30 seconds more or until aromatic. Add the chipotle powder, salt, black pepper, broth, and tomatoes to the pot. Cook, partially covered, for 45 minutes or until heated through. You can add ¼ cup of water during the cooking, as needed. Serve with the reserved bacon and other favorite toppings. Enjoy!

calories: 390 | fat: 29.8g | protein: 22.3g | carbs: 5.2g | net carbs: 3.7g | fiber: 1.5g

Spicy Pork and Spanish Onion

Prep time: 10 minutes | Cook time: 10 minutes | Serves 2

1 tablespoon olive oil
2 pork cutlets
1 bell pepper, seeded and sliced
1 Spanish onion, chopped
2 garlic cloves, minced

½ teaspoon hot sauce
½ teaspoon mustard
½ teaspoon paprika
Coarse sea salt and ground black pepper, to taste

Heat the olive oil in a large saucepan over medium-high heat. Then, fry the pork cutlets for 3 to 4 minutes until evenly golden and crispy on both sides. Decrease the temperature to medium and add the bell pepper, Spanish onion, garlic, hot sauce, and mustard; continue cooking until the vegetables have softened, for a further 3 minutes. Sprinkle with paprika, salt, and black pepper. Serve immediately and enjoy!

calories: 402 | fat: 24.2g | protein: 40.0g | carbs: 3.5g | net carbs: 2.7g | fiber: 0.8g

Pork Ragout

Prep time: 15 minutes | Cook time: 35 minutes | Serves 2

1 teaspoon lard, melted at room temperature
¾ pound (340 g) pork butt, cut into bite-sized cubes
1 red bell pepper, seeded and chopped
1 poblano pepper, seeded and chopped
2 cloves garlic, pressed

½ cup leeks, chopped
Sea salt and ground black pepper, to season
½ teaspoon mustard seeds
¼ teaspoon ground allspice
¼ teaspoon celery seeds
1 cup roasted vegetable broth
2 vine-ripe tomatoes, puréed

Melt the lard in a stockpot over moderate heat. Once hot, cook the pork cubes for 4 to 6 minutes, stirring occasionally to ensure even cooking. Then, stir in the vegetables and continue cooking until they are tender and fragrant. Add in the salt, black pepper, mustard seeds, allspice, celery seeds, roasted vegetable broth, and tomatoes. Reduce the heat to simmer. Let it simmer for 30 minutes longer or until everything is heated through. Ladle into individual bowls and serve hot. Bon appétit!

calories: 390 | fat: 24.2g | protein: 33.0g | carbs: 5.3g | net carbs: 4.1g | fiber: 1.2g

Bolognese Pork Zoodles

Prep time: 10 minutes | Cook time: 25 minutes | Serves 3

3 teaspoons olive oil
¾ pound (340 g) ground pork
2 cloves garlic, pressed

2 medium-sized tomatoes, puréed
2 zucchini, spiralized

Heat the olive oil in a saucepan over medium-high heat. Once hot, sear the pork for 3 to 4 minutes or until no longer pink. Stir in the garlic and cook for 30 seconds more or until fragrant. Fold in the puréed tomatoes and bring to a boil; immediately turn the heat to medium-low and continue simmering an additional 20 minutes. After that, fold in the zoodles and continue to cook for a further 1½ minutes until just al dente. Serve hot. Bon appétit!

calories: 358 | fat: 28.6g | protein: 20.2g | carbs: 4.0g | net carbs: 2.8g | fiber: 1.2g

Roasted Pork Shoulder

Prep time: 20 minutes | Cook time: 60 minutes | Serves 2

1 pound (454 g) pork shoulder
4 tablespoons red wine
1 teaspoon stone ground mustard
1 tablespoon coconut aminos
1 tablespoon lemon juice
1 tablespoon sesame oil
2 sprigs rosemary

1 teaspoon sage
1 shallot, peeled and chopped
½ celery stalk, chopped
½ head garlic, peeled and separated into cloves
Sea salt and freshly cracked black pepper, to season

Place the pork shoulder, red wine, mustard, coconut aminos, lemon juice, sesame oil, rosemary, and sage in a ceramic dish; cover and let it marinate in your refrigerator at least 3 hours. Discard the marinade and place the pork shoulder in a lightly greased baking dish. Scatter the vegetables around the pork shoulder and sprinkle with salt and black pepper. Roast in the preheated oven at 390ºF (199ºC) for 15 minutes. Now, reduce the temperature to 310ºF (154ºC) and continue baking an additional 40 to 45 minutes. Baste the meat with the reserved marinade once or twice. Place on cooling racks before carving and serving. Bon appétit!

calories: 500 | fat: 35.4g | protein: 40.1g | carbs: 2.6g | net carbs: 2.1g | fiber: 0.5g

Lemony Mustard Pork Roast

Prep time: 10 minutes | Cook time: 60 minutes | Serves 5

2 pounds (907 g) pork loin roast, trimmed
1½ tablespoons olive oil
1 tablespoon fresh lemon juice

1 tablespoon pork rub seasoning blend
1 tablespoon stone-ground mustard

Pat the pork loin roast dry. Massage the pork loin roast with the olive oil. Then, sprinkle the lemon juice, pork rub seasoning blend, and mustard over all sides of the roast. Prepare a grill for indirect heat. Grill the pork loin roast over indirect heat for about 1 hour. Let the grilled pork loin stand for 10 minutes before slicing and serving. Bon appétit!

calories: 385 | fat: 20.2g | protein: 48.0g | carbs: 0.1g | net carbs: 0g | fiber: 0.1g

Pulled Boston Butt

Prep time: 15 minutes | Cook time: 5 minutes | Serves 2

1 teaspoon lard, melted at room temperature
¾ pork Boston butt, sliced
2 garlic cloves, pressed
½ teaspoon red pepper flakes, crushed
½ teaspoon black peppercorns,

freshly cracked
Sea salt, to taste
2 bell peppers, seeded and sliced
1 tablespoon fresh mint leaves, snipped
4 tablespoons cream cheese

Melt the lard in a cast-iron skillet over a moderate flame. Once hot, brown the pork for 2 minutes per side until caramelized and crispy on the edges. Reduce the temperature to medium-low and continue cooking another 4 minutes, turning over periodically. Shred the pork with two forks and return to the skillet. Add the garlic, red pepper, black peppercorns, salt, and bell pepper and continue cooking for a further 2 minutes or until the peppers are just tender and fragrant. Serve with fresh mint and a dollop of cream cheese. Enjoy!

calories: 371 | fat: 21.8g | protein: 35.0g | carbs: 5.0g | net carbs: 4.0g | fiber: 1.0g

Creamy Pepper Loin Steaks

Prep time: 15 minutes | Cook time: 10 minutes | Serves 2

1 teaspoon lard, at room temperature
2 pork loin steaks
½ cup beef bone broth
2 bell peppers, deseeded and chopped
1 shallot, chopped

1 garlic clove, minced
Sea salt, to season
½ teaspoon cayenne pepper
¼ teaspoon paprika
1 teaspoon Italian seasoning mix
¼ cup Greek yogurt

Melt the lard in a cast-iron skillet over moderate heat. Once hot, cook the pork loin steaks until slightly browned or approximately 5 minutes per side; reserve. Add a splash of the beef bone broth to deglaze the pan. Now, cook the bell peppers, shallot, and garlic until tender and aromatic. Season with salt, cayenne pepper, paprika, and Italian seasoning mix. After that, decrease the temperature to medium-low, add the Greek yogurt to the skillet and let it simmer for 2 minutes more or until heated through. Serve immediately.

calories: 450 | fat: 19.1g | protein: 62.2g | carbs: 6.0g | net carbs: 4.9g | fiber: 1.1g

Pork Medallions

Prep time: 15 minutes | Cook time: 15 minutes | Serves 2

1 ounce (28 g) bacon, diced
2 pork medallions
2 garlic cloves, sliced
1 red onion, chopped
1 jalapeño pepper, deseeded and chopped
1 tablespoon apple cider vinegar

½ cup chicken bone broth
⅓ pound (136 g) red cabbage, shredded
1 bay leaf
1 sprig rosemary
1 sprig thyme
Kosher salt and ground black pepper, to taste

Heat a Dutch pot over medium-high heat. Once hot, cook the bacon until it is crisp or about 3 minutes; reserve. Now, cook the pork medallions in the bacon grease until they are browned on both sides. Add the remaining ingredients and reduce the heat to medium-low. Let it cook for 13 minutes more, gently stirring periodically to ensure even cooking. Taste and adjust the seasonings. Serve in individual bowls topped with the reserved fried bacon. Bon appétit!

calories: 529 | fat: 31.7g | protein: 51.1g | carbs: 6.2g | net carbs: 3.7g | fiber: 2.5g

Spicy Pork Meatballs with Seeds

Prep time: 15 minutes | Cook time: 20 minutes | Serves 2

1 tablespoon ground flax seeds
2 ounces (57 g) bacon rinds
½ pound (227 g) ground pork
1 garlic clove, minced
½ cup scallions, chopped
Sea salt and cayenne pepper, to taste

½ teaspoon smoked paprika
¼ teaspoon ground cumin
¼ teaspoon mustard seeds
½ teaspoon fennel seeds
½ teaspoon chili pepper flakes
2 tablespoons olive oil

In a mixing bowl, thoroughly combine all ingredients, except for the olive oil, until well combined. Form the mixture into balls and set aside. Heat the olive oil in a nonstick skillet and fry the meatballs for about 15 minutes or until cooked through. Serve with marinara sauce if desired. Bon appétit!

calories: 558 | fat: 50.0g | protein: 0.6g | carbs: 2.2g | net carbs: 1.4g | fiber: 0.8g

Paprika Pork Loin Shoulder

Prep time: 10 minutes | Cook time: 20 minutes | Serves 4

2 teaspoons olive oil
1 pound (454 g) pork loin shoulder, cut into bite-sized cubes
4 cloves garlic, minced

¼ cup red wine
½ teaspoon paprika
Sea salt and ground black pepper, to season
1 tablespoon hot sauce

Heat the olive oil in a saucepan over a moderate flame. Once hot, sear the pork for 5 to 6 minutes, stirring continuously to ensure even cooking; reserve. Now, sauté the garlic for 30 to 40 seconds or until just tender and aromatic. Add a splash of wine and stir, scraping the browned bits from the bottom of the saucepan. Add in the paprika, salt, pepper, and hot sauce; add the pork back to the saucepan. Turn the heat to simmer. Partially cover and simmer approximately 13 minutes until the sauce has thickened. Bon appétit!

calories: 301 | fat: 18.0g | protein: 30.2g | carbs: 2.5g | net carbs: 2.2g | fiber: 0.3g

Creamy Dijon Pork Filet Mignon

Prep time: 10 minutes | Cook time: 10 minutes | Serves 6

2 teaspoons lard, at room temperature
2 pounds (907 g) pork filet mignon, cut into bite-sized chunks

Flaky salt and ground black pepper, to season
1 tablespoon Dijon mustard
1 cup double cream

Melt the lard in a saucepan over moderate heat; now, sear the filet mignon for 2 to 3 minutes per side. Season with salt and pepper to taste. Fold in the Dijon mustard and cream. Reduce the heat to medium-low and continue to cook for a further 6 minutes or until the sauce has reduced slightly. Serve in individual plates, garnished with cauli rice if desired. Enjoy!

calories: 302 | fat: 16.5g | protein: 34.1g | carbs: 2.2g | net carbs: 2.1g | fiber: 0.1g

Herbed Pork and Turkey Meatloaf

Prep time: 20 minutes | Cook time: 60 minutes | Serves 6

1 pound (454 g)ground pork
½ pound (227 g) ground turkey
¼ cup flax seed meal
2 eggs, beaten
2 cloves garlic, minced
½ cup scallions, chopped
Sea salt and ground black pepper, to season
1 teaspoon dried oregano

½ teaspoon dried basil
½ teaspoon dried marjoram
½ teaspoon dried rosemary
1 tablespoon fresh chives, chopped
3 ounces (85 g) tomato paste
1 tablespoon coconut aminos
1 tablespoon brown mustard

Begin by preheating your oven to 360ºF (182ºC). Now, spritz the sides and bottom of a loaf pan with nonstick cooking oil. Thoroughly combine the ground meat with the flax seed meal, eggs, garlic, scallions, spices, and herbs. Press the mixture into the prepared loaf pan. Bake in the preheated oven for 30 minutes In a mixing bowl, whisk the tomato paste, coconut aminos, and mustard. Spread the mixture on top of the meatloaf. Return to the oven; bake for a further 30 minutes or until internal temperature reaches 165ºF (74ºC). Bon appétit!

calories: 345 | fat: 23.2g | protein: 30.1g | carbs: 2.7g | net carbs: 1.7g | fiber: 1.0g

St. Louis Ribs

Prep time: 10 minutes | Cook time: 2 hours | Serves 5

2 pounds (907 g) St. Louis-style pork ribs
1 teaspoon cayenne pepper
Flaky salt and ground black pepper, to season
4 tablespoons sesame oil
2 tablespoons Swerve

1 tablespoon coconut aminos soy sauce
1 teaspoon oyster sauce
1 cup tomato sauce, no sugar added
1 teaspoon Chinese five-spice
2 garlic cloves, pressed

Season the pork ribs with the cayenne pepper, salt, and black pepper. Arrange them on a tinfoil-lined baking pan. Cover with a piece of foil and bake in the preheated oven at 360ºF (182ºC) for 1 hour 30 minutes. In the meantime, thoroughly combine the remaining ingredients for the glaze; whisk to combine well and brush the glaze over the pork ribs. Continue to bake at 420ºF (216ºC) for 30 minutes longer. Bon appétit!

calories: 371 | fat: 21.1g | protein: 38.7g | carbs: 4.2g | net carbs: 3.0g | fiber: 1.2g

Texas Pulled Boston Butt

Prep time: 15 minutes | Cook time: 3 hours | Serves 4

Kosher salt, to season
1 teaspoon paprika
½ teaspoon oregano
½ teaspoon rosemary
1 teaspoon mustard seeds
½ teaspoon chipotle powder

1 teaspoon black peppercorns, whole
3 tablespoons apple cider vinegar
1 cup tomato sauce
1½ pounds (680 g) Boston butt

Thoroughly combine all ingredients, except for the Boston butt, in a big casserole dish. Now, place Boston butt on top skin-side up. Bake in the preheated oven at 300ºF (150ºC) for about 3 hours, checking and turning every 30 minutes. Cut the skin off and shred the pork with two forks; discard any fatty bits. Serve with coleslaw and the bowl of cooking juices on the side for dipping. Bon appétit!

calories: 340 | fat: 21.1g | protein: 30.7g | carbs: 4.3g | net carbs: 3.2g | fiber: 1.1g

Pork Cutlets with Juniper Berries

Prep time: 10 minutes | Cook time: 20 minutes | Serves 2

1 tablespoon lard, softened at room temperature
2 pork cutlets, 2-inch-thick
⅓ cup dry red wine
2 garlic cloves, sliced

½ teaspoon whole black peppercorns
4 tablespoons flaky salt
1 teaspoon juniper berries
½ teaspoon cayenne pepper

Melt the lard in a nonstick skillet over a moderate flame. Now, brown the pork cutlets for about 8 minutes, turning them over to ensure even cooking; reserve. Add a splash of wine to deglaze the pan. Stir in the remaining ingredients and continue to cook until fragrant or for a minute or so. Return the pork cutlets to the skillet, continue to cook until the sauce has thickened and everything is heated through about 10 minutes. Serve warm. Bon appétit!

calories: 370 | fat: 20.5g | protein: 40.2g | carbs: 1.2g | net carbs: 1.0g | fiber: 0.2g

Mediterranean Spiced Pork Roast

Prep time: 10 minutes | Cook time: 3 hours 50 minutes | Serves 4

2 pounds (907 g) pork shoulder	1 tablespoon Dijon mustard
2 tablespoons coconut aminos	1 tablespoon Mediterranean spice mix
½ cup red wine	

Place the pork shoulder, coconut aminos, wine, mustard, and Mediterranean spice mix in a ceramic dish. Cover and let it marinate in your refrigerator for 2 hours. Meanwhile, preheat your oven to 420ºF (216ºC). Place the pork shoulder on a rack set into a roasting pan. Roast for 15 to 20 minutes; reduce the heat to 330ºF (166ºC). Roast an additional 3 hours and 30 minutes, basting with the reserved marinade. Bon appétit!

calories: 610 | fat: 40.2g | protein: 57.0g | carbs: 0.7g | net carbs: 0.6g | fiber: 0.1g

Olla Podrida

Prep time: 15 minutes | Cook time: 40 minutes | Serves 4

2 tablespoons olive oil	½ cup Marsala wine
1½ pounds (680 g) pork ribs	8 ounces (227 g) button mushrooms, sliced
1 yellow onion, chopped	Sea salt and ground black pepper, to taste
2 garlic cloves, minced	
2 Spanish peppers, chopped	1 teaspoon cayenne pepper
1 Spanish Naga pepper, chopped	1 cup tomato purée
1 celery stalk, chopped	1 bay laurel

Heat 1 tablespoon of the olive oil in a stockpot over medium-high heat. Cook the pork ribs for 4 to 5 minutes per side or until brown; set aside. Heat the remaining olive oil and sauté the onion, garlic, peppers, and celery for 5 minutes until tender and fragrant. Add in a splash of red wine to deglaze the pot. Add the mushrooms, salt, black pepper, cayenne pepper, tomatoes, and bay laurel to the stockpot. When the mixture reaches boiling, turn the heat to a medium-low. Add the reserved pork back to the pot. Let it cook, partially covered, for 35 minutes. Serve warm.

calories: 360 | fat: 19.1g | protein: 38.2g | carbs: 4.9g | net carbs: 3.2g | fiber: 1.7g

Duo-Cheese Pork and Turkey Patties

Prep time: 15 minutes | Cook time: 15 minutes | Serves 6

1½ pounds (680 g) ground pork	½ cup Asiago cheese, shredded
½ pound (227 g) ground turkey	1 teaspoon mustard seeds
1 serrano pepper, deseeded and minced	½ teaspoon dried marjoram
	½ teaspoon dried basil
2 garlic cloves, finely minced	1 teaspoon paprika
½ cup onion, finely minced	Sea salt and ground black pepper, to taste
1 cup Romano cheese, grated	

Begin by preheating a gas grill to high. Mix all of the above ingredients until everything is well incorporated. Form the mixture into 6 patties with oiled hands. Place on the preheated grill and cook for 7 to 8 minutes on each side until slightly charred. Bon appétit!

calories: 514 | fat: 35.2g | protein: 44.2g | carbs: 2.5g | net carbs: 2.2g | fiber: 0.3g

Seared Pork Medallions

Prep time: 15 minutes | Cook time: 15 minutes | Serves 3

2 tablespoons olive oil	pepper, to taste
1 onion, sliced	½ teaspoon paprika
2 garlic cloves, sliced	1 tomato, sliced
2 cups button mushrooms, sliced	1 bell pepper, seeded and sliced
3 pork medallions	¼ cup fresh parsley, chopped
Sea salt and ground black	

Heat the olive oil in a frying pan over medium-high heat. Once hot, sauté the onion until tender and fragrant. Stir in the garlic and mushrooms and continue to sauté an additional minute or so. Add the pork medallions, salt, black pepper, paprika, tomato, and pepper to the frying pan; let it cook for 15 minutes or until heated through. Garnish with fresh parsley and serve. Bon appétit!

calories: 365 | fat: 17.2g | protein: 45.0g | carbs: 4.5g | net carbs: 3.6g | fiber: 0.9g

White Wine Pork with Cabbage

Prep time: 15 minutes | Cook time: 1 hour 15 minutes | Serves 6

2 tablespoons olive oil	¾ cup vegetable stock
2 pounds (907 g) pork stew meat, cubed	½ cup white wine
	3 carrots, chopped
Salt and black pepper, to taste	1 cabbage head, shredded
2 tablespoons butter	½ cup scallions, chopped
4 garlic cloves, minced	1 cup heavy cream

Set a pan over medium heat and warm butter and oil. Sear the pork until brown. Add garlic, scallions and carrots; sauté for 5 minutes. Pour in the cabbage, stock and wine, and bring to a boil. Reduce the heat and cook for 1 hour covered. Add in heavy cream as you stir for 1 minute, adjust seasonings and serve.

calories: 512 | fat: 32.6g | protein: 42.9g | carbs: 9.3g | net carbs: 5.9g | fiber: 3.4g

Pickle and Ham Stuffed Pork

Prep time: 20 minutes | Cook time: 35 minutes | Serves 4

Zest and juice from 2 limes	2 teaspoons cumin
2 garlic cloves, minced	4 pork loin steaks
¾ cup olive oil	2 pickles, chopped
1 cup fresh cilantro, chopped	4 ham slices
1 cup fresh mint, chopped	6 Swiss cheese slices
1 teaspoon dried oregano	2 tablespoons mustard
Salt and black pepper, to taste	
Salad:	
1 head red cabbage, shredded	3 tablespoons olive oil
2 tablespoons vinegar	Salt to taste

In a food processor, blitz the lime zest, oil, oregano, black pepper, cumin, cilantro, lime juice, garlic, mint, and salt. Rub the steaks with the mixture and toss well to coat; set aside for some hours in the fridge. Arrange the steaks on a working surface, split the pickles, mustard, cheese, and ham on them, roll, and secure with toothpicks. Heat a pan over medium heat, add in the pork rolls, cook each side for 2 minutes and remove to a baking sheet. Bake in the oven at 350ºF (180ºC) for 25 minutes. Prepare the red cabbage salad by mixing all salad ingredients and serve with the meat.

calories: 412 | fat: 37.1g | protein: 25.8g | carbs: 8.1g | net carbs: 3.1g | fiber: 5.0g

BBQ Pork Ribs

Prep time: 15 minutes | Cook time: 7 hours 5 minutes | Serves 6

3 racks pork ribs, silver lining removed
2 cups sugar-free BBQ sauce
2 tablespoons erythritol
2 teaspoons chili powder
2 teaspoons cumin powder
2 teaspoons onion powder
2 teaspoons smoked paprika
2 teaspoons garlic powder
Salt and black pepper to taste
1 teaspoon mustard powder

Preheat a smoker to 400ºF (205ºC) using mesquite wood to create flavor in the smoker. In a bowl, mix the erythritol, chili powder, cumin powder, black pepper, onion powder, smoked paprika, garlic powder, salt, and mustard powder. Rub the ribs and let marinate for 30 minutes. Place on the grill grate, and cook at reduced heat of 225ºF (107ºC) for 4 hours. Flip the ribs after and continue cooking for 4 hours. Brush the ribs with BBQ sauce on both sides and sear them in increased heat for 3 minutes per side. Remove and let sit for 4 minutes before slicing. Serve with red cabbage coleslaw.

calories: 581 | fat: 36.5g | protein: 44.6g | carbs: 1.8g | net carbs: 0g | fiber: 1.8g

Cumin Pork Chops

Prep time: 10 minutes | Cook time: 20 minutes | Serves 4

4 pork chops
Salt and black pepper, to taste
3 tablespoons paprika
¾ cup cumin powder
1 teaspoon chili powder

In a bowl, combine the paprika with black pepper, cumin, salt, and chili. Place in the pork chops and rub them well. Heat a grill over medium temperature, add in the pork chops, cook for 5 minutes, flip, and cook for 5 minutes. Serve with steamed veggies.

calories: 350 | fat: 18.6g | protein: 41.9g | carbs: 10.4g | net carbs: 3.9g | fiber: 6.5g

Italian Pork Sausage with Bell Peppers

Prep time: 15 minutes | Cook time: 20 minutes | Serves 6

¼ cup olive oil
2 pounds (907 g) Italian pork sausage, chopped
1 onion, sliced
4 sun-dried tomatoes, sliced thin
Salt and black pepper, to taste
½ pound (227 g) Gruyere
cheese, grated
3 yellow bell peppers, seeded and chopped
3 orange bell peppers, seeded and chopped
A pinch of red pepper flakes
½ cup fresh parsley, chopped

Set a pan over medium heat and warm oil, place in the sausage slices, cook each side for 3 minutes, remove to a bowl, and set aside. Stir in tomatoes, bell peppers, and onion, and cook for 5 minutes. Season with black pepper, pepper flakes, and salt and mix well. Cook for 1 minute, and remove from heat. Lay sausage slices onto a baking dish, place the bell pepper mixture on top, scatter with the Gruyere cheese, set in the oven at 340ºF (171ºC). Bake for 10 minutes, until the cheese melts. Serve topped with parsley.

calories: 566 | fat: 45.0g | protein: 34.0g | carbs: 9.7g | net carbs: 7.6g | fiber: 2.1g

Roasted Pork Loin with Collard

Prep time: 10 minutes | Cook time: 60 minutes | Serves 4

2 tablespoons olive oil
Salt and black pepper, to taste
1½ pounds (680 g) pork loin
A pinch of dry mustard
1 teaspoon hot red pepper flakes
½ teaspoon ginger, minced
1 cup collard greens, chopped
2 garlic cloves, minced
½ lemon, sliced
¼ cup water

In a bowl, combine the ginger with salt, mustard, and black pepper. Add in the meat, toss to coat. Heat the oil in a saucepan over medium heat, brown the pork on all sides, for 10 minutes. Transfer to the oven and roast for 40 minutes at 390ºF (199ºC). To the saucepan, add collard greens, lemon slices, garlic, and water; cook for 10 minutes. Serve on a platter and sprinkle pan juices on top.

calories: 431 | fat: 23.0g | protein: 45.0g | carbs: 3.6g | net carbs: 3.0g | fiber: 0.6g

Double Cheese BBQ Pork Pizza

Prep time: 10 minutes | Cook time: 25 minutes | Serves 4

1 low carb pizza bread
Olive oil for brushing
1 cup grated Manchego cheese
2 cups leftover pulled pork
½ cup sugar-free BBQ sauce
1 cup crumbled goat cheese

Preheat oven to 400ºF (205ºC) and put pizza bread on a pizza pan. Brush with olive oil and sprinkle the Manchego cheese all over. Mix the pork with BBQ sauce and spread over the cheese. Drop goat cheese on top and bake for 25 minutes until the cheese has melted. Slice the pizza with a cutter and serve.

calories: 345 | fat: 24.1g | protein: 17.9g | carbs: 6.9g | net carbs: 6.6g | fiber: 0.3g

Pork and Ricotta Bacon Wraps

Prep time: 15 minutes | Cook time: 35 minutes | Serves 6

6 bacon slices
2 tablespoons fresh parsley, chopped
1 pound (454 g) pork cutlets, sliced
⅓ cup ricotta cheese
1 tablespoon coconut oil
¼ cup onions, chopped
3 garlic cloves, peeled and
minced
2 tablespoons Parmesan cheese, grated
15 ounces (425 g) canned diced tomatoes
⅓ cup vegetable stock
Salt and black pepper, to taste
½ teaspoon Italian seasoning

Use a meat pounder to flatten the pork pieces. Set the bacon slices on top of each piece, then divide the parsley, ricotta cheese, and Parmesan cheese. Roll each pork piece and secure with a toothpick. Set a pan over medium heat and warm oil, cook the pork rolls until browned, and remove to a plate. Add in onions and garlic, and cook for 5 minutes. Place in the stock and cook for 3 minutes. Remove the toothpicks from the rolls and return to the pan. Stir in the pepper, salt, tomatoes, and Italian seasoning, bring to a boil, set heat to medium-low, and cook for 20 minutes covered. Split among bowls to serve.

calories: 436 | fat: 37.1g | protein: 33.9g | carbs: 3.8g | net carbs: 2.1g | fiber: 1.7g

Spicy Tomato Pork Chops

Prep time: 15 minutes | Cook time: 36 minutes | Serves 4

4 pork chops
1 tablespoon fresh oregano, chopped
2 garlic cloves, minced
1 tablespoon canola oil
15 ounces (425 g) canned

diced tomatoes
1 tablespoon tomato paste
Salt and black pepper, to taste
¼ cup tomato juice
1 red chili, finely chopped

Set a pan over medium heat and warm oil, place in the pork, season with pepper and salt, cook for 6 minutes on both sides; remove to a bowl. Add in the garlic, and cook for 30 seconds. Stir in the tomato paste, tomatoes, tomato juice, and chili; bring to a boil, and reduce heat to medium-low. Place in the pork chops, cover the pan and simmer everything for 30 minutes. Remove the pork to plates and sprinkle with fresh oregano to serve.

calories: 412 | fat: 21.0g | protein: 39.1g | carbs: 6.3g | net carbs: 3.5g | fiber: 2.8g

Spiralized Zucchini, Bacon, and Spinach Gratin

Prep time: 15 minutes | Cook time: 30 minutes | Serves 4

2 large zucchinis, spiralized
4 slices bacon, chopped
2 cups baby spinach
4 ounces (113 g) halloumi cheese, cut into cubes
2 cloves garlic, minced
1 cup heavy cream

½ cup sugar-free tomato sauce
1 cup grated Mozzarella cheese
½ teaspoon dried Italian mixed herbs
Salt and black pepper to taste

Preheat the oven to 350ºF (180ºC). Place the cast iron pan over medium heat and fry the bacon for 4 minutes, then add garlic and cook for 1 minute. In a bowl, mix the heavy cream, tomato sauce, and ⅙ cup water and add it to the pan. Stir in the zucchini, spinach, halloumi, Italian herbs, salt, and pepper. Sprinkle the Mozzarella cheese on top, and transfer the pan to the oven. Bake for 20 minutes or until the cheese is golden. Serve the gratin warm.

calories: 351 | fat: 27.2g | protein: 15.9g | carbs: 6.6g | net carbs: 5.2g | fiber: 1.4g

Pork and Mixed Vegetable Stir-Fry

Prep time: 10 minutes | Cook time: 20 minutes | Serves 4

1½ tablespoons butter
2 pounds (907 g) pork loin, cut into strips
Pink salt and chili pepper to taste
2 teaspoons ginger-garlic

paste
¼ cup chicken broth
5 tablespoons peanut butter
2 cups mixed stir-fry vegetables

Melt the butter in a wok and mix the pork with salt, chili pepper, and ginger-garlic paste. Pour the pork into the wok and cook for 6 minutes until no longer pink. Mix the peanut butter with some broth until smooth, add to the pork and stir; cook for 2 minutes. Pour in the remaining broth, cook for 4 minutes, and add the mixed veggies. Simmer for 5 minutes. Adjust the taste with salt and black pepper, and spoon the stir-fry to a side of cilantro cauli rice.

calories: 572 | fat: 49.1g | protein: 22.6g | carbs:5.3 g | net carbs: 1.1g | fiber: 4.2g

Pork and Cucumber Lettuce Cups

Prep time: 10 minutes | Cook time: 15 minutes | Serves 6

2 pounds (907 g) ground pork
1 tablespoon ginger- garlic paste
Pink salt and chili pepper to taste
1 teaspoon butter

1 head Iceberg lettuce
2 sprigs green onion, chopped
1 red bell pepper, seeded and chopped
½ cucumber, finely chopped

Put the pork with ginger-garlic paste, salt, and chili pepper seasoning in a saucepan. Cook for 10 minutes over medium heat while breaking any lumps until the pork is no longer pink. Drain liquid and add the butter, melt and brown the meat for 4 minutes, continuously stirring. Turn the heat off. Pat the lettuce dry with a paper towel and in each leaf, spoon two to three tablespoons of pork, top with green onions, bell pepper, and cucumber. Serve with soy drizzling sauce.

calories: 312 | fat: 24.2g | protein: 19.1g | carbs: 3.1g | net carbs: 1.0g | fiber: 2.1g

Mushroom and Pork Bake

Prep time: 10 minutes | Cook time: 45 minutes | Serves 6

1 onion, chopped
2 (10.5-ounce / 298-g) cans mushroom soup
6 pork chops

½ cup sliced mushrooms
Salt and ground pepper, to taste

Preheat the oven to 370ºF (188ºC). Season the pork chops with salt and black pepper, and place in a baking dish. Combine the mushroom soup, mushrooms, and onion, in a bowl. Pour this mixture over the pork chops. Bake for 45 minutes.

calories: 402 | fat: 32.5g | protein: 19.5g | carbs: 8.4g | net carbs: 7.9g | fiber: 0.5g

Roasted Stuffed Pork Loin Steak

Prep time: 15 minutes | Cook time: 30 minutes | Serves 4

1 tablespoon olive oil
Zest and juice from 1 lime
1 garlic clove, minced
1 tablespoon fresh cilantro, chopped
1 tablespoon fresh mint, chopped
Salt and black pepper, to taste

1 teaspoon cumin
2 pork loin steaks
1 pickle, chopped
2 ounces (57 g) smoked ham, sliced
2 ounces (57 g) Gruyere cheese sliced
1 tablespoon mustard

Start with making the marinade: combine the lime zest, oil, black pepper, cumin, cilantro, lime juice, garlic, mint and salt, in a food processor. Place the steaks in the marinade, and toss well to coat; set aside for some hours in the fridge. Arrange the steaks on a working surface, split the pickles, mustard, cheese, and ham on them, roll, and secure with toothpicks. Heat a pan over medium heat, add in the pork rolls, cook each side for 2 minutes and remove to a baking sheet. Bake in the oven at 350ºF (180ºC) for 25 minutes. Serve immediately.

calories: 433 | fat: 38g | protein: 30g | carbs: 5g | net carbs: 4g | fiber: 1g

Dijon Pork Loin Chops

Prep time: 15 minutes | Cook time: 10 minutes | Serves 4

4 pork loin chops	1 tablespoon water
1 teaspoon Dijon mustard	Salt and black pepper, to taste
1 tablespoon soy sauce	1 tablespoon butter
1 teaspoon lemon juice	A bunch of scallions, chopped

In a bowl, combine the water with lemon juice, mustard and soy sauce. Set aside. Set a pan over medium heat and melt butter, add in the pork chops, season with salt, and black pepper. Cook for 4 minutes, turn, and cook for an additional 4 minutes. Remove to a plate and keep warm. In the same pan, pour mustard sauce, and simmer for 5 minutes. Drizzle the sauce over the pork, top with scallions, and serve.

calories: 383 | fat: 21.6g | protein: 38.1g | carbs: 1.5g | net carbs: 1.1g | fiber: 0.4g

Rosemary Pork Chops with Kalamata Olives

Prep time: 10 minutes | Cook time: 40 minutes | Serves 4

4 pork chops, bone-in	minced
Salt and ground black pepper, to taste	½ cup kalamata olives, pitted and sliced
1 teaspoon dried rosemary	2 tablespoons olive oil
3 garlic cloves, peeled and	¼ cup vegetable broth

Season pork chops with black pepper and salt, and add in a roasting pan. Stir in the garlic, olives, olive oil, broth, and rosemary, set in the oven at 425ºF (220ºC), and bake for 10 minutes. Reduce heat to 350ºF (180ºC) and roast for 25 minutes. Slice the pork and sprinkle with pan juices all over to serve.

calories: 416 | fat: 25.1g | protein: 36.1g | carbs: 2.9g | net carbs: 2.1g | fiber: 0.8g

Pork and Cauliflower Goulash

Prep time: 15 minutes | Cook time: 10 minutes | Serves 4

1 red bell pepper, seeded and chopped	1 onion, chopped
2 tablespoons olive oil	14 ounces (397 g) canned diced tomatoes
1½ pounds (680 g) ground pork	¼ teaspoon garlic powder
Salt and black pepper, to taste	1 tablespoon tomato purée
2 cups cauliflower florets	1½ cups water

Heat olive oil in a pan over medium heat, stir in the pork, and brown for 5 minutes. Place in the bell pepper and onion, and cook for 4 minutes. Stir in the water, tomatoes, and cauliflower, bring to a simmer and cook for 5 minutes while covered. Place in the black pepper, tomato paste, salt, and garlic powder. Stir well, remove from the heat, split into bowls, and enjoy.

calories: 476 | fat: 36.9g | protein: 43.9g | carbs: 8.3g | net carbs: 4.4g | fiber: 3.9g

Pork Chops with Mushrooms

Prep time: 10 minutes | Cook time: 45 minutes | Serves 3

8 ounces (227 g) mushrooms, sliced	1 cup heavy cream
1 teaspoon garlic powder	3 pork chops, boneless
1 onion, peeled and chopped	1 teaspoon ground nutmeg
	¼ cup coconut oil

Set a pan over medium heat and warm the oil, add in the onion and mushrooms, and cook for 4 minutes. Stir in the pork chops, season with garlic powder, and nutmeg, and sear until browned. Put the pan in the oven at 350ºF (180ºC), and bake for 30 minutes. Remove pork chops to plates and maintain warm. Place the pan over medium heat, pour in the heavy cream over the mushroom mixture, and cook for 5 minutes; remove from heat. Sprinkle sauce over pork chops and enjoy.

calories: 610 | fat: 40.1g | protein: 41.9g | carbs: 16.6g | net carbs: 6.7g | fiber: 9.9g

Pork Medallions with Onions and Bacon

Prep time: 10 minutes | Cook time: 25 minutes | Serves 4

2 onions, chopped	Salt and black pepper, to taste
6 bacon slices, chopped	1 pound (454 g) pork
½ cup vegetable stock	tenderloin, cut into medallions

Set a pan over medium heat, stir in the bacon, cook until crispy, and remove to a plate. Add onions, black pepper, and salt, and cook for 5 minutes; set to the same plate with bacon. Add the pork medallions to the pan, season with black pepper and salt, brown for 3 minutes on each side, turn, reduce heat to medium, and cook for 7 minutes. Stir in the stock, and cook for 2 minutes. Return the bacon and onions to the pan and cook for 1 minute.

calories: 326 | fat: 17.9g | protein: 35.9g | carbs: 7.2g | net carbs: 5.9g | fiber: 1.3g

Avocado Pulled Pork Shoulder

Prep time: 10 minutes | Cook time: 2 hours 5 minutes | Serves 12

4 pounds (1.8 kg) pork shoulder	½ cup vegetable stock
1 tablespoon avocado oil	¼ cup jerk seasoning
	6 avocado, sliced

Rub the pork shoulder with jerk seasoning, and set in a greased baking dish. Pour in the stock, and cook for 1 hour 45 minutes in your oven at 350ºF (180ºC) covered with aluminium foil. Discard the foil and cook for another 20 minutes. Leave to rest for 30 minutes, and shred it with 2 forks. Serve topped with avocado slices.

calories: 566 | fat: 42.5g | protein: 41.9g | carbs: 11.4g | net carbs: 4.2g | fiber: 7.2g

Pesto Pork Chops with Pistachios

Prep time: 10 minutes | Cook time: 2 hours | Serves 4

1 cup parsley	5 tablespoons avocado oil
1 cup mint	Salt, to taste
1½ onions, chopped	4 pork chops
⅓ cup pistachios	5 garlic cloves, minced
1 teaspoon lemon zest	Juice from 1 lemon

In a food processor, combine the parsley with avocado oil, mint, pistachios, salt, lemon zest, and 1 onion. Rub the pork with this mixture, place in a bowl, and refrigerate for 1 hour while covered. Remove the chops and set to a baking dish, place in ½ onion, and garlic; sprinkle with lemon juice, and bake for 2 hours in the oven at 250ºF (121ºC). Split amongst plates and enjoy.

calories: 565 | fat: 40.1g | protein: 37.1g | carbs: 8.3g | net carbs: 5.4g | fiber: 2.9g

Easy Jamaican Pork Roast

Prep time: 10 minutes | Cook time: 4 hours | Serves 12

4 pounds (1.8 kg) pork roast
1 tablespoon olive oil
¼ cup jerk spice blend
½ cup vegetable stock
Salt and black pepper, to taste

Rub the pork with olive oil and the spice blend. Heat a dutch oven over medium heat and sear the meat well on all sides; add in the stock. Cover the pot, reduce the heat, and let cook for 4 hours.

calories: 283 | fat: 24.1g | protein: 23.1g | carbs: 0.4g | net carbs: 0g | fiber: 0.4g

Pork Tenderloin with Lemon Chimichurri

Prep time: 10 minutes | Cook time: 50 minutes | Serves 6

Lemon Chimichurri:
1 lemon, juiced
¼ cup chopped mint leaves
¼ cup chopped oregano leaves
2 cloves garlic, minced
¼ cup olive oil
Salt to taste
Pork:
1 (4-pound / 1.8-kg) pork tenderloin
Salt and black pepper to
season
Olive oil for rubbing

Make the lemon chimichurri to have the flavors incorporate while the pork cooks. In a bowl, mix the mint, oregano, and garlic. Then, add the lemon juice, olive oil, and salt, and combine well. Set the sauce aside at room temperature. Preheat the charcoal grill to 450ºF (235ºC) in medium heat creating a direct heat area and indirect heat area. Rub the pork with olive oil, season with salt and pepper. Place the meat over direct heat and sear for 3 minutes on each side, after which, move to the indirect heat area. Close the lid and cook for 25 minutes on one side, then open, turn the meat, and grill for 20 minutes on the other side. Remove the pork from the grill and let it sit for 5 minutes before slicing. Spoon lemon chimichurri over the pork and serve with fresh salad.

calories: 400 | fat: 17g | protein: 28g | carbs: 2g | net carbs: 2g | fiber: 0g

Bacon Smothered Pork with Thyme

Prep time: 10 minutes | Cook time: 20 minutes | Serves 6

7 strips bacon, chopped
6 pork chops
Pink salt and black pepper to taste
5 sprigs fresh thyme plus extra to garnish
¼ cup chicken broth
½ cup heavy cream

Cook bacon in a large skillet on medium heat for 5 minutes. Remove with a slotted spoon onto a paper towel-lined plate to soak up excess fat. Season pork chops with salt and black pepper, and brown in the bacon fat for 4 minutes on each side. Remove to the bacon plate. Stir in the thyme, chicken broth, and heavy cream and simmer for 5 minutes. Return the chops and bacon, and cook further for another 2 minutes. Serve chops and a generous ladle of sauce with cauli mash. Garnish with thyme leaves.

calories: 434 | fat: 37.1g | protein: 22.1g | carbs: 3.1g | net carbs: 2.9g | fiber: 0.2g

Pork and Butternut Squash Stew

Prep time: 15 minutes | Cook time: 45 minutes | Serves 6

1 cup butternut squash
2 pounds (907 g) pork, chopped
1 tablespoon peanut butter
1 tablespoon peanuts, chopped
1 garlic clove, minced
½ cup onion, chopped
½ cup white wine
1 tablespoon olive oil
1 teaspoon lemon juice
¼ cup sweetener, granulated
¼ teaspoon cardamom
¼ teaspoon all spice
2 cups chicken stock

Heat olive oil in a large pot. Add onions and sauté for 3 minutes until translucent. Add garlic, and cook for 30 more seconds. Add the pork, and cook until browned, about 5-6 minutes, stirring periodically. Pour in the wine, and cook for one minute. Throw in the remaining ingredients, except for the lemon juice and peanuts. Add two cups of water, bring the mixture to a boil, and cook for 5 minutes. Reduce the heat to low, cover the pot, and let cook for about 30 minutes. Adjust seasoning. Stir in the lemon juice before serving. Ladle into serving bowls, and serve topped with peanuts, and enjoy.

calories: 545 | fat: 33g | protein: 46g | carbs: 7g | net carbs: 4g | fiber: 3g

Cheesy Pork Nachos

Prep time: 5 minutes | Cook time: 10 minutes | Serves 4

1 bag low carb tortilla chips
2 cups leftover pulled pork
1 red bell pepper, seeded and chopped
1 red onion, diced
2 cups shredded Monterey Jack cheese

Preheat oven to 350ºF (180ºC). Arrange the chips in a medium cast iron pan, scatter pork over, followed by red bell pepper, and onion, and sprinkle with cheese. Place the pan in the oven and cook for 10 minutes until the cheese has melted. Allow cooling for 3 minutes and serve.

calories: 473 | fat: 25g | protein: 37g | carbs: 11g | net carbs: 9g | fiber: 2g

Tangy-Garlicky Pork Chops

Prep time: 10 minutes | Cook time: 15 minutes | Serves 4

1 pound (454 g) boneless center-cut pork chops, pounded to ¼ inch thick
Sea salt, for seasoning
Freshly ground black pepper, for seasoning
¼ cup good-quality olive oil, divided
¼ cup finely chopped fresh cilantro
1 tablespoon minced garlic
Juice of 1 lime

Pat the pork chops dry and season them lightly with salt and pepper. Place them in a large bowl, add 2 tablespoons of the olive oil, and the cilantro, garlic, and lime juice. Toss to coat the chops. Cover the bowl and marinate the chops at room temperature for 30 minutes. In a large skillet over medium-high heat, warm the remaining 2 tablespoons of olive oil. Add the pork chops in a single layer and fry them, turning them once, until they're just cooked through and still juicy, 6 to 7 minutes per side. Divide the chops between four plates and serve them immediately.

calories: 249 | fat: 16g | protein: 25g | carbs: 2g | net carbs: 2g | fiber: 0g

Lime Pork Chops with Dill Pickles

Prep time: 15 minutes | Cook time: 15 minutes | Serves 4

¼ cup lime juice
4 pork chops
1 tablespoon coconut oil, melted
2 garlic cloves, minced
1 tablespoon chili powder

1 teaspoon ground cinnamon
2 teaspoons cumin
Salt and black pepper, to taste
½ teaspoon hot pepper sauce
4 dill pickles, cut into spears and squeezed

In a bowl, combine the lime juice with oil, cumin, salt, hot pepper sauce, black pepper, cinnamon, garlic, and chili powder. Place in the pork chops, toss to coat, and refrigerate for 4 hours. Arrange the pork on a preheated grill over medium heat, cook for 7 minutes, turn, add in the dill pickles, and cook for another 7 minutes. Split among serving plates and enjoy.

calories: 316 | fat: 18.0g | protein: 36.0g | carbs: 3.9g | net carbs: 2.3g | fiber: 1.6g

Smoked Sausages with Peppers and Mushrooms

Prep time: 10 minutes | Cook time: 1 hour | Serves 6

3 yellow bell peppers, seeded and chopped
2 pounds (907 g) smoked sausage, sliced
Salt and black pepper, to taste
2 pounds (907 g) portobello

mushrooms, sliced
2 sweet onions, chopped
1 tablespoon Swerve
2 tablespoons olive oil
Arugula to garnish

In a baking dish, combine the sausages with Swerve, oil, black pepper, onion, bell peppers, salt, and mushrooms. Pour in 1 cup of water and toss well to ensure everything is coated, set in the oven at 320°F (160°C) to bake for 1 hour. To serve, divide the sausages between plates and scatter over the arugula.

calories: 524 | fat: 32.0g | protein: 28.9g | carbs: 14.4g | net carbs: 7.4g | fiber: 7.0g

Pork and Mashed Cauliflower Crust

Prep time: 15 minutes | Cook time: 1 hour | Serves 8

Crust:
1 egg
¼ cup butter
2 cups almond flour
Filling:
2 pounds (907 g) ground pork
⅓ cup onion, pureed
¾ teaspoon allspice

¼ teaspoon xanthan gum
¼ cup mozzarella, shredded
A pinch of salt

1 cup cauliflower, mashed
1 tablespoon ground sage
1 tablespoon butter

Preheat your oven to 350°F (180°C). Whisk together all of the crust ingredients in a bowl. Make two balls out of the mixture, and refrigerate for 10 minutes. Melt the butter in a pan over medium heat and add the ground pork. Cook for about 10minutes, stirring occasionally. Remove to a bowl. Add in the other ingredients and mix to combine. Roll out the tart crusts and place one at the bottom of a greased baking pan. Spread the filling over the crust. Top with the other coat. Bake for 50 minutes, then serve.

calories: 444 | fat: 19g | protein: 40g | carbs: 6g | net carbs: 4g | fiber: 2g

Pork Sausage with Spinach and Chili

Prep time: 10 minutes | Cook time: 30 minutes | Serves 6

1 onion, chopped
2 tablespoons olive oil
2 pounds (907 g) Italian pork sausage, sliced
1 red bell pepper, seeded and chopped
Salt and black pepper, to taste

4 pounds (1.8 kg) spinach, chopped
1 garlic, minced
¼ cup green chili peppers, chopped
1 cup water

Set pan over medium heat, warm oil and cook sausage for 10 minutes. Stir in onion, garlic and bell pepper and fry for 4 minutes. Place in spinach, salt, water, pepper, chili pepper, and cook for 10 minutes.

calories: 351 | fat: 27.9g | protein: 28.9g | carbs: 13.8g | net carbs: 6.3g | fiber: 7.5g

Pesto Pork Sausage Links

Prep time: 10 minutes | Cook time: 10 minutes | Serves 8

8 pork sausage links, sliced
1 pound (454 g) mixed cherry tomatoes, cut in half
4 cups baby spinach
1 tablespoon olive oil

1 pound (454 g) Monterrey Jack cheese, cubed
2 tablespoons lemon juice
1 cup basil pesto
Salt and black pepper, to taste

Warm oil in a pan and cook sausage links for 4 minutes per side. In a salad bowl, combine spinach, cheese, salt, pesto, pepper, cherry tomatoes, and lemon juice, and toss to coat. Mix in the sausage.

calories: 366 | fat: 26.1g | protein: 17.9g | carbs: 8.0g | net carbs: 6.7g | fiber: 1.3g

Pork Pie

Prep time: 15 minutes | Cook time: 1 hour | Serves 8

Crust:
1 egg
¼ cup butter
2 cups almond flour

¼ teaspoon xanthan gum
¼ cup shredded mozzarella
A pinch of salt

Filling:
2 pounds ground pork
½ cup water
⅓ cup pureed onion
¾ teaspoon allspice

1 cup cooked and mashed cauliflower
1 tablespoon ground sage
1 tablespoon butter

Preheat your oven to 350°F (180°C). Whisk together all crust ingredients in a bowl. Make two balls out of the mixture and refrigerate for 10 minutes. Combine the water, meat, and salt, in a pot over medium heat. Cook for about 15 minutes, place the meat along with the other ingredients in a bowl. Mix with your hands to combine. Roll out the pie crusts and place one at the bottom of a greased pie pan. Spread the filling over the crust. Top with the other coat. Bake in the oven for 50 minutes then serve.

calories: 435 | fat: 31g | protein: 31g | carbs: 5g | net carbs: 4g | fiber: 1g

Pork Chops with Tomatoes

Prep time: 10 minutes | Cook time: 37 minutes | Serves 4

4 pork chops
½ tablespoon fresh basil, chopped
1 garlic clove, minced
1 tablespoon olive oil

7 ounces (198 g) canned diced tomatoes
½ tablespoon tomato purée
Salt and black pepper, to taste
½ red chili, finely chopped

Season the pork with salt and black pepper. Set a pan over medium heat and warm oil, place in the pork chops, cook for 3 minutes, turn and cook for another 3 minutes; remove to a bowl. Add in the garlic and cook for 30 seconds. Stir in the tomato purée, tomatoes, and chili; bring to a boil, and reduce heat to medium-low. Place in the pork chops, cover the pan and simmer everything for 30 minutes. Remove the pork chops to plates and sprinkle with fresh oregano to serve.

calories: 372 | fat: 21g | protein: 40g | carbs: 3g | net carbs: 2g | fiber: 1g

Lemony Pork Chops with Veggies

Prep time: 10 minutes | Cook time: 12 minutes | Serves 4

1 tablespoon olive oil
1 tablespoon lemon juice
1 garlic clove, pureed
4 pork loin chops
⅓ head cabbage, shredded
1 tomato, chopped

1 tablespoon white wine
Salt and black pepper to taste
¼ teaspoon cumin
¼ teaspoon ground nutmeg
1 tablespoon parsley

In a bowl, mix the lemon juice, garlic, salt, pepper and olive oil. Brush the pork with the mixture. Preheat grill to high heat. Grill the pork for 2to 3 minutes on each side until cooked through. Remove to serving plates. Warm the remaining olive oil in a pan and cook in cabbage for 5 minutes. Drizzle with white wine, sprinkle with cumin, nutmeg, salt and pepper. Add in the tomatoes, cook for another 5 minutes, stirring occasionally. Ladle the sautéed cabbage to the side of the chops and serve sprinkled with parsley.

calories: 382 | fat: 21g | protein: 41g | carbs: 6g | net carbs: 4g | fiber: 2g

Pork Steaks with Chimichurri Sauce

Prep time: 10 minutes | Cook time: 5 minutes | Serves 4

1 garlic clove, minced
½ teaspoon white wine vinegar
1 tablespoon parsley leaves, chopped
1 tablespoon cilantro leaves, chopped
1 tablespoon extra-virgin olive

oil
16 ounces (454 g) pork loin steaks
Salt and black pepper to season
1 tablespoon sesame oil

To make the sauce: in a bowl, mix the parsley, cilantro and garlic. Add the vinegar, extra-virgin olive oil, and salt, and combine well. Preheat a grill pan over medium heat. Rub the pork with sesame oil, and season with salt and pepper. Grill the meat for 4 to 5 minutes on each side until no longer pink in the center. Put the pork on a serving plate and spoon chimichurri sauce over, to serve.

calories: 326 | fat: 21g | protein: 32g | carbs: 2g | net carbs: 2g | fiber: 0g

Pork Kofte with Cauliflower Mash

Prep time: 15 minutes | Cook time: 30 minutes | Serves 4

1 pound (454 g) ground pork
1 tablespoon olive oil
1 tablespoon pork rinds, crushed
1 garlic clove, minced
1 shallot, chopped
1 small egg
⅓ teaspoon paprika
Salt and black pepper to taste

1 tablespoon parsley, chopped
½ cup tomato purée, sugar-free
½ teaspoon oregano
⅓ cup Italian blend kinds of cheeses
1 tablespoon basil, chopped to garnish

In a bowl, mix the ground pork, shallot, pork rinds, garlic, egg, paprika, oregano, parsley, salt, and black pepper, just until combined. Form balls of the mixture and place them in an oiled baking pan; drizzle with olive oil. Bake in the oven for 18 minutes at 390ºF (199ºC). Pour the tomato purée all over the meatballs. Sprinkle with the Italian blend cheeses, and put it back in the oven to bake for 10 to 15 minutes until the cheese melts. Once ready, take out the pan and garnish with basil. Delicious when served with cauliflower mash.

calories: 458 | fat: 30g | protein: 34g | carbs: 8g | net carbs: 6g | fiber: 2g

Pork Steaks with Broccoli

Prep time: 10 minutes | Cook time: 25 minutes | Serves 4

1 tablespoon olive oil
1 tablespoon butter
4 pork steaks, bone-in
½ cup water
Salt and black pepper, to taste

2 garlic cloves, minced
1 tablespoon fresh parsley, chopped
½ head broccoli, cut into florets
½ lemon, sliced

Heat oil and butter over high heat. Add in the pork steaks, season with pepper and salt, and cook until browned; set to a plate. In the same pan, add garlic and broccoli and cook for 4 minutes. Pour the water, lemon slices, salt, and black pepper, and cook everything for 5 minutes. Return the pork steaks to the pan and cook for 10 minutes. Serve the steaks sprinkled with sauce with parsley.

calories: 561 | fat: 39g | protein: 47g | carbs: 3g | net carbs: 2g | fiber: 1g

Pork Loin Chops

Prep time: 10 minutes | Cook time: 13 minutes | Serves 2

½ tablespoon butter
½ tablespoon olive oil
4 pork loin chops
½ teaspoon Dijon mustard
½ tablespoon coconut aminos

½ teaspoon lemon juice
1 teaspoon cumin seeds
½ tablespoon water
Salt and black pepper, to taste
½ cup chives, chopped

Set a pan over medium heat and warm butter and olive oil, add in the pork chops, season with salt, and pepper, cook for 4 minutes, turn and cook for additional 4 minutes. Remove to a plate. In a bowl, mix the water with lemon juice, cumin seeds, mustard and coconut aminos. Pour the mustard sauce in the same pan and simmer for 5 minutes. Spread over pork, top with chives and serve.

calories: 382 | fat: 21g | protein: 38g | carbs: 1g | net carbs: 1g | fiber: 0g

Bacon and Cauliflower Stew

Prep time: 10 minutes | Cook time: 35 minutes | Serves 6

8 ounces (227 g) Mozzarella cheese, grated
2 cups chicken broth
½ teaspoon garlic powder
½ teaspoon onion powder
Salt and black pepper, to taste

4 garlic cloves, minced
¼ cup heavy cream
3 cups bacon, chopped
1 head cauliflower, cut into florets

In a pot, combine the bacon with broth, cauliflower, salt, heavy cream, black pepper, garlic powder, cheese, onion powder, and garlic, and cook for 35 minutes. Share into serving plates, and enjoy.

calories: 381 | fat: 25.1g | protein: 32.9g | carbs: 8.7g | net carbs: 6.0g | fiber: 2.7g

Hot Sausage with Pancetta and Kale

Prep time: 15 minutes | Cook time: 25 minutes | Serves 8

2 cups kale
8 cups chicken broth
A drizzle of olive oil
1 cup heavy cream
6 pancetta slices, chopped
1 pound (454 g)radishes, chopped

2 garlic cloves, minced
Salt and black pepper, to taste
A pinch of red pepper flakes
1 onion, chopped
1½ pounds (680 g) hot pork sausage, chopped

Set a pot over medium heat. Add in a drizzle of olive oil and warm. Stir in garlic, onion, pancetta, and sausage; cook for 5 minutes. Pour in broth, radishes, and kale, and simmer for 10 minutes. Stir in salt, red pepper flakes, black pepper, and heavy cream, and cook for about 5 minutes. Serve.

calories: 387 | fat: 28.9g | protein: 2.2g | carbs: 6.9g | net carbs: 5.5g | fiber: 1.4g

Pork Osso Bucco

Prep time: 15 minutes | Cook time: 1¾ hours | Serves 6

1 tablespoon butter, softened
6 (16-ounce / 454-g) pork shanks
1 tablespoon olive oil
3 cloves garlic, minced
1 cup diced tomatoes
Salt and black pepper to taste

½ cup chopped onions
½ cup chopped celery
2 cups Cabernet Sauvignon
5 cups vegetable broth
½ cup chopped parsley, extra to garnish
1 teaspoon lemon zest

Melt the butter in a saucepan over medium heat. Season the pork with salt and black pepper and brown it for 12 minutes; remove to a plate. In the same pan, sauté 2 cloves of garlic and onions in the oil, for 3 minutes; return the pork shanks. Stir in the Cabernet, celery, tomatoes, and vegetable broth; season with salt and pepper. Cover the pan and let simmer on low heat for 1½ hours, basting the pork every 15 minutes with the sauce. In a bowl, mix the remaining garlic, parsley, and lemon zest to make a gremolata, and stir the mixture into the sauce when it is ready. Turn the heat off and dish the Osso Bucco. Garnish with parsley and serve with creamy turnip mash.

calories: 533 | fat: 40g | protein: 34g | carbs: 4g | net carbs: 2g | fiber: 2g

Pork and Beef Meatballs

Prep time: 5 minutes | Cook time: 13 minutes | Serves 5

1 pound (454 g) ground pork
½ pound (227 g) ground beef
onion, chopped

garlic cloves, minced
1 teaspoon Hungarian spice blend

In a mixing bowl, thoroughly combine all ingredients until they are well incorporated. Form the mixture into meatballs with oiled hands. Place your meatballs on a tinfoil-lined baking sheet. Bake in the preheated oven at 395ºF (202ºC) for 12 to 14 minutes or until they are golden brown. Arrange on a nice serving platter and serve. Bon appétit!

calories: 377 | fat: 24g | protein: 36g | carbs: 2g | net carbs: 2g | fiber: og

Hearty Pork Stew Meat

Prep time: 10 minutes | Cook time: 1 hour | Serves 5

2 tablespoons olive oil
2 pounds pork stew meat
1 yellow onion, chopped
1 garlic cloves, minced
¼ cup dry sherry wine
4 cups chicken bone broth

1 cup tomatoes, pureed
1 bay laurel
Sea salt and ground black pepper, to taste
1 tablespoon fresh cilantro, chopped

Heat the olive oil in a soup pot over a moderate flame. Sear the pork for about 5 minutes, stirring continuously to ensure even cooking; reserve. Cook the yellow onion in the pan drippings until just tender and translucent. Stir in the garlic and continue to sauté for a further 30 seconds. Pour in a splash of dry sherry to deglaze the pan. Pour in the chicken bone broth and bring to a boil. Stir in the tomatoes and bay laurel. Season with salt and pepper to taste. Turn the heat to medium-low and continue to cook 10 minutes longer. Add the reserved pork back to the pot, partially cover, and continue to simmer for 45 minutes longer. Garnish with cilantro and serve hot.

calories: 332 | fat: 15g | protein: 41g | carbs: 4g | net carbs: 3g | fiber: 1g

Bacon and Pork Omelet

Prep time: 5 minutes | Cook time: 12 minutes | Serves 5

2 ounces (57 g) bacon, diced
1 pound (454 g) ground pork
1 shallot, chopped

1 teaspoon ginger-garlic paste
6 eggs, whisked

Heat up a nonstick skillet over a moderate flame. Now, cook the bacon until it releases easily from the bottom of the skillet. Then, add in the ground pork and shallot and cook for 4 to 5 minutes or until the pork is no longer pink; discard the excess fat. Fold in the ginger-garlic paste and whisked eggs; partially cover and let it cook on mediumlow temperature for 4 minutes. Flip your omelet and cook on the other side for 3 minutes longer. Slide your omelet onto a plate and serve right now. Bon appétit!

calories: 393 | fat: 28g | protein: 31g | carbs: 1g | net carbs: 1g | fiber: og

Pork and Veggies Burgers

Prep time: 10 minutes | Cook time: 5 minutes | Serves 6

2 pound (907 g) ground pork
Pink salt and chili pepper, to taste
1 tablespoon olive oil
1 tablespoon butter
1 white onion, sliced into rings

1 tablespoon balsamic vinegar
3 drops liquid stevia
6 low carb burger buns, halved
2 firm tomatoes, sliced into rings

Combine the pork, salt and chili pepper in a bowl, and mold out 6 patties. Heat the olive oil in a skillet over medium heat, and fry the patties for 4 to 5 minutes on each side until golden brown on the outside. Remove onto a plate, and sit for 3 minutes. Melt butter in a skillet over medium heat, sauté onions for 2 minutes, and stir in the balsamic vinegar and liquid stevia. Cook for 30 seconds stirring once, or twice until caramelized. In each bun, place a patty, top with some onion rings and 2 tomato rings. Serve the burgers with cheddar cheese dip.

calories: 315 | fat: 23g | protein: 16g | carbs: 7g | net carbs: 6g | fiber: 1g

Cheesy Pork and Veggies

Prep time: 10 minutes | Cook time: 40 minutes | Serves 4

1 pound (454 g) ground pork
1 onion, chopped
1 garlic clove, minced
½ green beans, chopped
Salt and black pepper to taste

1 zucchini, sliced
¼ cup heavy cream
5 eggs
½ cup Monterey Jack cheese, grated

In a bowl, mix onion, green beans, ground pork, garlic, black pepper and salt. Layer the meat mixture on the bottom of a small greased baking dish. Spread zucchini slices on top. In a separate bowl, combine cheese, eggs and heavy cream. Top with this creamy mixture and bake for 40 minutes at 360°F (182°C), until the edges and top become brown. Serve immediately.

calories: 335 | fat: 21g | protein: 28g | carbs: 4g | net carbs: 4g | fiber: 0g

Pork with Raspberry Sauce

Prep time: 10 minutes | Cook time: 15 minutes | Serves 4

1 tablespoon olive oil
2 pound pork chops
Salt and black pepper to taste
2 cups raspberries
¼ cup water

1½ tablespoon Italian herb mix
1 tablespoon balsamic vinegar
1 teaspoon Worcestershire sauce

Heat oil in a skillet over medium heat, season the pork with salt and black pepper and cook for 5 minutes on each side. Put in serving plates, and reserve the pork drippings. Mash raspberries with a fork in a bowl until jam-like. Pour into a saucepan, add water, and herb mix. Cook on low heat for 4 minutes. Stir in pork drippings, vinegar, and Worcestershire sauce. Simmer for 1 minute. Dish the pork chops, spoon sauce over, and serve with braised rapini.

calories: 413 | fat: 32g | protein: 26g | carbs: 5g | net carbs: 1g | fiber: 4g

Pork Lettuce Wraps

Prep time: 10 minutes | Cook time: 14 minutes | Serves 6

2 pound (907 g) ground pork
1 tablespoon ginger-garlic paste
Pink salt and chili pepper, to taste

1 teaspoon butter
1 fresh head iceberg lettuce
2 sprigs green onion, chopped
1 red bell pepper, chopped
½ cucumber, finely chopped

Put the pork with ginger-garlic, salt, and chili pepper seasoning in a saucepan. Cook for 10 minutes over medium heat while breaking any lumps until the beef is no longer pink. Drain liquid and add the butter, melt, and brown the meat for 4 minutes with continuous stirring. Pat the lettuce dry with paper towel and in each leaf spoon two to three tablespoons of pork, top with green onions, bell pepper, and cucumber. Serve with soy drizzling sauce.

calories: 311 | fat: 24g | protein: 19g | carbs: 3g | net carbs: 1g | fiber: 2g

Mustard Pork Meatballs

Prep time: 5 minutes | Cook time: 21 minutes | Serves 2

1 pound (454 g) ground pork
Salt and black pepper, to taste
1 tablespoon yellow mustard
½ cup almond flour

¼ cup mozzarella cheese, grated
¼ cup hot sauce
1 egg

Preheat oven to 400°F (205°C) and line a baking tray with parchment paper. In a bowl, combine the pork, pepper, mustard, flour, mozzarella cheese, salt, and egg. Form meatballs and arrange them on the baking tray. Cook for 16 minutes, then pour over the hot sauce and bake for 5 more minutes. Serve warm.

calories: 518 | fat: 22g | protein: 60g | carbs: 2g | net carbs: 1g | fiber: 1g

Parmesan Bacon-Stuffed Pork Roll

Prep time: 15 minutes | Cook time: 30 minutes | Serves 4

1 tablespoon olive oil
4 ounces (113 g) bacon, sliced
1 tablespoon fresh parsley, chopped
4 pork chops, boneless and flatten
1 cup ricotta cheese
1 tablespoon pine nuts
1 spring onion, chopped

1 garlic clove, minced
1 tablespoon Parmesan cheese, grated
5 ounces (142 g) canned diced tomatoes
Salt and black pepper to taste
½ teaspoon herbes de Provence

Put the pork chops on a flat surface. Set the bacon slices on top, then divide the ricotta cheese, pine nuts, and Parmesan cheese. Roll each pork piece and secure with a toothpick. Set a pan over medium heat and warm oil. Cook the pork rolls until browned, and remove to a plate. Add in the spring onion and garlic, and cook for 5 minutes. Place in the stock and cook for 3 minutes. Remove the toothpicks from the rolls and return them to the pan. Stir in the black pepper, salt, tomatoes and herbes de Provence. Bring to a boil, set heat to medium-low, and cook for 20 minutes while covered. Sprinkle with parsley to serve.

calories: 568 | fat: 38g | protein: 51g | carbs: 6g | net carbs: 3g | fiber: 2g

Grilled Pork Spare Ribs

Prep time: 10 minutes | Cook time: 50 minutes | Serves 4

1 tablespoon erythritol
Salt and black pepper, to taste
1 tablespoon olive oil
1 teaspoon chipotle powder
1 teaspoon garlic powder
1 pound (454 g) pork spare ribs
1 tablespoon sugar-free BBQ sauce + extra for serving

Mix the erythritol, salt, pepper, oil, chipotle, and garlic powder. Brush on the meaty sides of the ribs, and wrap in foil. Sit for 30 minutes to marinate. Preheat oven to 400ºF (205ºC), place wrapped ribs on a baking sheet, and cook for 40 minutes to be cooked through. Remove ribs and aluminum foil, brush with BBQ sauce, and brown under the broiler for 10 minutes on both sides. Slice and serve with extra BBQ sauce and lettuce tomato salad.

calories: 294 | fat: 18g | protein: 28g | carbs: 3g | net carbs: 3g | fiber: 0g

Spicy Pork and Capers with Olives

Prep time: 10 minutes | Cook time: 9 minutes | Serves 4

4 pork chops
1 tablespoon olive oil
1 garlic clove, minced
¼ tablespoon chili powder
¼ teaspoon cumin
Salt and black pepper, to taste
½ teaspoon hot pepper sauce
¼ cup capers
6 black olives, sliced

Preheat grill over medium heat. In a mixing bowl, combine olive oil, cumin, salt, hot pepper sauce, pepper, garlic and chili powder. Place in the pork chops, toss to coat, and refrigerate for 4 hours. Arrange the pork on a preheated grill, cook for 7 minutes, turn, add in the capers, and cook for another 2 minutes. Place onto serving plates and sprinkle with olives to serve.

calories: 300 | fat: 14g | protein: 40g | carbs: 2g | net carbs: 1g | fiber: 1g

Lemony Pork Chops and Brussel Sprouts

Prep time: 10 minutes | Cook time: 16 minutes | Serves 6

1 tablespoon lemon juice
3 cloves garlic, pureed
Salt and black pepper to taste
1 tablespoon olive oil
6 pork loin chops
1 tablespoon butter
1 pound (454 g) Brussel sprouts, halved
1 tablespoon white wine

Preheat grill to 400ºF (205ºC), and mix the lemon juice, garlic, salt, pepper, and oil in a bowl. Brush the pork with mixture, place onto a baking sheet, and cook for 6 minutes on each side until browned. Share into 6 plates, and make the side dish. Melt butter in a small wok, or pan and cook in Brussel sprouts for 5 minutes until tender. Drizzle with white wine, sprinkle with salt and black pepper, and cook for another 5 minutes. Ladle Brussel sprouts to the side of the chops, and serve with a hot sauce.

calories: 400 | fat: 22g | protein: 36g | carbs: 7g | net carbs: 4g | fiber: 3g

Golden Pork Burgers

Prep time: 10 minutes | Cook time: 10 minutes | Serves 4

1 tablespoon olive oil
1 pound (454 g) ground pork
Salt and black pepper to taste
½ teaspoon chili pepper
1 tablespoon parsley
1 white onion, sliced into rings
½ tablespoon balsamic vinegar
1 drop liquid stevia
1 tomato, sliced into rings
1 tablespoon mayonnaise

Warm half of the oil in a skillet over medium heat, sauté onions for 2 minutes, and stir in the balsamic vinegar and liquid stevia. Cook for 30 seconds stirring once or twice until caramelized; remove to a plate. Combine the pork, salt, black pepper and chili pepper in a bowl, and mold out 2 patties. Heat the remaining olive oil in a skillet over medium heat and fry the patties for 4 to 5 minutes on each side until golden brown on the outside. Remove to a plate and sit for 3 minutes. In each tomato slice, place half of the mayonnaise and a patty, and top with some onion rings. Cover with another tomato slice and serve.

calories: 380 | fat: 27g | protein: 29g | carbs: 2g | net carbs: 2g | fiber: 0g

Buttered Pork Chops

Prep time: 5 minutes | Cook time: 12 minutes | Serves 4

½ tablespoon olive oil
1 tablespoon butter
1 tablespoon rosemary
4 pork chops
Salt and black pepper, to taste
A pinch of paprika
½ teaspoon chili powder

Rub the pork chops with olive oil, salt, black pepper, paprika, and chili powder. Heat a grill over medium, add in the pork chops and cook for 10 minutes, flipping once halfway through. Remove to a serving plate. In a pan over low heat, warm the butter until it turns nutty brown. Pour over the pork chops, sprinkle with rosemary and serve. Serve immediately.

calories: 370 | fat: 22g | protein: 40g | carbs: 1g | net carbs: 1g | fiber: 0g

Balsamic Pork Loin Chops

Prep time: 5 minutes | Cook time: 15 minutes | Serves 4

4 pork loin chops, boneless
1 tablespoon rosemary, chopped
1 tablespoon balsamic vinegar
1 garlic clove, minced
1 tablespoon olive oil
Salt and black pepper to taste

Put the pork in a deep dish. Add in the balsamic vinegar, rosemary, garlic, olive oil, salt, and black pepper, and toss to coat. Cover the dish with plastic wrap and marinate the pork for 1 to 2 hours. Preheat grill to medium heat. Remove the pork when ready, reserve the marinade and grill covered for 10 minutes per side. Remove the pork chops and let them sit for 4 minutes on a serving plate. In a saucepan over medium heat, pour in the reserved marinade, add in 1 tablespoon water and bring to a boil for 2-3 minutes until the liquid becomes thickened. Top the chops with the sauce and serve.

calories: 363 | fat: 21g | protein: 40g | carbs: 1g | net carbs: 1g | fiber: 0g

Mediterranean Pork
Prep time: 10 minutes | Cook time: 35 minutes | Serves 4

1 garlic clove, minced
4 pork chops, bone-in
Salt and black pepper, to taste
1 teaspoon dried oregano
¼ cup kalamata olives, pitted

and sliced
1 tablespoon olive oil
1 tablespoon vegetable broth
¼ cup feta cheese, crumbled

Preheat the oven to 425°F (220°C). Rub pork chops with pepper and salt, and add in a roasting pan. Stir in the garlic, olives, olive oil, broth, and oregano, set in the oven and bake for 10 minutes. Reduce heat to 350°F (180°C) and roast for 25 minutes. Slice the pork, divide among plates, and sprinkle with pan juices and feta cheese all over. Serve immediately.

calories: 394 | fat: 24g | protein: 41g | carbs: 1g | net carbs: 1g | fiber: 0g

Lemony Peanuts Pork Chops
Prep time: 10 minutes | Cook time: 30 minutes | Serves 4

⅓ cup cilantro
⅓ cup mint
1 onion, chopped
¼ cup peanuts
1 tablespoon olive oil

Salt, to taste
4 pork chops
2 garlic cloves, minced
Juice and zest from 1 lemon

Preheat oven to 250°F (121°C). In a food processor, combine the cilantro with olive oil, mint, peanuts, salt, lemon zest, garlic, and onion. Rub the pork with this mixture, place in a bowl, and refrigerate for 1 hour while covered. Remove to a greased baking dish, sprinkle with lemon juice, and bake for 30 minutes in the oven. Serve immediately.

calories: 428 | fat: 26g | protein: 42g | carbs: 6g | net carbs: 5g | fiber: 1g

Pork Chops with Broccoli
Prep time: 10 minutes | Cook time: 51 minutes | Serves 4

1 shallot, chopped
2 (10½-ounce / 298-g) cans mushroom soup
4 pork chops

½ cup sliced mushrooms
Salt and black pepper to taste
1 tablespoon parsley
½ head broccoli, cut into florets

Steam the broccoli in salted water over medium heat for 6-8 minutes until tender. Set aside. Preheat the oven to 370°F (188°C). Season the pork chops with salt and pepper, and place in a greased baking dish. Combine the mushroom soup, mushrooms and onion, in a bowl. Pour this mixture over the pork chops. Bake for 45 minutes. Sprinkle with parsley and serve with broccoli.

calories: 434 | fat: 20g | protein: 40g | carbs: 7g | net carbs: 5g | fiber: 2g

Creamy Pork Chops and Canadian Ham
Prep time: 5 minutes | Cook time: 25 minutes | Serves 4

4 ounces (113 g) Canadian ham, chopped
4 pork chops
Salt and black pepper to taste

2 sprigs fresh thyme
1 tablespoon heavy cream
½ teaspoon Dijon mustard

Cook ham in a skillet over medium heat for 5 minutes. Remove to a plate. Season pork chops with salt and pepper, and brown in the bacon fat for 4 minutes on each side. Remove to the bacon plate. Stir in thyme, 1 tablespoon of water, mustard, and heavy cream and simmer for 5 minutes. Return the chops and bacon, and cook for another 10 minutes. Garnish with thyme leaves. Serve immediately.

calories: 373 | fat: 19g | protein: 40g | carbs: 1g | net carbs: 1g | fiber: 0g

Pork Wraps with Veggies
Prep time: 10 minutes | Cook time: 10 minutes | Serves 4

1 tablespoon avocado oil
1 pound (454 g) ground pork
1 tablespoon ginger paste
Salt and black pepper to taste
1 teaspoon butter

1 head Iceberg lettuce
½ onion, sliced
1 red bell pepper, seeded and chopped
2 dill pickles, finely chopped

Heat avocado oil in a pan over medium heat and put the in pork with ginger paste, salt, and pepper. Cook for 10 to 15 minutes over medium heat while breaking any lumps until the pork is no longer pink. Pat the lettuce dry with a paper towel and in each leaf, spoon two to three tablespoons of the pork mixture, top with onion slices, bell pepper, and dill pickles. Serve immediately.

calories: 424 | fat: 28g | protein: 31g | carbs: 4g | net carbs: 1g | fiber: 3g

Balsamic Pork Loin Chops
Prep time: 5 minutes | Cook time: 10 minutes | Serves 6

6 pork loin chops, boneless
1 tablespoon erythritol
¼ cup balsamic vinegar
3 cloves garlic, minced

¼ cup olive oil
⅓ teaspoon salt
Black pepper, to taste

Put the pork in a plastic bag. In a bowl, mix the erythritol, balsamic vinegar, garlic, olive oil, salt, pepper, and pour the sauce over the pork. Seal the bag, shake it, and place in the refrigerator. Marinate the pork for 2 hours. Preheat the grill to medium heat, remove the pork when ready, and grill covered for 10 minutes on each side. Remove and let sit for 4 minutes, and serve immediately.

calories: 419 | fat: 26g | protein: 40g | carbs: 2g | net carbs: 2g | fiber: 0g

Pork Medallions with Rosemary
Prep time: 10 minutes | Cook time: 20 minutes | Serves 4

2 onions, chopped
4 ounces (113 g) bacon, chopped
½ cup vegetable stock
Salt and black pepper, to taste

1 tablespoon fresh rosemary, chopped
1 pound (454 g) pork medallions

Fry the bacon in a pan over medium heat, until crispy, and remove to a plate. Add in onions, black pepper, and salt, and cook for 5 minutes; set to the same plate with bacon. Add pork to the pan, brown for 3 minutes, turn, and cook for 7 minutes. Stir in stock and cook for 2 minutes. Return bacon and onions to the pan and cook for 1 minute. Garnish with rosemary.

calories: 258 | fat: 15g | protein: 23g | carbs: 8g | net carbs: 6g | fiber: 2g

Herbed Pork Chops with Raspberry Sauce
Prep time: 10 minutes | Cook time: 10 minutes | Serves 4

1 tablespoon olive oil, extra for brushing
2 pound (907 g) pork chops
Pink salt and black pepper to taste
2 cups raspberries

¼ cup water
1½ tablespoon Italian Herb mix
1 tablespoon balsamic vinegar
1 teaspoon sugar-free Worcestershire sauce

Heat oil in a skillet over medium heat, season the pork with salt and black pepper and cook for 5 minutes on each side. Put on serving plates and reserve the pork drippings. Mash the raspberries with a fork in a bowl until jam-like. Pour into a saucepan, add the water, and herb mix. Bring to boil on low heat for 4 minutes. Stir in pork drippings, vinegar, and Worcestershire sauce. Simmer for 1 minute. Spoon sauce over the pork chops and serve with braised rapini.

calories: 413 | fat: 32g | protein: 26g | carbs: 5g | net carbs: 1g | fiber: 4g

Garlicky Pork and Bell Peppers
Prep time: 10 minutes | Cook time: 25 minutes | Serves 4

1 tablespoon butter
4 pork steaks, bone-in
1 cup chicken stock
Salt and black pepper, to taste
A pinch of lemon pepper
1 tablespoon olive oil

6 garlic cloves, minced
1 tablespoon fresh parsley, chopped
4 bell peppers, sliced
1 lemon, sliced

Heat a pan with 2 tablespoons oil and 2 tablespoons butter over medium heat. Add in the pork steaks, season with black pepper and salt, and cook until browned; remove to a plate. In the same pan, warm the rest of the oil and butter, add garlic and bell peppers and cook for 4 minutes. Pour the chicken stock, lemon slices, salt, lemon pepper, and black pepper, and cook everything for 5 minutes. Return the pork steaks to the pan and cook for 10 minutes. Split the sauce and steaks among plates and sprinkle with parsley to serve.

calories: 580 | fat: 39g | protein: 48g | carbs: 7g | net carbs: 6g | fiber: 1g

Lemony Pork Chops and Brussels Sprouts
Prep time: 10 minutes | Cook time: 15 minutes | Serves 6

1 tablespoon lemon juice
3 cloves garlic, pureed
1 tablespoon olive oil
6 pork loin chops
1 tablespoon butter

1 pound (454 g) brussels sprouts, trimmed and halved
1 tablespoon white wine
Salt and black pepper, to taste

Preheat broiler to 400ºF (205ºC) and mix the lemon juice, garlic, salt, black pepper, and oil in a bowl. Brush the pork with the mixture, place in a baking sheet, and cook for 6 minutes on each side until browned. Share into 6 plates and make the side dish. Melt butter in a small wok or pan and cook in brussels sprouts for 5 minutes until tender. Drizzle with white wine, sprinkle with salt and black pepper and cook for another 5 minutes. Ladle brussels sprouts to the side of the chops and serve with a hot sauce.

calories: 400 | fat: 25g | protein: 40g | carbs: 6g | net carbs: 3g | fiber: 3g

Lemony Pork Loin Roast
Prep time: 15 minutes | Cook time: 7 to 8 hours | Serves 6

3 tablespoons extra-virgin olive oil, divided
1 tablespoon butter
2 pounds pork loin roast
½ teaspoon salt
¼ teaspoon freshly ground

black pepper
¼ cup chicken broth
Juice and zest of 1 lemon
1 tablespoon minced garlic
½ cup heavy (whipping) cream

Lightly grease the insert of the slow cooker with 1 tablespoon of the olive oil. In a large skillet over medium-high heat, heat the remaining 2 tablespoons of the olive oil and the butter. Lightly season the pork with salt and pepper. Add the pork to the skillet and brown the roast on all sides for about 10 minutes. Transfer it to the insert. In a small bowl, stir together the broth, lemon juice and zest, and garlic. Add the broth mixture to the roast. Cover, and cook on low for 7 to 8 hours. Stir in the heavy cream and serve.

calories: 448 | fat: 31g | protein: 39g | carbs: 1g | net carbs: 1g | fiber: og

Cranberry Pork Roast
Prep time: 15 minutes | Cook time: 7 to 8 hours | Serves 6

3 tablespoons extra-virgin olive oil, divided
2 tablespoons butter
2 pounds (907 g) pork shoulder roast
1 teaspoon ground cinnamon
¼ teaspoon allspice
¼ teaspoon salt
⅛ teaspoon freshly ground

black pepper
½ cup cranberries
½ cup chicken broth
½ cup granulated erythritol
2 tablespoons dijon mustard
Juice and zest of ½ lemon
1 scallion, white and green parts, chopped, for garnish

Lightly grease the insert of the slow cooker with 1 tablespoon of the olive oil. In a large skillet over medium-high heat, heat the remaining 2 tablespoons of the olive oil and the butter. Lightly season the pork with cinnamon, allspice, salt, and pepper. Add the pork to the skillet and brown on all sides for about 10 minutes. Transfer to the insert. In a small bowl, stir together the cranberries, broth, erythritol, mustard, and lemon juice and zest, and add the mixture to the pork. Cover and cook on low for 7 to 8 hours. Serve topped with the scallion.

calories: 492 | fat: 40g | protein: 26g | carbs: 4g | net carbs: 3g | fiber: 1g

Pork Shoulder and Sauerkraut Casserole
Prep time: 15 minutes | Cook time: 9 to 10 hours | Serves 6

3 tablespoons extra-virgin olive oil, divided
2 tablespoons butter
2 pounds (907 g) pork shoulder roast

1 (28-ounce / 794-g) jar sauerkraut, drained
1 cup chicken broth
½ sweet onion, thinly sliced
¼ cup granulated erythritol

Lightly grease the insert of the slow cooker with 1 tablespoon of the olive oil. In a large skillet over medium-high heat, heat the remaining 2 tablespoons of the olive oil and the butter. Add the pork to the skillet and brown on all sides for about 10 minutes. Transfer to the insert and add the sauerkraut, broth, onion, and erythritol. Cover and cook on low for 9 to 10 hours. Serve warm.

calories: 516 | fat: 42g | protein: 28g | carbs: 7g | net carbs: 3g | fiber: 4g

Classic Carnitas

Prep time: 15 minutes | Cook time: 9 to 10 hours | Serves 8

3 tablespoons extra-virgin olive oil, divided
2 pounds pork shoulder, cut into 2-inch cubes
2 cups diced tomatoes
2 cups chicken broth
½ sweet onion, chopped
2 fresh chipotle peppers, chopped

Juice of 1 lime
1 teaspoon ground coriander
1 teaspoon ground cumin
½ teaspoon salt
1 avocado, peeled, pitted, and diced, for garnish
1 cup sour cream, for garnish
2 tablespoons chopped cilantro, for garnish

Lightly grease the insert of the slow cooker with 1 tablespoon of the olive oil. In a large skillet over medium-high heat, heat the remaining 2 tablespoons of the olive oil. Add the pork and brown on all sides for about 10 minutes. Transfer to the insert and add the tomatoes, broth, onion, peppers, lime juice, coriander, cumin, and salt. Cover and cook on low for 9 to 10 hours. Shred the cooked pork with a fork and stir the meat into the sauce. Serve topped with the avocado, sour cream, and cilantro.

calories: 508 | fat: 41g | protein: 29g | carbs: 7g | net carbs: 4g | fiber: 3g

Rosemary Lamb Chops

Prep time: 15 minutes | Cook time: 6 hours | Serves 4

3 tablespoons extra-virgin olive oil, divided
1½ pounds (1.1 kg) lamb shoulder chops
Salt, for seasoning
Freshly ground black pepper,

for seasoning
½ cup chicken broth
1 sweet onion, sliced
2 teaspoons minced garlic
2 teaspoons dried rosemary
1 teaspoon dried thyme

Lightly grease the insert of the slow cooker with 1 tablespoon of the olive oil. In a large skillet over medium-high heat, heat the remaining 2 tablespoons of the olive oil. Season the lamb with salt and pepper. Add the lamb to the skillet and brown for 6 minutes, turning once. Transfer the lamb to the insert, and add the broth, onion, garlic, rosemary, and thyme. Cover and cook on low for 6 hours. Serve warm.

calories: 380| fat: 27g | protein: 31g | carbs: 3g | net carbs: 2g | fiber: 1g

Pork Patties with Caramelized Onion Rings

Prep time: 10 minutes | Cook time: 10 minutes | Serves 6

2 pound (907 g) ground pork
Pink salt and chili pepper to taste
1 tablespoon olive oil
1 tablespoon butter
1 white onion, sliced into rings

1 tablespoon balsamic vinegar
3 drops liquid stevia
6 low carb burger buns, halved
2 firm tomatoes, sliced into rings

Combine the pork, salt and chili pepper in a bowl and mold out 6 patties. Heat the olive oil in a skillet over medium heat and fry the patties for 4 to 5 minutes on each side until golden brown on the outside. Remove onto a plate and sit for 3 minutes. Melt butter in a skillet over medium heat, sauté onions for 2 minutes, and stir in the balsamic vinegar and liquid stevia. Cook for 30 seconds stirring once or twice until caramelized. In each bun, place a patty, top with some onion rings and 2 tomato rings. Serve the burgers with cheddar cheese dip.

calories: 490 | fat: 35g | protein: 35g | carbs: 7g | net carbs: 7g | fiber: 0g

Stewed Pork and Veggies

Prep time: 15 minutes | Cook time: 30 minutes | Serves 4

1 tablespoon olive oil
1 red bell pepper, chopped
1 pound (454 g)stewed pork, cubed
Salt and black pepper, to taste
2 cups cauliflower florets
2 cups broccoli florets

1 onion, chopped
14 ounces (397 g) canned diced tomatoes
¼ teaspoon garlic powder
1 tablespoon tomato puree
1½ cups water
1 tablespoon parsley, chopped

In a pan, heat olive oil and cook the pork over medium heat for 5 minutes, until browned. Place in the bell pepper, and onion, and cook for 4 minutes. Stir in the water, tomatoes, broccoli, cauliflower, tomato purée, and garlic powder; bring to a simmer and cook for 20minutes while covered. Adjust the seasoning and serve sprinkled with parsley.

calories: 299 | fat: 13g | protein: 35g | carbs: 10g | net carbs: 6g | fiber: 4g

Baked Pork Sausage and Bell Pepper

Prep time: 10 minutes | Cook time: 45 minutes | Serves 4

12 pork sausages
5 large tomatoes, cut in rings
1 red bell pepper, seeded and sliced
1 yellow bell pepper, seeded and sliced
1 green bell pepper, seeded

and sliced
1 sprig thyme, chopped
1 sprig rosemary, chopped
4 cloves garlic, minced
2 bay leaves
1 tablespoon olive oil
1 tablespoon balsamic vinegar

Preheat the oven to 350ºF (180ºC). In the cast iron pan, add the tomatoes, bell peppers, thyme, rosemary, garlic, bay leaves, olive oil, and balsamic vinegar. Toss everything and arrange the sausages on top of the veggies. Put the pan in the oven and bake for 20 minutes. After, remove the pan shake it a bit and turn the sausages over with a spoon. Continue cooking for 25 minutes or until the sausages have browned to your desired color. Serve with the veggie and cooking sauce with cauli rice.

calories: 465 | fat: 41g | protein: 15g | carbs: 8g | net carbs: 4g | fiber: 4g

Pork Chops with Blackberry Gravy

Prep time: 10 minutes | Cook time: 10 minutes | Serves 4

1 tablespoon olive oil
1 pound (454 g) pork chops
Salt and black pepper to taste
1 cup blackberries
1 tablespoon chicken broth

½ tablespoon rosemary leaves, chopped
1 tablespoon balsamic vinegar
1 teaspoon Worcestershire sauce

Place the blackberries in a bowl and mash them with a fork until jam-like. Pour into a saucepan, add the chicken broth and rosemary. Bring to boil on low heat for 4 minutes. Stir in balsamic vinegar and Worcestershire sauce. Simmer for 1 minute. Heat oil in a skillet over medium heat, season the pork with salt and black pepper, and cook for 5 minutes on each side. Put on serving plates and spoon sauce over the pork chops.

calories: 302 | fat: 18g | protein: 28g | carbs: 4g | net carbs: 2g | fiber: 2g

Lemony Pork Loin and Brussels Sprouts

Prep time: 10 minutes | Cook time: 1¼ hours | Serves 4

½ pound (227 g) Brussels sprouts, chopped
1 tablespoon olive oil
Salt and black pepper, to taste
1½ pounds (680 g) pork loin
A pinch of dry mustard

1 teaspoon hot red pepper flakes
½ teaspoon ginger, minced
2 garlic cloves, minced
½ lemon sliced
¼ cup water

Preheat oven to 380ºF (193ºC). In a bowl, combine the ginger with salt, mustard, and black pepper. Add in meat, toss to coat. Heat the oil in a saucepan over medium heat, brown the pork on all sides, for 8 minutes. Transfer to the oven and roast for 1 hour. To the saucepan, add Brussels sprouts, lemon slices, garlic, and water; cook for 10 minutes. Serve on a platter, sprinkled with pan juices on top.

calories: 418 | fat: 22g | protein: 45g | carbs: 7g | net carbs: 4g | fiber: 3g

Pork Chops and Bacon

Prep time: 5 minutes | Cook time: 11 minutes | Serves 6

7 strips bacon, chopped
6 pork chops
Pink salt and black pepper to taste

5 sprigs fresh thyme
¼ cup chicken broth
½ cup heavy cream

Cook bacon in a large skillet over medium heat for 5 minutes to crispy. Remove with a slotted spoon onto a paper towel-lined plate to soak up excess fat. Season pork chops with salt and black pepper, and brown in the bacon grease for 4 minutes on each side. Remove to the bacon plate. Stir the thyme, chicken broth, and heavy cream in the same skillet, and simmer for 5 minutes. Season with salt and black pepper. Put the chops and bacon in the skillet, and cook further for another 2 minutes. Serve chops and a generous ladle of sauce with cauli mash.

calories: 435 | fat: 37g | protein: 22g | carbs: 4g | net carbs: 3g | fiber: 1g

Chapter 8 Beef and Lamb

Texas Chili

Prep time: 20 minutes | Cook time: 7 to 8 hours | Serves 4

¼ cup extra-virgin olive oil
1½ pounds (680 g) beef sirloin, cut into 1-inch chunks
1 sweet onion, chopped
2 green bell peppers, chopped
1 jalapeño pepper, seeded, finely chopped
2 teaspoons minced garlic
1 (28-ounce / 794-g) can diced

tomatoes
1 cup beef broth
3 tablespoons chili powder
½ teaspoon ground cumin
¼ teaspoon ground coriander
1 cup sour cream, for garnish
1 avocado, diced, for garnish
1 tablespoon cilantro, chopped, for garnish

Lightly grease the insert of the slow cooker with 1 tablespoon of the olive oil. In a large skillet over medium-high heat, heat the remaining 2 tablespoons of the olive oil. Add the beef and sauté until it is cooked through, about 8 minutes. Add the onion, bell peppers, jalapeño pepper, and garlic, and sauté for an additional 4 minutes. Transfer the beef mixture to the insert and stir in the tomatoes, broth, chili powder, cumin, and coriander. Cover and cook on low for 7 to 8 hours. Serve topped with the sour cream, avocado, and cilantro.

calories: 488 | fat: 38.1g | protein: 25.9g | carbs: 17.1g | net carbs: 10.2g | fiber: 6.9g

Simple Pesto Beef Chuck Roast

Prep time: 5 minutes | Cook time: 9 to 10 hours | Serves 8

1 tablespoon extra-virgin olive oil
2 pounds (907 g) beef chuck

roast
¾ cup prepared pesto
½ cup beef broth

Lightly grease the insert of the slow cooker with the olive oil. Slather the pesto all over the beef. Place the beef in the insert and pour in the broth. Cover and cook on low for 9 to 10 hours. Serve warm.

calories: 529 | fat: 42.9g | protein: 31.9g | carbs: 1.9g | net carbs: 1.9g | fiber: 0g

Chipotle Beef Spare Ribs

Prep time: 15 minutes | Cook time: 50 minutes | Serves 4

2 tablespoons erythritol
Pink salt and black pepper to taste
1 tablespoon olive oil
3 teaspoons chipotle powder

1 teaspoon garlic powder
1 pound (454 g) beef spare ribs
4 tablespoons sugar-free BBQ sauce plus extra for serving

Mix the erythritol, salt, pepper, oil, chipotle, and garlic powder. Brush on the meaty sides of the ribs and wrap in foil. Sit for 30 minutes to marinate. Preheat oven to 400°F (205°C), place wrapped ribs on a baking sheet, and cook for 40 minutes to be cooked through. Remove ribs and aluminium foil, brush with BBQ sauce, and brown under the broiler for 10 minutes on both sides. Slice and serve with extra BBQ sauce and lettuce tomato salad.

calories: 396 | fat: 32.8g | protein: 20.9g | carbs: 3.7g | net carbs: 3.0g | fiber: 0.7g

Beef and Mushrooms in Red Wine

Prep time: 15 minutes | Cook time: 10 minutes | Serves 4

3 tablespoons olive oil
1 tablespoon parsley, chopped
1 cup red wine
1 teaspoon dried thyme
Salt and black pepper, to taste
1 bay leaf
1 cup beef stock
1 pound (454 g) stewed beef,

cubed
12 pearl onions, halved
1 tomato, chopped
2 ounces (57 g) pancetta, chopped
2 garlic cloves, minced
½ pound (227 g) mushrooms, chopped

Heat a pan over high heat, stir in the pancetta and beef and cook until lightly browned; set aside. Place in the onions, mushrooms, and garlic, and cook for 5 minutes. Pour in the wine to deglaze the bottom of the pan and add beef stock, bay leaf, and tomato. Season with salt, black pepper and thyme. Return the meat and pancetta, cover and cook for 50 minutes. Serve sprinkled with parsley.

calories: 468 | fat: 22g | protein: 46g | carbs: 23g | net carbs: 18g | fiber: 5g

Grilled Lamb Kebabs

Prep time: 5 minutes | Cook time: 10 minutes | Serves 4

1 pound (454 g) ground lamb
¼ teaspoon cinnamon
1 egg

1 onion, grated
Salt and ground black pepper, to taste

Place all ingredients in a bowl. Mix with your hands to combine well. Divide the meat into 4 pieces. Shape all meat portions around previously-soaked skewers. Preheat grill to medium and grill the kebabs for about 5 minutes per side.

calories: 246 | fat: 15g | protein: 25g | carbs: 3g | net carbs: 2g | fiber: 1g

Basil Lamb Shoulder with Pine Nuts

Prep time: 10 minutes | Cook time: 50 minutes | Serves 4

1 pound (454 g) rolled lamb shoulder, boneless
1½ cups basil leaves, chopped
5 tablespoons pine nuts, chopped

½ cup green olives, pitted and chopped
3 cloves garlic, minced
Salt and black pepper, to taste

Preheat the oven to 450°F. In a bowl, combine the basil, pine nuts, olives, and garlic. Season with salt and pepper. Untie the lamb flat onto a chopping board, spread the basil mixture all over, and rub the spices onto the meat. Roll the lamb over the spice mixture and tie it together using 3 to 4 strings of butcher's twine. Place the lamb onto a baking dish and cook in the oven for 10 minutes. Reduce the heat to 350°F and continue cooking for 40 minutes. When ready, transfer the meat to a cleaned chopping board; let it rest for 10 minutes before slicing. Serve with roasted root vegetables.

calories: 391 | fat: 33g | protein: 21g | carbs: 3g | net carbs: 2g | fiber: 1g

Balsamic Mushroom Beef Meatloaf

Prep time: 15 minutes | Cook time: 1 hour 5 minutes | Serves 12

Meatloaf:

3 pounds (1.4 kg) ground beef	pepper
½ cup chopped onions	2 tablespoons chopped parsley
½ cup almond flour	¼ cup chopped bell peppers
2 garlic cloves, minced	⅓ cup grated Parmesan cheese
1 cup sliced mushrooms	1 teaspoon balsamic vinegar
3 eggs	1 teaspoon salt
¼ teaspoon ground black	

Glaze:

2 cups balsamic vinegar	2 tablespoons sugar-free ketchup
1 tablespoon Swerve	

Combine all meatloaf ingredients in a large bowl. Press this mixture into 2 greased loaf pans. Bake at 370ºF (188ºC) for about 30 minutes. Meanwhile, make the glaze by combining all ingredients in a saucepan over medium heat. Simmer for 20 minutes, until the glaze is thickened. Pour ¼ cup of the glaze over the meatloaf. Save the extra for future use. Put the meatloaf back in the oven and cook for 20 more minutes.

calories: 295 | fat: 18.9g | protein: 23.1g | carbs: 6.5g | net carbs: 6.1g | fiber: 0.4g

Simple Beef Burgers

Prep time: 15 minutes | Cook time: 20 minutes | Serves 6

2 pounds (907 g) ground beef	1 tablespoon chopped parsley
1 tablespoon onion flakes	1 tablespoon Worcestershire sauce
¾ cup almond flour	
¼ cup beef broth	

Combine all ingredients in a bowl. Mix well with your hands and make 6 patties out of the mixture. Arrange on a lined baking sheet. Bake at 370ºF (188ºC), for about 18 minutes, until nice and crispy.

calories: 355 | fat: 28.1g | protein: 27.1g | carbs: 3.2g | net carbs: 2.6g | fiber: 0.6g

Italian Veal Cutlets with Pecorino

Prep time: 15 minutes | Cook time: 1 hour 5 minutes | Serves 6

6 veal cutlets	A pinch of garlic salt
½ cup Pecorino cheese, grated	2 tablespoons butter
6 provolone cheese slices	2 tablespoons coconut oil, melted
Salt and black pepper, to taste	1 teaspoon Italian seasoning
4 cups tomato sauce	

Season the veal cutlets with garlic salt, black pepper, and salt. Set a pan over medium heat and warm oil and butter, place in the veal, and cook until browned on all sides. Spread half of the tomato sauce on the bottom of a baking dish that is coated with some cooking spray. Place in the veal cutlets then spread with Italian seasoning and sprinkle over the remaining sauce. Set in the oven at 360ºF (182ºC), and bake for 40 minutes. Scatter with the provolone cheese, then sprinkle with Pecorino cheese, and bake for another 5 minutes until the cheese is golden and melted. Serve.

calories: 363 | fat: 21.1g | protein: 26.1g | carbs: 8.4g | net carbs: 5.9g | fiber: 2.5g

Beef and Pimiento in Zucchini Boats

Prep time: 10 minutes | Cook time: 25 minutes | Serves 4

4 zucchinis	pimiento
2 tablespoons olive oil	Pink salt and black pepper to taste
1½ pounds (680 g) ground beef	1 cup grated yellow Cheddar cheese
1 medium red onion, chopped	
2 tablespoons chopped	

Preheat oven to 350ºF (180ºC). Lay the zucchinis on a flat surface, trim off the ends and cut in half lengthwise. Scoop out the pulp from each half with a spoon to make shells. Chop the pulp. Heat oil in a skillet; add the ground beef, red onion, pimiento, and zucchini pulp, and season with salt and black pepper. Cook for 6 minutes while stirring to break up lumps until beef is no longer pink. Turn the heat off. Spoon the beef into the boats and sprinkle with Cheddar cheese. Place on a greased baking sheet and cook to melt the cheese for 15 minutes until zucchini boats are tender. Take out, cool for 2 minutes, and serve warm with a mixed green salad.

calories: 334 | fat: 24.0g | protein: 17.9g | carbs: 7.6g | net carbs: 6.9g | fiber: 0.7g

Pinwheel Beef and Spinach Steaks

Prep time: 10 minutes | Cook time: 35 minutes | Serves 6

1½ pounds (680 g) beef flank steak	½ loose cup baby spinach
Salt and black pepper to taste	1 jalapeño pepper, chopped
1 cup crumbled Feta cheese	¼ cup chopped basil leaves

Preheat oven to 400ºF (205ºC) and grease a baking sheet with cooking spray. Wrap the steak in plastic wrap, place on a flat surface, and gently run a rolling pin over to flatten. Take off the wraps. Sprinkle with half of the Feta cheese, top with spinach, jalapeño, basil leaves, and the remaining cheese. Roll the steak over on the stuffing and secure with toothpicks. Place in the baking sheet and cook for 30 minutes, flipping once until nicely browned on the outside and the cheese melted within. Cool for 3 minutes, slice into pinwheels and serve with sautéed veggies.

calories: 491 | fat: 41.0g | protein: 28.0g | carbs: 2.1g | net carbs: 2.0g | fiber: 0.1g

Lemony Beef Rib Roast

Prep time: 15 minutes | Cook time: 35 minutes | Serves 6

5 pounds (2.3 kg) beef rib roast, on the bone	2 lemons, zested and juiced
3 heads garlic, cut in half	3 tablespoons mustard seeds
3 tablespoons olive oil	3 tablespoons Swerve
6 shallots, peeled and halved	Salt and black pepper to taste
	3 tablespoons thyme leaves

Preheat oven to 450ºF (235ºC). Place garlic heads and shallots in a roasting dish, toss with olive oil, and bake for 15 minutes. Pour lemon juice on them. Score shallow crisscrosses patterns on the meat and set aside. Mix Swerve, mustard seeds, thyme, salt, pepper, and lemon zest to make a rub; and apply it all over the beef. Place the beef on the shallots and garlic; cook in the oven for 15 minutes. Reduce the heat to 400ºF (205ºC), cover the dish with foil, and continue cooking for 5 minutes. Once ready, remove the dish, and let sit covered for 15 minutes before slicing.

calories: 555 | fat: 38.5g | protein: 58.3g | carbs: 7.7g | net carbs: 2.4g | fiber: 5.3g

Beef Tripe with Onions and Tomatoes

Prep time: 10 minutes | Cook time: 25 minutes | Serves 6

1½ pounds (680 g) beef tripe
4 cups buttermilk
Salt to taste
2 teaspoons creole seasoning

3 tablespoons olive oil
2 large onions, sliced
3 tomatoes, diced

Put the tripe in a bowl and cover with buttermilk. Refrigerate for 3 hours to extract bitterness and gamey taste. Remove from buttermilk, pat dry with a paper towel, and season with salt and creole seasoning. Heat 2 tablespoons of oil in a skillet over medium heat and brown the tripe on both sides for 6 minutes in total. Set aside. Add the remaining oil and sauté the onions for 3 minutes until soft. Include the tomatoes and cook for 10 minutes. Pour in a few tablespoons of water if necessary. Put the tripe in the sauce and cook for 3 minutes. Adjust taste with salt and serve with low carb rice.

calories: 341 | fat: 26.9g | protein: 21.9g | carbs: 2.7g | net carbs: 1.0g | fiber: 1.7g

Cauliflower and Tomato Beef Curry

Prep time: 10 minutes | Cook time: 21 minutes | Serves 6

1 tablespoon olive oil
1½ pounds (680 g) ground beef
1 tablespoon ginger-garlic paste
1 teaspoon garam masala
1 (7-ounce / 198-g) can whole

tomatoes
1 head cauliflower, cut into florets
Pink salt and chili pepper to taste
¼ cup water

Heat oil in a saucepan over medium heat, add the beef, ginger-garlic paste and season with garam masala. Cook for 5 minutes while breaking any lumps. Stir in the tomatoes and cauliflower, season with salt and chili pepper, and cook covered for 6 minutes. Add the water and bring to a boil over medium heat for 10 minutes or until the water has reduced by half. Adjust taste with salt. Spoon the curry into serving bowls and serve with shirataki rice.

calories: 373 | fat: 32.8g | protein: 21.9g | carbs: 4.0g | net carbs: 2.2g | fiber: 2.8g

Lamb Roast with Tomatoes

Prep time: 10 minutes | Cook time: 7 to 8 hours | Serves 6

1 tablespoon extra-virgin olive oil
2 pounds (907 g) lamb shoulder roast
Salt, for seasoning
Freshly ground black pepper, for seasoning
1 (14.5-ounce / 411-g) can

diced tomatoes
1 tablespoon cumin
2 teaspoons minced garlic
1 teaspoon paprika
1 teaspoon chili powder
1 cup sour cream
2 teaspoons chopped fresh parsley, for garnish

Lightly grease the insert of the slow cooker with the olive oil. Lightly season the lamb with salt and pepper. Place the lamb in the insert and add the tomatoes, cumin, garlic, paprika, and chili powder. Cover and cook on low for 7 to 8 hours. Stir in the sour cream. Serve topped with the parsley.

calories: 524 | fat: 43.1g | protein: 27.9g | carbs: 5.9g | net carbs: 4.9g | fiber: 1.0g

Zucchini and Beef Lasagna

Prep time: 15 minutes | Cook time: 45 minutes | Serves 4

1 pound (454 g) ground beef
2 large zucchinis, sliced lengthwise
3 cloves garlic
1 medium white onion, finely chopped
3 tomatoes, chopped
Salt and black pepper to taste

2 teaspoons sweet paprika
1 teaspoon dried thyme
1 teaspoon dried basil
1 cup shredded Mozzarella cheese
1 tablespoon olive oil
Cooking spray

Preheat the oven to 370ºF (188ºC) and lightly grease a baking dish with cooking spray. Heat the olive oil in a skillet and cook the beef for 4 minutes while breaking any lumps as you stir. Top with onion, garlic, tomatoes, salt, paprika, and pepper. Stir and continue cooking for 5 minutes. Then, lay ⅓ of the zucchini slices in the baking dish. Top with ⅓ of the beef mixture and repeat the layering process two more times with the same quantities. Season with basil and thyme. Finally, sprinkle the Mozzarella cheese on top and tuck the baking dish in the oven. Bake for 35 minutes. Remove the lasagna and let it rest for 10 minutes before serving.

calories: 346 | fat: 17.9g | protein: 40.2g | carbs: 5.5g | net carbs: 2.8g | fiber: 2.7g

Double Cheese Stuffed Venison

Prep time: 10 minutes | Cook time: 25 minutes | Serves 8

2 pounds (907 g) venison tenderloin
2 garlic cloves, minced
2 tablespoons chopped almonds

½ cup Gorgonzola cheese
½ cup Feta cheese
1 teaspoon chopped onion
½ teaspoon salt

Preheat your grill to medium. Slice the tenderloin lengthwise to make a pocket for the filling. Combine the rest of the ingredients in a bowl. Stuff the tenderloin with the filling. Shut the meat with skewers and grill for as long as it takes to reach your desired density.

calories: 196 | fat: 11.9g | protein: 25.1g | carbs: 2.1g | net carbs: 1.6g | fiber: 0.5g

Beef and Veggie Stuffed Butternut Squash

Prep time: 15 minutes | Cook time: 60 minutes | Serves 4

2 pounds (907 g) butternut squash, pricked with a fork
Salt and black pepper, to taste
3 garlic cloves, minced
1 onion, chopped
1 button mushroom, sliced
28 ounces (794 g) canned

diced tomatoes
1 teaspoon dried oregano
¼ teaspoon cayenne pepper
½ teaspoon dried thyme
1 pound (454 g) ground beef
1 green bell pepper, chopped

Lay the butternut squash on a lined baking sheet, set in the oven at 400ºF (205ºC), and bake for 40 minutes. After, cut in half, set aside to let cool, deseed, scoop out most of the flesh and let sit. Heat a greased pan over medium heat, add in the garlic, mushrooms, onion, and beef, and cook until the meat browns. Stir in the green pepper, salt, thyme, tomatoes, oregano, black pepper, and cayenne, and cook for 10 minutes; stir in the flesh. Stuff the squash halves with the beef mixture, and bake in the oven for 10 minutes. Split into plates and enjoy.

calories: 405 | fat: 14.5g | protein: 33.8g | carbs: 20.7g | net carbs: 12.3g | fiber: 8.4g

Beef and Broccoli Casserole

Prep time: 15 minutes | Cook time: 4 hours | Serves 6

1 tablespoon olive oil	diced tomatoes
2 pounds (907 g) ground beef	2 cups Mozzarella cheese,
1 head broccoli, cut into florets	grated
Salt and black pepper, to taste	16 ounces (454 g) tomato
2 teaspoons mustard	sauce
2 teaspoons Worcestershire	2 tablespoons fresh parsley,
sauce	chopped
28 ounces (794 g) canned	1 teaspoon dried oregano

Apply black pepper and salt to the broccoli florets, set them into a bowl, drizzle over the olive oil, and toss well to coat completely. In a separate bowl, combine the beef with Worcestershire sauce, salt, mustard, and black pepper, and stir well. Press on the slow cooker's bottom. Scatter in the broccoli, add the tomatoes, parsley, Mozzarella, oregano, and tomato sauce. Cook for 4 hours on low; covered. Split the casserole among bowls and enjoy while hot.

calories: 435 | fat: 21.1g | protein: 50.9g | carbs: 13.5g | net carbs: 5.5g | fiber: 8.0g

Pork Rind Crusted Beef Meatballs

Prep time: 10 minutes | Cook time: 40 minutes | Serves 5

½ cup pork rinds, crushed	1 tablespoon almond flour
1 egg	¼ cup free-sugar ketchup
Salt and black pepper, to taste	3 teaspoons Worcestershire
1½ pounds (680 g) ground	sauce
beef	½ teaspoon dry mustard
10 ounces (283 g) canned	¼ cup water
onion soup	

In a bowl, combine ⅓ cup of the onion soup with the beef, pepper, pork rinds, egg, and salt. Heat a pan over medium heat, shape the mixture into 12 meatballs. Brown in the pan for 12 minutes on both sides. In a separate bowl, combine the rest of the soup with the almond flour, dry mustard, ketchup, Worcestershire sauce, and water. Pour this over the beef meatballs, cover the pan, and cook for 20 minutes as you stir occasionally. Split among serving bowls and serve.

calories: 333 | fat: 18.1g | protein: 24.9g | carbs: 7.4g | net carbs: 6.9g | fiber: 0.5g

Beef and Fennel Provençal

Prep time: 10 minutes | Cook time: 45 minutes | Serves 4

12 ounces (340 g) beef steak	3 tablespoons olive oil
racks	½ cup apple cider vinegar
2 fennel bulbs, sliced	1 teaspoon herbs de Provence
Salt and black pepper, to taste	1 tablespoon Swerve

In a bowl, mix the fennel with 2 tablespoons of oil, Swerve, and vinegar, toss to coat well, and set to a baking dish. Season with herbs de Provence, pepper and salt, and cook in the oven at 400°F (205°C) for 15 minutes. Sprinkle black pepper and salt to the beef, place into an oiled pan over medium heat, and cook for a couple of minutes. Place the beef to the baking dish with the fennel, and bake for 20 minutes. Split everything among plates and enjoy.

calories: 231 | fat: 11.4g | protein: 19.1g | carbs: 8.7g | net carbs: 5.1g | fiber: 3.6g

Onion Sauced Beef Meatballs

Prep time: 15 minutes | Cook time: 30 minutes | Serves 5

2 pounds (907 g) ground beef	1 tablespoon fresh parsley,
Salt and black pepper, to taste	chopped
½ teaspoon garlic powder	1 tablespoon dried onion flakes
1¼ tablespoons coconut	1 onion, sliced
aminos	2 tablespoons butter
1 cup beef stock	¼ cup sour cream
¾ cup almond flour	

In a bowl, combine the beef with salt, garlic powder, almond flour, onion flakes, parsley, 1 tablespoon coconut aminos, black pepper, ¼ cup of beef stock. Form 6 patties, place them on a baking sheet, put in the oven at 370°F (188°C), and bake for 18 minutes. Set a pan with the butter over medium heat, stir in the onion, and cook for 3 minutes. Stir in the remaining beef stock, sour cream, and remaining coconut aminos, and bring to a simmer. Remove from heat, adjust the seasonings. Serve the meatballs topped with onion sauce.

calories: 434 | fat: 22.9g | protein: 32.1g | carbs: 6.9g | net carbs: 6.1g | fiber: 0.8g

Spicy Beef Brisket Roast

Prep time: 15 minutes | Cook time: 60 minutes | Serves 4

2 pounds (907 g) beef brisket	A pinch of cayenne pepper
½ teaspoon celery salt	½ teaspoon garlic powder
1 teaspoon chili powder	½ cup beef stock
1 tablespoon avocado oil	1 tablespoon garlic, minced
1 tablespoon sweet paprika	¼ teaspoon dry mustard

Preheat oven to 340°F (171°C). In a bowl, combine the paprika with dry mustard, chili powder, salt, garlic powder, cayenne pepper, and celery salt. Rub the meat with this mixture. Set a pan over medium heat and warm avocado oil, place in the beef, and sear until brown. Remove to a baking dish. Pour in the stock, add garlic and bake for 60 minutes. Set the beef to a cutting board, leave to cool before slicing and splitting in serving plates. Take the juices from the baking dish and strain, sprinkle over the meat, and enjoy.

calories: 481 | fat: 23.6g | protein: 54.8g | carbs: 4.2g | net carbs: 3.3g | fiber: 0.9g

Lemon-Mint Grilled Lamb Chops

Prep time: 10 minutes | Cook time: 6 minutes | Serves 4

8 lamb chops	mix
2 tablespoons favorite spice	2 tablespoons olive oil
Sauce:	
¼ cup olive oil	3 garlic cloves, pressed
1 teaspoon red pepper flakes	2 tablespoons lemon zest
2 tablespoons lemon juice	¼ cup parsley
2 tablespoons fresh mint	½ teaspoon smoked paprika

Rub lamb with olive oil and sprinkle with the seasoning. Preheat the grill to medium. Grill the lamb chops for about 3 minutes per side. Whisk together the sauce ingredients. Serve the lamb with sauce.

calories: 488 | fat: 31g | protein: 49g | carbs: 5g | net carbs: 3g | fiber: 2g

Mexican Beef and Tomato Chili

Prep time: 20 minutes | Cook time: 40 minutes | Serves 4

1 onion, chopped
2 tablespoons olive oil
2 pounds (907 g) ground beef
15 ounces (425 g) canned tomatoes with green chilies, chopped
3 ounces (85 g) tomato paste
½ cup pickled jalapeños, chopped
1 teaspoon chipotle chili paste

4 tablespoons garlic, minced
3 celery stalks, chopped
2 tablespoons coconut aminos
Salt and black pepper, to taste
A pinch of cayenne pepper
2 tablespoons cumin
1 teaspoon onion powder
1 teaspoon garlic powder
1 bay leaf
1 teaspoon chopped cilantro

Heat oil in a pan over medium heat, add in the onion, celery, garlic, beef, black pepper, and salt; cook until the meat browns. Stir in jalapeños, tomato paste, canned tomatoes with green chilies, salt, garlic powder, bay leaf, onion powder, cayenne, coconut aminos, chipotle chili paste, and cumin, and cook for 30 minutes while covered. Remove and discard bay leaf. Serve in bowls sprinkled with cilantro.

calories: 435 | fat: 25.9g | protein: 16.9g | carbs: 7.9g | net carbs: 5.1g | fiber: 2.8g

Russian Beef and Dill Pickle Gratin

Prep time: 15 minutes | Cook time: 40 minutes | Serves 5

2 teaspoons onion flakes
2 pounds (907 g) ground beef
2 garlic cloves, minced
Salt and black pepper, to taste
1 cup Mozzarella cheese, shredded
2 cups Fontina cheese,

shredded
1 cup Russian dressing
2 tablespoons sesame seeds, toasted
20 dill pickle slices
1 iceberg lettuce head, torn

Set a pan over medium heat, place in beef, garlic, salt, onion flakes, and pepper, and cook for 5 minutes. Remove to a baking dish, stir in Russian dressing, Mozzarella, and spread 1 cup of the Fontina cheese. Lay the pickle slices on top, spread over the remaining Fontina cheese and sesame seeds, place in the oven at 350ºF (180ºC), and bake for 20 minutes. Arrange the lettuce on a serving platter and top with the gratin.

calories: 585 | fat: 48.1g | protein: 40.9g | carbs: 8.5g | net carbs: 5.2g | fiber: 3.3g

Braised Beef Short Ribs with Sweet Onion

Prep time: 10 minutes | Cook time: 7 to 8 hours | Serves 8

1 tablespoon extra-virgin olive oil
2 pounds (907 g) beef short ribs
1 sweet onion, sliced
2 cups beef broth

2 tablespoons granulated erythritol
2 tablespoons balsamic vinegar
2 teaspoons dried thyme
1 teaspoon hot sauce

Lightly grease the insert of the slow cooker with the olive oil. Place the ribs, onion, broth, erythritol, balsamic vinegar, thyme, and hot sauce in the insert. Cover and cook on low for 7 to 8 hours. Serve warm.

calories: 475 | fat: 42.8g | protein: 17.9g | carbs: 2.0g | net carbs: 2.0g | fiber: 0g

Beef, Pancetta, and Mushroom Bourguignon

Prep time: 15 minutes | Cook time: 60 minutes | Serves 4

3 tablespoons coconut oil
1 tablespoon dried parsley flakes
1 cup red wine
1 teaspoon dried thyme
Salt and black pepper, to taste
1 bay leaf

⅓ cup coconut flour
2 pounds (907 g) beef, cubed
12 small white onions
4 pancetta slices, chopped
2 garlic cloves, minced
½ pound (227 g) mushrooms, chopped

In a bowl, combine the wine with bay leaf, olive oil, thyme, pepper, parsley, salt, and the beef cubes; set aside for 3 hours. Drain the meat, and reserve the marinade. Toss the flour over the meat to coat. Heat a pan over medium heat, stir in the pancetta, and cook until slightly browned. Place in the onions and garlic, and cook for 3 minutes. Stir-fry in the meat and mushrooms for 4-5 minutes. Pour in the marinade and 1 cup of water; cover and cook for 50 minutes. Season to taste and serve.

calories: 434 | fat: 25.9g | protein: 44.8g | carbs: 11.5g | net carbs: 6.9g | fiber: 4.6g

Italian Sausage and Okra Stew

Prep time: 20 minutes | Cook time: 30 minutes | Serves 6

1 pound (454 g) Italian sausage, sliced
1 red bell pepper, seeded and chopped
2 onions, chopped
Salt and black pepper, to taste
1 cup fresh parsley, chopped
6 green onions, chopped
¼ cup avocado oil

1 cup beef stock
4 garlic cloves
24 ounces (680 g) canned diced tomatoes
16 ounces (454 g) okra, trimmed and sliced
6 ounces (170 g) tomato sauce
2 tablespoons coconut aminos
1 tablespoon hot sauce

Set a pot over medium heat and warm oil, place in the sausages, and cook for 2 minutes. Stir in the onions, green onions, garlic, black pepper, bell pepper, and salt, and cook for 5 minutes. Add in the hot sauce, stock, tomatoes, coconut aminos, okra, and tomato sauce, bring to a simmer and cook for 15 minutes. Adjust the seasoning with salt and black pepper. Share into serving bowls and sprinkle with fresh parsley to serve.

calories: 315 | fat: 25.1g | protein: 16.1g | carbs: 16.8g | net carbs: 6.9g | fiber: 8.9g

Garlicky Lamb Chops with Sage

Prep time: 10 minutes | Cook time: 1 hour 10 minutes | Serves 6

6 lamb chops
1 tablespoon sage
1 teaspoon thyme
1 onion, sliced
1 cup water

3 garlic cloves, minced
2 tablespoons olive oil
½ cup white wine
Salt and black pepper, to taste

Heat the olive oil in a pan. Add onions and garlic, and cook for 4 minutes, until soft. Rub the sage and thyme over the lamb chops. Cook the lamb for about 3 minutes per side. Set aside. Pour the white wine and water into the pan, bring the mixture to a boil. Cook until the liquid is reduced by half. Add the chops in the pan, reduce the heat, and let simmer for 1 hour.

calories: 215 | fat: 13g | protein: 23g | carbs: 3g | net carbs: 2g | fiber: 1g

Caribbean Beef with Peppers

Prep time: 15 minutes | Cook time: 1 hour 5 minutes | Serves 8

2 onions, chopped
2 tablespoons avocado oil
2 pounds (907 g) beef stew meat, cubed
2 red bell peppers, seeded and chopped
1 habanero pepper, chopped
4 green chilies, chopped
14.5 ounces (411 g) canned

diced tomatoes
2 tablespoons fresh cilantro, chopped
4 garlic cloves, minced
½ cup vegetable broth
Salt and black pepper, to taste
1½ teaspoons cumin
½ cup black olives, chopped
1 teaspoon dried oregano

Set a pan over medium heat and warm avocado oil. Brown the beef on all sides; remove and set aside. Stir-fry in the red bell peppers, green chilies, oregano, garlic, habanero pepper, onions, and cumin, for about 5-6 minutes. Pour in the tomatoes and broth, and cook for 1 hour. Stir in the olives, adjust the seasonings and serve in bowls sprinkled with fresh cilantro.

calories: 304 | fat: 14.1g | protein: 25.1g | carbs: 10.9g | net carbs: 7.9g | fiber: 3.0g

Bacon and Beef Stew

Prep time: 15 minutes | Cook time: 1 hour 10 minutes | Serves 6

8 ounces (227 g) bacon, chopped
4 pounds (1.8 kg) beef meat for stew, cubed
4 garlic cloves, minced
2 brown onions, chopped
2 tablespoons olive oil
4 tablespoons red vinegar

4 cups beef stock
2 tablespoons tomato purée
2 cinnamon sticks
3 lemon peel strips
½ cup fresh parsley, chopped
4 thyme sprigs
2 tablespoons butter
Salt and black pepper, to taste

Set a saucepan over medium heat and warm oil, add in the garlic, bacon, and onion, and cook for 5 minutes. Stir in the beef, and cook until slightly brown. Pour in the vinegar, black pepper, butter, lemon peel strips, stock, salt, tomato purée, cinnamon sticks and thyme; stir for 3 minutes. Cook for 1 hour while covered. Get rid of the thyme, lemon peel, and cinnamon sticks. Split into serving bowls and sprinkle with parsley to serve.

calories: 591 | fat: 36.1g | protein: 63.1g | carbs: 8.1g | net carbs: 5.6g | fiber: 2.5g

Thai Beef Steak with Mushrooms

Prep time: 15 minutes | Cook time: 25 minutes | Serves 6

1 cup beef stock
4 tablespoons butter
¼ teaspoon garlic powder
¼ teaspoon onion powder
1 tablespoon coconut aminos
1½ teaspoons lemon pepper
1 pound (454 g) beef steak, cut

into strips
Salt and black pepper, to taste
1 cup shiitake mushrooms, sliced
3 green onions, chopped
1 tablespoon thai red curry paste

Melt butter in a pan over medium heat, add in the beef, season with garlic powder, black pepper, salt, and onion powder and cook for 4 minutes. Mix in the mushrooms and stir-fry for 5 minutes. Pour in the stock, coconut aminos, lemon pepper, and thai curry paste and cook for 15 minutes. Serve sprinkled with the green onions.

calories: 225 | fat: 15.1g | protein: 18.9g | carbs: 4.1g | net carbs: 2.9g | fiber: 1.2g

Butternut Squash and Beef Stew

Prep time: 15 minutes | Cook time: 35 minutes | Serves 4

3 teaspoons olive oil
1 pound (454 g) ground beef
1 cup beef stock
14 ounces (397 g) canned tomatoes with juice
1 tablespoon stevia
1 pound (454 g) butternut squash, chopped

1 tablespoon Worcestershire sauce
2 bay leaves
Salt and black pepper, to taste
1 onion, chopped
1 teaspoon dried sage
1 tablespoon garlic, minced

Set a pan over medium heat and heat olive oil, stir in the onion, garlic, and beef, and cook for 10 minutes. Add in butternut squash, Worcestershire sauce, bay leaves, stevia, beef stock, canned tomatoes, and sage, and bring to a boil. Reduce heat, and simmer for 30 minutes. Remove and discard the bay leaves and adjust the seasonings. Split into bowls and enjoy.

calories: 342 | fat: 17.1g | protein: 31.9g | carbs: 11.6g | net carbs: 7.4g | fiber: 4.2g

Herbed Veggie and Beef Stew

Prep time: 10 minutes | Cook time: 25 minutes | Serves 4

1 pound (454 g) ground beef
2 tablespoons olive oil
1 onion, chopped
2 garlic cloves, minced
14 ounces (397 g) canned diced tomatoes
1 tablespoon dried rosemary
1 tablespoon dried sage

1 tablespoon dried oregano
1 tablespoon dried basil
1 tablespoon dried marjoram
Salt and black pepper, to taste
2 carrots, sliced
2 celery stalks, chopped
1 cup vegetable broth

Set a pan over medium heat, add in the olive oil, onion, celery, and garlic, and sauté for 5 minutes. Place in the beef, and cook for 6 minutes. Stir in the tomatoes, carrots, broth, black pepper, oregano, marjoram, basil, rosemary, salt, and sage, and simmer for 15 minutes. Serve and enjoy!

calories: 254 | fat: 13.1g | protein: 29.9g | carbs: 10.1g | net carbs: 5.1g | fiber: 5.0g

Beef Chuck Roast with Mushrooms

Prep time: 15 minutes | Cook time: 3 hours 10 minutes | Serves 6

2 pounds (907 g) beef chuck roast, cubed
2 tablespoons olive oil
14.5 ounces (411 g) canned diced tomatoes
2 carrots, chopped
Salt and black pepper, to taste
½ pound (227 g) mushrooms,

sliced
2 celery stalks, chopped
2 yellow onions, chopped
1 cup beef stock
1 tablespoon fresh thyme, chopped
½ teaspoon dry mustard
3 tablespoons almond flour

Set an ovenproof pot over medium heat, warm olive oil and brown the beef on each side for a few minutes. Stir in the tomatoes, onions, salt, pepper, mustard, carrots, mushrooms, celery, and stock. In a bowl, combine 1 cup water with flour. Place this to the pot, stir then set in the oven, and bake for 3 hours at 325ºF (163ºC) stirring at intervals of 30 minutes. Scatter the fresh thyme over and serve warm.

calories: 326 | fat: 18.1g | protein: 28.1g | carbs: 10.4g | net carbs: 6.9g | fiber: 3.5g

Veal, Mushroom, and Green Bean Stew

Prep time: 15 minutes | Cook time: 1 hour 55 minutes | Serves 6

2 tablespoons olive oil
3 pounds (1.4 kg) veal shoulder, cubed
1 onion, chopped
1 garlic clove, minced
Salt and black pepper, to taste
1 cup water

1½ cups red wine
12 ounces (340 g) canned tomato sauce
1 carrot, chopped
1 cup mushrooms, chopped
½ cup green beans
2 teaspoons dried oregano

Set a pot over medium heat and warm the oil. Brown the veal for 5-6 minutes. Stir in the onion, and garlic, and cook for 3 minutes. Place in the wine, oregano, carrot, black pepper, salt, tomato sauce, water, and mushrooms, bring to a boil, reduce the heat to low. Cook for 1 hour and 45 minutes, then add in the green beans and cook for 5 minutes. Adjust the seasoning and split among serving bowls to serve.

calories: 416 | fat: 21.1g | protein: 44.2g | carbs: 7.3g | net carbs: 5.1g | fiber: 2.2g

Veal with Ham and Sauerkraut

Prep time: 15 minutes | Cook time: 55 minutes | Serves 4

1 pound (454 g) veal, cut into cubes
18 ounces (510 g) sauerkraut, rinsed and drained
Salt and black pepper, to taste
½ cup ham, chopped

1 onion, chopped
2 garlic cloves, minced
1 tablespoon butter
½ cup Parmesan cheese, grated
½ cup sour cream

Heat a pot with the butter over medium heat, add in the onion, and cook for 3 minutes. Stir in garlic, and cook for 1 minute. Place in the veal and ham, and cook until slightly browned. Place in the sauerkraut, and cook until the meat becomes tender, about 30 minutes. Stir in sour cream, pepper, and salt. Top with Parmesan cheese and bake for 20 minutes at 350°F (180°C).

calories: 431 | fat: 26.9g | protein: 28.6g | carbs: 10.1g | net carbs: 5.9g | fiber: 4.2g

Chimichurri Skirt Steak

Prep time: 10 minutes | Cook time: 10 minutes | Serves 2

¼ cup soy sauce
½ cup olive oil
Juice of 1 lime
2 tablespoons apple cider vinegar

1 pound (454 g) skirt steak
Pink Himalayan salt
Freshly ground black pepper
2 tablespoons butter
¼ cup chimichurri sauce

In a small bowl, mix together the soy sauce, olive oil, lime juice, and apple cider vinegar. Pour into a large zip-top bag, and add the skirt steak. Marinate for as long as possible: at least all day or, ideally, overnight. Dry the steak with a paper towel. Season both sides of the steak with pink Himalayan salt and pepper. In a large skillet over high heat, melt the butter. Add the steak and sear for about 4 minutes on each side, until well browned. Transfer the steak to a chopping board to rest for at least 5 minutes. Slice the skirt steak against the grain. Divide the slices between two plates, top with the chimichurri sauce, and serve.

calories: 715 | fat: 45.8g | protein: 69.8g | carbs: 5.9g | net carbs: 4.1g | fiber: 1.8g

Coffee Rib-Eye Steaks

Prep time: 5 minutes | Cook time: 15 minutes | Serves 2

Rub:
1 tablespoon ground coffee
1 tablespoon unsweetened cocoa powder
2 teaspoons kosher salt
Balsamic Butter:
3 tablespoons butter, softened
2 tablespoons balsamic vinegar (no sugar added)
1 teaspoon granulated

¼ teaspoon cayenne pepper
2 (8-ounce / 227-g) bone-in rib-eye steaks, room temperature

erythritol
For Garnish (optional):
Chopped fresh parsley

Preheat a grill to medium heat. Combine the coffee, cocoa powder, salt, and cayenne in a small bowl. Rub the steaks generously with the coffee mixture. Grill the steaks on direct heat for 6 minutes (for medium) to 8 minutes (for medium-well) per side, or until your desired doneness is reached. Remove the steaks from the grill and let rest for 5 minutes. Meanwhile, place the butter, balsamic vinegar, and sweetener in a small bowl and mix with a fork until blended. Serve the steaks with a generous dollop of balsamic butter. Garnish with chopped parsley, if desired.

calories: 584 | fat: 44.9g | protein: 52.8g | carbs: 3.9g | net carbs: 2.9g | fiber: 1.0g

Broccoli and Beef Roast

Prep time: 10 minutes | Cook time: 4 hours 30 minutes | Serves 2

1 pound (454 g) beef chuck roast
Pink Himalayan salt
Freshly ground black pepper
½ cup beef broth, plus more if needed

¼ cup soy sauce (or coconut aminos)
1 teaspoon toasted sesame oil
1 (16-ounce / 454-g) bag frozen broccoli

With the crock insert in place, preheat the slow cooker to low. On a cutting board, season the chuck roast with pink Himalayan salt and pepper, and slice the roast thin. Put the sliced beef in the slow cooker. In a small bowl, mix together the beef broth, soy sauce, and sesame oil. Pour over the beef. Cover and cook on low for 4 hours. Add the frozen broccoli, and cook for 30 minutes more. If you need more liquid, add additional beef broth. Serve hot.

calories: 805 | fat: 48.9g | protein: 73.8g | carbs: 18.1g | net carbs: 11.9g | fiber: 6.2g

Creole Beef Tripe Stew with Onions

Prep time: 5 minutes | Cook time: 22 minutes | Serves 6

1½ pounds (680 g) beef tripe
4 cups coconut milk
Pink salt
2 teaspoons Creole seasoning

3 tablespoons olive oil
2 onions, sliced
3 tomatoes, diced

Put tripe in a bowl, and cover with coconut milk. Refrigerate for 3 hours to extract bitterness and gamey taste. Remove from coconut milk, pat dry with paper towels, and season with salt and creole seasoning. Heat 2 tablespoons of oil in a skillet over medium heat and brown the tripe on both sides for 6 minutes in total. Remove, and set aside. Add the remaining oil, and sauté onions for 3 minutes. Include the tomatoes and cook for 10 minutes. Put the tripe in the sauce, and cook for 3 minutes.

calories: 284 | fat: 16g | protein: 20g | carbs: 14g | net carbs: 12g | fiber: 2g

Barbacoa Beef with Green Jalapeño

Prep time: 10 minutes | Cook time: 8 hours | Serves 2

1 pound (454 g) beef chuck roast
Pink Himalayan salt
Freshly ground black pepper
4 chipotle peppers in adobo sauce

1 (6-ounce / 170-g) can green jalapeño chiles
2 tablespoons apple cider vinegar
½ cup beef broth

With the crock insert in place, preheat the slow cooker to low. Season the beef chuck roast on both sides with pink Himalayan salt and pepper. Put the roast in the slow cooker. In a food processor (or blender), combine the chipotle peppers and their adobo sauce, jalapeños, and apple cider vinegar, and pulse until smooth. Add the beef broth, and pulse a few more times. Pour the chile mixture over the top of the roast. Cover and cook on low for 8 hours. Transfer the beef to a cutting board, and use two forks to shred the meat. Serve hot.

calories: 720 | fat: 45.8g | protein: 65.9g | carbs: 6.9g | net carbs: 2.1g | fiber: 4.8g

Lamb Chops with Fennel and Zucchini

Prep time: 10 minutes | Cook time: 6 hours | Serves 4

¼ cup extra-virgin olive oil, divided
1 pound (454 g) boneless lamb chops, about ½-inch thick
Salt, for seasoning
Freshly ground black pepper, for seasoning
½ sweet onion, sliced

½ fennel bulb, cut into 2-inch chunks
1 zucchini, cut into 1-inch chunks
¼ cup chicken broth
2 tablespoons chopped fresh basil, for garnish

Lightly grease the insert of the slow cooker with 1 tablespoon of the olive oil. Season the lamb with salt and pepper. In a medium bowl, toss together the onion, fennel, and zucchini with the remaining 3 tablespoons of the olive oil and then place half of the vegetables in the insert. Place the lamb on top of the vegetables, cover with the remaining vegetables, and add the broth. Cover and cook on low for 6 hours. Serve topped with the basil.

calories: 430 | fat: 36.9g | protein: 20.9g | carbs: 5.0g | net carbs: 3.0g | fiber: 2.0g

Ginger Beef Chuck Roast

Prep time: 15 minutes | Cook time: 9 to 10 hours | Serves 8

¼ cup extra-virgin olive oil, divided
2 pounds (907 g) beef boneless chuck roast
½ teaspoon salt
½ cup beef broth

¼ cup paleo or low-carb ketchup
2 tablespoons apple cider vinegar
2 tablespoons grated fresh ginger

Lightly grease the insert of the slow cooker with 1 tablespoon of the olive oil. In a large skillet over medium-high heat, heat the remaining 3 tablespoons of the olive oil. Season the beef with salt. Add the beef to the skillet and brown for 6 minutes. Transfer the beef to the insert. In a small bowl, stir together the broth, ketchup, apple cider vinegar, and ginger. Add the broth mixture to the beef. Cover and cook on low for 9 to 10 hours. Serve warm.

calories: 484 | fat: 38.9g | protein: 28.8g | carbs: 4.0g | net carbs: 4.0g | fiber: 0g

Beef Chuck and Pumpkin Stew

Prep time: 15 minutes | Cook time: 8 hours | Serves 6

3 tablespoons extra-virgin olive oil, divided
1 (2-pound / 907-g) beef chuck roast, cut into 1-inch chunks
½ teaspoon salt
¼ teaspoon freshly ground black pepper
2 cups beef broth
1 cup diced tomatoes

¼ cup apple cider vinegar
1½ cups cubed pumpkin, cut into 1-inch chunks
½ sweet onion, chopped
2 teaspoons minced garlic
1 teaspoon dried thyme
1 tablespoon chopped fresh parsley, for garnish

Lightly grease the insert of the slow cooker with 1 tablespoon of the olive oil. Lightly season the beef chucks with salt and pepper. In a large skillet over medium-high heat, heat the remaining 2 tablespoons of the olive oil. Add the beef and brown on all sides, about 7 minutes. Transfer the beef to the insert and stir in the broth, tomatoes, apple cider vinegar, pumpkin, onion, garlic, and thyme. Cover and cook on low heat for about 8 hours, until the beef is very tender. Serve topped with the parsley.

calories: 460 | fat: 33.9g | protein: 32.0g | carbs: 10.2g | net carbs: 7.3g | fiber: 2.9g

Easy Balsamic Beef Chuck Roast

Prep time: 15 minutes | Cook time: 7 to 8 hours | Serves 8

3 tablespoons of extra-virgin olive oil, divided
2 pounds (907 g) boneless beef chuck roast
1 cup beef broth
½ cup balsamic vinegar

1 tablespoon minced garlic
1 tablespoon granulated erythritol
½ teaspoon red pepper flakes
1 tablespoon chopped fresh thyme

Lightly grease the insert of the slow cooker with 1 tablespoon of the olive oil. In a large skillet over medium-high heat, heat the remaining 2 tablespoons of the olive oil. Add the beef and brown on all sides, about 7 minutes total. Transfer to the insert. In a small bowl, whisk together the broth, balsamic vinegar, garlic, erythritol, red pepper flakes, and thyme until blended. Pour the sauce over the beef. Cover and cook on low for 7 to 8 hours. Serve warm.

calories: 477 | fat: 39.0g | protein: 27.8g | carbs: 1.1g | net carbs: 1.1g | fiber: 0g

Hot Beef Curry with Bok Choy

Prep time: 10 minutes | Cook time: 7 to 8 hours | Serves 6

1 tablespoon extra-virgin olive oil
1 pound (454 g) beef chuck roast, cut into 2-inch pieces
1 sweet onion, chopped
1 red bell pepper, diced
2 cups coconut milk

2 tablespoons hot curry powder
1 tablespoon coconut aminos
2 teaspoons grated fresh ginger
2 teaspoons minced garlic
1 cup shredded baby bok choy

Lightly grease the insert of the slow cooker with the olive oil. Add the beef, onion, and bell pepper to the insert. In a medium bowl, whisk together the coconut milk, curry, coconut aminos, ginger, and garlic. Pour the sauce into the insert and stir to combine. Cover and cook on low for 7 to 8 hours. Stir in the bok choy and let stand 15 minutes. Serve warm.

calories: 505 | fat: 41.8g | protein: 22.9g | carbs: 9.8g | net carbs: 6.8g | fiber: 3.0g

Lamb Shanks with Wild Mushrooms
Prep time: 15 minutes | Cook time: 7 to 8 hours | Serves 6

3 tablespoons extra-virgin olive oil, divided
2 pounds (907 g) lamb shanks
½ pound (227 g) wild mushrooms, sliced
1 leek, thoroughly cleaned and chopped
2 celery stalks, chopped
1 carrot, diced
1 tablespoon minced garlic
1 (15-ounce / 425-g) can crushed tomatoes
½ cup beef broth
2 tablespoons apple cider vinegar
1 teaspoon dried rosemary
½ cup sour cream, for garnish

Lightly grease the insert of the slow cooker with 1 tablespoon of the olive oil. In a large skillet over medium-high heat, heat the remaining 2 tablespoons of the olive oil. Add the lamb; brown for 6 minutes, turning once; and transfer to the insert. In the skillet, sauté the mushrooms, leek, celery, carrot, and garlic for 5 minutes. Transfer the vegetables to the insert along with the tomatoes, broth, apple cider vinegar, and rosemary. Cover and cook on low for 7 to 8 hours. Serve topped with the sour cream.

calories: 474 | fat: 35.9g | protein: 30.9g | carbs: 11.1g | net carbs: 5.0g | fiber: 6.1g

Ground Beef and Cauliflower Curry
Prep time: 5 minutes | Cook time: 21 minutes | Serves 6

1 tablespoon olive oil
1½ pounds (680 g) ground beef
1 tablespoon ginger-garlic paste
1 teaspoon garam masala
1 (7-ounce / 198-g) can whole
tomatoes
1 small head cauliflower, cut into florets
Pink salt and chili pepper, to taste
¼ cup water

Heat oil in a saucepan over medium heat, add in beef, ginger-garlic paste and season with garam masala. Cook for 5 minutes while breaking any lumps. Stir in tomatoes and cauliflower, season with salt and chili pepper, and cook for 6 minutes. Add the water and bring to a boil over medium heat for 10 minutes, or until the liquid has reduced by half. Adjust taste with salt. Serve with shirataki rice.

calories: 255 | fat: 17g | protein: 23g | carbs: 4g | net carbs: 2g | fiber: 2g

Asian-Flavored Beef and Broccoli
Prep time: 10 minutes | Cook time: 24 minutes | Serves 4

½ cup coconut milk
2 tablespoons coconut oil
¼ teaspoon garlic powder
¼ teaspoon onion powder
½ tablespoon coconut aminos
1 pound (454 g) beef steak, cut into strips
Salt and black pepper, to taste
1 head broccoli, cut into florets
½ tablespoon Thai green curry paste
1 teaspoon ginger paste
1 tablespoon cilantro, chopped
½ tablespoon sesame seeds

Warm coconut oil in a pan over medium heat, add in beef, season with garlic powder, pepper, salt, ginger paste, and onion powder and cook for 4 minutes. Mix in the broccoli and stir-fry for 5 minutes. Pour in the coconut milk, coconut aminos, and Thai curry paste and cook for 15 minutes. Serve sprinkled with cilantro and sesame seeds.

calories: 350 | fat: 22g | protein: 30g | carbs: 13g | net carbs: 8g | fiber: 5g

Beef and Onion Stuffed Zucchinis
Prep time: 5 minutes | Cook time: 21 minutes | Serves 4

4 zucchinis
2 tablespoons olive oil
1½ pounds (680 g) ground beef
1 medium red onion, chopped
2 tablespoons pimiento rojo,
chopped
Pink salt and black pepper, to taste
1 cup yellow Cheddar cheese, grated

Preheat oven to 350ºF (180ºC). Lay the zucchinis on a flat surface, trim off the ends, and cut in half lengthwise. Scoop out pulp from each half with a spoon to make shells. Chop the flesh. Heat oil in a skillet; add the ground beef, red onion, pimiento, and zucchini pulp, and season with salt and black pepper. Cook for 6 minutes while stirring to break up lumps until beef is no longer pink. Spoon the beef into the boats, and sprinkle with Cheddar cheese. Place on a greased baking sheet, and cook to melt the cheese for 15 minutes until zucchini boats are tender. Take out, cool for 2 minutes, and serve warm with a mixed green salad.

calories: 535 | fat: 40g | protein: 42g | carbs: 4g | net carbs: 3g | fiber: 1g

Lamb Curry
Prep time: 15 minutes | Cook time: 7 to 8 hours | Serves 6

3 tablespoons extra-virgin olive oil, divided
1½ pounds (680 g) lamb shoulder chops
Salt, for seasoning
Freshly ground black pepper, for seasoning
3 cups coconut milk
½ sweet onion, sliced
¼ cup curry powder
1 tablespoon grated fresh ginger
2 teaspoons minced garlic
1 carrot, diced
2 tablespoons chopped cilantro, for garnish

Lightly grease the insert of the slow cooker with 1 tablespoon of the olive oil. In a large skillet over medium-high heat, heat the remaining 2 tablespoons of the olive oil. Season the lamb with salt and pepper. Add the lamb to the skillet and brown for 6 minutes, turning once. Transfer to the insert. In a medium bowl, stir together the coconut milk, onion, curry, ginger, and garlic. Add the mixture to the lamb along with the carrot. Cover and cook on low for 7 to 8 hours. Serve topped with the cilantro.

calories: 491 | fat: 41.2g | protein: 25.9g | carbs: 10.1g | net carbs: 5.2g | fiber: 4.9g

King Size Beef Burgers
Prep time: 5 minutes | Cook time: 18 minutes | Serves 4

2 tablespoons olive oil
1 pound (454 g) ground beef
2 green onions, chopped
1 garlic clove, minced
1 tablespoon thyme
2 tablespoons almond flour
2 tablespoons beef broth
½ tablespoon chopped parsley
½ tablespoon Worcestershire sauce

Grease a baking dish with the olive oil. Combine all ingredients except for the parsley in a bowl. Mix well with your hands and make 2 patties out of the mixture. Arrange on a lined baking sheet. Bake at 370ºF (188ºC), for about 18 minutes, until nice and crispy. Serve sprinkled with parsley.

calories: 371 | fat: 30g | protein: 20g | carbs: 5g | net carbs: 4g | fiber: 1g

Tunisian Lamb and Pumpkin Ragout

Prep time: 15 minutes | Cook time: 8 hours | Serves 6

¼ cup extra-virgin olive oil
1½ pounds (680 g) lamb shoulder, cut into 1-inch chunks
1 sweet onion, chopped
1 tablespoon minced garlic
4 cups pumpkin, cut into 1-inch pieces

2 carrots, diced
1 (14.5-ounce / 411-g) can diced tomatoes
3 cups beef broth
2 tablespoons ras el hanout
1 teaspoon hot chili powder
1 teaspoon salt
1 cup Greek yogurt

Lightly grease the slow cooker insert with 1 tablespoon olive oil. Place a large skillet over medium–high heat and add the remaining oil. Brown the lamb for 6 minutes, then add the onion and garlic. Sauté 3 minutes more, then transfer the lamb and vegetables to the insert. Add the pumpkin, carrots, tomatoes, broth, ras el hanout, chili powder, and salt to the insert and stir to combine. Cover and cook on low for 8 hours Serve topped with yogurt.

calories: 450 | fat: 34.9g | protein: 22.1g | carbs: 11.9g | net carbs: 8.8g | fiber: 3.1g

Sauerbraten

Prep time: 15 minutes | Cook time: 9 to 10 hours | Serves 6

3 tablespoons extra-virgin olive oil, divided
2 pounds (907 g) beef brisket
Salt, for seasoning
Freshly ground black pepper, for seasoning
1 sweet onion, cut into eighths

1 carrot, cut into chunks
2 celery stalks, cut into chunks
¾ cup beef broth
½ cup german-style mustard
¼ cup apple cider vinegar
½ teaspoon ground cloves
2 bay leaves

Lightly grease the insert of the slow cooker with 1 tablespoon of the olive oil. In a large skillet over medium-high heat, heat the remaining 2 tablespoons of the olive oil. Season the beef with salt and pepper. Add the beef to the skillet and brown on all sides for 6 minutes. Place the onion, carrot, and celery in the bottom of the insert and the beef on top of the vegetables. In a small bowl, whisk together the broth, mustard, apple cider vinegar, and cloves, and add to the beef along with the bay leaves. Cover and cook on low for 9 to 10 hours. Remove the bay leaves before serving.

calories: 505 | fat: 42.1g | protein: 28.9g | carbs: 3.2g | net carbs: 2.1g | fiber: 1.0g

Zoodles with Beef Bolognese Sauce

Prep time: 10 minutes | Cook time: 25 to 27 minutes | Serves 4

2 cups zoodles
1 pound (454 g) ground beef
2 garlic cloves
1 onion, chopped
1 teaspoon oregano

1 teaspoon sage
1 teaspoon rosemary
7 ounces (198 g) canned chopped tomatoes
2 tablespoons olive oil

Cook the zoodles in warm olive oil over medium heat for 3-4 minutes and remove to a serving plate. To the same pan, add onion and garlic and cook for 3 minutes. Add beef and cook until browned, about 4-5 minutes. Stir in the herbs and tomatoes. Cook for 15 minutes and serve over the zoodles.

calories: 371 | fat: 30g | protein: 20g | carbs: 5g | net carbs: 3g | fiber: 2g

Braised Beef Chuck Roast with Tomatoes

Prep time: 15 minutes | Cook time: 7 to 8 hours | Serves 4

3 tablespoons extra-virgin olive oil, divided
1 pound (454 g) beef chuck roast, cut into 1-inch cubes
Salt, for seasoning
Freshly ground black pepper, for seasoning
1 (15-ounce / 425-g) can diced tomatoes
2 tablespoons tomato paste

2 teaspoons minced garlic
2 teaspoons dried basil
1 teaspoon dried oregano
½ teaspoon whole black peppercorns
1 cup shredded Mozzarella cheese, for garnish
2 tablespoons chopped parsley, for garnish

Lightly grease the insert of the slow cooker with 1 tablespoon of the olive oil. In a large skillet over medium-high heat, heat the remaining 2 tablespoons of the olive oil. Season the beef with salt and pepper. Add the beef to the skillet and brown for 7 minutes. Transfer the beef to the insert. In a medium bowl, stir together the tomatoes, tomato paste, garlic, basil, oregano, and peppercorns, and add the tomato mixture to the beef in the insert. Cover and cook on low for 7 to 8 hours. Serve topped with the cheese and parsley.

calories: 540 | fat: 42.9g | protein: 29.8g | carbs: 6.9g | net carbs: 4.8g | fiber: 2.1g

Beef Chuck Roast with Veggies

Prep time: 15 minutes | Cook time: 1 hour 35 minutes | Serves 4

2 tablespoons olive oil
1 pound (454 g) beef chuck roast, cubed
1 cup canned diced tomatoes
Salt and black pepper, to taste
½ pound (227 g) mushrooms, sliced
1 celery stalk, chopped

1 bell pepper, sliced
1 onion, chopped
1 bay leaf
½ cup beef stock
1 tablespoon fresh rosemary, chopped
½ teaspoon dry mustard
1 tablespoon almond flour

Preheat oven to 350ºF (180ºC). Set a pot over medium heat, warm olive oil and brown the beef on each side for 4-5 minutes. Stir in tomatoes, onion, mustard, mushrooms, bell pepper, celery, and stock. Season with salt and pepper. In a bowl, combine ½ cup of water with flour and stir in the pot. Transfer to a baking dish and bake for 90 minutes, stirring at intervals of 30 minutes. Scatter the rosemary over and serve warm.

calories: 329 | fat: 17g | protein: 34g | carbs: 8g | net carbs: 4g | fiber: 4g

Seared Ribeye Steak with Shitake Mushrooms

Prep time: 5 minutes | Cook time: 12 minutes | Serves 1

6 ounces (170 g) ribeye steak
2 tablespoons butter
1 teaspoon olive oil

½ cup shitake mushrooms, sliced
Salt and black pepper, to taste

Heat the olive oil in a pan over medium heat. Rub the steak with salt and black pepper and cook about 4 minutes per side; set aside. Melt the butter in the pan and cook the shitakes for 4 minutes. Pour the butter and mushrooms over the steak to serve.

calories: 569 | fat: 47g | protein: 34g | carbs: 4g | net carbs: 3g | fiber: 1g

Cheesy Beef Gratin

Prep time: 15 minutes | Cook time: 25 minutes | Serves 4

2 tablespoons olive oil
1 onion, chopped
1 pound (454 g) ground beef
2 garlic cloves, minced
Salt and black pepper, to taste
1 cup Mozzarella cheese, shredded

1 cup fontina cheese, shredded
1 (14-ounce / 397-g) canned tomatoes, chopped
2 tablespoons sesame seeds, toasted
20 dill pickle slices

Preheat the oven to 390ºF (199ºC). Heat olive oil in a pan over medium heat, place in the beef, garlic, salt, onion, and black pepper, and cook for 5 minutes. Remove and set to a baking dish, stir in half of the tomatoes and Mozzarella cheese. Lay the pickle slices on top, spread over the fontina cheese and sesame seeds, and place in the oven to bake for 20 minutes.

calories: 620 | fat: 49g | protein: 36g | carbs: 9g | net carbs: 6g | fiber: 3g

Hot Beef Tenderloin with Bell Peppers

Prep time: 15 minutes | Cook time: 9 to 10 hours | Serves 6

3 tablespoons extra-virgin olive oil, divided
1 pound (454 g) beef tenderloin, cut into 1-inch chunks
½ sweet onion, chopped
2 teaspoons minced garlic
1 red bell pepper, diced
1 yellow bell pepper, diced

2 cups coconut cream
1 cup beef broth
3 tablespoons coconut aminos
1 tablespoon hot sauce
1 scallion, white and green parts, chopped, for garnish
1 tablespoon sesame seeds, for garnish

Lightly grease the insert of the slow cooker with 1 tablespoon of the olive oil. In a large skillet over medium-high heat, heat the remaining 2 tablespoons of the olive oil. Add the beef and brown for 6 minutes. Transfer to the insert. In the skillet, sauté the onion and garlic for 3 minutes. Transfer the onion and garlic to the insert along with the red pepper, yellow pepper, coconut cream, broth, coconut aminos, and hot sauce. Cover and cook on low for 9 to 10 hours. Serve topped with the scallion and sesame seeds.

calories: 442 | fat: 33.9g | protein: 24.8g | carbs: 10.9g | net carbs: 6.9g | fiber: 4.0g

Grilled Ribeye Steaks with Green Beans

Prep time: 5 minutes | Cook time: 12 to 13 minutes | Serves 4

4 ribeye steaks
2 tablespoons unsalted butter
1 teaspoon olive oil
½ cup green beans, sliced
Salt and ground pepper, to taste

1 tablespoon fresh thyme, chopped
1 tablespoon fresh rosemary, chopped
1 tablespoon fresh parsley, chopped

Brush the steaks with olive oil and season with salt and pepper. Preheat a grill pan over high heat and cook the steaks for about 4 minutes per side; set aside. Steam the green beans for 3-4 minutes until tender. Season with salt. Melt the butter in the pan and stir-fry the herbs for 1 minute; then mix in the green beans. Transfer over the steaks and serve.

calories: 516 | fat: 33g | protein: 49g | carbs: 6g | net carbs: 5g | fiber: 1g

Sour Cream Beef Carne Asada

Prep time: 15 minutes | Cook time: 9 to 10 hours | Serves 8

½ cup extra-virgin olive oil, divided
¼ cup lime juice
2 tablespoons apple cider vinegar
2 teaspoons minced garlic
1½ teaspoons paprika

1 teaspoon ground cumin
1 teaspoon chili powder
¼ teaspoon cayenne pepper
1 sweet onion, cut into eighths
2 pounds (907 g) beef rump roast
1 cup sour cream, for garnish

Lightly grease the insert of the slow cooker with 1 tablespoon of the olive oil. In a small bowl, whisk together the remaining olive oil, lime juice, apple cider vinegar, garlic, paprika, cumin, chili powder, and cayenne until well blended. Place the onion in the bottom of the insert and the beef on top of the vegetable. Pour the sauce over the beef. Cover and cook on low for 9 to 10 hours. Shred the beef with a fork. Serve topped with the sour cream.

calories: 540 | fat: 43.9g | protein: 30.9g | carbs: 2.9g | net carbs: 1.9g | fiber: 1.0g

Hungarian Beef and Carrot Goulash

Prep time: 15 minutes | Cook time: 9 to 10 hours | Serves 6

1 tablespoon extra-virgin olive oil
1½ pounds (680 g) beef, cut into 1-inch pieces
½ sweet onion, chopped
1 carrot, cut into ½-inch-thick slices
1 red bell pepper, diced
2 teaspoons minced garlic

1 cup beef broth
¼ cup tomato paste
1 tablespoon Hungarian paprika
1 bay leaf
1 cup sour cream
2 tablespoons chopped fresh parsley, for garnish

Lightly grease the insert of the slow cooker with the olive oil. Add the beef, onion, carrot, red bell pepper, garlic, broth, tomato paste, paprika, and bay leaf to the insert. Cover and cook on low for 9 to 10 hours. Remove the bay leaf and stir in the sour cream. Serve topped with the parsley.

calories: 550 | fat: 41.9g | protein: 31.8g | carbs: 7.9g | net carbs: 5.8g | fiber: 2.1g

Beef and cauliflower rice Casserole

Prep time: 5 minutes | Cook time: 26 minutes | Serves 6

2 pounds (907 g) ground beef
Pink salt and black pepper, to taste
1 cup cauliflower rice
2 cups cabbage, chopped

1 (14-ounce / 397-g) can diced tomatoes
¼ cup water
1 cup Colby Jack cheese, shredded

Preheat oven to 375ºF (190ºC) and grease a baking dish with cooking spray. Put beef in a pot and season with salt and pepper and cook over medium heat for 6 minutes until no longer pink. Drain grease. Add cauliflower rice, cabbage, tomatoes, and water. Stir and bring to boil covered for 5 minutes to thicken the sauce. Adjust taste with salt and black pepper. Spoon the beef mixture into the baking dish. Sprinkle with cheese, and bake in the oven for 15 minutes until cheese has melted and golden brown. Remove, cool for 4 minutes, and serve.

calories: 501 | fat: 38g | protein: 33g | carbs: 6g | net carbs: 3g | fiber: 3g

Beef and Cauliflower Stuffed Peppers
Prep time: 25 minutes | Cook time: 6 hours | Serves 4

3 tablespoons extra-virgin olive oil, divided
1 pound (454 g) ground beef
½ cup finely chopped cauliflower
1 tomato, diced
½ sweet onion, chopped
2 teaspoons minced garlic
2 teaspoons dried oregano
1 teaspoon dried basil
4 bell peppers, tops cut off and seeded
1 cup shredded Cheddar cheese
½ cup chicken broth
1 tablespoon basil, sliced into thin strips, for garnish

Lightly grease the insert of the slow cooker with 1 tablespoon of the olive oil. In a large skillet over medium-high heat, heat the remaining 2 tablespoons of the olive oil. Add the beef and sauté until it is cooked through, about 10 minutes. Add the cauliflower, tomato, onion, garlic, oregano, and basil. Sauté for an additional 5 minutes. Spoon the meat mixture into the bell peppers and top with the cheese. Place the peppers in the slow cooker and add the broth to the bottom. Cover and cook on low for 6 hours. Serve warm, topped with the basil.

calories: 572 | fat: 41.1g | protein: 38.2g | carbs: 11.9g | net carbs: 8.8g | fiber: 3.1g

Smoked Paprika Beef Ragout
Prep time: 15 minutes | Cook time: 1 hour 48 minutes | Serves 4

1 pound (454 g) chuck steak, trimmed and cubed
2 tablespoons olive oil
Salt and black pepper, to taste
2 tablespoons almond flour
1 medium onion, diced
½ cup dry white wine
1 red bell pepper, seeded and diced
2 teaspoons Worcestershire sauce
4 ounces (113 g) tomato purée
3 teaspoons smoked paprika
1 cup beef broth
Thyme leaves, for garnish

Lightly dredge the meat in the almond flour and set aside. Place a skillet over medium heat, add 1 tablespoon of oil and sauté the onion, and bell pepper for 3 minutes. Stir in the paprika, and add the remaining olive oil. Add the beef and cook for 10 minutes, turning halfway. Stir in white wine, let it reduce by half, about 3 minutes, and add Worcestershire sauce, tomato purée, and beef broth. Boil for 2 minutes, then reduce the heat to lowest and let simmer for 1½ hours; stirring now and then. Adjust the taste and dish the ragout. Serve garnished with thyme leaves.

calories: 299 | fat: 17g | protein: 27g | carbs: 11g | net carbs: 9g | fiber: 2g

Traditional Italian Bolognese Sauce
Prep time: 5 minutes | Cook time: 22 minutes | Serves 5

1 pound (454 g) ground beef
2 garlic cloves
1 onion, chopped
1 teaspoon oregano
1 teaspoon sage
1 teaspoon rosemary
7 ounces (198 g) canned chopped tomatoes
1 tablespoon olive oil

Heat olive oil in a saucepan. Add onion and garlic and cook for 3 minutes. Add beef and cook until browned, about 4-5 minutes. Stir in the herbs and tomatoes. Cook for 15 minutes. Serve with zoodles.

calories: 216 | fat: 14g | protein: 18g | carbs: 4g | net carbs: 3g | fiber: 1g

Hearty Beef and Pork Meatloaf
Prep time: 15 minutes | Cook time: 7 to 8 hours | Serves 8

3 tablespoons extra-virgin olive oil, divided
½ sweet onion, chopped
2 teaspoons minced garlic
1 pound (454 g) ground beef
1 pound (454 g) ground pork
½ cup almond flour
½ cup heavy whipping cream
2 eggs
2 teaspoons dried oregano
1 teaspoon dried basil
¼ teaspoon salt
¼ teaspoon freshly ground black pepper
¾ cup tomato purée
1 cup goat cheese

Lightly grease the insert of the slow cooker with 1 tablespoon of the olive oil. In a medium skillet over medium-high heat, heat the remaining 2 tablespoons of the olive oil. Add the onion and garlic and sauté until softened, about 3 minutes. In a bowl, mix the onion mixture, beef, pork, almond flour, heavy cream, eggs, oregano, basil, salt, and pepper until well combined. Transfer the meat mixture to the insert and form into a loaf with about ½-inch gap on the sides. Spread the tomato purée on top of the meatloaf and sprinkle with goat cheese. Cover and cook on low for 7 to 8 hours. Serve warm.

calories: 411 | fat: 28.9g | protein: 32.1g | carbs: 4.2g | net carbs: 1.1g | fiber: 3.1g

Three-Cheese Beef Sausage Casserole
Prep time: 20 minutes | Cook time: 25 minutes | Serves 8

⅓ cup almond flour
2 eggs
2 pounds (907 g) beef sausage, chopped
Salt and black pepper, to taste
1 tablespoon dried parsley
¼ teaspoon red pepper flakes
¼ cup Parmesan cheese, grated
¼ teaspoon onion powder
½ teaspoon garlic powder
¼ teaspoon dried oregano
1 cup ricotta cheese
1 cup sugar-free marinara sauce
1½ cups Cheddar cheese, shredded

In a bowl, combine the sausage, black pepper, pepper flakes, oregano, eggs, Parmesan cheese, onion powder, almond flour, salt, parsley, and garlic powder. Form balls, lay them on a greased baking sheet, place in the oven at 370ºF, and bake for 15 minutes. Remove the balls from the oven and cover with half of the marinara sauce. Pour ricotta cheese all over followed by the rest of the marinara sauce. Scatter the Cheddar cheese and bake in the oven for 10 minutes. Allow the meatballs casserole to cool before serving.

calories: 505 | fat: 36g | protein: 33g | carbs: 12g | net carbs: 11g | fiber: 1g

Italian Beef Roast with Jalapeño
Prep time: 5 minutes | Cook time: 1 hour 15 minutes | Serves 4

3½ pounds (1.5 kg) beef roast
4 ounces (113 g) mushrooms, sliced
12 ounces (340 g) beef stock
1 ounce (28 g) onion soup mix
½ cup Italian dressing
2 jalapeño peppers, shredded

In a bowl, combine the stock with the Italian dressing and onion soup mixture. Place the beef roast in a pan, stir in the stock mixture, mushrooms, and jalapeños; cover with aluminum foil. Set in the oven at 300ºF, and bake for 1 hour. Take out the foil and continue baking for 15 minutes. Allow the roast to cool, slice, and serve alongside a topping of the gravy.

calories: 616 | fat: 26g | protein: 88g | carbs: 9g | net carbs: 8g | fiber: 1g

Beef Chili

Prep time: 20 minutes | Cook time: 1 hour 20 minutes | Serves 10

1 tablespoon olive oil
½ large onion (5.5 ounces / 156 g), chopped
8 cloves garlic, minced
2½ pounds (1.1 kg) ground beef
2 (14.5-ounce / 411-g) cans diced tomatoes, with liquid
1 (6-ounce / 170-g) can tomato paste
1 (4-ounce / 113-g) can green chiles, with liquid
¼ cup chili powder
2 tablespoons ground cumin
1 tablespoon dried oregano
2 teaspoons sea salt
1 teaspoon black pepper
1 medium bay leaf (optional)

In a soup pot, heat the oil over medium-high heat. Add the onion and cook for 5 to 7 minutes until translucent. Add the garlic and cook for 1 minute until fragrant. Add the ground beef and cook for 8 to 10 minutes, breaking apart with a spatula, until browned. Add the remaining ingredients, except the bay leaf, and stir until combined. If desired, place the bay leaf in the middle and push down slightly. Reduce heat to low. Cover and cook for 1 hour, or until the flavors reach the desired intensity. Remove the bay leaf before serving.

calories: 430 | fat: 26.8g | protein: 32.9g | carbs: 10.1g | net carbs: 8.0g | fiber: 2.1g

Basil Feta Flank Steak Pinwheels

Prep time: 5 minutes | Cook time: 15 minutes | Serves 6

1½ pounds (680 g) beef flank steak
Salt and black pepper, to season
⅔ cup feta cheese, crumbled
½ loose cup baby spinach
1 jalapeño pepper, chopped
¼ cup basil leaves, chopped

Preheat oven to 400ºF (205ºC). Grease a baking sheet with cooking spray. Wrap the steak in plastic wrap, place on a flat surface, and gently run a rolling pin over to flatten. Take off the wraps. Sprinkle with half of the feta cheese, top with spinach, jalapeño, basil leaves, and the remaining cheese. Carefully roll the steak over on the stuffing and secure with toothpicks. Place in the greased baking sheet, and cook for 15 minutes, flipping once until nicely browned on the outside and the cheese melted within. Cool for 3 minutes, slice into pinwheels, and serve.

calories: 199 | fat: 9g | protein: 27g | carbs: 1g | net carbs: 1g | fiber: 0g

Beef Brisket with Red Wine

Prep time: 10 minutes | Cook time: 2 hours | Serves 4

1 tablespoon olive oil
1 pound (454 g) brisket
1 red onion, quartered
2 stalks celery, cut into chunks
1 garlic clove, minced
Salt and black pepper, to taste
1 bay leaf
1 tablespoon fresh thyme, chopped
1 cup red wine

Season the brisket with salt and pepper. Brown the meat on both sides in warm olive oil over medium heat for 6-8 minutes. Transfer to a deep casserole dish. In the dish, arrange the onion, garlic, celery, and bay leaf around the brisket and pour the wine all over it. Cover the pot and cook the ingredients in the oven for 2 hours at 370ºF (188ºC). When ready, remove the casserole. Transfer the beef to a chopping board and cut it into thick slices. Serve the beef and vegetables with a drizzle of the sauce.

calories: 203 | fat: 9g | protein: 25g | carbs: 3g | net carbs: 2g | fiber: 1g

Veggie cauliflower rice with Beef Steak

Prep time: 5 minutes | Cook time: 9 minutes | Serves 4

2 cups cauliflower rice
3 cups mixed vegetables
3 tablespoons butter
1 pound (454 g) beef skirt steak
Salt and black pepper, to taste
4 fresh eggs
Hot sauce (sugar-free) for topping (optional)

Mix the cauliflower rice with mixed vegetables in a bowl, sprinkle with a little water, and steam in the microwave for 1 minute to tender. Share into 4 serving bowls. Melt the butter in a skillet, season the beef with salt and pepper, and brown in the butter for 5 minutes on each side. Use a perforated spoon to ladle the meat onto the vegetables. Wipe out the skillet and return to medium heat, crack in an egg, season with salt and pepper, and cook until the egg white has set, but the yolk is still runny, for 3 minutes. Remove egg onto the vegetable bowl, and fry the remaining 3 eggs. Add to the other bowls. Drizzle the beef bowl with hot sauce (if desired) and serve.

calories: 791 | fat: 47g | protein: 65g | carbs: 22g | net carbs: 14g | fiber: 8g

Garlicky Lamb Chops in White Wine

Prep time: 5 minutes | Cook time: 1 hour 9 minutes | Serves 6

6 lamb chops
1 tablespoon sage
1 teaspoon thyme
1 onion, sliced
3 garlic cloves, minced
2 tablespoons olive oil
½ cup white wine
Salt and black pepper, to taste

Heat the olive oil in a pan. Add onion and garlic and cook for 3 minutes, until soft. Rub the sage and thyme over the lamb chops. Cook the lamb for about 3 minutes per side. Set aside. Pour the white wine and 1 cup of water into the pan, bring the mixture to a boil. Cook until the liquid is reduced by half. Add the chops in the pan, reduce the heat, and let simmer for 1 hour.

calories: 392 | fat: 35g | protein: 18g | carbs: 2g | net carbs: 1g | fiber: 1g

Balsamic Glazed Meatloaf

Prep time: 15 minutes | Cook time: 1 hour 10 minutes | Serves 12

3 pounds (1.4 kg) ground beef
½ cup onion, chopped
½ cup almond flour
2 garlic cloves, minced
1 cup mushrooms, sliced
3 eggs
Salt and black pepper, to taste
Glaze:
2 cups balsamic vinegar
1 tablespoon sweetener
2 tablespoons parsley, chopped
¼ cup bell peppers, chopped
⅓ cup Parmesan cheese, grated
1 teaspoon balsamic vinegar
2 tablespoons tomato purée

Combine all of the meatloaf ingredients in a large bowl. Press the mixture into greased loaf pan. Bake at 375ºF (190ºC) for about 30 minutes. Make the glaze by combining all of the ingredients in a saucepan over medium heat. Simmer for 20 minutes, until the glaze is thickened. Pour ¼ cup of the glaze over the meatloaf. Save the extra for future use. Put the meatloaf back in the oven, and cook for 20 more minutes.

calories: 375 | fat: 25g | protein: 23g | carbs: 13g | net carbs: 12g | fiber: 1g

Creamy Reuben Soup with Sauerkraut

Prep time: 10 minutes | Cook time: 20 minutes | Serves 6

1 onion, diced
7 cups beef stock
1 teaspoon caraway seeds
2 celery stalks, diced
2 garlic cloves, minced
¾ teaspoon black pepper
2 cups heavy cream

1 cup sauerkraut
1 pound (454 g) corned beef, chopped
3 tablespoons butter
1½ cups Swiss cheese
Salt and black pepper, to taste

Melt the butter in a large pot. Add onions and celery, and fry for 3 minutes until tender. Add garlic, and cook for another minute. Pour the broth over and stir in sauerkraut, salt, caraway seeds, and add a pinch of pepper. Bring to a boil. Reduce the heat to low, and add the corned beef. Cook for about 15 minutes. Adjust the seasoning. Stir in heavy cream and cheese, and cook for 1 minute.

calories: 567 | fat: 46g | protein: 29g | carbs: 12g | net carbs: 9g | fiber: 3g

Beef and Mushroom Cheeseburgers

Prep time: 5 minutes | Cook time: 11 to 13 minutes | Serves 4

2 tablespoons olive oil
1 pound (454 g) ground beef
½ teaspoon fresh parsley, chopped
½ teaspoon Worcestershire

sauce
Salt and black pepper, to taste
2 slices Mozzarella cheese
2 portobello mushroom caps

In a bowl, mix the beef, parsley, Worcestershire sauce, salt and black pepper with your hands until evenly combined. Make medium-sized patties out of the mixture. Preheat a grill to 400°F (205°C) and coat the mushroom caps with olive oil, salt and black pepper. Lay portobello caps, rounded side up and burger patties onto the hot grill pan and cook for 5 minutes. Turn the mushroom caps and continue cooking for 1 minute. Lay a Mozzarella slice on top of each patty. Continue cooking until the mushroom caps are softened, 4-5 minutes. Flip the patties and top with cheese. Cook for another 2-3 minutes until the cheese melts onto the meat. Remove the patties and sandwich into two mushroom caps each.

calories: 397 | fat: 32g | protein: 24g | carbs: 2g | net carbs: 1g | fiber: 1g

Beef-Cabbage Casserole

Prep time: 5 minutes | Cook time: 26 minutes | Serves 6

2 pounds (907 g) ground beef
Salt and black pepper, to taste
1 cup cauliflower rice
2 cups chopped cabbage

1 (14-ounce / 397-g) can diced tomatoes
1 cup shredded Colby jack cheese

Preheat oven to 370°F and grease a baking dish with cooking spray. Put beef in a pot and season with salt and black pepper and cook over medium heat for 6 minutes until no longer pink. Drain the grease. Add cauliflower rice, cabbage, tomatoes, and ¼ cup water. Stir and bring to boil covered for 5 minutes to thicken the sauce. Adjust taste with salt and black pepper. Spoon the beef mixture into the baking dish and spread evenly. Sprinkle with cheese and bake in the oven for 15 minutes until cheese has melted and it's golden brown. Remove and cool for 4 minutes and serve with low carb crusted bread.

calories: 402 | fat: 27g | protein: 36g | carbs: 6g | net carbs: 4g | fiber: 2g

Beef Casserole with Cauliflower

Prep time: 10 minutes | Cook time: 24 minutes | Serves 4

2 tablespoons olive oil
1 pound (454 g) ground beef
Salt and black pepper, to taste
½ cup cauliflower rice
1 tablespoon parsley, chopped
½ teaspoon dried oregano

1 cup kohlrabi, chopped
1 (5-ounce / 142-g) can diced tomatoes
¼ cup water
½ cup Mozzarella cheese, shredded

Put beef in a pot and season with salt and pepper; cook over medium heat for 6 minutes until no longer pink. Add cauliflower rice, kohlrabi, tomatoes, and water. Stir and bring to boil for 5 minutes to thicken the sauce. Spoon the beef mixture into the baking dish and spread evenly. Sprinkle with cheese and bake in the oven for 15 minutes at 380°F (193°C) until cheese has melted and it's golden brown. Remove and cool for 4 minutes, and serve sprinkled with parsley.

calories: 409 | fat: 33g | protein: 24g | carbs: 5g | net carbs: 3g | fiber: 2g

Beef and Cauliflower Curry with Cilantro

Prep time: 10 minutes | Cook time: 21 minutes | Serves 4

1 tablespoon olive oil
½ pound (227 g) ground beef
1 garlic clove, minced
1 teaspoon turmeric
1 tablespoon cilantro, chopped
1 tablespoon ginger paste
½ teaspoon garam masala

5 ounces (142 g) canned whole tomatoes
1 head cauliflower, cut into florets
Salt and chili pepper, to taste
¼ cup water

Heat oil in a saucepan over medium heat, add the beef, garlic, ginger paste, and garam masala. Cook for 5 minutes while breaking any lumps. Stir in the tomatoes and cauliflower, season with salt, turmeric, and chili pepper, and cook covered for 6 minutes. Add the water and bring to a boil over medium heat for 10 minutes or until the water has reduced by half. Spoon the curry into serving bowls and serve sprinkled with cilantro.

calories: 201 | fat: 15g | protein: 11g | carbs: 6g | net carbs: 4g | fiber: 2g

Beef Stew with Black Olives

Prep time: 15 minutes | Cook time: 1 hour 5 minutes | Serves 4

1 onion, chopped
2 tablespoons olive oil
1 teaspoon ginger paste
1 teaspoon coconut aminos
1 pound (454 g) beef stew meat, cubed
1 red bell pepper, seeded and chopped
½ scotch bonnet pepper, chopped

2 green chilies, chopped
1 cup tomatoes, chopped
1 tablespoon fresh cilantro, chopped
1 garlic clove, minced
¼ cup vegetable broth
Salt and black pepper, to taste
¼ cup black olives, chopped
1 teaspoon jerk seasoning

Brown the beef on all sides in warm olive oil over medium heat; remove and set aside. Stir-fry in the red bell peppers, green chilies, jerk seasoning, garlic, scotch bonnet pepper, onion, ginger paste, and coconut aminos, for about 5-6 minutes. Pour in the tomatoes and broth, and cook for 1 hour. Stir in the olives, adjust the seasonings and serve sprinkled with fresh cilantro.

calories: 254 | fat: 12g | protein: 27g | carbs: 11g | net carbs: 9g | fiber: 2g

Grilled Beef Skewers with Fresh Salad

Prep time: 10 minutes | Cook time: 13 minutes | Serves 4

1 pound (454 g) sirloin steak, boneless, cubed
¼ cup ranch dressing
1 red onion, sliced
½ tablespoon white wine vinegar
1 tablespoon extra-virgin olive

oil
2 ripe tomatoes, sliced
2 tablespoons fresh parsley, chopped
1 cucumber, sliced
Salt, to taste

Thread the beef cubes on the skewers, about 4-5 cubes per skewer. Brush half of the ranch dressing on the skewers (all around). Preheat grill to 400ºF (205ºC) and place the skewers on the grill grate to cook for 6 minutes. Turn the skewers once and cook further for 6 minutes. Brush the remaining ranch dressing on the meat and cook them for 1 more minute on each side. In a salad bowl mix together red onion, tomatoes, and cucumber, sprinkle with salt, vinegar, and extra-virgin olive oil; toss to combine. Top the salad with skewers and scatter the parsley all over.

calories: 357 | fat: 23g | protein: 25g | carbs: 12g | net carbs: 10g | fiber: 2g

Juicy Beef with Thyme and Rosemary

Prep time: 15 minutes | Cook time: 17 minutes | Serves 4

2 garlic cloves, minced
2 tablespoons butter
2 tablespoons olive oil
1 tablespoon fresh rosemary, chopped
1 pound (454 g) beef rump steak, sliced
Salt and black pepper, to taste
1 shallot, chopped

½ cup heavy cream
½ cup beef stock
1 tablespoon mustard
2 teaspoons coconut aminos
2 teaspoons lemon juice
1 teaspoon xylitol
A sprig of rosemary
A sprig of thyme

Set a pan to medium heat, warm in a tablespoon of olive oil and stir in the shallot; cook for 3 minutes. Stir in the stock, coconut aminos, xylitol, thyme sprig, cream, mustard and rosemary sprig, and cook for 8 minutes. Stir in butter, lemon juice, pepper and salt. Remove the rosemary and thyme. Set aside. In a bowl, combine the remaining oil with black pepper, garlic, rosemary, and salt. Toss in the beef to coat. Heat a pan over medium-high heat, place in the beef steak, cook for 6 minutes, flipping halfway through. Plate the beef slices, sprinkle over the sauce, and enjoy.

calories: 339 | fat: 25g | protein: 26g | carbs: 3g | net carbs: 2g | fiber: 1g

Sirloin Steak Skewers with Ranch Dressing

Prep time: 5 minutes | Cook time: 13 minutes | Serves 4

1 pound (454 g) sirloin steak, boneless, cubed

¼ cup ranch dressing, divided
Chopped scallions, for garnish

Preheat the grill on medium heat to 400ºF and thread the beef cubes on the skewers, about 4 to 5 cubes per skewer. Brush half of the ranch dressing on the skewers (all around) and place them on the grill grate to cook for 6 minutes. Turn the skewers once and cook further for 6 minutes. Brush the remaining ranch dressing on the meat and cook them for 1 more minute on each side. Plate, garnish with the scallions, and serve with a mixed veggie salad, and extra ranch dressing.

calories: 278 | fat: 19g | protein: 24g | carbs: 1g | net carbs: 1g | fiber: 0g

Juicy Beef Meatballs with Parsley

Prep time: 10 minutes | Cook time: 21 minutes | Serves 4

1 pound (454 g) ground beef
Salt and black pepper, to taste
½ teaspoon garlic powder
1¼ tablespoons coconut aminos
1 cup beef stock
¾ cup almond flour

1 tablespoon fresh parsley, chopped
1 onion, sliced
2 tablespoons butter
1 tablespoon olive oil
¼ cup sour cream

Preheat the oven to 390ºF (199ºC) and grease a baking dish. In a bowl, combine beef with salt, garlic powder, almond flour, parsley, 1 tablespoon of coconut aminos, black pepper, ¼ cup of beef stock. Form patties and place on the baking sheet. Bake for 18 minutes. Set a pan with the butter and olive oil over medium heat, stir in the onion, and cook for 3 minutes. Stir in the remaining beef stock, sour cream, and remaining coconut aminos, and bring to a simmer. Adjust the seasoning with black pepper and salt. Serve the meatballs topped with onion sauce.

calories: 519 | fat: 36g | protein: 24g | carbs: 18g | net carbs: 16g | fiber: 2g

Paprika Roast Beef Brisket

Prep time: 10 minutes | Cook time: 1 hour | Serves 4

2 pounds (907 g) beef brisket
½ teaspoon celery salt
1 teaspoon chili powder
2 tablespoons olive oil
1 tablespoon sweet paprika

Pinch of cayenne pepper
½ teaspoon garlic powder
½ cup beef stock
3 onions, cut into quarters
¼ teaspoon dry mustard

Grease a baking dish with cooking spray and preheat oven to 360ºF (182ºC). In a bowl, combine the paprika with dry mustard, chili powder, salt, garlic powder, cayenne pepper, and celery salt. Rub the meat with this mixture. Set a pan over medium heat and warm olive oil, place in the beef, and sear until brown. Remove to the baking dish. Pour in the stock, add onions and bake for 60 minutes. Set the beef to a cutting board, and leave to cool before slicing. Take the juices from the baking dish and strain, sprinkle over the meat to serve.

calories: 601 | fat: 41g | protein: 36g | carbs: 19g | net carbs: 16g | fiber: 3g

Beef and Egg cauliflower rice Bowls

Prep time: 5 minutes | Cook time: 14 minutes | Serves 4

2 cups cauliflower rice
3 cups frozen mixed vegetables
3 tablespoons butter
1 pound (454 g) skirt steak

Salt and black pepper, to taste
4 eggs
Hot sauce, for topping (optional)

Mix the cauliflower rice and mixed vegetables in a bowl, sprinkle with a little water, and steam in the microwave for 1 minute until tender. Share into 4 serving bowls. Melt the butter in a skillet, season the beef with salt and black pepper, and brown for 5 minutes on each side. Use a perforated spoon to ladle the meat onto the vegetables. Wipe out the skillet and return to medium heat, crack in an egg, season with salt and pepper and cook until the egg white has set, but the yolk is still runny 3 minutes. Remove egg onto the vegetable bowl and fry the remaining 3 eggs. Add to the other bowls. Drizzle the beef bowls with hot sauce (if desired) and serve.

calories: 470 | fat: 25g | protein: 42g | carbs: 21g | net carbs: 14g | fiber: 7g

Beef Lasagna with Zucchinis
Prep time: 15 minutes | Cook time: 44 minutes | Serves 4

2 tablespoons olive oil
½ red chili, chopped
1 pound (454 g) ground beef
3 large zucchinis, sliced lengthwise
2 garlic cloves, minced
1 shallot, chopped
1 cup tomato purée

Salt and black pepper, to taste
2 teaspoons sweet paprika
1 teaspoon dried thyme
1 teaspoon dried basil
1 cup Mozzarella cheese, shredded
1 cup chicken broth

Heat the oil in a skillet and cook the beef for 4 minutes while breaking any lumps as you stir. Top with shallot, garlic, chili, tomatoes, salt, paprika and black pepper. Stir and cook for 5 more minutes. Lay ⅓ of the zucchinis slices in a greased baking dish. Top with ⅓ of the beef mixture and repeat the layering process two more times with the same quantities. Season with basil and thyme. Pour in the chicken broth. Sprinkle the Mozzarella cheese on top and tuck the baking dish in the oven. Bake for 35 minutes at 380ºF (193ºC). Remove the lasagna and let it rest for 10 minutes before serving.

calories: 412 | fat: 30g | protein: 30g | carbs: 6g | net carbs: 4g | fiber: 2g

Skirt Steak with Green Beans
Prep time: 5 minutes | Cook time: 13 minutes | Serves 4

3 cups green beans, chopped
2 cups cauliflower rice
2 tablespoons butter
1 tablespoon olive oil
1 pound (454 g) skirt steak

Salt and black pepper. to taste
4 fresh eggs
Hot sauce (sugar-free) for topping (optional)

Put cauliflower rice and green beans in a bowl, sprinkle with a little water, and steam in the microwave for 90 seconds. Share into bowls. Warm butter and olive oil in a skillet, season the beef with salt and pepper, and brown for 5 minutes on each side. Ladle the meat onto the vegetables. Wipe out the skillet and return to medium heat, crack in an egg, season with salt and pepper and cook until the egg white has set, but the yolk is still runny, for 3 minutes. Remove egg onto the vegetable bowl and fry the remaining 3 eggs. Add to the other bowls. Drizzle with hot sauce (if desired) and serve.

calories: 409 | fat: 25g | protein: 40g | carbs: 8g | net carbs: 5g | fiber: 3g

Beef Sausage Casserole with Okra
Prep time: 15 minutes | Cook time: 25 minutes | Serves 4

1 cup okra, trimmed
1 tablespoon olive oil
1 celery stalk, chopped
¼ cup almond flour
1 egg
1 pound (454 g) beef sausage, chopped
Salt and black pepper, to taste
½ tablespoon dried parsley
¼ teaspoon red pepper flakes

¼ cup Parmesan cheese, grated
2 green onions, chopped
½ teaspoon garlic powder
¼ teaspoon dried oregano
½ cup ricotta cheese
½ cup marinara sauce, sugar-free
1 cup Cheddar cheese, shredded

In a bowl, combine the sausage, pepper, pepper flakes, oregano, egg, Parmesan cheese, green onions, almond flour, salt, parsley, celery, and garlic powder. Form balls, lay them on a lined baking sheet, place in the oven at 390ºF (199ºC), and bake for 15 minutes. Remove the balls from the oven and cover with half of the marinara sauce and okra. Pour ricotta cheese all over followed by the rest of the marinara sauce. Scatter the Cheddar cheese and bake in the oven for 10 minutes. Allow the meatballs casserole to cool before serving.

calories: 611 | fat: 44g | protein: 36g | carbs: 14g | net carbs: 12g | fiber: 2g

Flank Steak and Kale Roll
Prep time: 10 minutes | Cook time: 30 minutes | Serves 4

1 pound (454 g) flank steak
Salt and black pepper, to taste
½ cup ricotta cheese, crumbled
½ cup baby kale, chopped

1 serrano pepper, chopped
1 tablespoon basil leaves, chopped

Wrap the steak in plastic wraps, place on a flat surface, and gently run a rolling pin over to flatten. Take off the wraps. Sprinkle with half of the ricotta cheese, top with kale, serrano pepper, and the remaining cheese. Roll the steak over on the stuffing and secure with toothpicks. Place in the greased baking sheet and cook for 30 minutes at 390ºF (199ºC), flipping once until nicely browned on the outside and the cheese melted within. Cool for 3 minutes, slice and serve with basil.

calories: 211 | fat: 10g | protein: 28g | carbs: 1g | net carbs: 1g | fiber: 0g

Beef Steaks with Mushrooms and Bacon
Prep time: 10 minutes | Cook time: 40 minutes | Serves 4

2 ounces (57 g) bacon, chopped
1 cup mushrooms, sliced
1 garlic clove, chopped
1 shallot, chopped
1 cup heavy cream

1 pound (454 g) beef steaks
1 teaspoon ground nutmeg
¼ cup coconut oil
Salt and black pepper, to taste
1 tablespoon parsley, chopped

In a frying pan over medium heat, cook the bacon for 2-3 minutes and set aside. In the same pan, warm the oil, add in the onions, garlic and mushrooms, and cook for 4 minutes. Stir in the beef, season with salt, black pepper and nutmeg, and sear until browned, about 2 minutes per side. Preheat oven to 360ºF (182ºC) and insert the pan in the oven to bake for 25 minutes. Remove the beef steaks to a bowl and cover with foil. Place the pan over medium heat, pour in the heavy cream over the mushroom mixture, add in the reserved bacon and cook for 5 minutes; remove from heat. Spread the bacon/mushroom sauce over beef steaks, sprinkle with parsley and serve.

calories: 447 | fat: 37g | protein: 27g | carbs: 3g | net carbs: 2g | fiber: 1g

Beef Meatloaf with Balsamic Glaze

Prep time: 15 minutes | Cook time: 50 minutes | Serves 4

Meatloaf:
1 pound (454 g) ground beef
½ onion, chopped
1 tablespoon almond milk
1 tablespoon almond flour
1 garlic clove, minced
1 cup sliced mushrooms

1 small egg
Salt and black pepper, to taste
1 tablespoon parsley, chopped
⅓ cup Parmesan cheese, grated

Glaze:
⅓ cup balsamic vinegar
¼ tablespoon xylitol
¼ teaspoon garlic powder

¼ teaspoon onion powder
1 tablespoon plus ¼ teaspoon tomato purée

Grease a loaf pan with cooking spray and set aside. Preheat oven to 390ºF (199ºC). Combine all meatloaf ingredients in a large bowl. Press this mixture into the prepared loaf pan. Bake for about 30 minutes. To make the glaze, whisk all ingredients in a bowl. Pour the glaze over the meatloaf. Put the meatloaf back in the oven and cook for 20 more minutes. Let meatloaf sit for 10 minutes before slicing.

calories: 377 | fat: 26g | protein: 24g | carbs: 10g | net carbs: 9g | fiber: 1g

Beef Ragout with Green Beans

Prep time: 15 minutes | Cook time: 1 hour 48 minutes | Serves 4

2 tablespoons olive oil
1 pound (454 g) chuck steak, cubed
Salt and black pepper, to taste
2 tablespoons almond flour
4 green onions, diced
½ cup dry white wine
1 yellow bell pepper, diced

1 cup green beans, chopped
2 teaspoons Worcestershire sauce
4 ounces (113 g) tomato purée
3 teaspoons smoked paprika
1 cup beef broth
Parsley leaves, for garnish

Dredge the meat in the almond flour and set aside. Place a skillet over medium heat, add 1 tablespoon of oil andsauté the green onion, green beans, and bell pepper for 3 minutes. Stir in the paprika and the remaining olive oil. Add the beef and cook for 10 minutes, turning halfway. Stir in white wine, let it reduce by half, about 3 minutes, and add Worcestershire sauce, tomato purée, and beef broth. Boil for 2 minutes, then reduce the heat to lowest and let simmer for 1½ hours; stirring now and then. Adjust the taste and dish the ragout. Serve garnished with parsley leaves.

calories: 302 | fat: 17g | protein: 27g | carbs: 12g | net carbs: 9g | fiber: 3g

Balsamic Glazed Meatloaf

Prep time: 20 minutes | Cook time: 1 hour 10 minutes | Serves 6

1 cup white mushrooms, chopped
2 pounds (907 g) ground beef
2 tablespoons fresh parsley, chopped
2 garlic cloves, minced
1 onion, chopped
1 red bell pepper, seeded and chopped
½ cup almond flour

⅓ cup Parmesan cheese, grated
2 eggs
Salt and black pepper, to taste
1 teaspoon plus 2 cups balsamic vinegar, divided
1 tablespoon Swerve natural sweetener
1 tablespoon coconut aminos
2 tablespoons tomato purée

In a bowl, combine the beef with salt, mushrooms, bell pepper, Parmesan cheese, 1 teaspoon vinegar, parsley, garlic, black pepper, onion, almond flour, salt, and eggs. Set this into a loaf pan, and bake for 30 minutes in the oven at 370ºF (188ºC). Meanwhile, heat a small pan over medium heat, add in the 2 cups vinegar, Swerve, coconut aminos, and tomato purée, and cook for 20 minutes. Remove the meatloaf from the oven, spread the glaze over the meatloaf, and bake in the oven for 20 more minutes. Allow the meatloaf to cool, slice, and enjoy.

calories: 469 | fat: 22g | protein: 35g | carbs: 14g | net carbs: 12g | fiber: 2g

Beef-Stuffed Zucchini Boats

Prep time: 20 minutes | Cook time: 33 minutes | Serves 4

2 garlic cloves, minced
1 teaspoon cumin
1 tablespoon olive oil
1 pound (454 g) ground beef
½ cup onions, chopped
1 teaspoon smoked paprika
Salt and black pepper, to taste
4 zucchinis
¼ cup fresh cilantro, chopped

½ cup Monterey Jack cheese, shredded
1½ cups enchilada sauce
1 avocado, chopped, for serving
Green onions, chopped, for serving
Tomatoes, chopped, for serving

Set a pan over high heat and warm the oil. Add the onions, and cook for 2 minutes. Stir in the beef, and brown for 4-5 minutes. Stir in the paprika, pepper, garlic, cumin, and salt; cook for 2 minutes. Slice the zucchini in half lengthwise and scoop out the seeds. Set the zucchini in a greased baking pan, stuff each with the beef, scatter enchilada sauce on top, and spread with the Monterey cheese. Bake in the oven at 350ºF for 20 minutes while covered. Uncover, spread with cilantro, and bake for 5 minutes. Top with tomatoes, green onions and avocado, place on serving plates and enjoy.

calories: 520 | fat: 36g | protein: 34g | carbs: 20g | net carbs: 13g | fiber: 7g

Chapter 9 Fish and Seafood

Pistachio Nut Salmon with Shallot Sauce
Prep time: 15 minutes | Cook time: 30 minutes | Serves 4

4 salmon fillets
½ teaspoon pepper
1 teaspoon salt

¼ cup mayonnaise
½ cup pistachios, chopped

Sauce:
1 shallot, chopped
2 teaspoons lemon zest
1 tablespoon olive oil

A pinch of pepper
1 cup heavy cream

Preheat the oven to 375ºF (190ºC). Brush the salmon with mayonnaise and season with salt and pepper. Coat with pistachios. Place in a lined baking dish, and bake, for 15 minutes. Heat the olive oil in a saucepan, and sauté the shallots, for a few minutes. Stir in the rest of the sauce ingredients. Bring to a boil, and cook until thickened. Serve the salmon topped with the sauce.

calories: 564 | fat: 47.0g | protein: 34.0g | carbs: 8.1g | net carbs: 6.0g | fiber: 2.1g

Greek Tilapia with Tomatoes and Olives
Prep time: 10 minutes | Cook time: 15 minutes | Serves 4

4 tilapia fillets
2 garlic cloves, minced
2 teaspoons oregano
14 ounces (397 g) tomatoes, diced

1 tablespoon olive oil
½ red onion, chopped
2 tablespoons parsley
¼ cup kalamata olives

Heat olive oil in a skillet over medium heat, and cook onion, garlic, and oregano for 3 minutes. Stir in tomatoes and bring the mixture to a boil. Reduce the heat and simmer, for 5 minutes. Add olives and tilapia. Cook, for about 8 minutes. Serve the tilapia with the tomato sauce.

calories: 183 | fat: 15.0g | protein: 22.9g | carbs: 7.9g | net carbs: 6.2g | fiber: 1.7g

Coconut Shrimp Stew
Prep time: 15 minutes | Cook time: 15 minutes | Serves 6

1 cup coconut milk
2 tablespoons lime juice
¼ cup diced roasted peppers
1½ pounds (680 g) shrimp, peeled and deveined
¼ cup olive oil
1 garlic clove, minced

14 ounces (397 g) diced tomatoes
2 tablespoons sriracha sauce
¼ cup onions, chopped
¼ cup cilantro, chopped
Fresh dill, chopped to garnish
Salt and black pepper to taste

Heat the olive oil in a pot over medium heat. Add onions and, cook for 3 minutes, or until translucent.Add the garlic and cook, for another minute, until soft. Add tomatoes, shrimp, and cilantro. Cook until the shrimp becomes opaque, about 3-4 minutes. Stir in sriracha and coconut milk, and cook, for 2 more minutes. Do NOT bring to a boil. Stir in the lime juice, and season with salt and pepper to taste. Spoon the stew in bowls, garnish with fresh dill, and serve warm.

calories: 325 | fat: 20.9g | protein: 22.8g | carbs: 6.2g | net carbs: 5.1g | fiber: 1.1g

Smoked Salmon and Avocado Omelet
Prep time: 10 minutes | Cook time: 5 minutes | Serves 1

½ avocado, sliced
2 tablespoons chives, chopped
2 ounces (57 g) smoked salmon, cut into strips
1 spring onion, sliced

3 eggs
2 tablespoons cream cheese
1 tablespoon butter
Salt and black pepper to taste

In a small bowl, combine the chives and cream cheese. Set aside. Beat the eggs in a large bowl and season with salt and pepper. Melt the butter in a pan over medium heat. Add the eggs to the pan and cook, for about 3 minutes. Carefully flip the omelet over and continue cooking for 2 minutes until golden. Remove the omelet to a plate and spread the chive mixture over. Arrange the salmon, avocado, and onion slices. Wrap the omelet. Serve immediately.

calories: 512 | fat: 47.9g | protein: 36.8g | carbs: 12.9g | net carbs: 5.6g | fiber: 7.3g

Tilapia Tacos with Cabbage Slaw
Prep time: 10 minutes | Cook time: 5 minutes | Serves 4

1 tablespoon olive oil
1 teaspoon chili powder
2 tilapia fillets
1 teaspoon paprika
4 keto tortillas

Slaw:
½ cup red cabbage, shredded
1 tablespoon lemon juice
1 teaspoon apple cider vinegar
1 tablespoon olive oil

Season tilapia with chili powder and paprika. Heat the olive oil in a skillet over medium heat. Add tilapia, and cook until blackened, about 3 minutes per side. Cut into strips. Divide the tilapia between the tortillas. Combine all of the slaw ingredients in a bowl. Divide the slaw between the tortillas.

calories: 261 | fat: 20.1g | protein: 13.9g | carbs: 5.5g | net carbs: 3.6g | fiber: 1.9g

Halibut Tacos with Cabbage Slaw
Prep time: 15 minutes | Cook time: 6 minutes | Serves 4

1 tablespoon olive oil
1 teaspoon chili powder
Slaw:
2 tablespoons red cabbage, shredded
1 tablespoon lemon juice
Salt to taste

4 halibut fillets, skinless, sliced
2 low carb tortillas

½ tablespoon extra-virgin olive oil
½ carrot, shredded
1 tablespoon cilantro, chopped

Combine red cabbage with salt in a bowl; massage cabbage to tenderize. Add in the remaining slaw ingredient, toss to coat and set aside. Rub the halibut with olive oil, chili powder and paprika. Heat a grill pan over medium heat. Add halibut and cook until lightly charred and cooked through, about 3 minutes per side. Divide between the tortillas. Combine all slaw ingredients in a bowl. Split the slaw among the tortillas.

calories: 386 | fat: 25.9g | protein: 23.7g | carbs: 12.6g | net carbs: 6.4g | fiber: 6.2g

Tuna Shirataki Pad Thai

Prep time: 15 minutes | Cook time: 5 minutes | Serves 4

1 (7-ounce / 198-g) pack shirataki noodles
4 cups water
1 red bell pepper, sliced
2 tablespoons soy sauce, sugar-free
1 tablespoon ginger-garlic
paste
1 teaspoon chili powder
1 tablespoon water
4 tuna steaks
Salt and black pepper to taste
1 tablespoon olive oil
1 tablespoon parsley, chopped

In a colander, rinse the shirataki noodles with running cold water. Bring a pot of salted water to a boil; blanch the noodles for 2 minutes. Drain and set aside. Preheat a grill on medium-high. Season the tuna with salt and black pepper, brush with olive oil, and grill covered. Cook for 3 minutes on each side. In a bowl, whisk soy sauce, ginger-garlic paste, olive oil, chili powder, and water. Add bell pepper, and noodles and toss to coat. Assemble noodles and tuna in serving plate and garnish with parsley.

calories: 288 | fat: 16.1g | protein: 23.2g | carbs: 7.7g | net carbs: 6.7g | fiber: 1.0g

Tilapia and Riced Cauliflower Cabbage Tortillas

Prep time: 10 minutes | Cook time: 15 minutes | Serves 4

1 teaspoon avocado oil
1 cup cauli rice
4 tilapia fillets, cut into cubes
¼ teaspoon taco seasoning
Sea salt and hot paprika to
taste
2 whole cabbage leaves
2 tablespoons guacamole
1 tablespoon cilantro, chopped

Microwave the cauli rice in microwave safe bowl for 4 minutes. Fluff with a fork and set aside. Warm avocado oil in a skillet over medium heat, rub the tilapia with the taco seasoning, salt, and hot paprika, and fry until brown on all sides, for about 8 minutes in total. Divide the fish among the cabbage leaves, top with cauli rice, guacamole and cilantro.

calories: 171 | fat: 6.5g | protein: 24.4g | carbs: 2.8g | net carbs: 1.5g | fiber: 1.3g

Shirataki Noodles with Grilled Tuna

Prep time: 10 minutes | Cook time: 25 minutes | Serves 4

1 (7-ounce / 198-g) pack shirataki noodles
3 cups water
1 red bell pepper, seeded and halved
4 tuna steaks
Salt and black pepper to taste
Olive oil for brushing
2 tablespoons pickled ginger
2 tablespoons chopped cilantro

In a colander, rinse the shirataki noodles with running cold water. Bring a pot of salted water to a boil; blanch the noodles for 2 minutes. Drain and transfer to a dry skillet over medium heat. Dry roast for a minute until opaque. Grease a grill's grate with cooking spray and preheat on medium heat. Season the red bell pepper and tuna with salt and black pepper, brush with olive oil, and grill covered. Cook both for 3 minutes on each side. Transfer to a plate to cool. Dice bell pepper with a knife. Assemble the noodles, tuna, and bell pepper in serving plate. Top with pickled ginger and garnish with cilantro. Serve with roasted sesame sauce.

calories: 312 | fat: 18.3g | protein: 22.1g | carbs: 2.5g | net carbs: 1.8g | fiber: 0.7g

Salmon Fillets with Broccoli

Prep time: 10 minutes | Cook time: 30 minutes | Serves 4

4 salmon fillets
Salt and black pepper to taste
2 tablespoons mayonnaise
2 tablespoons fennel seeds, crushed
½ head broccoli, cut in florets
1 red bell pepper, sliced
1 tablespoon olive oil
2 lemon wedges

Brush the salmon with mayonnaise and season with salt and black pepper. Coat with fennel seeds, place in a lined baking dish and bake for 15 minutes at 370ºF (188ºC). Steam the broccoli and carrot for 3-4 minutes, or until tender, in a pot over medium heat. Heat the olive oil in a saucepan and sauté the red bell pepper for 5 minutes. Stir in the broccoli and turn off the heat. Let the pan sit on the warm burner for 2-3 minutes. Serve with baked salmon garnished with lemon wedges.

calories: 564 | fat: 36.8g | protein: 53.9g | carbs: 8.3g | net carbs: 5.9g | fiber: 2.4g

Dijon-Tarragon Salmon

Prep time: 10 minutes | Cook time: 10 minutes | Serves 4

4 salmon fillets
¾ teaspoon fresh thyme
1 tablespoon butter
Sauce:
¼ cup Dijon mustard
2 tablespoons white wine
¾ teaspoon tarragon
Salt and black pepper to taste

½ teaspoon tarragon
¼ cup heavy cream

Season the salmon with thyme, tarragon, salt, and black pepper. Melt the butter in a pan over medium heat. Add salmon and cook for about 4-5 minutes on both sides until the salmon is cooked through. Remove to a warm dish and cover. To the same pan, add the sauce ingredients over low heat and simmer until the sauce is slightly thickened, stirring continually. Cook for 60 seconds to infuse the flavors and adjust the seasoning. Serve the salmon, topped with the sauce.

calories: 538 | fat: 26.5g | protein: 66.9g | carbs: 2.1g | net carbs: 1.4g | fiber: 0.7g

Coconut and Pecorino Fried Shrimp

Prep time: 15 minutes | Cook time: 10 minutes | Serves 4

2 teaspoons coconut flour
2 tablespoons grated Pecorino cheese
1 egg, beaten in a bowl
¼ teaspoon curry powder
Sauce:
2 tablespoons butter
2 tablespoons cilantro leaves, chopped
½ onion, diced
1 pound (454 g) shrimp, shelled
3 tablespoons coconut oil
Salt to taste

½ cup coconut cream
½ ounce (14 g) Paneer cheese, grated

Combine coconut flour, Pecorino cheese, curry powder, and salt in a bowl. Melt the coconut oil in a skillet over medium heat. Dip the shrimp in the egg first, and then coat with the dry mixture. Fry until golden and crispy, about 5 minutes. In another skillet, melt the butter. Add onion and cook for 3 minutes. Add curry and cilantro and cook for 30 seconds. Stir in coconut cream and Paneer cheese and cook until thickened. Add the shrimp and coat well. Serve warm.

calories: 740 | fat: 63.8g | protein: 34.2g | carbs: 5.2g | net carbs:4.2 g | fiber: 1.0g

Chive-Sauced Chili Cod

Prep time: 10 minutes | Cook time: 20 minutes | Serves 4

1 teaspoon chili powder
4 cod fillets
Salt and black pepper to taste
1 tablespoon olive oil

1 garlic clove, minced
⅓ cup lemon juice
2 tablespoons vegetable stock
2 tablespoons chives, chopped

Preheat oven to 400ºF (205ºC) and grease a baking dish with cooking spray. Rub the cod fillets with chili powder, salt, and pepper and lay in the dish. Bake for 10-15 minutes. In a skillet over low heat, warm olive oil and sauté garlic for 1 minute. Add lemon juice, vegetable stock, and chives. Season with salt, pepper, and cook for 3 minutes until the stock slightly reduces. Divide fish into 2 plates, top with sauce, and serve.

calories: 450 | fat: 35.2g | protein: 20.1g | carbs: 7.0g | net carbs: 6.4g | fiber: 0.6g

Hazelnut Haddock Bake

Prep time: 15 minutes | Cook time: 25 minutes | Serves 4

1 tablespoon butter
1 shallot, sliced
1 pound (454 g) haddock fillet
2 eggs, hard-boiled, chopped
½ cup water
3 tablespoons hazelnut flour

2 cups sour cream
1 tablespoon parsley, chopped
½ cup pork rinds, crushed
1 cup Mozzarella cheese, grated
Salt and black pepper to taste

Melt butter in a saucepan over medium heat and sauté the shallots for about 3 minutes. Reduce the heat to low and stir the hazelnut flour into it to form a roux. Cook the roux to be golden brown and stir in the sour cream until the mixture is smooth. Season with salt and pepper, and stir in the parsley. Spread the haddock fillet in a greased baking dish, sprinkle the eggs on top, and spoon the sauce over. In a bowl, mix the pork rinds with the Mozzarella cheese, and sprinkle it over the sauce. Bake in the oven for 20 minutes at 370ºF (188ºC) until the top is golden and the sauce and cheese are bubbly.

calories: 786 | fat: 56.9g | protein: 64.9g | carbs: 9.5g | net carbs: 8.4g | fiber: 1.1g

Asparagus and Trout Foil Packets

Prep time: 15 minutes | Cook time: 15 minutes | Serves 4

1 pound (454 g) asparagus spears
1 tablespoon garlic purée
1 pound (454 g) deboned trout, butterflied
Salt and black pepper to taste

3 tablespoons olive oil
2 sprigs rosemary
2 sprigs thyme
2 tablespoons butter
½ medium red onion, sliced
2 lemon slices

Preheat the oven to 400ºF (205ºC). Rub the trout with garlic purée, salt and black pepper. Prepare two aluminum foil squares. Place the fish on each square. Divide the asparagus and onion between the squares, top with a pinch of salt and pepper, a sprig of rosemary and thyme, and 1 tablespoon of butter. Also, lay the lemon slices on the fish. Wrap and close the fish packets securely, and place them on a baking sheet. Bake in the oven for 15 minutes, and remove once ready.

calories: 495 | fat: 39.2g | protein: 26.9g | carbs: 7.5g | net carbs: 4.9g | fiber: 2.6g

Parsley-Lemon Salmon

Prep time: 10 minutes | Cook time: 20 minutes | Serves 4

4 salmon fillets
½ cup heavy cream
1 tablespoon mayonnaise
½ tablespoon parsley, chopped
½ lemon, zested and juiced

Salt and black pepper to season
1 tablespoon Parmesan cheese, grated

In a bowl, mix the heavy cream, parsley, mayonnaise, lemon zest, lemon juice, salt and pepper, and set aside. Season the fish with salt and black pepper, drizzle lemon juice on both sides of the fish and arrange them in a parchment paper–lined baking sheet. Spread the parsley mixture and sprinkle with Parmesan cheese. Bake in the oven for 15 minutes at 400ºF (205ºC). Great served with steamed broccoli.

calories: 555 | fat: 30.3g | protein: 56.1g | carbs: 2.2g | net carbs: 2.1g | fiber: 0.1g

Lobster and Cauliflower Salad Rolls

Prep time: 15 minutes | Cook time: 0 minutes | Serves 4

5 cups cauliflower florets
⅓ cup celery, diced
2 cups large shrimp, cooked
1 tablespoon dill, chopped
½ cup mayonnaise

1 teaspoon apple cider vinegar
¼ teaspoon celery seeds
2 tablespoons lemon juice
2 teaspoons Swerve
Salt and black pepper to taste

Combine cauliflower, celery, shrimp, and dill in a large bowl. Whisk mayonnaise, vinegar, celery seeds, sweetener, and lemon juice in another bowl. Season with salt. Pour the dressing over the salad, and gently toss to combine. Serve cold.

calories: 181 | fat: 15.1g | protein: 11.9g | carbs: 5.4g | net carbs: 1.9g | fiber: 3.5g

Provençal Lemony Fish Stew

Prep time: 15 minutes | Cook time: 6 minutes | Serves 2

1 tablespoon olive oil
1 shallot, sliced
3 garlic cloves, minced
1 cup tomato purée
5 cups white fish stock
1 teaspoon basil
½ teaspoon rosemary
½ California bay leaf
⅓ teaspoon saffron threads,

crumbled
Sea salt and freshly cracked black pepper, to taste
1 pound (454 g) grouper fish
⅓ pound (151 g) cockles, scrubbed
⅓ pound (151 g) prawns
1 tablespoon fresh lemon juice

Heat the olive oil in a stockpot over a moderate flame. Sauté the shallot for 3 minutes or until tender; add in the garlic and cook for 30 seconds or until aromatic. Pour in the tomato purée and white fish stock; bring everything to a boil. Stir in the basil, rosemary, California bay leaf, saffron threads, salt, and black pepper. Turn the heat to medium-low. Fold in the grouper and cockles; gently stir to combine and simmer for 2 to 3 minutes. Add in the prawns; continue to simmer for 3 minutes more or until thoroughly warmed. Drizzle each serving with fresh lemon juice and enjoy!

calories: 176 | fat: 5g | protein: 24g | carbs: 5g | net carbs: 4g | fiber: 1g

Catalan Shrimp

Prep time: 5 minutes | Cook time: 20 minutes | Serves 4

¼ cup olive oil, divided
1 pound (454 g) shrimp, deveined
Salt to taste

¼ teaspoon cayenne pepper
3 garlic cloves, sliced
2 tablespoons chopped parsley

Warm olive oil in a large skillet over medium heat. Reduce the heat and add the garlic; cook for 6-8 minutes, but make sure it doesn't brown or burn. Add the shrimp, season with salt and cayenne pepper, stir for one minute and turn off the heat. Let the shrimp finish cooking with the heat of the hot oil for about 8-10 minutes. Serve garnished with parsley.

calories: 442 | fat: 28.9g | protein: 43.2g | carbs: 1.2g | net carbs: 1.1g | fiber: 0.1g

Salmon with Radish and Arugula Salad

Prep time: 15 minutes | Cook time: 10 minutes | Serves 4

1 pound (454 g) salmon, cut into 4 steaks each
1 cup radishes, sliced
Salt and black pepper to taste
8 green olives, pitted and chopped
1 cup arugula

2 large tomatoes, diced
3 tablespoons red wine vinegar
2 green onions, sliced
3 tablespoons olive oil
2 slices zero carb bread, cubed
¼ cup parsley, chopped

In a bowl, mix the radishes, olives, black pepper, arugula, tomatoes, wine vinegar, green onion, olive oil, bread, and parsley. Let sit for the flavors to incorporate. Season the salmon steaks with salt and pepper; grill on both sides for 8 minutes in total. Serve the salmon on a bed of the radish salad.

calories: 339 | fat: 21.6g | protein: 28.4g | carbs: 5.3g | net carbs: 3.0g | fiber: 2.3g

Baked Tilapia with Black Olives

Prep time: 15 minutes | Cook time: 25 minutes | Serves 4

4 tilapia fillets
2 garlic cloves, minced
1 teaspoon basil, chopped
1 cup canned tomatoes
¼ tablespoon chili powder
2 tablespoons white wine

1 tablespoon olive oil
½ red onion, chopped
2 tablespoons parsley
10 black olives, pitted and halved

Preheat oven to 350ºF (180ºC). Heat the olive oil in a skillet over medium heat and cook the onion and garlic for about 3 minutes. Stir in tomatoes, olives, chili powder, and white wine and bring the mixture to a boil. Reduce the heat and simmer for 5 minutes. Put the tilapia in a baking dish, pour over the sauce and bake in the oven for 10-15 minutes. Serve garnished with basil.

calories: 281 | fat: 15.0g | protein: 23.0g | carbs: 7.2g | net carbs: 6.0g | fiber: 1.2g

Dijon Crab Cakes

Prep time: 10 minutes | Cook time: 5 minutes | Serves 4

1 tablespoon coconut oil
1 pound (454 g) lump crab meat
1 teaspoon Dijon mustard

1 egg
¼ cup mayonnaise
1 tablespoon coconut flour
1 tablespoon cilantro, chopped

In a bowl, add crab meat, mustard, mayonnaise, coconut flour, egg, cilantro, salt, and pepper; mix to combine. Make patties out of the mixture. Melt coconut oil in a skillet over medium heat. Add crab patties and cook for 2-3 minutes per side. Remove to kitchen paper. Serve.

calories: 316 | fat: 24.3g | protein: 15.2g | carbs: 1.8g | net carbs: 1.5g | fiber: 0.3g

Sardines with Zoodles

Prep time: 10 minutes | Cook time: 15 minutes | Serves 4

2 tablespoons olive oil
4 cups zoodles (spiralized zucchini)
1 pound (454 g) whole fresh sardines, gutted and cleaned

½ cup sundried tomatoes, chopped
1 tablespoon dill
1 garlic clove, minced

Preheat the oven to 350ºF (180ºC) and line a baking sheet with parchment paper. Arrange the sardines on the dish, drizzle with olive oil, sprinkle with salt and pepper. Bake for 10 minutes until the skin is crispy. Warm oil in a skillet and stir-fry zucchini, garlic and tomatoes for 5 minutes. Transfer the sardines to a plate and serve with the veggie pasta.

calories: 432 | fat: 28.2g | protein: 32.3g | carbs: 7.1g | net carbs: 5.4g | fiber: 1.7g

Tuna Omelet Wraps

Prep time: 10 minutes | Cook time: 10 minutes | Serves 4

1 avocado, sliced
1 tablespoon chopped chives
1 cup canned tuna, drained
2 spring onions, sliced
8 eggs, beaten

4 tablespoons mascarpone cheese
1 tablespoon butter
Salt and black pepper, to taste

In a small bowl, combine the chives and mascarpone cheese; set aside. Melt the butter in a pan over medium heat. Add the eggs to the pan and cook for about 3 minutes. Flip the omelet over and continue cooking for another 2 minutes until golden. Season with salt and black pepper. Remove the omelet to a plate and spread the chive mixture over. Arrange the tuna, avocado, and onion slices. Wrap the omelet and serve immediately.

calories: 480 | fat: 37.8g | protein: 26.8g | carbs: 9.9g | net carbs: 6.3g | fiber: 3.6g

Tomato and Olive Tilapia Flillets

Prep time: 10 minutes | Cook time: 25 minutes | Serves 4

4 tilapia fillets
2 garlic cloves, minced
2 teaspoons oregano
14 ounces (397 g) diced tomatoes

1 tablespoon olive oil
½ red onion, chopped
2 tablespoons parsley
¼ cup kalamata olives

Heat olive oil in a skillet over medium heat and cook the onion for 3 minutes. Add garlic and oregano and cook for 30 seconds. Stir in tomatoes and bring the mixture to a boil. Reduce the heat and simmer for 5 minutes. Add olives and tilapia, and cook for about 8 minutes. Serve the tilapia with tomato sauce.

calories: 283 | fat: 15.1g | protein: 22.9g | carbs: 7.9g | net carbs: 5.9g | fiber: 2.0g

Seared Scallops with Sausage

Prep time: 10 minutes | Cook time: 10 minutes | Serves 4

2 tablespoons butter
12 fresh scallops, rinsed
8 ounces (227 g) sausage, chopped

1 red bell pepper, sliced
1 red onion, finely chopped
1 cup Grana Padano, grated
Salt and black pepper to taste

Melt half of the butter in a skillet over medium heat, and cook the onion and bell pepper for 5 minutes until tender. Add the sausage and stir-fry for another 5 minutes. Remove and set aside. Pat dry scallops with paper towels, and season with salt and pepper. Add the remaining butter to the skillet and sear scallops for 2 minutes on each side to have a golden brown color. Add the sausage mixture back, and warm through. Transfer to serving platter and top with Grana Padano cheese.

calories: 835 | fat: 61.9g | protein: 55.9g | carbs: 10.5g | net carbs: 9.4g | fiber: 1.1g

Tiger Shrimp with Chimichurri

Prep time: 15 minutes | Cook time: 35 minutes | Serves 4

1 pound (454 g) tiger shrimp, peeled and deveined
2 tablespoons olive oil
Chimichurri:
Salt and black pepper to taste
¼ cup extra-virgin olive oil
2 garlic cloves, minced
1 lime, juiced

1 garlic clove, minced
Juice of 1 lime
Salt and black pepper to taste

¼ cup red wine vinegar
2 cups parsley, minced
¼ teaspoon red pepper flakes

Combine the shrimp, olive oil, garlic, and lime juice, in a bowl, and let marinate in the fridge for 30 minutes. To make the chimichurri dressing, blitz the chimichurri ingredients in a blender until smooth; set aside. Preheat your grill to medium. Add shrimp and cook about 2 minutes per side. Serve shrimp drizzled with the chimichurri dressing.

calories: 524 | fat: 30.2g | protein: 48.8g | carbs: 8.3g | net carbs: 7.1g | fiber: 1.2g

Asian Scallop and Vegetable

Prep time: 10 minutes | Cook time: 5 minutes | Serves 4

4 teaspoons sesame oil
½ cup yellow onion, sliced
1 cup asparagus spears, sliced
½ cup celery, chopped
½ cup enoki mushrooms
1 pound (454 g) bay scallops
1 tablespoon fresh parsley, chopped

Kosher salt and ground black pepper, to taste
½ teaspoon red pepper flakes, crushed
1 tablespoon coconut aminos
2 tablespoons rice wine
½ cup dry roasted peanuts, roughly chopped

Heat 1 teaspoon of the sesame oil in a wok over a medium-high flame. Now, fry the onion until crisp-tender and translucent; reserve. Heat another teaspoon of the sesame oil and fry the asparagus and celery for about 3 minutes until crisp-tender; reserve. Then, heat another teaspoon of the sesame oil and cook the mushrooms for 2 minutes more or until they start to soften; reserve. Lastly, heat the remaining teaspoon of sesame oil and cook the bay scallops just until they are opaque. Return all reserved vegetables to the wok. Add in the remaining ingredients and toss to combine. Serve warm and enjoy!

calories: 236 | fat: 13g | protein: 27g | carbs: 6g | net carbs: 4g | fiber: 2g

Coconut Mussel Curry

Prep time: 15 minutes | Cook time: 20 minutes | Serves 4

2 tablespoons cup coconut oil
2 green onions, chopped
1 pound (454 g) mussels, cleaned, de-bearded
1 shallot, chopped
1 garlic clove, minced

½ cup coconut milk
½ cup white wine
1 teaspoon red curry powder
2 tablespoons parsley, chopped

Cook the shallots and garlic in the wine over low heat. Stir in the coconut milk and red curry powder and cook for 3 minutes. Add the mussels and steam for 7 minutes or until their shells are opened. Then, use a slotted spoon to remove to a bowl leaving the sauce in the pan. Discard any closed mussels at this point. Stir the coconut oil into the sauce, turn the heat off, and stir in the parsley and green onions. Serve the sauce immediately with a butternut squash mash.

calories: 354 | fat: 20.4g | protein: 21.0g | carbs: 2.2g | net carbs: 0.2g | fiber: 2.0g

Fennel and Trout Parcels

Prep time: 10 minutes | Cook time: 15 minutes | Serves 4

½ pound (227 g) deboned trout, butterflied
Salt and black pepper to season
3 tablespoons olive oil plus extra for tossing
4 sprigs rosemary

4 sprigs thyme
4 butter cubes
1 cup thinly sliced fennel
1 medium red onion, sliced
8 lemon slices
3 teaspoons capers to garnish

Preheat the oven to 400°F (205°C). Cut out parchment paper wide enough for each trout. In a bowl, toss the fennel and onion with a little bit of olive oil and share into the middle parts of the papers. Place the fish on each veggie mound, top with a drizzle of olive oil each, a pinch of salt and black pepper, a sprig of rosemary and thyme, and 1 cube of butter. Also, lay the lemon slices on the fish. Wrap and close the fish packets securely, and place them on a baking sheet. Bake in the oven for 15 minutes, and remove once ready. Plate them and garnish the fish with capers and serve with a squash mash.

calories: 235 | fat: 9.1g | protein: 17.1g | carbs: 3.7g | net carbs: 2.7g | fiber: 1.0g

Salmon and Cucumber Panzanella

Prep time: 15 minutes | Cook time: 10 minutes | Serves 4

1 pound (454 g) skinned salmon, cut into 4 steaks each
1 cucumber, peeled, seeded, cubed
Salt and black pepper to taste
8 black olives, pitted and chopped

1 tablespoon capers, rinsed
2 large tomatoes, diced
3 tablespoons red wine vinegar
¼ cup thinly sliced red onion
3 tablespoons olive oil
2 slices zero carb bread, cubed
¼ cup thinly sliced basil leaves

Preheat a grill to 350°F (180°C) and prepare the salad. In a bowl, mix the cucumbers, olives, pepper, capers, tomatoes, wine vinegar, onion, olive oil, bread, and basil leaves. Let sit for the flavors to incorporate. Season the salmon steaks with salt and pepper; grill them on both sides for 8 minutes in total. Serve the salmon steaks warm on a bed of the veggies' salad.

calories: 339 | fat: 21.6g | protein: 28.6g | carbs: 5.3g | net carbs: 3.2g | fiber: 2.1g

Blackened Tilapia Tacos

Prep time: 10 minutes | Cook time: 5 minutes | Serves 4

1 tablespoon olive oil
1 teaspoon chili powder
2 tilapia fillets
Slaw:
½ cup red cabbage, shredded
1 tablespoon lemon juice
1 teaspoon apple cider vinegar

1 teaspoon paprika
4 low carb tortillas

1 tablespoon olive oil
Salt and black pepper to taste

Season the tilapia with chili powder and paprika. Heat the olive oil in a skillet over medium heat. Add tilapia and cook until blackened, about 3 minutes per side. Cut into strips. Divide the tilapia between the tortillas. Combine all slaw ingredients in a bowl and top the fish to serve.

calories: 269 | fat: 20.1g | protein: 13.7g | carbs: 5.3g | net carbs: 3.4g | fiber: 1.9g

Tilapia and Red Cabbage Taco Bowl

Prep time: 10 minutes | Cook time: 15 minutes | Serves 4

2 cups cauli rice
2 teaspoons butter
4 tilapia fillets, cut into cubes
¼ teaspoon taco seasoning

Salt and chili pepper to taste
¼ head red cabbage, shredded
1 ripe avocado, pitted and chopped

Sprinkle cauli rice in a bowl with a little water and microwave for 3 minutes. Fluff after with a fork and set aside. Melt butter in a skillet over medium heat, rub the tilapia with the taco seasoning, salt, and chili pepper, and fry until brown on all sides, for about 8 minutes in total. Transfer to a plate and set aside. In 4 serving bowls, share the cauli rice, cabbage, fish, and avocado. Serve with chipotle lime sour cream dressing.

calories: 270 | fat: 23.5g | protein: 16.6g | carbs: 9.1g | net carbs: 3.9g | fiber: 5.2g

Sicilian Zoodle and Sardine Spaghetti

Prep time: 5 minutes | Cook time: 10 minutes | Serves 2

4 cups zoodles (spiralled zucchini)
2 ounces (57 g) cubed bacon
4 ounces (113 g) canned sardines, chopped

½ cup canned chopped tomatoes
1 tablespoon capers
1 tablespoon parsley
1 teaspoon minced garlic

Pour some of the sardine oil in a pan. Add garlic and cook for 1 minute. Add the bacon and cook for 2 more minutes. Stir in the tomatoes and let simmer for 5 minutes. Add zoodles and sardines and cook for 3 minutes.

calories: 356 | fat: 31.2g | protein: 20.1g | carbs: 8.8g | net carbs: 5.9g | fiber: 2.9g

Sour Cream Salmon Steaks

Prep time: 10 minutes | Cook time: 20 minutes | Serves 4

1 cup sour cream
½ tablespoon minced dill
½ lemon, zested and juiced
Pink salt and black pepper to

season
4 salmon steaks
½ cup grated Parmesan cheese

Preheat oven to 400ºF (205ºC) and line a baking sheet with parchment paper; set aside. In a bowl, mix the sour cream, dill, lemon zest, juice, salt and black pepper, and set aside. Season the fish with salt and black pepper, drizzle lemon juice on both sides of the fish and arrange them in the baking sheet. Spread the sour cream mixture on each fish and sprinkle with Parmesan. Bake the fish for 15 minutes and after broil the top for 2 minutes with a close watch for a nice a brown color. Plate the fish and serve with buttery green beans.

calories: 289 | fat: 23.5g | protein: 16.1g | carbs: 1.5g | net carbs: 1.3g | fiber: 0.2g

Sriracha Shrimp Sushi Rolls

Prep time: 10 minutes | Cook time: 0 minutes | Serves 5

2 cups cooked and chopped shrimp
1 tablespoon sriracha sauce

¼ cucumber, julienned
5 hand roll nori sheets
¼ cup mayonnaise

Combine shrimp, mayonnaise, cucumber and sriracha sauce in a bowl. Lay out a single nori sheet on a flat surface and spread about ⅕ of the shrimp mixture. Roll the nori sheet as desired. Repeat with the other ingredients. Serve with sugar-free soy sauce.

calories: 220 | fat: 10.2g | protein: 18.6g | carbs: 2.0g | net carbs: 0.9g | fiber: 1.1g

Chimichurri Grilled Shrimp

Prep time: 10 minutes | Cook time: 35 minutes | Serves 4

1 pound (454 g)shrimp, peeled and deveined
Chimichurri:
½ teaspoon salt
¼ cup olive oil
2 garlic cloves
¼ cup red onions, chopped

2 tablespoons olive oil
Juice of 1 lime

¼ cup red wine vinegar
½ teaspoon pepper
2 cups parsley
¼ teaspoon red pepper flakes

Process the chimichurri ingredients in a blender until smooth; set aside. Combine shrimp, olive oil, and lime juice, in a bowl, and let marinate in the fridge for 30 minutes. Preheat your grill to medium. Add shrimp and cook about 2 minutes per side. Serve shrimp drizzled with the chimichurri sauce.

calories: 284 | fat: 20.4g | protein: 15.8g | carbs: 4.8g | net carbs: 3.6g | fiber: 1.2g

Crab Patties

Prep time: 10 minutes | Cook time: 5 minutes | Serves 8

2 tablespoons coconut oil
1 tablespoon lemon juice
1 cup lump crab meat

2 teaspoons Dijon mustard
1 egg, beaten
1½ tablespoons coconut flour

In a bowl to the crabmeat, add all the ingredients, except for the oil; mix well to combine. Make patties out of the mixture. Melt the coconut oil in a skillet over medium heat. Add the crab patties and cook for about 2-3 minutes per side.

calories: 216 | fat: 11.6g | protein: 15.2g | carbs: 3.6g | net carbs: 3.5g | fiber: 0.1g

Parmesan Shrimp with Curry Sauce

Prep time: 10 minutes | Cook time: 5 minutes | Serves 2

½ ounce (14 g) grated
Parmesan cheese
1 egg, beaten
¼ teaspoon curry powder
Sauce:
2 tablespoons curry leaves
2 tablespoons butter
½ onion, diced

2 teaspoons almond flour
12 shrimp, shelled
3 tablespoons coconut oil

½ cup heavy cream
½ ounce (14 g) Cheddar
cheese, shredded

Combine all dry ingredients for the batter. Melt the coconut oil in a skillet over medium heat. Dip the shrimp in the egg first, and then coat with the dry mixture. Fry until golden and crispy. In another skillet, melt butter. Add onion and cook for 3 minutes. Add curry leaves and cook for 30 seconds. Stir in heavy cream and Cheddar and cook until thickened. Add shrimp and coat well. Serve.

calories: 561 | fat: 40.9g | protein: 24.3g | carbs: 5.0g | net carbs: 4.2g | fiber: 0.8g

Lemony Paprika Shrimp

Prep time: 10 minutes | Cook time: 20 minutes | Serves 6

½ cup butter, divided
2 pounds (907 g) shrimp,
peeled and deveined
Salt and black pepper to taste
¼ teaspoon sweet paprika

1 tablespoon minced garlic
3 tablespoons water
1 lemon, zested and juiced
2 tablespoons chopped parsley

Melt half of the butter in a large skillet over medium heat, season the shrimp with salt, black pepper, paprika, and add to the butter. Stir in the garlic and cook the shrimp for 4 minutes on both sides until pink. Remove to a bowl and set aside. Put the remaining butter in the skillet; include the lemon zest, juice, and water. Add the shrimp, parsley, and adjust the taste with salt and pepper. Cook for 2 minutes. Serve shrimp and sauce with squash pasta.

calories: 256 | fat: 22.1g | protein: 12.9g | carbs: 2.0g | net carbs: 1.9g | fiber: 0.1g

Seared Scallops with Chorizo

Prep time: 10 minutes | Cook time: 10 minutes | Serves 4

2 tablespoons butter
16 fresh scallops
8 ounces (227 g) chorizo,
chopped
1 red bell pepper, seeds

removed, sliced
1 cup red onions, finely
chopped
1 cup Asiago cheese, grated
Salt and black pepper to taste

Melt half of the butter in a skillet over medium heat, and cook the onion and bell pepper for 5 minutes until tender. Add the chorizo and stir-fry for another 3 minutes. Remove and set aside. Pat dry the scallops with paper towels, and season with salt and pepper. Add the remaining butter to the skillet and sear the scallops for 2 minutes on each side to have a golden brown color. Add the chorizo mixture back and warm through. Transfer to serving platter and top with Asiago cheese.

calories: 490 | fat: 32.1g | protein: 35.8g | carbs: 6.0g | net carbs: 4.9g | fiber: 1.1g

Pistachio Salmon with Shallot Sauce

Prep time: 15 minutes | Cook time: 20 minutes | Serves 4

4 salmon fillets
½ teaspoon pepper
1 teaspoon salt

Sauce:
1 chopped shallot
2 teaspoons lemon zest
1 tablespoon olive oil

¼ cup mayonnaise
½ cup chopped pistachios

A pinch of black pepper
1 cup heavy cream

Preheat the oven to 370ºF (188ºC). Brush the salmon with mayonnaise and season with salt and pepper. Coat with pistachios, place in a lined baking dish and bake for 15 minutes. Heat olive oil in a saucepan and sauté the shallot for 3 minutes. Stir in the rest of the sauce ingredients. Bring the mixture to a boil and cook until thickened. Serve the fish with the sauce.

calories: 562 | fat: 46.8g | protein: 34.1g | carbs: 8.1g | net carbs: 5.9g | fiber: 2.2g

Mussels and Coconut Milk Curry

Prep time: 10 minutes | Cook time: 20 minutes | Serves 6

3 pounds (1.4 kg) mussels,
cleaned, de-bearded
1 cup minced shallots
3 tablespoons minced garlic
1½ cups coconut milk

2 cups dry white wine
2 teaspoons red curry powder
⅓ cup coconut oil
⅓ cup chopped green onions
⅓ cup chopped parsley

Pour the wine into a large saucepan and cook the shallots and garlic over low heat. Stir in the coconut milk and red curry powder and cook for 3 minutes. Add the mussels and steam for 7 minutes or until their shells are opened. Then, use a slotted spoon to remove to a bowl leaving the sauce in the pan. Discard any closed mussels at this point. Stir the coconut oil into the sauce, turn the heat off, and stir in the parsley and green onions. Serve the sauce immediately with a butternut squash mash.

calories: 355 | fat: 20.5g | protein: 21.0g | carbs: 2.5g | net carbs: 0.2g | fiber: 2.3g

Alaska Cod with Butter Garlic Sauce

Prep time: 10 minutes | Cook time: 15 minutes | Serves 6

2 teaspoons olive oil
6 Alaska cod fillets
Salt and black pepper to taste
4 tablespoons salted butter

4 cloves garlic, minced
⅓ cup lemon juice
3 tablespoons white wine
2 tablespoons chopped chives

Heat the oil in a skillet over medium heat and season the cod with salt and black pepper. Fry the fillets in the oil for 4 minutes on one side, flip and cook for 1 minute. Take out, plate, and set aside. In another skillet over low heat, melt the butter and sauté the garlic for 3 minutes. Add the lemon juice, wine, and chives. Season with salt, black pepper, and cook for 3 minutes until the wine slightly reduces. Put the fish in the skillet, spoon sauce over, cook for 30 seconds and turn the heat off. Divide fish into 6 plates, top with sauce, and serve with buttered green beans.

calories: 265 | fat: 17.1g | protein: 19.9g | carbs: 2.5g | net carbs: 2.4g | fiber: 0.1g

Creamy Herbed Salmon

Prep time: 10 minutes | Cook time: 10 minutes | Serves 2

2 salmon fillets
¾ teaspoon dried tarragon
Sauce:
2 tablespoons butter
½ teaspoon dill
½ teaspoon tarragon

2 tablespoons olive oil
¾ teaspoon dried dill

¼ cup heavy cream
Salt and black pepper to taste

Season the salmon with dill and tarragon. Warm the olive oil in a pan over medium heat. Add salmon and cook for about 4 minutes on both sides. Set aside. To make the sauce: melt the butter and add the dill and tarragon. Cook for 30 seconds to infuse the flavors. Whisk in the heavy cream, season with salt and black pepper, and cook for 2-3 minutes. Serve the salmon topped with the sauce.

calories: 467 | fat: 40.1g | protein: 22.1g | carbs: 1.9g | net carbs: 1.6g | fiber: 0.3g

Parmesan Baked Salmon with Broccoli

Prep time: 10 minutes | Cook time: 30 minutes | Serves 4

2 salmon fillets, cubed
3 white fish, cubed
1 head broccoli, cut into florets
1 tablespoon butter, melted
Salt and black pepper to taste

1 cup crème fraiche
¼ cup grated Parmesan cheese
Grated Parmesan cheese for topping

Preheat oven to 400ºF (205ºC) and grease an 8 x 8 inches casserole dish with cooking spray. Toss the fish cubes and broccoli in butter and season with salt and pepper to taste. Spread in the greased dish. Mix the crème fraiche with Parmesan cheese, pour and smear the cream on the fish, and sprinkle with some more Parmesan cheese. Bake for 25 to 30 minutes until golden brown on top, take the dish out, sit for 5 minutes and spoon into plates. Serve with lemon-mustard asparagus.

calories: 355 | fat: 17.2g | protein: 28.1g | carbs: 4.9g | net carbs: 3.9g | fiber: 1.0g

Tuna Cakes with Seeds

Prep time: 10 minutes | Cook time: 10 minutes | Serves 4

3 tablespoons sugar-free mayonnaise
1 tablespoon Sriracha sauce
1 teaspoon wheat-free soy sauce
1 teaspoon coconut flour
1 pound (454 g) fresh tuna, cut into ½-inch cubes

2 tablespoons white sesame seeds
1 tablespoon black sesame seeds
2 tablespoons avocado oil or other light-tasting oil, for the pan

In a mixing bowl, whisk together the mayonnaise, Sriracha, soy sauce, and flour until smooth. Add the tuna and stir to combine. Combine the white and black sesame seeds and spread on a small plate. Using your hands, form the tuna mixture into 12 small cakes about 2 inches in diameter. Gently dip both sides of the cakes in the sesame seeds to lightly coat them. Heat the oil in a medium-sized nonstick sauté pan over medium heat. Cook the cakes in batches, 1 to 2 minutes per side, until golden brown. Serve warm.

calories: 300 | fat: 18.9g | protein: 26.9g | carbs: 2.0g | net carbs: 1.0g | fiber: 1.0g

Sriracha Shrimp Stuffed Avocados

Prep time: 5 minutes | Cook time: 0 minutes | Serves 4

1 pound (454 g) large shrimp, peeled, deveined, and cooked (tails removed)
⅓ cup sugar-free mayonnaise
2 tablespoons Sriracha sauce

1 teaspoon chopped fresh cilantro, plus more for garnish if desired
1 teaspoon lime juice
2 large ripe Hass avocados

Chop the shrimp into bite-sized pieces and place in a medium-sized bowl. Add the mayonnaise, Sriracha, cilantro, and lime juice. Mix until well combined. Place in the refrigerator to chill for 10 minutes. Just before serving, cut the avocados in half and remove the pits. Spoon ½ cup of the spicy shrimp mixture into each avocado half. Serve immediately, garnished with extra cilantro, if desired. If not consuming it right away, store the spicy shrimp mixture in the refrigerator for up to 5 days.

calories: 335 | fat: 29.1g | protein: 14.9g | carbs: 7.9g | net carbs: 2.8g | fiber: 5.1g

Macadamia Tilapia

Prep time: 5 minutes | Cook time: 15 minutes | Serves 2

2 (4-ounce / 113-g) tilapia fillets
½ cup unsalted macadamia nuts
1 tablespoon chopped fresh parsley

1 tablespoon fresh lemon juice
2 teaspoons coconut oil
¼ teaspoon garlic powder
Lemon wedges, for serving

Preheat the oven to 400ºF (205ºC). Line a rimmed baking sheet with parchment paper. Rinse the tilapia with cold water, pat dry with a paper towel, and place on the lined baking sheet. Place the macadamia nuts, parsley, and lemon juice in a food processor and pulse/chop until the mixture is slightly chunkier than breadcrumb consistency. Be sure not to overblend, or you will end up with nut butter. Top each fillet with 1 teaspoon of the coconut oil and then the macadamia nut mixture, pressing it into the fish. Bake for 10 to 15 minutes, until the top is crisp and slightly golden brown. Serve with lemon wedges on the side.

calories: 382 | fat: 32.6g | protein: 22.6g | carbs: 5.4g | net carbs: 2.6g | fiber: 2.8g

White Tuna Patties

Prep time: 5 minutes | Cook time: 20 minutes | Serves 3

2 large eggs
1 tablespoon fresh lemon juice
¼ cup grated Parmesan cheese
¼ cup golden flaxseed meal
2 tablespoons chopped fresh parsley
2 teaspoons Old Bay

seasoning
1 (12-ounce / 340-g) can white tuna, in water
¼ cup finely chopped onions
¼ teaspoon salt
¼ cup avocado oil, for frying
Lemon wedges, for serving (optional)

In a bowl, beat the eggs with the lemon juice. Stir in the Parmesan cheese, flaxseed meal, parsley, and Old Bay seasoning. Drain the tuna well, removing as much of the water as possible. Add the drained tuna and onions to the Parmesan mixture and mix well. Season with salt and pepper to taste. Shape the tuna mixture into 6 patties. Heat the oil in a large skillet over medium heat. When hot, add half of the patties and fry until golden brown, 3 to 5 minutes per side, then set on a paper towel–lined dish to soak up any excess oil. Repeat with the remaining patties. Serve with lemon wedges, if desired.

calories: 306 | fat: 18.1g | protein: 30.9g | carbs: 5.0g | net carbs: 2.0g | fiber: 3.0g

Anchovies and Veggies Wraps

Prep time: 10 minutes | Cook time: 0 minutes | Serves 4

2 (2-ounce / 57-g) can anchovies in olive oil, drained
1 cucumber, sliced
2 cups red cabbage, shredded
1 red onion, chopped
1 teaspoon Dijon mustard
4 tablespoons mayonnaise
¼ teaspoon ground black pepper
1 large-sized tomato, diced
12 lettuce leaves

In a mixing bowl, combine the anchovies with the cucumber, cabbage, onion, mustard, mayonnaise, black pepper, and tomatoes. Arrange the lettuce leaves on a tray. Spoon the anchovy/vegetable mixture into the center of a lettuce leaf, taco-style. Repeat until you run out of ingredients. Bon appétit!

calories: 191 | fat: 13g | protein: 3g | carbs: 10g | net carbs: 7g | fiber: 3g

Haddock with Mediterranean Sauce

Prep time: 10 minutes | Cook time: 20 minutes | Serves 4

1 pound haddock fillets
Sea salt and freshly cracked black pepper, to taste
Mediterranean Sauce:
2 scallions, chopped
½ teaspoon dill weed
½ teaspoon oregano
1 teaspoon basil
1 tablespoon olive oil
¼ cup mayonnaise
¼ cup cream cheese, at room temperature

Start by preheating your oven to 360ºF (182ºC). Toss the haddock fillets with the olive oil, salt, and black pepper. Cover with foil and bake for 20 to 25 minutes. In the meantime, make the sauce by whisking all ingredients until well combined. Serve with the warm haddock fillets and enjoy!

calories: 260 | fat: 19g | protein: 20g | carbs: 1g | net carbs: 1g | fiber: 0g

Cod Fillet with Summer Salad

Prep time: 10 minutes | Cook time: 10 minutes | Serves 5

4 tablespoons extra-virgin olive oil
5 cod fillets
¼ cup balsamic vinegar
1 tablespoon stone-ground mustard
Sea salt and ground black pepper, to season
½ pound (227 g) green cabbage, shredded
2 cups lettuce, cut into small pieces
1 red onion, sliced
1 garlic clove, minced
1 teaspoon red pepper flakes

Heat 1 tablespoon of the olive oil in a large frying pan over medium-high heat. Once hot, fry the fish fillets for 5 minutes until golden brown; flip them and cook on the other side for 4 to 5 minutes more; work in batches to avoid overcrowding the pan. Flake the cod fillets with two forks and reserve. To make the dressing, whisk the remaining tablespoon of olive oil with the balsamic vinegar, mustard, salt, and black pepper. Combine the green cabbage, lettuce, onion, and garlic in a salad bowl. Dress the salad and top with the reserved fish. Garnish with red pepper flakes and serve. Enjoy!

calories: 276 | fat: 7g | protein: 43g | carbs: 6g | net carbs: 4g | fiber: 2g

Seafood Chowder

Prep time: 10 minutes | Cook time: 20 minutes | Serves 4

2 tablespoons coconut oil
2 garlic cloves, pressed
1 shallot, chopped
1 cup broccoli, broken into small florets
1 bell peppers, chopped
4 cups fish broth
4 tablespoons dry sherry
6 ounces (170 g) scallops
6 ounces (170 g) shrimp, peeled and deveined
1 cup heavy cream
1 tablespoon fresh chives, chopped

Melt the coconut oil in a soup pot over a moderate flame. Now, cook the garlic and shallot for 3 to 4 minutes or until they have softened. Stir in the broccoli florets, bell peppers, and fish broth; bring to a boil. Turn the heat to medium-low, partially cover, and let it cook for 12 minutes more. Add in the dry sherry, scallops, shrimp, and heavy cream. Continue to cook an additional 7 minutes or until heated through. Taste and adjust the seasonings. Serve garnished with fresh chives. Bon appétit!

calories: 272 | fat: 20g | protein: 17g | carbs: 7g | net carbs: 6g | fiber: 1g

Gambas al Ajillo

Prep time: 5 minutes | Cook time: 3 minutes | Serves 5

2 tablespoons butter
2 cloves garlic, minced
2 small cayenne pepper pods
2 pounds (907 g) shrimp,
peeled and deveined
¼ cup Manzanilla
Sea salt and ground black pepper, to taste

Melt the butter in a sauté pan over moderate heat. Add the garlic and cayenne peppers and cook for 40 seconds. Add the shrimp and cook for about a minute. Pour in the Manzanilla; season with salt and black pepper. Continue to cook for a minute or so, until the shrimp are cooked through. Add lemon slices to each serving if desired. Enjoy!

calories: 203 | fat: 6g | protein: 37g | carbs: 2g | net carbs: 2g | fiber: 0g

Curry White Fish Fillet

Prep time: 10 minutes | Cook time: 15 minutes | Serves 6

2 tablespoons sesame oil
1 shallot, chopped
2 bell peppers, seeded and sliced
1 teaspoon coriander, ground
1 teaspoon cumin, ground
4 tablespoons red curry paste
1 teaspoon ginger-garlic paste
1 ½ pounds (680 g) white fish
fillets, skinless, boneless
½ cup tomato purée
½ cup haddi ka shorba (Indian bone broth)
1 cup coconut milk
½ teaspoon red chili powder
Kosher salt and ground black pepper, to taste

Heat the sesame oil in a saucepan over moderate heat; then, sauté the shallot and peppers until they have softened or about 4 minutes. Now, stir in the coriander, cumin, red curry paste, and ginger-garlic paste; continue to sauté an additional 4 minutes, stirring frequently. After that, fold in the fish and tomato purée; pour in the haddi ka shorba and coconut milk. Season with red chili powder, salt, and black pepper. Turn the heat to simmer and let it cook for 5 minutes longer or until everything is cooked through. Enjoy!

calories: 349 | fat: 25g | protein: 23g | carbs: 6g | net carbs: 3g | fiber: 4g

Garlicky Mackerel Fillet

Prep time: 5 minutes | Cook time: 5 minutes | Serves 2

1 tablespoon olive oil
2 mackerel fillets
2 garlic cloves, minced
Sea salt and ground black

pepper, to taste
½ teaspoon thyme
1 teaspoon rosemary
½ teaspoon basil

Heat the olive oil in a frying pan over a moderate flame and swirl to coat the bottom of the pan. Pat dry the mackerel fillets. Now, brown the fish fillets for 5 minutes per side until golden and crisp, shaking the pan lightly. During the last minutes, add the garlic, salt, black pepper, and herbs. Bon appétit!

calories: 481 | fat: 15g | protein: 80g | carbs: 1g | net carbs: 1g | fiber: 0g

Sardine Burgers

Prep time: 10 minutes | Cook time: 6 minutes | Serves 3

2 (5.5-ounce / 156-g) canned sardines, drained
2 ounces (57 g) Romano cheese, preferably freshly grated
1 egg, beaten
3 tablespoons flaxseed meal
1 tablespoon dry Italian seasoning blend

1 teaspoon fresh garlic, peeled and minced
½ onion, chopped
½ teaspoon celery salt
Freshly ground black pepper, to taste
½ teaspoon smoked paprika
2 tablespoons butter

In a mixing dish, thoroughly combine the sardines with the cheese, egg, flaxseed meal, dry Italian seasoning blend, garlic, and onion. Season with the celery salt, black pepper, and smoked paprika. Form the mixture into six equal patties. Melt the butter in a frying pan over a moderate flame. Once hot, fry the fish burgers for 4 to 6 minutes on each side. Serve garnished with fresh lemon slices. Bon appétit!

calories: 267 | fat: 21g | protein: 14g | carbs: 6g | net carbs: 2g | fiber: 3g

Cheesy Shrimp Stuffed Mushrooms

Prep time: 10 minutes | Cook time: 17 minutes | Serves 6

1 tablespoon butter
1 yellow onion, finely minced
1 cloves garlic, minced
Flaky salt and ground black pepper, to taste
16 ounces (454 g) fresh Bay shrimp, chopped

8 ounces (227 g) ricotta cheese, softened
6 tablespoons mayonnaise
1½ pounds (680 g) large-sized button mushroom cups
1 cup cheddar cheese, shredded

Melt the butter in a frying pan over moderate heat. Then, sauté the onion and garlic for 2 to 3 minutes or until just tender and fragrant. Stir in the salt, black pepper, fresh Bay shrimp, ricotta cheese, and mayo; gently stir to combine well. Bake the mushroom cups in the preheated oven at 390°F (199°C) until they have softened slightly. Spoon the shrimp mixture into each mushroom cup. Return to the oven and bake for 8 to 11 minutes more. Top each mushroom cup with cheddar cheese. Bake for a further 7 minutes or until bubbly. Bon appétit!

calories: 354 | fat: 24g | protein: 28g | carbs: 5g | net carbs: 3g | fiber: 2g

Tuna Fillet Salade Niçoise

Prep time: 5 minutes | Cook time: 7 minutes | Serves 2

¾ pound (340 g) tuna fillet, skinless
1 white onion, sliced
1 teaspoon Dijon mustard

8 Niçoise olives, pitted and sliced
½ teaspoon anchovy paste

Brush the tuna with nonstick cooking oil; season with salt and freshly cracked black pepper. Then, grill your tuna on a lightly oiled rack approximately 7 minutes, turning over once or twice. Let the fish stand for 3 to 4 minutes and break into bite-sized pieces. Transfer to a nice salad bowl. Toss the tuna pieces with the white onion, Dijon mustard, Niçoise olives, and anchovy paste. Serve well chilled and enjoy!

calories: 194 | fat: 3g | protein: 37g | carbs: 1g | net carbs: 1g | fiber: 0g

Anchovies with Caesar Dressing

Prep time: 5 minutes | Cook time: 3 minutes | Serves 3

6 anchovies, cleaned and deboned
1 fresh garlic clove, peeled

1 teaspoon Dijon mustard
2 egg yolks
⅓ cup extra-virgin olive oil

Place the anchovies onto a lightly oiled grill pan; place under the grill for 2 minutes. Turn them over and cook for a further minute or so; remove from the grill. Process the garlic, Dijon mustard, egg yolks, and extra-virgin olive oil in your blender. Blend until creamy and uniform. Serve the warm grilled anchovies with the Caesar dressing on the side. Bon appétit!

calories: 449 | fat: 34g | protein: 33g | carbs: 1g | net carbs: 1g | fiber: 0g

Haddock and Turkey Smoked Sausage

Prep time: 15 minutes | Cook time: 17 minutes | Serves 4

2 tablespoons butter, at room temperature
1 onion, chopped
2 cloves garlic, sliced
1 bell pepper, sliced
1 celery stalk, chopped
1 cup broccoli florets
4 ounces (113 g) turkey smoked sausage, sliced
Sea salt and ground black pepper, to taste

2 tomatoes, pureed
2 cups fish broth
1 teaspoon chili powder
¼ teaspoon ground allspice
16 ounces (454 g) haddock steak, cut into bite-sized chunks
2 tablespoons fresh coriander, minced
1 teaspoon Creole seasoning blend

Melt the butter in a heavy-bottomed pot over moderate heat. Now, sauté the onion, garlic, and pepper, for 2 minutes until just tender and aromatic. Add in the celery, broccoli, turkey smoked sausage, salt, black pepper, pureed tomatoes, and broth. Bring to a rolling boil and immediately reduce the heat to simmer. Add in the remaining ingredients, partially cover, and continue simmering for 15 minutes. Ladle into soup bowls and serve immediately.

calories: 236 | fat: 9g | protein: 27g | carbs: 6g | net carbs: 4g | fiber: 2g

Catfish Flakes and Cauliflower Casserole

Prep time: 10 minutes | Cook time: 25 minutes | Serves 4

1 tablespoon sesame oil	1 sprigs dried thyme, crushed
11 ounces (312 g) cauliflower	1 sprig rosemary, crushed
4 scallions	24 ounces (680 g) catfish, cut
1 garlic clove, minced	into pieces
1 teaspoon fresh ginger root,	½ cup cream cheese
grated	½ cup heavy cream
Salt and ground black pepper,	1 egg
to taste	1 ounce (28 g) butter, cold
Cayenne pepper, to taste	

Preheat the oven to 390ºF (199ºC). Lightly grease a casserole dish with cooking spray. Heat the oil in a pan over medium-high heat. Cook the cauliflower and scallions until tender or 5 to 6 minutes. Add the garlic and ginger; continue to sauté 1 minute more. Transfer the vegetables to the casserole dish. Sprinkle with seasonings. Add catfish to the top. In a bowl, thoroughly combine the cream cheese, heavy cream, and egg. Spread this creamy mixture over the top of your casserole. Top with slices of butter. Bake in for 18 to 22 minutes or until the fish flakes easily with a fork. Serve.

calories: 510 | fat: 40g | protein: 31g | carbs: 6g | net carbs: 4g | fiber: 2g

White Chowder

Prep time: 5 minutes | Cook time: 15 minutes | Serves 4

2 teaspoons butter, at room	seasoning
temperature	¾ pound (340 g) sea bass,
½ white onion, chopped	broken into chunks
1 tablespoon Old Bay	1 cup heavy cream

Melt the butter in a soup pot over a moderate flame. Now, sweat the white onion until tender and translucent. Then, add in the Old Bay seasoning and 3 cups of water; bring to a rapid boil. Reduce the heat to medium-low and let it simmer, covered, for 9 to 12 minutes. Fold in the sea bass and heavy cream; continue to cook until everything is thoroughly heated or about 5 minutes. Serve warm and enjoy!

calories: 257 | fat: 18g | protein: 21g | carbs: 4g | net carbs: 4g | fiber: 0g

Cajun Tilapia Fish Burgers

Prep time: 5 minutes | Cook time: 46 minutes | Serves 5

1½ pounds tilapia fish, broken	½ cup almond flour
into chunks	1 tablespoon Cajun seasoning
2 eggs, whisked	mix
½ cup shallots, chopped	

Mix all of the above ingredients in a bowl. Shape the mixture into 10 patties and place in your refrigerator for about 40 minutes. Cook in the preheated frying pan that is previously greased with nonstick cooking spray. Cook for 3 minutes until golden brown on the bottom. Carefully flip over and cook the other side for a further 3 minutes. Remove to a paper towel-lined plate until ready to serve. Serve with fresh lettuce, if desired. Bon appétit!

calories: 238 | fat: 11g | protein: 33g | carbs: 3g | net carbs: 2g | fiber: 1g

Shrimp Jambalaya

Prep time: 5 minutes | Cook time: 20 minutes | Serves 4

1 shallot, chopped	1½ cups tomatoes, crushed
1 cup ham, cut into 1/2-inch	1½ cups vegetable broth
cubes	¾ pound (340 g) shrimp

Heat up a lightly greased soup pot over a moderate flame. Now, sauté the shallots until they have softened or about 4 minutes. Add in the ham, tomatoes, and vegetable broth and bring to a boil. Turn the heat to simmer, cover and continue to cook for 13 minutes longer. Fold in the shrimp and continue to simmer until they are thoroughly cooked and the cooking liquid has thickened slightly, about 3 to 4 minutes. Serve in individual bowls and enjoy!

calories: 170 | fat: 5g | protein: 26g | carbs: 6g | net carbs: 5g | fiber: 1g

Swedish Herring and Spinach Salad

Prep time: 10 minutes | Cook time: 0 minutes | Serves 3

6 ounces (170 g) pickled	1 teaspoon garlic, minced
herring pieces, drained and	1 bell pepper, chopped
flaked	1 red onion, chopped
½ cup baby spinach	2 tablespoons key lime juice,
2 tablespoons fresh basil	freshly squeezed
leaves	Sea salt and ground black
2 tablespoons fresh chives,	pepper, to taste
chopped	

In a salad bowl, combine the herring pieces with spinach, basil leaves, chives, garlic, bell pepper, and red onion. Then, drizzle key lime juice over the salad; add salt and pepper to taste and toss to combine. Smaklig maltid! Bon appétit!

calories: 134 | fat: 8g | protein: 10g | carbs: 5g | net carbs: 4g | fiber: 1g

Asian Salmon and Veggies Salad

Prep time: 20 minutes | Cook time: 5 minutes | Serves 2

Salad:

¼ cup water	2 radishes, sliced
¼ cup Sauvignon Blanc	1 bell pepper, sliced
½ pound salmon fillets	1 medium-sized white onion,
1 cup Chinese cabbage, sliced	sliced Salad
1 tomato, sliced	

Dressing:

½ teaspoon fresh garlic,	1 tablespoon sesame oil
minced	1 tablespoon tamari sauce
1 fresh chili pepper, seeded	1 teaspoon xylitol
and minced	1 tablespoon fresh mint,
½ teaspoon fresh ginger,	roughly chopped
peeled and grated	Sea salt and freshly ground
2 tablespoons fresh lime juice	black pepper, to taste

Place the water and Sauvignon Blanc in a sauté pan; bring to a simmer over moderate heat. Place the salmon fillets, skin-side down in the pan and cover with the lid. Cook for 5 to 8 minutes or to your desired doneness; do not overcook the salmon; reserve. Place the Chinese cabbage, tomato, radishes, bell pepper, and onion in a serving bowl. Prepare the salad dressing by whisking all ingredients. Dress your salad, top with the salmon fillets and serve immediately!

calories: 277 | fat: 15g | protein: 24g | carbs: 5g | net carbs: 4g | fiber: 1g

Tuna, Ham and Avocado Wraps

Prep time: 10 minutes | Cook time: 3 minutes | Serves 3

½ cup dry white wine
½ cup water
½ teaspoon mixed peppercorns
½ teaspoon dry mustard powder

½ pound Ahi tuna steak
6 slices of ham
½ Hass avocado, peeled, pitted and sliced
1 tablespoon fresh lemon juice
6 lettuce leaves

Add wine, water, peppercorns, and mustard powder to a skillet and bring to a boil. Add the tuna and simmer gently for 3 minutes to 5 minutes per side. Discard the cooking liquid and slice tuna into bite-sized pieces. Divide the tuna pieces between slices of ham. Add avocado and drizzle with fresh lemon. Roll the wraps up and place each wrap on a lettuce leaf. Serve well chilled. Bon appétit!

calories: 308 | fat: 20g | protein: 28g | carbs: 4g | net carbs: 1g | fiber: 3g

Alaskan Cod Fillet

Prep time: 10 minutes | Cook time: 2 minutes | Serves 4

1 tablespoon coconut oil
4 Alaskan cod fillets
Salt and freshly ground black pepper, to taste
6 leaves basil, chiffonade
Mustard Cream Sauce:
1 teaspoon yellow mustard
1 teaspoon paprika
¼ teaspoon ground bay leaf

3 tablespoons cream cheese
½ cup Greek-style yogurt
1 garlic clove, minced
1 teaspoon lemon zest
1 tablespoon fresh parsley, minced
Sea salt and ground black pepper, to taste

Heat coconut oil in a pan over medium heat. Sear the fish for 2 to 3 minutes per side. Season with salt and ground black pepper. Mix all ingredients for the sauce until everything is well combined. Top the fish fillets with the sauce and serve garnished with fresh basil leaves. Bon appétit!

calories: 166 | fat: 8g | protein: 20g | carbs: 3g | net carbs: 3g | fiber: 0g

Smoked Haddock Burgers

Prep time: 10 minutes | Cook time: 6 minutes | Serves 4

2 tablespoons extra virgin olive oil
8 ounces (227 g) smoked haddock
1 egg
¼ cup Parmesan cheese, grated

1 teaspoon chili powder
1 teaspoon dried parsley flakes
¼ cup scallions, chopped
1 teaspoon fresh garlic, minced
Salt and ground black pepper, to taste
4 lemon wedges

Heat 1 tablespoon of oil in a pan over medium-high heat. Cook the haddock for 6 minutes or until just cooked through; discard the skin and bones and flake into small pieces. Mix the smoked haddock, egg, cheese, chili powder, parsley, scallions, garlic, salt, and black pepper in a large bowl. Heat the remaining tablespoon of oil and cook fish burgers until they are well cooked in the middle or about 6 minutes. Garnish each serving with a lemon wedge.

calories: 174 | fat: 11g | protein: 15g | carbs: 2g | net carbs: 2g | fiber: 0g

Grilled Salmon Steak

Prep time: 5 minutes | Cook time: 10 minutes | Serves 4

4 (5-ounce / 142-g) salmon steaks
2 cloves garlic, pressed
4 tablespoons olive oil

1 tablespoon Taco seasoning mix
2 tablespoons fresh lemon juice

Place all of the above ingredients in a ceramic dish; cover and let it marinate for 40 minutes in your refrigerator. Place the salmon steaks onto a lightly oiled grill pan; place under the grill for 6 minutes. Turn them over and cook for a further 5 to 6 minutes, basting with the reserved marinade; remove from the grill. Serve immediately and enjoy!

calories: 331 | fat: 21g | protein: 30g | carbs: 2g | net carbs: 2g | fiber: 0g

Thai Tuna Fillet

Prep time: 15 minutes | Cook time: 20 minutes | Serves 4

1 tablespoon peanut oil
4 tuna fillets
1 teaspoon freshly grated ginger
Kosher salt and freshly ground
Sauce:
1 scallions, chopped
2 garlic cloves, minced
1 tablespoon fresh cilantro, chopped
1 teaspoon Sriracha sauce

black pepper, to taste
1 teaspoon cayenne pepper
½ teaspoon cumin seeds
¼ teaspoon ground cinnamon

4 tablespoons mayonnaise
½ cup sour cream
1 teaspoon stone-ground mustard

Preheat your oven to 375°F (190°C). Line a baking sheet with foil. Place the tuna fillets onto the prepared baking sheet; now, fold up all 4 sides of the foil. Add peanut oil, grated ginger, salt, black pepper, cayenne pepper, cumin, and cinnamon. Fold the sides of the foil over the fish fillets, sealing the packet. Bake until cooked through, approximately 20 minutes. To make the sauce, whisk together all of the sauce ingredients. Serve immediately and enjoy!

calories: 389 | fat: 18g | protein: 50g | carbs: 4g | net carbs: 4g | fiber: 0g

Cod Fillet with Parsley Pistou

Prep time: 15 minutes | Cook time: 10 minutes | Serves 4

1 cup packed roughly chopped fresh flat-leaf Italian parsley
1 to 2 small garlic cloves, minced
Zest and juice of 1 lemon
1 teaspoon salt

½ teaspoon freshly ground black pepper
1 cup extra-virgin olive oil, divided
1 pound (454 g) cod fillets, cut into 4 equal-sized pieces

In a food processor, combine the parsley, garlic, lemon zest and juice, salt, and pepper. Pulse to chop well. While the food processor is running, slowly stream in ¾ cup olive oil until well combined. Set aside. In a large skillet, heat the remaining ¼ cup olive oil over medium-high heat. Add the cod fillets, cover, and cook 4 to 5 minutes on each side, or until cooked through. Thicker fillets may require a bit more cooking time. Remove from the heat and keep warm. Add the pistou to the skillet and heat over medium-low heat. Return the cooked fish to the skillet, flipping to coat in the sauce. Serve warm, covered with pistou.

calories: 581 | fat: 55g | protein: 21g | carbs: 3g | net carbs: 2g | fiber: 1g

Goan Sole Fillet Stew

Prep time: 5 minutes | Cook time: 20 minutes | Serves 3

1 tablespoon butter, at room temperature
1 shallot, chopped
1 teaspoon curry paste

1 cup tomatoes, pureed
¾ pound (340 g) sole fillets, cut into 1-inch pieces

Melt the butter in a stockpot over a medium-high flame. Sauté the shallot until softened. Add the curry paste and pureed tomatoes along with 2 cups of water to the pot; bring to a rolling boil. Immediately reduce the heat to medium-low and continue to simmer, covered, for 12 minutes longer; make sure to stir periodically. Fold in the chopped sole fillets; continue to cook for a further 8 minutes or until the fish flakes easily with a fork. Enjoy!

calories: 191 | fat: 9g | protein: 24g | carbs: 3g | net carbs: 2g | fiber: 1g

Spanish Cod à La Nage

Prep time: 5 minutes | Cook time: 15 minutes | Serves 5

2 tablespoons olive oil
1 Spanish onion, chopped
1 medium-sized zucchini, diced

1 vine-ripe tomatoes, pureed
1½ pounds (680 g) cod fish fillets

Heat the olive oil in a stockpot over medium-high flame. Now, cook the Spanish onion until tender and translucent. Pour in the pureed tomatoes along with 2 cups of water. Bring to a boil and reduce the heat to medium-low. Let it simmer an additional 10 to 13 minutes. Now, fold in the cod fish fillets. Cook, covered, an additional 5 to 6 minutes or until the codfish is just cooked through and an instant-read thermometer registers 140 °F (60°C). Place the fish in individual bowls; ladle the fish broth over each serving, and serve hot. Enjoy!

calories: 177 | fat: 6g | protein: 25g | carbs: 4g | net carbs: 3g | fiber: 1g

Cod Patties with Creamed Horseradish

Prep time: 10 minutes | Cook time: 13 minutes | Serves 4

1 pound (454 g) cod fillets
2 eggs, beaten
1 tablespoon flax seeds meal
Sauce:
4 tablespoons mayonnaise
4 tablespoons Ricotta cheese
1 teaspoon creamed horseradish

4 tablespoons Parmesan cheese, grated
2 tablespoons olive oil

2 green onions, chopped
1 tablespoon fresh basil, chopped

Steam the cod fillets until done and cooked through, approximately 10 minutes. Flake the fish with a fork; add in the beaten eggs, flax seeds meal, and Parmesan. Shape the mixture into 4 equal patties. Heat the olive oil in a nonstick skillet. Fry the fish patties over moderate heat for 3 minutes per side. In the meantime, whisk the sauce ingredients until everything is well incorporated. Bon appétit!

calories: 346 | fat: 23g | protein: 26g | carbs: 7g | net carbs: 6g | fiber: 1g

Old Bay Sea Bass Fillet

Prep time: 10 minutes | Cook time: 15 minutes | Serves 6

2 tablespoons butter, at room temperature
1 leek, chopped
1 bell pepper, chopped
1 serrano pepper, chopped
2 garlic cloves, minced
2 tablespoons fresh coriander, chopped
2 vine-ripe tomatoes, pureed

4 cups fish stock
2 pounds (907 g) sea bass fillets, chopped into small chunks
1 tablespoon Old Bay seasoning
½ teaspoon sea salt, to taste
1 bay laurels

Melt the butter in a heavy-bottomed pot over moderate heat. Stir in the leek and peppers and sauté them for about 5 minutes or until tender. Stir in the garlic and continue to sauté for 30 to 40 seconds more. Add in the remaining ingredients; gently stir to combine. Turn the heat to medium-low and partially cover the pot. Now, let it cook until thoroughly heated, approximately 10 minutes longer. Lastly, discard the bay laurels and serve warm. Bon appétit!

calories: 227 | fat: 8g | protein: 32g | carbs: 5g | net carbs: 4g | fiber: 1g

Red Snapper Fillet and Salad

Prep time: 10 minutes | Cook time: 18 minutes | Serves 4

1 pound (454 g) red snapper fillets
5 eggs
1 bell pepper, deseeded and sliced
1 tomato, sliced
1 cucumber, sliced
2 scallions, sliced

½ cup radishes, sliced
4 cups lettuce salad
4 tablespoons olive oil
4 tablespoons apple cider vinegar
½ cup Kalamata olives, pitted and halved

Steam the red snapper fillets until done and cooked through, approximately 10 minutes. Slice the fish fillets into bite-sized strips. Cook the eggs in a saucepan for about 8 minutes; peel the eggs under running water and carefully slice them. Place your veggies in a salad bowl; add the olive oil and vinegar and toss to combine. Top with the fish and boiled eggs. Salt to taste. Garnish with Kalamata olives and serve well-chilled or at room temperature. Bon appétit!

calories: 300 | fat: 19g | protein: 27g | carbs: 4g | net carbs: 3g | fiber: 1g

Lemony Shrimp and Veggie Bowl

Prep time: 10 minutes | Cook time: 4 minutes | Serves 4

2 pounds (907 g) large shrimp, peeled and deveined
1 teaspoon cayenne pepper
Sea salt and freshly ground black pepper, to taste
1 red onion, sliced

2 garlic cloves, sliced
2 Italian peppers, sliced
1 tablespoon fresh lemon juice
2 tablespoons olive oil
1 cup arugula

Gently pat the shrimp dry with a paper towel. Add the cayenne pepper, salt, black pepper, and toss to evenly coat. Grill the shrimp over medium-high heat for 2 minutes; flip them and cook for a further 2 minutes. Transfer to a bowl; add in the remaining ingredients and toss to combine. Serve immediately.

calories: 268 | fat: 8g | protein: 46g | carbs: 4g | net carbs: 3g | fiber: 1g

Italian Haddock Fillet

Prep time: 5 minutes | Cook time: 10 minutes | Serves 6

2 pounds (907 g) haddock fillets
1 tablespoon Italian seasoning blend

Sea salt and freshly ground black pepper, to taste
2 tablespoons olive oil
½ cup marinara sauce

Season the haddock fillets and brush them on all sides with olive oil and marinara sauce. Grill over medium heat for 9 to 11 minutes until golden with brown edges. Use a metal spatula to gently lift the haddock fillets, place them on serving plates and serve with the remaining marinara sauce. Bon appétit!

calories: 226 | fat: 6g | protein: 38g | carbs: 2g | net carbs: 1g | fiber: 1g

Salmon Fillet

Prep time: 10 minutes | Cook time: 19 minutes | Serves 6

2 tablespoons peanut oil
2 bell peppers, deseeded and sliced
½ cup scallions, chopped
2 cloves garlic, minced
4 tablespoons Marsala wine

2 ripe tomatoes, pureed
2½ pounds salmon fillets
Sea salt and ground black pepper, to taste
¼ teaspoon ground bay leaf
1 teaspoon paprika

Heat the peanut oil in a large frying pan over a moderate flame. Now, sauté the bell peppers and scallions for 3 minutes. Add in the garlic and continue to sauté for 30 seconds more or until aromatic but not until it's browned. Add a splash of wine to deglaze the pan. Stir in the remaining ingredients and turn the heat to simmer. Let it cook, partially covered, for 15 minutes or until the salmon is cooked through. Bon appétit!

calories: 347 | fat: 19g | protein: 40g | carbs: 4g | net carbs: 3g | fiber: 1g

Herbed Monkfish Fillet

Prep time: 10 minutes | Cook time: 17 minutes | Serves 6

2 tablespoons olive oil
6 monkfish fillets
Sea salt and ground black pepper, to taste
2 green onions, sliced
2 green garlic stalks, sliced
½ cup sour cream

1 teaspoon oregano
1 teaspoon basil
1 teaspoon rosemary
½ cup cheddar cheese, shredded
2 tablespoons fresh chives, chopped

Heat the olive oil in a frying pan over a medium-high flame. Once hot, sear the monkfish fillets for 3 minutes until golden brown; flip them and cook on the other side for 3 to 4 minutes more. Season with salt and black pepper. Transfer the monkfish fillets to a lightly greased casserole dish. Add the green onions and green garlic. In a mixing dish, thoroughly combine the sour cream with the oregano, basil, rosemary, and cheddar cheese. Spoon the mixture into your casserole dish and bake at 360°F (182°C) for about 11 minutes or until golden brown on top. Garnish with fresh chives and serve. Bon appétit!

calories: 229 | fat: 13g | protein: 26g | carbs: 2g | net carbs: 2g | fiber: 0g

Tilapia and Shrimp Soup

Prep time: 10 minutes | Cook time: 21 minutes | Serves 5

1 tablespoon butter
4 scallions, chopped
1 cup celery, chopped
1 Italian pepper, deseeded and chopped
1 poblano pepper, deseeded and chopped
2 cups cauliflower, grated
2 Roma tomatoes, pureed

4 cups chicken broth
1 pound (454 g) tilapia, skinless and chopped into small chunks
½ pound (227 g) medium shrimp, deveined
2 tablespoons balsamic vinegar

Melt the butter in a heavy-bottomed pot over a moderate flame. Once hot, cook your veggies until crisp-tender or about 4 minutes, stirring periodically to ensure even cooking. Add in the pureed tomatoes and chicken broth. When the soup reaches boiling, turn the heat to a simmer. Add in the tilapia and let it cook, partially covered, for 12 minutes. Stir in the shrimp, partially cover, and continue to cook for 5 minutes more. Afterwards, stir in the balsamic vinegar. Ladle into individual bowls and serve warm.

calories: 194 | fat: 6g | protein: 26g | carbs: 6g | net carbs: 4g | fiber: 2g

Curry Tilapia

Prep time: 10 minutes | Cook time: 15 minutes | Serves 4

1 tablespoon peanut oil
3 green cardamoms
1 teaspoon cumin seeds
1 shallot, chopped
1 red chili pepper, chopped
1 red bell pepper, chopped
1 teaspoon ginger-garlic paste

1 cup tomato puree 1 cup chicken broth
1 tablespoon curry paste
1½ pounds (680 g) tilapia
1 cinnamon stick
Sea salt and ground black pepper, to taste

Heat the peanut oil in a saucepan over medium-heat. Now, toast the cardamoms and cumin for 2 minutes until aromatic. Add in the shallot, red chili, bell pepper and continue to sauté for 2 minutes more or until just tender and translucent. Add in the ginger-garlic paste and continue to sauté an additional 30 seconds. Pour the tomato puree and chicken broth into the saucepan. Bring to a boil. Turn the heat to medium-low and stir in the curry paste, tilapia, cinnamon, salt, and black pepper. Let it simmer, partially covered, for 10 minutes more. Flake the fish and serve in individual bowls. Enjoy!

calories: 209 | fat: 7g | protein: 35g | carbs: 3g | net carbs: 2g | fiber: 1g

Mediterranean Halibut Fillet

Prep time: 5 minutes | Cook time: 30 minutes | Serves 4

1½ pounds (680 g) halibut fillets
2 tablespoons olive oil
2 tablespoons fresh lemon juice

1 tablespoon Greek seasoning blend
½ cup Kalamata olives, pitted and sliced

Start by preheating your oven to 380°F (193°C). Toss the halibut fillets with the olive oil, fresh lemon juice, and Greek seasoning blend. Arrange the halibut fillets in a baking pan and cover with foil. Bake approximately 30 minutes, flipping once or twice. Garnish with Kalamata olives and serve warm. Bon appétit!

calories: 397 | fat: 32g | protein: 25g | carbs: 2g | net carbs: 1g | fiber: 1g

Chepala Vepudu

Prep time: 10 minutes | Cook time: 10 minutes | Serves 3

3 carp fillets
1 teaspoon chili powder
1 teaspoon cumin powder
1 teaspoon turmeric powder
1 coriander powder
½ teaspoon garam masala
½ teaspoon flaky salt

¼ teaspoon cayenne pepper
3 tablespoons full-fat coconut milk
1 egg
2 tablespoons olive oil
6 curry leaves, for garnish

Pat the fish fillets with kitchen towels and add to a large resealable bag. Add the spices to the bag and shake to coat on all sides. In a shallow dish, whisk the coconut milk and egg until frothy and well combined. Dip the fillets into the egg mixture. Then, heat the oil in a large frying pan. Fry the fish fillets on both sides until they are cooked through and the coating becomes crispy. Serve with curry leaves and enjoy!

calories: 443 | fat: 28g | protein: 43g | carbs: 3g | net carbs: 2g | fiber: 1g

Stir-Fried Scallops with Cauliflower

Prep time: 10 minutes | Cook time: 6 minutes | Serves 5

1 tablespoon butter
2 medium Italian peppers, seeded and sliced
2 cups cauliflower florets
½ teaspoon fresh ginger, minced
1 teaspoon garlic, minced
2 pounds (907 g) sea scallops

½ cup dry white wine
½ teaspoon cayenne pepper
½ teaspoon oregano
½ teaspoon marjoram
½ teaspoon rosemary
Sea salt and ground black pepper, to taste
½ cup chicken broth

Melt the butter in a large frying pan over medium-high heat. Stir in the Italian peppers, cauliflower, ginger, and garlic. Cook for about 3 minutes or until the vegetables have softened. Stir in the sea scallops and continue to cook for 3 minutes. Stir to coat with the vegetable mixture. Add in the remaining ingredients and let it simmer, partially covered, for a few minutes longer. Bon appétit!

calories: 217 | fat: 4g | protein: 24g | carbs: 5g | net carbs: 4g | fiber: 1g

Sea Bass Fillet with Dill Sauce

Prep time: 10 minutes | Cook time: 20 minutes | Serves 2

1 tablespoon olive oil
1 cup red onions, sliced
2 bell peppers, seeded and sliced
Dill Sauce:
1 tablespoon mayonnaise
¼ cup Greek yogurt
1 tablespoon fresh dill,

Se salt and cayenne pepper, to taste
1 teaspoon paprika
1 pound sea bass fillets

chopped
½ teaspoon garlic powder
½ fresh lemon, juiced

Toss the onions, peppers, and sea bass fillets with the olive oil, salt, cayenne pepper, and paprika. Line a baking pan with a piece of parchment paper. Preheat your oven to 400°F (205°C). Arrange your fish and vegetables on the prepared baking pan. Bake for 10 minutes; turn them over and bake for a further 10 to 12 minutes. Meanwhile, make the sauce by mixing all ingredients until well combined. Serve the fish and vegetables with the dill sauce on the side. Bon appétit!

calories: 374 | fat: 17g | protein: 43g | carbs: 6g | net carbs: 4g | fiber: 2g

Old Bay Prawns

Prep time: 10 minutes | Cook time: 10 minutes | Serves 2

¾ pound (340 g) prawns, peeled and deveined
1 teaspoon Old Bay seasoning mix
½ teaspoon paprika
Coarse sea salt and ground black pepper, to taste
1 habanero pepper, seeded and minced

1 bell pepper, seeded and minced
1 cup pound broccoli florets
2 teaspoons olive oil
1 tablespoon fresh chives, chopped2 slices lemon, for garnish
2 dollops of sour cream, for garnish

Toss the prawns with the Old Bay seasoning mix, paprika, salt, and black pepper. Arrange them on a parchment-lined roasting pan. Add the bell pepper and broccoli. Drizzle olive oil over everything and transfer the pan to a preheated oven. Roast at 390°F (199°C) for 8 to 11 minutes, turning the pan halfway through the cooking time. Bake until the prawns are pink and cooked through. Serve with fresh chives, lemon, and sour cream. Bon appétit!

calories: 269 | fat: 10g | protein: 38g | carbs: 7g | net carbs: 4g | fiber: 3g

Halászlé with Paprikash

Prep time: 15 minutes | Cook time: 10 minutes | Serves 2

1 tablespoon extra virgin olive oil
2 bell peppers, chopped
1 Hungarian wax pepper, chopped
1 garlic clove, minced
1 red onion, chopped
½ pound (227 g) tilapia, cut into bite-sized pieces
1½ cups fish broth
2 vine-ripe tomatoes, pureed

1 teaspoon sweet paprika
½ teaspoon mixed peppercorns, crushed
1 bay laurel
½ teaspoon sumac
½ teaspoon dried thyme
¼ teaspoon dried rosemary
Kosher salt, to season
½ teaspoon garlic, minced
2 tablespoons sour cream

Heat the extra virgin olive oil in a Dutch oven over medium-high heat. Now, sauté the peppers, garlic, and onion until tender and aromatic. Now, stir in the tilapia, broth, tomatoes, and spices. Reduce the heat to medium-low. Let it simmer, covered, for 9 to 13 minutes. Meanwhile, mix ½ teaspoon of minced garlic with the sour cream. Serve with the warm paprikash and enjoy!

calories: 252 | fat: 13g | protein: 28g | carbs: 5g | net carbs: 3g | fiber: 2g

Baked Halibut Steaks

Prep time: 10 minutes | Cook time: 13 minutes | Serves 2

2 tablespoons olive oil
2 halibut steaks
1 red bell pepper, sliced
1 yellow onion, sliced
1 teaspoon garlic, smashed

½ teaspoon hot paprika
Sea salt cracked black pepper, to your liking
1 dried thyme sprig, leaves crushed

Start by preheating your oven to 390°F (199°C). Then, drizzle olive oil over the halibut steaks. Place the halibut in a baking dish that is previously greased with a nonstick spray. Top with the bell pepper, onion, and garlic. Sprinkle hot paprika, salt, black pepper, and dried thyme over everything. Bake in the preheated oven for 13 to 15 minutes and serve immediately. Enjoy!

calories: 502 | fat: 19g | protein: 72g | carbs: 6g | net carbs: 5g | fiber: 1g

Sole Fish Jambalaya

Prep time: 15 minutes | Cook time: 8 minutes | Serves 2

1 teaspoon extra virgin olive oil	cut into bite-sized strips
1 jalapeno pepper, minced	1 large-sized ripe tomato, pureed
1 small-sized leek, chopped	½ cup water
½ teaspoon ginger garlic paste	½ cup clam juice
¼ teaspoon ground cumin	Kosher salt, to season
¼ teaspoon ground allspice	1 bay laurel
½ teaspoon oregano	5-6 black peppercorns
¼ teaspoon thyme	1 cup spinach, torn into pieces
¼ teaspoon marjoram	
1 pound (454 g) sole fish fillets,	

Heat the oil in a Dutch oven over a moderate flame. Sauté the pepper and leek until softened. Stir in the ginger-garlic paste, cumin, allspice, oregano, thyme, and marjoram. Add in the fish, tomatoes, water, clam juice, salt, bay laurel, and black peppercorns. Cover and decrease the temperature to medium-low. Let it simmer for 4 to 6 minutes or until the liquid has reduced slightly. Stir in the spinach and let it simmer, covered, for about 2 minutes more or until it wilts. Ladle into serving bowls and serve warm.

calories: 232 | fat: 4g | protein: 38g | carbs: 6g | net carbs: 4g | fiber: 2g

Cod Fillet and Mustard Greens

Prep time: 10 minutes | Cook time: 13 minutes | Serves 2

1 tablespoon olive oil	½ cup fish broth
1 bell pepper, seeded and sliced	2 cod fish fillets
1 jalapeno pepper, seeded and sliced	½ teaspoon paprika
2 stalks green onions, sliced	Sea salt and ground black pepper, to season
1 stalk green garlic, sliced	1 cup mustard greens, torn into bite-sized pieces

Heat the olive oil in a Dutch pot over a moderate flame. Now, sauté the peppers, green onions, and garlic until just tender and aromatic. Add in the broth, fish fillets, paprika, salt, black pepper, and mustard greens. Reduce the temperature to medium-low, cover, and let it cook for 11 to 13 minutes or until heated through. Serve immediately garnished with lemon slices if desired. Bon appétit!

calories: 171 | fat: 8g | protein: 20g | carbs: 5g | net carbs: 3g | fiber: 2g

Cheesy Cod Fillet

Prep time: 10 minutes | Cook time: 5 minutes | Serves 3

3 cod fillets	½ teaspoon shallot powder
½ cup almond meal	1 teaspoon dried rosemary, crushed
1 teaspoon cayenne pepper	1 cup Romano cheese, preferably freshly grated
Sea salt and ground black pepper, to season	2 tablespoons butter
1 teaspoon garlic powder	
1 teaspoon porcini powder	

Pat the cod fillets dry with paper towels. Add the fish, almond meal, and spices to the bag and shake to coat on all sides. Coat them with grated Romano cheese. Melt the butter in a frying pan over medium-high heat. Now pan-fry the fish fillets until flesh flakes easily and it is nearly opaque, about 4 to 5 minutes per side. Serve on warm plates. Bon appétit!

calories: 406 | fat: 30g | protein: 32g | carbs: 4g | net carbs: 2g | fiber: 2g

Shrimp and Sea Scallop

Prep time: 10 minutes | Cook time: 5 minutes | Serves 2

1 tablespoon olive oil	½ cup fish broth
½ cup scallions, chopped	¼ teaspoon Cajun seasoning mix
1 garlic clove, minced	Sea salt and ground black pepper, to taste
½ pound (227 g) shrimp, deveined	1 tablespoon fresh parsley, chopped
½ pound (227 g) sea scallops	
2 tablespoons rum	

In a sauté pan, heat the olive oil until sizzling. Now, sauté your scallions and garlic until they are just tender and fragrant. Now, sear the shrimp and sea scallops for 2 to 3 minutes or until they are firm. Add a splash of rum to deglaze the pan. Now, pour in the fish broth. Add in the Cajun seasoning mix, salt, and black pepper; stir and remove from heat. Serve warm garnished with fresh parsley. Enjoy!

calories: 305 | fat: 9g | protein: 47g | carbs: 3g | net carbs: 2g | fiber: 1g

Dijon Sea Bass Fillet

Prep time: 10 minutes | Cook time: 10 minutes | Serves 3

2 tablespoons olive oil	peppercorns, crushed
3 sea bass fillets	3 tablespoons butter
¼ teaspoon red pepper flakes, crushed	1 tablespoon Dijon mustard
Sea salt, to taste	2 cloves garlic, minced
⅓ teaspoon mixed	1 tablespoon fresh lime juice

Heat the olive oil in a skillet over medium-high heat. Pat dry the sea bass fillets with paper towels. Now pan-fry the fish fillets for about 4 minutes on each side until flesh flakes easily and it is nearly opaque. Season your fish with red pepper, salt, and mixed peppercorns. To make the sauce, melt the 3 tablespoons of butter in a saucepan over low heat; stir in the Dijon mustard, garlic, and lime juice. Let it simmer for 2 minutes. To serve, spoon the Dijon butter sauce over the fish fillets. Bon appétit!

calories: 314 | fat: 23g | protein: 24g | carbs: 1g | net carbs: 1g | fiber: 0g

Mackerel Fillet and Clam

Prep time: 10 minutes | Cook time: 12 minutes | Serves 3

2 teaspoons olive oil	pepper, to taste
2 mackerel fillets, patted dry	½ teaspoon cayenne pepper
1 shallot, finely chopped	½ teaspoon fennel seeds
2 cloves garlic, minced	½ teaspoon mustard seeds
½ cup dry white wine	1 teaspoon celery seeds
9 littleneck clams, scrubbed	1 teaspoon coriander, minced
Flaky salt and ground black	

In a large skillet, heat 1 teaspoon of the olive oil until sizzling; now, cook the mackerel fillets for about 6 minutes until cooked all the way through. Make sure to shake the skillet occasionally to prevent sticking; reserve, keeping warm. Heat the remaining teaspoon of olive oil and sauté the shallot and garlic for 1 to 2 minutes or until fragrant. Add in the wine and remaining seasonings; cook until almost evaporated. Fold in the clams and cook for 5 to 6 minutes until they open. Return the fish to the skillet and serve warm. Bon appétit!

calories: 379 | fat: 9g | protein: 60g | carbs: 4g | net carbs: 4g | fiber: 0g

Monkfish Mayonnaise Salad

Prep time: 10 minutes | Cook time: 9 minutes | Serves 5

2 pounds (57 g) monkfish
1 bell pepper, sliced
½ cup radishes, sliced
1 red onion, chopped
1 garlic clove, minced

1 tablespoon balsamic vinegar
½ cup mayonnaise
1 teaspoon stone-ground mustard
Flaky salt, to season

Pat the fish dry with paper towels and brush on both sides with nonstick cooking oil. Grill over medium-high heat, flipping halfway through for about 9 minutes or until opaque. Flake the fish with a fork and toss with the remaining ingredients; gently toss to combine well. Serve at room temperature or well-chilled. Bon appétit!

calories: 306 | fat: 19g | protein: 27g | carbs: 4g | net carbs: 3g | fiber: 1g

Spicy Tiger Prawns

Prep time: 10 minutes | Cook time: 10 minutes | Serves 6

2 tablespoons olive oil
1 teaspoon butter
2 scallions, chopped
2 cloves garlic, pressed
2 bell peppers, chopped
2½ pounds (1.1 kg) tiger prawns, deveined
¼ teaspoon ground black

pepper
1 teaspoon paprika
1 teaspoon red chili flakes
½ teaspoon mustard seeds
½ teaspoon fennel seeds
Sea salt, to taste
½ cup Marsala wine

Heat the olive oil and butter in a frying pan over a medium-high flame. Now, sweat the scallions, garlic, and peppers until they are crisp-tender about 2 minutes. Add in the tiger prawns and cook for 1½ minutes on each side until they are opaque. Stir in the remaining ingredients and continue to cook for 5 minutes more over low heat. Taste and adjust seasonings. Bon appétit!

calories: 219 | fat: 7g | protein: 39g | carbs: 3g | net carbs: 2g | fiber: 1g

Cod Fillet with Lemony Sesame Sauce

Prep time: 10 minutes | Cook time: 7 minutes | Serves 6

6 cod fillets, skin-on
3 tablespoons olive oil
Sea salt and ground black pepper, to season
1 lemon, freshly squeezed
½ teaspoon fresh ginger, minced

1 garlic clove, minced
1 red chili pepper, minced
3 tablespoons toasted sesame seeds
3 tablespoons toasted sesame oil

Prepare a grill for medium-high heat. Rub the cod fillets with olive oil; season both sides with salt and black pepper. Next, place the cod fillets on the grill skin side down. Grill approximately 7 minutes until the skin is lightly charred. To make the sauce, whisk the remaining ingredients until well combined; season with lots of black pepper. Divide the cod fillets among serving plates. Spoon the sauce over them and enjoy!

calories: 341 | fat: 17g | protein: 42g | carbs: 3g | net carbs: 2g | fiber: 1g

Tilapia Fillet

Prep time: 5 minutes | Cook time: 10 minutes | Serves 6

6 tilapia fillets, patted dry
Sea salt and ground black pepper, to taste
1 teaspoon cayenne pepper

6 tablespoons butter
1 teaspoon garlic, minced
1 tablespoon parsley, chopped
1 teaspoon fresh lime juice

Brush a nonstick skillet with cooking oil. Heat the skillet over medium-high heat. Once the oil is heated, pan-fry the tilapia until both sides turn golden brown; gently flip them with a tong. Season with salt, black pepper, and cayenne pepper. Prepare the garlic butter sauce by whisking the remaining ingredients. Serve the tilapia with a dollop of garlic butter if desired. Bon appétit!

calories: 215 | fat: 14g | protein: 24g | carbs: 1g | net carbs: 1g | fiber: 0g

Mahi Mahi Ceviche

Prep time: 10 minutes | Cook time: 10 minutes | Serves 4

1½ pounds mahi-mahi fish, cut into bite-sized cubes
Sea salt and ground black pepper, to taste
1 teaspoon hot paprika
2 garlic cloves, minced

4 scallions, chopped
2 Roma tomatoes, sliced
1 bell pepper, sliced
4 tablespoons olive oil
2 tablespoons fresh lemon juice

Season the haddock fillets with salt, black pepper, and paprika. Brush them on all sides with nonstick cooking oil. Grill over medium heat for 9 to 11 minutes until golden with brown edges. Use a metal spatula to gently lift the haddock fillets. Toss your fish with the remaining ingredients in a large bowl. Taste and adjust seasonings. Divide between four serving bowls and serve.

calories: 424 | fat: 30g | protein: 33g | carbs: 6g | net carbs: 4g | fiber: 2g

Salmon Tacos with Guajillo Sauce

Prep time: 10 minutes | Cook time: 10 minutes | Serves 5

2 pounds (907 g) salmon
Flaky salt and ground black pepper, to taste
10 lettuce leaves
2 bell peppers, chopped
1 cucumber, chopped
1 avocado, pitted and peeled

1 tomato, halved
2 tablespoons extra-virgin olive oil
1 tablespoon lemon juice
4 tablespoons green onions
1 teaspoon garlic
1 guajillo chili pepper

Season your salmon with salt and black pepper. Brush the salmon on all sides with nonstick cooking oil. Grill over medium heat for 13 minutes until golden and opaque in the middle. Flake the fish with two forks. Divide the fish among the lettuce leaves; add the bell peppers and cucumber. Pulse the remaining ingredients in your blender 8 to 10 times or until smooth with several small chunks of tomatoes and scallions. Top each lettuce taco with the guajillo sauce and serve.

calories: 342 | fat: 17g | protein: 40g | carbs: 7g | net carbs: 3g | fiber: 4g

Swordfish with Greek Yogurt Sauce

Prep time: 10 minutes | Cook time: 25 minutes | Serves 6

2 tablespoons butter
4 swordfish steaks
1 teaspoon paprika
½ teaspoon ground bay leaf
½ teaspoon mustard seeds
Sea salt and ground black pepper, to season
1 yellow onion, sliced

1 teaspoon garlic, minced
1 cup Greek yogurt
4 tablespoons mayonnaise
2 tablespoons fresh basil, chopped
2 tablespoons fresh dill, chopped
1 teaspoon urfa biber chile

Butter the bottom and sides of your casserole dish. Toss the swordfish steaks with the seasonings. Arrange the swordfish steaks in the prepared casserole dish. Scatter the onion and garlic around the swordfish steaks. Bake in the preheated oven at 390°F (199°C) for about 25 minutes. Meanwhile, whisk the Greek yogurt with the remaining ingredients to make the sauce. Serve the warm fish steaks with the sauce on the side. Bon appétit!

calories: 346 | fat: 23g | protein: 32g | carbs: 3g | net carbs: 3g | fiber: 0g

Goat Cheese Stuffed Squid

Prep time: 15 minutes | Cook time: 30 minutes | Serves 4

8 ounces (227 g) frozen spinach, thawed and drained
4 ounces (113 g) crumbled goat cheese
½ cup chopped pitted olives
½ cup extra-virgin olive oil, divided
¼ cup chopped sun-dried

tomatoes
¼ cup chopped fresh flat-leaf Italian parsley
2 garlic cloves, finely minced
¼ teaspoon freshly ground black pepper
2 pounds (907 g) baby squid, cleaned and tentacles removed

Preheat the oven to 350°F (180°C). In a medium bowl, combine the spinach, goat cheese, olives, ¼ cup olive oil, sun-dried tomatoes, parsley, garlic, and pepper. Pour 2 tablespoons olive oil in the bottom of a baking dish and spread to coat the bottom. Stuff each cleaned squid with 2 to 3 tablespoons of the cheese mixture, depending on the size of squid, and place in the baking dish. Drizzle the tops with the remaining 2 tablespoons olive oil and bake until the squid are cooked through, 25 to 30 minutes. Remove from the oven and allow to cool 5 to 10 minutes before serving.

calories: 469 | fat: 37g | protein: 24g | carbs: 10g | net carbs: 7g | fiber: 3g

Rosemary-Lemon Snapper Fillet

Prep time: 15 minutes | Cook time: 15 minutes | Serves 4

1¼ pounds (567 g) fresh red snapper fillet, cut into two equal pieces
2 lemons, thinly sliced
6 to 8 sprigs fresh rosemary, stems removed

½ cup extra-virgin olive oil
6 garlic cloves, thinly sliced
1 teaspoon salt
½ teaspoon freshly ground black pepper

Preheat the oven to 425°F (220°C). Place two large sheets of parchment on the counter. Place 1 piece of fish in the center of each sheet. Top the fish pieces with lemon slices and rosemary leaves. In a small bowl, combine the olive oil, garlic, salt, and pepper. Drizzle the oil over each piece of fish. Top each piece of fish with a second large sheet of parchment and starting on a long side, fold the paper up to about 1 inch from the fish. Repeat on the remaining sides, going in a clockwise direction. Fold in each corner once to secure. Place both parchment pouches on a baking sheet and bake until the fish is cooked through, 10 to 12 minutes.

calories: 390 | fat: 29g | protein: 29g | carbs: 3g | net carbs: 3g | fiber: 0g

Scallops and Calamari

Prep time: 5 minutes | Cook time: 10 minutes | Serves 4

8 ounces (227 g) calamari steaks, cut into ½-inch-thick strips or rings
8 ounces (227 g) sea scallops
1½ teaspoons salt, divided

1 teaspoon freshly ground black pepper
1 teaspoon garlic powder
⅓ cup extra-virgin olive oil
2 tablespoons butter

Place the calamari and scallops on paper towels and pat dry. Sprinkle with 1 teaspoon salt and allow to sit for 15 minutes at room temperature. Pat dry with additional paper towels. Sprinkle with pepper and garlic powder. In a skillet, heat the olive oil and butter over medium-high heat. Add the scallops and calamari in a single layer to the skillet and sprinkle with the remaining ½ teaspoon salt. Cook 2 to 4 minutes on each side, until just golden but still slightly opaque in center. Using a slotted spoon, transfer to a serving platter. Allow the cooking oil to cool slightly and drizzle over the seafood before serving.

calories: 309 | fat: 25g | protein: 18g | carbs: 3g | net carbs: 3g | fiber: 0g

Chapter 10 Salads

Chicken Thigh Green Salad

Prep time: 10 minutes | Cook time: 15 minutes | Serves 2

2 chicken thighs, skinless
Sea salt and cayenne pepper, to season
½ teaspoon Dijon mustard
1 tablespoon red wine vinegar
¼ cup mayonnaise

1 small-sized celery stalk, chopped
2 spring onion stalks, chopped
½ head Romaine lettuce, torn into pieces
½ cucumber, sliced

Fry the chicken thighs until thoroughly heated and crunchy on the outside; an instant-read thermometer should read about 165°F (74°C). Discard the bones and chop the meat. Place the other ingredients in a serving bowl and stir until everything is well incorporated. Layer the chopped chicken thighs over the salad. Serve well chilled and enjoy!

calories: 455 | fat: 29.1g | protein: 40.2g | carbs: 6.6g | net carbs: 2.8g | fiber: 3.8g

Arugula and Avocado Salad

Prep time: 15 minutes | Cook time: 0 minutes | Serves 4

Salad:
6 cups baby arugula
1 avocado, diced
½ cup cherry tomatoes, halved
⅓ cup shaved Parmesan

cheese
¼ cup thinly sliced red onions
¼ cup pili nuts or pine nuts

Dressing:
3 tablespoons extra-virgin olive oil
1 tablespoon red wine vinegar

1 small clove garlic, pressed or minced
Salt and pepper, to taste

Place all the salad ingredients in a large bowl and gently toss. In a small bowl, stir together the dressing ingredients. Toss the salad with the dressing right before serving.

calories: 274 | fat: 23.9g | protein: 8.7g | carbs: 9.0g | net carbs: 4.0g | fiber: 5.0g

Caprese Salad

Prep time: 15 minutes | Cook time: 0 minutes | Serves 5

2 medium tomatoes, each cut into 5 slices
Coarse salt to taste
6 ounces (170 g) fresh Mozzarella, cut into 10 slices
2 avocados, cut into 30 thin slices
3 to 4 large basil leaves,

chopped, plus additional leaves for garnish
¼ cup extra-virgin olive oil or avocado oil
1 lime, halved
Ground black pepper
Italian seasoning (optional)

Lay the tomato slices on a serving plate and sprinkle with salt. On top of each tomato, stack a Mozzarella slice, 3 avocado slices, and some chopped basil. Drizzle with the oil and squeeze some lime juice over the top. Sprinkle with pepper and Italian seasoning, if using. Garnish each stack with a basil leaf, if desired.

calories: 284 | fat: 25.7g | protein: 7.5g | carbs: 8.0g | net carbs: 3.5g | fiber: 4.5g

Feta Cucumber Salad

Prep time: 10 minutes | Cook time: 0 minutes | Serves 5

2 medium-large cucumbers
½ cup thinly sliced red onions
4 ounces (113 g) Feta cheese,

crumbled
Salt and pepper to taste

Dressing:
¼ cup extra-virgin olive oil
1 tablespoon red wine vinegar
1 tablespoon Swerve

confectioners'-style sweetener
½ teaspoon dried ground oregano

Peel the cucumbers as desired and cut in half lengthwise, then slice. In a medium-sized bowl, toss the cucumbers with the onions. Add the Feta and gently toss to combine. Make the dressing: Place all the ingredients in a small bowl and whisk to combine. Serve right away or place in the refrigerator to chill before serving. To serve, gently toss the salad with the dressing and season to taste with salt and pepper.

calories: 172 | fat: 15.2g | protein: 4.5g | carbs: 6.5g | net carbs: 3.7g | fiber: 2.8g

Spinach and Bacon Salad

Prep time: 15 minutes | Cook time: 0 minutes | Serves 4

8 cups baby spinach
4 slices bacon, pan-fried and chopped
3 large eggs, hard-boiled and sliced
10 grape tomatoes, halved
2 avocados, sliced or cubed

½ medium red onion, thinly sliced
½ cup sliced white mushrooms
⅓ cup chopped pecans
Ground black pepper
¾ cup ranch or blue cheese dressing

In a large bowl, gently toss the spinach, bacon, hard-boiled eggs, tomatoes, avocados, onion, mushrooms, and pecans. Season with pepper to taste. Top with the dressing just before serving.

calories: 402 | fat: 34.6g | protein: 12.9g | carbs: 11.1g | net carbs: 7.4g | fiber: 3.7g

Kale and Smoked Salmon Salad

Prep time: 15 minutes | Cook time: 0 minutes | Serves 4

¼ cup extra virgin olive oil
1 tablespoon lemon juice
½ teaspoon garlic powder
½ teaspoon sea salt
¼ teaspoon black pepper
6 ounces (170 g) chopped and deribbed kale (from 8

to 10 ounces / 227 to 283 g untrimmed)
¼ cup salted roasted sunflower seeds
8 ounces (227 g) smoked salmon, cut into pieces

In a large bowl, whisk together the olive oil, lemon juice, garlic powder, sea salt, and black pepper. Add the chopped kale. Use your hands to massage the kale with the dressing mixture. Grab a bunch, squeeze with the dressing, release, and repeat. Do this for a couple of minutes, until the kale starts to soften. Add the sunflower seeds and smoked salmon. Toss together.

calories: 258 | fat: 20.0g | protein: 14.0g | carbs: 6.0g | net carbs: 6.0g | fiber: 0g

Greek Caper Salad

Prep time: 10 minutes | Cook time: 0 minutes | Serves 4

5 tomatoes, chopped
1 large cucumber, chopped
1 green bell pepper, chopped
1 small red onion, chopped
16 Kalamata olives, chopped
4 tablespoons capers

7 ounces (198 g) Feta cheese, chopped
1 teaspoon oregano, dried
4 tablespoons olive oil
Salt to taste

Place tomatoes, pepper, cucumber, onion, Feta and olives in a bowl. Mix to combine. Season with salt. Combine the capers, olive oil and oregano in a small bowl. Drizzle the dressing over the salad.

calories: 324 | fat: 27.8g | protein: 9.4g | carbs: 11.9g | net carbs: 8.0g | fiber: 3.9g

Beef and Spinach Salad

Prep time: 15 minutes | Cook time: 20 minutes | Serves 4

3 tablespoons olive oil
½ pound (227 g) beef rump steak, cut into strips
Salt and black pepper, to taste
1 teaspoon cumin
A pinch of dried thyme
2 garlic cloves, minced

4 ounces (113 g) Feta cheese, crumbled
½ cup pecans, toasted
2 cups spinach
1½ tablespoons lemon juice
¼ cup fresh mint, chopped

Season the beef with salt, 1 tablespoon of olive oil, garlic, thyme, pepper, and cumin. Place on a preheated to medium heat grill, and cook for 10 minutes, flip once. Remove the grilled beef to a cutting board, leave to cool, and slice into strips. Sprinkle the pecans on a lined baking sheet, place in the oven at 350ºF (180ºC), and toast for 10 minutes. In a salad bowl, combine the spinach with black pepper, mint, remaining olive oil, salt, lemon juice, Feta cheese, and pecans, and toss well to coat. Top with the beef slices and enjoy.

calories: 435 | fat: 43.1g | protein: 17.1g | carbs: 5.3g | net carbs: 3.4g | fiber: 1.9g

Spanish Chicken and Pepper Salad

Prep time: 10 minutes | Cook time: 15 minutes | Serves 6

1½ pounds (680 g) chicken breasts
½ cup dry white wine
1 onion, chopped
2 Spanish peppers, seeded and chopped
1 Spanish naga chili pepper, chopped

2 garlic cloves, minced
2 cups arugula
¼ cup mayonnaise
1 tablespoon balsamic vinegar
1 tablespoon stone-ground mustard
Sea salt and freshly ground black pepper, to season

Place the chicken breasts in a saucepan. Add the wine to the saucepan and cover the chicken with water. Bring to a boil over medium-high heat. Reduce to a simmer and cook partially covered for 10 to 14 minutes (an instant-read thermometer should register 165ºF (74ºC)). Transfer the chicken from the poaching liquid to a cutting board; cut into bite-sized pieces and transfer to a salad bowl. Add the remaining ingredients to the salad bowl and gently stir to combine. Serve well chilled.

calories: 280 | fat: 16.2g | protein: 27.2g | carbs: 4.9g | net carbs: 4.0g | fiber: 0.9g

Egg and Avocado Salad in Lettuce Cups

Prep time: 15 minutes | Cook time: 15 minutes | Serves 2

4 large eggs
1 avocado, halved
Pink Himalayan salt
Freshly ground black pepper
½ teaspoon lemon juice

4 butter lettuce cups, washed and patted dry with paper towels
2 radishes, thinly sliced

In a medium saucepan, cover the eggs with water. Place over high heat, and bring the water to a boil. Once it is boiling, turn off the heat, cover, and leave on the burner for 10 to 12 minutes. Remove the eggs with a slotted spoon and run them under cold water for 1 minute. Then gently tap the shells and peel. In a medium bowl, chop the hardboiled eggs. Add the avocado to the bowl, and mash the flesh with a fork. Season with pink Himalayan salt and pepper, add the lemon juice, and stir to combine. Place the 4 lettuce cups on two plates. Top the lettuce cups with the egg salad and the slices of radish and serve.

calories: 259 | fat: 20.1g | protein: 15.1g | carbs: 8.0g | net carbs: 2.9g | fiber: 5.1g

Shrimp Salad with Lemony Mayonnaise

Prep time: 10 minutes | Cook time: 0 minutes | Serves 4

1 small head cauliflower, cut into florets
⅓ cup diced celery
Dressing:
½ cup mayonnaise
1 teaspoon apple cider vinegar
¼ teaspoon celery seeds
A pinch of black pepper

½ cup sliced black olives
2 cups cooked large shrimp
1 tablespoon dill, chopped

1 tablespoon lemon juice
1 teaspoon Swerve
Salt to taste

Combine the cauliflower, celery, shrimp, and dill in a large bowl. Whisk together the mayonnaise, vinegar, celery seeds, black pepper, sweetener, and lemon juice in another bowl. Season with salt to taste. Pour the dressing over and gently toss to combine; refrigerate for 1 hour. Top with olives to serve.

calories: 182 | fat: 15g | protein: 12g | carbs: 4g | net carbs: 2g | fiber: 2g

Caesar Salad with Salmon and Egg

Prep time: 5 minutes | Cook time: 27 minutes | Serves 4

2 cups water
8 eggs
2 cups torn romaine lettuce
½ cup smoked salmon,

chopped
6 slices bacon
1 tablespoon Heinz low carb Caesar dressing

Boil the water in a pot over medium heat for 5 minutes and bring to simmer. Crack each egg into a small bowl and gently slide into the water. Poach for 2 to 3 minutes, remove with a perforated spoon, transfer to a paper towel to dry, and plate. Poach the remaining 7 eggs. Put the bacon in a skillet and fry over medium heat until browned and crispy, about 6 minutes, turning once. Remove, allow cooling, and chop in small pieces. Toss the lettuce, smoked salmon, bacon, and Caesar dressing in a salad bowl. Divide the salad into 4 plates, top with two eggs each, and serve immediately or chilled.

calories: 260 | fat: 21g | protein: 8g | carbs: 6g | net carbs: 5g | fiber: 1g

Charred Broccoli and Sardine Salad
Prep time: 5 minutes | Cook time: 5 minutes | Serves 4

1 pound (454 g) broccoli florets
½ white onion, thinly sliced
2 (4-ounce / 113-g) cans sardines in oil, drained
2 tablespoons fresh lime juice
1 teaspoon stone-ground mustard

Heat a lightly greased cast-iron skillet over medium-high heat. Cook the broccoli florets for 5 to 6 minutes until charred; work in batches. In salad bowls, place the charred broccoli with onion and sardines. Toss with the lime juice and mustard. Serve at room temperature. Bon appétit!

calories: 160 | fat: 7.2g | protein: 17.6g | carbs: 5.6g | net carbs: 2.6g | fiber: 3.0g

Spicy Leek and Green Cabbage Salad
Prep time: 15 minutes | Cook time: 40 minutes | Serves 4

3 tablespoons extra-virgin olive oil
1 medium-sized leek, chopped
½ pound (227 g) green cabbage, shredded
½ teaspoon caraway seeds
Sea salt, to taste
4-5 black peppercorns
1 garlic clove, minced
1 teaspoon yellow mustard
1 tablespoon balsamic vinegar
½ teaspoon Sriracha sauce

Drizzle 2 tablespoons of the olive oil over the leek and cabbage; sprinkle with caraway seeds, salt, black peppercorns. Roast in the preheated oven at 420ºF (216ºC) for 37 to 40 minutes. Place the roasted mixture in a salad bowl. Toss with the remaining tablespoon of olive oil garlic, mustard, vinegar, and Sriracha sauce. Serve immediately and enjoy!

calories: 116 | fat: 10.1g | protein: 1.0g | carbs: 6.5g | net carbs: 4.7g | fiber: 1.8g

Zucchini and Bell Pepper Slaw
Prep time: 15 minutes | Cook time: 0 minutes | Serves 3

1 zucchini, shredded
1 yellow bell pepper, sliced
1 red onion, thinly sliced
2 tablespoons extra-virgin olive oil
1 tablespoon balsamic vinegar
1 teaspoon Dijon mustard
¼ teaspoon cumin seeds
¼ teaspoon ground black pepper
Sea salt, to taste

Thoroughly combine all ingredients in a salad bowl. Refrigerate for 1 hour before serving or serve right away. Enjoy!

calories: 97 | fat: 9.5g | protein: 0.8g | carbs: 2.7g | net carbs: 2.4g | fiber: 0.3g

Asparagus and Mozzarella Caprese Salad
Prep time: 15 minutes | Cook time: 0 minutes | Serves 2

1 teaspoon fresh lime juice
1 tablespoon hot Hungarian paprika infused oil
½ teaspoon kosher salt
¼ teaspoon red pepper flakes
½ pound (227 g) asparagus spears, trimmed
1 cup grape tomatoes, halved
2 tablespoon red wine vinegar
1 garlic clove, pressed 1-2 drops liquid stevia
1 tablespoon fresh basil
1 tablespoon fresh chives
½ cup Mozzarella, grated

Heat your grill to the hottest setting. Toss your asparagus with the lime juice, hot Hungarian paprika infused oil, salt, and red pepper flakes. Place the asparagus spears on the hot grill. Grill until one side chars; then, grill your asparagus on the other side. Cut the asparagus spears into bite-sized pieces and transfer to a salad bowl. Add the grape tomatoes, red wine, garlic, stevia, basil, and chives; toss to combine well. Top with freshly grated Mozzarella cheese and serve immediately.

calories: 190 | fat: 13.2g | protein: 9.6g | carbs: 7.5g | net carbs: 4.2g | fiber: 3.3g

Mediterranean Tomato and Zucchini Salad
Prep time: 15 minutes | Cook time: 10 minutes | Serves 4

½ pound (227 g) Roma tomatoes, sliced
½ pound (227 g) zucchini, sliced
1 Lebanese cucumber, sliced
1 cup arugula
½ teaspoon oregano
½ teaspoon basil
½ teaspoon rosemary
½ teaspoon ground black
pepper
Sea salt, to season
4 tablespoons extra-virgin olive oil
2 tablespoons fresh lemon juice
½ cup Kalamata olives, pitted and sliced
4 ounces (113 g) Feta cheese, cubed

Arrange the Roma tomatoes and zucchini slices on a roasting pan; spritz cooking oil over your vegetables. Bake in the preheated oven at 350ºF (180ºC) for 6 to 7 minutes. Let them cool slightly, then, transfer to a salad bowl. Add in the cucumber, arugula, herbs, and spices. Drizzle olive oil and lemon juice over your veggies; toss to combine well. Top with Kalamata olives and Feta cheese. Serve at room temperature and enjoy!

calories: 242 | fat: 22.1g | protein: 6.4g | carbs: 6.9g | net carbs: 5.1g | fiber: 1.8g

Tangy Squid and Veggies Salad
Prep time: 15 minutes | Cook time: 5 minutes | Serves 4

4 medium squid tubes, cut into strips
½ cup mint leaves
2 medium cucumbers, halved and cut in strips
½ cup coriander leaves, reserve the stems
½ red onion, finely sliced
Salt and black pepper, to taste
1 teaspoon fish sauce
1 red chili, roughly chopped
1 clove garlic
2 limes, juiced
1 tablespoon chopped coriander
1 teaspoon olive oil

In a salad bowl, mix mint leaves, cucumber strips, coriander leaves, and red onion. Season with salt, black pepper and some olive oil; set aside. In the mortar, pound the coriander stems, and red chili to form a paste using the pestle. Add the fish sauce and lime juice, and mix with the pestle. Heat a skillet over high heat on a stovetop and sear the squid on both sides to lightly brown, about 5 minutes. Pour the squid on the salad and drizzle with the chili dressing. Toss the ingredients with two spoons, garnish with coriander, and serve the salad as a single dish or with some more seafood.

calories: 318 | fat: 23g | protein: 25g | carbs: 3g | net carbs: 2g | fiber: 1g

Roasted Asparagus Salad

Prep time: 15 minutes | Cook time: 15 minutes | Serves 5

14 ounces (397 g) asparagus spears, trimmed
2 tablespoons olive oil
½ teaspoon oregano
½ teaspoon rosemary
Sea salt and freshly ground
black pepper, to taste
5 tablespoons mayonnaise
3 tablespoons sour cream
1 tablespoon wine vinegar
1 teaspoon fresh garlic, minced
1 cup cherry tomatoes, halved

In a lightly greased roasting pan, toss the asparagus with the olive oil, oregano, rosemary, salt, and black pepper. Roast in the preheated oven at 425ºF (220ºC) for 13 to 15 minutes until just tender. Meanwhile, in a mixing bowl, thoroughly combine the mayonnaise, sour cream, vinegar, and garlic; dress the salad and top with the cherry tomato halves. Serve at room temperature. Bon appétit!

calories: 180 | fat: 17.6g | protein: 2.6g | carbs: 4.5g | net carbs: 2.5g | fiber: 2.0g

Bell Pepper, Cabbage, and Arugula Coleslaw

Prep time: 15 minutes | Cook time: 0 minutes | Serves 4

2 teaspoons balsamic vinegar
1 teaspoon fresh garlic, minced
2 tablespoons tahini (sesame paste)
1 tablespoon yellow mustard
Sea salt and ground black pepper, to taste
¼ teaspoon paprika
1 red bell pepper, seeded and sliced
1 green bell pepper, seeded and sliced
½ pound (227 g) Napa cabbage, shredded
2 cups arugula, torn into pieces
1 Spanish onion, thinly sliced into rings
4 tablespoons sesame seeds, lightly toasted

Make a dressing by whisking the balsamic vinegar, garlic, tahini, mustard, salt, black pepper, and paprika. In a salad bowl, combine the bell peppers, cabbage, arugula, and Spanish onion. Dress the salad and toss until everything is well incorporated. Garnish with sesame seeds just before serving. Serve well chilled and enjoy!

calories: 123 | fat: 9.2g | protein: 4.6g | carbs: 5.8g | net carbs: 2.8g | fiber: 3.0g

Chicken and Sunflower Seed Salad

Prep time: 15 minutes | Cook time: 15 minutes | Serves 3

1 chicken breast, skinless
¼ mayonnaise
¼ cup sour cream
2 tablespoons Cottage cheese, room temperature
Salt and black pepper, to taste
¼ cup sunflower seeds, hulled
and roasted
½ avocado, peeled and cubed
½ teaspoon fresh garlic, minced
2 tablespoons scallions, chopped

Bring a pot of well-salted water to a rolling boil. Add the chicken to the boiling water; now, turn off the heat, cover, and let the chicken stand in the hot water for 15 minutes. Then, drain the water; chop the chicken into bite-sized pieces. Add the remaining ingredients and mix well. Place in the refrigerator for at least one hour. Serve well chilled. Enjoy!

calories: 401 | fat: 35.2g | protein: 16.2g | carbs: 5.7g | net carbs: 2.9g | fiber: 2.8g

Roasted Asparagus and Cherry Tomato Salad

Prep time: 15 minutes | Cook time: 20 minutes | Serves 3

1 pound (454 g) asparagus, trimmed
¼ teaspoon ground black pepper
Flaky salt, to season
3 tablespoons sesame seeds
1 tablespoon Dijon mustard
½ lime, freshly squeezed
3 tablespoons extra-virgin olive oil
2 garlic cloves, minced
1 tablespoon fresh tarragon, snipped
1 cup cherry tomatoes, sliced

Start by preheating your oven to 400ºF (205ºC). Spritz a roasting pan with nonstick cooking spray. Roast the asparagus for about 13 minutes, turning the spears over once or twice. Sprinkle with salt, pepper, and sesame seeds; roast an additional 3 to 4 minutes. To make the dressing, whisk the Dijon mustard, lime juice, olive oil, and minced garlic. Chop the asparagus spears into bite-sized pieces and place them in a nice salad bowl. Add the tarragon and tomatoes to the bowl; gently toss to combine. Dress your salad and serve at room temperature. Enjoy!

calories: 160 | fat: 12.4g | protein: 5.7g | carbs: 6.2g | net carbs: 2.2g | fiber: 4.0g

Herbed Chicken Salad

Prep time: 15 minutes | Cook time: 15 minutes | Serves 4

Poached Chicken:
2 chicken breasts, skinless and boneless
½ teaspoon salt
Salad:
4 scallions, trimmed and thinly sliced
1 tablespoon fresh coriander, chopped
1 teaspoon Dijon mustard
2 bay laurels
1 thyme sprig
1 rosemary sprig

2 teaspoons freshly squeezed lemon juice
1 cup mayonnaise, preferably homemade

Place all ingredients for the poached chicken in a stockpot; cover with water and bring to a rolling boil. Turn the heat to medium-low and let it simmer for about 15 minutes or until a meat thermometer reads 165ºF (74ºC). Let the poached chicken cool to room temperature. Cut into strips and transfer to a nice salad bowl. Toss the poached chicken with the salad ingredients; serve well chilled and enjoy!

calories: 540 | fat: 48.9g | protein: 18.9g | carbs: 3.2g | net carbs: 2.8g | fiber: 0.4g

Grilled Chicken and Cucumber Salad

Prep time: 10 minutes | Cook time: 15 minutes | Serves 2

2 chicken breasts
2 tablespoons extra-virgin olive oil
4 tablespoons apple cider
vinegar
1 cup grape tomatoes, halved
1 Lebanese cucumber, thinly sliced

Preheat your grill to medium-high temperature. Now, grill the chicken breasts for 5 to 7 minutes on each side. Slice the chicken into strips and transfer them to a nice salad bowl. Toss with the olive oil, vinegar, grape tomatoes, and cucumber. Garnish with fresh snipped chives if desired. Bon appétit!

calories: 402 | fat: 18.1g | protein: 51.5g | carbs: 5.2g | net carbs: 3.7g | fiber: 1.5g

Skirt Steak, Veggies, and Pecan Salad
Prep time: 15 minutes | Cook time: 10 minutes | Serves 2

8 ounces (227 g) skirt steak
Pink Himalayan salt
Freshly ground black pepper
1 tablespoon butter
2 romaine hearts or 2 cups

chopped romaine
½ cup halved grape tomatoes
¼ cup crumbled blue cheese
¼ cup pecans
1 tablespoon olive oil

Heat a large skillet over high heat. Pat the steak dry with a paper towel, and season both sides with pink Himalayan salt and pepper. Add the butter to the skillet. When it melts, put the steak in the skillet. Sear the steak for about 3 minutes on each side, for medium-rare. Transfer the steak to a cutting board and let it rest for at least 5 minutes. Meanwhile, divide the romaine between two plates, and top with the grape tomato halves, blue cheese, and pecans. Drizzle with the olive oil. Slice the skirt steak across the grain, top the salads with it, and serve.

calories: 451 | fat: 36g | protein: 30g | carbs: 7g | net carbs: 5g | fiber: 2g

Mediterranean Tomato and Avocado Salad
Prep time: 5 minutes | Cook time: 0 minutes | Serves 4

3 tomatoes, sliced
1 large avocado, sliced
8 kalamata olives
¼ pound (113 g) buffalo

mozzarella cheese, sliced
1 tablespoon pesto sauce
1 tablespoon olive oil

Arrange the tomato slices on a serving platter and place the avocado slices in the middle. Arrange the olives around the avocado slices and drop pieces of mozzarella on the platter. Drizzle the pesto sauce all over, and drizzle olive oil as well.

calories: 290 | fat: 25g | protein: 9g | carbs: 9g | net carbs: 4g | fiber: 5g

Tuna Cheese Caprese Salad
Prep time: 10 minutes | Cook time: 0 minutes | Serves 4

2 (10 ounce / 283-g) cans tuna chunks in water, drained
2 tomatoes, sliced
8 ounces (283 g) fresh mozzarella cheese, sliced
6 basil leaves

½ cup black olives, pitted and sliced
1 tablespoon extra virgin olive oil
½ lemon, juiced

Place the tuna in the center of a serving platter. Arrange the cheese and tomato slices around the tuna. Alternate a slice of tomato, cheese, and a basil leaf. To finish, scatter the black olives over the top, drizzle with olive oil and lemon juice and serve.

calories: 360 | fat: 31g | protein: 21g | carbs: 3g | net carbs: 1g | fiber: 2g

Tuna Salad with Olives and Lettuce
Prep time: 5 minutes | Cook time: 0 minutes | Serves 2

1 cup canned tuna, drained
1 teaspoon onion flakes
1 tablespoon mayonnaise
1 cup shredded romaine

lettuce
1 tablespoon lime juice
Sea salt, to taste
6 black olives, pitted and sliced

Combine the tuna, mayonnaise, lime juice, and salt in a small bowl; mix to combine well. In a salad platter, arrange the shredded lettuce and onion flakes. Spread the tuna mixture over; top with black olives to serve.

calories: 248 | fat: 20g | protein: 19g | carbs: 3g | net carbs: 2g | fiber: 1g

Lemony Prawn and Arugula Salad
Prep time: 10 minutes | Cook time: 3 minute | Serves 4

4 cups baby arugula
½ cup garlic mayonnaise
1 tablespoon olive oil
1 pound (454 g) tiger prawns,

peeled and deveined
1 teaspoon Dijon mustard
Salt and chili pepper to season
2 tablespoons lemon juice

First, make the dressing: add the mayonnaise, lemon juice and mustard in a small bowl. Mix until smooth and creamy. Set aside until ready to use. Heat 1 tablespoon of olive oil in a skillet over medium heat, add the prawns, season with salt, and chili pepper, and fry for 3 minutes on each side until prawns are pink. Set aside to a plate. Place the arugula in a serving bowl and pour half of the dressing on the salad. Toss with 2 spoons until mixed, and add the remaining dressing. Divide salad onto 4 plates and top with prawns.

calories: 215 | fat: 20g | protein: 8g | carbs: 3g | net carbs: 2g | fiber: 1g

Mackerel and Green Bean Salad
Prep time: 10 minutes | Cook time: 11 minutes | Serves 2

2 mackerel fillets
2 hard-boiled eggs, sliced
1 tablespoon coconut oil
2 cups green beans
1 avocado, sliced

4 cups mixed salad greens
1 tablespoon olive oil
1 tablespoon lemon juice
1 teaspoon Dijon mustard
Salt and black pepper, to taste

Fill a saucepan with water and add the green beans and salt. Cook over medium heat for about 3 minutes. Drain and set aside. Melt the coconut oil in a pan over medium heat. Add the mackerel fillets and cook for about 4 minutes per side, or until opaque and crispy. Divide the green beans between two salad bowls. Top with mackerel, eggs, and avocado slices. In a bowl, whisk together the lemon juice, olive oil, mustard, salt, and pepper, and drizzle over the salad.

calories: 525 | fat: 42g | protein: 27g | carbs: 22g | net carbs: 8g | fiber: 14g

Dijon Broccoli Slaw Salad
Prep time: 10 minutes | Cook time: 0 minutes | Serves 6

1 tablespoon granulated Swerve
1 tablespoon Dijon mustard
1 tablespoon olive oil
4 cups broccoli slaw

⅓ cup mayonnaise, sugar-free
1 teaspoon celery seeds
1½ tablespoon apple cider vinegar
Salt and black pepper, to taste

Whisk together all ingredients except the broccoli slaw. Place broccoli slaw in a large salad bowl. Pour the dressing over. Mix with your hands to combine well.

calories: 110 | fat: 10g | protein: 3g | carbs: 5g | net carbs: 2g | fiber: 3g

Mustard Eggs Salad

Prep time: 10 minutes | Cook time: 10 minutes | Serves 8

10 eggs
¾ cup mayonnaise
1 teaspoon sriracha sauce
1 tablespoon mustard
½ cup scallions
½ stalk celery, minced

½ teaspoon fresh lemon juice
½ teaspoon sea salt
½ teaspoon black pepper
1 head romaine lettuce, torn into pieces

Add the eggs in a pan and cover with enough water and boil. Get them from the heat and allow to set for 10 minutes while covered. Chop the eggs and add to a salad bowl. Stir in the remaining ingredients until everything is well combined. Refrigerate until ready to serve.

calories: 174 | fat: 13g | protein: 7g | carbs: 10g | net carbs: 8g | fiber: 2g

Balsamic Brussels Sprouts Cheese Salad

Prep time: 10 minutes | Cook time: 20 minutes | Serves 6

2 pound (907 g) Brussels sprouts, halved
1 tablespoon olive oil
Salt and black pepper to taste
2½ tablespoon balsamic

vinegar
¼ head red cabbage, shredded
1 tablespoon Dijon mustard
1 cup Pecorino Romano cheese, grated

Preheat oven to 400ºF (205ºC) and line a baking sheet with foil. Toss the brussels sprouts with olive oil, a little salt, black pepper, and balsamic vinegar, in a bowl, and spread on the baking sheet in an even layer. Bake until tender on the inside and crispy on the outside, about 20 to 25 minutes. Transfer to a salad bowl and add the red cabbage, Dijon mustard and half of the cheese. Mix until well combined. Sprinkle with the remaining cheese, share the salad onto serving plates, and serve with the salmon.

calories: 210 | fat: 18g | protein: 4g | carbs: 12g | net carbs: 6g | fiber: 6g

Spring Vegetable Salad with Cheese Balls

Prep time: 15 minutes | Cook time: 10 minutes | Serves 6

Cheese balls:
3 eggs
1 cup feta cheese, crumbled
½ cup pecorino cheese, shredded
Salad:
1 head iceberg lettuce, leaves separated
½ cup cucumber, thinly sliced
2 tomatoes, seeded and chopped
½ cup red onion, thinly sliced

1 cup almond flour
1 tablespoon flax meal
1 teaspoon baking powder
Salt and black pepper, to taste

½ cup radishes, thinly sliced
⅓ cup mayonnaise
1 teaspoon mustard
1 teaspoon paprika
1 teaspoon oregano
Salt, to taste

Set oven to 390ºF (199ºC). Line a piece of parchment paper to a baking sheet. In a mixing dish, mix all ingredients for the cheese balls; form balls out of the mixture. Set the balls on the prepared baking sheet. Bake for 10 minutes until crisp. Arrange lettuce leaves on a large salad platter; add in radishes, tomatoes, cucumbers, and red onion. In a small mixing bowl, mix the mayonnaise, paprika, salt, oregano, and mustard. Sprinkle this mixture over the vegetables. Add cheese balls on top and serve.

calories: 234 | fat: 17g | protein: 12g | carbs: 11g | net carbs: 8g | fiber: 3g

Tuscan Kale Salad with Lemony Anchovies

Prep time: 15 minutes | Cook time: 0 minutes | Serves 4

1 large bunch lacinato or dinosaur kale
¼ cup toasted pine nuts
1 cup shaved or coarsely shredded fresh Parmesan cheese
¼ cup extra-virgin olive oil

8 anchovy fillets, roughly chopped
2 to 3 tablespoons freshly squeezed lemon juice (from 1 large lemon)
2 teaspoons red pepper flakes (optional)

Remove the rough center stems from the kale leaves and roughly tear each leaf into about 4-by-1-inch strips. Place the torn kale in a large bowl and add the pine nuts and cheese. In a small bowl, whisk together the olive oil, anchovies, lemon juice, and red pepper flakes (if using). Drizzle over the salad and toss to coat well. Let sit at room temperature 30 minutes before serving, tossing again just prior to serving.

calories: 337 | fat: 25g | protein: 16g | carbs: 12g | net carbs: 10g | fiber: 2g

Lush Greek Salad

Prep time: 10 minutes | Cook time: 0 minutes | Serves 4

2 large English cucumbers
4 Roma tomatoes, quartered
1 green bell pepper, cut into 1- to 1½-inch chunks
¼ small red onion, thinly sliced
4 ounces pitted Kalamata olives
¼ cup extra-virgin olive oil
2 tablespoons freshly

squeezed lemon juice
1 tablespoon red wine vinegar
1 tablespoon chopped fresh oregano or 1 teaspoon dried oregano
¼ teaspoon freshly ground black pepper
4 ounces (113 g) crumbled traditional feta cheese

Cut the cucumbers in half lengthwise and then into ½-inch-thick half-moons. Place in a large bowl. Add the quartered tomatoes, bell pepper, red onion, and olives. In a small bowl, whisk together the olive oil, lemon juice, vinegar, oregano, and pepper. Drizzle over the vegetables and toss to coat. Divide between salad plates and top each with 1 ounce of feta.

calories: 278 | fat: 22g | protein: 8g | carbs: 12g | net carbs: 8g | fiber: 4g

Cheesy Green Salad with Bacon

Prep time: 5 minutes | Cook time: 6 minutes | Serves 4

2 (8-ounce / 227-g) pack mixed salad greens
8 strips bacon
1½ cups crumbled blue cheese
1 tablespoon white wine

vinegar
1 tablespoon extra virgin olive oil
Salt and black pepper to taste

Pour the salad greens in a salad bowl; set aside. Fry bacon strips in a skillet over medium heat for 6 minutes, until browned and crispy. Chop the bacon and scatter over the salad. Add in half of the cheese, toss and set aside. In a small bowl, whisk the white wine vinegar, olive oil, salt, and black pepper until dressing is well combined. Drizzle half of the dressing over the salad, toss, and top with remaining cheese. Divide salad into four plates and serve with crusted chicken fries along with the remaining dressing.

calories: 205 | fat: 20g | protein: 4g | carbs: 5g | net carbs: 2g | fiber: 3g

Cheesy Pork Patties Salad

Prep time: 5 minutes | Cook time: 20 minutes | Serves 4

1 pound (454 g) ground pork
Salt and black pepper to
season
1 tablespoon olive oil
2 hearts romaine lettuce, torn

into pieces
2 firm tomatoes, sliced
¼ red onion, sliced
3 ounces (85 g) yellow cheddar
cheese, shredded

Season the pork with salt and black pepper, mix and make medium-sized patties out of them. Heat the oil in a skillet over medium heat and fry the patties on both sides for 10 minutes until browned and cook within. Transfer to a wire rack to drain oil. When cooled, cut into quarters. Mix the lettuce, tomatoes, and red onion in a salad bowl, season with a little oil, salt, and black pepper. Toss and add the pork on top. Melt the cheese in the microwave for about 90 seconds. Drizzle the cheese over the salad and serve.

calories: 310 | fat: 23g | protein: 22g | carbs: 9g | net carbs: 2g | fiber: 7g

Bacon, Avocado, and Veggies Salad

Prep time: 10 minutes | Cook time: 0 minutes | Serves 4

2 large avocados, 1 chopped
and 1 sliced
1 spring onion, sliced
4 cooked bacon slices,
Vinaigrette:
1 tablespoon olive oil
1 teaspoon Dijon mustard

crumbled
2 cups spinach
2 small lettuce heads, chopped
2 hard-boiled eggs, chopped

1 tablespoon apple cider
vinegar

Combine the spinach, lettuce, eggs, chopped avocado, and spring onion, in a large bowl. Whisk together the vinaigrette ingredients in another bowl. Pour the dressing over, toss to combine and top with the sliced avocado and bacon.

calories: 350 | fat: 33g | protein: 7g | carbs: 11g | net carbs: 3g | fiber: 8g

Caesar Salad with Chicken and Cheese

Prep time: 10 minutes | Cook time: 11 minutes | Serves 4

4 boneless, skinless chicken
thighs
¼ cup lemon juice
2 garlic cloves, minced
1 tablespoon olive oil
½ cup Caesar salad dressing,

sugar-free
12 bok choy leaves
3 Parmesan crisps
Parmesan cheese, grated for
garnishing

Mix chicken, lemon juice, 1 tablespoon olive oil and garlic in a ziploc bag. Seal the bag, shake well, and refrigerate for 1 hour. Preheat the grill to medium and grill the chicken for 4 minutes per side. Cut bok choy lengthwise, and brush with the remaining oil. Grill the bok choy for about 3 minutes. Place on a bowl. Top with chicken and Parmesan; drizzle the dressing over. Top with Parmesan crisps to serve.

calories: 529 | fat: 39g | protein: 33g | carbs: 6g | net carbs: 5g | fiber: 1g

Shrimp, Cauliflower and Avocado Salad

Prep time: 10 minutes | Cook time: 13 minutes | Serves 6

1 cauliflower head, florets only
1 pound (454 g) medium
shrimp
¼ cup plus 1 tablespoon olive
oil

1 avocado, chopped
1 tablespoon chopped dill
¼ cup lemon juice
1 tablespoon lemon zest
Salt and black pepper to taste

Heat 1 tablespoon olive oil in a skillet and cook shrimp for 8 minutes. Microwave cauliflower for 5 minutes. Place shrimp, cauliflower, and avocado in a bowl. Whisk the remaining olive oil, lemon zest, juice, dill, and salt, and pepper, in another bowl. Pour the dressing over, toss to combine and serve immediately.

calories: 214 | fat: 17g | protein: 15g | carbs: 9g | net carbs: 5g | fiber: 4g

Dijon Cauliflower Salad

Prep time: 10 minutes | Cook time: 10 minutes | Serves 6

1 large cauliflower
Sea salt and freshly ground
black pepper, to taste
3 hard-boiled eggs, diced
¾ cup avocado oil mayonnaise
2 tablespoons Dijon mustard

¼ cup dill pickle, diced
3 celery stalks, diced
1 tablespoon apple cider
vinegar
1 teaspoon garlic powder

Remove the stem and cut the cauliflower into florets. Put 1 to 2 inches water in a large pot, add a pinch of salt, and bring to a boil. Add the cauliflower, reduce the heat to low, and cover the pot. Steam the cauliflower for 10 minutes, or until fork-tender. Drain the cauliflower and let it cool for 15 minutes.
Mix the remaining ingredients in a large bowl. When cooled, add the cauliflower and mix together. Cover and refrigerate for 1 to 2 hours, until chilled. Serve cold.

calories: 305 | fat: 30g | protein: 6g | carbs: 4g | net carbs: 3g | fiber: 1g

Skirt Steak and Pickled Peppers Salad

Prep time: 10 minutes | Cook time: 10 minutes | Serves 4

1 pound (454 g) skirt steak,
sliced
Salt and black pepper to
season
1 teaspoon olive oil

1½ cups mixed salad greens
3 chopped pickled peppers
1 tablespoon red wine
vinaigrette
½ cup crumbled queso fresco

Brush the steak slices with olive oil and season with salt and black pepper on both sides. Heat pan over high heat and cook the steaks on each side for about 5-6 minutes. Remove to a bow. Mix the salad greens, pickled peppers, and vinaigrette in a salad bowl. Add the beef and sprinkle with queso fresco.

calories: 315 | fat: 26g | protein: 18g | carbs: 3g | net carbs: 2g | fiber: 1g

Classic Greek Salad

Prep time: 10 minutes | Cook time: 0 minutes | Serves 4

5 tomatoes, chopped
1 large cucumber, chopped
1 green bell pepper, chopped
1 small red onion, chopped
16 kalamata olives, chopped

1 tablespoon capers
1 cup feta cheese, chopped
1 teaspoon oregano, dried
1 tablespoon olive oil
Salt to taste

Place tomatoes, bell pepper, cucumber, onion, feta cheese and olives in a bowl; mix to combine well. Season with salt. Combine capers, olive oil, and oregano, in a bowl. Drizzle with the dressing to serve.

calories: 323 | fat: 28g | protein: 9g | carbs: 12g | net carbs: 8g | fiber: 4g

Garlicky Chicken Salad

Prep time: 10 minutes | Cook time: 8 minutes | Serves 4

2 chicken breasts, boneless, skinless, flattened
Salt and black pepper, to taste
1 tablespoon garlic powder

1 teaspoon olive oil
1½ cups mixed salad greens
1 tablespoon red wine vinegar
1 cup crumbled blue cheese

Season the chicken with salt, black pepper, and garlic powder. Heat oil in a pan over high heat and fry the chicken for 4 minutes on both sides until golden brown. Remove chicken to a cutting board and let cool before slicing. Toss salad greens with red wine vinegar and share the salads into 4 plates. Divide chicken slices on top and sprinkle with blue cheese. Serve.

calories: 286 | fat: 23g | protein: 14g | carbs: 5g | net carbs: 4g | fiber: 1g

Israeli Veggies, Nut, and Seed Salad

Prep time: 15 minutes | Cook time: 0 minutes | Serves 4

¼ cup pine nuts
¼ cup shelled pistachios
¼ cup coarsely chopped walnuts
¼ cup shelled pumpkin seeds
¼ cup shelled sunflower seeds
2 large English cucumbers, unpeeled and finely chopped
1 pint cherry tomatoes, finely chopped
½ small red onion, finely

chopped
½ cup finely chopped fresh Italian parsley
¼ cup extra-virgin olive oil
2 to 3 tablespoons freshly squeezed lemon juice
1 teaspoon salt
¼ teaspoon freshly ground black pepper
4 cups baby arugula

In a skillet, toast the pine nuts, pistachios, walnuts, pumpkin seeds, and sunflower seeds over medium-low heat until golden and fragrant, 5 to 6 minutes. Remove from the heat and set aside. In a large bowl, combine the cucumber, tomatoes, red onion, and parsley. In a small bowl, whisk together olive oil, lemon juice, salt, and pepper. Pour over the chopped vegetables and toss to coat. Add the toasted nuts and seeds and arugula and toss with the salad to blend well. Serve at room temperature or chilled.

calories: 414 | fat: 34g | protein: 10g | carbs: 17g | net carbs: 11g | fiber: 6g

Strawberry and Spinach Salad

Prep time: 5 minutes | Cook time: 10 minutes | Serves 2

4 cups spinach
4 strawberries, sliced
½ cup flaked almonds
1½ cups grated hard goat

cheese
1 tablespoon raspberry vinaigrette
Salt and black pepper, to taste

Preheat your oven to 400ºF (205ºC). Arrange the grated goat cheese in two circles on two pieces of parchment paper. Place in the oven and bake for 10 minutes. Find two same bowls, place them upside down, and carefully put the parchment paper on top to give the cheese a bowl-like shape. Let cool that way for 15 minutes. Divide spinach among the bowls stir in salt, pepper and drizzle with vinaigrette. Top with almonds and strawberries.

calories: 445 | fat: 34g | protein: 33g | carbs: 7g | net carbs: 5g | fiber: 2g

Mozzarella Bacon and Tomato Salad

Prep time: 5 minutes | Cook time: 5 minutes | Serves 2

1 large tomato, sliced
4 basil leaves
8 mozzarella cheese slices
1 teaspoon olive oil

4 bacon slices, chopped
1 teaspoon balsamic vinegar
Salt, to taste

Place the bacon in a skillet over medium heat and cook until crispy, about 5 minutes. Divide the tomato slices between two serving plates. Arrange the mozzarella slices over and top with the basil leaves. Add the crispy bacon on top, drizzle with olive oil and vinegar. Sprinkle with salt and serve.

calories: 279 | fat: 26g | protein: 21g | carbs: 3g | net carbs: 2g | fiber: 1g

Baby Arugula and Walnuts Salad

Prep time: 10 minutes | Cook time: 0 minutes | Serves 4

4 tablespoons extra-virgin olive oil
Zest and juice of 2 lemon (2 to 3 tablespoons)
1 tablespoon red wine vinegar
½ teaspoon salt
¼ teaspoon freshly ground

black pepper
8 cups baby arugula
1 cup coarsely chopped walnuts
1 cup crumbled goat cheese
½ cup pomegranate seeds

In a small bowl, whisk together the olive oil, zest and juice, vinegar, salt, and pepper and set aside. To assemble the salad for serving, in a large bowl, combine the arugula, walnuts, goat cheese, and pomegranate seeds. Drizzle with the dressing and toss to coat.

calories: 444 | fat: 40g | protein: 10g | carbs: 11g | net carbs: 8g | fiber: 3g

Homemade Albacore Tuna Salad
Prep time: 5 minutes | Cook time: 0 minutes | Serves 4

2 (5-ounce / 142-g) cans albacore tuna packed in water, drained
¼ cup avocado oil mayonnaise
2 teaspoons Dijon mustard
3 teaspoons dried dill
2 teaspoons lime juice
½ cup diced bell pepper

In a small bowl, combine the tuna, mayonnaise, mustard, dill, lime juice, and bell pepper. Serve on a bed of mixed greens.

calories: 294 | fat: 21g | protein: 13g | carbs: 19g | net carbs: 12g | fiber: 7g

Classic Caprese Salad
Prep time: 10 minutes | Cook time: 0 minutes | Serves 8

8 ounces (227 g) fresh mozzarella cheese
4 tomatoes
¼ cup balsamic vinegar
¼ cup extra virgin olive oil
1 cup fresh basil
1 teaspoon sea salt
½ teaspoon freshly ground black pepper

Cut the mozzarella and tomatoes into ¼-inch-thick slices and arrange in an alternating pattern on a plate. In a small bowl, mix the balsamic vinegar and olive oil. Drizzle on top of the mozzarella and tomatoes. Stack the fresh basil and roll it into a tight log. Carefully cut into thin julienne slices, and toss over the salad. Sprinkle the salt and pepper on top and enjoy.

calories: 148 | fat: 11g | protein: 9g | carbs: 4g | net carbs: 3g | fiber: 1g

Turkey and Walnuts Salad
Prep time: 10 minutes | Cook time: 0 minutes | Serves 4

1 pound (454 g) turkey breast, cooked
3 green onions, sliced
2 celery stalks, diced
½ cup chopped walnuts
½ cup avocado oil mayonnaise
1 teaspoon fresh lemon juice
¼ teaspoon sea salt
¼ teaspoon freshly ground black pepper
Mixed greens

Chop the turkey breast into small pieces. In a large bowl, combine the turkey, onions, celery, walnuts, mayonnaise, lemon juice, salt, and pepper, and mix well. Serve on a bed of mixed greens.

calories: 351 | fat: 23g | protein: 32g | carbs: 5g | net carbs: 3g | fiber: 2g

Vinegary Cucumber Salad
Prep time: 5 minutes | Cook time: 0 minutes | Serves 2

1 large hothouse or English cucumber
¼ red onion, finely sliced
2 tablespoons organic apple cider vinegar
2 tablespoons extra virgin olive oil
5 drops liquid stevia
1 teaspoon sea salt

Slice the cucumber and place in a medium bowl. Add the red onion. In a small bowl, mix the apple cider vinegar, olive oil, stevia, and salt together. Pour over the cucumbers and onion. Stir together well to combine and refrigerate for 30 minutes. Serve chilled.

calories: 151 | fat: 14g | protein: 1g | carbs: 7g | net carbs: 6g | fiber: 1g

Dijon Egg Salad
Prep time: 5 minutes | Cook time: 0 minutes | Serves 4

6 hard boiled eggs, finely chopped
1 celery stalk, diced
½ cup cashews, finely diced
¼ cup olive oil mayonnaise
1 tablespoon Dijon mustard
1½ teaspoons curry powder
¼ teaspoon salt
¼ teaspoon freshly ground black pepper
8 butter lettuce leaves

In a medium mixing bowl, combine the eggs with the celery and cashews. Add the mayonnaise, mustard, curry powder, salt, and pepper, and stir until thoroughly combined. Divide the salad into four equal servings and serve on top of the butter lettuce leaves.

calories: 600 | fat: 50g | protein: 23g | carbs: 15g | net carbs: 13g | fiber: 2g

Avocado and Egg Salad
Prep time: 5 minutes | Cook time: 0 minutes | Serves 4

½ avocado, mashed
1 tablespoon freshly squeezed lemon juice
¼ teaspoon salt
¼ teaspoon freshly ground
black pepper
6 hard boiled eggs, finely chopped
2 radishes, sliced

In a medium bowl, combine the avocado with the lemon juice, salt, and pepper. Add the chopped eggs to the avocado mixture and stir gently to combine. Serve topped with the radish slices.

calories: 272 | fat: 20g | protein: 18g | carbs: 5g | net carbs: 2g | fiber: 3g

Chapter 11 Soups

Chicken and Cabbage Soup
Prep time: 15 minutes | Cook time: 40 minutes | Serves 6

1 rotisserie chicken, shredded
6 cups water
2 tablespoons butter
2 celery stalks, chopped
½ onion, chopped
1 bay leaf

Sea salt and ground black pepper, to taste
1 tablespoon fresh cilantro, chopped
2 cups green cabbage, sliced into strips

Cook the bones and carcass from a leftover chicken with water over medium-high heat for 15 minutes. Then, reduce to a simmer and cook an additional 15 minutes. Reserve the chicken along with the broth. Let it cool enough to handle, shred the meat into bite-size pieces. Melt the butter in a large stockpot over medium heat. Sauté the celery and onion until tender and fragrant. Add bay leaf, salt, pepper, and broth, and let it simmer for 10 minutes. Add the reserved chicken, cilantro, and cabbage. Simmer for an additional 10 to 11 minutes, until the cabbage is tender. Bon appétit!

calories: 266 | fat: 23.6g | protein: 9.4g | carbs: 4.2g | net carbs: 2.6g | fiber: 1.6g

Cauliflower and Lamb Soup
Prep time: 10 minutes | Cook time: 4 hours | Serves 6

1 pound (454 g) ground lamb
5 cups beef broth
1 cauliflower head, cut into florets
1 cup heavy cream
1 yellow onion, chopped

2 cloves garlic, chopped
1 tablespoon freshly chopped thyme
½ teaspoon cracked black pepper
½ teaspoon salt

Add the ground lamb and cauliflower to the base of a stockpot. Add in the remaining ingredients minus the heavy cream, and cook on high for 4 hours. Warm the heavy cream before adding to the soup. Use an immersion blender to blend the soup until creamy.

calories: 264 | fat: 14.0g | protein: 26.9g | carbs: 5.9g | net carbs: 3.9g | fiber: 2.0g

Lamb and Cheddar Taco Soup
Prep time: 10 minutes | Cook time: 4 to 6 hours | Serves 6

1 pound (454 g) ground lamb
4 cups beef broth
1 cup shredded Cheddar cheese
1 cup diced tomatoes
1 green bell pepper, chopped
1 yellow onion, chopped

2 cloves garlic, chopped
1 teaspoon ground cumin
1 teaspoon ground coriander
1 teaspoon paprika
½ teaspoon cayenne pepper
Salt and pepper, to taste

Add all the ingredients to a slow cooker minus the shredded cheese and cook on high for 4 to 6 hours. Stir in the shredded cheese and serve.

calories: 266 | fat: 12.9g | protein: 30.1g | carbs: 5.9g | net carbs: 4.8g | fiber: 1.1g

Lemony Chicken and Chive Soup
Prep time: 10 minutes | Cook time: 4 hours | Serves 4

2 boneless, skinless chicken breasts
6 cups chicken broth
¼ cup freshly squeezed lemon juice

2 tablespoons chives, chopped
1 yellow onion, chopped
2 cloves garlic, chopped
Salt and pepper, to taste

Add all the ingredients to a slow cooker and cook on high for 4 hours. Once cooked, shred the chicken and stir back into the soup.

calories: 172 | fat: 5.9g | protein: 22.1g | carbs: 6.0g | net carbs: 5.0g | fiber: 1.0g

Pork Soup
Prep time: 10 minutes | Cook time: 25 minutes | Serves 5

2 teaspoons olive oil
1 pound (454 g)ground pork
2 shallots, chopped
1 celery stalk, chopped
1 fresh Italian pepper, seeded

and chopped
5 cups beef bone broth
2 tablespoons fresh cilantro, roughly chopped

Heat 1 teaspoon of the olive oil in a soup pot over a medium-high flame. Brown the ground pork until no longer pink or about 4 minutes, crumbling with a spatula; reserve. In the same pot, heat the remaining teaspoon of olive oil. Sauté the shallot until just tender and fragrant. Add in the chopped celery and Italian pepper along with the reserved cooked pork. Pour in the beef bone broth. When it comes to a boil, turn the heat to simmer. Let it simmer, partially covered, for 25 minutes until everything is cooked through. Season with salt to taste, ladle into soup bowls, and garnish each serving with fresh cilantro. Bon appétit!

calories: 293 | fat: 20.5g | protein: 23.5g | carbs: 1.5g | net carbs: 1.3g | fiber: 0.2g

Turkeyand Green Bean Soup
Prep time: 20 minutes | Cook time: 7 to 8 hours | Serves 8

1 tablespoon extra-virgin olive oil
4 cups chicken broth
½ pound (227 g) skinless turkey breast, cut into ½-inch chunks
2 celery stalks, chopped
1 carrot, diced
1 sweet onion, chopped
2 teaspoons minced garlic

2 teaspoons chopped fresh thyme
1 cup cream cheese, diced
2 cups heavy whipping cream
1 cup green beans, cut into 1-inch pieces
Salt, for seasoning
Freshly ground black pepper, for seasoning

Lightly grease the insert of the slow cooker with the olive oil. Place the broth, turkey, celery, carrot, onion, garlic, and thyme in the insert. Cover and cook on low for 7 to 8 hours. Stir in the cream cheese, heavy cream, and green beans. Season with salt and pepper and serve.

calories: 416 | fat: 35.1g | protein: 19.8g | carbs: 7.0g | net carbs: 5.0g | fiber: 2.0g

Pork and Mustard Green Soup

Prep time: 15 minutes | Cook time: 20 minutes | Serves 2

1 tablespoon olive oil
1 bell pepper, seeded and chopped
2 garlic cloves, pressed
½ cup scallions, chopped
½ pound (227 g) ground pork (84% lean)
1 cup beef bone broth
1 cup water
½ teaspoon crushed red

pepper flakes
Sea salt and freshly cracked black pepper, to season
1 bay laurel
1 teaspoon fish sauce
2 cups mustard greens, torn into pieces
1 tablespoon fresh parsley, chopped

Heat the olive oil in a stockpot over a moderate flame. Coat, once hot, sauté the pepper, garlic, and scallions until tender or about 3 minutes. After that, stir in the ground pork and cook for 5 minutes more or until well browned, stirring periodically. Add in the beef bone broth, water, red pepper, salt, black pepper, and bay laurel. Reduce the temperature to simmer and cook, covered, for 10 minutes. Afterwards, stir in the fish sauce and mustard greens. Remove from the heat; let it stand until the greens are wilted. Ladle into individual bowls and serve garnished with fresh parsley.

calories: 345 | fat: 25.1g | protein: 23.2g | carbs: 6.2g | net carbs: 3.2g | fiber: 3.0g

Easy Chicken and Onion Soup

Prep time: 10 minutes | Cook time: 30 minutes | Serves 2

2 chicken drumsticks, skinless and boneless
½ white onion, chopped
1 stalk celery, chopped

1 teaspoon poultry seasoning mix
1 tablespoon fresh cilantro, chopped

Place the chicken in a stockpot. Add enough water to cover by about an inch. Now, add in the chopped onion, celery and poultry seasoning mix. Bring to a boil over medium-high heat. Turn the temperature to medium-low and cook for 35 to 40 minutes. As for the chicken, the meat thermometer should register 165°F (74°C). Make sure to add extra water during the cooking as needed to keep the ingredients covered. Season to taste and serve with fresh cilantro. Bon appétit!

calories: 167 | fat: 4.8g | protein: 25.5g | carbs: 3.2g | net carbs: 2.6g | fiber: 0.6g

Creamy Beef Soup

Prep time: 10 minutes | Cook time: 4 hours | Serves 6

1 pound (454 g) lean ground beef
1 cup beef broth
1 cup heavy cream
½ cup shredded Mozzarella cheese

½ cup diced tomatoes
1 yellow onion, chopped
2 cloves garlic, chopped
1 tablespoon Italian seasoning
Salt and pepper, to taste

Add all the ingredients to a slow cooker minus the heavy cream and Mozzarella cheese. Cook on high for 4 hours. Warm the heavy cream, and then add the warmed cream and cheese to the soup. Stir well and serve.

calories: 242 | fat: 14.0g | protein: 24.8g | carbs: 4.0g | net carbs: 3.0g | fiber: 1.0g

Leek and Turkey Soup

Prep time: 15 minutes | Cook time: 1 hour 10 minutes | Serves 2

3 cups water
½ pound (227 g) turkey thighs
1 cup cauliflower, broken into small florets
1 large-sized leek, chopped
1 small-sized stalk celery, chopped
½ head garlic, split horizontally
¼ teaspoon turmeric powder

¼ teaspoon Turkish sumac
¼ teaspoon fennel seeds
½ teaspoon mustard seeds
1 bay laurel
Sea salt and freshly ground black pepper, to season
1 teaspoon coconut aminos
1 whole egg

Add the water and turkey thighs to a pot and bring it to a rolling boil. Cook for about 40 minutes; discard the bones and shred the meat using two forks. Stir in the cauliflower, leeks, celery, garlic, and spices. Reduce the heat to simmer and let it cook until everything is heated through, about 30 minutes. Afterwards, add the coconut aminos and egg; whisk until the egg is well incorporated into the soup. Serve hot and enjoy!

calories: 217 | fat: 8.2g | protein: 25.1g | carbs: 6.7g | net carbs: 4.5g | fiber: 2.2g

Beef and Mushroom Soup

Prep time: 10 minutes | Cook time: 40 minutes | Serves 6

1 pound (454 g) beef chuck, cubed
1½ cups cremini mushrooms
6 cups beef broth
½ cup heavy cream
½ cup whipped cream cheese

1 yellow onion, chopped
2 cloves garlic, chopped
Salt and pepper, to taste
1 tablespoon coconut oil, for cooking

Add the coconut oil to a skillet and brown the beef. Once cooked, add the beef to the base of a stockpot with all of the ingredients minus the heavy cream. Mix well. Bring to a simmer and whisk again until the cream cheese is mixed evenly into the soup. Cook for 30 minutes. Warm the heavy cream, and then add to the soup.

calories: 316 | fat: 18.9g | protein: 30.1g | carbs: 5.0g | net carbs: 4.0g | fiber: 1.0g

Herbed Beef Soup

Prep time: 15 minutes | Cook time: 40 minutes | Serves 6

1 pound (454 g) beef chuck roast, cubed
6 cups beef bone broth (you can also use regular beef broth)
1 yellow onion, chopped
2 cloves garlic, chopped
2 carrots, chopped
2 stalks celery, sliced

1 teaspoon fresh thyme, chopped
½ teaspoon dried oregano
1 handful fresh basil, chopped
Salt and pepper, to taste

1 tablespoon coconut oil, for cooking

Add the coconut oil to a skillet and brown the beef over medium heat. Add the beef and the remaining ingredients minus the basil to a stockpot and bring to a boil. Reduce to a simmer and cook for about 30 minutes or until the vegetables are tender. Serve with freshly chopped basil.

calories: 220 | fat: 9.0g | protein: 29.0g | carbs: 6.0g | net carbs: 5.0g | fiber: 1.0g

Turkey Taco Soup

Prep time: 10 minutes | Cook time: 4 hours | Serves 6

1 pound (454 g) ground turkey
5 cups chicken bone broth (you can also use regular chicken broth)
1 cup canned diced tomatoes (no sugar added)

1 cup whipped cream cheese
1 yellow onion, chopped
1 tablespoon chili powder
1 teaspoon cumin
1 teaspoon garlic powder
1 teaspoon onion powder

Add all the ingredients to the base of a Crock-Pot minus the cream cheese and cover with the chicken broth. Set on high and cook for 4 hours adding in the cream cheese at the 3.5 hour mark. Stir well before serving.

calories: 336 | fat: 22.9g | protein: 27.9g | carbs: 5.9g | net carbs: 4.8g | fiber: 1.1g

Italian Tomato Soup

Prep time: 15 minutes | Cook time: 30 minutes | Serves 4

1½ tablespoons olive oil
½ cup scallions, chopped
1 teaspoon fresh garlic, minced
1 teaspoon dried oregano
½ teaspoon dried rosemary
1½ pounds (680 g) Roma tomatoes, diced
2 cups Brodo di Pollo (Italian

broth)
2 tablespoons tomato paste
2 cups mustard greens, torn into pieces
Sea salt and ground black pepper, to taste
2 tablespoons fresh Italian parsley, roughly chopped

Heat the olive oil in a soup pot over a moderate flame. Now, sauté the scallions until softened or 3 to 4 minutes. Then, stir in the garlic, oregano, and rosemary, and continue to sauté an additional 30 seconds. Then, stir in the Roma tomatoes, Italian broth, and tomato paste; bring to a boil. Now, reduce the heat to medium-low and let it cook, partially covered, for 20 to 25 minutes. Puree the soup in your blender and return it to the pot. Add in the mustard greens; season with salt and black pepper. Next, cook over a moderate flame until the greens wilt. Garnish with fresh Italian parsley and serve immediately.

calories: 105 | fat: 7.3g | protein: 2.5g | carbs: 6.1g | net carbs: 2.9g | fiber: 3.2g

Cream of Broccoli Soup

Prep time: 15 minutes | Cook time: 20 minutes | Serves 4

3 tablespoons olive oil
1 celery rib, chopped
½ white onion, finely chopped
1 teaspoon ginger-garlic paste
1 (1-pound / 454-g) head

broccoli, broken into florets
4 cups vegetable broth
½ cup double cream
1½ cups Monterey Jack cheese, grated

Heat the olive oil in a soup pot over moderate heat. Now, sauté the celery rib and onion until they have softened. Fold in the ginger-garlic paste and broccoli; pour in the vegetable broth and bring to boil. Turn the heat to simmer. Continue to cook for a further 13 minutes or until the broccoli is cooked through. Fold in the cream, stir and remove from heat. Divide your soup between four ramekins and top them with the Monterey Jack cheese. Broil for about 5 minutes or until cheese is bubbly and golden. Bon appétit!

calories: 324 | fat: 28.1g | protein: 13.3g | carbs: 4.3g | net carbs: 3.8g | fiber: 0.5g

Zucchini and Celery Soup

Prep time: 10 minutes | Cook time: 15 minutes | Serves 3

2 teaspoons extra-virgin olive oil
½ pound (227 g) zucchini, peeled and diced
½ shallot, chopped

½ cup celery, chopped
½ teaspoon garlic powder
¼ teaspoon red pepper flakes
2 cups vegetable broth

Heat 1 teaspoon of the olive oil in a soup pot over medium-high heat; cook your zucchini for 1 to 2 minutes or until just tender; reserve. In the same pot, heat the remaining teaspoon of olive oil; sauté the shallot until tender and translucent. Add the remaining ingredients to the sautéed vegetables in the soup pot. Reduce the heat to medium-low, cover and let it cook for 15 minutes or until thoroughly heated. Ladle into serving bowls and serve warm. Bon appétit!

calories: 57 | fat: 3.2g | protein: 2.2g | carbs: 3.6g | net carbs: 2.5g | fiber: 1.1g

Bacon Green Soup

Prep time: 15 minutes | Cook time: 15 minutes | Serves 4

2 slices bacon, chopped
2 tablespoons scallions, chopped
1 carrot, chopped
1 celery, chopped
Salt and ground black pepper, to taste
1 teaspoon garlic, finely chopped
½ teaspoon dried rosemary

1 sprig thyme, stripped and chopped
½ head green cabbage, shredded
½ head broccoli, broken into small florets
3 cups water
1 cup chicken stock
½ cup full-fat yogurt

Heat a stockpot over medium heat; now, sear the bacon until crisp. Reserve the bacon and 1 tablespoon of fat. Then, cook scallions, carrots, and celery in 1 tablespoon of reserved fat. Add salt, pepper, and garlic; cook an additional 1 minute or until fragrant. Now, stir in rosemary, thyme, cabbage, and broccoli. Pour in water and stock, bringing to a rapid boil; reduce heat and let it simmer for 10 minutes more. Add yogurt and cook an additional 5 minutes, stirring occasionally. Use an immersion blender, to purée your soup until smooth. Taste and adjust the seasonings. Garnish with the cooked bacon just before serving.

calories: 96 | fat: 7.7g | protein: 3.0g | carbs: 4.2g | net carbs: 3.2g | fiber: 1.0g

Beef Hamburger Soup

Prep time: 10 minutes | Cook time: 4 hours | Serves 6

1 pound (454 g) lean ground beef
½ cup no-sugar added marinara sauce
½ cup beef broth

½ cup shredded Cheddar cheese
1 yellow onion, chopped
2 cloves garlic, chopped
Salt and pepper, to taste

Add all the ingredients to a slow cooker minus the shredded cheese and cook on high for 4 hours. Stir in the cheese and serve.

calories: 210 | fat: 9.1g | protein: 25.8g | carbs: 5.0g | net carbs: 4.0g | fiber: 1.0g

Herbed Beef and Zucchini Soup
Prep time: 10 minutes | Cook time: 4 to 6 hours | Serves 6

1 pound (454 g) lean ground beef
4 cups beef broth
1 zucchini, diced
2 stalks celery, chopped
½ cup diced tomatoes
1 yellow onion, chopped

2 cloves garlic, chopped
1 teaspoon freshly chopped thyme
1 teaspoon freshly chopped rosemary
Salt and pepper, to taste

Add all the ingredients to a slow cooker and cook on high for 4 to 6 hours. Stir well before serving.

calories: 186 | fat: 6.0g | protein: 7.1g | carbs: 5.0g | net carbs: 4.0g | fiber: 1.0g

Coconut Carrot Soup
Prep time: 15 minutes | Cook time: 40 minutes | Serves 8

6 cups vegetable broth
¼ cup full-fat unsweetened coconut milk
¾ pound (340 g) carrots, peeled and chopped
2 teaspoons grated ginger

1 teaspoon ground turmeric
1 sweet yellow onion, chopped
2 cloves garlic, chopped
Pinch of sea salt and pepper, to taste

Add all the ingredients minus the coconut milk to a stockpot over medium heat and bring to a boil. Reduce to a simmer and cook for 40 minutes or until the carrots are tender. Use an immersion blender and blend the soup until smooth. Stir in the coconut milk. Enjoy right away and freeze any leftovers.

calories: 74 | fat: 3.0g | protein: 4.1g | carbs: 7.1g | net carbs: 4.9g | fiber: 2.2g

Cream Cheese Chicken Soup
Prep time: 20 minutes | Cook time: 40 minutes | Serves 6

2 boneless, skinless chicken breasts
2 cups chicken broth
2 cups water
1 cup whipped cream cheese
½ cup shredded Cheddar cheese
1 yellow onion, chopped

2 cloves garlic, chopped
1 teaspoon chili powder
½ teaspoon cumin
½ teaspoon salt
¼ teaspoon black pepper
1 tablespoon coconut oil, for cooking

Heat a large skillet over medium heat with a ½ tablespoon of the coconut oil. Brown the chicken breasts until cooked through. Set aside. Add the garlic and onion to a large stockpot with the remaining 1 tablespoon of the coconut oil and sauté until translucent over low to medium heat. This should take about 3 to 5 minutes. Add this chicken broth and water. Whisk in the cream cheese and keep whisking over low to medium heat until combined. Add in the spices and bring to a boil. While the water is boiling, cut the chicken into bite-sized pieces and add to the stockpot. Reduce to a simmer and cook for 30 to 35 minutes. Stir in the Cheddar cheese and serve.

calories: 158 | fat: 6.9g | protein: 17.2g | carbs: 5.1g | net carbs: 3.9g | fiber: 1.2g

Garlicky Coconut Milk and Tomato Soup
Prep time: 15 minutes | Cook time: 30 minutes | Serves 6

6 cups vegetable broth
½ cup full-fat unsweetened coconut milk
1½ cups canned diced tomatoes
1 yellow onion, chopped

3 cloves garlic, chopped
1 teaspoon Italian seasoning
1 bay leaf
Pinch of salt and pepper, to taste
Fresh basil, for serving

Add all the ingredients minus the coconut milk and fresh basil to a stockpot over medium heat and bring to a boil. Reduce to a simmer and cook for 30 minutes. Remove the bay leaf, and then use an immersion blender to blend the soup until smooth. Stir in the coconut milk. Garnish with fresh basil and serve.

calories: 105 | fat: 6.9g | protein: 6.1g | carbs: 5.8g | net carbs: 4.8g | fiber: 1.0g

Avocado and Cucumber Soup
Prep time: 10 minutes | Cook time: 0 minutes | Serves 4

1 ripe avocado
½ cucumber, sliced
1 cup full-fat unsweetened coconut milk
1 tablespoon freshly chopped

mint leaves
1 tablespoon freshly squeezed lemon juice
Pinch of salt

Add all the ingredients to a high-speed blender and blend until creamy. Chill in the refrigerator for 1 hour before serving.

calories: 250 | fat: 24.1g | protein: 2.9g | carbs: 8.9g | net carbs: 4.1g | fiber: 4.8g

Guacamole and Tomato Soup
Prep time: 10 minutes | Cook time: 0 minutes | Serves 4

3 cups chicken broth
½ cup heavy cream
2 ripe avocados pitted

½ cup freshly chopped cilantro
1 tomato, chopped
Salt and black pepper, to taste

Add all the ingredients to a high-speed blender and blend until creamy. Chill in the refrigerator for 1 hour before serving.

calories: 290 | fat: 25.9g | protein: 6.1g | carbs: 10.1g | net carbs: 3.0g | fiber: 7.1g

Coconut Milk and Pumpkin Soup
Prep time: 15 minutes | Cook time: 30 minutes | Serves 6

6 cups vegetable broth
1 cup canned pumpkin
1 cup full-fat coconut milk
1 teaspoon freshly chopped

sage
2 cloves garlic, chopped
Pinch of salt and pepper, to taste

Add all the ingredients minus the coconut milk to a stockpot over medium heat and bring to a boil. Reduce to a simmer and cook for 30 minutes. Add the coconut milk and stir.

calories: 145 | fat: 10.8g | protein: 6.2g | carbs: 6.9g | net carbs: 5.0g | fiber: 1.9g

Beef and Bacon Soup

Prep time: 15 minutes | Cook time: 40 minutes | Serves 6

1 pound (454 g) of lean ground beef
6 slices uncured bacon
6 cups beef broth
1 cup heavy cream
1 cup shredded Cheddar cheese
1 yellow onion, chopped

1 teaspoon garlic powder
½ teaspoon onion powder
½ teaspoon cumin
½ teaspoon paprika
½ cup sour cream, for serving
1 tablespoon coconut oil, for cooking

Add the coconut oil to a skillet and cook the bacon until crispy. Allow the bacon to cool and chop into small pieces. Set aside. Once cooked, add the lean ground beef to the same skillet with the bacon fat and cook until browned. Add the onions and cook for another 2 to 3 minutes. Add all the ingredients minus the bacon, heavy cream, sour cream and cheese to a stockpot and stir. Cook for 25 minutes. Warm the heavy cream, and then add the warmed cream and cheese and serve with the bacon and a dollop of sour cream.

calories: 500 | fat: 34.0g | protein: 41.0g | carbs: 5.0g | net carbs: 4.0g | fiber: 1.0g

Chicken Garlic Soup

Prep time: 10 minutes | Cook time: 15 minutes | Serves 6

2 boneless, skinless chicken breasts
4 cups chicken broth
½ cup whipped cream cheese
3 cloves garlic, chopped

1 teaspoon thyme
1 teaspoon salt
¼ teaspoon black pepper
1 tablespoon butter

Preheat a stockpot over medium heat with the butter. Add the chicken and brown until completely cooked through. Remove from heat. Shred the chicken and add it back to the stockpot along with the remaining ingredients minus the cream cheese. Bring to a simmer. Add in the cream cheese and whisk until there are no more clumps. Simmer for 10 minutes and serve.

calories: 130 | fat: 6.1g | protein: 15.9g | carbs: 2.1g | net carbs: 2.1g | fiber: 0g

Sausage and Shrimp Jambalaya Soup

Prep time: 15 minutes | Cook time: 6 to 7 hours | Serves 8

1 tablespoon extra-virgin olive oil
6 cups chicken broth
1 (28-ounce / 794-g) can diced tomatoes
1 pound (454 g) spicy organic sausage, sliced
1 cup chopped cooked chicken
1 red bell pepper, chopped
½ sweet onion, chopped

1 jalapeño pepper, chopped
2 teaspoons minced garlic
3 tablespoons Cajun seasoning
½ pound (227 g) medium shrimp, peeled, deveined, and chopped
½ cup sour cream, for garnish
1 avocado, diced, for garnish
2 tablespoons chopped cilantro, for garnish

Lightly grease the insert of the slow cooker with the olive oil. Add the broth, tomatoes, sausage, chicken, red bell pepper, onion, jalapeño pepper, garlic, and Cajun seasoning. Cover and cook on low for 6 to 7 hours. Stir in the shrimp and leave on low for 30 minutes, or until the shrimp are cooked through. Serve topped with the sour cream, avocado, and cilantro.

calories: 401 | fat: 30.8g | protein: 24.2g | carbs: 8.9g | net carbs: 4.9g | fiber: 4.0g

Chicken and Jalapeño Soup

Prep time: 10 minutes | Cook time: 4 hours | Serves 6

6 cups chicken broth
3 boneless, skinless chicken breasts
Juice from 1 lime
1 yellow onion, chopped

2 cloves garlic, chopped
1 jalapeño pepper, seeded and sliced
1 handful fresh cilantro
Salt and black pepper, to taste

Add all the ingredients minus the cilantro, salt and black pepper to the base of a slow cooker and cook on high for 4 hours. Add the cilantro and season with salt and black pepper. Shred the chicken and serve.

calories: 110 | fat: 3.0g | protein: 16.0g | carbs: 4.0g | net carbs: 3.0g | fiber: 1.0g

Chicken Lemon Soup

Prep time: 10 minutes | Cook time: 4 hours | Serves 6

6 cups chicken broth
3 boneless, skinless chicken breasts
Juice from 1 lemon
1 yellow onion, chopped
2 cloves garlic, chopped

1 teaspoon cayenne pepper
1 teaspoon dried thyme
1 handful of fresh parsley, minced
Salt and black pepper, to taste

Add all the ingredients minus the salt, black pepper and parsley to the base of a slow cooker minus the parsley and cook on high for 4 hours. Add the parsley and season with salt and black pepper. Shred the chicken and serve.

calories: 110 | fat: 3.0g | protein: 15.9g | carbs: 4.1g | net carbs: 2.9g | fiber: 1.2g

Creamy-Lemony Chicken Soup

Prep time: 10 minutes | Cook time: 30 minutes | Serves 6

½ cup grass-fed butter
½ onion, chopped
2 celery stalks, chopped
2 teaspoons minced garlic
¼ cup arrowroot
5 cups chicken stock
3 cups shredded cooked chicken

Zest and juice of 1 lemon
1 cup heavy (whipping) cream
Sea salt, for seasoning
Freshly ground black pepper, for seasoning
1 tablespoon chopped fresh oregano

Sauté the vegetables. In a medium stockpot over medium-high heat, melt the butter. Add the onion, celery, and garlic and sauté until they've softened, about 5 minutes. Make the soup base. Add the arrowroot and whisk until it forms a paste. Whisk in the chicken stock. Thicken the soup. Bring the soup to a boil, then reduce the heat to low and simmer, stirring it from time to time, until the soup thickens, about 15 minutes. Add the remaining ingredients. Stir in the chicken, lemon zest, lemon juice, and cream and simmer until the chicken is heated through, about 10 minutes. Season and serve. Season the soup with salt and pepper. Ladle the soup into bowls, garnish with the oregano, and serve it hot.

calories: 501 | fat: 36g | protein: 28g | carbs: 13g | net carbs: 10g | fiber: 3g

Italian Mozzarella Chicken Soup

Prep time: 10 minutes | Cook time: 4 hours | Serves 6

6 cups chicken broth
3 boneless, skinless chicken breasts
1 cup canned diced tomatoes
1 yellow onion, chopped
2 cloves garlic, chopped
1 cup shredded Mozzarella

cheese
1 jalapeño pepper, seeded and sliced
1 teaspoon dried thyme
1 teaspoon dried oregano
Salt and black pepper, to taste

Add all the ingredients minus the salt and black pepper to the base of a slow cooker minus the cheese and cook on high for 4 hours. Stir in the cheese and season with salt and black pepper. Shred the chicken and serve.

calories: 126 | fat: 4.0g | protein: 16.9g | carbs: 4.9g | net carbs: 3.8g | fiber: 1.1g

Shrimp Jalapeño Soup

Prep time: 10 minutes | Cook time: 35 minutes | Serves 6

4 cups chicken broth
Juice from 1 lime
1 pound (454 g) peeled, deveined shrimp
1 yellow onion, chopped
1 shallot, chopped

3 cloves garlic, chopped
1 jalapeño pepper, seeded and sliced
Salt and black pepper, to taste
1 tablespoon coconut oil for cooking

Add the coconut oil to a large stockpot over medium heat. Add the shrimp, onion, shallot and garlic and cook until the shrimp are cooked through and pink. Add the remaining ingredients minus the salt and black pepper, and bring to a boil. Reduce the heat to a simmer and cook for 30 minutes. Season with salt and black pepper and serve.

calories: 154 | fat: 4.9g | protein: 21.2g | carbs: 5.9g | net carbs: 4.8g | fiber: 1.1g

Cucumber Cream Soup

Prep time: 10 minutes | Cook time: 0 minutes | Serves 6

2 cups heavy cream
1 cup sour cream
1 cucumber, diced
1 tablespoon spicy brown mustard
1 tablespoon horseradish
2 tablespoons freshly chopped

parsley
2 tablespoons freshly chopped dill
2 tablespoons freshly chopped mint
Salt and black pepper, to taste

Add all the ingredients to a large mixing bowl minus the cucumber. Use an immersion blender and blend until smooth. Stir in the cucumber, and chill in the refrigerator for at least 1 hour before serving.

calories: 234 | fat: 22.9g | protein: 3.1g | carbs: 5.9g | net carbs: 4.7g | fiber: 1.2g

Easy Egg Drop Soup

Prep time: 5 minutes | Cook time: 5 minutes | Serves 4

4 cups chicken broth
2 tablespoons unsalted butter
3 large eggs

Salt and pepper
1 green onion, sliced, for garnish

In a medium-sized pot over high heat, bring the chicken broth and butter to a boil. Crack the eggs into a bowl, beat with a fork, and set aside. Once the broth is boiling, slowly stir in the beaten eggs, then remove the pot from the heat. Season with salt and pepper to taste. Serve garnished with the sliced green onion.

calories: 156 | fat: 9.4g | protein: 9.6g | carbs: 1.1g | net carbs: 1.1g | fiber: 0g

Broccoli Cheddar Soup

Prep time: 10 minutes | Cook time: 20 minutes | Serves 6

4 cloves garlic, minced
3½ cups chicken broth
1 cup heavy cream

4 cups broccoli florets
3 cups shredded Cheddar cheese

In a large pot, cook the garlic over medium heat for 1 minute, until fragrant. Add the chicken broth, cream, and broccoli. Increase the heat to bring to a boil, then reduce the heat and simmer for 10 to 20 minutes, until the broccoli is tender. Use a slotted spoon to remove about one-third of the broccoli pieces and set aside. Use an immersion blender to purée the mixture, or transfer to a regular blender in batches if you don't have an immersion blender. Reduce the heat to low. Add the Cheddar ½ cup at a time, stirring constantly, and continue to stir until melted. Puree again until smooth. Remove from the heat. Return the reserved broccoli florets to the soup.

calories: 395 | fat: 33.1g | protein: 16.9g | carbs: 7.2g | net carbs: 5.9g | fiber: 1.3g

Spinach Mozzarella Soup

Prep time: 10 minutes | Cook time: 15 minutes | Serves 4

2 cups chicken broth
1 cup heavy cream
1 cup shredded mozzarella cheese
1 cup fresh spinach, chopped

3 cloves garlic, chopped
1 teaspoon onion powder
1 teaspoon dried thyme
Salt and black pepper, to taste

Add all the ingredients minus the heavy cream and mozzarella to the base of a stockpot. Bring to a boil, and then simmer for 10 minutes. Warm the heavy cream, and then add to the soup along with mozzarella. Stir until the cheese has melted.

calories: 151 | fat: 13g | protein: 6g | carbs: 3g | net carbs: 3g | fiber: 0g

Asparagus Parmesan Soup

Prep time: 10 minutes | Cook time: 15 minutes | Serves 4

2 cups chicken broth
1 cup heavy cream
1 cup shredded Parmesan cheese
1 cup asparagus finely

chopped
1 yellow onion, chopped
3 cloves garlic, chopped
1 teaspoon dried thyme
Salt and black pepper, to taste

Add all the ingredients minus the heavy cream and Parmesan cheese to the base of a stockpot. Bring to a boil, and then simmer for 10 minutes. Warm the heavy cream, and then add to the soup along with the Parmesan cheese. Stir until the cheese has melted and serve.

calories: 228 | fat: 17g | protein: 12g | carbs: 7g | net carbs: 5g | fiber: 2g

Italian Pork Sausage and Zoodle Soup

Prep time: 15 minutes | Cook time: 25 minutes | Serves 8

1 tablespoon olive oil
4 cloves garlic, minced
1 pound (454 g) pork sausage (no sugar added)
½ tablespoon Italian seasoning
3 cups regular beef broth
3 cups beef bone broth
2 medium zucchini (6 ounces / 170 g each), spiralized

In a large soup pot, heat the oil over medium heat. Add the garlic and cook for about 1 minute, until fragrant. Add the sausage, increase the heat to medium-high, and cook for about 10 minutes, stirring occasionally and breaking apart into small pieces, until browned. Add the seasoning, regular broth, and bone broth, and simmer for 10 minutes. Add the zucchini. Bring to a simmer again, then simmer for about 2 minutes, until the zucchini is soft.

calories: 215 | fat: 16.8g | protein: 12.2g | carbs: 2.1g | net carbs: 2.1g | fiber: 0g

Chicken, Carrot and Cauliflower Soup

Prep time: 15 minutes | Cook time: 7 to 8 hours | Serves 6

1 tablespoon extra-virgin olive oil
4 cups chicken broth
2 cups coconut milk
2 cups diced chicken breast
½ sweet onion, chopped
2 celery stalks, chopped
1 carrot, diced
½ cup chopped cauliflower
2 teaspoons minced garlic
1 teaspoon chopped thyme
1 teaspoon chopped oregano
¼ teaspoon freshly ground black pepper

Lightly grease the insert of the slow cooker with the olive oil. Add the broth, coconut milk, chicken, onion, celery, carrot, cauliflower, garlic, thyme, oregano, and pepper. Cover and cook on low for 7 to 8 hours. Serve warm.

calories: 300 | fat: 25.1g | protein: 13.9g | carbs: 8.1g | net carbs: 4.9g | fiber: 3.2g

Creamy Cauliflower Soup with Sausage

Prep time: 10 minutes | Cook time: 35 minutes | Serves 4

1 cauliflower head, chopped
1 turnip, chopped
1 tablespoon butter
1 chorizo sausage, sliced
2 cups chicken broth
1 small onion, chopped
2 cups water
Salt and black pepper, to taste

Melt 1 tablespoon of the butter in a large pot over medium heat. Stir in onion and cook until soft and golden, about 3-4 minutes. Add cauliflower and turnip, and cook for another 5 minutes. Pour the broth and water over. Bring to a boil, simmer covered, and cook for about 20 minutes until the vegetables are tender. Remove from heat. Melt the remaining butter in a skillet. Add the chorizo sausage and cook for 5 minutes until crispy. Puree the soup with a hand blender until smooth. Taste and adjust the seasonings. Serve the soup in deep bowls topped with the chorizo sausage.

calories: 251 | fat: 19g | protein: 10g | carbs: 8g | net carbs: 6g | fiber: 2g

Cheesy Coconut Carrot Soup

Prep time: 15 minutes | Cook time: 6 hours | Serves 6

1 tablespoon butter
5 cups chicken broth
1 cup coconut milk
2 celery stalks, chopped
1 carrot, chopped
½ sweet onion, chopped
Pinch cayenne pepper
8 ounces (227 g) cream
cheese, cubed
2 cups shredded Cheddar cheese
Salt, for seasoning
Freshly ground black pepper, for seasoning
1 tablespoon chopped fresh thyme, for garnish

Lightly grease the insert of the slow cooker with the butter. Place the broth, coconut milk, celery, carrot, onion, and cayenne pepper in the insert. Cover and cook on low for 6 hours. Stir in the cream cheese and Cheddar, then season with salt and pepper. Serve topped with the thyme.

calories: 405 | fat: 36.0g | protein: 14.9g | carbs: 6.9g | net carbs: 5.9g | fiber: 1.0g

Sauerkraut and Organic Sausage Soup

Prep time: 15 minutes | Cook time: 6 hours | Serves 6

1 tablespoon extra-virgin olive oil
6 cups beef broth
1 pound (454 g) organic sausage, cooked and sliced
2 cups sauerkraut
2 celery stalks, chopped
1 sweet onion, chopped
2 teaspoons minced garlic
2 tablespoons butter
1 tablespoon hot mustard
½ teaspoon caraway seeds
½ cup sour cream
2 tablespoons chopped fresh parsley, for garnish

Lightly grease the insert of the slow cooker with the olive oil. Place the broth, sausage, sauerkraut, celery, onion, garlic, butter, mustard, and caraway seeds in the insert. Cover and cook on low for 6 hours. Stir in the sour cream. Serve topped with the parsley.

calories: 333 | fat: 27.9g | protein: 15.2g | carbs: 5.9g | net carbs: 2.0g | fiber: 3.9g

Spicy Chicken and Tomato Taco Soup

Prep time: 15 minutes | Cook time: 6 hours | Serves 8

3 tablespoons extra-virgin olive oil, divided
1 pound (454 g) ground chicken
1 sweet onion, diced
1 red bell pepper, chopped
2 teaspoons minced garlic
2 tablespoons taco seasoning
4 cups chicken broth
2 cups coconut milk
1 tomato, diced
1 jalapeño pepper, chopped
2 cups shredded Cheddar cheese
½ cup sour cream, for garnish
1 scallion, white and green parts, chopped, for garnish

Lightly grease the insert of the slow cooker with 1 tablespoon of the olive oil. In a large skillet over medium-high heat, heat the remaining 2 tablespoons of the olive oil. Add the chicken and sauté until it is cooked through, about 6 minutes. Add the onion, red bell pepper, garlic, and taco seasoning, and sauté for an additional 3 minutes. Transfer the chicken mixture to the insert, and stir in the broth, coconut milk, tomato, and jalapeño pepper. Cover and cook on low for 6 hours. Stir in the cheese. Serve topped with the sour cream and scallion.

calories: 435 | fat: 35.1g | protein: 21.9g | carbs: 9.1g | net carbs: 7.2g | fiber: 1.9g

Cauliflower and Double-Cheese Soup

Prep time: 15 minutes | Cook time: 6 hours | Serves 6

1 tablespoon extra-virgin olive oil
4 cups chicken broth
2 cups coconut milk
2 cups chopped cooked chicken
1 cup chopped cooked bacon

2 cups chopped cauliflower
1 sweet onion, chopped
3 teaspoons minced garlic
½ cup cream cheese, cubed
2 cups shredded Cheddar cheese

Lightly grease the insert of the slow cooker with the olive oil. Place the broth, coconut milk, chicken, bacon, cauliflower, onion, and garlic in the insert. Cover and cook on low for 6 hours. Stir in the cream cheese and Cheddar and serve.

calories: 541 | fat: 44.1g | protein: 35.1g | carbs: 6.9g | net carbs: 5.9g | fiber: 1.0g

Chicken and Pumpkin Soup

Prep time: 15 minutes | Cook time: 6 hours | Serves 6

1 tablespoon extra-virgin olive oil
4 cups chicken broth
2 cups coconut milk
1 pound (454 g) pumpkin, diced
½ sweet onion, chopped
1 tablespoon grated fresh ginger
2 teaspoons minced garlic

½ teaspoon ground cinnamon
¼ teaspoon ground nutmeg
¼ teaspoon freshly ground black pepper
¼ teaspoon salt
Pinch ground allspice
1 cup heavy whipping cream
2 cups chopped cooked chicken

Lightly grease the insert of the slow cooker with the olive oil. Place the broth, coconut milk, pumpkin, onion, ginger, garlic, cinnamon, nutmeg, pepper, salt, and allspice in the insert. Cover and cook on low for 6 hours. Using an immersion blender or a regular blender, purée the soup. If you removed the soup from the insert to purée, add it back to the pot, and stir in the cream and chicken. Keep heating the soup on low for 15 minutes to heat the chicken through, and then serve warm.

calories: 390 | fat: 32.1g | protein: 16.1g | carbs: 10.2g | net carbs: 5.1g | fiber: 5.1g

Beef, Tomato, and Zucchini Soup

Prep time: 20 minutes | Cook time: 6 hours | Serves 6

3 tablespoons extra-virgin olive oil, divided
1 pound (454 g) ground beef
½ sweet onion, chopped
2 teaspoons minced garlic
4 cups beef broth
1 (28-ounce / 794-g) can diced

tomatoes, undrained
1 zucchini, diced
1½ tablespoons dried basil
2 teaspoons dried oregano
4 ounces (113 g) cream cheese
1 cup shredded Mozzarella

Lightly grease the insert of the slow cooker with 1 tablespoon of the olive oil. In a large skillet over medium-high heat, heat the remaining 2 tablespoons of the olive oil. Add the ground beef and sauté until it is cooked through, about 6 minutes. Add the onion and garlic and sauté for an additional 3 minutes. Transfer the meat mixture to the insert. Stir in the broth, tomatoes, zucchini, basil, and oregano. Cover and cook on low for 6 hours. Stir in the cream cheese and Mozzarella and serve.

calories: 473 | fat: 36.1g | protein: 29.9g | carbs: 8.9g | net carbs: 6.0g | fiber: 2.9g

Bacon and Chicken Soup

Prep time: 15 minutes | Cook time: 8 hours | Serves 8

1 tablespoon extra-virgin olive oil
6 cups chicken broth
3 cups cooked chicken, chopped
1 sweet onion, chopped
2 celery stalks, chopped
1 carrot, diced

2 teaspoons minced garlic
1½ cups heavy whipping cream
1 cup cream cheese
1 cup cooked chopped bacon
1 tablespoon chopped fresh parsley, for garnish

Lightly grease the insert of the slow cooker with the olive oil. Add the broth, chicken, onion, celery, carrot, and garlic. Cover and cook on low for 8 hours. Stir in the heavy cream, cream cheese, and bacon. Serve topped with the parsley.

calories: 489 | fat: 36.9g | protein: 26.9g | carbs: 10.9g | net carbs: 9.8g | fiber: 1.1g

Sausage and Leek Soup

Prep time: 15 minutes | Cook time: 6 hours | Serves 6

3 tablespoons olive oil, divided
1½ pounds (680 g) sausage, without casing
6 cups chicken broth
2 celery stalks, chopped
1 carrot, diced

1 leek, thoroughly cleaned and chopped
2 teaspoons minced garlic
2 cups chopped kale
1 tablespoon chopped fresh parsley, for garnish

Lightly grease the insert of the slow cooker with 1 tablespoon of the olive oil. In a large skillet over medium-high heat, heat the remaining 2 tablespoons of the olive oil. Add the sausage and sauté until it is cooked through, about 7 minutes. Transfer the sausage to the insert, and stir in the broth, celery, carrot, leek, and garlic. Cover and cook on low for 6 hours. Stir in the kale. Serve topped with the parsley.

calories: 385 | fat: 31.2g | protein: 20.9g | carbs: 5.1g | net carbs: 3.9g | fiber: 1.2g

Beef and Tomato Cheeseburger Soup

Prep time: 15 minutes | Cook time: 6 hours | Serves 8

3 tablespoons olive oil, divided
1 pound (454 g) ground beef
1 sweet onion, chopped
2 teaspoons minced garlic
6 cups beef broth
1 (28-ounce / 794-g) can diced tomatoes
2 celery stalks, chopped

1 carrot, chopped
1 cup heavy whipping cream
2 cups shredded Cheddar cheese
½ teaspoon freshly ground black pepper
1 scallion, white and green parts, chopped, for garnish

Lightly grease the insert of the slow cooker with 1 tablespoon of the olive oil. In a large skillet over medium-high heat, heat the remaining 2 tablespoons of the olive oil. Add the ground beef and sauté until it is cooked through, about 6 minutes. Add the onion and garlic and sauté for an additional 3 minutes. Transfer the beef mixture to the insert, and stir in the broth, tomatoes, celery, and carrot. Cover and cook on low for 6 hours. Stir in the heavy cream, cheese, and pepper. Serve hot, topped with the scallion.

calories: 414 | fat: 32.2g | protein: 25.9g | carbs: 7.9g | net carbs: 5.8g | fiber: 2.1g

Chicken and Cauliflower Soup

Prep time: 15 minutes | Cook time: 7 to 8 hours | Serves 6

1 tablespoon extra-virgin olive oil
4 cups chicken broth
2 cups coconut milk
2 cups diced chicken breast
½ sweet onion, chopped
2 celery stalks, chopped

1 carrot, diced
½ cup chopped cauliflower
2 teaspoons minced garlic
1 teaspoon chopped thyme
1 teaspoon chopped oregano
¼ teaspoon freshly ground black pepper

Lightly grease the insert of the slow cooker with the olive oil. Add the broth, coconut milk, chicken, onion, celery, carrot, cauliflower, garlic, thyme, oregano, and pepper. Cover and cook on low for 7 to 8 hours. Serve warm.

calories: 300 | fat: 24.9g | protein: 13.8g | carbs: 7.9g | net carbs: 5.1g | fiber: 2.8g

Creamy-Cheesy Cauliflower Soup

Prep time: 5 minutes | Cook time: 20 minutes | Serves 4

1 tablespoon butter
½ onion, chopped
2 cups riced/shredded cauliflower (I buy it pre-riced at Trader Joe's)
1 cup chicken broth

2 ounces (57 g) cream cheese
1 cup heavy (whipping) cream
Pink Himalayan salt
Freshly ground pepper
½ cup shredded Cheddar cheese (I use sharp Cheddar)

In a medium saucepan over medium heat, melt the butter. Add the onion and cook, stirring occasionally, until softened, about 5 minutes. Add the cauliflower and chicken broth, and allow the mixture to come to a boil, stirring occasionally. Lower the heat to medium-low and simmer until the cauliflower is soft enough to mash, about 10 minutes. Add the cream cheese, and mash the mixture. Add the cream and purée the mixture with an immersion blender. Season the soup with pink Himalayan salt and pepper. Pour the soup into four bowls, top each with the shredded Cheddar cheese, and serve.

calories: 372 | fat: 35g | protein: 9g | carbs: 9g | net carbs: 6g | fiber: 3g

Spiced-Pumpkin Soup

Prep time: 15 minutes | Cook time: 6 hours | Serves 6

1 tablespoon extra-virgin olive oil
4 cups chicken broth
2 cups coconut milk
1 pound pumpkin, diced
½ sweet onion, chopped
1 tablespoon grated fresh ginger
2 teaspoons minced garlic

½ teaspoon ground cinnamon
¼ teaspoon ground nutmeg
¼ teaspoon freshly ground black pepper
¼ teaspoon salt
pinch ground allspice
1 cup heavy (whipping) cream
2 cups chopped cooked chicken

Lightly grease the insert of the slow cooker with the olive oil. Place the broth, coconut milk, pumpkin, onion, ginger, garlic, cinnamon, nutmeg, pepper, salt, and allspice in the insert. Cover and cook on low for 6 hours. Using an immersion blender or a regular blender, purée the soup. If you removed the soup from the insert to purée, add it back to the pot, and stir in the cream and chicken. Keep heating the soup on low for 15 minutes to heat the chicken through, and then serve warm.

calories: 389 | fat: 32g | protein: 16g | carbs: 10g | net carbs: 5g | fiber: 5g

Rich Taco Soup

Prep time: 5 minutes | Cook time: 4¼ hours | Serves 4

1 pound (454 g) ground beef
Pink Himalayan salt, to taste
Freshly ground black pepper, to taste
2 cups beef broth

1 (10-ounce / 283-g) can diced tomatoes
1 tablespoon taco seasoning
8 ounces (227 g) cream cheese

With the crock insert in place, preheat the slow cooker to low. On the stove top, in a medium skillet over medium-high heat, sauté the ground beef until browned, about 8 minutes, and season with pink Himalayan salt and pepper. Add the ground beef, beef broth, tomatoes, taco seasoning, and cream cheese to the slow cooker. Cover and cook on low for 4 hours, stirring occasionally. Ladle into four bowls and serve.

calories: 422 | fat: 33g | protein: 25g | carbs: 6g | net carbs: 5g | fiber: 1g

Rich Cheesy Bacon-Cauliflower Soup

Prep time: 15 minutes | Cook time: 6 hours | Serves 6

1 tablespoon extra-virgin olive oil
4 cups chicken broth
2 cups coconut milk
2 cups chopped cooked chicken
1 cup chopped cooked bacon

2 cups chopped cauliflower
1 sweet onion, chopped
3 teaspoons minced garlic
½ cup cream cheese, cubed
2 cups shredded cheddar cheese

Lightly grease the insert of the slow cooker with the olive oil. Place the broth, coconut milk, chicken, bacon, cauliflower, onion, and garlic in the insert. Cover and cook on low for 6 hours. Stir in the cream cheese and Cheddar and serve.

calories: 540 | fat: 44g | protein: 35g | carbs: 7g | net carbs: 6g | fiber: 1g

Nacho Soup

Prep time: 15 minutes | Cook time: 6 hours | Serves 8

3 tablespoons extra-virgin olive oil, divided
1 pound (454 g) ground chicken
1 sweet onion, diced
1 red bell pepper, chopped
2 teaspoons minced garlic
2 tablespoons taco seasoning
4 cups chicken broth

2 cups coconut milk
1 tomato, diced
1 jalapeño pepper, chopped
2 cups shredded cheddar cheese
½ cup sour cream, for garnish
1 scallion, white and green parts, chopped, for garnish

Lightly grease the insert of the slow cooker with 1 tablespoon of the olive oil. In a large skillet over medium-high heat, heat the remaining 2 tablespoons of the olive oil. Add the chicken and sauté until it is cooked through, about 6 minutes. Add the onion, red bell pepper, garlic, and taco seasoning, and sauté for an additional 3 minutes. Transfer the chicken mixture to the insert, and stir in the broth, coconut milk, tomato, and jalapeño pepper. Cover and cook on low for 6 hours. Stir in the cheese. Serve topped with the sour cream and scallion.

calories: 434 | fat: 35g | protein: 22g | carbs: 9g | net carbs: 7g | fiber: 2g

Slow Cooked Faux Lasagna Soup
Prep time: 20 minutes | Cook time: 6 hours | Serves 6

3 tablespoons extra-virgin olive oil, divided
1 pound (454 g) ground beef
½ sweet onion, chopped
2 teaspoons minced garlic
4 cups beef broth
1 (28-ounce / 794-g) can diced tomatoes, undrained
1 zucchini, diced
1½ tablespoons dried basil
2 teaspoons dried oregano
4 ounces (113 g) cream cheese
1 cup shredded mozzarella

Lightly grease the insert of the slow cooker with 1 tablespoon of the olive oil. In a large skillet over medium-high heat, heat the remaining 2 tablespoons of the olive oil. Add the ground beef and sauté until it is cooked through, about 6 minutes. Add the onion and garlic and sauté for an additional 3 minutes. Transfer the meat mixture to the insert. Stir in the broth, tomatoes, zucchini, basil, and oregano. Cover and cook on low for 6 hours. Stir in the cream cheese and mozzarella and serve.

calories: 472 | fat: 36g | protein: 30g | carbs: 9g | net carbs: 6g | fiber: 3g

Pork and Vegetable Soup
Prep time: 5 minutes | Cook time: 20 minutes | Serves 5

1½ pounds (680 g) pork stew meat, cubed
5 cups vegetable broth
½ cup scallions, chopped
2 bell peppers, chopped
1 celery stalk, chopped

Spritz the bottom of a large soup pot with nonstick cooking spray. Heat up the pot over medium-high heat. Now, brown the meat for 5 minutes, stirring frequently. Deglaze the skillet with a splash of vegetable broth, scraping up any brown bits stuck to the bottom. After that, stir in the remaining ingredients and bring to a rolling boil. Turn the heat to simmer; cover and let it simmer for 15 minutes until everything is thoroughly warmed. Ladle into individual bowls and serve hot. Bon appétit!

calories: 303 | fat: 18g | protein: 29g | carbs: 4g | net carbs: 3g | fiber: 1g

Colden Gazpacho Soup
Prep time: 15 minutes | Cook time: 0 minutes | Serves 6

2 small green peppers, roasted
2 large red peppers, roasted
2 medium avocados, flesh scoped out
2 garlic cloves
2 spring onions, chopped
1 cucumber, chopped
1 cup olive oil
1 tablespoon lemon juice
4 tomatoes, chopped
7 ounces (198 g) goat cheese
1 small red onion, chopped
1 tablespoon apple cider vinegar
Salt, to taste

Place the peppers, tomatoes, avocados, red onion, garlic, lemon juice, olive oil, vinegar, and salt, in a food processor. Pulse until your desired consistency is reached. Taste and adjust the seasoning. Transfer the mixture to a pot. Stir in cucumber and spring onions. Cover and chill in the fridge at least 2 hours. Divide the soup between 6 bowls. Serve topped with goat cheese and an extra drizzle of olive oil.

calories: 528 | fat: 46g | protein: 8g | carbs: 7g | net carbs: 4g | fiber: 3g

Creamy Tomato Soup
Prep time: 10 minutes | Cook time: 14 minutes | Serves 6

1 tablespoon butter
2 large red onions, diced
½ cup raw cashew nuts, diced
2 (28-ounce / 794-g) cans tomatoes
1 teaspoon fresh thyme leaves, extra to garnish
1½ cups water
Salt and black pepper to taste
1 cup heavy cream

Melt butter in a pot over medium heat and sauté the onions for 4 minutes until softened. Stir in the tomatoes, thyme, water, cashews, and season with salt and black pepper. Cover and bring to simmer for 10 minutes until thoroughly cooked. Open, turn the heat off, and puree the ingredients with an immersion blender. Adjust to taste and stir in the heavy cream. Spoon into soup bowls and serve.

calories: 310 | fat: 27g | protein: 11g | carbs: 12g | net carbs: 10g | fiber: 2g

Green Minestrone Soup
Prep time: 10 minutes | Cook time: 12 minutes | Serves 4

1 tablespoon butter
1 tablespoon onion-garlic puree
2 heads broccoli, cut in florets
2 stalks celery, chopped
5 cups vegetable broth
1 cup baby spinach
Salt and black pepper to taste
1 tablespoon Gruyere cheese, grated

Melt the butter in a saucepan over medium heat and sauté the onion-garlic puree for 3 minutes until softened. Mix in the broccoli and celery, and cook for 4 minutes until slightly tender. Pour in the broth, bring to a boil, then reduce the heat to medium-low and simmer covered for about 5 minutes. Drop in the spinach to wilt, adjust the seasonings, and cook for 4 minutes. Ladle soup into serving bowls. Serve with a sprinkle of grated Gruyere cheese.

calories: 227 | fat: 20g | protein: 8g | carbs: 9g | net carbs: 2g | fiber: 7g

Cheesy Cauliflower Soup
Prep time: 10 minutes | Cook time: 17 minutes | Serves 4

1 tablespoon butter
1 onion, chopped
2 head cauliflower, cut into florets
2 cups water
Salt and black pepper to taste
3 cups almond milk
1 cup shredded white cheddar cheese
3 bacon strips

Melt the butter in a saucepan over medium heat and sauté the onion for 3 minutes until fragrant. Include the cauli florets, sauté for 3 minutes to slightly soften, add the water, and season with salt and black pepper. Bring to a boil, and then reduce the heat to low. Cover and cook for 10 minutes. Puree cauliflower with an immersion blender until the ingredients are evenly combined and stir in the almond milk and cheese until the cheese melts. Adjust taste with salt and black pepper. In a non-stick skillet over high heat, fry the bacon, until crispy. Divide soup between serving bowls, top with crispy bacon, and serve hot.

calories: 402 | fat: 37g | protein: 8g | carbs: 9g | net carbs: 6g | fiber: 3g

Power Green Soup

Prep time: 10 minutes | Cook time: 14 minutes | Serves 6

1 broccoli head, chopped	5 cups veggie stock
1 cup spinach	1 cup coconut milk
1 onion, chopped	1 tablespoon butter
2 garlic cloves, minced½ cup	1 bay leaf
watercress	Salt and black pepper, to taste

Melt the butter in a large pot over medium heat. Add onion and garlic, and cook for 3 minutes. Add broccoli and cook for an additional 5 minutes. Pour the stock over and add the bay leaf. Close the lid, bring to a boil, and reduce the heat. Simmer for about 3 minutes. At the end, add spinach and watercress, and cook for 3 more minutes. Stir in the coconut cream, salt and black pepper. Discard the bay leaf, and blend the soup with a hand blender.

calories: 392 | fat: 37g | protein: 5g | carbs: 11g | net carbs: 6g | fiber: 5g

Reuben Beef Soup

Prep time: 10 minutes | Cook time: 20 minutes | Serves 6

1 onion, diced	1 pound (454 g) corned beef, chopped
6 cups beef stock	1 tablespoon butter
1 teaspoon caraway seeds	1½ cup swiss cheese, shredded
2 celery stalks, diced	
2 garlic cloves, minced	Salt and black pepper, to taste
2 cups heavy cream	
1 cup sauerkraut, shredded	

Melt the butter in a large pot. Add onion and celery, and fry for 3 minutes until tender. Add garlic and cook for another minute. Pour the beef stock over and stir in sauerkraut, salt, caraway seeds, and add a pinch of black pepper. Bring to a boil. Reduce the heat to low, and add the corned beef. Cook for about 15 minutes, adjust the seasoning. Stir in heavy cream and cheese and cook for 1 minute.

calories: 450 | fat: 37g | protein: 23g | carbs: 9g | net carbs: 8g | fiber: 1g

Coconut Cheesy Cauliflower Soup

Prep time: 10 minutes | Cook time: 15 minutes | Serves 4

½ head cauliflower, chopped	1½ tablespoon flax seed meal
1 tablespoon coconut oil	2 cups water
½ cup leeks, chopped	1½ cups coconut milk
1 celery stalk, chopped	6 ounces (170 g) Monterey
1 serrano pepper, finely chopped	Jack cheese, shredded
	Salt and black pepper, to taste
1 teaspoon garlic puree	Fresh parsley, chopped

In a deep pan over medium heat, melt the coconut oil and sauté the serrano pepper, celery and leeks until soft, for about 5 minutes. Add in coconut milk, garlic puree, cauliflower, water and flax seed. While covered partially, allow simmering for 10 minutes or until cooked through. Whizz with a immersion blender until smooth. Fold in the shredded cheese, and stir to ensure the cheese is completely melted and you have a homogenous mixture. Season with pepper and salt to taste. Divide among serving bowls, decorate with parsley and serve while warm.

calories: 312 | fat: 16g | protein: 13g | carbs: 9g | net carbs: 7g | fiber: 2g

Curry Green Beans and Shrimp Soup

Prep time: 10 minutes | Cook time: 10 minutes | Serves 4

1 tablespoon butter	1 tablespoon red curry paste
1 pound (454 g) jumbo shrimp, peeled and deveined	6 ounces (170 g) coconut milk
	Salt and chili pepper to taste
1 teaspoon ginger-garlic puree	1 bunch green beans, halved

Melt butter in a medium saucepan over medium heat. Add the shrimp, season with salt and black pepper, and cook until they are opaque, 2 to 3 minutes. Remove shrimp to a plate. Add the ginger-garlic puree and red curry paste to the butter and sauté for 2 minutes until fragrant. Stir in the coconut milk; add the shrimp, salt, chili pepper, and green beans. Cook for 4 minutes. Reduce the heat to a simmer and cook an additional 3 minutes, occasionally stirring. Adjust taste with salt, fetch soup into serving bowls, and serve with cauli rice.

calories: 375 | fat: 35g | protein: 9g | carbs: 4g | net carbs: 2g | fiber: 2g

Cheesy Broccoli Soup

Prep time: 10 minutes | Cook time: 14 minutes | Serves 4

¾ cup heavy cream	1 tablespoon butter
1 onion, diced	3 cups grated cheddar cheese
1 teaspoon minced garlic	Salt and black pepper, to taste
4 cups chopped broccoli	½ bunch fresh mint, chopped
4 cups veggie broth	

Melt the butter in a large pot over medium heat. Sauté onion and garlic for 3 minutes or until tender, stirring occasionally. Season with salt and black pepper. Add the broth, broccoli and bring to a boil. Reduce the heat and simmer for 10 minutes. Puree the soup with a hand blender until smooth. Add in 2¾ cups of the cheddar cheese and cook about 1 minute. Taste and adjust the seasoning. Stir in the heavy cream. Serve in bowls with the remaining cheddar cheese and sprinkled with fresh mint.

calories: 561 | fat: 52g | protein: 24g | carbs: 11g | net carbs: 7g | fiber: 4g

Salsa Verde Chicken Soup

Prep time: 10 minutes | Cook time: 5 minutes | Serves 4

½ cup salsa verde	cheese
2 cups cooked and shredded chicken	½ teaspoon chili powder
2 cups chicken broth	½ teaspoon ground cumin
1 cup shredded cheddar cheese	½ teaspoon fresh cilantro, chopped
4 ounces (113 g) cream	Salt and black pepper, to taste

Combine the cream cheese, salsa verde, and broth, in a food processor; pulse until smooth. Transfer the mixture to a pot and place over medium heat. Cook until hot, but do not bring to a boil. Add chicken, chili powder, and cumin and cook for about 3-5 minutes, or until it is heated through. Stir in cheddar cheese and season with salt and pepper to taste. If it is very thick, add a few tablespoons of water and boil for 1-3 more minutes. Serve hot in bowls sprinkled with fresh cilantro.

calories: 346 | fat: 23g | protein: 25g | carbs: 4g | net carbs: 3g | fiber: 1g

Creamy Chicken Soup
Prep time: 10 minutes | Cook time: 2 minutes | Serves 4

2 cups cooked and shredded chicken
1 tablespoon butter, melted
4 cups chicken broth
1 tablespoon chopped cilantro
⅓ cup buffalo sauce
½ cup cream cheese
Salt and black pepper, to taste

Blend the butter, buffalo sauce, and cream cheese, in a food processor, until smooth. Transfer to a pot, add chicken broth and heat until hot but do not bring to a boil. Stir in chicken, salt, black pepper and cook until heated through. When ready, remove to soup bowls and serve garnished with cilantro.

calories: 406 | fat: 29g | protein: 27g | carbs: 5g | net carbs: 5g | fiber: 0g

Tangy Cucumber and Avocado Soup
Prep time: 10 minutes | Cook time: 0 minutes | Serves 4

4 large cucumbers, seeded, chopped
1 large avocado, peeled and pitted
Salt and black pepper to taste
2 cups water
1 tablespoon cilantro, chopped
1 tablespoon olive oil
2 limes, juiced
1 teaspoon minced garlic
2 tomatoes, chopped
1 chopped avocado for garnish

Pour the cucumbers, avocado halves, salt, black pepper, olive oil, lime juice, cilantro, water, and garlic in the food processor. Puree the ingredients for 2 minutes or until smooth. Pour the mixture in a bowl and top with avocado and tomatoes. Serve chilled with zero-carb bread.

calories: 170 | fat: 7g | protein: 4g | carbs: 10g | net carbs: 4g | fiber: 6g

Spicy Chicken Soup
Prep time: 10 minutes | Cook time: 20 minutes | Serves 4

1 tablespoon coconut oil
1 pound (454 g) chicken thighs
¾ cup red enchilada sauce
¼ cup water
¼ cup onion, chopped
3 ounces (85 g) canned diced green chilis
1 avocado, sliced
1 cup cheddar cheese, shredded
¼ cup pickled jalapeños, chopped
½ cup sour cream
1 tomato, diced

Put a large pan over medium heat. Add coconut oil and warm. Place in the chicken and cook until browned on the outside. Stir in onion, chilies, water, and enchilada sauce, then close with a lid. Allow simmering for 20 minutes until the chicken is cooked through. Spoon the soup on a serving bowl and top with the sauce, cheese, sour cream, tomato, and avocado.

calories: 643 | fat: 44g | protein: 46g | carbs: 12g | net carbs: 10g | fiber: 2g

Almond Soup with Sour Cream and Cilantro
Prep time: 10 minutes | Cook time: 21 minutes | Serves 4

1 tablespoon olive oil
1 cup onion, chopped
1 celery, chopped
2 cloves garlic, minced
2 turnips, peeled and chopped
4 cups vegetable broth
Salt and white pepper, to taste
¼ cup ground almonds
1 cup almond milk
1 tablespoon fresh cilantro, chopped
1 teaspoon sour cream

Warm oil in a pot over medium heat and sauté celery, garlic, and onion for 6 minutes. Stir in white pepper, broth, salt, and ground almonds. Bring to the boil and simmer for 15 minutes. Transfer soup to an immersion blender and puree. Serve garnished with sour cream and cilantro.

calories: 125 | fat: 7g | protein: 5g | carbs: 12g | net carbs: 8g | fiber: 4g

Lush Vegetable Soup
Prep time: 15 minutes | Cook time: 25 minutes | Serves 4

1 teaspoon olive oil
1 onion, chopped
1 garlic clove, minced
½ celery stalk, chopped
1 cup mushrooms, sliced
½ head broccoli, chopped
1 cup spinach, torn into pieces
Salt and black pepper, to taste
2 thyme sprigs, chopped
3 cups vegetable stock
1 tomato, chopped
½ cup almond milk

Heat olive oil in a saucepan. Add onion, celery and garlic; sauté until translucent, stirring occasionally, about 5 minutes. Place in spinach, mushrooms, salt, rosemary, tomatoes, bay leaves, black pepper, thyme, and vegetable stock. Simmer the mixture for 15 minutes while the lid is slightly open. Stir in almond milk and cook for 5 more minutes.

calories: 140 | fat: 6g | protein: 3g | carbs: 4g | net carbs: 1g | fiber: 3g

Red Curry Shrimp and Bean Soup
Prep time: 10 minutes | Cook time: 11 minutes | Serves 4

1 onion, chopped
1 tablespoon red curry paste
1 tablespoon butter
1 pound jumbo shrimp, deveined
1 teaspoon ginger-garlic puree
1 cup coconut milk
Salt and chili pepper, to taste
1 bunch green beans, halved
1 tablespoon cilantro, chopped

Add the shrimp to melted butter in a saucepan over medium heat, season with salt and pepper, and cook until they are opaque, 2 to 3 minutes. Remove to a plate. Add in the ginger-garlic puree, onion, and red curry paste and sauté for 2 minutes until fragrant. Stir in the coconut milk; add the shrimp, salt, chili pepper, and green beans. Cook for 4 minutes. Reduce the heat to a simmer and cook an additional 3 minutes, occasionally stirring. Adjust taste with salt, fetch soup into serving bowls, and serve sprinkled with cilantro.

calories: 351 | fat: 32g | protein: 8g | carbs: 4g | net carbs: 3g | fiber: 1g

Spiced Cucumber Soup
Prep time: 15 minutes | Cook time: 0 minutes | Serves 6

4 cups chicken broth
1 cup heavy cream
2 cucumbers, sliced
1 teaspoon freshly chopped rosemary
1 teaspoon freshly chopped thyme
1 pinch of Salt and black pepper, to taste

Add all the ingredients to a large mixing bowl and whisk well. Use an immersion blender and blend until smooth. Chill for 1 hour before serving.

calories: 111 | fat: 9g | protein: 4g | carbs: 5g | net carbs: 4g | fiber: 1g

Turnip and Soup with Pork Sausage

Prep time: 10 minutes | Cook time: 32 minutes | Serves 4

3 turnips, chopped
2 celery sticks, chopped
1 tablespoon butter
1 tablespoon olive oil
1 pork sausage, sliced

2 cups vegetable broth
½ cup sour cream
3 green onions, chopped
2 cups water
Salt and black pepper, to taste

Sauté green onions in melted butter over medium heat until soft and golden, about 3 minutes. Add celery and turnip, and cook for another 5 minutes. Pour over the vegetable broth and water over. Bring to a boil, simmer covered, and cook for about 20 minutes until the vegetables are tender. Remove from heat. Puree the soup with a hand blender until smooth. Add sour cream and adjust the seasoning. Warm the olive oil in a skillet. Add the pork sausage and cook for 5 minutes. Serve the soup in deep bowls topped with pork sausage.

calories: 275 | fat: 23g | protein:7 g | carbs: 10g | net carbs: 6g | fiber: 4g

Creamy Turkey and Celery Soup

Prep time: 15 minutes | Cook time: 4 hours | Serves 7

1 pound (454 g) turkey breast, cubed
5 cups chicken broth
1 cup cream cheese
1 stalk celery, chopped

3 cloves garlic, chopped
1 teaspoon freshly chopped rosemary
Salt and black pepper, to taste

Add all the ingredients minus the cream cheese to the base of a slow cooker. Cook on high for 4 hours. Stir in the cream cheese until well combined.

calories: 216 | fat: 14g | protein: 17g | carbs: 3g | net carbs: 2g | fiber: 1g

Butternut Squash Soup

Prep time: 15 minutes | Cook time: 4 to 6 hours | Serves 8

1½ cups butternut squash, cubed
1 cup heavy cream
5 cups chicken broth
3 cloves garlic, chopped

2 teaspoons ground cinnamon
½ teaspoon ground nutmeg
½ teaspoon ground cloves
Salt and black pepper, to taste

Add all the ingredients minus the heavy cream to the base of a slow cooker. Cook on high for 4 to 6 hours. Warm the heavy cream, and then add to the soup. Use an immersion blender and blend until smooth.

calories: 95 | fat: 7g | protein: 4g | carbs: 3g | net carbs: 2g | fiber: 1g

Heavy Cream-Cheese Broccoli Soup

Prep time: 10 minutes | Cook time: 13 minutes | Serves 4

1 tablespoon olive oil
1 tablespoon peanut butter
¾ cup heavy cream
1 onion, diced
1 garlic, minced
4 cups chopped broccoli
4 cups veggie broth

2¾ cups cheddar cheese, grated
¼ cup cheddar cheese to garnish
Salt and black pepper, to taste
½ bunch fresh mint, chopped

Warm olive oil and peanut butter in a pot over medium heat. Sauté onion and garlic for 3 minutes, stirring occasionally.

Season with salt and pepper. Add the broth and broccoli and bring to a boil. Reduce the heat and simmer for 10 minutes. Puree the soup with a hand blender until smooth. Add in the cheese and cook about 1 minute. Stir in the heavy cream. Serve in bowls with the reserved grated cheddar cheese and sprinkled with fresh mint.

calories: 508 | fat: 28g | protein: 26g | carbs: 11g | net carbs: 7g | fiber: 4g

Spiced Pumpkin Soup

Prep time: 15 minutes | Cook time: 4 to 6 hours | Serves 8

1½ cups pumpkin, cubed
1 cup heavy cream
5 cups chicken broth
3 cloves garlic, chopped

2 teaspoons ground cinnamon
½ teaspoon ground nutmeg
½ teaspoon ground cloves
Salt and black pepper, to taste

Add all the ingredients minus the heavy cream to the base of a slow cooker. Cook on high for 4 to 6 hours. Warm the heavy cream, and then add to the soup. Use an immersion blender and blend until smooth.

calories: 96 | fat: 7g | protein: 4g | carbs: 6g | net carbs: 4g | fiber: 2g

Cheesy Broccoli and Spinach Soup

Prep time: 10 minutes | Cook time: 16 minutes | Serves 4

1 tablespoon butter
1 onion, chopped
1 garlic clove, minced
2 heads broccoli, cut in florets
2 stalks celery, chopped
4 cups vegetable broth

1 cup baby spinach
Salt and black pepper, to taste
1 tablespoon basil, chopped
Parmesan cheese, shaved to serve

Melt the butter in a saucepan over medium heat. Sauté the garlic and onion for 3 minutes until softened. Mix in the broccoli and celery, and cook for 4 minutes until slightly tender. Pour in the broth, bring to a boil, then reduce the heat to medium-low and simmer covered for about 5 minutes. Drop in the spinach to wilt, adjust the seasonings, and cook for 4 minutes. Ladle soup into serving bowls. Serve with a sprinkle of grated Parmesan cheese and chopped basil.

calories: 123 | fat: 11g | protein: 1g | carbs: 4g | net carbs: 3g | fiber: 1g

Creamy Cauliflower and Leek Soup

Prep time: 10 minutes | Cook time: 35 minutes | Serves 4

4 cups vegetable broth
2 heads cauliflower, cut into florets
1 celery stalk, chopped
1 onion, chopped

1 cup leeks, chopped
1 tablespoon butter
1 tablespoon olive oil
1 cup heavy cream
½ teaspoon red pepper flakes

Warm butter and olive oil in a pot set over medium heat and sauté onion, leeks, and celery for 5 minutes. Stir in vegetable broth and cauliflower and bring to a boil; simmer for 30 minutes. Transfer the mixture to an immersion blender and puree; add in the heavy cream and stir. Decorate with red pepper flakes to serve.

calories: 231 | fat: 18g | protein: 4g | carbs: 9g | net carbs: 5g | fiber: 4g

White Mushroom Cream Soup with Herbs

Prep time: 10 minutes | Cook time: 23 minutes | Serves 4

1 onion, chopped
½ cup crème fraiche
¼ cup butter
12 ounces (340 g) white mushrooms, chopped
1 teaspoon thyme leaves, chopped
1 teaspoon parsley leaves, chopped
2 garlic cloves, minced
4 cups vegetable broth
Salt and black pepper, to taste

Add butter, onion and garlic to a pot over high heat and cook for 3 minutes. Add in mushrooms, salt and pepper, and cook for 10 minutes. Pour in broth and bring to a boil. Reduce heat and simmer for 10 minutes. Puree soup with a hand blender. Stir in crème fraiche. Garnish with herbs before serving.

calories: 190 | fat: 15g | protein: 3g | carbs: 6g | net carbs: 4g | fiber: 2g

Creamy Tomato Soup with Basil

Prep time: 10 minutes | Cook time: 14 minutes | Serves 4

1 tablespoon olive oil
1 onion, diced
1 garlic clove, minced
¼ cup raw cashew nuts, diced
14 ounces canned tomatoes
1 teaspoon fresh basil leaves
Salt and black pepper, to taste
1 cup crème fraîche

Warm olive oil in a pot over medium heat and sauté the onion and garlic for 4 minutes until softened. Stir in the tomatoes, basil, 1 cup water, cashew nuts, and season with salt and black pepper. Cover and bring to simmer for 10 minutes until thoroughly cooked. Puree the ingredients with an immersion blender. Adjust to taste and stir in the crème fraîche. Serve sprinkled with basil.

calories: 189 | fat: 14g | protein: 5g | carbs: 4g | net carbs: 2g | fiber: 2g

Buffalo Cheese Chicken Soup

Prep time: 10 minutes | Cook time: 7 minutes | Serves 4

1 onion, chopped
2 cups cooked, shredded chicken
1 tablespoon butter
4 cups chicken broth
1 tablespoon cilantro, chopped
⅓ cup buffalo sauce
½ cup cream cheese
Salt and black pepper, to taste

In a skillet over medium heat, warm butter and sauté the onion until tender, about 5 minutes. Add to a food processor and blend with buffalo sauce and cream cheese, until smooth. Transfer to a pot, add chicken broth and heat until hot but do not bring to a boil. Stir in chicken, salt, pepper and cook until heated through. When ready, remove to soup bowls and serve garnished with cilantro.

calories: 487 | fat: 41g | protein: 16g | carbs: 5g | net carbs: 3g | fiber: 2g

Turkey and Veggies Soup

Prep time: 10 minutes | Cook time: 25 minutes | Serves 4

1 onion, chopped
1 garlic clove, minced
3 celery stalks, chopped
2 leeks, chopped
1 tablespoon butter
4 cups chicken stock
Salt and black pepper, to taste
¼ cup fresh parsley, chopped
1 large zucchini, spiralized
2 cups turkey meat, cooked and chopped

In a pot over medium heat, add in leeks, celery, onion, and garlic and cook for 5 minutes. Place in the turkey meat, black pepper, salt, and stock, and cook for 20 minutes. Stir in the zucchini, and cook turkey soup for 5 minutes. Serve in bowls sprinkled with parsley.

calories: 312 | fat: 13g | protein: 16g | carbs: 9g | net carbs: 4g | fiber: 5g

Cheesy Broccoli and Bacon Soup

Prep time: 10 minutes | Cook time: 10 minutes | Serves 6

2 cups chicken broth
1 cup broccoli florets finely chopped
1 cup heavy cream
1 cup shredded cheddar cheese
½ white onion, chopped
2 cloves garlic, chopped
3 slices cooked bacon, crumbled for serving
½ teaspoon salt
¼ teaspoon black pepper

Add all the ingredients minus the heavy cream, cheddar cheese and bacon to a stockpot over medium heat. Bring to a simmer and cook for 5 minutes. Warm the cream, and then add the warm cream and cheddar cheese. Whisk until smooth. Serve with crumbled bacon.

calories: 220 | fat: 18g | protein: 11g | carbs: 4g | net carbs: 3g | fiber: 1g

Creamy Tomato Soup

Prep time: 10 minutes | Cook time: 40 minutes | Serves 6

3 cups canned whole, peeled tomatoes
4 cups chicken broth
1 cup heavy cream
3 cloves garlic, chopped
2 tablespoons butter
1 teaspoon freshly chopped thyme
Salt and black pepper, to taste

Add the butter to the bottom of a stockpot. Add in all the remaining ingredients minus the heavy cream. Bring to a boil, and then simmer for 40 minutes. Warm the heavy cream, and then stir into the soup.

calories: 144 | fat: 12g | protein: 4g | carbs: 4g | net carbs: 3g | fiber: 1g

Cheesy Tomato and Onion Soup

Prep time: 15 minutes | Cook time: 30 minutes | Serves 6

4 cups vegetable broth
1 cup heavy cream
1 cup canned diced tomatoes
1 yellow onion, chopped
2 cloves garlic, chopped
1 cup shredded mozzarella cheese
Freshly chopped basil, for serving

Add all of the ingredients minus the heavy cream, cheese and fresh basil to a stockpot over medium heat. Bring to a boil, and then reduce to a simmer. Simmer for 30 minutes. While the soup is cooking, warm the heavy cream over low heat and add to the soup once cooked. Use an immersion blender and blend until smooth. Stir in the mozzarella cheese and top with fresh basil.

calories: 122 | fat: 9g | protein: 6g | carbs: 5g | net carbs: 4g | fiber: 1g

Chapter 12 Snacks and Appetizers

Turkey Stuffed Mini Peppers
Prep time: 10 minutes | Cook time: 10 minutes | Serves 5

2 teaspoons olive oil
1 teaspoon mustard seeds
5 ounces (142 g) ground turkey
Salt and ground black pepper, to taste
10 mini bell peppers, cut in half

lengthwise, stems and seeds removed
2 ounces (57 g) garlic and herb seasoned chevre goat cheese, crumbled

Heat the oil in a skillet over medium-high heat. Once hot, cook mustard seeds with ground turkey until the turkey is no longer pink. Crumble with a fork. Season with salt and black pepper. Lay the pepper halves cut-side-up on a parchment-lined baking sheet. Spoon the meat mixture into the center of each pepper half. Top each pepper with cheese. Bake in the preheated oven at 400ºF (205ºC) for 10 minutes. Bon appétit!

calories: 200 | fat: 17.1g | protein: 7.8g | carbs: 2.9g | net carbs: 2.0g | fiber: 0.9g

Cheese Bites with Pickle
Prep time: 15 minutes | Cook time: 0 minutes | Serves 10

10 ounces (283 g) Swiss cheese, shredded
10 ounces (283 g) cottage cheese
¼ cup sour cream

1 tablespoon pickle, minced
Sea salt and ground black pepper, to season
1 teaspoon granulated garlic
¾ cup pecans, finely chopped

Beat the Swiss cheese, cottage cheese, sour cream, minced pickles, and seasonings until everything is well incorporated. Place the mixture for 2 hours in your refrigerator. Form the mixture into bite-sized balls using your hands and a spoon. Roll the cheese balls over the chopped pecans to coat them evenly. Bon appétit!

calories: 200 | fat: 15.6g | protein: 11.4g | carbs: 4.8g | net carbs: 3.8g | fiber: 1.0g

Romano and Asiago Cheese Crisps
Prep time: 15 minutes | Cook time: 30 minutes | Serves 8

1¼ cups Romano cheese, grated
½ cup Asiago cheese, grated
2 ripe tomatoes, peeled
½ teaspoon sea salt

½ teaspoon chili powder
1 teaspoon dried oregano
1 teaspoon dried basil
1 teaspoon dried parsley flakes
1 teaspoon garlic powder

Mix the cheese in a bowl. Place tablespoon-sized heaps of the mixture onto parchmentlined baking pans. Bake in the preheated oven at 380ºF (193ºC) approximately 7 minutes until beginning to brown around the edges. Let them stand for about 15 minutes until crisp. Meanwhile, purée the tomatoes in your food processor. Bring the puréed tomatoes to a simmer, add the remaining ingredients and cook for 30 minutes or until it has thickened and cooked through. Serve the cheese crisps with the spicy tomato sauce on the side. Bon appétit!

calories: 110 | fat: 7.5g | protein: 8.4g | carbs: 2.0g | net carbs: 1.6g | fiber: 0.4g

Cheese and Shrimp Stuffed Celery
Prep time: 10 minutes | Cook time: 5 minutes | Serves 6

5 ounces (142 g) shrimp
10 ounces (283 g) cottage cheese, at room temperature
4 ounces (113 g) Coby cheese, shredded

2 scallions, chopped
1 teaspoon yellow mustard
Sea salt, to taste
½ teaspoon oregano
6 stalks celery, cut into halves

Gently pat the shrimp dry with a paper towel. Cook the shrimp in a lightly greased skillet over medium-high heat for 2 minutes; turn them over and cook for a further 2 minutes. Chop the shrimp and transfer to a mixing bowl. Add in the cheese, scallions, mustard, and spices. Mix to combine well. Divide the shrimp mixture between the celery stalks and serve. Bon appétit!

calories: 127 | fat: 6.1g | protein: 13.4g | carbs: 4.2g | net carbs: 3.7g | fiber: 0.5g

Wrapped Shrimp with Bacon
Prep time: 15 minutes | Cook time: 15 minutes | Serves 8

24 medium shrimp, deveined
8 slices of thick-cut bacon, cut into thirds
1 teaspoon mustard powder
1 teaspoon onion powder

½ teaspoon granulated garlic
½ teaspoon red pepper flakes, crushed
Sea salt and ground black pepper, to taste

Start by preheating your oven to 400ºF (205ºC). Line a large-sized baking sheet with Silpat mat or aluminum foil. Wrap each shrimp with a piece of bacon; secure with a toothpick. Place the wrapped shrimp on the prepared baking sheet. Sprinkle with mustard, onion powder, garlic, red pepper, salt, and black pepper. Bake for about 13 minutes or until the shrimp is thoroughly cooked. Bon appétit!

calories: 120 | fat: 10.4g | protein: 5.6g | carbs: 0.4g | net carbs: 0.4g | fiber: 0g

Cocktail Meatballs
Prep time: 15 minutes | Cook time: 20 minutes | Serves 2

¼ pound (113 g) ground turkey
¼ pound (113 g) ground pork
1 ounce (28 g) bacon, chopped
¼ cup flaxseed meal
½ teaspoon garlic, pressed
1 egg, beaten
½ cup Cheddar cheese,

shredded
Sea salt, to season
¼ teaspoon ground black pepper
¼ teaspoon cayenne pepper
¼ teaspoon marjoram

Start by preheating your oven to 400ºF (205ºC). Thoroughly combine all ingredients in a mixing bowl. Now, form the mixture into meatballs. Place your meatballs in a parchment-lined baking sheet. Bake in the preheated oven for about 18 minutes, rotating the pan halfway through. Serve with toothpicks and enjoy!

calories: 570 | fat: 42.3g | protein: 40.2g | carbs: 6.4g | net carbs: 0.8g | fiber: 5.6g

Bacon Fat Bombs

Prep time: 15 minutes | Cook time: 0 minutes | Serves 8

½ stick butter, at room temperature
8 ounces (227 g) cottage cheese, at room temperature
8 ounces (227 g) Mozzarella

cheese, crumbled
1 teaspoon shallot powder
1 teaspoon Italian seasoning blend
2 ounces (57 g) bacon bits

Mix the butter, cheese, shallot powder, and Italian seasoning blend until well combined. Place the mixture in your refrigerator for about 60 minutes. Shape the mixture into 18 balls. Roll each ball in the bacon bits until coated on all sides. Enjoy!

calories: 150 | fat: 9.4g | protein: 13.0g | carbs: 2.1g | net carbs: 1.6g | fiber: 0.5g

Meaty Jalapeños

Prep time: 15 minutes | Cook time: 40 minutes | Serves 10

2 ounces (57 g) bacon, chopped
½ pound (227 g) ground pork
½ pound (227 g) ground beef
½ cup red onion, chopped
2 garlic cloves, minced
1 teaspoon taco seasoning mix
Sea salt and ground black pepper, to season

½ cup tomato purée
1 teaspoon stone-ground mustard
20 jalapeño peppers, seeded and halved lengthwise
4 ounces (113 g) Parmesan cheese, preferably freshly grated

Preheat a nonstick skillet over medium-high heat. Now, cook the bacon, pork, and beef for about 4 minutes until no longer pink. Add in the onion and garlic and cook an additional 3 minutes until they are tender. Sprinkle with the taco seasoning mix, salt, and black pepper. Fold in the tomato purée and mustard. Continue to cook over medium-low heat for 4 minutes more. Spoon the mixture into jalapeño peppers. Bake in the preheated oven at 390°F (199°C) for about 20 minutes. Top with Parmesan cheese and bake an additional 6 minutes or until cheese is golden on the top. Bon appétit!

calories: 190 | fat: 13.3g | protein: 12.6g | carbs: 4.8g | net carbs: 3.6g | fiber: 1.2g

Caprese Sticks

Prep time: 10 minutes | Cook time: 0 minutes | Serves 8

2 tablespoons extra-virgin olive oil
2 tablespoons red wine vinegar
1 tablespoon Italian seasoning blend
8 pieces Prosciutto
8 pieces Soppressata
16 grape tomatoes

8 black olives, pitted
8 ounces (227 g) Mozzarella, cubed
2 tablespoons fresh basil leaves, chopped
1 red bell pepper, sliced
1 yellow bell pepper, sliced
Coarse sea salt, to taste

In a small mixing bowl, make the vinaigrette by whisking the oil, vinegar, and Italian seasoning blend. Set aside. Slide the ingredients on the prepared skewers. Arrange the sticks on serving platter. Season with salt to taste. Serve the vinaigrette on the side and enjoy!

calories: 142 | fat: 8.3g | protein: 12.8g | carbs: 3.2g | net carbs: 2.2g | fiber: 1.0g

Bacon-Wrapped Poblano Poppers

Prep time: 15 minutes | Cook time: 30 minutes | Serves 16

10 ounces (283 g) cottage cheese, at room temperature
6 ounces (170 g) Swiss cheese, shredded
Sea salt and ground black pepper, to taste
½ teaspoon shallot powder

½ teaspoon cumin powder
⅓ teaspoon mustard seeds
16 poblano peppers, seeded and halved
16 thin slices bacon, sliced lengthwise

Mix the cheese, salt, black pepper, shallot powder, cumin, and mustard seeds until well combined. Divide the mixture between the pepper halves. Wrap each pepper with 2 slices of bacon; secure with toothpicks. Arrange the stuffed peppers on the rack in the baking sheet. Bake in the preheated oven at 390°F (199°C) for about 30 minutes until the bacon is sizzling and browned. Bon appétit!

calories: 184 | fat: 14.1g | protein: 8.9g | carbs: 5.8g | net carbs: 5.0g | fiber: 0.8g

BLT Cups

Prep time: 10 minutes | Cook time: 10 minutes | Serves 10

5 ounces (142 g) bacon, chopped
5 tablespoons Parmigiano-Reggiano cheese, grated
1 teaspoon adobo sauce
2 tablespoons mayonnaise
Sea salt and ground black

pepper, to taste
2 tablespoons green onions, minced
10 pieces lettuce
10 tomatoes cherry tomatoes, discard the insides

Preheat a frying pan over moderate heat. Cook the bacon in the frying pan until crisp, about 7 minutes; reserve. In a mixing bowl, thoroughly combine the cheese, adobo sauce, mayo, salt, black pepper, and green onions. Divide the mayo mixture between the cherry tomatoes. Divide the cooked bacon between the cherry tomatoes. Top with the lettuce and serve immediately. Bon appétit!

calories: 93 | fat: 8.2g | protein: 2.6g | carbs: 1.5g | net carbs: 1.1g | fiber: 0.4g

Chicken and Spinach Meatballs

Prep time: 15 minutes | Cook time: 25 minutes | Serves 10

1½ pounds (680 g) ground chicken
8 ounces (227 g) Parmigiano-Reggiano cheese, grated
1 teaspoon garlic, minced
1 tablespoon Italian seasoning mix

1 egg, whisked
8 ounces (227 g) spinach, chopped
½ teaspoon mustard seeds
Sea salt and ground black pepper, to taste
½ teaspoon paprika

Mix the ingredients until everything is well incorporated. Now, shape the meat mixture into 20 meatballs. Transfer your meatballs to a baking sheet and brush them with a nonstick cooking oil. Bake in the preheated oven at 390°F (199°C) for about 25 minutes or until golden brown. Serve with cocktail sticks and enjoy!

calories: 210 | fat: 12.4g | protein: 19.4g | carbs: 4.5g | net carbs: 4.0g | fiber: 0.5g

Cream Cheese Stuffed Mushrooms

Prep time: 15 minutes | Cook time: 40 minutes | Serves 10

20 button mushrooms, stalks removed
6 ounces (170 g) cream cheese
¼ cup mayonnaise
¼ teaspoon mustard seeds
½ teaspoon celery seeds
Sea salt and black pepper, to taste

Adjust an oven rack to the center position. Brush your mushrooms with nonstick cooking spray and arrange them on a baking sheet. Roast your mushrooms in the preheated oven at 375°F (190°C) for 40 minutes until the mushrooms release liquid. In the meantime, mix the remaining ingredients until well combined. Spoon the mixture into the roasted mushroom caps. Bon appétit!

calories: 104 | fat: 9.8g | protein: 2.6g | carbs: 2.0g | net carbs: 1.5g | fiber: 0.5g

Wrapped Asparagus with Prosciutto

Prep time: 15 minutes | Cook time: 20 minutes | Serves 6

1½ pounds (680 g) asparagus spears, trimmed
1 teaspoon shallot powder
½ teaspoon granulated garlic
½ teaspoon paprika
Kosher salt and ground black pepper, to taste
1 tablespoon sesame oil
10 slices prosciutto

Toss the asparagus spears with the shallot powder, garlic, paprika, salt, and black pepper. Drizzle sesame oil all over the asparagus spears. Working one at a time, wrap a prosciutto slice on each asparagus spear; try to cover the entire length of the asparagus spear. Place the wrapped asparagus spears on a parchment-lined roasting pan. Bake in the preheated oven at 390°F (199°C) for about 18 minutes or until thoroughly cooked. Bon appétit!

calories: 120 | fat: 6.5g | protein: 10.1g | carbs: 6.2g | net carbs: 3.2g | fiber: 3.0g

Hot Spare Ribs

Prep time: 20 minutes | Cook time: 2 hours | Serves 2

1 pound (454 g) spare ribs
1 teaspoon Dijon mustard
1 tablespoon rice wine
Salt and ground black pepper, to season
Hot Sauce:
1 teaspoon Sriracha sauce
1 tablespoon olive oil
1 cup tomato sauce, sugar-free
1 teaspoon garlic, pressed
½ shallot powder
1 teaspoon cayenne pepper
½ teaspoon ground allspice
1 tablespoon avocado oil

1 teaspoon garlic, minced
Salt, to season

Arrange the spare ribs on a parchment-lined baking pan. Add the remaining ingredients for the ribs and toss until well coated. Bake in the preheated oven at 360°F (182°C) for 1 hour. Rotate the pan and roast an additional 50 to 60 minutes. Baste the ribs with the cooking liquid periodically. In the meantime, whisk the sauce ingredients until well mixed. Pour the hot sauce over the ribs. Place under the broiler and broil for 7 to 9 minutes or until an internal temperature reaches 145°F (63°C). Brush the sauce onto each rib and serve warm. Bon appétit!

calories: 471 | fat: 27.1g | protein: 48.6g | carbs: 6.6g | net carbs: 4.6g | fiber: 2.0g

Caribbean Baked Wings

Prep time: 15 minutes | Cook time: 45 minutes | Serves 2

4 chicken wings
1 tablespoon coconut aminos
2 tablespoons rum
2 tablespoons butter
1 tablespoon onion powder
1 tablespoon garlic powder
½ teaspoon salt
¼ teaspoon freshly ground black pepper
½ teaspoon red pepper flakes
¼ teaspoon dried dill
2 tablespoons sesame seeds

Pat dry the chicken wings. Toss the chicken wings with the remaining ingredients until well coated. Arrange the chicken wings on a parchment-lined baking sheet. Bake in the preheated oven at 420°F (216°C) for 45 minutes until golden brown. Serve with your favorite sauce for dipping. Bon appétit!

calories: 287 | fat: 18.6g | protein: 15.5g | carbs: 5.1g | net carbs: 3.3g | fiber: 1.8g

Sardine Pepper Boats

Prep time: 10 minutes | Cook time: 10 minutes | Serves 3

2 eggs
½ red onion, chopped
½ teaspoon garlic clove, minced
2 ounces (57 g) canned boneless sardines, drained and chopped
¼ freshly ground black pepper
½ cup tomatoes, chopped
¼ cup mayonnaise
3 tablespoons Ricotta cheese
3 bell peppers, seeded and halved

Place the eggs and water in a saucepan; bring to a rapid boil; immediately remove from the heat. Allow it to sit, covered, for 10 minutes. Then, discard the shells, rinse the eggs under cold water, and chop them. Thoroughly combine the onion, garlic, sardines, black pepper, tomatoes, mayonnaise, and cheese. Stuff the pepper halves and serve well chilled. Bon appétit!

calories: 372 | fat: 31.2g | protein: 16.1g | carbs: 5.9g | net carbs: 4.5g | fiber: 1.4g

Pork Skewers with Greek Dipping Sauce

Prep time: 15 minutes | Cook time: 10 minutes | Serves 2

½ pound (227 g) pork loin, cut into bite-sized pieces
2 garlic cloves, pressed
1 scallion stalk, chopped
¼ cup dry red wine
1 thyme sprig
Dipping Sauce:
½ cup Greek yogurt
½ teaspoon dill, ground
½ Lebanese cucumber, grated
1 teaspoon garlic, minced
Sea salt, to taste
1 rosemary sprig
1 tablespoon lemon juice
1 teaspoon stone ground mustard
1 tablespoon olive oil

½ teaspoon ground black pepper
2 tablespoons cilantro leaves, roughly chopped

Place the pork loin in a ceramic dish; add in the garlic, scallions, wine, thyme, rosemary, lemon juice, mustard, and olive oil. Let them marinate in your refrigerator for 2 to 3 hours Thread the pork pieces onto bamboo skewers. Grill them for 5 to 6 minutes per side. Meanwhile, whisk the remaining ingredients until well mixed. Serve the pork skewers with the sauce for dipping and enjoy!

calories: 313 | fat: 20.0g | protein: 29.2g | carbs: 2.2g | net carbs: 1.6g | fiber: 0.6g

Zucchini Chips

Prep time: 10 minutes | Cook time: 20 minutes | Serves 2

1 tablespoon extra-virgin olive oil	½ pound (227 g) zucchini, sliced into rounds
¼ teaspoon sea salt	2 tablespoons Parmesan cheese, grated
1 teaspoon hot paprika	

Gently toss the sliced zucchini with the olive oil, salt, and paprika. Place them on a tinfoillined baking sheet. Sprinkle the Parmesan cheese evenly over each zucchini round. Bake in the preheated oven at 400ºF (205ºC) for 15 to 20 minutes or until your chips turns a golden-brown color.

calories: 53 | fat: 4.5g | protein: 1.6g | carbs: 1.5g | net carbs: 0.9g | fiber: 0.6g

Kale Chips

Prep time: 15 minutes | Cook time: 15 minutes | Serves 2

2 cups kale, torn into pieces	½ teaspoon garlic powder
1 tablespoons olive oil	½ teaspoon fresh dill, minced
Sea salt, to taste	½ tablespoon fresh parsley, minced
¼ teaspoon pepper	
½ teaspoon onion powder	

Start by preheating your oven to 320ºF (160ºC). Toss the kale leaves with all other ingredients until well coated. Bake for 10 to 14 minutes, depending on how crisp you like them. Store the kale chips in an airtight container for up to a week. Bon appétit!

calories: 69 | fat: 6.5g | protein: 0.5g | carbs: 1.5g | net carbs: 1.0g | fiber: 0.5g

Cauliflower Bites

Prep time: 10 minutes | Cook time: 30 minutes | Serves 2

1½ cups cauliflower florets	pepper, to taste
1 tablespoon butter, softened	1 teaspoon Italian seasoning mix
1 egg, whisked	½ cup Asiago cheese, grated
Sea salt and ground black	

Pulse the cauliflower in your food processor; now, heat the butter in a nonstick skillet and cook the cauliflower until golden. Add the remaining ingredients and blend together until well incorporated. Form the mixture into balls and flatten them with the palm of your hand. Arrange on a tinfoil-lined baking pan. Bake in the preheated oven at 400ºF (205ºC) for 25 to 30 minutes. Serve with homemade ketchup. Bon appétit!

calories: 235 | fat: 19.1g | protein: 12.4g | carbs: 4.4g | net carbs: 2.9g | fiber: 1.5g

Anchovy Fat Bombs

Prep time: 15 minutes | Cook time: 0 minutes | Serves 10

8 ounces (227 g) Cheddar cheese, shredded	anchovies, chopped
6 ounces (170 g) cream cheese, at room temperature	½ yellow onion, minced
4 ounces (113 g) canned	1 teaspoon fresh garlic, minced
	Sea salt and ground black pepper, to taste

Mix all of the above ingredients in a bowl. Place the mixture in your refrigerator for 1 hour. Then, shape the mixture into bite-sized balls. Serve immediately.

calories: 123 | fat: 8.8g | protein: 7.4g | carbs: 3.3g | net carbs: 3.3g | fiber: 0g

Bakery Mini Almond Muffins

Prep time: 15 minutes | Cook time: 20 minutes | Serves 9

3 eggs	½ teaspoon baking soda
2 tablespoons coconut oil	½ teaspoon baking powder
3 ounces (85 g) double cream	A pinch of salt
1 cup almond meal	½ teaspoon ground cloves
½ cup flax seed meal	1 teaspoon ground cinnamon
½ teaspoon monk fruit powder	1 teaspoon vanilla essence

In a mixing bowl, whisk the eggs with the coconut milk and double cream. In another bowl, mix the remaining ingredients. Now, add the wet mixture to the dry mixture. Mix again to combine well. Spoon the batter into small silicone molds. Bake in the preheated oven at 360ºF (182ºC) for 13 to 17 minutes. Bon appétit!

calories: 86 | fat: 6.5g | protein: 4.2g | carbs: 3.2g | net carbs: 3.2g | fiber: 0g

Onions Rings

Prep time: 15 minutes | Cook time: 20 minutes | Serves 4

½ cup coconut flour	3 ounces (85 g) Parmesan cheese, grated
3 eggs	2 onions, cut into ½-inch thick rings
2 tablespoons water	
2 tablespoons double cream	
4 ounces (113 g) pork rinds	

Place the coconut flour in a shallow dish. In another dish, mix the eggs, water, and cream; place the pork rinds and Parmesan in the third dish. Dip the onion rings into the coconut flour; then, dip them into the egg mixture; lastly, roll the onion rings in the Parmesan mixture. Place the coated rings on a lightly greased baking rack; bake at 420ºF (216ºC) for 13 to 16 minutes. Enjoy!

calories: 323 | fat: 27.7g | protein: 10.2g | carbs: 5.6g | net carbs: 4.5g | fiber: 1.1g

Cheesy Bacon-Stuffed Jalapeño Poppers

Prep time: 15 minutes | Cook time: 20 minutes | Serves 3

5 slices bacon	¼ cup shredded Cheddar cheese
6 jalapeño peppers	¼ teaspoon garlic powder
3 ounces (85 g) cream cheese, softened	

In a skillet over medium heat, fry the bacon until crispy. Set aside on a paper towel–lined plate to cool. When cool enough to handle, chop the bacon into bits. Preheat the oven to 400ºF (205ºC). Line a rimmed baking sheet with parchment paper. Slice the jalapeño peppers in half lengthwise. Use a spoon to scrape out the seeds and membranes. In a medium-sized bowl, use a fork to combine the cream cheese, Cheddar cheese, garlic powder, and bacon bits. Spoon some of the mixture into each jalapeño half and set the peppers cheese side up on the lined baking sheet. Bake for 18 to 20 minutes, until the cheese is melted and slightly crisp on top.

calories: 203 | fat: 16g | protein: 9g | carbs: 3g | net carbs: 2g | fiber: 1g

Mediterranean Cheese Sticks

Prep time: 10 minutes | Cook time: 15 minutes | Serves 4

2 eggs, beaten
1½ cups Romano cheese, grated
2 cups Mozzarella, shredded
2 garlic cloves, crushed
1 teaspoon dried rosemary
1 teaspoon dried parsley flakes

Mix all of the ingredients until everything is well incorporated. Roll the dough out on a parchment-lined baking pan. Bake in the preheated oven at 360°F (182°C) for about 13 minutes until golden brown. Cut into sticks and serve at room temperature. Enjoy!

calories: 257 | fat: 12.3g | protein: 32.7g | carbs: 4.0g | net carbs: 3.0g | fiber: 1.0g

Cheese Biscuits

Prep time: 15 minutes | Cook time: 20 minutes | Serves 10

1 cup coconut flour
½ cup flaxseed meal
1½ cups almond meal
½ teaspoon baking soda
1 teaspoon baking powder
½ teaspoon salt
1 teaspoon paprika
2 eggs
1 stick butter
1 cup Romano cheese, grated
1½ cups Colby cheese, grated

Mix the flour with the baking soda, baking powder, salt, and paprika. In a separate bowl, beat the eggs and butter. Stir the wet mixture into the flour mixture. Fold in the grated cheese. Mix again until everything is well incorporated. Roll the batter into 16 balls and place them on a lightly greased cookie sheet. Flatten them slightly with the palms of your hands. Bake at 350°F (180°C) for about 17 minutes. Bon appétit!

calories: 380 | fat: 33.6g | protein: 14.0g | carbs: 6.6g | net carbs: 1.6g | fiber: 5.0g

Spanish Sausage and Cheese Stuffed Mushrooms

Prep time: 15 minutes | Cook time: 25 minutes | Serves 6

30 button mushrooms, stalks removed and cleaned
8 ounces (227 g) Chorizo sausage, crumbled
2 scallions, chopped
2 green garlic stalks, chopped
2 tablespoons fresh parsley, chopped
10 ounces (283 g) goat cheese, crumbled
Sea salt and ground black pepper, to season
½ teaspoon red pepper flakes, crushed

Place the mushroom caps on a lightly greased baking sheet. Mix the remaining ingredients until well combined. Divide this stuffing between the mushroom caps. Bake in the preheated oven at 340°F (171°C) for 25 minutes or until thoroughly cooked. Serve with cocktail sticks. Bon appétit!

calories: 325 | fat: 23.6g | protein: 23.0g | carbs: 5.0g | net carbs: 3.8g | fiber: 1.2g

Italian Sausage and Eggplant Pie

Prep time: 15 minutes | Cook time: 40 minutes | Serves 6

6 eggs
12 ounces (340 g) raw sausage rolls
10 cherry tomatoes, halved
2 tablespoons heavy cream
2 tablespoons Parmesan
cheese
Salt and black pepper to serve
2 tablespoons parsley, chopped
5 eggplant slices

Preheat your oven to 375°F (190°C). Grease a pie dish with cooking spray. Press the sausage roll at the bottom of a pie dish. Arrange the eggplant slices on top of the sausage. Top with cherry tomatoes. Whisk together the eggs along with the heavy cream, salt, Parmesan cheese, and black pepper. Spoon the egg mixture over the sausage. Bake for about 40 minutes until it is browned around the edges. Serve warm, and scatter with chopped parsley.

calories: 341 | fat: 28.0g | protein: 1.7g | carbs: 5.9g | net carbs: 3.0g | fiber: 2.9g

Cheese and Ham Egg Cakes

Prep time: 15 minutes | Cook time: 25 minutes | Serves 8

2 cups ham, chopped
⅓ cup Parmesan cheese, grated
1 tablespoon parsley, chopped
¼ cup almond flour
9 eggs
⅓ cup mayonnaise, sugar-free
¼ teaspoon garlic powder
¼ cup onion, chopped
Sea salt to taste
Cooking spray

Preheat your oven to 375°F (190°C). Lightly grease nine muffin pans with cooking spray, and set aside. Place the onion, ham, garlic powder, and salt, in a food processor, and pulse until ground. Stir in the mayonnaise, almond flour, and Parmesan cheese. Press this mixture into the muffin cups. Press for 5 minutes. Crack an egg into each muffin cup. Return to the oven and bake for 20 more minutes or until the tops are firm to the touch and eggs are cooked. Leave to cool slightly before serving.

calories: 266 | fat: 18.0g | protein: 13.5g | carbs: 1.6g | net carbs: 1.0g | fiber: 0.6g

Simple Butter Broccoli

Prep time: 5 minutes | Cook time: 5 minutes | Serves 6

1 broccoli head, florets only
¼ cup butter
Salt to taste

Place the broccoli in a pot filled with salted water, and bring to a boil. Cook for about 3 minutes, or until tender. Melt the butter in a microwave. Drain the broccoli and transfer to a plate. Drizzle the butter over and season with some salt and pepper.

calories: 115 | fat: 7.8g | protein: 4.0g | carbs: 5.7g | net carbs: 5.6g | fiber: 0.1g

Chorizo and Asparagus Traybake

Prep time: 15 minutes | Cook time: 15 minutes | Serves 4

2 tablespoons olive oil
A bunch of asparagus, ends trimmed and chopped
4 ounces (113 g) Spanish
chorizo, sliced
Salt and black pepper to taste
¼ cup chopped parsley

Preheat your oven to 325°F (163°C) and grease a baking dish with olive oil. Add in the asparagus and season with salt and black pepper. Stir in the chorizo slices. Bake for 15 minutes until the chorizo is crispy. Arrange on a serving platter and serve sprinkled with parsley.

calories: 412 | fat: 36.6g | protein: 14.6g | carbs: 4.3g | net carbs: 3.3g | fiber: 1.0g

Chicken Wrapped Provolone and Prosciutto

Prep time: 10 minutes | Cook time: 10 minutes | Serves 8

¼ teaspoon garlic powder
8 ounces (227 g) provolone cheese

8 raw chicken tenders
Black pepper to taste
8 prosciutto slices

Pound the chicken until half an inch thick. Season with salt, pepper, and garlic powder. Cut the provolone cheese into 8 strips. Place a slice of prosciutto on a flat surface. Place one chicken tender on top. Top with a provolone strip. Roll the chicken, and secure with previously soaked skewers. Preheat the grill. Grill the wraps for about 3 minutes per side.

calories: 175 | fat: 10.1g | protein: 16.9g | carbs: 0g | net carbs: 0.7g | fiber: 0g

Fried Baby Artichoke

Prep time: 10 minutes | Cook time: 10 minutes | Serves 4

12 fresh baby artichokes
2 tablespoons lemon juice

2 tablespoons olive oil
Salt to taste

Slice the artichokes vertically into narrow wedges. Drain them on paper towels before frying. Heat the olive oil in a cast-iron skillet over high heat. Fry the artichokes until browned and crispy. Drain excess oil on paper towels. Sprinkle with salt and lemon juice.

calories: 36 | fat: 2.5g | protein: 2.0g | carbs: 23.8g | net carbs: 3.0g | fiber: 20.8g

Deviled Eggs

Prep time: 10 minutes | Cook time: 20 minutes | Serves 6

6 eggs
1 tablespoon green tabasco

⅓ cup sugar-free mayonnaise

Place the eggs in a saucepan, and cover with salted water. Bring to a boil over medium heat. Boil for 8 minutes. Place the eggs in an ice bath and let cool for 10 minutes. Peel and slice them in. Whisk together the tabasco, mayonnaise, and salt in a small bowl. Spoon this mixture on top of every egg.

calories: 180 | fat: 17.0g | protein: 6.0g | carbs: 5.0g | net carbs: 5.0g | fiber: 0g

Cauliflower Fritters

Prep time: 15 minutes | Cook time: 15 minutes | Serves 4

1 pound (454 g) cauliflower, grated
½ cup Parmesan cheese
3 ounces (85 g) onion, finely chopped

½ teaspoon baking powder
½ cup almond flour
3 eggs
½ teaspoon lemon juice
Olive oil, for frying

Sprinkle the salt over the cauliflower in a bowl, and let it stand for 10 minutes. Place the other ingredients in the bowl. Mix with your hands to combine. Put a skillet over medium heat, and heat some olive oil in it. Shape fritters out of the cauliflower mixture. Fry for 3 minutes per side. Serve.

calories: 70 | fat: 5.3g | protein: 4.5g | carbs: 6.0g | net carbs: 3.0g | fiber: 3.0g

Parsnip Chips

Prep time: 15 minutes | Cook time: 15 minutes | Serves 4

3 tablespoons olive oil
⅓ cup natural yogurt
1 teaspoon lime juice
1 tablespoon parsley, chopped

Salt and black pepper, to taste
1 garlic clove, minced
2 cups parsnips, sliced

Preheat the oven to 300ºF (150ºC). Set parsnip on a baking sheet; toss with garlic powder, 1 tablespoon of olive oil, and salt. Bake for 15 minutes, tossing once halfway through, until slices are crisp and browned. In a bowl, mix yogurt, lime juice, black pepper, 2 tablespoons of olive oil, garlic, and salt until well combined. Serve the chips with yogurt dip.

calories: 175 | fat: 12.6g | protein: 2.0g | carbs: 11.9g | net carbs: 8.6g | fiber: 3.3g

Prosciutto Wrapped Basil Mozzarella

Prep time: 10 minutes | Cook time: 0 minutes | Serves 6

6 thin prosciutto slices
18 basil leaves

18 Mozzarella ciliegine (about 8½ ounces / 241 g in total)

Cut the prosciutto slices into three strips. Place basil leaves at the end of each strip. Top with Mozzarella. Wrap the Mozzarella in prosciutto. Secure with toothpicks.

calories: 164 | fat: 12.0g | protein: 13.1g | carbs: 0.6g | net carbs: 0.6g | fiber: 0g

Liverwurst Truffles

Prep time: 10 minutes | Cook time: 0 minutes | Serves 8

8 bacon slices, cooked and chopped
8 ounces (227 g) Liverwurst
¼ cup pistachios, chopped

1 teaspoon Dijon mustard
6 ounces (170 g) cream cheese

Combine liverwurst and pistachios in the bowl of your food processor. Pulse until smooth. Whisk the cream cheese and mustard in another bowl. Make 12 balls out of the liverwurst mixture. Make a thin cream cheese layer over. Coat with bacon pieces. Arrange on a plate and refrigerate for 30 minutes.

calories: 146 | fat: 11.9g | protein: 7.1g | carbs: 2.7g | net carbs: 1.6g | fiber: 1.1g

Jalapeño and Zucchini Frittata Cups

Prep time: 15 minutes | Cook time: 30 minutes | Serves 4

2 tablespoons olive oil
2 green onions, chopped
1 garlic clove, minced
½ jalapeño pepper, chopped
½ carrot, chopped
1 zucchini, shredded

2 tablespoons Mozzarella cheese, shredded
8 eggs, whisked
Salt and black pepper, to taste
½ teaspoon dried oregano

Sauté green onions and garlic in warm olive oil over medium heat for 3 minutes. Stir in carrot, zucchini, and jalapeño pepper, and cook for 4 more minutes. Remove the mixture to a lightly greased baking pan with a nonstick cooking spray. Top with Mozzarella cheese. Cover with the whisked eggs; season with oregano, black pepper, and salt. Bake in the oven for about 20 minutes at 360ºF (182ºC).

calories: 336 | fat: 27.9g | protein: 14.1g | carbs: 5.3g | net carbs: 4.8g | fiber: 0.5g

Bacon and Mortadella Sausage Almond Balls

Prep time: 15 minutes | Cook time: 0 minutes | Serves 4

6 ounces (170 g) Mortadella sausage
6 bacon slices, cooked and crumbled

2 tablespoons almonds, chopped
½ teaspoon Dijon mustard
3 ounces (85 g) cream cheese

Combine the mortadella and almonds in the bowl of your food processor. Pulse until smooth. Whisk the cream cheese and mustard in another bowl. Make balls out of the mortadella mixture. Make a thin cream cheese layer over. Coat with bacon, arrange on a plate and chill before serving.

calories: 548 | fat: 51.2g | protein: 21.6g | carbs: 4.4g | net carbs: 3.5g | fiber: 0.9g

Monterrey Jack Cheese Chips

Prep time: 10 minutes | Cook time: 15 minutes | Serves 4

2 cups Monterrey Jack cheese, grated
Salt to taste

½ teaspoon garlic powder
½ teaspoon cayenne pepper
½ teaspoon dried rosemary

Mix grated cheese with spices. Create 2 tablespoons of cheese mixture into small mounds on a lined baking sheet. Bake for about 15 minutes at 425°F (220°C); then allow to cool to harden the chips.

calories: 439 | fat: 36.9g | protein: 26.9g | carbs: 1.8g | net carbs: 1.7g | fiber: 0.1g

Lettuce Wrapped Duo-Cheese and Tomato

Prep time: 10 minutes | Cook time: 0 minutes | Serves 4

1 pound (454 g) Gruyere cheese, grated
¼ pound (113 g) Feta cheese, crumbled

½ teaspoon oregano
1 tomato, chopped
½ cup buttermilk
1 head lettuce

In a bowl, mix Feta and Gruyere cheese, oregano, tomato, and buttermilk. Separate the lettuce leaves and put them on a serving platter. Divide the mixture between them, roll up, folding in the ends to secure and serve.

calories: 434 | fat: 32.6g | protein: 27.6g | carbs: 7.6g | net carbs: 6.7g | fiber: 0.9g

Salami Omelet

Prep time: 10 minutes | Cook time: 10 minutes | Serves 1

2 tablespoons butter
8 eggs
6 basil, chopped
½ cup Mozzarella cheese

2 tablespoons water
4 slices salami
2 tomatoes, sliced
Salt and black pepper, to taste

In a bowl, whisk the eggs with a fork. Add in the water, salt, and black pepper. Melt the butter in a skillet and cook the eggs for 30 seconds. Spread the salami slices over. Arrange the sliced tomato and Mozzarella over the salami. Cook for about 3 minutes. Cover the skillet and continue cooking for 3 more minutes until omelet is completely set. When ready, remove the pan from heat; run a spatula around the edges of the omelet and flip it onto a warm plate, folded side down. Serve garnished with basil leaves.

calories: 442 | fat: 34.1g | protein: 29.4g | carbs: 6.9g | net carbs: 2.7g | fiber: 4.2g

Bacon and Avocado Muffin Sandwiches

Prep time: 10 minutes | Cook time: 5 minutes | Serves 2

¼ cup flax meal
1 egg
2 tablespoons heavy cream
2 tablespoons pesto
¼ cup almond flour
¼ teaspoon baking soda

Salt and black pepper to taste
Filling:
2 tablespoons cream cheese
4 slices of bacon
½ medium avocado, sliced

Mix together the dry muffin ingredients in a bowl. Add egg, heavy cream, and pesto, and whisk well with a fork. Season with salt and pepper. Divide the mixture between two ramekins. Place in the microwave and cook for 60-90 seconds. Leave to cool before filling. Meanwhile, in a nonstick skillet, over medium heat, cook the bacon slices until crispy. Transfer to paper towels to soak up excess fat. Set aside.Invert the muffins onto a plate and cut in half, crosswise. Make sandwiches by spreading cream cheese and topping with bacon and avocado.

calories: 512 | fat: 38.1g | protein: 16.5g | carbs: 8.7g | net carbs: 4.6g | fiber: 4.1g

Avocado and Zucchini Eggs

Prep time: 15 minutes | Cook time: 20 minutes | Serves 4

½ red onion, sliced
1 teaspoon canola oil
4 ounces (113 g) pork sausage, sliced
1 cup zucchinis, chopped

1 avocado, pitted, peeled, chopped
6 eggs
Salt and black pepper to season

Warm canola oil in a pan over medium heat and sauté the onion for 3 minutes. Add the smoked sausage and cook for 3-4 minutes more, flipping once. Introduce the zucchinis, season lightly with salt, stir and cook for 5 minutes. Mix in the avocado and turn the heat off. Create 3 holes in the mixture, crack the eggs into each hole, sprinkle with salt and black pepper, and slide the pan into the preheated oven and bake for 6 minutes until the egg whites are set or firm but with the yolks still runny.

calories: 401 | fat: 31.1g | protein: 24.9g | carbs: 6.9g | net carbs: 3.5g | fiber: 3.4g

Mexican Chorizo and Squash Omelet

Prep time: 10 minutes | Cook time: 5 minutes | Serves 4

8 eggs, beaten
8 ounces (227 g) chorizo sausages, chopped
½ cup cotija cheese, crumbled
8 ounces (227 g) roasted

squash, mashed
2 tablespoons olive oil
Salt and black pepper, to taste
Cilantro to garnish

Season the eggs with salt and pepper and stir in the cotija cheese and squash. Heat half of olive oil in a pan over medium heat. Add chorizo sausage and cook until browned on all sides, turning occasionally. Drizzle the remaining olive oil and pour the egg mixture over. Cook for 4 minutes until the eggs are cooked and lightly browned. Remove the pan and run a spatula around the edges of the omelet; slide onto a platter. Fold in half; serve sprinkled with cilantro.

calories: 684 | fat: 52.1g | protein: 38.2g | carbs: 9.3g | net carbs: 8.4g | fiber: 0.9g

Paprika Veggie Bites
Prep time: 5 minutes | Cook time: 0 minutes | Serves 3

1 teaspoon Dijon mustard
½ cup cream cheese
¼ cup mayonnaise
1 cucumber, cut into rounds

1 bell pepper, seeded and cut into 4 pieces lengthwise
1 teaspoon paprika

Mix the Dijon mustard, cream cheese, and mayonnaise in a bowl; stir to combine. Place the cucumber and bell peppers on a serving platter. Divide the cheese mixture between the vegetables. Sprinkle paprika over the vegetable bites. Serve well chilled.

calories: 164 | fat: 17g | protein: 2g | carbs: 3g | net carbs: 2g | fiber: 1g

Cheesy Ham-Egg Cups
Prep time: 5 minutes | Cook time: 13 minutes | Serves 9

9 slices ham
Coarse salt and ground black pepper, to season
1 teaspoon jalapeño pepper,

seeded and minced
½ cup Swiss cheese, shredded
9 eggs

Begin by preheating your oven to 390°F (199°C). Lightly grease a muffin pan with cooking spray. Line each cup with a slice of ham; add salt, black pepper, jalapeño, and cheese. Crack an egg into each ham cup. Bake in the preheated oven about 13 minutes or until the eggs are cooked through. Bon appétit!

calories: 137 | fat: 9g | protein: 12g | carbs: 2g | net carbs: 1g | fiber: 1g

Whiskey-Glazed Chicken Wings
Prep time: 5 minutes | Cook time: 50 to 55 minutes | Serves 5

2 tablespoons extra-virgin olive oil
2 pounds (907 g) chicken wings

1 tablespoon whiskey
1 tablespoon Taco seasoning mix
1 cup tomato purée

Start by preheating your oven to 410°F (210°C). Toss the chicken wings with the other ingredients until well coated. Place the wings onto a rack in the baking pan. Bake in the preheated oven for 50 to 55 minutes until a meat thermometer reads 165°F (74°C). Serve with dipping sauce, if desired. Enjoy!

calories: 293 | fat: 12g | protein: 41g | carbs: 4g | net carbs: 3g | fiber: 1g

Avocado and Ham Stuffed Eggs
Prep time: 5 minutes | Cook time: 12 minutes | Serves 4

4 large eggs
½ avocado, mashed
½ teaspoon yellow mustard

1 garlic clove, minced
2 ounces (57 g) cooked ham, chopped

Place the eggs in a saucepan and fill with enough water. Bring the water to a rolling boil; heat off. Cover and allow the eggs to sit for about 12 minutes; let them cool. Slice the eggs into halves; mix the yolks with the avocado, mustard and garlic. Divide the avocado filling among the egg whites. Top with the chopped ham. Bon appétit!

calories: 128 | fat: 9g | protein: 9g | carbs: 3g | net carbs: 1g | fiber: 2g

Fajita Spareribs
Prep time: 5 minutes | Cook time: 2 hours 30 minutes | Serves 4

2 pounds (907 g) St. Louis-style spareribs
1 tablespoon Fajita seasoning mix

2 cloves garlic, pressed
½ cup chicken bone broth
1 cup tomato purée

Toss the spareribs with the Fajita seasoning mix, garlic, chicken bone broth, and tomato purée until well coated. Arrange the spare ribs on a tinfoil-lined baking sheet. Bake in the preheated oven at 260°F (127°C) for 2 hours and 30 minutes. Place under the preheated broiler for about 8 minutes until the sauce is lightly caramelized. Bon appétit!

calories: 344 | fat: 14g | protein: 50g | carbs: 5g | net carbs: 4g | fiber: 1g

Cheesy Prosciutto Balls
Prep time: 5 minutes | Cook time: 0 minutes | Serves 4

2 ounces (57 g) goat cheese, crumbled
2 ounces (57 g) feta cheese crumbled
3 ounces (85 g) prosciutto,

chopped
1 red bell pepper, seeded and finely chopped
2 tablespoons sesame seeds, toasted

Thoroughly combine the cheese, prosciutto and pepper until everything is well incorporated. Shape the mixture into balls. Arrange these keto balls on a platter and place them in the refrigerator until ready to serve. Roll the keto balls in toasted sesame seeds before serving. Bon appétit!

calories: 176 | fat: 13g | protein: 13g | carbs: 2g | net carbs: 1g | fiber: 1g

Cheddar Anchovies Fat Bombs
Prep time: 5 minutes | Cook time: 0 minutes | Serves 2

2 (2-ounce / 57-g) cans anchovies, drained
⅓ cup cream cheese, chilled
⅓ cup Cheddar cheese,

shredded
1 tablespoon Dijon mustard
2 scallions, chopped

Mix all of the above ingredients until everything is well incorporated. Shape the mixture into bite-sized balls. Serve well chilled and enjoy!

calories: 391 | fat: 27g | protein: 34g | carbs: 3g | net carbs: 2g | fiber: 1g

Baked Cocktail Franks
Prep time: 5 minutes | Cook time: 12 minutes | Serves 10

2 tablespoons olive oil
18 ounces (510 g) cocktail franks
Sea salt and red pepper flakes,

to taste
2 tablespoons wholegrain mustard

Start by preheating your oven to 360°F (182°C). Then, brush a baking pan with olive oil. Place the cocktail franks on the baking pan. Sprinkle them with the salt and red pepper; add in the mustard and toss to combine. Bake approximately 12 minutes until they are golden brown. Serve warm and enjoy!

calories: 155 | fat: 12g | protein: 9g | carbs: 5g | net carbs: 4g | fiber: 1g

Mini Bacon and Kale Muffins

Prep time: 5 minutes | Cook time: 30 minutes | Serves 6

2 slices cooked bacon, chopped
½ cup scallions, chopped
1 garlic clove, minced
1 cup kale, torn into small

pieces
4 eggs, well whisked
4 tablespoons Greek yogurt
Kosher salt and ground white pepper, to season

Add cupcake liners to a mini muffin tin. Mix the bacon with the scallions, garlic, and kale. Fold in the eggs and yogurt. Mix to combine well. Season with salt and ground white pepper; divide the mixture between the cupcake liners. Bake in the preheated oven at 360ºF (182ºC) for 30 minutes or until your muffins are thoroughly cooked and firm. Let cool for about 5 minutes; lastly, run a butter knife around the edges of each muffin to loosen it. Serve warm or at room temperature. Enjoy!

calories: 88 | fat: 7g | protein: 6g | carbs: 2g | net carbs: 1g | fiber: 1g

Blue Cheese and Ranch Dip

Prep time: 5 minutes | Cook time: 0 minutes | Serves 10

½ cup Greek-style yogurt
1 cup blue cheese, crumbled
½ cup mayonnaise
1 tablespoon lime juice

Freshly ground black pepper, to taste
2 tablespoons ranch seasoning

In a mixing bowl, thoroughly combine all ingredients until well incorporated. Serve well chilled with your favorite keto dippers. Bon appétit!

calories: 94 | fat: 8g | protein: 4g | carbs: 1g | net carbs: 1g | fiber: 0g

Traditional Walnut Fat Bombs

Prep time: 5 minutes | Cook time: 1 minute | Serves 10

2 tablespoons keto chocolate protein powder
¼ cup erythritol

5 ounces (142 g) butter
3 ounces (85 g) walnut butter
10 whole walnuts, halved

In a sauté pan, melt the butter, protein powder, and Erythritol over a low flame, for 1 minute. Stir until smooth and well mixed. Spoon the mixture into a piping bag and pipe into mini cupcake liners. Add the walnut halves to each mini cupcake. Place in your refrigerator for at least 2 hours. Bon appétit!

calories: 260 | fat: 27g | protein: 5g | carbs: 3g | net carbs: 1g | fiber: 2g

Avocado-Bacon Sushi

Prep time: 5 minutes | Cook time: 0 minutes | Serves 8

1 teaspoon garlic paste
2 scallions, finely chopped
4 ounces (113 g) cream cheese, softened
1 teaspoon adobo sauce
1 avocado, mashed

2 tablespoons fresh lemon juice
8 bacon slices
1 tablespoon toasted sesame seeds

In a mixing bowl, thoroughly combine the garlic paste, scallions, cream cheese, adobo sauce, avocado, and fresh lemon juice. Divide the mixture evenly between the bacon slices. Roll up tightly and garnish with toasted sesame seeds. Enjoy!

calories: 350 | fat: 37g | protein: 2g | carbs: 4g | net carbs: 2g | fiber: 2g

Herbed Prawn and Veggie Skewers

Prep time: 10 minutes | Cook time: 8 to 9 minutes | Serves 4

2 tablespoons olive oil
1 pound (454 g) king prawns, deveined and cleaned
Sea salt and ground black pepper, to taste
1 teaspoon garlic powder
1 tablespoon fresh sage,

minced
1 teaspoon fresh rosemary
2 tablespoons fresh lime juice
2 tablespoons cilantro, chopped
2 bell peppers, diced
1 cup cherry tomatoes

Heat the olive oil in a wok over a moderately high heat. Now, cook the prawns for 7 to 8 minutes, until they have turned pink. Stir in the seasonings and cook an additional minute, stirring frequently. Remove from the heat and toss with the lime juice and fresh cilantro. Tread the prawns onto bamboo skewers, alternating them with peppers and cherry tomatoes. Serve on a serving platter. Bon appétit!

calories: 179 | fat: 8g | protein:20 g | carbs: 5g | net carbs: 4g | fiber: 1g

Deviled Eggs with Roasted Peppers

Prep time: 5 minutes | Cook time: 9 t0 10 minutes | Serves 10

10 eggs
¼ cup sour cream
¼ cup roasted red pepper, chopped
2 tablespoons olive oil

1 teaspoon stone-ground mustard
1 garlic clove, minced
Sea salt, to taste
1 teaspoon red pepper flakes

Arrange the eggs in a saucepan. Pour in water (1-inch above the eggs) and bring to a boil. Heat off and let it sit, covered, for 9 to 10 minutes. When the eggs are cool enough to handle, peel away the shells; rinse the eggs under running water. Separate egg whites and yolks. Mix the egg yolks with the sour cream, roasted pepper, olive oil, mustard, garlic, and salt. Stuff the eggs, arrange on a nice serving platter, and garnish with red pepper flakes! Enjoy!

calories: 97 | fat: 8g | protein: 6g | carbs: 1g | net carbs: 1g | fiber:0 g

Chicken Wings with Ranch Dressing

Prep time: 10 minutes | Cook time: 50 minutes | Serves 6

2 pounds (907 g) chicken wings, pat dry
Nonstick cooking spray
Sea salt and cayenne pepper, to taste
Ranch Dressing:
¼ cup sour cream
¼ cup coconut milk
½ cup mayonnaise

½ teaspoon lemon juice
1 tablespoon fresh parsley, minced
1 clove garlic, minced
2 tablespoons onion, finely chopped
¼ teaspoon dry mustard
Sea salt and ground black pepper, to taste

Start by preheating your oven to 420ºF (216ºC). Spritz the chicken wings with a cooking spray. Sprinkle the chicken wings with salt and cayenne pepper. Arrange the chicken wings on a parchment-lined baking pan. Bake in the preheated oven for 50 minutes or until the wings are golden and crispy. In the meantime, make the dressing by mixing all of the above ingredients. Serve with warm wings.

calories: 466 | fat: 37g | protein: 27g | carbs: 2g | net carbs: 2g | fiber: 0g

Beef-Stuffed Peppers

Prep time: 5 minutes | Cook time: 30 minutes | Serves 6

¾ pound (340 g) ground beef
½ cup onion, chopped
2 garlic cloves, minced

12 mini peppers, seeded
½ cup Cheddar cheese,
shredded

Heat up a lightly oiled sauté pan over a moderate flame. Brown the ground beef for 3 to 4 minutes, crumbling with a fork. Stir in the onions and garlic; continue to sauté an additional 2 minutes or until tender and aromatic. Cook the peppers in boiling water until just tender or approximately 7 minutes. Arrange the stuffed peppers on a tinfoil-lined baking pan. Divide the beef mixture among the peppers. Top with the shredded Cheddar cheese. Bake in the preheated oven at 360ºF (182ºC) approximately 17 minutes. Serve at room temperature. Bon appétit!

calories: 207 | fat: 10g | protein: 20g | carbs: 7g | net carbs: 5g | fiber: 2g

Turkey and Avocado Roll-Ups

Prep time: 5 minutes | Cook time: 0 minutes | Serves 8

½ fresh lemon, juiced
2 avocados, pitted, peeled and
diced
16 slices cooked turkey

breasts, deli-sliced
Salt and black pepper, to taste
16 slices Swiss cheese

Drizzle fresh lemon juice over your avocados. Place 1-2 avocado pieces on the turkey breast slice. Season with salt and black pepper to taste. Add the slice of Swiss cheese; repeat with the remaining ingredients. Roll them up and arrange on a nice serving platter. Bon appétit!

calories: 332 | fat: 24g | protein: 23g | carbs: 7g | net carbs: 3g | fiber: 4g

Cheesy Ham and Chicken Bites

Prep time: 5 minutes | Cook time: 22 to 24 minutes | Serves 5

5 slices ham
5 chicken fillets, about ¼-inch
thin

3 ounces (85 g) Ricotta cheese
⅓ cup Colby cheese, grated
½ cup tomato purée

Place a slice of ham on each chicken fillet. Thoroughly combine the Ricotta cheese and Colby cheese until everything is well incorporated. Then, divide the cheese mixture between the chicken fillets. Roll them up and secure with toothpicks. Transfer them to a lightly oiled baking tray. Bake in the preheated oven at 390ºF (199ºC) for 18 minutes, flipping them once or twice. Pour the spicy tomato purée over the chicken roll-ups and bake another 4 to 6 minutes or until everything is thoroughly cooked. Bon appétit!

calories: 289 | fat: 11g | protein:37 g | carbs: 7g | net carbs: 5g | fiber: 2g

Spicy Chicken Drumettes

Prep time: 5 minutes | Cook time: 23 minutes | Serves 6

2 pounds (907 g) chicken
drumettes
Sea salt and ground black
pepper, to taste
½ teaspoon paprika
1 teaspoon cayenne pepper

1 teaspoon dried oregano
⅓ cup hot sauce
1 tablespoon stone-ground
mustard
1 teaspoon garlic powder

Pat dry the chicken drumettes with paper towels. Season them with salt, black pepper, paprika, cayenne pepper, and oregano. Brush the drumettes with cooking oil and transfer to a roasting pan. Bake at 420ºF (216ºC) for 18 minutes. Toss with the hot sauce, mustard and garlic powder; broil for 5 minutes more or until the chicken drumettes are golden brown and thoroughly cooked. Bon appétit!

calories: 179 | fat: 3g | protein: 34g | carbs: 2g | net carbs: 1g | fiber: 1g

Romano Cheese Meatballs

Prep time: 5 minutes | Cook time: 20 minutes | Serves 10

½ ground turkey
1 pound (454 g) ground beef
4 ounces (113 g) pork rinds
¼ cup coconut milk
1 shallot, chopped

2 garlic cloves, minced
Sea salt and ground black
pepper, to taste
½ cup Romano cheese, grated

Thoroughly combine all ingredients in a mixing bowl; shape the mixture into bite-sized meatballs. Place your meatballs on a parchment-lined baking sheet; brush your meatballs with olive oil. Bake for 10 minutes; rotate the pan and bake for a further 10 minutes. Serve with cocktail sticks and enjoy!

calories: 247 | fat: 18g | protein: 19g | carbs: 1g | net carbs: 1g | fiber: 0g

Chicken Wings in Spicy Tomato Sauce

Prep time: 10 minutes | Cook time: 45 minutes | Serves 6

3 pounds (1.4 kg) chicken
wings
Sea salt and ground black
Sauce:
2 vine-ripe tomatoes
1 onion

pepper, to taste
½ teaspoon paprika
½ teaspoon cayenne pepper

2 garlic cloves
1 teaspoon chili pepper

Start by preheating your oven to 400ºF (205ºC). Set a wire rack inside a rimmed baking sheet. Season the chicken wings with salt, black pepper, paprika, and cayenne pepper. Bake the wings approximately 45 minutes or until the skin is crispy. To make the sauce, purée all ingredients in your food processor. Bon appétit!

calories: 309 | fat: 8g | protein: 50g | carbs: 5g | net carbs: 4g | fiber: 1g

Baked Romano Zucchini Rounds

Prep time: 5 minutes | Cook time: 15 minutes | Serves 6

2 tablespoons olive oil
2 eggs
½ teaspoon smoked paprika
Sea salt and ground black
pepper, to taste

2 pounds (907 g) zucchini,
sliced into rounds
½ cup Romano cheese,
shredded

Begin by preheating an oven to 420ºF (216ºC). Coat a rimmed baking sheet with Silpat mat or parchment paper. In a mixing bowl, whisk the olive oil with eggs. Add in the paprika, salt, and black pepper. Now, dip the zucchini slices into the egg mixture. Top with the shredded Romano cheese. Arrange the zucchini rounds on the baking sheet; bake for 15 minutes until they are golden. Serve at room temperature.

calories: 137 | fat: 10g | protein: 9g | carbs: 6g | net carbs: 4g | fiber: 2g

Crab Egg Scramble

Prep time: 15 minutes | Cook time: 0 minutes | Serves 4

1 tablespoon olive oil
8 eggs
Sauce:
¾ cup crème fraiche
½ cup chives, chopped

6 ounces (170 g) crabmeat
Salt and black pepper to taste

½ teaspoon garlic powder
Salt to taste

Whisk the eggs with a fork in a bowl, and season with salt and black pepper. Set a sauté pan over medium heat and warm olive oil. Add in the eggs and scramble them. Stir in crabmeat and cook until cooked thoroughly. In a mixing dish, combine crème fraiche and garlic powder. Season with salt and sprinkle with chives. Serve the eggs with the white sauce.

calories: 406 | fat: 32.6g | protein: 23.3g | carbs: 4.3g | net carbs: 4.2g | fiber: 0.1g

Greek-Style Ricotta Olive Dip

Prep time: 5 minutes | Cook time: 0 minutes | Serves 8

10 ounces (284 g) ricotta cheese
4 tablespoons Greek yogurt
½ teaspoon cayenne pepper
4 tablespoons olives, sliced

½ teaspoon shallot powder
½ teaspoon garlic salt
½ teaspoon black pepper
4 tablespoons cilantro, minced

Thoroughly combine the ricotta cheese, Greek yogurt, cayenne pepper, olives, shallot powder, garlic salt, and black pepper in a mixing bowl. Transfer to a nice serving bowl. Garnish with cilantro, serve and enjoy your party!

calories: 72 | fat: 6g | protein: 4g | carbs: 2g | net carbs: 2g | fiber: 0g

Lettuce Wraps with Ham and Tomato

Prep time: 10 minutes | Cook time: 0 minutes | Serves 5

10 Boston lettuce leaves, washed and rinsed well
1 tablespoon lemon juice, freshly squeezed

10 tablespoons cream cheese
10 thin ham slices
1 tomato, chopped
1 red chili pepper, chopped

Drizzle lemon juice over the lettuce leaves. Spread cream cheese over the lettuce leaves. Add a ham slice on each leaf. Divide chopped tomatoes between the lettuce leaves. Top with chili peppers and arrange on a nice serving platter. Bon appétit!

calories: 148 | fat: 10g | protein: 11g | carbs: 4g | net carbs: 3g | fiber: 1g

Mozzarella Meatballs

Prep time: 10 minutes | Cook time: 18 to 25 minutes | Serves 8

½ pound (227 g) ground pork
1 pound (454 g) ground turkey
1 garlic clove, minced
4 tablespoons pork rinds, crushed
2 tablespoons shallots,

chopped
4 ounces (113 g) Mozzarella string cheese, cubed
1 ripe tomato, puréed
Salt and ground black pepper, to taste

In a mixing bowl, thoroughly combine all ingredients, except for the cheese. Shape the mixture into bite-sized balls. Press 1 cheese cube into the center of each ball. Place the meatballs on a parchment-lined baking sheet. Bake in the preheated oven at 350°F (180°C) for 18 to 25 minutes. Bon appétit!

calories: 389 | fat: 31g | protein: 24g | carbs: 2g | net carbs:1 g | fiber: 1g

Deviled Eggs with Chives

Prep time: 5 minutes | Cook time: 15 minutes | Serves 8

8 eggs
2 tablespoons cream cheese
1 teaspoon Dijon mustard
1 tablespoon mayonnaise
1 tablespoon tomato purée, no sugar added

1 teaspoon balsamic vinegar
Sea salt and freshly ground black pepper, to taste
¼ teaspoon cayenne pepper
2 tablespoons chives, chopped

Place the eggs in a single layer in a saucepan. Add water to cover the eggs and bring to a boil. Cover, turn off the heat, and let the eggs stand for 15 minutes. Drain the eggs and peel them under cold running water. Slice the eggs in half lengthwise; remove the yolks and thoroughly combine them with cream cheese, mustard, mayo, tomato purée, vinegar, salt, black, and cayenne pepper. Next, divide the yolk mixture among egg whites. Garnish with fresh chives and enjoy!

calories: 149 | fat: 11g | protein: 10g | carbs: 2g | net carbs: 2g | fiber: 0g

Italian Cheddar Cheese Crisps

Prep time: 5 minutes | Cook time: 8 minutes | Serves 4

1 cup sharp Cheddar cheese, grated
¼ teaspoon ground black

pepper
½ teaspoon cayenne pepper
1 teaspoon Italian seasoning

Start by preheating an oven to 400°F (205°C). Line a baking sheet with a parchment paper. Mix all of the above ingredients until well combined. Then, place tablespoon-sized heaps of the mixture onto the prepared baking sheet. Bake at the preheated oven for 8 minutes, until the edges start to brown. Allow the cheese crisps to cool slightly; then, place them on paper towels to drain the excess fat. Enjoy!

calories: 134 | fat: 11g | protein: 5g | carbs: 1g | net carbs: 1g | fiber: 0g

Hearty Burger Dip

Prep time: 10 minutes | Cook time: 1 hour 30 minutes | Serves 2

¼ pound (113 g) ground pork
¼ pound (113 g) ground turkey
½ red onion, chopped
1 garlic clove, minced
1 serrano pepper, chopped
1 bell pepper, chopped
2 ounces (57 g) sour cream

½ cup Provolone cheese, grated
2 ounces (57 g) tomato purée
½ teaspoon mustard
½ teaspoon dried oregano
½ teaspoon dried basil
¼ teaspoon dried marjoram

Place all of the above ingredients, except for the sour cream and Provolone cheese in your slow cooker. Cook for 1 hour 30 minutes at Low setting. Afterwards, fold in sour cream and cheese. Serve warm with celery sticks if desired. Bon appétit!

calories: 423 | fat: 29g | protein: 32g | carbs: 5g | net carbs: 4g | fiber: 1g

Lemony Bacon Chips

Prep time: 5 minutes | Cook time: 10 minutes | Serves 12

1½ pounds (680 g) bacon, cut into 1-inch squares
¼ cup lemon juice

1 teaspoon Ranch seasoning mix
1 tablespoon hot sauce

Toss the bacon squares with the lemon juice, Ranch seasoning mix, and hot sauce. Arrange the bacon squares on a parchment-lined baking sheet. Roast in the preheated oven at 375°F (190°C) approximately 10 minutes or until crisp. Let it cool completely before storing. Bon appétit!

calories: 232 | fat: 23g | protein: 7g | carbs: 1g | net carbs: 1g | fiber: 0g

Ranch Chicken-Bacon Dip

Prep time: 10 minutes | Cook time: 20 minutes | Serves 6

3 slices bacon
1½ cups shredded cooked chicken
1 (8-ounce / 227-g) package cream cheese, softened

½ cup Buffalo sauce
½ cup ranch dressing
Chopped green onions, for garnish (optional)

Preheat the oven to 375°F (190°C). In a skillet over medium heat, fry the bacon until crispy. Set aside on a paper towel-lined plate to cool, then chop. In a large bowl, combine the shredded chicken, cream cheese, Buffalo sauce, ranch dressing, and bacon; mix well. Transfer the chicken mixture to a shallow 1-quart baking dish and bake for 20 minutes, until warm throughout. Garnish with chopped green onions, if desired.

calories: 286 | fat: 25g | protein: 11g | carbs: 3g | net carbs: 3g | fiber: 0g

Lime Brussels Sprout Chips

Prep time: 15 minutes | Cook time: 10 minutes | Serves 2

3 cups Brussels sprouts leaves
Juice of ½ lime
2½ tablespoons avocado oil or

melted coconut oil
Pink Himalayan salt

Preheat the oven to 400°F (205°C). Line a rimmed baking sheet with parchment paper. Trim off the flat stem ends of the Brussels sprouts and separate the leaves. You should end up with 2 to 3 cups of leaves. Place the separated leaves in a large bowl and add the lime juice. Add the oil and season with salt to taste. Toss until the leaves are evenly coated. Spread the leaves evenly on the prepared baking sheet and bake for 7 to 10 minutes, until lightly golden brown.

calories: 173 | fat: 18g | protein: 2g | carbs: 4g | net carbs: 2g | fiber: 2g

Classic Caprese Skewers

Prep time: 15 minutes | Cook time: 0 minutes | Serves 6

8 ounces (227 g) ciliegini Mozzarella balls, drained and halved
Marinade:
¼ cup extra-virgin olive oil
1 clove garlic, pressed or minced
1 tablespoon chopped fresh parsley

9 grape tomatoes, halved
18 fresh basil leaves

1 tablespoon dried ground oregano
1 tablespoon fresh lemon juice
Kosher salt and ground black pepper, to taste

In a medium-sized bowl, combine the Mozzarella balls with the marinade ingredients. Stir well and cover; place in the refrigerator to marinate for 1 hour. To assemble, place a Mozzarella ball, a basil leaf (folded in half lengthwise if needed), and a grape tomato half on a toothpick. Serve right away or store in the refrigerator until ready to serve.

calories: 174 | fat: 16g | protein: 8g | carbs: 2g | net carbs: 2g | fiber: 0g

Cheesy Charcuterie Board

Prep time: 15 minutes | Cook time: 0 minutes | Serves 6 to 8

4 ounces (113 g) prosciutto, sliced
4 ounces (113 g) Calabrese salami, sliced
4 ounces (113 g) capicola, sliced
7 ounces (198 g) Parrano Gouda cheese
7 ounces (198 g) aged

Manchego cheese
7 ounces (198 g) Brie cheese
½ cup roasted almonds
½ cup mixed olives
12 cornichons (small, tart pickles)
1 sprig fresh rosemary or other herbs of choice, for garnish

Arrange the meats, cheeses, and almonds on a large wooden cutting board. Place the olives and pickles in separate bowls and set them on or alongside the cutting board. Garnish with a spring of rosemary or other fresh herbs of your choice.

calories: 445 | fat: 35g | protein: 31g | carbs: 3g | net carbs: 2g | fiber: 1g

Cheese Crisps with Basil

Prep time: 5 minutes | Cook time: 8 minutes | Serves 2

½ cup shredded Cheddar cheese
½ cup shredded Parmesan

cheese
½ teaspoon dried basil
¼ teaspoon garlic powder

Preheat the oven to 400°F (205°C). Line a baking sheet with parchment paper. In a medium-sized bowl, mix together all the ingredients. Scoop up a heaping tablespoon of the mixture and place it on the parchment paper. Repeat, making a total of 8 small piles, spacing them 2 inches apart to prevent the cheese from running together. Bake for 8 minutes, until golden brown. Let cool for 5 minutes before removing from the parchment paper.

calories: 195 | fat: 13g | protein: 15g | carbs: 3g | net carbs: 3g | fiber: 0g

Creamy Herb Dip

Prep time: 15 minutes | Cook time: 5 minutes | Serves 7

1 (8-ounce / 227-g) package cream cheese
½ cup heavy whipping cream
¼ cup sour cream
3 tablespoons finely chopped fresh chives

2 tablespoons finely chopped onions
2 tablespoons finely chopped fresh parsley
½ teaspoon garlic powder

Place the cream cheese and heavy whipping cream in a microwave-safe bowl and microwave on high for 1 minute; stir and repeat until the texture is smooth. Add the remaining ingredients and stir to combine. Place in the refrigerator to chill for at least 30 minutes before serving.

calories: 156 | fat: 14g | protein: 3g | carbs: 2g | net carbs: 2g | fiber: 1g

Crispy Fried Dill Pickles

Prep time: 5 minutes | Cook time: 5 minutes | Serves 2

¼ cup avocado oil or coconut oil
3 tablespoons mayonnaise
¼ cup finely grated Parmesan cheese

3 tablespoons golden flaxseed meal
⅛ teaspoon garlic powder
12 dill pickle rounds

Heat the oil in a small skillet over medium-high heat. Place the mayonnaise in a bowl. In another bowl, mix together the Parmesan cheese, flaxseed meal, and garlic powder. Place the pickle slices on a paper towel and cover with another paper towel to dry the tops. Dip each pickle slice into the mayonnaise and then into the Parmesan and flaxseed "breading," making sure to coat the slices evenly. When the temperature of the oil reaches 400°F (205°C), gently place the breaded pickles in the hot oil and fry until golden and crispy, 1 to 2 minutes per side. Place the fried pickles on a paper towel-lined plate to absorb the excess oil before serving.

calories: 376 | fat: 38g | protein: 8g | carbs: 5g | net carbs: 1g | fiber: 4g

Fresh Homemade Guacamole

Prep time: 15 minutes | Cook time: 0 minutes | Serves 4

2 ripe avocados
½ tomato, chopped
¼ cup minced red onions
2 tablespoons finely chopped fresh cilantro

1 tablespoon fresh lime juice
½ teaspoon minced garlic
½ teaspoon salt
1 tablespoon sour cream (optional)

Slice the avocados in half lengthwise, remove the pits, and scoop the flesh into a medium-sized serving bowl. Mash the avocado flesh. Stir in the tomato, onions, cilantro, lime juice, garlic, and salt. Fold in the sour cream, if using. Serve right away or place in the refrigerator to chill until ready to serve.

calories: 133 | fat: 12g | protein: 2g | carbs: 8g | net carbs: 3g | fiber: 5g

Oven-Baked Prosciutto-Wrapped Asparagus

Prep time: 5 minutes | Cook time: 12 minutes | Serves 6

18 asparagus spears, ends trimmed
2 tablespoons coconut oil, melted

6 slices prosciutto
1 teaspoon garlic powder

Preheat the oven to 400°F (205°C). Line a rimmed baking sheet with parchment paper. Place the asparagus and coconut oil in a large zip-top plastic bag. Seal and toss until the asparagus is evenly coated. Wrap a slice of prosciutto around 3 grouped asparagus spears. Repeat with the remaining prosciutto and asparagus, making a total of 6 bundles. Arrange the bundles in a single layer on the lined baking sheet. Sprinkle the garlic powder over the bundles. Bake for 8 to 12 minutes, until the asparagus is tender.

calories: 122 | fat: 10g | protein: 8g | carbs: 3g | net carbs: 2g | fiber: 1g

Bacon-Wrapped Enoki Mushrooms

Prep time: 10 minutes | Cook time: 40 minutes | Serves 5

½ pound (227 g) enoki mushrooms
5 slices bacon, cut into halves
Dipping Sauce:
½ cup water
2 tablespoons sesame oil
2 tablespoons coconut aminos
1 teaspoon monk fruit powder

1 large clove garlic, minced
½ teaspoon ground ginger
1 teaspoon Chinese five-spice powder
Kosher salt and ground black pepper, to taste

Wrap the mushrooms with the bacon and secure with toothpicks. Arrange on a parchment-lined baking tray and bake at 380°F (193°C) for 40 minutes, flipping once halfway through cooking. In the meantime, make the sauce by whisking all ingredients in a wok or deep saucepan. Cook over medium heat until thickened and reduced. Serve the bacon dippers with the sauce on the side.

calories: 323 | fat: 33g | protein: 2g | carbs: 5g | net carbs: 3g | fiber: 2g

Mexican Shrimp-Stuffed Avocados

Prep time: 10 minutes | Cook time: 15 minutes | Serves 4

2 avocados, halved and pitted
12 large cooked shrimp, peeled and deveined
3 tablespoons salsa

¼ cup shredded Mexican cheese blend
Finely chopped fresh cilantro, for garnish (optional)
Sour cream, for garnish (optional)

Preheat the oven to 350ºF (180ºC). Line a rimmed baking sheet with parchment paper. Rinse the shrimp and halve lengthwise. Place in a bowl and top with the salsa. Stir to coat the shrimp evenly with the salsa. Place the avocado halves cut side up on the lined baking sheet. Fill each half with salsa-coated shrimp and top with the cheese. Bake for 15 minutes, until the cheese is melted. Serve garnished with cilantro and/or topped with sour cream, if desired.

calories: 185 | fat: 13g | protein: 11g | carbs: 7g | net carbs: 6g | fiber: 1g

Margherita Pizza with Mushrooms

Prep time: 5 minutes | Cook time: 18 minutes | Serves 4

4 medium portobello mushroom caps, stemmed
Dash of salt
¼ cup no-sugar-added marinara sauce
4 tomato slices

4 ounces (113 g) fresh Mozzarella, cut into 4 slices
4 teaspoons extra-virgin olive oil or avocado oil
2 small cloves or 1 large clove garlic, minced
1 tablespoon chopped fresh basil, for garnish

Preheat the oven to 375ºF (190ºC). Place a wire rack in a rimmed baking sheet. Set the mushroom caps on top of the wire rack. Place 1 tablespoon of marinara and a slice of tomato in each cap, then a Mozzarella slice. Drizzle with olive oil, then top with the minced garlic. Bake for 15 to 18 minutes, until the cheese is melted and the mushrooms are tender. Remove from the oven and top with the basil before serving.

calories: 141 | fat: 10g | protein: 8g | carbs: 6g | net carbs: 4g | fiber: 2g

Herbed Provolone Cheese Chips

Prep time: 5 minutes | Cook time: 9 minutes | Serves 5

6 ounces (170 g) (170 g) provolone cheese, grated
½ teaspoon garlic powder
½ teaspoon shallot powder
¼ teaspoon ground black pepper

1 teaspoon dried dill
½ teaspoon dried oregano
1 teaspoon paprika

Place the grated provolone cheese in small heaps on a roasting pan lined with Silpat mat. Make sure to leave enough room in between them. Sprinkle the herbs and spices over them. Bake in the preheated oven at 395ºF (202ºC) for about 9 minutes, Transfer to a cooling rack and let it sit for 20 minutes before serving. Serve with a homemade salsa sauce if desired.

calories: 119 | fat: 9g | protein: 9g | carbs: 1g | net carbs: 1g | fiber: 0g

Crispy Five Seed Crackers

Prep time: 5 minutes | Cook time: 1 hour | Serves 12

¼ cup chia seeds
¼ cup sesame seeds
¼ cup flax seeds
¼ cup sunflower seeds
¼ cup pumpkin seeds
¼ cup almond meal

1 teaspoon psyllium husk powder
Coarse sea salt, to taste
¼ teaspoon ground cumin
¾ cup boiling water
4 tablespoons coconut oil, melted

Thoroughly combine the seeds, almond meal, psyllium husk powder, salt, and ground cumin until well mixed. Pour the boiling water over the seed mixture; add in the melted coconut oil. Spread out the batter thinly on a tinfoil-lined baking pan. Bake in the preheated oven at 310ºF (154ºC) for 30 minutes. Rotate the pan and continue to bake an additional 25 to 30 minutes. Heat off. Allow your crackers to dry in the warm oven for 50 to 60 minutes longer. Bon appétit!

calories: 128 | fat: 13g | protein: 4g | carbs: 3g | net carbs: 1g | fiber: 2g

Chapter 13 Desserts

Chocolate Almond Bark
Prep time: 10 minutes | Cook time: 0 minutes | Makes 15 pieces

¾ cup coconut oil
¼ cup confectioners' erythritol–monk fruit blend; less sweet: 3 tablespoons

3 tablespoons dark cocoa powder
½ cup slivered almonds
¾ teaspoon almond extract

Line the baking pan with parchment paper and set aside. In the microwave-safe bowl, melt the coconut oil in the microwave in 10-second intervals. In the medium bowl, whisk together the melted coconut oil, confectioners' erythritol–monk fruit blend, and cocoa powder until fully combined. Stir in the slivered almonds and almond extract. Pour the mixture into the prepared baking pan and spread evenly. Put the pan in the freezer for about 20 minutes, or until the chocolate bark is solid. Once the chocolate bark is solid, break apart into 15 roughly even pieces to serve. Store the chocolate bark in an airtight container in the freezer. Allow to slightly thaw about 5 minutes before eating. Thaw only what you will be eating.

calories: 118 | fat: 13.0g | protein: 1.0g | carbs: 1.0g | net carbs: 0g | fiber: 1.0g

Chocolate Popsicles
Prep time: 5 minutes | Cook time: 0 minutes | Serves 8

1¾ cups plain yogurt
4 tablespoons full-fat milk
5 tablespoons cocoa powder

½ teaspoon pure vanilla essence
¾ cup Swerve

Place all ingredients in a bowl of your food processor. Pour into popsicle molds and freeze. Bon appétit!

calories: 60 | fat: 2.5g | protein: 3.0g | carbs: 5.4g | net carbs: 4.1g | fiber: 1.3g

Cinnamon Crusted Almonds
Prep time: 5 minutes | Cook time: 45 minutes | Makes 2½ cups

2½ cups whole raw almonds
2 tablespoons unsalted butter, melted
1 large egg white
½ teaspoon vanilla extract

¼ cup brown or golden erythritol–monk fruit blend; less sweet: 2 tablespoons
1 teaspoon ground cinnamon
¼ teaspoon sea salt

Preheat the oven to 275°F (135°C). Line the baking sheet with parchment paper and set aside. In a large bowl, toss the almonds in the melted butter. In another large bowl, using an electric mixer on medium high, lightly beat the egg white for about 1 minute, until frothy. Add the vanilla to the egg white and mix until just combined. Add the almonds and stir until well coated. In the small bowl, combine the brown erythritol–monk fruit blend, cinnamon, and salt and sprinkle over the nut mixture. Toss to coat and spread evenly on the prepared baking sheet. Bake for 45 minutes, stirring occasionally, until golden. Allow to cool fully, 15 to 20 minutes, before eating. Store in an airtight container at room temperature for up to 1 week.

calories: 385 | fat: 33.9g | protein: 13.0g | carbs: 13.0g | net carbs: 4.9g | fiber: 8.1g

Coconut Brownies
Prep time: 10 minutes | Cook time: 20 minutes | Serves 10

½ cup butter, melted
1¼ cups coconut flour
1 teaspoon baking powder

⅓ cup cocoa powder, unsweetened
1 cup Xylitol

Mix all ingredients in the order listed above. Scrape the batter into a parchment-lined baking pan. Bake in the preheated oven at 360°F (182°C) approximately 20 minutes or until a tester comes out clean. Transfer to a cooling rack for 1 hour before slicing and serving. Bon appétit!

calories: 124 | fat: 12.8g | protein: 0.8g | carbs: 3.2g | net carbs: 1.4g | fiber: 1.8g

Pecan Pralines
Prep time: 5 minutes | Cook time: 15 minutes | Makes 18 clusters

4 tablespoons (½ stick) unsalted butter, at room temperature
¼ cup granulated erythritol–monk fruit blend

1½ cups pecan halves
½ teaspoon salt
2 tablespoons heavy whipping cream

Line the baking sheet with parchment paper and set aside. In the skillet, melt the butter over medium-high heat. Using the silicone spatula, stir in the erythritol–monk fruit blend and combine well, making sure to dissolve the sugar in the butter. Stir in the pecan halves and salt. Once the pecans are completely covered in the glaze, add the heavy cream and quickly stir. When the heavy cream bubbles and evaporates, remove from the heat immediately. Quickly spoon the clusters of 4 to 5 pecan halves each onto the prepared baking sheet and allow to fully cool and set, 15 to 20 minutes, before enjoying. Store leftovers in an airtight container on the counter or in the refrigerator for up 5 days.

calories: 86 | fat: 9.0g | protein: 1.0g | carbs: 1.0g | net carbs: 0g | fiber: 1.0g

Strawberries Coated with Chocolate Chips
Prep time: 10 minutes | Cook time: 5 minutes | Makes 15

5 ounces (142 g) sugar-free dark chocolate chips
1 tablespoon vegetable

shortening or lard
15 medium whole strawberries, fresh or frozen

Line the baking sheet with parchment paper and set aside. In the microwave-safe bowl, combine the chocolate and shortening. Melt in the microwave in 30-second intervals, stirring in between. Dip the strawberries into the melted chocolate mixture and place them on the prepared baking sheet. Put the strawberries in the freezer for 10 to 15 minutes to set before serving. Store leftovers in an airtight container in the refrigerator for up to 3 days.

calories: 216 | fat: 18.0g | protein: 4.0g | carbs: 11.0g | net carbs: 6.0g | fiber: 5.0g

Cream Cheese Fat Bombs

Prep time: 10 minutes | Cook time: 0 minutes | Makes 30 bombs

8 ounces (227 g) full-fat cream cheese, at room temperature
8 tablespoons (1 stick) unsalted butter, at room temperature

3 tablespoons confectioners' erythritol–monk fruit blend
3 tablespoons coconut oil
½ teaspoon vanilla extract

In the large mixing bowl, using an electric mixer on high, beat the cream cheese and butter for 2 to 3 minutes, until light and fluffy, stopping and scraping the bowl once or twice, as needed. Add the confectioners' erythritol–monk fruit blend, coconut oil, and vanilla and mix until well combined. Scoop the mixture into a pastry bag and pipe into the molds or cupcake liners. Put the molds in the freezer for 1 hour to firm. Pop out the fat bombs to serve. Store in an airtight container in the freezer for up to 3 weeks.

calories: 66 | fat: 6.9g | protein: 0g | carbs: 0g | net carbs: 0g | fiber: 0g

Peanut Butter and Chocolate Fat Bombs

Prep time: 5 minutes | Cook time: 5 minutes | Makes 24 bombs

½ cup no-sugar-added peanut butter
½ cup coconut oil
¼ cup unsweetened cocoa powder

⅓ cup confectioners' erythritol–monk fruit blend; less sweet: 2½ tablespoons
¼ teaspoon sea salt

In the small microwave-safe bowl, melt the peanut butter, coconut oil, and cocoa powder in the microwave in 30-second intervals, mixing in between. Once the peanut butter mixture is completely melted, stir in the confectioners' erythritol–monk fruit blend and salt. Pour the mixture into the silicone molds and put in the freezer for about 30 minutes, or until they are completely set. Remove the bombs from the silicone molds to serve. To store, transfer to an airtight container and put in the freezer for up to 3 weeks.

calories: 70 | fat: 7.1g | protein: 1.0g | carbs: 1.9g | net carbs: 1.9g | fiber: 0g

Posset

Prep time: 5 minutes | Cook time: 10 minutes | Serves 4

2½ cups heavy whipping cream
½ cup granulated erythritol–monk fruit blend
¼ cup freshly squeezed lemon juice

2 tablespoons freshly squeezed lime juice
½ teaspoon orange extract
¼ teaspoon sea salt
¼ cup blueberries, for garnish (optional)

In the small saucepan, cook the heavy cream and erythritol–monk fruit blend over medium heat for 6 minutes, or until the sweetener has dissolved. Stir constantly so the mixture does not boil over. Remove the cream mixture from the heat and stir in the lemon juice, lime juice, orange extract, and salt. Pour the mixture into the ramekins and cover with plastic wrap. Chill for at least 6 hours or overnight to allow the mixture to fully set before serving. Garnish with the blueberries (if using). Store leftovers in an airtight container for up to 5 days in the refrigerator.

calories: 520 | fat: 54.8g | protein: 3.0g | carbs: 6.0g | net carbs: 6.0g | fiber: 0g

Strawberry Mousse

Prep time: 10 minutes | Cook time: 0 minutes | Serves 6

8 ounces (227 g) strawberries, sliced
¼ cup granulated erythritol–monk fruit blend
½ ounce (14 g) full-fat cream

cheese, at room temperature
1 cup heavy whipping cream, divided
⅛ teaspoon vanilla extract
⅛ teaspoon salt

Put the large metal bowl in the freezer to chill for at least 5 minutes. In a blender, purée the strawberries and erythritol–monk fruit blend. Set aside. In the chilled large bowl, using an electric mixer on medium high, beat the cream cheese and ¼ cup of heavy cream until well combined. Add the vanilla and salt and mix to combine. Add the remaining ¾ cup of heavy cream and beat on high for 1 to 3 minutes, until very stiff peaks form. Gently fold the purée into the whipped cream. Refrigerate for at least 1 hour and up to overnight before serving. Serve in short glasses or small mason jars.

calories: 160 | fat: 15.9g | protein: 0.9g | carbs: 4.0g | net carbs: 3.0g | fiber: 1.0g

Mocha Mousse

Prep time: 10 minutes | Cook time: 0 minutes | Serves 6

1 (13.5-ounce / 383-g) can coconut cream, chilled overnight
3 tablespoons granulated erythritol–monk fruit blend; less sweet: 2 tablespoons

2 tablespoons unsweetened cocoa powder, plus more for dusting
1 teaspoon instant espresso powder
¼ teaspoon salt

Put the large metal bowl in the freezer to chill for at least 1 hour. In the chilled large bowl, using an electric mixer on high, combine the coconut cream (adding it by the spoonful and reserving the water that has separated), erythritol–monk fruit blend, the cocoa powder, espresso powder, and salt and beat for 3 to 5 minutes, until stiff peaks form, stopping and scraping the bowl once or twice, as needed. If the consistency is too thick, add the reserved water from the coconut cream 1 tablespoon at a time to thin. Serve immediately in a cold glass, dusted with cocoa powder. Store leftovers in an airtight container for up to 5 days in the refrigerator.

calories: 126 | fat: 11.9g | protein: 0g | carbs: 3.1g | net carbs: 2.0g | fiber: 1.1g

Super Coconut Cupcakes

Prep time: 15 minutes | Cook time: 15 minutes | Serves 9

6 eggs, beaten
½ cup coconut oil, melted
3 tablespoons granulated Swerve
2 tablespoons flaxseed meal
⅓ cup coconut flour

1 teaspoon baking powder
A pinch of salt
A pinch of freshly grated nutmeg
1 teaspoon lemon zest
1 teaspoon coconut extract

Start by preheating your oven to 360°F (182°C). Coat a muffin pan with cupcake liners. Beat the eggs with the coconut oil and granulated Swerve until frothy. In another mixing bowl, thoroughly combine the remaining ingredients. Stir this dry mixture into the wet mixture; mix again to combine. Spoon the batter into the prepared muffin pan. Bake for 13 to 15 minutes, or until a tester comes out dry and clean. To serve, sprinkle with some extra granulated Swerve if desired. Bon appétit!

calories: 164 | fat: 16.8g | protein: 2.2g | carbs: 1.6g | net carbs: 0.7g | fiber: 0.9g

Anise Cookies

Prep time: 5 minutes | Cook time: 20 minutes | Serves 8

2 tablespoons coconut oil
1 tablespoon coconut milk
1 egg, whisked
1 cup coconut flour
1 cup almond flour
1 teaspoon baking powder

¼ cup monk fruit powder
1 teaspoon pure anise extract
¼ teaspoon ground cloves
½ teaspoon ground cinnamon
A pinch of salt

In a mixing bowl, beat the coconut oil, coconut milk, and egg. In a separate bowl, mix the flour, baking powder, monk fruit, anise extract, ground cloves, cinnamon, and salt. Add the dry mixture to the wet mixture; mix to combine well. Shape the mixture into small balls and arrange them on a parchment-lined baking pan. Bake at 360°F (182°C) for 13 minutes. Transfer to cooling racks for 10 minutes. Bon appétit!

calories: 143 | fat: 12.9g | protein: 3.6g | carbs: 5.1g | net carbs: 2.7g | fiber: 2.4g

Chocolate Lava Cake

Prep time: 15 minutes | Cook time: 10 minutes | Serves 4

2 tablespoons coconut flour
4 tablespoons cocoa powder, unsweetened
½ teaspoon baking powder
3 eggs
1½ ounces (43 g) butter, melted

1½ ounces (43 g) heavy cream
A pinch of Himalayan salt
¼ teaspoon cardamom
½ teaspoon cinnamon
½ teaspoon rum extract
½ teaspoon vanilla extract
6 tablespoons xylitol

Thoroughly combine the flour, cocoa powder, and baking powder. In another mixing bowl, whisk the eggs with the butter and heavy cream; fold this wet mixture into the dry mixture. Add in the remaining ingredients; mix until everything is well blended. Spritz 4 ceramic mugs with nonstick cooking spray; pour the batter into the prepared mugs. Bake in the preheated oven at 350°F (180°C) for 10 minutes or until the edges have set but the middle is still soft. Lift each lava cake onto a serving plate with a spatula. Bon appétit!

calories: 169 | fat: 15.7g | protein: 4.4g | carbs: 6.0g | net carbs: 3.4g | fiber: 2.6g

Rum Brownies

Prep time: 15 minutes | Cook time: 22 minutes | Serves 8

⅔ cup almond flour
½ cup coconut flour
1 teaspoon baking powder
1 cup xylitol
½ cup cocoa powder, unsweetened
2 eggs
6 ounces (170 g) butter, melted

3 ounces (85 g) baking chocolate, unsweetened and melted
2 tablespoons rum
A pinch of salt
A pinch of freshly grated nutmeg
¼ teaspoon ground cinnamon

In a mixing bowl, thoroughly combine dry ingredients. In a separate bowl, mix all the wet ingredients until well combined. Stir dry mixture into wet ingredients. Evenly spread the batter into a parchment-lined baking dish. Bake in the preheated oven at 360°F (182°C) for 20 to 22 minutes, until your brownies are set. Cut into squares and serve.

calories: 321 | fat: 30.1g | protein: 5.7g | carbs: 6.2g | net carbs: 2.6g | fiber: 3.6g

Penuche Bars

Prep time: 15 minutes | Cook time: 0 minutes | Serves 10

½ stick butter
2 tablespoons tahini (sesame paste)
½ cup almond butter
1 teaspoon Stevia

2 ounces (57 g) baker's chocolate, sugar-free
A pinch of salt
A pinch of grated nutmeg
½ teaspoon cinnamon powder

Microwave the butter for 30 to 35 seconds. Fold in the tahini, almond butter, Stevia, and chocolate. Sprinkle with salt, nutmeg, and cinnamon; whisk to combine well. Scrape the mixture into a parchment-lined baking tray. Transfer to the freezer for 40 minutes. Cut into bars and enjoy!

calories: 180 | fat: 18.4g | protein: 1.7g | carbs: 3.1g | net carbs: 2.0g | fiber: 1.1g

Hazelnut Pudding

Prep time: 15 minutes | Cook time: 0 minutes | Serves 4

1 cup double cream
½ teaspoon Swerve
4 tablespoons cream cheese

½ teaspoon vanilla extract
4 ounces (113 g) hazelnuts, ground

Place a mixing bowl in your freezer for 5 to 10 minutes to chill. In the mixing bowl, beat the cream at high speed until the cream starts to thicken. Slowly add in the Swerve and continue beating until stiff peaks form. Add in the cream cheese and vanilla extract; continue to mix an additional minute or so. Fold in the hazelnuts and carefully stir to combine. Serve well chilled and enjoy!

calories: 342 | fat: 33.1g | protein: 6.5g | carbs: 7.4g | net carbs: 4.4g | fiber: 3.0g

Peanut and Chocolate Balls

Prep time: 15 minutes | Cook time: 0 minutes | Serves 6

½ cup coconut oil
½ cup peanut butter, no sugar added
¼ cup cocoa powder,

unsweetened
¼ cup Xylitol
4 tablespoons roasted peanuts, ground

Microwave the coconut oil until melted; add in the peanut butter and stir until well combined. Add the cocoa powder and Xylitol to the batter. Transfer to your freezer for about 1 hour. Shape the batter into bite-sized balls and roll them over the ground peanuts. Bon appétit!

calories: 330 | fat: 32.5g | protein: 6.8g | carbs: 7.5g | net carbs: 4.9g | fiber: 2.6g

Almond Fudge Bars

Prep time: 10 minutes | Cook time: 0 minutes | Serves 7

1 cup almonds
4 tablespoons coconut flakes
4 tablespoons cacao powder,

no sugar added
3 tablespoons coconut oil
¼ cup monk fruit powder

Process all ingredients in your blender until everything is well combined, scraping down the sides as needed. Press firmly into a parchment lined rectangular pan. Cut into squares and serve your bars well chilled. Bon appétit!

calories: 80 | fat: 6.9g | protein: 0.6g | carbs: 4.6g | net carbs: 3.5g | fiber: 1.1g

Cream Mousse

Prep time: 10 minutes | Cook time: 0 minutes | Serves 4

2 cups double cream
4 egg yolks
½ teaspoon instant coffee

1 teaspoon pure coconut extract
6 tablespoons Xylitol

Heat the cream in a pan over low heat; let it cool slightly. Then, whisk the egg yolks with the instant coffee, coconut extract, and Xylitol until well combined. Add the egg mixture to the lukewarm cream. Warm the mixture over low heat until it has reduced and thickened. Refrigerate for 3 hours before serving. Enjoy!

calories: 290 | fat: 27.7g | protein: 6.0g | carbs: 5.0g | net carbs: 5.0g | fiber: 0g

Coconut-Fudge Ice Pops

Prep time: 5 minutes | Cook time: 0 minutes | Serves 4

½ (13.5-ounce / 383-g) can coconut cream
2 teaspoons Swerve natural sweetener

2 tablespoons unsweetened cocoa powder
2 tablespoons sugar-free chocolate chips

In a food processor (or blender), mix together the coconut cream, sweetener, and unsweetened cocoa powder. Pour into ice pop molds, and drop chocolate chips into each mold. Freeze for at least 2 hours before serving.

calories: 193 | fat: 20g | protein: 2g | carbs: 9g | net carbs: 3g | fiber: 6g

Creamsicle Float

Prep time: 5 minutes | Cook time: 0 minutes | Serves 2

1 can diet lemon lime soda
4 tablespoons heavy (whipping) cream

1 teaspoon vanilla extract
6 ice cubes

In a food processor (or blender), combine the lemon lime soda, cream, vanilla, and ice. Blend well, pour into two tall glasses, and serve.

calories: 56 | fat: 6g | protein: 1g | carbs: 3g | net carbs: 1g | fiber: 2g

Creamy Strawberry Shake

Prep time: 10 minutes | Cook time: 0 minutes | Serves 2

¾ cup heavy (whipping) cream
2 ounces (57 g) cream cheese, at room temperature
1 tablespoon Swerve natural

sweetener
¼ teaspoon vanilla extract
6 strawberries, sliced
6 ice cubes

In a food processor (or blender), combine the heavy cream, cream cheese, sweetener, and vanilla. Mix on high to fully combine. Add the strawberries and ice, and blend until smooth. Pour into two tall glasses and serve.

calories: 407 | fat: 42g | protein: 4g | carbs: 13g | net carbs: 6g | fiber: 7g

Cheesecake

Prep time: 15 minutes | Cook time: 25 minutes | Serves 8

3 tablespoons coconut oil
⅓ cup coconut flour
⅔ cup almond flour
½ teaspoon cardamom
A pinch of salt 3 tablespoons xylitol Filling:
8 ounces (227 g) cream

cheese, at room temperature
6 tablespoons xylitol
1 teaspoon vanilla extract
⅓ cup sour cream
2 egg
½ teaspoon cinnamon powder
1 teaspoon ground anise

Mix all of the crust ingredients until everything is well incorporated. Press the crust mixture into a lightly greased springform pan. Bake in the preheated oven at 320°F (160°C) for 8 minutes. In a mixing bowl, mix the cheese and xylitol until well combined. Add in the remaining ingredients and mix until smooth using a mixer set at low-medium speed. Spread the filling over the prepared crust. Cover with strips of aluminum foil. Bake at 300°F (150°C) approximately 16 minutes or until the edges are set. Bon appétit!

calories: 260 | fat: 24.2g | protein: 6.1g | carbs: 5.0g | net carbs: 3.5g | fiber: 1.5g

Almond Chocolate Squares

Prep time: 10 minutes | Cook time: 0 minutes | Serves 10

½ cup coconut flour ½ cup almond meal
1 cup almond butter
¼ cup erythritol

2 tablespoons coconut oil
½ cup sugar-free bakers' chocolate, chopped into small chunks

Mix the coconut flour, almond meal, butter, and erythritol until smooth. Press the mixture into a parchment-lined square pan. Place in your freezer for 30 minutes. Meanwhile, microwave the coconut oil and bakers' chocolate for 40 seconds. Pour the glaze over the cake and transfer to your freezer until the chocolate is set or about 20 minutes. Cut into squares and enjoy!

calories: 235 | fat: 25.2g | protein: 1.6g | carbs: 3.5g | net carbs: 2.2g | fiber: 1.3g

Crispy Strawberry Chocolate Bark

Prep time: 10 minutes | Cook time: 1 minute | Serves 2

½ (2.8-ounce / 79-g) keto-friendly chocolate bar
1 tablespoon heavy (whipping)

cream
2 tablespoons salted almonds
1 fresh strawberry, sliced

Line a baking sheet with parchment paper. Break up the chocolate bar half into small pieces, and put them in a microwave-safe bowl with the cream. Heat in the microwave for 45 seconds at 50 percent power. Stir the chocolate, and cook for 20 seconds more at 50 percent power. Stir again, making sure the mixture is fully melted and combined. If not, microwave for another 20 seconds. Pour the chocolate mixture onto the parchment paper and spread it in a thin, uniform layer. Sprinkle on the almonds, then add the strawberry slices. Refrigerate until hardened, about 2 hours. Once the bark is nice and hard, break it up into smaller pieces to nibble on. The bark will keep for up to 4 days in a sealed container in the refrigerator.

calories: 111 | fat: 10g | protein: 3g | carbs: 9g | net carbs: 4g | fiber: 5g

Chocolate Brownie Cake

Prep time: 10 minutes | Cook time: 3 hours | Serves 12

½ cup plus 1 tablespoon unsalted butter, melted, divided
1½ cups almond flour
¾ cup cocoa powder
¾ cup granulated erythritol
1 teaspoon baking powder
¼ teaspoon fine salt
1 cup heavy (whipping) cream
3 eggs, beaten
2 teaspoons pure vanilla extract
1 cup whipped cream

Generously grease the insert of the slow cooker with 1 tablespoon of the melted butter. In a large bowl, stir together the almond flour, cocoa powder, erythritol, baking powder, and salt. In a medium bowl, whisk together the remaining ½ cup of the melted butter, heavy cream, eggs, and vanilla until well blended. Whisk the wet ingredients into the dry ingredients and spoon the batter into the insert. Cover and cook on low for 3 hours, and then remove the insert from the slow cooker and let the cake sit for 1 hour. Serve warm with the whipped cream.

calories: 185 | fat: 16g | protein: 5g | carbs: 7g | net carbs: 6g | fiber: 1g

Citrus Raspberry Custard Cake

Prep time: 15 minutes | Cook time: 3 hours | Serves 8

1 teaspoon coconut oil
6 eggs, separated
2 cups heavy (whipping) cream
¾ cup granulated erythritol
½ cup coconut flour
¼ teaspoon salt
Juice and zest of 2 limes
½ cup raspberries

Lightly grease a springform pan with the coconut oil. In a large bowl, using a handheld mixer, beat the egg whites until stiff peaks form, about 5 minutes. In a large bowl, whisk together the yolks, heavy cream, erythritol, coconut flour, salt, and lime juice and zest. Fold the egg whites into the mixture. Transfer the batter to the springform pan and sprinkle the raspberries over the top. Place a wire rack in the insert of the slow cooker and place the springform pan on the wire rack. Cover and cook on low for 3 hours, or until a toothpick inserted in the center comes out clean. Remove the cover and allow the cake to cool to room temperature. Place the springform pan in the refrigerator for at least 2 hours, until the cake is firm. Carefully remove the sides of the springform pan. Slice and serve.

calories: 165 | fat: 15g | protein: 6g | carbs: 4g | net carbs: 3g | fiber: 1g

Coconut Lemon Truffles with Pecans

Prep time: 30 minutes | Cook time: 0 minutes | Makes 16 truffles

3 cups shredded unsweetened coconut, divided
½ cup pecans
2 tablespoons coconut oil
Zest and juice of 1 lemon
½ cup monk fruit sweetener, granulated form
Pinch sea salt

Put 2 cups of the coconut and the pecans in a food processor and pulse until the mixture looks like a paste, about 5 minutes. Add the coconut oil, lemon zest, lemon juice, sweetener, and salt to the processor and pulse until the mixture forms a big ball, about 2 minutes. Scoop the mixture out with a tablespoon and roll it into 16 balls. Roll the truffles in the remaining 1 cup of coconut. Store the truffles in a sealed container in the refrigerator for up to one week or in the freezer for up to one month.

calories: 160 | fat:16 g | protein: 2g | carbs: 5g | net carbs: 2g | fiber: 3g

Easy Dark Chocolate Fudge

Prep time: 15 minutes | Cook time: 0 minutes | Makes 30 pieces

1 cup coconut oil, melted
1 cup cocoa powder
1 teaspoon vanilla extract
½ cup monk fruit sweetener, granulated form
Pinch sea salt

Line a 9-by-9-inch glass baking dish with plastic wrap and set it aside. Place the coconut oil, cocoa powder, vanilla, sweetener, and salt in a blender and process until the mixture is smooth and blended. Pour the mixture into the baking dish and place more plastic wrap over it. Place the fudge in the refrigerator for at least 4 hours, until it is set up and firm. Remove the fudge from the baking dish, cut it into roughly 1½-inch squares and store in the freezer in a sealed container for up to one month.

calories: 139 | fat: 15g | protein: 1g | carbs: 3g | net carbs: 1g | fiber: 2g

Blueberry-Vanilla Pudding

Prep time: 10 minutes | Cook time: 10 minutes | Serves 6

3 cups coconut milk
⅓ cup monk fruit sweetener, granulated form
¼ cup arrowroot flour
1 egg
1 tablespoon coconut oil
1 tablespoon pure vanilla extract
1 cup fresh blueberries

In a large saucepan, whisk together the coconut milk, sweetener, and arrowroot. Bring the mixture to a boil then reduce the heat to low, whisking constantly, until the pudding is thick, about 5 minutes. Whisk the egg into the pudding and cook, while still whisking, for about 30 seconds. Whisk the coconut oil and vanilla into the pudding until it's smooth. Transfer the pudding to a medium bowl and cover it with plastic wrap, pressing the wrap down to the surface of the pudding, then place it in the refrigerator to cool completely, about 2 hours. Spoon the pudding into bowls and top with the blueberries.

calories: 286 | fat: 27g | protein: 3g | carbs: 9g | net carbs: 7g | fiber: 2g

Hazelnut Shortbread Cookies

Prep time: 10 minutes | Cook time: 10 minutes | Makes 18 cookies

½ cup butter, at room temperature, plus more for greasing
½ cup granulated sweetener
1 teaspoon alcohol-free pure
vanilla extract
1½ cups almond flour
½ cup ground hazelnuts
Pinch sea salt

In a medium bowl, cream together the butter, sweetener, and vanilla until well blended. Stir in the almond four, ground hazelnuts, and salt until a firm dough is formed. Roll the dough into a 2-inch cylinder and wrap it in plastic wrap. Place the dough in the refrigerator for at least 30 minutes until firm. Preheat the oven to 350ºF (180ºC). Line a baking sheet with parchment paper and lightly grease the paper with butter; set aside. Unwrap the chilled cylinder, slice the dough into 18 cookies, and place the cookies on the baking sheet. Bake the cookies until firm and lightly browned, about 10 minutes. Allow the cookies to cool on the baking sheet for 5 minutes and then transfer them to a wire rack to cool completely.

calories: 105 | fat: 10g | protein: 3g | carbs: 2g | net carbs: 1g | fiber: 1g

Pumpkin-Almond Fat Bombs

Prep time: 10 minutes | Cook time: 0 minutes | Makes 16 fat bombs

½ cup butter, at room temperature
½ cup cream cheese, at room temperature
⅓ cup pure pumpkin purée

3 tablespoons chopped almonds
4 drops liquid stevia
½ teaspoon ground cinnamon
¼ teaspoon ground nutmeg

Line an 8-by-8-inch pan with parchment paper and set aside. In a small bowl, whisk together the butter and cream cheese until very smooth. Add the pumpkin purée and whisk until blended. Stir in the almonds, stevia, cinnamon, and nutmeg. Spoon the pumpkin mixture into the pan. Use a spatula or the back of a spoon to spread it evenly in the pan, then place it in the freezer for about 1 hour. Cut into 16 pieces and store the fat bombs in a tightly sealed container in the freezer until ready to serve.

calories: 87 | fat: 9g | protein: 1g | carbs: 1g | net carbs: 1g | fiber: 0g

Coffee-Coconut Ice Pops

Prep time: 5 minutes | Cook time: 0 minutes | Serves 4

2 cups brewed coffee, cold
¾ cup coconut cream
2 teaspoons Swerve natural sweetener or 2 drops liquid

stevia
2 tablespoons sugar-free chocolate chips

In a food processor (or blender), mix together the coffee, coconut cream, and sweetener until thoroughly blended. Pour into ice pop molds, and drop a few chocolate chips into each mold. Freeze for at least 2 hours before serving.

calories: 105 | fat: 10g | protein: 1g | carbs: 7g | net carbs: 2g | fiber: 5g

Blackberry Cobbler with Almonds

Prep time: 15 minutes | Cook time: 3 to 4 hours | Serves 10

For the Filling:
1 tablespoon coconut oil
6 cups blackberries
For the Topping:
2 cups ground almonds
½ cup granulated erythritol
1 tablespoon baking powder

½ cup granulated erythritol
1 teaspoon ground cinnamon

½ teaspoon salt
1 cup heavy (whipping) cream
½ cup butter, melted

Lightly grease the insert of a 4-quart slow cooker with the coconut oil. Add the blackberries, erythritol, and cinnamon to the insert. Mix to combine. In a large bowl, stir together the almonds, erythritol, baking powder, and salt. Add the heavy cream and butter and stir until a thick batter forms. Drop the batter by the tablespoon on top of the blackberries. Cover and cook on low for 3 to 4 hours. Serve warm.

calories: 281 | fat: 31g | protein: 8g | carbs: 10g | net carbs: 4g | fiber: 6g

Chocolate Pecan-Berry Mascarpone Bowl

Prep time: 5 minutes | Cook time: 0 minutes | Serves 2

1 cup chopped pecans
1 teaspoon Swerve natural sweetener or 1 drop liquid stevia

¼ cup mascarpone
30 Lily's dark-chocolate chips
6 strawberries, sliced

Divide the pecans between two dessert bowls. In a small bowl, mix the sweetener into the mascarpone cheese. Top the nuts with a dollop of the sweetened mascarpone. Sprinkle in the chocolate chips, top each dish with the strawberries, and serve.

calories: 462 | fat: 47g | protein: 6g | carbs: 15g | net carbs: 6g | fiber: 9g

Chocolate-Coconut Shake

Prep time: 10 minutes | Cook time: 0 minutes | Serves 2

¾ cup heavy (whipping) cream
4 ounces (113 g) coconut milk
1 tablespoon Swerve natural sweetener

¼ teaspoon vanilla extract
2 tablespoons unsweetened cocoa powder

Pour the cream into a medium cold metal bowl, and with your hand mixer and cold beaters, beat the cream just until it forms peaks. Slowly pour in the coconut milk, and gently stir it into the cream. Add the sweetener, vanilla, and cocoa powder, and beat until fully combined. Pour into two tall glasses, and chill in the freezer for 1 hour before serving. I usually stir the shakes twice during this time.

calories: 444 | fat: 47g | protein: 4g | carbs: 15g | net carbs: 7g | fiber: 8g

Fresh Strawberry Cheesecake Mousse

Prep time: 10 minutes | Cook time: 0 minutes | Serves 2

4 ounces (113 g) cream cheese, at room temperature
1 tablespoon heavy (whipping) cream
1 teaspoon Swerve natural

sweetener or 1 drop liquid stevia
1 teaspoon vanilla extract
4 fresh strawberries, sliced

Break up the cream cheese block into smaller pieces and distribute evenly in a food processor (or blender). Add the cream, sweetener, and vanilla. Mix together on high. I usually stop and stir twice and scrape down the sides of the bowl with a small rubber scraper to make sure everything is mixed well. Add the strawberries to the food processor, and mix until combined. Divide the strawberry cheesecake mixture between two small dishes, and chill for 1 hour before serving.

calories: 221 | fat: 21g | protein: 4g | carbs: 11g | net carbs: 4g | fiber: 7g

Avocado-Chocolate Pudding

Prep time: 5 minutes | Cook time: 0 minutes | Serves 2

1 ripe medium avocado, cut into chunks
2 ounces (57 g) cream cheese, at room temperature
1 tablespoon Swerve natural

sweetener
4 tablespoons unsweetened cocoa powder
¼ teaspoon vanilla extract
Pinch pink Himalayan salt

In a food processor (or blender), combine the avocado with the cream cheese, sweetener, cocoa powder, vanilla, and pink Himalayan salt. Blend until completely smooth. Pour into two small dessert bowls, and chill for 30 minutes before serving.

calories: 281 | fat: 27g | protein: 8g | carbs: 27g | net carbs: 12g | fiber: 15g

Cheesy Lemonade Fat Bomb

Prep time: 10 minutes | Cook time: 0 minutes | Serves 2

½ lemon
4 ounces (113 g) cream cheese, at room temperature
2 ounces (57 g) butter, at room temperature

2 teaspoons Swerve natural sweetener or 2 drops liquid stevia
Pinch pink Himalayan salt

Zest the lemon half with a very fine grater into a small bowl. Squeeze the juice from the lemon half into the bowl with the zest. In a medium bowl, combine the cream cheese and butter. Add the sweetener, lemon zest and juice, and pink Himalayan salt. Using a hand mixer, beat until fully combined. Spoon the mixture into the fat bomb molds. Freeze for at least 2 hours, unmold, and eat! Keep extras in your freezer in a zip-top bag so you and your loved ones can have them anytime you are craving a sweet treat. They will keep in the freezer for up to 3 months.

calories: 404 | fat: 43g | protein: 4g | carbs: 8g | net carbs: 4g | fiber: 4g

Coconut-Chocolate Treats

Prep time: 10 minutes | Cook time: 3 minutes | Makes 16 treats

⅓ cup coconut oil
¼ cup unsweetened cocoa powder
4 drops liquid stevia

Pinch sea salt
¼ cup shredded unsweetened coconut

Line a 6-by-6-inch baking dish with parchment paper and set aside. In a small saucepan over low heat, stir together the coconut oil, cocoa, stevia, and salt for about 3 minutes. Stir in the coconut and press the mixture into the baking dish. Place the baking dish in the refrigerator until the mixture is hard, about 30 minutes. Cut into 16 pieces and store the treats in an airtight container in a cool place.

calories: 43 | fat: 5g | protein: 1g | carbs: 1g | net carbs: 1g | fiber: 0g

Slow Cooker Chocolate Pot De Crème

Prep time: 10 minutes | Cook time: 3 hours | Serves 6

6 egg yolks
2 cups heavy (whipping) cream
⅓ cup cocoa powder
1 tablespoon pure vanilla extract

½ teaspoon liquid stevia
Whipped coconut cream, for garnish (optional)
Shaved dark chocolate, for garnish (optional)

In a medium bowl, whisk together the yolks, heavy cream, cocoa powder, vanilla, and stevia. Pour the mixture into a 1½-quart baking dish and place the dish in the insert of the slow cooker. Pour in enough water to reach halfway up the sides of the baking dish. Cover and cook on low for 3 hours. Remove the baking dish from the insert and cool to room temperature on a wire rack. Chill the dessert completely in the refrigerator and serve, garnished with the whipped coconut cream and shaved dark chocolate (if desired).

calories: 198 | fat: 18g | protein: 5g | carbs: 4g | net carbs: 3g | fiber: 1g

Cheesecake Fat Bomb with Berries

Prep time: 10 minutes | Cook time: 0 minutes | Serves 2

4 ounces (113 g) cream cheese, at room temperature
4 tablespoons butter, at room temperature
2 teaspoons Swerve natural

sweetener or 2 drops liquid stevia
1 teaspoon vanilla extract
¼ cup berries, fresh or frozen

In a medium bowl, use a hand mixer to beat the cream cheese, butter, sweetener, and vanilla. In a small bowl, mash the berries thoroughly. Fold the berries into the cream-cheese mixture using a rubber scraper. Spoon the cream-cheese mixture into fat bomb molds. Freeze for at least 2 hours, unmold them, and eat! Leftover fat bombs can be stored in the freezer in a zip-top bag for up to 3 months. It's nice to have some in your freezer for when you are craving a sweet treat.

calories: 414 | fat: 43g | protein: 4g | carbs: 9g | net carbs: 4g | fiber: 5g

Simple Peanut Butter Fat Bomb

Prep time: 10 minutes | Cook time: 1 minute | Serves 2

1 tablespoon butter, at room temperature
1 tablespoon coconut oil
2 tablespoons all-natural

peanut butter or almond butter
2 teaspoons Swerve natural sweetener or 2 drops liquid stevia

In a microwave-safe medium bowl, melt the butter, coconut oil, and peanut butter in the microwave for 1 minute on 50 percent power. Mix in the sweetener. Pour the mixture into fat bomb molds. Freeze for 30 minutes, unmold them, and eat! Keep some extras in your freezer so you can eat them anytime you are craving a sweet treat.

calories: 196 | fat: 20g | protein: 3g | carbs: 8g | net carbs: 3g | fiber: 5g

Baked Cheesecake Bites

Prep time: 10 minutes | Cook time: 30 minutes | Serves 4

4 ounces (113 g) cream cheese, at room temperature
¼ cup sour cream
2 large eggs

⅓ cup Swerve natural sweetener
¼ teaspoon vanilla extract

Preheat the oven to 350°F (180°C). In a medium mixing bowl, use a hand mixer to beat the cream cheese, sour cream, eggs, sweetener, and vanilla until well mixed. Place silicone liners (or cupcake paper liners) in the cups of a muffin tin. Pour the cheesecake batter into the liners, and bake for 30 minutes. Refrigerate until completely cooled before serving, about 3 hours. Store extra cheesecake bites in a zip-top bag in the freezer for up to 3 months.

calories: 169 | fat: 15g | protein: 5g | carbs: 18g | net carbs: 2g | fiber: 16g

Pumpkin Cheesecake Bites
Prep time: 10 minutes | Cook time: 30 minutes | Serves 4

4 ounces (113 g) pumpkin purée
4 ounces (113 g) cream cheese, at room temperature
2 large eggs
⅓ cup Swerve natural sweetener
2 teaspoons pumpkin pie spice

Preheat the oven to 350ºF (180ºC). In a medium mixing bowl, use a hand mixer to mix the pumpkin purée, cream cheese, eggs, sweetener, and pumpkin pie spice until thoroughly combined. Place silicone liners (or cupcake paper liners) into the cups of a muffin tin. Pour the batter into the liners, and bake for 30 minutes. Refrigerate until completely cooled before serving, about 3 hours. Put leftover cheesecake bites in a zip-top plastic bag and store in the freezer for up to 3 months.

calories: 156 | fat: 12g | protein: 5g | carbs: 21g | net carbs: 4g | fiber: 17g

Keto Peanut Butter Cookies
Prep time: 5 minutes | Cook time: 10 minutes | Makes 15 cookies

1 cup natural crunchy peanut butter
½ cup Swerve natural
sweetener
1 egg

Preheat the oven to 350ºF (180ºC). Line a baking sheet with a silicone baking mat or parchment paper. In a medium bowl, use a hand mixer to mix together the peanut butter, sweetener, and egg. Roll up the batter into small balls about 1 inch in diameter. Spread out the cookie-dough balls on the prepared pan. Press each dough ball down with the tines of a fork, then repeat to make a crisscross pattern. Bake for about 12 minutes, or until golden. Let the cookies cool for 10 minutes on the lined pan before serving. If you try to move them too soon, they will crumble. Store leftover cookies covered in the refrigerator for up to 5 days.

calories: 98 | fat: 8g | protein: 4g | carbs: 10g | net carbs: 3g | fiber: 7g

Creamy Chocolate Mousse
Prep time: 10 minutes | Cook time: 0 minutes | Serves 2

1½ tablespoons heavy (whipping) cream
4 tablespoons butter, at room temperature
1 tablespoon unsweetened
cocoa powder
4 tablespoons cream cheese, at room temperature
1 tablespoon Swerve natural sweetener

In a medium chilled bowl, use a whisk or fork to whip the cream. Refrigerate to keep cold. In a separate medium bowl, use a hand mixer to beat the butter, cocoa powder, cream cheese, and sweetener until thoroughly combined. Take the whipped cream out of the refrigerator. Gently fold the whipped cream into the chocolate mixture with a rubber scraper. Divide the pudding between two dessert bowls. Cover and chill for 1 hour before serving.

calories: 460 | fat: 50g | protein: 4g | carbs: 10g | net carbs: 4g | fiber: 6g

Lemon Custard
Prep time: 10 minutes | Cook time: 3 hours | Serves 4

5 egg yolks
¼ cup freshly squeezed lemon juice
1 tablespoon lemon zest
1 teaspoon pure vanilla extract
⅓ teaspoon liquid stevia
2 cups heavy (whipping) cream
1 cup whipped coconut cream

In a medium bowl, whisk together the yolks, lemon juice and zest, vanilla, and liquid stevia. Whisk in the heavy cream and divide the mixture between 4 ramekins. Place a rack at the bottom of the insert of the slow cooker and place the ramekins on it. Pour in enough water to reach halfway up the sides of the ramekins. Cover and cook on low for 3 hours. Remove the ramekins from the insert and cool to room temperature. Chill the ramekins completely in the refrigerator and serve topped with whipped coconut cream.

calories: 319 | fat: 30g | protein: 7g | carbs: 3g | net carbs: 3g | fiber: 0g

Ginger-Pumpkin Pudding
Prep time: 5 minutes | Cook time: 3 to 4 hours | Serves 8

1 tablespoon coconut oil
2 cups pumpkin purée
1½ cups coconut milk
2 eggs
½ cup almond flour
1 ounce (28 g) protein powder
1 tablespoon grated fresh ginger
¾ teaspoon liquid stevia
Pinch ground cloves
1 cup whipped coconut cream

Lightly grease the insert of the slow cooker with coconut oil. In a large bowl, stir together pumpkin, coconut milk, eggs, almond flour, protein powder, ginger, liquid stevia, and cloves. Transfer the mixture to the insert. Cover and cook on low 3 to 4 hours. Serve warm with whipped coconut cream.

calories: 217 | fat: 19g | protein: 8g | carbs: 7g | net carbs: 3g | fiber: 4g

Pumpkin Compote with Mix Berries
Prep time: 10 minutes | Cook time: 3 to 4 hours | Serves 10

1 tablespoon coconut oil
2 cups diced pumpkin
1 cup cranberries
1 cup blueberries
½ cup granulated erythritol
Juice and zest of 1 lemon
½ cup coconut milk
1 teaspoon ground cinnamon
½ teaspoon ground allspice
¼ teaspoon ground nutmeg
1 cup whipped cream

Lightly grease the insert of the slow cooker with the coconut oil. Place the pumpkin, cranberries, blueberries, erythritol, lemon juice and zest, coconut milk, cinnamon, allspice, and nutmeg in the insert. Cover and cook on low for 3 to 4 hours. Let the compote cool for 1 hour and serve warm with a generous scoop of whipped cream.

calories: 113 | fat: 9g | protein: 4g | carbs: 7g | net carbs: 4g | fiber: 3g

Blueberry-Pecan Crisp

Prep time: 10 minutes | Cook time: 3 to 4 hours | Serves 8

5 tablespoons coconut oil, melted, divided
4 cups blueberries
¾ cup plus 2 tablespoons granulated erythritol
1 cup ground pecans
1 teaspoon baking soda
½ teaspoon ground cinnamon
2 tablespoons coconut milk
1 egg

Lightly grease a 4-quart slow cooker with 1 tablespoon of the coconut oil. Add the blueberries and 2 tablespoons of erythritol to the insert. In a large bowl, stir together the remaining ¾ cup of the erythritol, ground pecans, baking soda, and cinnamon until well mixed. Add the coconut milk, egg, and remaining coconut oil, and stir until coarse crumbs form. Top the contents in the insert with the pecan mixture. Cover and cook on low for 3 to 4 hours. Serve warm.

calories: 222 | fat: 19g | protein: 9g | carbs: 9g | net carbs: 5g | fiber: 4g

Tender Almond Pound Cake

Prep time: 10 minutes | Cook time: 5 to 6 hours | Serves 8

1 tablespoon coconut oil
2 cups almond flour
1 cup granulated erythritol
½ teaspoon cream of tartar
Pinch salt
1 cup butter, melted
5 eggs
2 teaspoons pure vanilla extract

Lightly grease an 8-by-4-inch loaf pan with the coconut oil. In a large bowl, stir together the almond flour, erythritol, cream of tartar, and salt, until well mixed. In a small bowl, whisk together the butter, eggs, and vanilla. Add the wet ingredients to the dry ingredients and stir to combine. Transfer the batter to the loaf pan. Place the loaf pan in the insert of the slow cooker. Cover and cook until a toothpick inserted in the center comes out clean, about 5 to 6 hours on low. Serve warm.

calories: 281 | fat: 29g | protein: 5g | carbs: 1g | net carbs: 1g | fiber: 0g

Classic Almond Golden Cake

Prep time: 15 minutes | Cook time: 3 hours | Serves 8

½ cup coconut oil, divided
1½ cups almond flour
½ cup coconut flour
½ cup granulated erythritol
2 teaspoons baking powder
3 eggs
½ cup coconut milk
2 teaspoons pure vanilla extract
½ teaspoon almond extract

Line the insert of a 4-quart slow cooker with aluminum foil and grease the aluminum foil with 1 tablespoon of the coconut oil. In a medium bowl, mix the almond flour, coconut flour, erythritol, and baking powder. In a large bowl, whisk together the remaining coconut oil, eggs, coconut milk, vanilla, and almond extract. Add the dry ingredients to the wet ingredients and stir until well blended. Transfer the batter to the insert and use a spatula to even the top. Cover and cook on low for 3 hours, or until a toothpick inserted in the center comes out clean. Remove the cake from the insert and cool completely before serving.

calories: 234 | fat: 22g | protein: 6g | carbs: 3g | net carbs: 2g | fiber: 1g

Peanut Butter Cupcake

Prep time: 15 minutes | Cook time: 3 to 4 hours | Serves 8

2 tablespoons coconut oil, divided
1 cup almond flour
1 cup granulated erythritol, divided
1 teaspoon baking powder
¼ teaspoon salt
¾ cup natural peanut butter
½ cup heavy (whipping) cream
1 teaspoon pure vanilla extract
1 cup boiling water
¼ cup cocoa powder

Lightly grease the insert of a 4-quart slow cooker with 1 tablespoon of the coconut oil. In a large bowl, stir together the almond flour, ½ cup of the erythritol, baking powder, and salt. In a medium bowl, whisk together the peanut butter, heavy cream, and vanilla until smooth. Add the peanut butter mixture to the dry ingredients and stir to combine. Transfer the batter to the insert and spread it out evenly. In a small bowl, stir together the remaining ½ cup of the erythritol, boiling water, and cocoa powder. Pour the chocolate mixture over the batter. Cover and cook on low for 3 to 4 hours. Let the cake stand for 30 minutes and serve warm.

calories: 244 | fat: 20g | protein: 11g | carbs: 6g | net carbs: 3g | fiber: 3g

Old-fashioned Gingerbread Cake

Prep time: 10 minutes | Cook time: 3 hours | Serves 8

1 tablespoon coconut oil
2 cups almond flour
¾ cup granulated erythritol
2 tablespoons coconut flour
2 tablespoons ground ginger
2 teaspoons baking powder
2 teaspoons ground cinnamon
½ teaspoon ground nutmeg
¼ teaspoon ground cloves
Pinch salt
¾ cup heavy (whipping) cream
½ cup butter, melted
4 eggs
1 teaspoon pure vanilla extract

Lightly grease the insert of the slow cooker with coconut oil. In a large bowl, stir together the almond flour, erythritol, coconut flour, ginger, baking powder, cinnamon, nutmeg, cloves, and salt. In a medium bowl, whisk together the heavy cream, butter, eggs, and vanilla. Add the wet ingredients to the dry ingredients and stir to combine. Spoon the batter into the insert. Cover and cook on low for 3 hours, or until a toothpick inserted in the center comes out clean. Serve warm.

calories: 259 | fat: 23g | protein: 7g | carbs: 6g | net carbs: 3g | fiber: 3g

Banana Fat Bombs

Prep time: 10 minutes | Cook time: 0 minutes | Makes 12 fat bombs

1¼ cups cream cheese, at room temperature
¾ cup heavy (whipping) cream
1 tablespoon pure banana extract
6 drops liquid stevia

Line a baking sheet with parchment paper and set aside. In a medium bowl, beat together the cream cheese, heavy cream, banana extract, and stevia until smooth and very thick, about 5 minutes. Gently spoon the mixture onto the baking sheet in mounds, leaving some space between each mound, and place the baking sheet in the refrigerator until firm, about 1 hour. Store the fat bombs in an airtight container in the refrigerator for up to 1 week.

calories: 134 | fat: 12g | protein: 3g | carbs: 1g | net carbs: 1g | fiber: 0g

Simple Blueberry Fat Bombs

Prep time: 10 minutes | Cook time: 0 minutes | Makes 12 fat bombs

½ cup coconut oil, at room temperature
½ cup cream cheese, at room temperature
½ cup blueberries, mashed with a fork
6 drops liquid stevia
Pinch ground nutmeg

Line a mini muffin tin with paper liners and set aside. In a medium bowl, stir together the coconut oil and cream cheese until well blended. Stir in the blueberries, stevia, and nutmeg until combined. Divide the blueberry mixture into the muffin cups and place the tray in the freezer until set, about 3 hours. Place the fat bombs in an airtight container and store in the freezer until you wish to eat them.

calories: 115 | fat: 12g | protein: 1g | carbs: 1g | net carbs: 1g | fiber: 0g

Almond Butter Fat Bombs

Prep time: 10 minutes | Cook time: 4 minutes | Makes 12 fat bombs

¾ cup coconut oil
¼ cup cocoa powder
¼ cup almond butter
⅛ teaspoon chili powder
3 drops liquid stevia

Line a mini muffin tin with paper liners and set aside. Put a small saucepan over low heat and add the coconut oil, cocoa powder, almond butter, chili powder, and stevia. Heat for 4 minutes until the coconut oil is melted, then whisk to blend. Spoon the mixture into the muffin cups and place the tin in the refrigerator until the bombs are firm, about 15 minutes. Transfer the cups to an airtight container and store the fat bombs in the freezer until you want to serve them.

calories: 117 | fat: 12g | protein: 2g | carbs: 2g | net carbs: 2g | fiber: 0g

Keto Almond Butter Fudge

Prep time: 10 minutes | Cook time: 0 minutes | Makes 36 pieces

1 cup coconut oil, at room temperature
1 cup almond butter
¼ cup heavy (whipping) cream
10 drops liquid stevia
Pinch sea salt

Line a 6-by-6-inch baking dish with parchment paper and set aside. In a medium bowl, whisk together the coconut oil, almond butter, heavy cream, stevia, and salt until very smooth. Spoon the mixture into the baking dish and smooth the top with a spatula. Place the dish in the refrigerator until the fudge is firm, about 2 hours. Cut into 36 pieces and store the fudge in an airtight container in the freezer for up to 2 weeks.

calories: 204 | fat: 22g | protein: 3g | carbs: 3g | net carbs: 2g | fiber: 1g

Vanilla-Raspberry Cheesecake

Prep time: 10 minutes | Cook time: 25 to 30 minutes | Serves 12

⅔ cup coconut oil, melted
½ cup cream cheese, at room temperature
6 eggs
3 tablespoons granulated
sweetener
1 teaspoon alcohol-free pure vanilla extract
½ teaspoon baking powder
¾ cup raspberries

Preheat the oven to 350ºF (180ºC). Line an 8-by-8-inch baking dish with parchment paper and set aside. In a large bowl, beat together the coconut oil and cream cheese until smooth. Beat in the eggs, scraping down the sides of the bowl at least once. Beat in the sweetener, vanilla, and baking powder until smooth. Spoon the batter into the baking dish and use a spatula to smooth out the top. Scatter the raspberries on top. Bake until the center is firm, about 25 to 30 minutes. Allow the cheesecake to cool completely before cutting into 12 squares.

calories: 176 | fat: 18g | protein: 6g | carbs: 3g | net carbs: 2g | fiber: 1g

Coconut-Vanilla Ice Pops

Prep time: 10 minutes | Cook time: 5 minutes | Makes 8 ice pops

2 cups almond milk
1 cup heavy (whipping) cream
1 vanilla bean, halved
lengthwise
1 cup shredded unsweetened coconut

Place a medium saucepan over medium heat and add the almond milk, heavy cream, and vanilla bean. Bring the liquid to a simmer and reduce the heat to low. Continue to simmer for 5 minutes. Remove the saucepan from the heat and let the liquid cool. Take the vanilla bean out of the liquid and use a knife to scrape the seeds out of the bean into the liquid. Stir in the coconut and divide the liquid between the ice pop molds. Freeze until solid, about 4 hours, and enjoy.

calories: 166 | fat: 15g | protein: 3g | carbs: 4g | net carbs: 2g | fiber: 2g

Super Easy Peanut Butter Mousse

Prep time: 10 minutes | Cook time: 0 minutes | Serves 4

1 cup heavy (whipping) cream
¼ cup natural peanut butter
1 teaspoon alcohol-free pure
vanilla extract
4 drops liquid stevia

In a medium bowl, beat together the heavy cream, peanut butter, vanilla, and stevia until firm peaks form, about 5 minutes. Spoon the mousse into 4 bowls and place in the refrigerator to chill for 30 minutes. Serve.

calories: 280 | fat: 28g | protein: 6g | carbs: 4g | net carbs: 3g | fiber: 1g

Blueberry-Almond Muffins

Prep time: 5 minutes | Cook time: 25 minutes | Makes 10 muffins

2½ cups blanched almond flour
½ cup erythritol
1½ teaspoons baking powder
¼ teaspoon sea salt
⅓ cup coconut oil, melted
⅓ cup unsweetened almond milk
3 large eggs
½ teaspoon vanilla extract
¾ cup blueberries

Preheat the oven to 350ºF (180ºC). Line 10 cups of a muffin tin with silicone or parchment paper liners. In a large bowl, stir together the almond flour, erythritol, baking powder, and sea salt. Stir in the melted coconut oil, almond milk, eggs, and vanilla. Fold in the blueberries. Distribute the batter evenly among the muffin cups. Bake for about 25 minutes, until the tops are golden and an inserted toothpick comes out clean.

calories: 254 | fat: 23g | protein: 8g | carbs: 11g | net carbs: 5g | fiber: 6g

Chapter 14 Seasonings, Dressings, and Sauces

Cajun Seasoning
Prep time: 5 minutes | Cook time: 0 minutes | Makes ⅓ cup

1 tablespoon garlic powder
1 tablespoon kosher salt
1 tablespoon paprika
2 teaspoons cayenne pepper
2 teaspoons dried oregano leaves

2 teaspoons dried thyme leaves
2 teaspoons onion powder
1 teaspoon ground black pepper

Place all of the ingredients in a small bowl and mix well. Store in an airtight container for up to 6 months.

calories: 5 | fat: 0g | protein: 0g | carbs: 1.0g | net carbs: 1.0g | fiber: 0g

Dill Feta Dressing
Prep time: 5 minutes | Cook time: 0 minutes | Makes 1 cup

¼ cup sugar-free mayonnaise
⅓ cup crumbled Feta cheese
2 tablespoons full-fat sour cream
2 tablespoons heavy whipping cream

1 tablespoon chopped fresh dill
1 tablespoon white vinegar
⅛ teaspoon ground black pepper
⅛ teaspoon onion powder

Place all of the ingredients in a small blender and blend for 30 seconds, until creamy and nearly entirely smooth. Store in an airtight container in the refrigerator for up to 1 week.

calories: 75 | fat: 8.1g | protein: 1.2g | carbs: 0.3g | net carbs: 0.3g | fiber: 0g

Tahini Dressing
Prep time: 5 minutes | Cook time: 0 minutes | Makes ⅓ cup

3 tablespoons filtered water
2 tablespoons tahini
1 tablespoon lemon juice

1 teaspoon minced garlic
½ teaspoon kosher salt

Place all of the ingredients in a small blender and blend until smooth. Store in an airtight container in the refrigerator for up to 1 week.

calories: 62 | fat: 5.0g | protein: 2.0g | carbs: 3.0g | net carbs: 1.0g | fiber: 2.0g

Chicken Seasoning
Prep time: 5 minutes | Cook time: 0 minutes | Makes ¾ cup

2 tablespoons dried parsley
2 tablespoons kosher salt
2 tablespoons onion powder
2 tablespoons smoked paprika
1 tablespoon dried rosemary leaves

1 tablespoon dried thyme leaves
1 tablespoon garlic powder
2 teaspoons ground black pepper

Place all of the ingredients in a small bowl and mix well. Store in an airtight container for up to 6 months.

calories: 5 | fat: 0g | protein: 0g | carbs: 1.6g | net carbs: 1.0g | fiber: 0.6g

Blackened Seasoning
Prep time: 5 minutes | Cook time: 0 minutes | Makes 1 cup

3 tablespoons cayenne pepper
3 tablespoons chili powder
3 tablespoons paprika
2 tablespoons ground black pepper
1 tablespoon chipotle powder

1 tablespoon dried oregano leaves
1 tablespoon dried thyme leaves
1 tablespoon garlic powder
1 tablespoon onion powder

Place all of the ingredients in a small bowl and mix well. Store in an airtight container for up to 6 months.

calories: 7 | fat: 0g | protein: 0g | carbs: 1.5g | net carbs: 1.0g | fiber: 0.5g

Jerk Seasoning
Prep time: 5 minutes | Cook time: 0 minutes | Makes ⅓ cup

1 tablespoon cayenne pepper
1 tablespoon granulated erythritol
2 teaspoons dried parsley
2 teaspoons garlic powder
2 teaspoons kosher salt
2 teaspoons onion powder
1 teaspoon dried thyme leaves

1 teaspoon ground allspice
1 teaspoon smoked paprika
½ teaspoon ginger powder
½ teaspoon ground cinnamon
½ teaspoon ground nutmeg
½ teaspoon ground black pepper

Place all of the ingredients in a small bowl and mix well. Store in an airtight container for up to 6 months.

calories: 6 | fat: 0g | protein: 0g | carbs: 1.5g | net carbs: 1.0g | fiber: 0.5g

Beef Seasoning
Prep time: 5 minutes | Cook time: 0 minutes | Makes ½ cup

2 tablespoons kosher salt
1 tablespoon garlic powder
1 tablespoon ground black pepper
1 tablespoon onion powder

1 tablespoon smoked paprika
1 teaspoon dried thyme leaves
1 teaspoon ground coriander
1 teaspoon ground cumin

Place all of the ingredients in a small bowl and mix well. Store in an airtight container for up to 6 months.

calories: 4 | fat: 0g | protein: 0g | carbs: 1.5g | net carbs: 1.0g | fiber: 0.5g

Blue Cheese Dressing
Prep time: 5 minutes | Cook time: 0 minutes | Makes 1 cup

⅓ cup sugar-free mayonnaise
¼ cup crumbled blue cheese
1 ounce (28 g) cream cheese (2 tablespoons), softened

2 tablespoons heavy whipping cream
1 teaspoon lemon juice

Place all of the ingredients in a small blender and blend for 30 seconds, until creamy and nearly entirely smooth. Store in an airtight container in the refrigerator for up to 1 week.

calories: 101 | fat: 10.2g | protein: 1.0g | carbs: 0.5g | net carbs: 0.5g | fiber: 0g

Seafood Seasoning

Prep time: 5 minutes | Cook time: 0 minutes | Serves ½ cup

3 tablespoons dried parsley
1 tablespoon dried chives
1 tablespoon dried dill weed
1 tablespoon grated lemon zest
2 teaspoons celery salt
1 teaspoon dried marjoram leaves

1 teaspoon garlic powder
1 teaspoon ground coriander
1 teaspoon kosher salt
1 teaspoon onion powder
1 teaspoon paprika
½ teaspoon ground white pepper

Place all of the ingredients in a small bowl and mix well. Store in an airtight container for up to 6 months.

calories: 2 | fat: 0g | protein: 0g | carbs: 1.5g | net carbs: 1.0g | fiber: 0.5g

Basic Syrup

Prep time: 2 minutes | Cook time: 3 minutes | Makes 2 cups

2 cups filtered water
1 cup granulated erythritol

⅛ teaspoon xanthan gum

To make basic simple syrup, combine all of the ingredients in a small saucepan. Cook over medium heat for 3 minutes, stirring occasionally, until all of the sweetener has dissolved. Let cool to room temperature. Pour the syrup into a clean jar with an airtight lid and store in the refrigerator for up to 1 month.

calories: 0 | fat: 0g | protein: 0g | carbs: 0g | net carbs: 0g | fiber: 0g

Parmesan Basil Vinaigrette

Prep time: 5 minutes | Cook time: 0 minutes | Makes ¾ cup

¼ cup fresh basil leaves
¼ cup sugar-free mayonnaise
2 tablespoons extra-virgin olive oil
2 tablespoons full-fat sour cream
1 tablespoon apple cider vinegar

1 tablespoon lemon juice
1 tablespoon granulated erythritol
1 tablespoon grated Parmesan cheese
½ teaspoon kosher salt
¼ teaspoon ground black pepper

Place all of the ingredients in a small blender and blend until mostly smooth. Store in an airtight container in the refrigerator for up to 1 week.

calories: 124 | fat: 14.0g | protein: 0g | carbs: 0g | net carbs: 0g | fiber: 0g

Raspberry Coulis

Prep time: 3 minutes | Cook time: 5 minutes | Makes 1½ cups

2 cups fresh or frozen red raspberries
2 tablespoons granulated erythritol

Combine the raspberries and sweetener in a small saucepan and cook over medium heat for 5 minutes, or until bubbling. Blend with an immersion blender for 30 seconds or until liquefied, then pour the sauce through a fine-mesh strainer to remove any seed fragments. Let cool before using. Store in an airtight container in the refrigerator for up to 1 week or in the freezer for up to 3 months.

calories: 13 | fat: 0g | protein: 0g | carbs: 2.6g | net carbs: 1.0g | fiber: 1.6g

Strawberry Vinaigrette

Prep time: 5 minutes | Cook time: 0 minutes | Makes ½ cup

¼ cup chopped fresh strawberries
2 tablespoons avocado oil or other light-tasting oil
1 tablespoon chopped fresh basil
1 tablespoon filtered water

2 teaspoons red wine vinegar
½ teaspoon granulated erythritol
⅛ teaspoon kosher salt
⅛ teaspoon ground black pepper

Place all of the ingredients in a small blender and blend until mostly smooth. Store in an airtight container in the refrigerator for up to 1 week.

calories: 66 | fat: 7.0g | protein: 0g | carbs: 1.0g | net carbs: 1.0g | fiber: 0g

Scallion Ginger Dressing

Prep time: 8 minutes | Cook time: 0 minutes | Makes ¾ cup

¼ cup chopped scallions
3 tablespoons avocado oil or other light-tasting oil
2 tablespoons filtered water
2 tablespoons fish sauce (no sugar added)
2 tablespoons granulated

erythritol
1 tablespoon lime juice
1 tablespoon white vinegar
1 tablespoon peeled and minced fresh ginger
1 teaspoon toasted sesame oil

Place all of the ingredients in a small blender and blend until mostly smooth. Store in an airtight container in the refrigerator for up to 1 week.

calories: 76 | fat: 8.0g | protein: 1.0g | carbs: 1.0g | net carbs: 1.0g | fiber: 0g

Tomato and Bacon Dressing

Prep time: 8 minutes | Cook time: 0 minutes | Makes ¾ cup

¼ cup sugar-free mayonnaise
5 cherry tomatoes
3 slices bacon, cooked and chopped
1 clove garlic, peeled
2 tablespoons chopped fresh

parsley
½ teaspoon granulated erythritol
¼ teaspoon kosher salt
⅛ teaspoon ground black pepper

Place all of the ingredients in a small blender and blend until mostly smooth. Store in an airtight container in the refrigerator for up to 1 week.

calories: 95 | fat: 10.0g | protein: 2.0g | carbs: 1.0g | net carbs: 1.0g | fiber: 0g

Lemony Caper Dressing

Prep time: 5 minutes | Cook time: 0 minutes | Makes ¾ cup

½ cup sugar-free mayonnaise
2 tablespoons extra-virgin olive oil
1 tablespoon capers, drained

1 tablespoon lemon juice
1 tablespoon white vinegar
1 teaspoon grated lemon zest
½ teaspoon dried dill weed

Place all of the ingredients in a small blender and blend for 30 seconds, until creamy and nearly entirely smooth. Store in an airtight container in the refrigerator for up to 1 week.

calories: 106 | fat: 13.0g | protein: 0g | carbs: 0g | net carbs: 0g | fiber: 0g

Basil Pesto

Prep time: 5 minutes | Cook time: 0 minutes | Makes ¾ cup

1 cup fresh basil leaves
¼ cup extra-virgin olive oil
¼ cup grated Parmesan cheese
¼ cup pine nuts

1 tablespoon chopped garlic
¼ teaspoon kosher salt
⅛ teaspoon ground black pepper

Put all of the ingredients in a small blender or mini food processor. Pulse until fully combined but not quite smooth. Store in an airtight container in the refrigerator for up to 1 week or in the freezer for up to 3 months.

calories: 140 | fat: 14.0g | protein: 2.9g | carbs: 1.4g | net carbs: 1.0g | fiber: 0.4g

Remoulade

Prep time: 5 minutes | Cook time: 0 minutes | Makes ½ cup

⅓ cup sugar-free mayonnaise
1 tablespoon dill pickle relish
1 teaspoon Cajun Seasoning
1 teaspoon capers, drained
1 teaspoon Dijon mustard

1 teaspoon lemon juice
1 teaspoon prepared horseradish
½ teaspoon minced garlic

Place all of the ingredients in a small bowl and mix well. Serve immediately or store in an airtight container in the refrigerator for up to 5 days.

calories: 161 | fat: 18.8g | protein: 0g | carbs: 1.1g | net carbs: 1.1g | fiber: 0g

Creamy Duo-Cheese Dipping Sauce

Prep time: 10 minutes | Cook time: 0 minutes | Serves 10

4 ounces (113 g) Feta cheese
1 cup Asiago cheese, shredded

1 cup double cream
1 tablespoon paprika

Melt the cheese and cream in a saucepan over medium-low heat. Transfer to a serving bowl and top with paprika. Serve with fresh celery sticks if desired. Enjoy!

calories: 127 | fat: 10.8g | protein: 5.5g | carbs: 1.3g | net carbs: 1.3g | fiber: 0g

Homemade Dijon Vinaigrette

Prep time: 5 minutes | Cook time: 0 minutes | Serves 4

2 tablespoons Dijon mustard
Juice of ½ lemon
1 garlic clove, finely minced
1½ tablespoons red wine vinegar

Pink Himalayan salt
Freshly ground black pepper, to taste
3 tablespoons olive oil

In a small bowl, whisk the mustard, lemon juice, garlic, and red wine vinegar until well combined. Season with pink Himalayan salt and pepper, and whisk again. Slowly add the olive oil, a little bit at a time, whisking constantly. Keep in a sealed glass container in the refrigerator for up to 1 week

calories: 99 | fat: 11g | protein: 1g | carbs: 1g | net carbs: 1g | fiber:0g

Raita

Prep time: 8 minutes | Cook time: 0 minutes | Makes 1 cup

⅓ cup full-fat Greek yogurt
⅓ cup full-fat sour cream
¼ cup finely chopped cucumbers
1 tablespoon chopped fresh cilantro

1 tablespoon chopped fresh mint
1 teaspoon granulated erythritol
1 teaspoon minced red onions
¼ teaspoon ground cumin

Place all of the ingredients in a small bowl and mix well. Serve immediately or store in an airtight container in the refrigerator for up to 3 days.

calories: 30 | fat: 2.1g | protein: 0.9g | carbs: 1.0g | net carbs: 1.0g | fiber: 0g

Sriracha Sauce

Prep time: 5 minutes | Cook time: 0 minutes | Makes ¾ cup

½ cup sugar-free mayonnaise
1½ tablespoons lime juice
1½ tablespoons Sriracha

sauce
1 tablespoon granulated erythritol

Place all of the ingredients in a small bowl and stir well until combined. Store in an airtight container in the refrigerator for up to 1 week.

calories: 140 | fat: 15.8g | protein: 0g | carbs: 1.0g | net carbs: 1.0g | fiber: 0g

Tangy Avocado Crema

Prep time: 5 minutes | Cook time: 0 minutes | Serves 4

½ cup sour cream
½ avocado
1 garlic clove, finely minced
¼ cup fresh cilantro leaves

Juice of ½ lime
Pinch pink Himalayan salt
Pinch freshly ground black pepper

In a food processor (or blender), mix the sour cream, avocado, garlic, cilantro, lime juice, pink Himalayan salt, and pepper until smooth and fully combined. Spoon the sauce into an airtight glass jar and keep in the refrigerator for up to 3 days.

calories: 87 | fat: 8g | protein: 1g | carbs: 4g | net carbs: 2g | fiber: 2g

Orange Chili Sauce

Prep time: 5 minutes | Cook time: 0 minutes | Makes 1¼ cup

1 cup sugar-free orange marmalade
1 tablespoon filtered water
1 tablespoon fish sauce (no sugar added)

1 tablespoon lime juice
1 teaspoon granulated erythritol
1 teaspoon red pepper flakes
1 teaspoon toasted sesame oil

Place all of the ingredients in a small bowl and mix well. Store in an airtight container in the refrigerator for up to 2 weeks.

calories: 21 | fat: 0g | protein: 0g | carbs: 5.9g | net carbs: 4.9g | fiber: 1.0g

BBQ Sauce

Prep time: 8 minutes | Cook time: 0 minutes | Makes ¾ cup

½ cup reduced-sugar ketchup, store-bought or homemade
2 tablespoons apple cider vinegar
2 tablespoons granulated erythritol
1 tablespoon filtered water
1½ teaspoons ground allspice
1½ teaspoons ground mustard powder

1 teaspoon blackstrap molasses (optional; see note)
½ teaspoon liquid smoke
½ teaspoon onion powder
½ teaspoon Worcestershire sauce
¼ teaspoon ground cloves
¼ teaspoon xanthan gum (optional, to thicken)

Place all of the ingredients in a medium-sized bowl and whisk together. Store in an airtight container in the refrigerator for up to 2 weeks.

calories: 15 | fat: 0g | protein: 0g | carbs: 2.8g | net carbs: 2.8g | fiber: 0g

Marinara

Prep time: 5 minutes | Cook time: 0 minutes | Makes 4 cups

1 (28-ounce / 794-g) can peeled whole San Marzano tomatoes
¼ cup extra-virgin olive oil
2 tablespoons red wine vinegar
1 teaspoon dried basil leaves
1 teaspoon dried oregano leaves

1 teaspoon dried parsley leaves
1 teaspoon garlic powder
1 teaspoon kosher salt
1 teaspoon onion powder
½ teaspoon red pepper flakes
¼ teaspoon ground black pepper

Place the tomatoes and olive oil in a blender and blend for 30 seconds, or until the desired consistency is reached. If you prefer a chunkier sauce, pulse instead of blending for about 15 seconds. Stir in the remaining ingredients. Store in an airtight container for up to 1 week in the refrigerator or 6 months in the freezer.

calories: 85 | fat: 6.8g | protein: 1.0g | carbs: 5.0g | net carbs: 3.0g | fiber: 2.0g

Ketchup

Prep time: 5 minutes | Cook time: 1 hour | Makes 2 cups

1 (28-ounce / 794-g) can tomato purée
⅓ cup granulated erythritol
¼ teaspoon cayenne pepper
½ cup white vinegar
1½ teaspoons dehydrated

onions
½ teaspoon celery salt
½ teaspoon whole cloves
1 (1-inch) piece of cinnamon stick, broken

Combine the tomato purée, sweetener, and cayenne pepper in a medium-sized saucepan and bring to a boil over medium heat, then reduce the heat to low. Simmer until it reduces by half, about 30 minutes, stirring occasionally. Meanwhile, in another small saucepan, combine the vinegar, onions, celery salt, cloves, and cinnamon stick pieces. Bring to a boil, then remove from the heat. Strain out the solids. Add the flavored vinegar to the tomato mixture. Simmer for another 20 minutes, or until the ketchup reaches the desired consistency. Remove from the heat and let cool. Blend the cooled ketchup with an immersion blender or in a small blender until smooth. Store in a clean jar with an airtight lid for up to 1 month in the refrigerator.

calories: 15 | fat: 0g | protein: 0g | carbs: 3.8g | net carbs: 2.8g | fiber: 1.0g

Alfredo Sauce

Prep time: 5 minutes | Cook time: 1 minutes | Makes 1½ cups

½ cup mascarpone cheese (4 ounces / 113 g)
¼ cup grated Parmesan cheese
¼ cup (½ stick) butter

½ cup heavy whipping cream
½ teaspoon kosher salt
¼ teaspoon ground black pepper

Place the mascarpone, Parmesan, and butter in a medium-sized microwave-safe bowl. Microwave on high for 30 seconds, then stir. Microwave on high for 30 seconds more. Add the cream, salt, and pepper to the bowl. Whisk together until smooth. Serve immediately.

calories: 240 | fat: 23.9g | protein: 3.1g | carbs: 1.2g | net carbs: 1.2g | fiber: 0g

Creamy Caesar Dressing

Prep time: 5 minutes | Cook time: 0 minutes | Serves 4

½ cup mayonnaise
1 tablespoon Dijon mustard
Juice of ½ lemon
½ teaspoon Worcestershire sauce

Pinch pink Himalayan salt
Pinch freshly ground black pepper
¼ cup grated Parmesan cheese

In a medium bowl, whisk together the mayonnaise, mustard, lemon juice, Worcestershire sauce, pink Himalayan salt, and pepper until fully combined. Add the Parmesan cheese, and whisk until creamy and well blended. Keep in a sealed glass container in the refrigerator for up to 1 week.

calories: 222 | fat: 23g | protein: 2g | carbs: 2g | net carbs: 2g | fiber: 0g

Lemony Chunky Blue Cheese

Prep time: 5 minutes | Cook time: 0 minutes | Serves 4

½ cup sour cream
½ cup mayonnaise
Juice of ½ lemon
½ teaspoon Worcestershire sauce

Pink Himalayan salt, to taste
Freshly ground black pepper, to taste
2 ounces (57 g) crumbled blue cheese

In a medium bowl, whisk the sour cream, mayonnaise, lemon juice, and Worcestershire sauce. Season with pink Himalayan salt and pepper, and whisk again until fully combined. Fold in the crumbled blue cheese until well combined. Keep in a sealed glass container in the refrigerator for up to 1 week.

calories: 306 | fat: 32g | protein: 7g | carbs: 3g | net carbs: 3g | fiber: 0g

Sriracha Mayonnaise

Prep time: 5 minutes | Cook time: 0 minutes | Serves 4

½ cup mayonnaise
2 tablespoons Sriracha sauce
½ teaspoon garlic powder

½ teaspoon onion powder
¼ teaspoon paprika

In a small bowl, whisk together the mayonnaise, Sriracha, garlic powder, onion powder, and paprika until well mixed. Pour into an airtight glass container, and keep in the refrigerator for up to 1 week.

calories: 201 | fat: 22g | protein: 1g | carbs: 2g | net carbs: 1g | fiber: 1g

Avocado Mayonnaise

Prep time: 5 minutes | Cook time: 0 minutes | Serves 4

1 medium avocado, cut into chunks
½ teaspoon ground cayenne pepper
Juice of ½ lime

2 tablespoons fresh cilantro leaves (optional)
Pinch pink Himalayan salt
¼ cup olive oil

In a food processor (or blender), blend the avocado, cayenne pepper, lime juice, cilantro, and pink Himalayan salt until all the ingredients are well combined and smooth. Slowly incorporate the olive oil, adding 1 tablespoon at a time, pulsing the food processor in between. Keep in a sealed glass container in the refrigerator for up to 1 week.

calories: 58 | fat: 5g | protein: 1g | carbs: 4g | net carbs: 1g | fiber: 3g

Fettuccine Alfredo

Prep time: 5 minutes | Cook time: 10 minutes | Serves 2

4 tablespoons butter
2 ounces (57-g) cream cheese
1 cup heavy (whipping) cream
½ cup grated Parmesan cheese
1 garlic clove, finely minced

1 teaspoon dried Italian seasoning
Pink Himalayan salt, to taste
Freshly ground black pepper, to taste

In a heavy medium saucepan over medium heat, combine the butter, cream cheese, and heavy cream. Whisk slowly and constantly until the butter and cream cheese melt. Add the Parmesan, garlic, and Italian seasoning. Continue to whisk until everything is well blended. Turn the heat to medium-low and simmer, stirring occasionally, for 5 to 8 minutes to allow the sauce to blend and thicken. Season with pink Himalayan salt and pepper, and stir to combine. Toss with your favorite hot, precooked, keto-friendly noodles and serve. Keep this sauce in a sealed glass container in the refrigerator for up to 4 days.

calories: 294 | fat: 30g | protein: 5g | carbs: 2g | net carbs: 2g | fiber: 0g

Bolognese Sauce

Prep time: 15 minutes | Cook time: 7 to 8 hours | Serves 10

3 tablespoons extra-virgin olive oil, divided
1 pound (454 g) ground pork
½ pound (227 g) ground beef
½ pound (227 g) bacon, chopped
1 sweet onion, chopped

1 tablespoon minced garlic
2 celery stalks, chopped
2 (28-ounce / 794-g) cans diced tomatoes
½ cup coconut milk
¼ cup apple cider vinegar

Lightly grease the insert of the slow cooker with 1 tablespoon of the olive oil. In a large skillet over medium-high heat, heat the remaining 2 tablespoons of the olive oil. Add the pork, beef, and bacon, and sauté until cooked through, about 7 minutes. Stir in the onion and garlic and sauté for an additional 2 minutes. Transfer the meat mixture to the insert and add the celery, tomatoes, coconut milk, and apple cider vinegar. Cover and cook on low for 7 to 8 hours. Serve, or cool completely, and store in the refrigerator in a sealed container for up to 4 days or in the freezer for 1 month.

calories: 333 | fat: 23g | protein: 25g | carbs: 5g | net carbs: 2g | fiber: 3g

Asian Peanut Sauce

Prep time: 5 minutes | Cook time: 0 minutes | Serves 4

½ cup creamy peanut butter (I use Justin's)
2 tablespoons coconut aminos

1 teaspoon Sriracha sauce
1 teaspoon toasted sesame oil
1 teaspoon garlic powder

In a food processor (or blender), blend the peanut butter, coconut aminos, Sriracha sauce, sesame oil, and garlic powder until thoroughly mixed. Pour into an airtight glass container and keep in the refrigerator for up to 1 week.

calories: 185 | fat: 15g | protein: 7g | carbs: 8g | net carbs: 6g | fiber: 2g

Basil Dressing

Prep time: 10 minutes | Cook time: 0 minutes | Makes 1 cup

1 avocado, peeled and pitted
¼ cup sour cream
¼ cup extra-virgin olive oil
¼ cup chopped fresh basil
1 tablespoon freshly squeezed

lime juice
1 teaspoon minced garlic
Sea salt, to taste
Freshly ground black pepper, to taste

Place the avocado, sour cream, olive oil, basil, lime juice, and garlic in a food processor and pulse until smooth, scraping down the sides of the bowl once during processing. Season the dressing with salt and pepper. Keep the dressing in an airtight container in the refrigerator for 1 to 2 weeks.

calories: 173 | fat: 17g | protein: 5g | carbs: 1g | net carbs: 1g | fiber: 0g

Garlicky Mayonnaise

Prep time: 10 minutes | Cook time: 0 minutes | Serves 8

1 large egg
2 teaspoons Dijon mustard
1½ teaspoons minced garlic
1 cup olive oil

1 tablespoon freshly squeezed lemon juice
Sea salt, for seasoning

In a medium bowl, whisk together the egg, mustard, and garlic until they're well blended, about 2 minutes. Slowly add the olive oil in a thin, continuous stream, whisking constantly until the aioli is thick. Whisk in the lemon juice and season the aioli with salt. Store the aioli in an airtight container in the refrigerator for up to four days.

calories: 124 | fat: 14g | protein: 0g | carbs: 0g | net carbs: 0g | fiber: 0g

Spanish Queso Sauce

Prep time: 10 minutes | Cook time: 3 to 4 hours | Makes 4 cups

1 tablespoon extra-virgin olive oil
12 ounces (340-g) cream cheese

1 cup sour cream
2 cups salsa verde
1 cup monterey jack cheese, shredded

Lightly grease the insert of the slow cooker with the olive oil. In a large bowl, stir together the cream cheese, sour cream, salsa verde, and Monterey Jack cheese, until blended. Transfer the mixture to the insert. Cover and cook on low for 3 to 4 hours. Serve warm.

calories: 278 | fat: 25g | protein: 9g | carbs: 4g | net carbs: 4g | fiber: 0g

Garlic Aioli Sauce

Prep time: 5 minutes | Cook time: 0 minutes | Serves 4

½ cup mayonnaise
2 garlic cloves, minced
Juice of 1 lemon
1 tablespoon chopped fresh flat-leaf Italian parsley

1 teaspoon chopped chives
Pink Himalayan salt, to taste
Freshly ground black pepper, to taste

In a food processor (or blender), combine the mayonnaise, garlic, lemon juice, parsley, and chives, and season with pink Himalayan salt and pepper. Blend until fully combined. Pour into a sealed glass container and chill in the refrigerator for at least 30 minutes before serving. (This sauce will keep in the fridge for up to 1 week.)

calories: 204 | fat: 22g | protein: 1g | carbs: 3g | net carbs: 2g | fiber: 1g

Cheesy Hot Crab Sauce

Prep time: 10 minutes | Cook time: 5 to 6 hours | Makes 4 cups

8 ounces (227-g) cream cheese
8 ounces (227-g) goat cheese
1 cup sour cream
½ cup grated Asiago cheese
1 sweet onion, finely chopped

1 tablespoon granulated erythritol
2 teaspoons minced garlic
12 ounces (340-g) crabmeat, flaked
1 scallion, white and green parts, chopped

In a large bowl, stir together the cream cheese, goat cheese, sour cream, Asiago cheese, onion, erythritol, garlic, crabmeat, and scallion until well mixed. Transfer the mixture to an 8-by-4-inch loaf pan and place the pan in the insert of the slow cooker. Cover and cook on low for 5 to 6 hours. Serve warm.

calories: 361 | fat: 28g | protein: 17g | carbs: 10g | net carbs: 8g | fiber: 2g

Marinara Sauce

Prep time: 10 minutes | Cook time: 7 to 8 hours | Serves 12

3 tablespoons extra-virgin olive oil, divided
2 (28-ounce / 794-g) cans crushed tomatoes
½ sweet onion, finely chopped
2 teaspoons minced garlic

½ teaspoon salt
1 tablespoon chopped fresh basil
1 tablespoon chopped fresh oregano

Lightly grease the insert of the slow cooker with 1 tablespoon of the olive oil. Add the remaining 2 tablespoons of the olive oil, tomatoes, onion, garlic, and salt to the insert, stirring to combine. Cover and cook on low for 7 to 8 hours. Remove the cover and stir in the basil and oregano. Store the cooled sauce in a sealed container in the refrigerator for up to 1 week.

calories: 66 | fat: 5g | protein: 1g | carbs: 7g | net carbs: 5g | fiber: 2g

Cheesy Spinach Basil Pesto

Prep time: 10 minutes | Cook time: 0 minutes | Makes 2 cups

2 cups fresh spinach
1 cup fresh basil leaves
3 garlic cloves, smashed
¼ cup pecans

¼ cup grated Parmesan cheese
½ cup good-quality olive oil
Sea salt, for seasoning
Freshly ground black pepper, for seasoning

Blend the base. Put the spinach, basil, garlic, pecans, and Parmesan in a blender and pulse until the mixture is finely chopped, scraping down the sides of the blender once. Finish the pesto. While the blender is running, pour in the olive oil in a thin stream and blend until the pesto is smooth. Season it with salt and pepper. Store. Store in a sealed container in the refrigerator for up to one week.

calories: 60 | fat: 6g | protein: 1g | carbs: 1g | net carbs: 1g | fiber: 0g

Bolognese Sauce

Prep time: 15 minutes | Cook time: 40 minutes | Serves 4

2 tablespoons olive oil
1 pound (454 g) ground beef
1 onion, chopped
2 celery stalks, chopped
2 tablespoons minced garlic
1 (28-ounce / 794-g) can diced tomatoes
¼ cup red wine

¼ cup tomato purée
2 teaspoons dried oregano
2 teaspoons dried basil
1 teaspoon dried parsley
½ teaspoon sea salt
¼ teaspoon red pepper flakes

In a large pot over medium-high heat, warm the olive oil. Brown the ground beef, stirring it occasionally, until cooked through, about 6 minutes. Stir in the onion, celery, and garlic and sauté until softened, about 3 minutes. Add the remaining ingredients. Cook the sauce. Bring the sauce to a boil, then reduce the heat to low and simmer it for 25 to 30 minutes, stirring occasionally. Cool the sauce completely and store in a sealed container in the refrigerator for up to four days.

calories: 457 | fat: 35g | protein: 21g | carbs: 13g | net carbs: 8g | fiber: 5g

Herbed Balsamic Vinegar

Prep time: 4 minutes | Cook time: 0 minutes | Makes 1 cup

1 cup extra-virgin olive oil
¼ cup balsamic vinegar
2 tablespoons chopped fresh oregano
1 teaspoon chopped fresh basil

1 teaspoon minced garlic
Sea salt, to taste
Freshly ground black pepper, to taste

Whisk the olive oil and vinegar in a small bowl until emulsified, about 3 minutes. Whisk in the oregano, basil, and garlic until well combined, about 1 minute. Season the dressing with salt and pepper. Transfer the dressing to an airtight container, and store it in the refrigerator for up to 1 week. Give the dressing a vigorous shake before using it.

calories: 83 | fat: 9g | protein: 0g | carbs: 0g | net carbs: 0g | fiber: 0g

Herbed Kale Pesto

Prep time: 15 minutes | Cook time: 0 minutes | Makes 1½ cups

1 cup chopped kale
1 cup fresh basil leaves
3 garlic cloves

2 teaspoons nutritional yeast
¼ cup extra-virgin olive oil

Place the kale, basil, garlic, and yeast in a food processor and pulse until the mixture is finely chopped, about 3 minutes. With the food processor running, drizzle the olive oil into the pesto until a thick paste forms, scraping down the sides of the bowl at least once. Add a little water if the pesto is too thick. Store the pesto in an airtight container in the refrigerator for up to 1 week

calories: 44 | fat: 4g | protein: 1g | carbs: 1g | net carbs: 1g | fiber: 0g

Spicy Enchilada Sauce

Prep time: 10 minutes | Cook time: 7 to 8 hours | Makes 4 cups

¼ cup extra-virgin olive oil, divided
2 cups puréed tomatoes
1 cup water
1 sweet onion, chopped

2 jalapeño peppers, chopped
2 teaspoons minced garlic
2 tablespoons chili powder
1 teaspoon ground coriander

Lightly grease the insert of the slow cooker with 1 tablespoon of the olive oil. Place the remaining 3 tablespoons of the olive oil, tomatoes, water, onion, jalapeño peppers, garlic, chili powder, and coriander in the insert. Cover and cook on low 7 to 8 hours. Serve over poultry or meat. After cooling, store the sauce in a sealed container in the refrigerator for up to 1 week.

calories: 92 | fat: 8g | protein: 2g | carbs: 4g | net carbs: 2g | fiber: 2g

Chapter 15 Egg and Dairy

Double Cheese Stuffed Bell Peppers

Prep time: 10 minutes | Cook time: 17 minutes | Serves 4

4 summer bell peppers, divined and halved
1 clove garlic, minced
4 ounces (113 g) cream cheese
2 ounces (57 g) Mozzarella cheese, crumbled
2 tablespoons Greek-style yogurt

Cook the peppers in boiling water in a Dutch oven until just tender or approximately 7 minutes. Mix the garlic, cream cheese, mozzarella, and yogurt until well combined. Then, stuff the peppers with the cheese mixture. Arrange the stuffed peppers on a tinfoil-lined baking pan. Bake in the preheated oven at 360°F (182°C) for 10 to 12 minutes. Serve at room temperature. Bon appétit!

calories: 140 | fat: 10g | protein: 8g | carbs: 6g | net carbs: 5g | fiber: 1g

Cheesy Omelet and Vegetables

Prep time: 15 minutes | Cook time: 5 minutes | Serves 2

2 teaspoons olive oil
2 scallion stalks, chopped
2 garlic cloves, minced
bell peppers, chopped
½ cup cauliflower florets
eggs
½ teaspoon cayenne pepper
Kosher salt and ground black
pepper, to season
½ teaspoon dried Mexican oregano
½ teaspoon chili pepper flakes
½ teaspoon dried parsley flakes
2 ounces (57 g) Cotija cheese, crumbled

Heat the olive oil in a medium-sized pan over moderate heat. Sauté the scallions and garlic until just tender and fragrant. Now, stir in the peppers and cauliflower and continue sautéing an additional 2 to 3 minutes. Meanwhile, mix the eggs with the cayenne pepper, salt, black pepper, oregano, chili pepper flakes, and parsley. Pour the egg mixture over the sautéed vegetables. Let it cook, tilting your pan so the raw parts can cook. Add the Cotija cheese, fold over and leave for 1 minute before slicing and serving. Enjoy!

calories: 287 | fat: 20g | protein: 17g | carbs: 7g | net carbs: 4g | fiber: 3g

Scrambled Eggs and Baby Spinach

Prep time: 5 minutes | Cook time: 2 minutes | Serves 2

2 teaspoons olive oil
4 cups baby spinach
½ teaspoon garlic powder
4 eggs, well whisked
Sea salt cayenne pepper, to taste, to taste

Heat the olive oil in a frying pan over medium-high heat. Add in the baby spinach and garlic powder; cook, until wilted, about 1 minute or so. Now, add the whisked eggs to the pan and cook for 1 minute, stirring continuously to ensure even cooking. Season with salt and cayenne pepper and serve immediately. Enjoy!

calories: 183 | fat: 13g | protein: 13g | carbs: 3g | net carbs: 2g | fiber: 1g

Spicy Brown Mushroom Omelet

Prep time: 10 minutes | Cook time: 5 minutes | Serves 2

1 tablespoon olive oil
½ brown onion, thinly sliced
1 garlic clove, thinly sliced
1 green chili, minced
½ pound (227 g) brown mushrooms, sliced
4 eggs, whisked
1 tablespoon fresh coriander, chopped
Sea salt and ground black pepper, to taste
½ teaspoon Kashmiri chili powder
½ teaspoon garam masala

In a nonstick skillet, heat the olive oil until sizzling. Then, sauté the onion until translucent. Now, stir in the garlic, chili pepper, and mushrooms and continue sautéing until just tender and fragrant or about 2 minutes. Reserve. Add in the whisked eggs, fresh coriander, salt, black pepper, Kashmiri chili powder, and garam masala. Give it a quick swirl to distribute the eggs evenly across the skillet. Cook for 2 to 3 minutes. Flip your omelet over and cook an additional minute or so. Fill with the mushroom mixture, fold and serve immediately. Bon appétit!

calories: 217 | fat: 16g | protein: 14g | carbs: 5g | net carbs: 4g | fiber: 1g

Egg, Scallion, Jalapeño Pepper Salad

Prep time: 10 minutes | Cook time: 10 minutes | Serves 2

3 eggs
¼ cup scallions, chopped
1 jalapeño pepper, deseeded and minced
¼ cup mayonnaise
1 teaspoon Dijon mustard
Kosher salt and ground black pepper, to taste
1 tablespoon fresh parsley, roughly chopped
½ teaspoon sweet paprika

Arrange the eggs in a small saucepan. Pour in water (1-inch above the eggs) and bring to a boil. Heat off and let it sit, covered, for 9 to 10 minutes. When the eggs are cool enough to handle, peel away the shells, and rinse the eggs under running water. Chop the eggs and transfer them to a serving bowl. Add in the scallions, jalapeno pepper, mayonnaise, mustard, salt, and black pepper. Sprinkle fresh parsley and paprika over the salad and serve well chilled.

calories: 398 | fat: 35g | protein: 15g | carbs: 5g | net carbs: 4g | fiber: 1g

Yogurt and Swiss Cheese Soup

Prep time: 10 minutes | Cook time: 13 minutes | Serves 2

2 tablespoons butter, at room temperature
½ cup shallots, chopped
½ cup cream of onion soup
½ cup water
1 cup yogurt
4 ounces (113 g) Swiss cheese, shredded

Melt the butter in a pot over a moderate flame; now, sauté the shallots until just tender and fragrant or about 3 minutes. Stir in the cream of onion soup and water. Turn the heat to simmer and let it cook for 10 minutes more or until everything is heated through. Heat off; fold in the yogurt and cheese. Whisk until everything is well incorporated and the cheese completely melts. Ladle into individual bowls. Bon appétit!

calories: 365 | fat: 27g | protein: 21g | carbs: 7g | net carbs: 6g | fiber: 1g

Egg Muffins

Prep time: 20 minutes | Cook time: 15 minutes | Serves 4

6 tablespoons almond flour
2 tablespoons flaxseed meal
¼ teaspoon baking soda
4 eggs
4 ounces (113 g) cheddar cheese, shredded

In a mixing bowl, thoroughly combine all of the above ingredients until well incorporated. Line a muffin tin with non-stick baking cups. Scrape the batter into the prepared baking cups. Bake in the preheated oven at 350ºF (180ºC) for 15 to 17 minutes. Transfer to a wire rack to cool slightly before unmolding and serving. Bon appétit!

calories: 292 | fat: 23g | protein: 16g | carbs: 5g | net carbs: 2g | fiber: 3g

Bacon Frittata with Olives and Herbs

Prep time: 10 minutes | Cook time: 19 minutes | Serves 4

6 eggs
½ cup heavy cream
2 tablespoons Greek-style yogurt
2 ounces (57 g) bacon, chopped
Sea salt and freshly ground black pepper, to taste
1 tablespoon olive oil
½ cup red onions, peeled and
sliced
1 garlic clove, finely chopped
8 Kalamata olives, pitted and sliced
1 teaspoon dried oregano
½ teaspoon dried rosemary
½ teaspoon dried marjoram
4 ounces (113 g) feta cheese, crumbled

Preheat your oven to 360ºF (182ºC). Sprits a baking pan with a nonstick cooking spray. Mix the eggs, cream, yogurt, bacon, salt, and black pepper. Heat the oil in a skillet over medium-high heat. Now, cook the onion and garlic until tender and fragrant, about 3 minutes. Transfer the mixture to the prepared baking pan. Pour the egg mixture over the vegetables. Add olives, oregano, rosemary, and marjoram. Bake approximately 13 minutes, until the eggs are set. Scatter feta cheese over the top and bake an additional 3 minutes. Let it sit for 5 minutes; slice into wedges and serve.

calories: 345 | fat: 29g | protein: 18g | carbs: 4g | net carbs: 3g | fiber: 1g

Paprika Egg Salad with Mayo

Prep time: 5 minutes | Cook time: 13 minutes | Serves 5

7 eggs
2 scallions, chopped
1 cup radishes, thinly sliced
1 bell pepper, chopped
⅓ cup mayonnaise
1 teaspoon stone-ground mustard
Kosher salt and ground black pepper, to taste
1 teaspoon paprika

Arrange the eggs in a saucepan. Pour in water (1-inch above the eggs) and bring to a boil. Heat off and let it sit, covered, for 13 minutes. When the eggs are cool enough to handle, peel away the shells, and rinse the eggs under running water. Chop the eggs and transfer them to a salad bowl. Add in the scallions, radishes, bell peppers, mayo, and mustard. Season with salt and black pepper to taste. Gently stir until everything is well incorporated. Sprinkle paprika on top and serve well chilled. Bon appétit!

calories: 172 | fat: 14g | protein: 8g | carbs: 3g | net carbs: 2g | fiber: 1g

Italian Bacon Omelet

Prep time: 10 minutes | Cook time: 5 minutes | Serves 3

3 ounces (85 g) bacon, diced
2 garlic cloves, minced
1 Italian pepper, chopped
6 eggs, whisked
1 teaspoon Italian seasoning
blend
Sea salt and ground black pepper, to season
½ cup goat cheese, shredded

Preheat a nonstick skillet over a medium-high flame. Now, cook the bacon until crisp or about 4 minutes; reserve. Add in the garlic and Italian pepper; continue to sauté for a minute or so until aromatic. Pour the eggs into the skillet. Sprinkle with the Italian seasoning blend, salt, and black pepper. Cook until the eggs are golden brown on top. Add the reserved bacon and goat cheese. Fold your omelet in half and serve immediately. Bon appétit!

calories: 481 | fat: 43g | protein: 17g | carbs: 5g | net carbs: 4g | fiber: 1g

Mediterranean Shakshuka

Prep time: 10 minutes | Cook time: 0 minutes | Serves 3

1 tablespoon avocado oil
½ cup diced onion
2 cloves garlic, minced
1 (10-ounce / 283-g) can diced tomatoes with green chilies
½ cup tomato purée
1 teaspoon paprika
1 teaspoon ground cumin
½ teaspoon sea salt
6 large eggs
2 tablespoons chopped fresh parsley

In a sauté pan, heat the oil over medium-low heat. Add the diced onion and cook for about 10 minutes, until browned. Add the minced garlic and sauté for about 1 minute, until fragrant. Add the diced tomatoes (with juices), tomato purée, paprika, and cumin and mix. Add the sea salt. Cover and simmer 12 to 15 minutes, until the tomato mixture has thickened and most of the liquid is gone. Crack the eggs into the pan so that each egg is surrounded by tomato mixture. Sprinkle the eggs lightly with more sea salt. Cover and cook for 4 to 6 minutes, until the egg whites are opaque, but the yolks are still runny. Sprinkle with parsley to serve.

calories: 248 | fat: 15g | protein: 16g | carbs: 10g | net carbs: 8g | fiber: 2g

Broccoli and Cauliflower Omelet

Prep time: 10 minutes | Cook time: 10 minutes | Serves 6

2 tablespoons butter
1 medium-sized leek, chopped
1 cup broccoli florets
1 cup cauliflower florets
8 eggs
4 tablespoons sour cream
¼ teaspoon garlic powder
½ teaspoon cayenne pepper
Sea salt and freshly ground black pepper, to taste
½ cup Greek feta cheese, crumbled

Melt the butter in a nonstick aluminum pan over a moderate flame. Now, sauté the leeks, broccoli and cauliflower for 5 minutes, until they've softened. Thoroughly combine the eggs, sour cream, garlic powder, cayenne pepper, salt, and black pepper. Pour the egg mixture over the vegetables in the pan. Move the pan around to spread it out evenly. Continue to cook for about 5 minutes until the eggs are fully set and the surface is smooth. Top with feta cheese and serve immediately. Bon appétit!

calories: 266 | fat: 20g | protein: 15g | carbs: 6g | net carbs: 5g | fiber: 1g

Egg and Bacon Muffins with Kale

Prep time: 10 minutes | Cook time: 16 minutes | Serves 4

½ cup bacon
1 shallot, chopped
1 garlic clove, minced
1 cup kale
1 ripe tomato, chopped
6 eggs

1 cup Asiago cheese, shredded
Salt and black pepper, to taste
1 teaspoon dried rosemary
½ teaspoon dried basil
½ teaspoon dried marjoram

Start by preheating your oven to 390ºF (199ºC). Add muffin liners to a muffin tin. Preheat your pan over medium heat. Cook the bacon for 3 to 4 minutes; now, chop the bacon and reserve. Now, cook the shallots and garlic in the bacon fat until they are tender. Add the remaining ingredients and mix to combine well. Pour the batter into muffin cups and bake for 13 minutes or until the edges are slightly browned. Allow your muffins to stand for 5 minutes before removing from the tin. Bon appétit!

calories: 384 | fat: 30g | protein: 24g | carbs: 5g | net carbs: 4g | fiber: 1g

Two-Cheese Sausage Balls

Prep time: 5 minutes | Cook time: 18 minutes | Serves 3

½ pound (227 g) breakfast
sausage
½ cup almond flour
½ cup Colby cheese, shredded
4 tablespoons Romano

cheese, freshly grated
1 egg
1 garlic clove, pressed
2 tablespoons fresh chives,
minced

Thoroughly combine all ingredients in a mixing bowl; mix until everything is well incorporated. Shape the mixture into balls and arrange them on a parchment-lined cookie sheet. Bake in the preheated oven at 360ºF (182ºC) for about 18 minutes. Serve warm or cold. Bon appétit!

calories: 412 | fat: 35g | protein: 20g | carbs: 5g | net carbs: 5g | fiber: 0g

Herbed Cheese Balls

Prep time: 10 minutes | Cook time: 0 minutes | Serves 10

2 tablespoons mayonnaise
8 ounces (227 g) extra-sharp
Cheddar cheese, shredded
6 ounces (170 g) cream
cheese, softened
½ cup sour cream
½ teaspoon paprika

¼ teaspoon granulated garlic
powder
1 teaspoon oregano
1 teaspoon basil
1 teaspoon rosemary
1 teaspoon mint
2 tablespoons chives, chopped

In a mixing bowl, thoroughly combine the mayonnaise, Cheddar cheese, cream cheese, and sour cream until smooth and uniform. Wrap the cheese mixture in a plastic wrap and form into a ball. Refrigerate the cheese ball at least 2 hours. Meanwhile, mix the remaining ingredients until well combined. Roll the cheese ball over the herb mixture. Serve well chilled with assorted keto veggies. Bon appétit!

calories: 176 | fat: 16g | protein: 7g | carbs: 2g | net carbs: 1g | fiber: 1g

Old-Fashioned Greek Tirokroketes

Prep time: 10 minutes | Cook time: 11 minutes | Serves 5

2 ounces (57 g) feta cheese,
crumbled
3 ounces (85 g) smoked gouda
cheese, grated
2 ounces (57 g) Cheddar
cheese, grated
¼ teaspoon oregano

½ teaspoon basil
¼ teaspoon garlic powder
3 eggs, lightly beaten
¼ cup flaxseed meal
¼ cup almond flour
1 teaspoon baking powder

In a mixing bowl, combine all ingredients until everything is well incorporated. Cover the bowl with a plastic wrap and place in your refrigerator at least 30 minutes. Grab about a spoonful of the mixture and roll it into a ball using your hands. Bake in the preheated oven at 390ºF (199ºC) for about 11 minutes. Serve immediately and enjoy!

calories: 247 | fat: 20g | protein: 14g | carbs: 5g | net carbs: 2g | fiber: 3g

Greek Scrambled Eggs

Prep time: 6 minutes | Cook time: 6 minutes | Serves 3

2 tablespoons butter
4 tablespoons Greek yogurt
6 eggs
½ teaspoon cayenne pepper
½ teaspoon oregano

½ teaspoon basil
Sea salt and freshly ground
black pepper, to taste
3 ounces (85 g) halloumi
cheese, crumbled

Melt the butter in a frying pan over moderate heat. Then, thoroughly combine the Greek yogurt, eggs, cayenne pepper, oregano, basil, salt, and black pepper. Pour the yogurt/egg mixture into the frying pan. Continue to cook, stirring with a spatula, for about 6 minutes until thick and creamy curds form. Top with halloumi cheese and serve warm. Enjoy!

calories: 313 | fat: 25g | protein: 19g | carbs: 2g | net carbs: 2g | fiber: 0g

Sausage Frittatas with Goat Cheese

Prep time: 10 minutes | Cook time: 25 to 27 minutes | Serves 6

6 ounces (170 g) pork
sausage, sliced
1 teaspoon fresh garlic
4 tablespoons green onions,
chopped
1 bell pepper, chopped
⅓ cup heavy whipping cream

5 eggs
Flaky salt and ground black
pepper, to season
½ teaspoon basil
½ teaspoon oregano
1⅓ cups goat cheese,
crumbled

Heat up a lightly oiled nonstick skillet over a moderate flame. Sear the sausage, crumbling with a fork. Cook the garlic, onions, and bell pepper in the pan drippings, stirring frequently to ensure even cooking. Add the sausage back to the skillet and stir to combine. Heat off. In a mixing dish, thoroughly combine the heavy whipping cream with the eggs; fold in the sausage/vegetable mixture. Season with salt, black pepper, basil, and oregano. Divide the mixture between lightly greased muffin cups. Bake in the preheated oven at 360ºF (182ºC) approximately 20 minutes. Top with the cheese and bake for 5 to 7 minutes longer or until they starting to get slightly browned on top. Bon appétit!

calories: 287 | fat: 24g | protein: 16g | carbs: 2g | net carbs: 2g | fiber: 0g

Cheesy Tomato Frittata

Prep time: 5 minutes | Cook time: 25 to 33 minutes | Serves 4

⅓ cup Greek-style yogurt
6 eggs
⅔ cup Cheddar cheese, shredded

1 tomato, sliced
2 scallions, chopped

Start by preheating your oven to 355°F (179°C). Then, mix the Greek-style yogurt and eggs until frothy. Add in ½ of cheese, tomato, and scallions. Spoon the mixture into a lightly oiled baking pan. Scatter the remaining Cheddar cheese over the top. Bake in the preheated oven for 25 to 33 minutes or until the edges appear cooked and the center jiggles just a bit. Remove your frittata to a cooling rack before slicing and serving. Slice into four wedges and serve. Bon appétit!

calories: 299 | fat: 23g | protein: 20g | carbs: 3g | net carbs: 3g | fiber: 0g

Dilled Egg Salad with Dijon Mayo

Prep time: 5 minutes | Cook time: 12 minutes | Serves 3

4 eggs
1 teaspoon Dijon mustard
4 tablespoons mayonnaise

1 scallion, chopped
1 tablespoon fresh dill, minced

Place the eggs in a saucepan and fill with enough water. Bring the water to a rolling boil; heat off. Cover and allow the eggs to sit for about 12 minutes; let them cool. Peel and chop the eggs; place them in a salad bowl; add in the mustard, mayonnaise, scallions, and dill. Salt and pepper to taste. Serve well-chilled and enjoy!

calories: 212 | fat: 20g | protein: 8g | carbs: 1g | net carbs: 1g | fiber: 0g

French Scrambled Eggs

Prep time: 5 minutes | Cook time: 8 minutes | Serves 3

6 large eggs
1 tablespoon butter, at room temperature
¼ teaspoon ground black pepper

Sea salt, to taste
4 tablespoons crème fraîche

Crack the eggs into a bowl and beat them with a wire whisk until the yolks and whites are fully incorporated into each other. Then, melt the butter in a nonstick skillet over a moderate flame. Once hot, add the egg mixture to the skillet. The eggs will start to form curds. Stir until just set but still slightly wet or 8 to 10 minutes. Add in the black pepper, salt, and crème fraiche. Remove from the heat. Enjoy!

calories: 257 | fat: 21g | protein: 13g | carbs: 1g | net carbs: 1g | fiber: 0g

Goat Cheese Omelet

Prep time: 5 minutes | Cook time: 7 minutes | Serves 2

2 teaspoons butter, at room temperature
4 eggs, whisked
4 tablespoons goat cheese

1 teaspoon paprika
Sea salt and ground black pepper, to taste

Melt the butter in a pan over medium heat. Add the whisked eggs to the pan and cover with the lid; reduce the heat to medium-low. Cook for 4 minutes; now, stir in the cheese and paprika; continue to cook an additional 3 minutes or until cheese has melted. Season with salt and pepper and serve immediately. Enjoy!

calories: 287 | fat: 23g | protein: 20g | carbs: 1g | net carbs: 1g | fiber: 0g

Mangalore-Style Egg Curry

Prep time: 15 minutes | Cook time: 20 minutes | Serves 4

2 tablespoons olive oil
½ cup scallions, chopped
1 teaspoon Kashmiri chili powder
¼ teaspoon carom seeds
¼ teaspoon methi seeds
Kosher salt and ground black pepper, to taste
2 ripe tomatoes, puréed
2 teaspoons tamarind paste

½ cup chicken stock
4 boiled egg, peeled
1 teaspoon curry paste
2 tablespoons curry leaves
½ teaspoon cinnamon powder
½ cup coconut milk
1 tablespoon cilantro leaves

Heat the oil in a pan over medium heat. Now, cook the scallions and chili for 3 minutes, until tender and fragrant. Add carom seeds, methi seeds, salt, pepper, and tomatoes; cook for a further 8 minutes. Then, add the tamarind paste and chicken stock. Reduce the heat to medium-low and cook for 3 minutes more. Add the eggs, curry paste, curry leaves, cinnamon powder, and coconut milk. Let it simmer for 6 minutes more. Garnish with cilantro leaves. Bon appétit!

calories: 305 | fat: 16g | protein: 32g | carbs: 6g | net carbs: 5g | fiber: 1g

Ham, Cheese and Egg Cups

Prep time: 10 minutes | Cook time: 5 minutes | Serves 6

6 thin slices ham
1 teaspoon mustard
6 eggs
4 ounces (113 g) cream cheese

½ teaspoon red pepper flakes, crushed
Garlic salt and ground black pepper, to taste
6 ounces (170 g) Colby cheese, shredded
2 tablespoons green onions, chopped

Spritz a muffin tin with nonstick cooking spray. Place the ham slices over each muffin cup and gently press down until a cup shape forms. In a mixing dish, whisk the mustard, eggs, cream cheese, red pepper, garlic salt, and black pepper. Divide the egg mixture between the cups. Top with the shredded Colby cheese. Bake in the preheated oven at 360ºF (182ºC) approximately 25 minutes. Transfer the muffin tin to a wire rack before serving. Garnish with green onions and serve. Bon appétit!

calories: 258 | fat: 19g | protein: 18g | carbs: 3g | net carbs: 3g | fiber: 0g

Mediterranean Aïoli

Prep time: 10 minutes | Cook time: 0 minutes | Serves 6

2 egg yolks
1 teaspoon stone-ground mustard
½ teaspoon sea salt
A pinch of ground black pepper

1 teaspoon garlic, crushed
1 tablespoon lemon juice
½ cup extra-virgin olive oil
1 tablespoon fresh chives

Whisk the egg yolks and add them to your food processor. Add in the mustard, salt, black pepper, garlic, and lemon juice; continue mixing until everything is well incorporated. Now, with the machine running, add the oil to the egg yolk mixture in a steady stream. Mix until you reach your desired thickness. Garnish with chives. Keep for about 1 week in the refrigerator. Bon appétit!

calories: 94 | fat: 9g | protein: 2g | carbs: 1g | net carbs: 1g | fiber: 0g

Fried Eggs with Canadian Bacon

Prep time: 5 minutes | Cook time: 5 minutes | Serves 2

2 slices Canadian bacon
4 eggs
¼ teaspoon ground black pepper

Salt, to season
8 cherry tomatoes, halves

Heat up a nonstick aluminum pan over a medium-high flame. Once hot, fry the bacon for 5 minutes until crispy; reserve, living the rendered fat in the pan. Turn the heat to medium-low. Crack the eggs into the bacon grease. Cover the pan with a lid and fry the eggs until they are cooked through. Salt and pepper to taste. Serve with the reserved bacon and cherry tomatoes on the side. Enjoy!

calories: 326 | fat: 13g | protein: 46g | carbs: 5g | net carbs: 4g | fiber: 1g

Boiled Eggs with Lemony Avocado

Prep time: 5 minutes | Cook time: 6 minutes | Serves 3

6 eggs
½ teaspoon kosher salt
½ teaspoon ground black pepper
½ teaspoon cayenne pepper

½ teaspoon dried dill weed
1 avocado, pitted and sliced
1 tablespoon lemon juice

Place the eggs in a pan of boiling water; then, cook over low heat for 6 minutes. Peel and halve the eggs. Sprinkle the eggs with salt, black pepper, cayenne pepper, and dill. Serve on individual plates; drizzle the avocado slices with fresh lemon juice and serve with eggs. Enjoy!

calories: 222 | fat: 17g | protein: 12g | carbs: 6g | net carbs: 2g | fiber: 4g

Chapter 16 Side Dishes

Roasted Cauliflower with Serrano Ham
Prep time: 5 minutes | Cook time: 20 minutes | Serves 6

1 head cauliflower, cut into 1-inch slices
2 tablespoons olive oil
Salt and chili pepper, to taste
1 teaspoon garlic powder
10 slices Serrano ham, chopped
¼ cup pine nuts, chopped
1 teaspoon capers
1 teaspoon parsley

Preheat oven to 450ºF (235ºC) and line a baking sheet with foil. Brush the cauli steaks with olive oil and season with chili pepper, garlic, and salt. Spread the cauli slices on the baking sheet. Roast in the oven for 10 minutes until tender and lightly browned. Remove the sheet and sprinkle the ham and pine nuts all over the cauli. Bake for another 10 minutes until the ham is crispy and a nutty aroma is perceived. Take out, sprinkle with capers and parsley and serve.

calories: 180 | fat: 13g | protein: 11g | carbs: 8g | net carbs: 5g | fiber: 3g

Roasted Brussels Sprouts with Balsamic Glaze
Prep time: 5 minutes | Cook time: 30 minutes | Serves 4

3 tablespoons balsamic vinegar
1 tablespoon erythritol
½ tablespoon olive oil
Salt and black pepper, to taste
1 pound (454 g) Brussels sprouts, halved
5 slices prosciutto, chopped

Preheat oven to 400ºF and line a baking sheet with parchment paper. Mix balsamic vinegar, erythritol, olive oil, salt, and black pepper and combine with the Brussels sprouts in a bowl. Spread the mixture on the baking sheet and roast for 30 minutes until tender on the inside and crispy on the outside. Toss with prosciutto, share among 4 plates, and serve with chicken breasts.

calories: 143 | fat: 5g | protein: 10g | carbs: 16g | net carbs: 11g | fiber: 5g

Mashed Cauliflower with Bacon and Chives
Prep time: 5 minutes | Cook time: 16 minutes | Serves 6

6 slices bacon
3 heads cauliflower, leaves removed
2 cups water
2 tablespoons melted butter
½ cup coconut milk
Salt and black pepper, to taste
¼ cup grated yellow Cheddar cheese
2 tablespoons chopped chives

Preheat oven to 350ºF (180ºC). Fry bacon in a heated skillet over medium heat for 5 minutes until crispy. Remove to a paper towel-lined plate, allow to cool, and crumble. Set aside and keep bacon fat. Boil cauli heads in water in a pot over high heat for 7 minutes, until tender. Drain and put in a bowl. Include butter, coconut milk, salt, black pepper, and purée using a hand blender until smooth and creamy. Lightly grease a casserole dish with the bacon fat and spread the mash on it. Sprinkle with Cheddar cheese and place under the broiler for 4 minutes on high until the cheese melts. Remove and top with bacon and chopped chives. Serve with pan-seared scallops.

calories: 206 | fat: 17g | protein: 8g | carbs: 8g | net carbs: 5g | fiber: 3g

Baked Zucchini Sticks with Garlic Aioli
Prep time: 5 minutes | Cook time: 15 minutes | Serves 4

¼ cup pork rind crumbs
1 teaspoon sweet paprika
¼ cup shredded Parmesan cheese
Aioli:
½ cup mayonnaise
1 garlic clove, minced
Salt and chili pepper, to taste
3 fresh eggs
2 zucchinis, cut into strips

Juice and zest from ½ lemon

Preheat oven to 425ºF and line a baking sheet with foil. Grease with cooking spray and set aside. Mix the pork rinds, paprika, Parmesan cheese, salt, and chili pepper in a bowl. Beat the eggs in another bowl. Coat zucchini strips in eggs, then in Parmesan mixture, and arrange on the baking sheet. Grease lightly with cooking spray and bake for 15 minutes to be crispy. To make the aioli, combine in a bowl mayonnaise, lemon juice, and garlic, and gently stir until everything is well incorporated. Add the lemon zest, adjust the seasoning and stir again. Cover and place in the refrigerator until ready to serve. Serve the zucchini strips with garlic aioli for dipping.

calories: 186 | fat: 11g | protein: 8g | carbs: 7g | net carbs: 5g | fiber: 2g

Baked Spinach Cheese Balls
Prep time: 10 minutes | Cook time: 10 to 12 minutes | Serves 8

⅓ cup crumbled ricotta cheese
¼ teaspoon nutmeg
¼ teaspoon pepper
3 tablespoons heavy cream
1 teaspoon garlic powder
1 tablespoon onion powder
2 tablespoons butter, melted
⅓ cup Parmesan cheese, shredded
2 eggs
1 cup spinach
1 cup almond flour

Place all ingredients in a food processor. Process until smooth. Place in the freezer for about 10 minutes. Make balls out of the mixture and arrange them on a lined baking sheet. Bake in the oven at 350ºF for about 10-12 minutes.

calories: 149 | fat: 9g | protein: 6g | carbs: 3g | net carbs: 1g | fiber: 2g

Cheddar Buffalo Chicken Bake
Prep time: 5 minutes | Cook time: 28 minutes | Serves 6

2 tablespoons olive oil
8 ounces (227 g) cream cheese
1 pound (454 g) ground chicken
1 cup buffalo sauce
1 cup ranch dressing
3 cups grated yellow Cheddar cheese

Preheat oven to 350ºF. Lightly grease a baking sheet with a cooking spray. Warm the oil in a skillet over medium heat and brown the chicken for 5 minutes, take off the heat, and set aside. Spread cream cheese at the bottom of the baking sheet, top with chicken, pour buffalo sauce over, add ranch dressing, and sprinkle with Cheddar cheese. Bake for 23 minutes until cheese has melted and golden brown on top. Remove and serve with veggie sticks.

calories: 618 | fat: 49g | protein: 33g | carbs: 14g | net carbs: 12g | fiber: 2g

Grilled Prosciutto-Chicken Wraps

Prep time: 5 minutes | Cook time: 6 minutes | Serves 8

¼ teaspoon garlic powder
8 ounces (227 g) Provolone
cheese

8 raw chicken tenders
Salt and black pepper, to taste
8 prosciutto slices

Pound the chicken until half an inch thick. Season with salt, black pepper, and garlic powder. Cut the provolone cheese into 8 strips. Place a slice of prosciutto on a flat surface. Place one chicken tender on top. Top with a provolone strip. Roll the chicken and secure with previously soaked skewers. Grill the wraps for 3 minutes per side.

calories: 271 | fat: 13g | protein: 35g | carbs: 2g | net carbs: 1g | fiber: 1g

Simple Boiled Stuffed Eggs

Prep time: 5 minutes | Cook time: 10 minutes | Serves 6

6 eggs
1 tablespoon Sriracha

⅓ cup mayonnaise
Salt, to taste

Place the eggs in a saucepan and cover with salted water. Bring to a boil over medium heat. Boil for 10 minutes. Place the eggs in an ice bath and let cool for 10 minutes. Peel and slice in half lengthwise. Scoop out the yolks to a bowl; mash with a fork. Whisk together the Sriracha, mayonnaise, mashed yolks, and salt, in a bowl. Spoon this mixture into egg whites.

calories: 92 | fat: 6g | protein: 6g | carbs: 3g | net carbs: 3g | fiber: 0g

Avocado Crostini Nori with Walnuts

Prep time: 5 minutes | Cook time: 2 minutes | Serves 4

8 slices low carb bread
(baguette)
4 nori sheets
1 cup mashed avocado
⅓ teaspoon salt

1 teaspoon lemon juice
1½ tablespoons coconut oil
⅓ cup chopped raw walnuts
1 tablespoon chia seeds

In a bowl, flake the nori sheets into the smallest possible pieces. In another bowl, mix the avocado, salt, and lemon juice, and stir in half of the nori flakes. Set aside. Place the bread slices on a baking sheet and toast in a broiler on medium heat for 2 minutes, making sure not to burn. Remove the crostini after and brush with coconut oil on both sides. Top each crostini with the avocado mixture and garnish with the chia seeds, chopped walnuts, Serve.

calories: 317 | fat: 18g | protein: 9g | carbs: 10g | net carbs: 3g | fiber: 7g

Tuna-Mayo Topped Dill Pickles

Prep time: 5 minutes | Cook time: 0 minutes | Serves 12

18 ounces (510 g) canned and
drained tuna
6 large dill pickles

¼ teaspoon garlic powder
⅓ cup sugar-free mayonnaise
1 tablespoon onion flakes

Combine the mayonnaise, tuna, onion flakes, and garlic powder in a bowl. Cut the pickles in half lengthwise. Top each half with tuna mixture. Place in the fridge for 30 minutes before serving.

calories: 59 | fat: 2g | protein: 9g | carbs: 3g | net carbs: 2g | fiber: 1g

Spiced Baked Gruyere Crisps

Prep time: 5 minutes | Cook time: 6 minutes | Serves 4

2 cups Gruyere cheese,
shredded
½ teaspoon garlic powder

¼ teaspoon onion powder
1 rosemary sprig, minced
½ teaspoon chili powder

Set oven to 400ºF (205ºC). Coat two baking sheets with parchment paper. Mix Gruyere cheese with the seasonings. Take 1 tablespoon of cheese mixture and form small mounds on the baking sheets. Bake for 6 minutes. Leave to cool. Serve.

calories: 276 | fat: 21g | protein: 20g | carbs: 1g | net carbs: 1g | fiber: 0g

Oven Baked String Beans and Mushrooms

Prep time: 10 minutes | Cook time: 20 to 25 minutes | Serves 4

2 cups string beans, cut in
halves
1 pound (454 g) cremini
mushrooms, quartered
3 tomatoes, quartered
2 cloves garlic, minced

3 tablespoons olive oil
3 shallots, julienned
½ teaspoon dried thyme
Salt and black pepper, to
season

Preheat oven to 450ºF (235ºC). In a bowl, mix the strings beans, mushrooms, tomatoes, garlic, olive oil, shallots, thyme, salt, and pepper. Pour the vegetables in a baking sheet and spread them all around. Place the baking sheet in the oven and bake the veggies for 20 to 25 minutes.

calories: 154 | fat: 11g | protein: 4g | carbs: 13g | net carbs: 9g | fiber: 4g

Mozzarella Prosciutto Wraps with Basil

Prep time: 5 minutes | Cook time: 0 minutes | Serves 6

6 thin prosciutto slices
18 basil leaves
18 ciliegine Mozzarella balls

2 tablespoons extra-virgin olive
oil

Cut the prosciutto slices into three strips each. Place basil leaves at the end of each strip. Top with a ciliegine Mozzarella ball. Wrap the Mozzarella in prosciutto. Secure with toothpicks. Arrange on a platter, drizzle with olive oil, and serve.

calories: 211 | fat: 16g | protein: 14g | carbs: 2g | net carbs: 1g | fiber: 1g

Baked Broccoli Bites

Prep time: 10 minutes | Cook time: 20 minutes | Serves 4

1½ pounds (680 g) broccoli,
cut into bite-sized florets
¼ cup extra-virgin olive oil
Juice of ½ lemon

2 cloves garlic, minced
Salt and pepper, to taste
Red pepper flakes (optional)

Preheat the oven to 400ºF (205ºC). In a large mixing bowl, combine the broccoli, oil, lemon juice, and garlic and toss until well coated. Season lightly with salt, black pepper, and red pepper flakes, if using. Pour onto a rimmed baking sheet and spread out in a single layer. Bake for 18 to 20 minutes, until lightly golden brown.

calories: 133 | fat: 14g | protein: 1g | carbs: 4g | net carbs: 3g | fiber: 1g

Pecorino Mushroom Burgers

Prep time: 15 minutes | Cook time: 13 minutes | Serves 4

2 tablespoons butter, softened
2 tablespoons olive oil
2 garlic cloves, minced
2 cups portobello mushrooms, chopped
4 tablespoons blanched almond flour
4 tablespoons ground flax

seeds
4 tablespoons hemp seeds
4 tablespoons sunflower seeds
1 tablespoon Cajun seasoning
1 teaspoon mustard
2 eggs, whisked
½ cup Pecorino cheese, shredded

Set a pan over medium heat and warm the olive oil. Add in mushrooms and garlic and sauté until there is no more water in mushrooms. Remove to a plate and let cool for a few minutes. In a bowl, place Pecorino cheese, almond flour, hemp seeds, mustard, eggs, sunflower seeds, flax seeds, mushrooms, and Cajun seasoning. Create 4 burgers from the mixture. To the same pan, add and warm the butter; fry the burgers for 7 minutes. Flip them over with a wide spatula and cook for 6 more minutes. Serve with guacamole.

calories: 368 | fat: 30g | protein: 14g | carbs: 15g | net carbs: 11g | fiber: 4g

Avocado-Bacon Stuffed Eggs

Prep time: 15 minutes | Cook time: 15 minutes | Serves 3

1 ripe avocado
4 large hard-boiled eggs
4 slices bacon, cooked and crumbled
1 red chili pepper, seeded and

minced
1 garlic clove, minced
2 tablespoons lemon juice
Salt and black pepper, to taste

Peel the eggs, halve them lengthwise and transfer the yolks to a mixing bowl. Add the avocado, chili pepper, garlic and lemon juice to the bowl. Mash with a fork until well combined. Season with salt and black pepper. Scoop the mixture into the egg whites and top with the crumbled bacon. Refrigerate until cold or serve right away.

calories: 455 | fat: 37g | protein: 25g | carbs: 8g | net carbs: 3g | fiber: 5g

Cheesy Cauli Bake with Mayo

Prep time: 5 minutes | Cook time: 25 minutes | Serves 6

2 heads cauliflower, cut into florets
¼ cup melted butter
Salt and black pepper to taste
1 pinch red pepper flakes

½ cup mayonnaise
¼ teaspoon Dijon mustard
3 tablespoons grated pecorino cheese

Preheat oven to 400ºF (205ºC) and grease a baking dish with cooking spray. Combine the cauli florets, butter, salt, black pepper, and red pepper flakes in a bowl until well mixed. Mix the mayonnaise and Dijon mustard in a bowl, and set aside until ready to serve. Arrange cauliflower florets on the prepared baking dish. Sprinkle with grated pecorino cheese and bake for 25 minutes until the cheese has melted and golden brown on the top. Remove, let sit for 3 minutes to cool, and serve with the mayo sauce.

calories: 171 | fat: 13g | protein: 5g | carbs: 13g | net carbs: 9g | fiber: 4g

Cheesy Ham Pizza Rolls

Prep time: 15 minutes | Cook time: 30 minutes | Serves 5

Dough:
½ cup Parmesan cheese
1 cup Mozzarella cheese
3 egg whites
Filling:
2 cups cooked ham, sliced
1 cup Gouda cheese, sliced
5 tablespoons tomato purée

¾ cup coconut flour
1 cup heavy cream

1 teaspoon crushed black pepper, for topping

Preheat the oven to 400ºF (205ºC), and line a baking sheet with parchment paper. In a food processor, combine the ingredients for the crust and process until a smooth dough forms. Flatten the dough into a rectangular shape onto the prepared baking sheet. Bake for about 15 minutes. Remove from the oven and allow to cool slightly. Spread the tomato purée evenly across the dough. Top with the sliced ham and Gouda cheese. Roll the dough carefully into a log. Slice the log into 5 even pieces and place each one back onto the baking sheet. Sprinkle with crushed black pepper. Bake again for about 10 minutes until the dough is golden brown and the cheese is bubbly.

calories: 492 | fat: 35g | protein: 35g | carbs: 6g | net carbs: 4g | fiber: 2g

Duo-Cheese Lettuce Rolls

Prep time: 5 minutes | Cook time: 5 minutes | Serves 6

½ pound (227 g) gouda cheese, grated
½ pound (227 g) feta cheese, crumbled
1 teaspoon taco seasoning mix

2 tablespoons olive oil
1½ cups guacamole
1 cup coconut milk
A head lettuce

Mix both types of cheese with taco seasoning mix. Set a pan over medium heat and warm the olive oil. Spread the shredded cheese mixture all over the pan. Fry for 5 minutes, turning once. Arrange some of the cheese mixture on each lettuce leaf, top with coconut milk and guacamole, then roll up folding in the ends to secure and serve.

calories: 401 | fat: 30g | protein: 18g | carbs: 10g | net carbs: 5g | fiber: 5g

Prosciutto-Wrapped Piquillo Peppers

Prep time: 15 minutes | Cook time: 0 minutes | Serves 8

8 canned roasted piquillo peppers
1 tablespoon olive oil
Filling:
8 ounces (227 g) goat cheese
3 tablespoons heavy cream
3 tablespoons chopped parsley

3 slices prosciutto, cut into thin slices
1 tablespoon balsamic vinegar

½ teaspoon minced garlic
1 tablespoon olive oil
1 tablespoon chopped mint

Mix all filling ingredients in a bowl. Place in a freezer bag, press down and squeeze, and cut off the bottom. Drain and deseed the peppers. Squeeze about 2 tablespoons of the filling into each pepper. Wrap a prosciutto slice onto each pepper. Secure with toothpicks. Arrange them on a serving platter. Sprinkle the olive oil and vinegar over.

calories: 216 | fat: 17g | protein: 11g | carbs: 6g | net carbs: 5g | fiber: 1g

Chicken-Stuffed Cucumber Bites
Prep time: 5 minutes | Cook time: 0 minutes | Serves 6

2 cucumbers, sliced with a
3-inch thickness
2 cups small dices leftover
chicken
¼ jalapeño pepper, seeded

and minced
1 tablespoon Dijon mustard
⅓ cup mayonnaise
Salt and black pepper, to taste

Cut mid-level holes in cucumber slices with a knife and set aside. Combine chicken, jalapeño pepper, mustard, mayonnaise, salt, and black pepper to be evenly mixed. Fill cucumber holes with chicken mixture and serve.

calories: 115 | fat: 14g | protein: 14g | carbs: 5g | net carbs: 4g | fiber: 1g

Mascarpone Turkey Pastrami Pinwheels
Prep time: 5 minutes | Cook time: 0 minutes | Serves 4

Cooking spray
8 ounces (227 g) mascarpone
cheese
10 ounces (284 g) turkey

pastrami, sliced
10 canned pepperoncini
peppers, sliced and drained

Lay a 12 x 12 plastic wrap on a flat surface and arrange the pastrami all over slightly overlapping each other. Spread the cheese on top of the salami layers and arrange the pepperoncini on top. Hold two opposite ends of the plastic wrap and roll the pastrami. Twist both ends to tighten and refrigerate for 2 hours. Unwrap the salami roll and slice into 2-inch pinwheels. Serve.

calories: 549 | fat: 49g | protein: 29g | carbs: 10g | net carbs: 7g | fiber: 3g

Creamy Keto Beans
Prep time: 5 minutes | Cook time: 2 minutes | Serves 4

11 ounces (312 g) green beans
1 cup coconut cream

2 teaspoons butter

Combine all the ingredients in the Instant Pot. Secure the lid. Select the Manual mode and set the cooking time for 2 minutes at High Pressure. Once cooking is complete, do a quick pressure release. Carefully open the lid. Serve warm.

calories: 184 | fat: 16.6g | protein: 2.9g | carbs: 8.4g | net carbs: 4.4g | fiber: 4.0g

Crispy Chorizo with Parsley
Prep time: 5 minutes | Cook time: 15 minutes | Serves 6

7 ounces (198 g) Spanish
chorizo, sliced
4 ounces (113 g) cream

cheese
¼ cup chopped parsley

Preheat oven to 325ºF (163ºC). Line a baking dish with waxed paper. Bake chorizo for 15 minutes until crispy. Remove and let cool. Arrange on a serving platter. Top with cream cheese. Serve sprinkled with parsley.

calories: 207 | fat: 18g | protein: 9g | carbs: 1g | net carbs: 1g | fiber: 0g

Classic Devilled Eggs with Sriracha Mayo
Prep time: 5 minutes | Cook time: 10 minutes | Serves 4

8 large eggs
3 cups water
3 tablespoons sriracha sauce

4 tablespoons mayonnaise
Salt, to taste
¼ teaspoon smoked paprika

Bring eggs to boil in salted water in a pot over high heat, and then reduce the heat to simmer for 10 minutes. Transfer eggs to an ice water bath, let cool completely and peel the shells. Slice the eggs in half height wise and empty the yolks into a bowl. Smash with a fork and mix in sriracha sauce, mayonnaise, and half of the paprika until smooth. Spoon filling into a piping bag with a round nozzle and fill the egg whites to be slightly above the brim. Garnish with remaining paprika and serve.

calories: 180 | fat: 12g | protein: 13g | carbs: 4g | net carbs: 4g | fiber: 0g

Feta Zucchini and Pepper Gratin
Prep time: 5 minutes | Cook time: 30 to 40 minutes | Serves 6

2 pounds (907 g) zucchinis,
sliced
2 red bell peppers, seeded and
sliced

Salt and black pepper, to taste
1½ cups crumbled feta cheese
2 tablespoons butter, melted
½ cup heavy whipping cream

Preheat oven to 370ºF (188ºC). Place the sliced zucchinis in a colander over the sink, sprinkle with salt and let sit for 20 minutes. Transfer to paper towels to drain the excess liquid. Grease a baking dish with cooking spray and make a layer of zucchini and bell peppers overlapping one another. Season with pepper, and sprinkle with feta cheese. Repeat the layering process a second time. Combine the butter and whipping cream in a bowl, stir to mix completely, and pour over the vegetables. Bake for 30-40 minutes or until golden brown on top.

calories: 211 | fat: 16g | protein: 10g | carbs: 9g | net carbs: 6g | fiber: 3g

Garlicky Roasted Vegetable Mix
Prep time: 10 minutes | Cook time: 15 to 20 minutes | Serves 4

1 butternut squash, cut into
chunks
¼ pound (113 g) shallots,
peeled
¼ pound (113 g) Brussels
sprouts

1 sprig rosemary, chopped
1 sprig thyme, chopped
4 cloves garlic, peeled only
3 tablespoons olive oil
Salt and black pepper, to taste

Preheat the oven to 450ºF (235ºC). Pour the butternut squash, shallots, garlic cloves, and Brussels sprouts in a bowl. Season with salt, black pepper, olive oil, and toss. Pour the mixture on a baking sheet and sprinkle with the chopped thyme and rosemary. Roast the vegetables for 15–20 minutes. Once ready, remove and spoon into a serving bowl. Serve with oven roasted chicken thighs.

calories: 159 | fat: 10g | protein: 3g | carbs: 14g | net carbs: 10g | fiber: 4g

Colby Bacon-Wrapped Jalapeño Peppers

Prep time: 5 minutes | Cook time: 25 minutes | Serves 6

12 jalapeño peppers
¼ cup shredded Colby cheese
6 ounces (170 g) cream

cheese, softened
6 slices bacon, halved

Cut the jalapeño peppers in half, and then remove the membrane and seeds. Combine cheeses and stuff into the pepper halves. Wrap each pepper with a bacon strip and secure with toothpicks. Place the filled peppers on a baking sheet lined with a piece of foil. Bake at 350ºF for 25 minutes until bacon has browned, and crispy and cheese is golden brown on the top. Remove to a paper towel lined plate to absorb grease, arrange on a serving plate, and serve warm.

calories: 219 | fat: 20g | protein: 7g | carbs: 3g | net carbs: 2g | fiber: 1g

Creamy Spinach

Prep time: 5 minutes | Cook time: 4 minutes | Serves 4

2 cups chopped spinach
2 ounces (57 g) Monterey Jack
cheese, shredded
1 cup almond milk

1 tablespoon butter
1 teaspoon minced garlic
½ teaspoon salt

Combine all the ingredients in the Instant Pot. Secure the lid. Select the Manual mode and set the cooking time for 4 minutes at High Pressure. Once cooking is complete, do a quick pressure release. Carefully open the lid. Give the mixture a good stir and serve warm.

calories: 101 | fat: 8.1g | protein: 4.2g | carbs: 2.6g | net carbs: 2.3g | fiber: 0.3g

Lemon-Butter Mushrooms

Prep time: 10 minutes | Cook time: 4 minutes | Serves 2

1 cup cremini mushrooms,
sliced
½ cup water
1 tablespoon lemon juice

1 teaspoon almond butter
1 teaspoon grated lemon zest
½ teaspoon salt
½ teaspoon dried thyme

Combine all the ingredients in the Instant Pot. Secure the lid. Select the Manual mode and set the cooking time for 4 minutes at High Pressure. Once cooking is complete, do a natural pressure release for 5 minutes, then release any remaining pressure. Carefully open the lid. Serve warm.

calories: 63 | fat: 4.8g | protein: 2.9g | carbs: 3.3g | net carbs: 2.1g | fiber: 1.2g

Simple Buttery Broccoli

Prep time: 5 minutes | Cook time: 3 minutes | Serves 6

1 broccoli head, florets only
Kosher salt and black pepper,

to taste
¼ cup butter

Place the broccoli in a pot filled with salted water and bring to a boil. Cook for about 3 minutes until crisp-tender. Drain the broccoli and transfer to a plate. Melt the butter in a microwave. Drizzle the butter over and season with some salt and black pepper.

calories: 102 | fat: 8g | protein: 3g | carbs: 7g | net carbs: 4g | fiber: 3g

Parmesan Cauliflower Fritters

Prep time: 5 minutes | Cook time: 6 minutes | Serves 4

1 pound (454 g) grated
cauliflower
½ cup Parmesan cheese,
grated
3 ounces (85 g) chopped onion
½ teaspoon baking powder

½ cup almond flour
2 eggs
½ teaspoon lemon juice
2 tablespoons olive oil
⅓ teaspoon salt

Sprinkle the salt over the cauliflower in a bowl, and let it stand for 10 minutes. Add in the other ingredients. Mix with your hands to combine. Place a skillet over medium heat, and heat olive oil. Shape fritters out of the cauliflower mixture. Fry in batches, for about 3 minutes per side.

calories: 231 | fat: 13g | protein: 11g | carbs: 10g | net carbs: 6g | | fiber: 4g

Cauli Rice with Cheddar and Bacon

Prep time: 10 minutes | Cook time: 8 to 10 minutes | Serves 8

1 head cauliflower, cut into
florets
2 tablespoons butter
¼ cup sour cream
2 tablespoons heavy cream
3 cloves garlic, minced

1 teaspoon sea salt
1½ cups shredded Cheddar
cheese
⅓ cup cooked bacon bits
¼ cup chopped green onions

Bring a large pot of water to a boil on the stove top. Add the cauliflower florets and cook for 8 to 10 minutes, until very soft. Drain well and pat dry. Meanwhile, in a microwave-safe bowl or in a saucepan, combine the butter, sour cream, heavy cream, garlic, and sea salt, and heat in the microwave or on the stove until hot and melted. Transfer the cauliflower florets to a food processor. Add the butter-cream mixture and purée until smooth. Transfer the cauliflower to a serving dish. Immediately stir in most of the Cheddar, bacon bits, and green onions, reserving a little of each for the topping. To serve, garnish with the reserved Cheddar, bacon, and green onions.

calories: 180 | fat: 13g | protein: 9g | carbs: 5g | net carbs: 3g | fiber: 2g

Ricotta Spinach Gnocchi

Prep time: 5 minutes | Cook time: 7 minutes | Serves 4

1 cup ricotta cheese
1 cup Parmesan cheese,
grated
¼ teaspoon nutmeg powder
1 egg, cracked into a bowl

Salt and black pepper, to taste
3 cups chopped spinach
1½ cups almond flour
2½ cups water
2 tablespoons butter

To a bowl, add the ricotta cheese, half of the Parmesan cheese, egg, nutmeg powder, salt, spinach, almond flour, and black pepper. Mix well. Make gnocchi of the mixture using 2 tablespoons and set aside. Bring the water to a boil over high heat on a stovetop, about 5 minutes. Place one gnocchi onto the water, if it breaks apart; add some more flour to the other gnocchi to firm it up. Put the remaining gnocchi in the water to poach and rise to the top, about 2 minutes. Remove the gnocchi with a perforated spoon to a serving plate. Melt the butter in a microwave and pour over the gnocchi. Sprinkle with the remaining Parmesan cheese and serve with green salad.

calories: 238 | fat: 16g | protein: 18g | carbs: 9g | net carbs: 4g | fiber: 5g

Liverwurst and Pistachio Balls

Prep time: 10 minutes | Cook time: 0 minutes | Serves 8

8 bacon slices, cooked and chopped
8 ounces (227 g) Liverwurst
¼ cup chopped pistachios

1 teaspoon Dijon mustard
6 ounces (170 g) cream cheese

Combine the liverwurst and pistachios in the bowl of food the processor. Pulse until smooth. Whisk the cream cheese and mustard in another bowl. Make 12 balls out of the liverwurst mixture. Make a thin cream cheese layer over. Coat with bacon, arrange on a plate and chill for 30 minutes.

calories: 227 | fat: 25g | protein: 9g | carbs: 4g | net carbs: 3g | fiber: 1g

Spicy Onion Rings

Prep time: 15 minutes | Cook time: 20 minutes | Serves 4

1 large onion, sliced into rings
½ cup almond flour
1 egg
½ teaspoon garlic powder

1 teaspoon paprika
1 teaspoon cayenne pepper
1 teaspoon salt

Preheat the oven to 400ºF (205ºC), and line a baking sheet with parchment paper. Add the egg to a mixing bowl and then add the almond flour and seasoning to another bowl. Stir the almond flour mixture well. Dip the sliced onions into the egg mixture, followed by the almond flour mix, covering both sides of the sliced onions. Add the onion rings to the baking sheet and bake for about 10 minutes on each side or until crispy.

calories: 51 | fat: 3g | protein: 3g | carbs: 4g | net carbs: 3g | fiber: 1g

Roasted Brussels Sprouts with Balsamic Glaze

Prep time: 5 minutes | Cook time: 20 to 30 minutes | Serves 8

¼ cup olive oil
2 tablespoons balsamic vinegar
½ teaspoon garlic powder

1 teaspoon sea salt
¼ teaspoon black pepper
1 pound (454 g) Brussels sprouts, trimmed and halved

Preheat the oven to 450ºF (235ºC). Line a large baking sheet with foil. In a large bowl, whisk together the oil, balsamic vinegar, garlic powder, sea salt, and black pepper, until smooth. Add the Brussels sprouts and toss to coat. Spread the Brussels sprouts over the baking sheet in a single layer, so that all the sprouts touch the pan. Roast for 10 to 15 minutes, until browned on the bottom. Flip and repeat for another 10 to 15 minutes.

calories: 88 | fat: 6g | protein: 1g | carbs: 5g | net carbs: 3g | fiber: 2g

Herbed Roasted Radishes

Prep time: 5 minutes | Cook time: 16 to 26 minutes | Serves 6

3 tablespoons avocado oil
3 cloves garlic, minced
1 tablespoon fresh thyme, chopped
1 tablespoon fresh rosemary,

chopped
1½ teaspoons sea salt
¼ teaspoon black pepper
2 pounds (907 g) radishes, trimmed and halved

Preheat the oven to 425ºF (220ºC). Line a baking sheet with foil and grease it. In a large bowl, whisk together the oil, garlic, thyme, rosemary, sea salt, and black pepper. Add the radishes and toss to coat. Arrange the radishes in a single layer on the pan, making sure each one touches the pan. Spread them out as much as possible. Roast for 8 to 13 minutes, until golden on the bottom. Flip and roast for 8 to 13 more minutes.

calories: 98 | fat: 7g | protein: 1g | carbs: 6g | net carbs: 4g | fiber: 2g

Garlicky Roasted Broccoli

Prep time: 5 minutes | Cook time: 20 to 30 minutes | Serves 6

¼ cup olive oil
1 teaspoon lemon zest
1 tablespoon lemon juice
6 cloves garlic, minced

½ teaspoon sea salt
¼ teaspoon black pepper
1 pound (454 g) broccoli florets

Preheat the oven to 400ºF (205ºC). Grease a 20 × 14-inch baking sheet or two 10 × 14-inch pans. In a large bowl, whisk together the oil, lemon zest, lemon juice, garlic, sea salt, and black pepper. Add the broccoli florets and toss to coat. Arrange the broccoli florets in a single layer on the baking sheet so that each piece is touching the baking sheet. Roast for 20 to 30 minutes, until the edges of the florets are browned.

calories: 109 | fat: 9g | protein: 2g | carbs: 5g | net carbs: 3g | fiber: 2g

Smoked Mackerel and Turnip Patties

Prep time: 5 minutes | Cook time: 14 minutes | Serves 6

1 turnip, diced
1½ cups water
Salt and chili pepper, to taste
3 tablespoons olive oil, plus more for rubbing
4 smoked mackerel steaks,

bones removed, flaked
3 eggs, beaten
2 tablespoons mayonnaise
1 tablespoon pork rinds, crushed

Bring the turnip to boil in salted water in a saucepan over medium heat for 8 minutes or until tender. Drain the turnip through a colander, transfer to a mixing bowl, and mash the lumps. Add the mackerel, eggs, mayonnaise, pork rinds, salt, and chili pepper; mix and make 6 compact patties. Heat olive oil in a skillet over medium heat and fry the patties for 3 minutes on each side until golden brown. Remove onto a wire rack to cool. Serve with sesame lime dipping sauce.

calories: 348 | fat: 22g | protein: 33g | carbs: 3g | net carbs: 2g | fiber: 1g

Scrambled Eggs with Swiss Chard Pesto

Prep time: 10 minutes | Cook time: 3 minutes | Serves 4

3 tablespoons butter
8 eggs, beaten
¼ cup almond milk
Salt and black pepper, to taste
Swiss Chard Pesto:
2 cups Swiss chard

1 cup Parmesan cheese, grated
2 garlic cloves, minced
½ cup olive oil
2 tablespoons lime juice
½ cup walnuts, chopped

Set a pan over medium heat and warm butter. Mix eggs, black pepper, salt, and almond milk. Cook the egg mixture while stirring gently, until eggs are set but still tender and moist, for 3 minutes. In your blender, place all the ingredients for the pesto, excluding the olive oil. Pulse until roughly blended. While the machine is still running, slowly add in the olive oil until the desired consistency is attained. Serve alongside warm scrambled eggs.

calories: 626 | fat: 58g | protein: 20g | carbs: 8g | net carbs: 7g | fiber: 1g

Parmesan Creamed Spinach

Prep time: 5 minutes | Cook time: 5 minutes | Serves 4

1 tablespoon unsalted butter
1 clove garlic, minced
9 ounces (255 g) fresh spinach, chopped
2 ounces (57 g) cream cheese

½ cup grated Parmesan cheese
2 tablespoons heavy whipping cream
Salt and pepper, to taste

In a large pot over medium heat, combine the butter and garlic. Sauté, stirring frequently, for 3 to 4 minutes, until fragrant. Add the spinach and cream cheese and use a spatula to combine. Stir in the Parmesan cheese and cream. Bring to a simmer and cook, stirring, for about 1 minute to reduce a bit. Remove from the heat and season with salt and pepper to taste before serving.

calories: 172 | fat: 14g | protein: 7g | carbs: 4g | net carbs: 3g | fiber: 1g

Baked Keto Granola

Prep time: 10 minutes | Cook time: 27 minutes | Serves 10

⅓ cup sunflower seeds
⅓ cup flaxseed meal
1 cup coconut, shredded, unsweetened
½ cup pecans, chopped
½ cup walnuts, chopped
½ stick butter

¼ cup water
½ teaspoon cinnamon ground
½ teaspoon grated nutmeg
A pinch of coarse sea salt
1 teaspoon vanilla paste

Thoroughly combine all ingredients until well combined. Place the mixture on a parchment-lined roasting pan. Bake in the preheated oven at 300ºF (150ºC) for about 27 minutes. Let it cool completely before storing. Bon appétit!

calories: 162 | fat: 16g | protein: 3g | carbs: 5g | net carbs: 2g | fiber: 3g

Chili Broccoli Sprouts

Prep time: 5 minutes | Cook time: 10 minutes | Serves 4

1 cup water
1 pound (454 g) broccoli sprouts
1 teaspoon sesame oil
1 teaspoon coconut aminos

1 teaspoon minced garlic
½ teaspoon chopped chili pepper
½ teaspoon salt

Pour the water into the Instant Pot. Lock the lid and bring the water to a boil on Sauté mode for about 10 minutes. Open the lid and add the broccoli sprouts to the Instant Pot. Let sit in the hot water for 1 minute, then transfer to a bowl. Whisk together the remaining ingredients in a separate bowl until combined. Pour the mixture over the broccoli sprouts and gently toss to combine. Serve immediately.

calories: 55 | fat: 1.3g | protein: 4.3g | carbs: 4.5g | net carbs: 0.5g | fiber: 4.0g

Chapter 17 Smoothies

Avocado and Berry Smoothie
Prep time: 5 minutes | Cook time: 0 minutes | Serves 2

1 cup unsweetened full-fat coconut milk
1 scoop Perfect Keto Exogenous Ketone Powder in chocolate sea salt
½ avocado

2 tablespoons almond butter
½ cup berries, fresh or frozen (no sugar added if frozen)
½ cup ice cubes
¼ teaspoon liquid stevia (optional)

In a blender, combine the coconut milk, protein powder, avocado, almond butter, berries, ice, and stevia (if using). Blend until thoroughly mixed and frothy. Pour into two glasses and enjoy.

calories: 446 | fat: 43g | protein: 7g | carbs: 16g | net carbs: 9g | fiber: 7g

Easy Peanut Butter Smoothie
Prep time: 5 minutes | Cook time: 0 minutes | Serves 2

1 cup water
¾ cup coconut cream
1 scoop chocolate protein powder

2 tablespoons natural peanut butter
3 ice cubes

Put the water, coconut cream, protein powder, peanut butter, and ice in a blender and blend until smooth. Pour into 2 glasses and serve immediately.

calories: 486 | fat: 40g | protein: 30g | carbs: 11g | net carbs: 6g | fiber: 5g

Raspberry and Kale Smoothie
Prep time: 10 minutes | Cook time: 0 minutes | Serves 2

1 cup water
½ cup raspberries
½ cup shredded kale

¾ cup cream cheese
1 tablespoon coconut oil
1 scoop vanilla protein powder

Put the water, raspberries, kale, cream cheese, coconut oil, and protein powder in a blender and blend until smooth. Pour into 2 glasses and serve immediately.

calories: 436 | fat: 36g | protein: 28g | carbs: 11g | net carbs: 6g | fiber: 5g

Spinach and Hemp Heart Smoothie
Prep time: 5 minutes | Cook time: 0 minutes | Serves 1

1 cup frozen spinach
1 cup unsweetened almond milk
2 tablespoons hemp hearts

1 tablespoon MCT oil
1 scoop chocolate-flavored protein powder

Put all the ingredients in a blender and blend until smooth, 30 to 45 seconds. Pour into a glass and serve immediately.

calories: 416 | fat: 27g | protein: 35g | carbs: 7g | net carbs: 4g | fiber: 3g

Creamy Cashew Lemon Smoothie
Prep time: 5 minutes | Cook time: 0 minutes | Serves 1

1 cup unsweetened cashew milk
¼ cup heavy (whipping) cream
¼ cup freshly squeezed lemon

juice
1 scoop plain protein powder
1 tablespoon coconut oil
1 teaspoon Swerve

Put the cashew milk, heavy cream, lemon juice, protein powder, coconut oil, and sweetener in a blender and blend until smooth. Pour into a glass and serve immediately.

calories: 503 | fat: 45g | protein: 29g | carbs: 15g | net carbs: 11g | fiber: 4g

Spinach-Cucumber Smoothie
Prep time: 5 minutes | Cook time: 0 minutes | Serves 2

1 cup coconut milk
1 cup spinach
½ English cucumber, chopped
½ cup blueberries

1 scoop plain protein powder
2 tablespoons coconut oil
4 ice cubes
Mint sprigs, for garnish

Put the coconut milk, spinach, cucumber, blueberries, protein powder, coconut oil, and ice in a blender and blend until smooth. Pour into 2 glasses, garnish each with the mint, and serve immediately.

calories: 353 | fat: 32g | protein: 15g | carbs: 9g | net carbs: 6g | fiber: 3g

Creamy Vanilla Smoothie
Prep time: 5 minutes | Cook time: 0 minutes | Serves 2

2 cups coconut milk
1 scoop vanilla protein powder
5 drops liquid stevia

1 teaspoon ground cinnamon
½ teaspoon alcohol-free vanilla extract

Put the coconut milk, protein powder, stevia, cinnamon, and vanilla in a blender and blend until smooth. Pour into 2 glasses and serve immediately.

calories: 492 | fat: 47g | protein: 18g | carbs: 8g | net carbs: 6g | fiber: 2g

Avocado Smoothie with Mixed Berries
Prep time: 5 minutes | Cook time: 0 minutes | Serves 4

1 avocado, pitted and sliced
3 cups mixed blueberries and strawberries
2 cups unsweetened almond milk

6 tablespoons heavy cream
2 teaspoons erythritol
1 cup ice cubes
⅓ cup nuts and seeds mix

Combine the avocado slices, blueberries, strawberries, almond milk, heavy cream, erythritol, ice cubes, nuts and seeds in a smoothie maker; blend in high-speed until smooth and uniform. Pour the smoothie into drinking glasses, and serve immediately.

calories: 336 | fat: 25g | protein: 8g | carbs: 18g | net carbs: 12g | fiber: 6g

Morning Five Greens Smoothie
Prep time: 5 minutes | Cook time: 0 minutes | Serves 4

6 kale leaves, chopped
3 stalks celery, chopped
1 ripe avocado, skinned, pitted, sliced
1 cup ice cubes

2 cups spinach, chopped
1 large cucumber, peeled and chopped
Chia seeds, for garnish

In a blender, add the kale, celery, avocado, and ice cubes, and blend for 45 seconds. Add the spinach and cucumber, and process for another 45 seconds until smooth. Pour the smoothie into glasses, garnish with chia seeds and serve the drink immediately.

calories: 133 | fat: 9g | protein: 5g | carbs: 13g | net carbs: 6g | fiber: 7g

Double-Berry Coconut Smoothie
Prep time: 5 minutes | Cook time: 0 minutes | Serves 4

½ cup water
1½ cups coconut milk
1 cup frozen strawberries

2 cups fresh blueberries
¼ teaspoon vanilla extract
1 tablespoon protein powder

Using a blender, combine all the ingredients and blend well until you attain a uniform and creamy consistency. Divide in glasses and serve!

calories: 281 | fat: 22g | protein: 4g | carbs: 21g | net carbs: 16g | fiber: 5g

Lemony Berry Smoothie
Prep time: 5 minutes | Cook time: 0 minutes | Serves 5

2 cups unsweetened vanilla almond milk
2 cups raspberries, fresh or frozen
1 cup blueberries, fresh or frozen
½ cup monk fruit/erythritol

sweetener blend (1:1 sugar replacement)
½ cup almond butter, no sugar added
½ cup lemon juice
¼ cup chia seeds

In a blender, combine all the ingredients and blend until smooth. If using fresh berries, chill the smoothie for 30 minutes.

calories: 256 | fat: 18g | protein: 8g | carbs: 39g | net carbs: 11g | fiber: 28g

Classic PB and J Smoothie
Prep time: 5 minutes | Cook time: 0 minutes | Serves 2

¾ cup frozen mixed berries (blueberries, raspberries, and blackberries)
¼ cup full-fat sour cream
½ cup full-fat coconut milk
¼ cup water

1½ tablespoons all-natural peanut butter (no added sugar)
½ tablespoon granulated erythritol/monk fruit blend (optional)

In a blender, blend the frozen mixed berries, sour cream, coconut milk, water, peanut butter, and erythritol/monk fruit blend (if using). Pulse a few times to get the ingredients to fall to the bottom, and blend for about 1 minute, or until smooth. If the blender struggles, add a few tablespoons of water and try again. Serve and enjoy immediately.

calories: 266 | fat: 23g | protein: 5g | carbs: 11g | net carbs: 9g | fiber: 2g

Spinach and Cucumber Smoothie
Prep time: 5 minutes | Cook time: 0 minutes | Serves 1

1 small very ripe avocado, peeled and pitted
1 cup almond milk or water, plus more as needed
1 cup tender baby spinach leaves, stems removed
½ medium cucumber, peeled

and seeded
1 tablespoon extra-virgin olive oil or avocado oil
8 to 10 fresh mint leaves, stems removed
Juice of 1 lime (about 1 to 2 tablespoons)

In a blender or a large wide-mouth jar, if using an immersion blender, combine the avocado, almond milk, spinach, cucumber, olive oil, mint, and lime juice and blend until smooth and creamy, adding more almond milk or water to achieve your desired consistency.

calories: 330 | fat: 30g | protein: 4g | carbs: 19g | net carbs:10 g | fiber: 9g

Blueberry-Almond Butter Smoothie
Prep time: 5 minutes | Cook time: 0 minutes | Serves 1

1 cup unsweetened almond milk, plus more as needed
¼ cup frozen blueberries
2 tablespoons unsweetened almond butter
1 tablespoon ground flaxseed or chia seeds

1 tablespoon extra-virgin olive oil or avocado oil
1 to 2 teaspoons stevia or monk fruit extract (optional)
½ teaspoon vanilla extract
¼ teaspoon ground cinnamon

In a blender or a large wide-mouth jar, if using an immersion blender, combine the almond milk, blueberries, almond butter, flaxseed, olive oil, stevia (if using), vanilla, and cinnamon and blend until smooth and creamy, adding more almond milk to achieve your desired consistency.

calories: 460 | fat: 40g | protein: 9g | carbs: 20g | net carbs: 10g | fiber: 10g

Blueberry-Spinach Smoothie
Prep time: 5 minutes | Cook time: 0 minutes | Serves 1

½ cup full-fat coconut milk
½ cup fresh baby spinach
½ cup frozen wild blueberries

1 scoop keto collagen powder
1 tablespoon almond butter

Place all the ingredients in a high-speed blender and blend until smooth.

calories: 454 | fat: 36g | protein: 20g | carbs: 16g | net carbs: 12g | fiber: 4g

Apple-Almond Butter Smoothie
Prep time: 5 minutes | Cook time: 0 minutes | Serves 1

½ Granny Smith apple, cored
¼ cup almond butter
½ cup coconut cream
½ cup unsweetened almond milk

½ tablespoon cinnamon
¼ teaspoon powdered ginger
5 to 10 drops liquid stevia
1 cup ice

Place all the ingredients in a high-speed blender and blend until smooth.

calories: 388 | fat: 33g | protein: 5g | carbs: 26g | net carbs: 18g | fiber: 8g

Spiced Pistachio-Lemon Smoothie

Prep time: 5 minutes | Cook time: 0 minutes | Serves 1

½ cup plain whole-milk Greek yogurt
½ cup unsweetened almond milk, plus more as needed
Zest and juice of 1 lemon
1 tablespoon extra-virgin olive oil
1 tablespoon shelled pistachios, coarsely chopped

1 to 2 teaspoons monk fruit extract or stevia (optional)
¼ to ½ teaspoon ground allspice or unsweetened pumpkin pie spice
¼ teaspoon ground cinnamon
¼ teaspoon vanilla extract

In a blender or a large wide-mouth jar, if using an immersion blender, combine the yogurt, ½ cup almond milk, lemon zest and juice, olive oil, pistachios, monk fruit extract (if using), allspice, cinnamon, and vanilla and blend until smooth and creamy, adding more almond milk to achieve your desired consistency.

calories: 264 | fat: 22g | protein: 6g | carbs: 12g | net carbs: 10g | fiber: 2g

Turmeric Avocado Smoothie

Prep time: 5 minutes | Cook time: 0 minutes | Serves 1

¾ cup full-fat coconut milk
¼ cup unsweetened almond milk
1 teaspoon ground turmeric
½ teaspoon ground ginger
¼ teaspoon cinnamon

¼ teaspoon freshly ground black pepper
1 scoop collagen protein
5 drops liquid stevia
5 to 6 ice cubes
½ avocado

Place all the ingredients, except the ice cubes and avocado, in a high-speed blender. Pulse several times. Add the ice cubes and avocado and blend at high speed until smooth.

calories: 536 | fat: 51g | protein: 11g | carbs: 17g | net carbs: 10g | fiber: 7g

Vanilla Coconut Smoothie

Prep time: 5 minutes | Cook time: 0 minutes | Serves 1

1 cup full-fat coconut milk
½ teaspoon vanilla extract
1 scoop vanilla bone broth protein
½ cup water

1 cup ice
Pinch of sea salt
2 to 3 drops liquid stevia (optional)

Place all the ingredients in a high-speed blender and blend until smooth.

calories: 549 | fat: 49g | protein: 25g | carbs: 9g | net carbs: 9g | fiber: 0g

Refreshing Green Smoothie

Prep time: 5 minutes | Cook time: 0 minutes | Serves 1

1 cup unsweetened almond, cashew, or coconut milk
½ medium cucumber, peeled and halved lengthwise
1 tablespoon vanilla protein powder
½ lime, peeled and seeded
1 tablespoon hemp seeds

1 avocado, sliced
1 cup frozen kale, stems removed
1 tablespoon coconut oil, melted
5 to 6 stevia drops
1 cup ice cubes

In a high-powered blender, combine the milk, cucumber, protein powder, lime, hemp seeds, avocado, kale, and coconut oil. Blend for 30 seconds. Add the stevia and ice cubes, and then blend on high for 1 minute. Pour into a glass and serve.

calories: 634 | fat: 46g | protein: 21g | carbs: 32g | net carbs: 14g | fiber: 18g

Creamy Flaxseed-Ginger Smoothie

Prep time: 5 minutes | Cook time: 0 minutes | Serves 1

1 cup full-fat coconut milk
1 tablespoon coconut cream
1 teaspoon finely diced fresh ginger
½ teaspoon spirulina powder
¼ teaspoon ground cardamom

¼ teaspoon ground cinnamon
1 tablespoon vanilla protein powder
1 cup ice cubes
1 teaspoon flaxseed

In a high-powered blender, combine the coconut milk, coconut cream, ginger, spirulina, cardamom, and cinnamon. Blend for 30 seconds. Add the protein powder and ice cubes, and blend on high for 1 minute. Pour the smoothie into a glass, sprinkle the flaxseed on top, and enjoy.

calories: 708 | fat: 60g | protein: 15g | carbs: 27g | net carbs: 19g | fiber: 8g

Coconut Strawberry Smoothie

Prep time: 5 minutes | Cook time: 0 minutes | Serves 1

¾ cup fresh strawberries, hulled, plus extra for garnish (optional)
1 cup coconut milk, chilled
2 tablespoons heavy whipping cream
2 tablespoons unsweetened coconut flakes

1 scoop unflavored collagen peptides
¼ teaspoon liquid stevia
¼ teaspoon pink Himalayan salt

Put all the ingredients in a blender and blend until smooth, 30 to 45 seconds. Pour into a glass and serve immediately, garnished with strawberries, if desired.

calories: 294 | fat: 23g | protein: 12g | carbs: 13g | net carbs: 9g | fiber: 4g

Avocado and Almond Smoothie

Prep time: 5 minutes | Cook time: 0 minutes | Serves 2

⅓ ripe avocado, peeled and pitted
3 teaspoons cacao powder, unsweetened
¼ teaspoon grated nutmeg

2 teaspoons granulated erythritol
1 cup almond milk
½ cup water

Purée all ingredients in a blender until smooth and uniform. Spoon into two glasses and enjoy!

calories: 140 | fat: 9g | protein: 4g | carbs: 7g | net carbs: 4g | fiber: 3g

Avocado and Seed Smoothie Bowl

Prep time: 5 minutes | Cook time: 0 minutes | Serves 2

½ ripe avocado, peeled and pitted
½ cup canned coconut milk
½ cup water
2 teaspoons sunflower seeds

2 tablespoons sesame seeds
2 teaspoons granulated erythritol
1 teaspoon ground cinnamon

Purée all the ingredients in your blender or food processor. Divide the mixture between two serving bowls and serve well-chilled.

calories: 286 | fat: 28g | protein: 5g | carbs: 8g | net carbs: 5g | fiber: 3g

Appendix 1 Measurement Conversion Chart

VOLUME EQUIVALENTS(DRY)

US STANDARD	METRIC (APPROXIMATE)
1/8 teaspoon	0.5 mL
1/4 teaspoon	1 mL
1/2 teaspoon	2 mL
3/4 teaspoon	4 mL
1 teaspoon	5 mL
1 tablespoon	15 mL
1/4 cup	59 mL
1/2 cup	118 mL
3/4 cup	177 mL
1 cup	235 mL
2 cups	475 mL
3 cups	700 mL
4 cups	1 L

VOLUME EQUIVALENTS(LIQUID)

US STANDARD	US STANDARD (OUNCES)	METRIC (APPROXIMATE)
2 tablespoons	1 fl.oz.	30 mL
1/4 cup	2 fl.oz.	60 mL
1/2 cup	4 fl.oz.	120 mL
1 cup	8 fl.oz.	240 mL
1 1/2 cup	12 fl.oz.	355 mL
2 cups or 1 pint	16 fl.oz.	475 mL
4 cups or 1 quart	32 fl.oz.	1 L
1 gallon	128 fl.oz.	4 L

TEMPERATURES EQUIVALENTS

FAHRENHEIT(F)	CELSIUS(C) (APPROXIMATE)
225 °F	107 °C
250 °F	120 °C
275 °F	135 °C
300 °F	150 °C
325 °F	160 °C
350 °F	180 °C
375 °F	190 °C
400 °F	205 °C
425 °F	220 °C
450 °F	235 °C
475 °F	245 °C
500 °F	260 °C

WEIGHT EQUIVALENTS

US STANDARD	METRIC (APPROXIMATE)
1 ounce	28 g
2 ounces	57 g
5 ounces	142 g
10 ounces	284 g
15 ounces	425 g
16 ounces (1 pound)	455 g
1.5 pounds	680 g
2 pounds	907 g

Appendix 2 The Dirty Dozen and Clean Fifteen

The Environmental Working Group (EWG) is a nonprofit, nonpartisan organization dedicated to protecting human health and the environment Its mission is to empower people to live healthier lives in a healthier environment. This organization publishes an annual list of the twelve kinds of produce, in sequence, that have the highest amount of pesticide residue-the Dirty Dozen-as well as a list of the fifteen kinds ofproduce that have the least amount of pesticide residue-the Clean Fifteen.

THE DIRTY DOZEN

- The 2016 Dirty Dozen includes the following produce. These are considered among the year's most important produce to buy organic:

Strawberries	Spinach
Apples	Tomatoes
Nectarines	Bell peppers
Peaches	Cherry tomatoes
Celery	Cucumbers
Grapes	Kale/collard greens
Cherries	Hot peppers

- *The Dirty Dozen list contains two additional itemskale/collard greens and hot peppers-because they tend to contain trace levels of highly hazardous pesticides.*

THE CLEAN FIFTEEN

- The least critical to buy organically are the Clean Fifteen list. The following are on the 2016 list:

Avocados	Papayas
Corn	Kiw
Pineapples	Eggplant
Cabbage	Honeydew
Sweet peas	Grapefruit
Onions	Cantaloupe
Asparagus	Cauliflower
Mangos	

- *Some of the sweet corn sold in the United States are made from genetically engineered (GE) seedstock. Buy organic varieties of these crops to avoid GE produce.*

Appendix 3 Index

My body is less judgmental of my diet than my mind is.

Made in the USA
Monee, IL
19 February 2021